SECRETARIES OF DEFENSE HISTORICAL SERIES

MELVIN LAIRD

and the Foundation of the Post-Vietnam Military

—— 1969–1973 ——

SECRETARIES OF DEFENSE HISTORICAL SERIES

ERIN R. MAHAN, GENERAL EDITOR

SECRETARIES OF DEFENSE HISTORICAL SERIES

Volume VII

MELVIN LAIRD

and the Foundation of the Post-Vietnam Military

—— 1969–1973 ——

Richard A. Hunt

Historical Office
Office of the Secretary of Defense
Washington, DC • 2015

Use of ISBN

This is the official U.S. Government edition of this publication and is herein identified to certify its authenticity. Use of 978-0-16-092757-7 is for the U.S. Government Publishing Office editions only. The Superintendent of Documents of the U.S. Government Publishing Office requests that any reprinted edition clearly be labeled a copy of the authentic work with a new ISBN.

Library of Congress Cataloging-in-Publication Data

Hunt, Richard A., 1942–

  Melvin Laird and the foundation of the post-Vietnam military, 1969–1973 / Richard A. Hunt.

    pages cm. — (Secretaries of Defense historical series ; volume VII)

  Includes bibliographical references and index.

  ISBN 978-0-16-092757-7 (alk. paper)

  1. Laird, Melvin R. 2. United States. Department of Defense—Officials and employees—Biography. 3. Vietnam War, 1961–1975—United States. 4. United States—Politics and government—1969–1974. 5. United States—Military policy—History—20th century. 6. United States. Department of Defense—History. 7. Cabinet officers—United States—Biography. I. United States. Department of Defense. Historical Office. II. Title.

  UA23.6.H86 2015

  355'.03357309047—dc23

                        2015009197

⊚The paper used in this publication meets the requirements for permanence established by the American National Standard for Information Sciences "Permanence of Paper for Printed Library Materials" (ANSI Z39.48-1984).

For sale by the Superintendent of Documents, U.S. Government Publishing Office
Internet: bookstore.gpo.gov   Phone: toll free (866) 512-1800;   DC area (202) 512-1800
Fax: (202) 512-2104 Mail: Stop IDCC, Washington, DC 20402-0001

ISBN 978-0-16-092757-7

CONTENTS

Charts and Maps

Tables

FOREWORD

VOLUME VII OF THE SECRETARIES OF DEFENSE Historical Series covers President Richard Nixon's first term, January 1969–January 1973, when Melvin Laird served as secretary of defense. The Vietnam War was the dominant issue during his tenure, affecting every aspect of Defense Department operations, planning, programming, and budgeting. Secretary Laird entered office intent upon disengaging from the conflict and helping Nixon reach the peace settlement that had eluded President Lyndon Johnson's administration. Laird implicitly recognized that U.S. involvement in the war had to end because it diverted resources and attention from matters vital to U.S. national interests, such as the Cold War rivalry with the Soviet Union. Despite the conflict's burden on Laird and the Pentagon, the secretary and his immediate staff began shaping the department for the postwar era. They sought to rebuild traditional alliances, replenish weapons and ammunition inventories, develop and procure advanced weapon systems, and adequately fund research and development projects. The success of these initiatives required stable spending in the years to come, but during Laird's tenure the defense program came under sharp attack from Congress and domestic critics. They pressed the administration to spend a greater share of the federal budget on housing, education, the environment, and Medicare. With the end of conscription and the adoption of the All-Volunteer Force (AVF), the department also faced rising personnel costs to attract future recruits. The military services and the secretary of defense confronted serious threats to the morale and cohesion of the armed forces. Racial tensions, inequality, and the use of illegal drugs among service members, in particular, required innovative approaches. The effort to launch the AVF likewise demanded basic changes to the way the military traditionally handled personnel issues.

Laird's tenure as secretary coincided with significant changes in national security policy. The Nixon Doctrine, which encouraged U.S. allies to contribute more in terms of funding and troop levels in defense of their own nations, was part of the framework of Laird's efforts. Nixon also scaled back the national security strategy to an affordable level that could be realistically implemented.

Laird improved collaboration and consultations between his office and the Joint Chiefs of Staff, reducing tensions that had built up during the McNamara years. The secretary also improved congressional relations that had soured during the long years of the Vietnam War. Faced with an NSC system that consolidated policymaking in the White House, Laird used his political canniness and bureaucratic skill to stymie the attempts of Nixon and National Security Adviser Henry A. Kissinger to assert greater control over the defense program.

Two interrelated themes frame this volume and are examined within the context of the often competing policymaking perspectives of the secretary, the president, and his national security adviser. The first is the policy to withdraw U.S. forces from Vietnam while improving and modernizing South Vietnam's military so it could defend the country and continue the struggle to remain independent of North Vietnam. How to withdraw and how quickly to do so proved contentious. Preparing for the postwar period is the second major theme of this volume. Vietnam proved costly in expending lives and resources, in weakening relations with allies, and in delaying modernization of weapons and equipment. Laird and Nixon agreed on the necessity of reversing these negative trends but differed over the amount of money required. As part of building for the future, Laird lobbied to end conscription and provide equal and expanded opportunities for women and minorities. He left office after achieving the two major goals he set: withdrawing U.S. troops from Vietnam and ending the draft. His successors would not have to wage war in Vietnam but would have to make sure the All-Volunteer Force was viable, prepared to fight, and offered equal opportunities for all.

Given that the Vietnam War was front and center during Laird's tenure, the author's scholarly background made him a logical selection by my predecessors, General Editors Alfred Goldberg and Stuart Rochester. Richard A. Hunt holds a Ph.D. in history from the University of Pennsylvania and served as a historian with the Army. While on active duty, he was assigned to the Military Assistance Command, Vietnam history office. Subsequently, as a civilian historian for the U.S. Army Center of Military History, he worked on historical studies of the Vietnam War and helped establish and manage the Center's Army-wide oral history program. His most notable book, *Pacification: The American Struggle for Vietnam's*

Hearts and Minds, analyzes the U.S.-South Vietnamese effort to stem the Viet Cong insurgency. He has also published numerous reviews and articles on the Vietnam War and has frequently presented papers at academic conferences in the United States and overseas.

Dr. Hunt wrote much of this manuscript under the supervision of my immediate predecessors. I encouraged the author to shift from a broad analysis of U.S. national security policy during the Nixon administration to an account more focused on Melvin Laird and the Office of the Secretary of Defense. This new emphasis was in keeping with the change I envisioned when the office renamed its official history series. I believe that Dr. Hunt succeeded in this endeavor and has provided an eminently readable and distinctive account of a secretary of defense whose tenure has had such far-reaching effects on today's military.

Interested government agencies reviewed Volume VII and cleared its contents for public release. Although the text has been declassified, some of the official sources cited in the volume may remain classified. The volume was prepared in the Office of the Secretary of Defense, but the views expressed are those of the author and do not necessarily represent those of the Office of the Secretary of Defense.

Erin R. Mahan
Chief Historian, OSD

————— PREFACE —————

MELVIN LAIRD BECAME SECRETARY OF DEFENSE in January 1969 facing a formidable agenda—to withdraw the U.S. military from Vietnam and to reshape the armed forces. The United States remained mired in the war in Southeast Asia that the outgoing administration had failed to resolve. Newly inaugurated President Richard Nixon and his secretary of defense knew that they needed to extricate the nation from this unpopular, stalemated struggle. To facilitate the withdrawal of U.S. forces, the new secretary pushed Vietnamization, the policy of improving the capabilities of South Vietnam's military and withdrawing U.S. forces. The new secretary of defense intended to achieve his goals before leaving office at the end of Richard Nixon's first presidential term, his intended departure date.

At the same time Laird worked to ensure the future strength and readiness of the U.S. military, then beset by personnel turbulence and materiel problems aggravated in part by the massive buildup of troops and equipment in Vietnam. Laird also aimed to strengthen U.S. alliances in Asia. In addition, he confronted intense presidential, public, and congressional pressure to cut defense spending. To ready the armed forces for the future, he sought to end an unpopular and inequitable conscription system that tore at the fabric of American society and to replace the existing draftee military with an all-volunteer force of regulars, robustly supported by the National Guard and reserve components. Challenged by the growing Soviet strategic missile arsenal, Laird advocated the antiballistic missile (ABM) system to defend the United States from the threat of Soviet offensive missiles. In his judgment, the ABM was a prerequisite for a strategic arms limitation agreement with the Soviet Union.

From the start, the new secretary set out to improve relations between military and civilian leaders in the Pentagon. Robert McNamara's uncompromising management style as secretary of defense had antagonized military leaders and eroded trust between the uniformed services and the civilians running the Pentagon. Laird championed participatory management, his self-described practice for increasing the role of the Joint Chiefs of Staff in the decision-making process and improving civilian-military relations within the Department of Defense (DoD). The secretary also hoped to mend fences with the legislative branch. Some congressional members had found McNamara arrogant and abrasive.

Foremost a politician, Laird drew on his experience and contacts in the House of Representatives and as a prominent Republican Party leader to gain congressional support for many of his goals. He proved to be a pragmatist capable of building alliances with the opposing party throughout his tenure as secretary of defense. He also had a strong sense for what the public wanted and what policies could actually be implemented. The hand of the former congressman was evident in the way he withdrew U.S. forces from Vietnam, handled the Defense budget, championed the end conscription, and established the All-Volunteer Force (AVF). His political instincts also helped him address emerging social problems in the armed forces, such as illegal drug use and the lack of equal opportunity for minorities and women. Nixon and Henry Kissinger, his national security adviser, tried to limit the secretary of defense's control of the Defense budget. Their efforts proved a minor impediment to Laird, whose continued political support in Congress and deft bureaucratic moves often allowed him to bypass White House restrictions.

This book describes the interplay of five major topics. The chapters on Vietnam detail the prolonged and often acrimonious struggle within the administration to shape and execute policy. A strong and resourceful leader, Laird outmaneuvered Nixon and Kissinger on the pace of withdrawals. The budget chapters assess Laird's efforts to protect the defense program from immediate, sometimes drastic cuts and to begin preparing the armed forces for post-Vietnam era requirements. These chapters focus on internal administration struggles and the battles with Congress to build a sound Defense budget. One common theme is the impact of rising spending on entitlement programs and the growing concern for social issues on the defense program. As usual, the peace "dividend" proved illusory. The chapters on NATO, East Asian allies, and military assistance present Laird's efforts to keep U.S. alliances viable through military assistance, direct U.S. support, and efforts encouraging allies to provide more resources for their defense while the U.S. moved to reduce its forces stationed overseas. The chapter on the All-Volunteer Force and a separate one on the military's social problems highlight Laird's reform efforts to keep the armed forces cohesive and prepared for the future. Two chapters on

DoD organization and management provide necessary institutional and historical context. Laird's role in handling the issue of prisoners of war and those missing in action is not covered in this work because the topic is thoroughly and ably assessed in two books published by the Office of the Secretary of Defense, Historical Office: *The Long Road Home* (2000), by Vernon Davis, which traces the development of U.S. policy on POWs; and *Honor Bound* (1998), by Stuart Rochester and Frederick Kiley, which examines North Vietnam's harsh treatment of the POWs.

Like most secretaries of defense, Laird has not received the recognition he deserves, particularly among scholars writing about Nixon's first term. His contributions have been overlooked in part because of the almost exclusive focus of historians on the fascinating, complex partnership between Nixon and Kissinger. In the mid-1990s Joan Hoff in her *Nixon Reconsidered* (1994) emphasizes Laird's singular importance, characterizing him as the most understudied and underestimated influential figure in the first Nixon administration. She notes Laird's critical role in pushing Vietnamization and ending the draft, but her book has little to say about his leadership of the Pentagon. Studies of Nixon's presidency, such as Robert Dallek's *Nixon and Kissinger* (2007), tend to present Laird as a secondary figure, without fully appreciating his vital contributions. Even recent works on Vietnam, Jeffrey Kimball's *Nixon's Vietnam War* (1998), James Willbanks' *Abandoning Vietnam* (2004), and John Prados' *Vietnam: History of an Unwinnable War* (2009), refer to Laird but without fully assessing his importance. Henry Kissinger's *Ending the Vietnam War* (2003) rehearses the familiar story of his own role. The relative neglect of Laird changed somewhat with the 2008 publication of a full-scale authorized biography. Dale Van Atta's *With Honor* includes much material on Laird as secretary but little about his management of the Pentagon or his role in shaping the Defense budget. Internal debates about Vietnam policy, the conduct of the war, and relations with U.S allies do not receive systematic coverage.

The present volume examines Melvin Laird as a major figure in Nixon's administration, highlighting the tensions within an administration grappling with difficult interrelated issues: ending a war fought on foreign soil, and strengthening alliances and the armed forces during a period of fiscal retrenchment and antimilitary sentiment in the country. Laird accomplished the broad goals he set at the start of his tenure: remove U.S. forces from Vietnam and end conscription. His efforts to expand opportunities for minorities and women and to deal with drug use represent early steps to address unfolding, intricate personnel issues. Laird saw the birth of the AVF, but the all-volunteer concept had to endure many trials in the 1970s and 1980s that threatened its existence. Laird departed the Pentagon in January 1973, as he intended, before South Vietnam's total military defeat in 1975. Still, Laird's efforts established a foundation for future secretaries to build a postwar military that could cope with emerging political, economic, and social conditions.

—————— ACKNOWLEDGMENTS ——————

I WISH TO THANK THE MANY PEOPLE who provided invaluable assistance and advice over the course of researching and writing this book. Foremost are the three OSD chief historians who directed this project. I am grateful to Alfred Goldberg for initially giving me the opportunity to write this volume. Along the way he offered encouragement as well as insightful and constructive criticism, and in countless ways helped improve this manuscript. The late Stuart Rochester upheld Dr. Goldberg's high standards. Dr. Erin Mahan, the current chief historian provided unwavering support, a keen eye, and sage advice. Our meticulously attentive senior editor, Sandra Doyle, shepherded this manuscript through production and transformed it into an inviting book. Other historians from the OSD Historical Office offered much helpful advice: Glen Asner, Jon Hoffman, Edward Keefer, and Walter Poole as well as former colleagues Nancy Berlage, John Carland, Edward Drea, Ronald Granieri, David Humphrey, Ronald Landa, Diane Putney, and Winifred Thompson. All raised probing questions about draft chapters and suggested numerous improvements. My primary research assistant, Corbin Williamson, helped format the endnotes and tables as well as answer editorial queries; research assistants Matthew Ambrose, Doug Bell, and Anthony Crain helped in preparing the bibliography. Matthew Ambrose, Sarah Barksdale, Ryan Carpenter, and Joel Christenson were invaluable in locating photographs. Cameron Morse and Patricia Skinner facilitated the security review. John Glennon did superb work reviewing and fact-checking the manuscript and the notes. Carolyn Thorne ably handled innumerable administrative issues. Special thanks go to Jamie Harvey in Creative Services at the U.S. Government Printing Office for designing the dust jacket and text layout. Retired Lt. Gen. Robert Pursley, Secretary Laird's military assistant, provided counsel and the singular perspective of a participant. The Nixon Presidential Materials office guided me through the uniquely rich collection of Nixon presidential papers and tapes when they were located at the National Archives and Records Administration, College Park, Maryland. Project director Karl Weissenbach helped clear numerous administrative hurdles. Mark Fischer, Sahr Conway-Lanz, William Joyner, David Mengel, John Powers, Robert Reed, and Samuel W. Rushay Jr. steered me to important files and made me more productive. Ryan Pettigrew, the audio visual archivist at the Nixon Presidential Library in Yorba Linda, California, simplified the task of locating appropriate photographs from the collection. At the Ford Presidential Library in Ann Arbor, Michigan, where Melvin Laird's papers reside, Geir Gunderson, Karen Holzhauser, Donna Lehman, and Helmi Raaska made my frequent visits efficient and enjoyable.

I wish to thank also the archivists at NARA II who led me through Vietnam War records: Richard Boylan, Susan Francis-Houghton, Jeannine Jeffrey, and Clifford Snyder. The late Herb Rawlings-Milton and Victoria Washington assisted my research in classified records. At the JCS Information Management Division, I thank Michael Johnson and John Krysa for their assistance. At the Historical Office of the Department of State, John Carland, David Humphrey, and Edward Keefer offered crucial advice about accessing documents. The members of the Pentagon Library also provided helpful reference assistance. At the U.S. Army Center of Military History, Joel Meyerson and Frank Shirer facilitated my research in the center's archival collection.

Despite the valiant efforts of so many knowledgeable people, any errors of fact or judgment remain solely my responsibility.

SECRETARIES OF DEFENSE HISTORICAL SERIES

MELVIN LAIRD

and the Foundation of the Post-Vietnam Military

—— 1969–1973 ——

CHAPTER 1

Change Comes to the Pentagon

WHEN MELVIN R. LAIRD took the reins of the Department of Defense (DoD) in the newly installed administration of President Richard M. Nixon on 20 January 1969, he inherited a host of troubling issues from his immediate predecessors, Robert S. McNamara and Clark M. Clifford. Most difficult was the intractable war in Vietnam that continued to divide the American public. McNamara, a towering secretary of defense, had left office in the middle of the seemingly stalemated war from which he and President Lyndon Johnson could not disentangle the nation. As a candidate Nixon had pledged to end the divisive Vietnam War. In selecting Laird, a Republican representative from Wisconsin for 16 years, he had found the right man to do it. Although the president and secretary did not always see eye to eye on how to end American involvement, Laird tenaciously held to his plan to withdraw U.S. forces.

The Vietnam War was the driving issue of Laird's tenure. It exacted a high toll on the U.S. economy in the form of inflation and budget deficits and consumed nearly one-third ($28.5 billion) of DoD's fiscal year (FY) 1968 outlays. Mounting U.S. casualties intensified public opposition to the draft and boosted support for an all-volunteer military force. During his campaign Nixon had promised to end military conscription, and Laird embraced this policy. The termination of the draft and the attainment of a nonconscripted force at the time of Laird's departure from office in 1973 represented a fundamental shift in personnel policy with broad political and social ramifications.

In addition to the Vietnam War, other national security problems awaited the Nixon administration. The Soviet occupation of Czechoslovakia in 1968 had strained relations with the Soviet Union, making it more difficult to reach arms control agreements between the superpowers. Yet the increase in Soviet strategic missiles made the pursuit of arms control more urgent. The deep U.S. immersion in Vietnam also negatively affected relations with the North Atlantic Treaty Organization (NATO). America's allies remained reluctant to increase their conventional military forces or provide greater support for U.S. units in Western Europe while U.S. forces fought in Southeast Asia, thereby aggravating U.S. economic woes, particularly the shortfall in the balance of payments.

Entering office, Nixon had a good grasp of the problems that would complicate the pursuit of his long-term agenda: reshaping America's post–Vietnam War relationships with the Soviet Union, Europe, and Asia. Laird would support Nixon's ambitious foreign policy agenda, taking steps to ensure that the armed forces remained prepared and capable of carrying out that agenda in a period of shrinking Defense budgets.

As secretary of defense Laird led the largest federal department and arguably the most complex and most costly enterprise in the world. From congressional experience, Laird had learned the magnitude of the establishment he inherited. Defense outlays of nearly $82 billion for FY 1968, which ended 30 June 1968, represented almost half (46 percent) of all federal expenditures (over $178 billion) for that year. The Defense budget financed a wide array of functions: more than $20 billion for operations and maintenance; $23 billion for procurement; $7.7 billion for research, development, and test and evaluation (RDT&E); $1.776 billion for military construction and family housing; $601 million for military grants and sales; and $108 million for civil defense. During FY 1968 the department awarded more than $44 billion in contracts for goods and services and held property (real and personal) valued at $202.5 billion.[1]

In FY 1968 the armed forces counted in their ranks over 3.5 million men and women serving in the United States and throughout the world. The Army, organized into 19 divisions, had 1,570,000 soldiers; the Navy, 932 ships and 765,000 sailors; the Marine Corps, 4 divisions and 307,000 marines; and the Air Force, 184 wings and 905,000 airmen. On the department's payrolls as well were 1,352,000 civilian employees. An additional 3,174,000 people worked in defense-related industries.[2]

The defense establishment of the late 1960s—both DoD and the industries that supported it—was immense, too much so for critics of the Pentagon, who feared its power and oversized influence. By its sheer size, worldwide span of its installations, personnel, large number of component organizations, and economic impact of billions of dollars in expenditures, DoD posed a unique and formidable management challenge.[3]

Laird also inherited the managerial system of former Defense Secretary McNamara. Although Laird's immediate predecessor was Clark Clifford, who served for less than a year, the Defense Department still bore McNamara's unmistakable imprint. During his seven years in office, McNamara had transformed both the institution and the relationships between its civilian and military leaders, earning his reputation as master of the department by dint of his strong personality, dominating presence, and innovative management practices that centralized control of the Pentagon in the Office of the Secretary of Defense (OSD). His management approach, manifested in the Planning, Programming, and Budgeting System (PPBS) that linked PPB with systems analysis (assessments of cost effectiveness in allocating funds) firmly established OSD's budget authority over the services. In his quest for centralized management McNamara diminished the role of the service secretaries and the stature of the Joint Chiefs of Staff (JCS). He used the service chiefs as sounding boards for positions that he and OSD advocated. The JCS, upset by having civilian experts second guess their professional judgments, resented this intrusion into traditional military roles. Their frustration had little effect on McNamara. At congressional hearings Laird had clashed with McNamara over the cost and strategy of the Vietnam War. He believed that McNamara's arrogance and failure to understand the political needs of the members of Congress had strained DoD relations with the House and Senate. In Laird's view, McNamara had stayed too long in this demanding position and was losing effectiveness. Laird intended to undo the negative aspects of his predecessor's legacy: strained relations with Congress, the JCS, and the service secretaries.[4]

At the start of Laird's tenure, OSD had a deputy secretary, seven assistant secretaries, a director of research and engineering, and other officials of assistant secretary rank—all reporting to him (see chart, page 4). The Joint Chiefs of Staff were also responsible to the secretary. Three agencies—Defense Intelligence, Defense Atomic Support, and Defense Communications—reported to the JCS. The three military departments—Army, Navy, and Air Force—operated under the direction and authority of the defense secretary, as did the Defense Contract Audit Agency (DCAA) and the Defense Supply Agency (DSA). Commanders of the unified and

Department of Defense, 1968

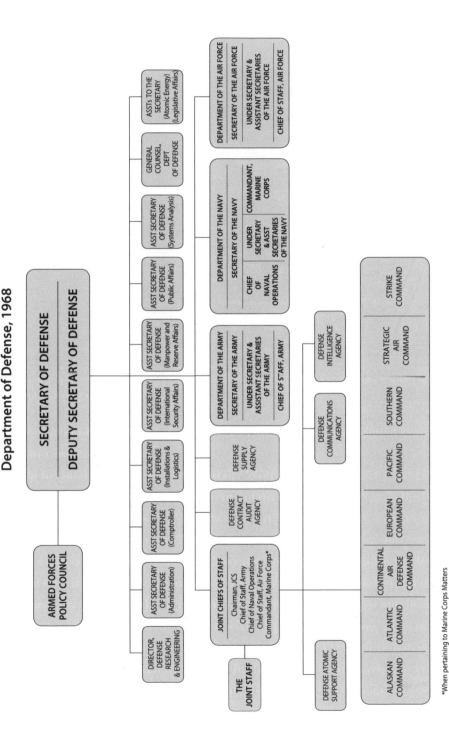

*When pertaining to Marine Corps Matters

Source: DoD Brief of the Organization and Functions, ASD (Administration), April 1968, Subject Files, OSD Historical Office.

specified commands—Alaskan, Atlantic, Continental Air Defense, European, Pacific, Southern, Strategic Air, and Strike—were responsible to the president and the secretary for carrying out the missions assigned to them. The commands reported to the secretary through the JCS, while the secretary served as the principal assistant to the president in all matters relating to DoD.[5]

Laird sought to put his own mark on the organization of the Defense Department. In Congress he had worked on the 1958 Defense Reorganization Act that had strengthened the secretary's authority and elevated the status of the JCS chairman. As the defense secretary-designate he considered it appropriate to take a fresh look at defense organization as well as policy.

A Reluctant and Independent Secretary

Laird did not seek the post of secretary of defense. He enjoyed prominence and respect as a Wisconsin congressman and as a leading figure in the Republican Party. In the fifties Laird supported Nixon in 1952 and 1956 as vice presidential candidate on the Republican ticket. Laird was a member of the "Chowder and Marching Society," a select group of young Republican politicians that rallied to Nixon. In Congress Nixon had been a charter member of the society, along with Gerald R. Ford (R–MI). Nixon relied on Laird as a presidential campaign adviser in 1968, and after Nixon's narrow victory Laird became deeply involved in reviewing candidates for positions in the new administration. He suggested that Nixon nominate Senator Henry M. "Scoop" Jackson (D–WA), an expert in military affairs, for the post of secretary of defense. Bringing Jackson into the cabinet, Laird argued, would be a welcome gesture of bipartisanship after a divisive election and Nixon agreed. After consultation with Democratic Party leaders, Jackson turned down the offer. He had been warned that serving in a Republican administration would likely foreclose any chance of his becoming a future Democratic presidential nominee.[6]

Once Jackson withdrew, Nixon, who self-imposed a deadline for selecting and announcing his cabinet nominees, pressed Laird, known for his political shrewdness, strong character, and expertise on defense appropriations, to accept the position. Laird had declined Nixon's previous offer to serve as secretary of health, education and welfare. He also declined the defense post, remaining reluctant to give up his seat in the House. Nixon, who would not accept no for an answer, and his political adviser, Bryce Harlow, concluded that Laird was "the best man for the job." The president-elect later wrote that he "made the hard sell" to persuade Laird. But in turn Laird drove a hard bargain. As a condition of taking the post, he insisted on authority to make civilian and military appointments, hoping that the president-elect would balk at such a stipulation. To Laird's surprise, Nixon agreed, pledging not to overrule Laird's choice of civilian or military personnel appointments. As Laird later described it, he would have "no interference from anybody on military and civilian personnel. I did not want to have to answer to anybody on the appointments I made." He also made clear that he would serve only four years as secretary, believing McNamara had made a serious mistake by staying too long. From the start Laird exercised a high degree of independence from the White House.[7]

Nixon knew from personal experience that Laird, with a reputation for being independent and even wily, would be hard to control. Eisenhower, with whom Nixon discussed his cabinet picks, agreed that Laird might be devious, but added that such a trait was a valuable asset "for anyone who has to run the Pentagon and get along with Congress."[8] Over the course of his tenure, Laird's insistence on autonomy in running the Pentagon would clash with the White House's predisposition to exercise full control of the national security organization.

Laird stepped into his Pentagon office with relatively untested executive and administrative skills. Unlike McNamara, who came from the executive ranks of the Ford Motor Company, Laird brought his considerable experience as a legislator and politician. A native of Nebraska and a graduate of Carleton College in Minnesota, he had enlisted in the U.S. Navy in May 1942 at age 20, was commissioned in March 1944, and served in the Pacific during World War II. Following his military service, Laird was elected in 1946 to the Wisconsin State Senate to succeed his father. In 1952 he won election to the House of Representatives from Wisconsin's seventh district and returned to Washington for another seven terms until nominated late in 1968 to be Nixon's secretary of defense. Laird devoted much of his congressional career to defense, education, and health issues, serving on the House Committee on Appropriations and subcommittees on Agriculture, Commerce, Defense, Military Construction, Labor, and Health, Education, and Welfare.[9]

In Congress, Laird earned a reputation for being hawkish on defense issues. In 1962 he wrote *The House Divided: America's Strategy Gap* to focus public attention

Secretary of Defense Laird welcomes President Richard M. Nixon to the Pentagon.
(OSD Historical Office)

on international communism and the requirements for U.S. national security. The book traced the relationship between the American economy and defense spending. The Soviet Union, because of its centralized economy and the absence of political accountability to its citizens, Laird argued, could devote whatever portion of its GNP (Gross National Product) it wanted to defense. U.S. defense spending, in contrast, was constrained by what the nation's economy and political will would support. As the official preparing Defense budgets he would come to a greater appreciation of these constraints on defense outlays.[10]

At the outset of his tenure, Laird had in mind priorities that would make it possible to achieve his overarching goal of strengthening the military establishment for the coming post–Vietnam War period. First, he planned to reduce the U.S. role in Vietnam so that the armed forces could enjoy continued public support for their other responsibilities. He believed that public backing for the military was "at the breaking point," making it necessary to "wind down the war." Second, he wanted to change the defense personnel system by ending the draft and instituting a more equitable lottery system. As a congressman he had favored universal military training so that all would have an obligation to serve.[11] Third on the priority list was to replenish defense stores, equipment, and ammunition that had been transferred from NATO and other stocks to support the Vietnam War.[12] Fourth, he believed in what he called "participatory-type management" in the Pentagon, a clear repudiation of McNamara's imperious style. He wanted to involve the military services, the JCS, and the OSD assistant secretaries in the decision-making process to a greater extent than McNamara had allowed and to enhance their stature. Fifth, in a related initiative, he set fiscal guidance to services in advance so that they could develop programs within that guidance and help shape the budget in a meaningful way.

Finally, he wanted to ensure his control over DoD field agencies. To run DoD intelligence agencies, he appointed generals loyal to him with whom he could meet frequently, selecting Army Lt. Gen. Donald V. Bennett to head the Defense Intelligence Agency (DIA) and Vice Adm. Noel A. M. Gayler for the National Security Agency (NSA). Laird deemed it essential that they realize "that they are responsible to the Secretary of Defense." Control of these two agencies he regarded as "perhaps the most important tool the Secretary has." The DIA came under the authority of the secretary, but it reported to him through the JCS and thus appeared on organization charts as subordinate to the JCS.[13]

The strongest attribute Laird brought to the Pentagon was his knowledge of Congress and his close personal ties with many of its leaders on both sides of the political aisle. Alluding to McNamara's difficult relations with the legislative branch and the military's "disdain and contempt" for Congress, Laird wanted the Pentagon to recognize "that the Congress is just as important as the presidency as far as defense policy is concerned." Accordingly, Laird paid particular attention to maintaining good relations on Capitol Hill. He preferred that the Pentagon carry out its own liaison with legislative members and committees without relying on the White House as an intermediary. Although Laird had an assistant secretary for legislative affairs, he personally remained heavily involved in congressional relations, having lunch regularly with key members of Congress, meeting with the Speaker of the House, testifying before congressional committees, and, for a man with little hair, traveling to Capitol Hill for an unusual number of haircuts at the House barbershop. Keeping the White House informed but at arm's length, he wanted no White House official to lobby for him or to tutor him in how to sway members of Congress. He asserted that "the Secretary of Defense should be in charge of congressional liaison and work with the Congress and there should be no interference from anybody in the White House at any time."[14]

A New Team

Having insisted that President Nixon give him a free hand in making DoD appointments, Laird exercised this prerogative from the start. He sought talented, experienced people who would complement his strengths. For his most important selection, that of deputy, Laird looked for someone with credentials in business management and defense technology.[15] He chose David Packard, chairman of the board, president, and chief executive officer of the Hewlett-Packard (HP) Company, which did a substantial amount of business with DoD. Laird had known Packard for years and believed that he possessed the executive and technical skills to take charge of weapons development as well as help oversee the Defense budget. Laird expected Packard to run the department and be its chief operating officer. Initially reluctant to take the position because his affiliation with HP created a conflict of interest, Packard relented, conceding that Laird "used a lot of salesmanship on me."[16] Laird selected Packard without notifying the president-elect. Realizing that as a courtesy he should have informed Nixon prior to Packard's acceptance, he hastily arranged a meeting between Nixon and Packard in Florida. Laird apologized for the oversight and Nixon supported the selection. The irony was that the president-elect had tried unsuccessfully to entice Packard to take a cabinet position. Later Nixon paid tribute to Laird's skill as a recruiter: "I struck out. I could not have been more amazed when you . . . told me that he had agreed to come aboard as your Deputy."[17]

Packard's ties with HP threatened his confirmation. The firm sold data processing and electronic testing equipment to DoD laboratories and defense subcontractors. Domestic sales for HP in 1968 totaled $207 million, of which

$34 million came from DoD and $60 million from defense contractors. Packard also served on the board of directors of other corporations with defense business, such as General Dynamics and U.S. Steel. At the time, federal law required a public official only to disclose his interest in a firm or corporation with a government contract and to promise not to participate in contract negotiations with that firm. The Senate Committee on Armed Services went further, requiring a nominee to sever associations with any corporation having a contract of $10,000 or more with DoD.[18]

Before his confirmation hearings began, Packard voluntarily devised a plan to resolve the conflict of interest. He would resign as chairman and CEO of HP and from the boards of all other organizations doing business with DoD and sell all of his shares of stock in corporations doing business with DoD, except for his $200 million in HP holdings. Liquidating that many shares at one time, about 30 percent of the company's outstanding shares, would significantly reduce the stock's price and harm other shareholders. Packard offered to place his and his wife's HP stock into a short-term trust managed by an independent board to exist as long as he served in public office. The trust would distribute the dividends and other income to educational and charitable organizations. After leaving office, he and his wife would receive, at most, the market value of the stocks at the time he entered public office. The Packards would have to bear any losses should the stock lose value. Packard agreed to make a huge financial sacrifice for a government position that paid him $30,000 per annum.[19] The committee accepted Packard's plan, and the Senate confirmed him on 23 January with only Senator Albert A. Gore Sr. (D–TN) opposing the appointment.[20]

Laird brought key members of his congressional staff, Carl S. Wallace and William J. Baroody Jr., to his immediate office in the Pentagon: Wallace, a Wisconsin native, had served in the Army during World War II. After the war he was the veterans' employment representative to the Wisconsin State Employment Service. He had been Laird's administrative assistant from 1965 to 1969 and joined DoD as special assistant to the secretary, mainly handling politically sensitive issues. Baroody, Laird's legislative and press assistant in the House and research director of the House Republican Conference, also became a special assistant to the secretary. A U.S. Navy veteran, he prepared the secretary's congressional testimony and drafted a number of position papers on defense strategy and policy.[21]

Preparing for the changing of the guard. Left to right: Defense Secretary Clark Clifford,
Defense Secretary-designate Melvin Laird, Deputy Defense Secretary-designate David Packard,
and Deputy Defense Secretary Paul Nitze. (OSD Historical Office)

Laird called on Robert F. Froehlke, a close friend since childhood and lifelong confidant, to help him sort through lists of prospective appointees, especially applicants referred by the White House. A presidential endorsement was no guarantee of a defense job, for Laird did not compromise his veto power on appointments. He took a decidedly nonpartisan, practical approach. For the sake of continuity and to capitalize on the experience and talents of critical incumbents, he retained a number of high-ranking officials appointed by his predecessors, many of whom he knew personally from his service in Congress. He kept Robert C. Moot, a Democrat, as comptroller. Moot had served in that capacity for Secretary Clifford and earlier as comptroller for the Defense Supply Agency and administrator of the Small Business Administration. Laird knew Moot from his appearances before the House Appropriations Committee. Familiar with Leonard Niederlehner, a former Navy Reserve officer and the deputy general counsel for DoD since 1953, Laird appointed him acting DoD general counsel. Niederlehner, a civil servant, held the position until August 1970, when J. Fred Buzhardt Jr. replaced him. Laird was acquainted with John S. Foster Jr. and retained him as director of defense research and engineering (DDR&E), a position

Director of Defense Research and Engineering John Foster. (NARA)

in which he had served since 1965. Foster had broad experience—he joined the Lawrence Radiation Laboratory in Livermore, California, in 1952 and rose to become its director from 1961 to 1965. In the 1950s he had served on the Air Force Scientific Advisory Board and the Army Scientific Advisory Panel. Jack L. Stempler, the assistant secretary of defense (ASD) for legislative affairs since December 1965, remained in that job until January 1970. An attorney and former Marine Corps officer, Stempler had served as assistant general counsel in DoD before assuming his post as head of legislative affairs. Richard G. Capen Jr. replaced him in January 1970, moving up from principal deputy assistant secretary. Capen, a former naval officer and journalist, also served on the Defense Prisoner of War Policy Committee that advised the secretary on POW/MIA (prisoner of war/missing in action) issues.[22]

Laird kept Air Force Col. Robert E. Pursley, who had become Secretary McNamara's deputy military assistant in April 1966 and served continuously as military assistant to McNamara and Clifford. Military assistants had a critical role functioning as executive officers, setting up meetings, preparing agendas, taking notes, and even drafting memoranda for the secretary. Laird retained Pursley for the sake of continuity to help with his transition, and on Clifford's recommendation. Before joining OSD, Pursley had earned an MBA from Harvard University, was a member of the OSD Systems Analysis staff (1963–1965), and a faculty member of the Air War College. Astute, bureaucratically skilled, and loyal, Pursley earned Laird's full confidence as a trusted adviser. Henry A. Kissinger, Nixon's national security adviser, and his deputy, Alexander M. "Al" Haig Jr., regarded Pursley as Laird's abettor in resisting White House pressure, believing he exercised undue influence over the secretary.[23]

Laird made no immediate changes in the military leadership of the armed services. He persuaded General Earle G. Wheeler, first appointed as chairman of the JCS in July 1964, to a stay sixth year; Chief of Naval Operations Admiral Thomas H. Moorer replaced him in July 1970. Admiral Elmo R. Zumwalt Jr. took over as chief of naval operations. The former commander of U.S. forces in Vietnam, General William C. Westmoreland, continued as chief of staff of the Army until 30 June 1972. General John D. Ryan succeeded General John P. McConnell as Air Force chief of staff in August 1969. Marine Corps Commandant General Leonard F. Chapman Jr. served from January 1968 to December 1971, when he gave way to General Robert E. Cushman Jr.[24]

Laird selected new civilian leadership for the services. John H. Chafee, an attorney and outgoing governor of Rhode Island, became secretary of the Navy in January 1969, even though he and Laird had clashed over the Republican platform in 1964. Chafee, who served as a Marine Corps lieutenant in World War II,

Armed Forces Policy Council, 17 February 1969. Seated at the table, left to right: Air Force Chief of Staff General John McConnell, Air Force Secretary Robert Seamans, Army Chief of Staff General William Westmoreland, Army Secretary Stanley Resor, Deputy Defense Secretary Packard, Defense Secretary Laird, Navy Secretary John Chafee (hidden), Chief of Naval Operations Admiral Thomas Moorer, Chairman of the Joint Chiefs of Staff General Earle Wheeler, and Marine Corps Commandant General Leonard Chapman. Laird continued the practice of holding weekly meeting throughout his tenure. The service secretaries, the chairman and the JCS, assistant secretaries of defense, and Laird's speechwriter, political adviser, and military assistant were regular attendees. (OSD Historical Office)

was a well-liked liberal member of the GOP. Laird persuaded a hesitant Robert C. Seamans Jr., former deputy administrator of National Aeronautics and Space Administration (NASA) and professor at Massachusetts Institute of Technology (MIT), to become secretary of the Air Force, even suggesting that he might replace Packard who planned to leave in two years. Harold Brown stayed on as Air Force secretary until Seamans came on board on 15 February 1969. Seamans had a reputation as a strong manager with good contacts on Capitol Hill. The only holdover, Stanley R. Resor, served as secretary of the Army from July 1965 to June 1971 when Laird replaced him with Robert Froehlke. Laird expected his service secretaries to "ride two horses at once." They were to be aware of his priorities and to represent their services' interests. Laird, his special assistants, and Chafee, all experienced politicians, gave the Pentagon leadership a level of Washington political seasoning equal to McNamara's team.[25]

To help manage the department, Laird called on Froehlke, to be assistant secretary of defense for administration. Froehlke, a lawyer and former insurance company executive, had served in the Army during World War II. In March 1969 Laird brought in Roger T. Kelley, vice president for personnel and public affairs of the Caterpillar Tractor Company, as assistant secretary of defense for manpower. Former editor of the *Armed Forces Journal* Daniel Z. Henkin became assistant secretary of defense for public affairs in May 1969. Assistant Secretary of Defense for Installations and Logistics Barry J. Shillito, appointed in February 1969, had previously served as assistant secretary of the Navy for logistics, director of materiel for Hughes Aircraft, and president of the Logistics Management Institute, a not-for-profit consulting organization advising DoD and other government departments. The Office of

Secretary of the Navy John Chafee, 13 February 1969. (OSD Historical Office)

Assistant Secretary of Defense for Health and Environment, created by legislation in November 1968, was established in June 1970 to serve as the principal staff adviser and coordinator for the secretary on health and sanitation matters and environmental quality. Dr. Louis M. Rousselot assumed the position effective 22 July 1970.[26]

Systems Analysis and International Security Affairs

Prompted by political considerations and a desire to involve the armed services more actively in shaping the Defense budget, Laird adjusted the roles of the Systems Analysis (SA) and International Security Affairs (ISA) offices. McNamara had established Systems Analysis under his comptroller, Charles J. Hitch, in 1961 to help evaluate the Defense budget and spending, elevating the office to the assistant secretary level in 1965. Systems Analysis performed an important management function, providing independent reviews of each military service's budget. Prior to SA's establishment, each service separately set forth in its budget the requirements it believed it needed to meet identified threats. Under this new system, no service could be expected to assess objectively its own proposals. Individual members of the JCS naturally represented their own services and tended to resolve interservice budget issues through bargaining and logrolling. Before SA, no single office or agency in DoD had responsibility for analyzing the Defense budget as a whole or for assessing the costs and benefits of specific programs. No office existed to evaluate for the secretary the question of whether acquiring additional aircraft or ground forces or ships would better improve national security. McNamara used SA to strengthen civilian oversight of military spending by subjecting service budgets and weapon systems to an intense study of their relative costs and benefits, a business-world practice that he imposed on the largely unreceptive military services.[27]

Yet by the end of 1968 the Systems Analysis office was under siege. Congressional and military critics, who objected to OSD civilians overruling or ignoring professional military judgments rendered by the JCS and the civilian service chiefs, decried the office as too arrogant and dominant. After Laird became secretary, Representative L. Mendel Rivers (D–SC), a longtime vocal critic of systems analysis, attacked it with vehemence. On 27 March 1969 he warned Laird, who was testifying at the committee's hearings on military posture and authorizations for FY 1970, "as sure as the sun rises in the heavens and you are sitting on that seat, if you retain this organization you are headed for trouble, and with this committee." Systems

Analysis, Rivers thundered at the hearing, "will not run this country any longer, like it did in the other administration."[28] In May Rivers asserted that SA civilians had usurped the traditional role of the military, injected their views into strategic and tactical decisions, and "negated the statutory functions" of the JCS. Proposals from SA were implemented despite "the most carefully considered professional military judgment that they were unsound." Rivers demanded "absolute proof in my hands that that office has not wittingly or unwittingly taken over the functions of the Joint Chiefs of Staff." He wanted assurance from Packard that SA would provide advice only when requested.[29]

Packard told Rivers that he and Ivan Selin, whom Laird appointed merely as an acting assistant secretary to appease critics, would change the way the SA office functioned. Packard would not discard systems analysis as a discipline. Instead, he would work with the services "in helping them strengthen their own capability to use analytical procedures." Taking a firm position, Packard defended systems analysis, averring that he could not manage the department "without the benefit of independent analysis provided by ASD(SA)" or without "giving full recognition and consideration to the advice of our professional military people."[30] Not at all mollified by Packard's response, Rivers threatened in November to eliminate the position of assistant secretary for systems analysis from the authorization bill because, the congressman wildly and erroneously asserted, "at this very moment the Office of Systems Analysis is designing a new force structure, without regard to any recommendations" of the JCS and military departments. "January is approaching," Rivers railed, "and the Office of Systems Analysis will be abolished."[31]

To calm down Rivers, Packard reminded him in December that DoD had instituted fundamental changes to preclude SA from redesigning force structure, issuing in October 1969 a new version of the Planning, Programming, and Budgeting System. This new PPBS was the fruit of consultation among OSD staff, the JCS, and the service secretaries. Under the new system, the military departments, the JCS, and defense agencies would first comment on the initial fiscal guidance. Then, "with the participation of the Secretaries of the military departments," Laird and Packard would "issue revised fiscal guidance," the budget numbers that the military departments and JCS would use. In the next step, OSD, including the Office of Systems Analysis, would review the force structure plans. The new procedures called for greater involvement of the JCS and services at the beginning

Representative Mendel Rivers (D–SC), arch foe of systems analysis under defense secretaries Robert McNamara and Melvin Laird. (LBJ Presidential Library)

of the process and abolished the Draft Presidential Memoranda (DPM), which had been the basic force planning documents that SA prepared for McNamara. Packard reminded Rivers that "responsibility for initiating analytical documents analogous to the DPM's (called Program Objective Memoranda [POM] under the new system) has been given to the military departments," a change that gave them "more responsibility for program development." The OSD staff would review the POMs before Laird or Packard made decisions. The FY 1972 budget would be the first one formulated under the new system.[32]

The new DoD procedures derived from an agreement reached in July 1969 between OSD, JCS, and the services. Under the new arrangement, SA would remain at the assistant secretary level but have no authority to initiate proposals. The JCS and the services would design the organization of forces. Systems Analysis would retain the responsibility of reviewing quantitative requirements for forces, weapons, equipment, and personnel recommended by the services and JCS; review the quantitative and cost implications of service and JCS recommendations; and participate in reviews of the Five-Year Defense Program (FYDP).[33]

The Systems Analysis office thus had a continuing but still critical role. As a congressman Laird had been skeptical of the office, but, like Packard, he saw it as providing an essential advisory function and retained it, while enhancing the prerogatives of the services.[34] Although he favored a strong systems analysis staff, Laird, in contrast to McNamara, tried to keep its work behind the scenes and away from direct congressional scrutiny. Laird's position found support in the White House. Kissinger, the president's influential national security adviser, believed the problem was not the concept of systems analysis per se, but "how it was used."[35] The arrival of a permanent appointee, Gardiner L. Tucker, on 30 January 1970, to replace Ivan Selin in effect signaled the end of the political dispute over systems analysis and a reaffirmation of its importance. Educated as a physicist, Tucker had worked for IBM, becoming its director of research before joining DoD in 1967. He had served as the principal deputy DDR&E before taking over Systems Analysis.

Owing to its influential policy role in political-military affairs, the Office of International Security Affairs was regarded as DoD's "State Department." McNamara had considered ISA one of the most significant posts in DoD, because it supported the department's participation in National Security Council (NSC) affairs and analyzed international political-military issues and their relation with national strategy. ISA also managed the Military Assistance Program (MAP). Laird relied on ISA for analysis and counsel behind the scenes, expecting ISA to provide policy ideas, apprise him of major trends bearing on U.S. defense posture, and ameliorate civil-military friction. Under Laird, ISA remained prominent but less influential, especially within the context of Nixon's national security system, which envisioned a greater role for the president and a diminished role for the Department of State.[36]

Laird also wanted to reduce conflicts between ISA and State. Initially he retained in office for a few months the incumbent assistant secretary, Paul C. Warnke, who was persona non grata in the Nixon White House, to help prepare him for trips to Vietnam and Europe. Laird brought in Paul H. Nitze as special assistant for arms control and intended to appoint him to run ISA, but strong objections from Senator Barry M. Goldwater (R–AZ) forced Nitze's withdrawal. Laird then selected G. Warren Nutter, chairman of the economics department at the University of Virginia, to head ISA. Nutter had worked on the Republican platforms of 1960 and 1964 and served also as a foreign policy adviser during Nixon's 1968

Secretary Laird with members of his team. Left to right: ASD for International Security
Affairs Warren Nutter, Comptroller Robert Moot, and ASD for Installations and Logistics
Barry Shillito. (OSD Historical Office)

presidential campaign. He proved less influential than his predecessors at ISA.[37]
Laird later mused that Nutter's forte "was not necessarily in the foreign affairs area,
but in the foreign economic area." In October 1970 Laird recruited Armistead I.
Selden Jr., a former Democratic congressman from Alabama, as Nutter's deputy.
Having served on the House Committee on Armed Services (HCAS), Selden was
familiar with foreign affairs and defense matters and helped the department gain
backdoor access to the committees.[38]

Laird made ISA the Defense Department's focal point for overseeing Vietnamization, the program for withdrawing U.S. forces from Vietnam and increasing the
size and quality of South Vietnam's military. Largely composed of ISA personnel,
the Vietnamization Task Force oversaw the program, but the meetings covered
more than Vietnamization, including discussions of the pacification program,
South Vietnam's economy, bombing and military operations, budget issues, and
measurements of progress in almost all aspects of the war. Laird held regular
meetings with Nutter and his staff to review the war effort, important sessions in
helping the secretary to refine his thinking about the conflict. ISA also chaired a
policy committee on POW/MIA affairs and had a special assistant responsible for
implementing defense policy on POWs. It was Laird's conviction that DoD had
to strengthen its efforts on behalf of the prisoners and their families and openly
advocate prisoners' rights.[39]

Acquisition Reform

Most of Laird's predecessors as secretary had struggled to find an acquisition system that would procure materiel in minimum time at a high level of cost effectiveness. By the time Laird arrived at Defense, the escalating cost of new weapon systems threatened to make national security unaffordable. Major defense programs, such as the Army's main battle tank (MBT–70), the Navy's Mark 48 submarine torpedo, and the Air Force's F–111 jet fighter and C–5A air transport, suffered from cost overruns and developmental problems, provoking criticism from Congress and the press. Concerned by the C–5A's runaway costs, in March 1969 Laird asked trusted assistants John Foster, Barry Shillito, and Robert Moot to ascertain the extent of the overruns, what was being done to control them, and how best to inform Congress and the public of the actual situation. Overruns, more than a public relations issue, represented a serious drain on the shrinking DoD budget. In April Nixon cut DoD's FY 1970 expenditures by more than a billion dollars and then lopped off another $3 billion in August. Despite McNamara's management changes, acquisition remained troublesome. To fend off critics, save money, and make more effective use of dwindling defense dollars reform became a necessity.[40]

Deputy Secretary Packard assumed responsibility for reforming the acquisition system for new weapon systems. Convinced that DoD needed better acquisition management and procurement policies, he believed that "the unsatisfactory way" the department had handled development and acquisition of new weapon systems was one of the most serious problems DoD faced in 1969. Packard found the record of the 1960s worrisome: Despite high acquisition and development budgets, only a small amount of new equipment had become available to the services. As he saw it, "the American taxpayer had not received very good value for the vast sums of money being spent by the Defense Department." Believing that under McNamara OSD had usurped decision-making authority that more appropriately belonged to the services, Packard wanted the armed forces to strengthen their management of weapon programs.[41] On the basis of several studies, he concluded that the primary reason for rising costs was "over-optimism in cost estimates" by contractors and the military services, the result of competition between the contractors and within the services for limited resources. The services needed, in his view, to define more explicitly what they really required in a weapon system, and do a better job in evaluating contractors' cost estimates and making them aware of the need for "cost realism" in devising their proposals. He also pushed OSD to improve its capability to validate estimates. For their part, contractors needed to identify more clearly the risks of developing a weapon system, before beginning production.[42]

In April 1969 Packard told the service secretaries that he would personally review information submitted quarterly to the Senate Preparedness Investigating Subcommittee on 31 major weapons, including the Safeguard antiballistic missile (ABM), CVAN 69 (a new nuclear aircraft carrier), Poseidon nuclear submarine, F–15 fighter, and C–5A cargo plane. He would require briefings from project officers when a troubled program warranted a more thorough examination. In May Packard set up the Defense Systems Acquisition Review Council (DSARC) to advise him on the status of each project from design to full-scale production. The services retained primary responsibility for acquiring and managing weapon systems, but Packard wanted the council to evaluate each system before it entered a new phase in the process. The council—comprising the director of research and engineering, the assistant secretary for installations and logistics, the assistant secretary for systems analysis, and the comptroller—would evaluate each system at three milestones: contract initiation, the transition from contract to development, and the shift from development to production. DSARC would review all issues and program thresholds three or more times during the acquisition cycle, augmenting the decision-making process within DoD. Packard encouraged the services "to accept the responsibility [for developing weapon systems] on the basis that they would not be bothered by OSD staff interference as long as the project was being managed well."[43]

Blue Ribbon Defense Panel

Laird and others understood that the need for reform went beyond the acquisition process. As a congressman Laird had paid close attention to DoD organization. As defense secretary-designate he declared in December 1968 that he would establish an independent commission to "reappraise the defense establishment and defense policy, and the organization of the Department of Defense." Such a broad reappraisal would give the new administration a chance to reshape the department, curtail rising defense costs, and improve management. On 30 June 1969 Laird announced that President Nixon had appointed Gilbert W. Fitzhugh, chairman of the board of Metropolitan Life Insurance Company, to head the Blue Ribbon

Defense Panel. It would focus on four areas: organization and management of DoD, research and development (R&D), procurement policies and practices, and other matters that the secretary might raise. National security policy was specifically excluded from review. Laird expected the panel to complete its study in a year and hoped the review would help restore public confidence in DoD.[44] The panel of 13 men and 2 women consisted of eight businessmen, three academics, two attorneys, a labor union leader, and even a representative of the National Football League. Fred Buzhardt, a lawyer and former administrative assistant to Senator James Strom Thurmond (D–SC), who later became DoD general counsel, served as Fitzhugh's special assistant and the panel's liaison with DoD.[45]

Barely three months after the panel had convened, it came under attack. Senator William Proxmire (D–WI) welcomed the high-level review, but he voiced skepticism about the panel's independence, because 8 of its 15 members came from firms that had business ties with DoD. Fitzhugh's Metropolitan Life held more than $34 million in common stock in 24 of the largest defense contractor firms. Four panel members, the senator alleged, had little expertise in defense issues. He judged that a mere three members had both relevant expertise and were untainted by conflicts of interest. Given the panel's flawed composition and its ties to the Pentagon, Proxmire expected the group's final report to be "mere 'window dressing'—designed to hide the areas of glaring inefficiency."[46]

Proxmire's prediction proved far off the mark. The panel's recommendations were so bold that the White House and Pentagon viewed them with alarm and quickly distanced themselves from the chief recommendations. Haig characterized them as "earth-shaking," At the end of May 1970, well before the panel released its report, Laird warned Kissinger that Fitzhugh's reorganization proposals might well diminish the role of the JCS. Admiral Moorer, who would become chairman in July 1970, complained that the panel "would cut me right out of the picture." After meeting with Fitzhugh on 15 June, Kissinger sent Nixon a memorandum urging him to look at "some of the more controversial of the panel's recommendations" before Fitzhugh issued his report. A wary Nixon met with Fitzhugh on 17 June, but only to discuss the forthcoming report in general terms. He even balked at formally receiving the document. He wrote in the margins of Kissinger's memorandum, "Shouldn't Laird just receive this? Hasn't P[resident] already done his bit?" Fearing the panel's recommendations would leak to the press, Laird persuaded

Chairman of the Blue Ribbon Defense Panel Gilbert Fitzhugh officially presents the study group's final report to President Nixon and Secretary Laird in the Oval Office, 15 July 1970. (Nixon Presidential Library)

Nixon to meet again with Fitzhugh on 15 July to receive the panel's final product. Not wanting to appear to endorse the panel's controversial recommendations, the president insisted that no member of the press be present during the ten-minute session. Laird also dissociated himself from the report's findings, telling Kissinger, "We won't endorse it, but let Fitzhugh make it public."[47] The report, containing 157 major recommendations, was officially released at the Pentagon on 29 July, two days after Fitzhugh briefed the congressional committees that would study the panel's conclusions. At a news conference, Laird termed the Blue Ribbon Defense Panel report the most far-reaching defense review since 1958 and stated that he would immediately implement some of the report's provisions, such as changes in contracting procedures. In general these provisions aroused no controversy.[48]

The Blue Ribbon Defense Panel found numerous flaws in DoD's organization and management, contending that the department was so large and cumbersome it fostered adversarial relations among its components. With 27 organizations reporting to it, OSD had difficulty managing the department. The many layers of military and civilian staffs created excessive paperwork and duplication of effort that bogged down the department's top echelon in reviewing details. Too much decision-making authority was centralized at the secretary's level, and differences of judgment were "submerged or compromised at lower levels of the Department of Defense."[49]

Implementation of the central recommendations indeed could have a seismic effect, as Haig had suggested. The panel proposed a complete restructuring of OSD, the JCS, the military secretariats, and the combatant commands (see chart, page 25). The OSD staff would be pared to 2,000 people from its current level of 3,500. Reporting to the secretary of defense would be three deputy secretaries, the JCS, the ASD for public affairs, the general counsel, the assistants for legislative affairs and atomic energy, and a director of Pentagon services. The panel recommended creating a "net assessment" group that would also report to the secretary. The plan would divide DoD into three functional elements: military operations, personnel and resource management, and evaluation (weapon testing, cost analysis, and financial controls), each run by a civilian deputy secretary of defense who would outrank all officials save the secretary. The civilian service secretaries would come under the deputy secretary of defense for resource management. The deputy secretary of defense for operations would have responsibility for military operations, the unified commands, operational requirements, intelligence, telecommunications, international security affairs, defense communications, and civil defense. He would issue orders to a four-star officer with a separate staff. The panel concluded that the Joint Chiefs could better serve as military advisers to the president and secretary "if they were relieved of the necessity of performing delegated duties in the field of military operations and Defense Agency supervision." Removed from the operational chain of command, the JCS would have only an advisory role. Two panel members, Wilfred J. McNeil and Robert C. Jackson, opposed changing the JCS role. McNeil, a former DoD comptroller and the panel member with the most experience in defense issues, believed the Fitzhugh reorganization would not decentralize DoD, but would further concentrate command and management.[50]

The panel proposed three new unified commands (Strategic Forces, Tactical or General Purpose Forces, and Logistics). Strategic Command would include Strategic Air Command (SAC), Continental Air Defense (CONAD), and Fleet Ballistic Missile Operations. Tactical Command would include European Command (EUCOM), Pacific Command (PACOM), and a merged Atlantic Command (LANTCOM), Southern Command (SOUTHCOM), and Strike Command (STRICOM). Logistics

**Blue Ribbon Defense Panel
Proposal for DoD Reorganization, 1970**

Secretary of Defense

Deputy for Resources   Deputy for Evaluation   Deputy for Operations   Joint Chiefs of Staff

Army   Comptroller   Asst Secretaries (4)

Navy   Test & Evaluation   Requirements

Air Force   Program Analysis   Intelligence

Asst Secretaries (5)   Strategic Command

Tactical Command

Logistics Command

Source: "Report to the President and the Secretary of Defense on the Department of Defense," by the Blue Ribbon Defense Panel, 1 July 1970, 61, box 555, Subject Files, OSD Historical Office.

Command would control the Theater Logistics commands.[51] This core reorganization proposal found little support among the uniformed leadership of the military, which opposed their removal from operational matters. Admiral Moorer thought the proposed structure created unsolvable budgetary and organizational problems, allowing unified commanders to switch funds "between services without involving the Service Secretaries." Army General Andrew J. Goodpaster, then commander in chief of European forces, believed the reform would add several layers of communication between the president and the unified commanders.[52]

Warned by the chief counsel of the House Armed Services Committee that the reorganization proposal would likely split the committee and "engender serious animosities toward the Administration," the White House decided not to advocate the plan. It chose to let Congress take up the issue. Although the White House agreed with some ideas, such as the need for an independent office of test and evaluation, it rejected the primary one. Kissinger warned Nixon that central reform would separate the JCS chairman from his ties with the military, and the top military officer would become "an extension of the authority and influence of the Secretary." Removing the chairman from the operational chain, Kissinger argued, would also deprive the president of the independent military analysis that had helped him decide to launch the secret 1969 Operation Menu bombings and the 1970 Cambodian incursion "against the mainstream of bureaucratic opinion," a euphemism for the opposition of Laird and Rogers. To prevent Laird from taking preemptive action, Nixon instructed the secretary in November to discuss any reorganization plans with him and the JCS.[53]

Laird needed no restraining. Like the White House, he was unwilling to implement any of the report's major features or even to comment on the proposal to remove the JCS from operational decisions. He faulted the concept of three deputy secretaries as "concentrating more authority at the top level." Laird knew the president wanted to deal with one senior military officer, the JCS chairman, not the heads of three separate commands. Laird rejected the Blue Ribbon Defense Panel's main recommendations but adopted some of the suggested technical changes in budgeting and weapons acquisition.[54] Some were broad, cosmetic recommendations that lacked explicit implementing guidance. As Wayne K. Smith of the National Security Council noted, Laird was proceeding cautiously in implementing the panel's recommendations, thus allaying White House concerns that he would try to act unilaterally.[55]

The Blue Ribbon study pointed to the growing management burden on the secretary and his deputy, a problem that Laird also recognized. More frequent hearings before committees on Capitol Hill increased the demands on the secretary and his deputy. In February 1971 Laird sought Nixon's support for establishing a second deputy of defense, arguing that another deputy would ease the management burden on him and Packard and allow him to spend more time with the service secretaries and JCS. Laird stressed that neither deputy would impede direct contact between the secretary and the service secretaries or the Joint Chiefs. The JCS chairman would not be the subordinate of a civilian deputy, as the Fitzhugh report advocated. Nixon supported Laird's request. In October 1972 Congress passed legislation creating a second deputy, but Laird did not fill the position. Because he planned to leave in January 1973, he recalled later, "I felt that it would be better if I recommended to the new Secretary of Defense that he fill that position."[56]

The Fitzhugh panel offered proposals on cost overruns and acquisition reform, seeking to make the acquisition process easier to manage. According to the panel, a defense contractor faced a monumental, if not impossible task trying to prepare a single contract to design and manufacture a new weapon or plane that no one had ever built—and that might even prove impossible to produce. Therefore, the panel recommended that the department discontinue the practice of negotiating one fixed-price procurement contract for the acquisition of a major weapon system over a 7- to 10-year period, divide the total development process into phases, shorten the contracting period, and require the contractor to build and test prototypes before moving into full production. Since these proposals accorded with the new DSARC procedures, Laird accepted the Blue Ribbon Defense Panel's contract reform proposals and put them into effect immediately. Rather than negotiate a single long-term, all-inclusive contract, Laird instituted what he called the "fly before you buy" procedure, which required periodic tests and evaluations before proceeding to the next stage of development or before purchasing equipment. The new procedure gave DoD the options of making reviews, canceling production, and increasing or decreasing the number of weapons purchased. With this change, Laird hoped to avoid repeating the pitfalls of the C–5A contract that attempted to project the entire cost of building the transport.[57]

The panel wanted to establish an assistant secretary position for test and evaluation, arguing that an independent office would fulfill a widely recognized need for evaluating weapons in a simulated combat environment. The existing process of allowing the services to control the testing and evaluation of the weapons they desired represented a conflict of interest. Facing opposition from weapons developers, Laird established a new testing office under a deputy director for test and evaluation "to coordinate and establish policy for all test and evaluation matters." The deputy would serve under the director of defense research and engineering, traditionally an advocate of weapons development.[58]

The Blue Ribbon Defense Panel also advocated substantial reorganization of intelligence in its July 1970 report, concluding that management of defense intelligence was fragmented and poorly coordinated. In marked contrast to its advocacy of decentralizing decision making in other areas of DoD, the panel wanted to centralize intelligence at the OSD level to improve the management of resources and the analysis of information.[59] Panel members believed that the services had excessive influence over NSA and DIA and their personnel, budgets, R&D, and intelligence products, thus calling into question the objectivity of the intelligence those agencies produced. The panel advocated setting up a defense intelligence service that reported "to the Secretary directly and not through the JCS."[60]

To make the DoD intelligence community more responsive to its consumers, the Fitzhugh panel wanted a clear chain of command from the secretary to the organizations producing intelligence through an assistant secretary of defense for intelligence (ASD[I]) responsible for coordinating and directing the entire system. Serving under the proposed deputy secretary for operations, the ASD(I) would represent the secretary on intelligence issues and direct all defense intelligence activities, including national programs managed in the department.[61]

As with the recommendations on the broader reorganization of DoD, the group's ideas on intelligence reform met a cool reception. The White House thought that the panel focused too much on administrative and management issues and gave insufficient attention to improving the quality of reports.[62] On behalf of the JCS, Admiral Moorer vigorously opposed any change to military intelligence, especially the proposal to remove the director of DIA from the chain of command and no longer require the director to report to the JCS chairman. The Joint Chiefs insisted that the "operational direction of intelligence" should remain with the operating agencies. They considered it an inappropriate function for OSD.[63]

The experience of the Blue Ribbon Defense Panel confirmed the difficulty of bringing about large-scale organizational change in the Defense Department without legislative action. Laird's major organizational study changed little. In devising a plan for reorganizing the Pentagon, the panel seemed naïve in not realizing the political and bureaucratic obstacles to such dramatic changes. Despite Laird's initial support of the panel's work, "not a single major recommendation was adopted," noted one later evaluation.[64]

UNDER HIS PHILOSOPHY of participatory management, Laird sought to undo what he considered the negative aspects of McNamara's practices. He expected a more collegial relationship between the civilian leadership of the department and the military services. Thus he gave the services more involvement in decision making and a greater voice in designing force structure and shaping the budget than they had enjoyed under McNamara. Laird also deftly reduced the once highly visible role and influence of systems analysis, an outcome that the armed services and influential members of Congress welcomed.

Laird's efforts led to smoother relations between the military and civilian sides of the Pentagon. His relations with the White House and JCS would at times be complicated and characterized by mutual mistrust. The secretary, the White House, and the JCS would deliberately keep each other in the dark about their actions or intentions. Laird would sometimes delay forwarding JCS memoranda to the White House, and the JCS and White House knew it because the White House and Chairman Moorer employed direct channels of communication that excluded Laird. Moorer's NSC liaison officer in the White House, Rear Adm. Rembrandt C. Robinson, provided him directly, and at times secretly, inside information on deliberations between the White House and OSD.

Laird delegated to Packard much of the day-to-day management of the Defense Department and major responsibility for working out the details of the budget and the acquisition program with the services. Laird retained final decision authority and represented the department in its budget and policy battles with the White House and Congress. The secretary did little to change the structure of the department. The White House made the decision to set up the position of ASD for intelligence. Congress imposed the post of assistant secretary for health affairs by legislation.

As secretary Laird would contend with political and economic pressure to shrink the DoD budget, a constant complicating factor. Already on a downward trajectory at the start of Laird's tenure, the department's declining finances and political support caused by the Vietnam War would affect decisions on force structure, development and procurement of weapons and equipment, and the size of the U.S. military presence overseas. Nixon wrote the secretary of his deep concern that the growing proportion of the Defense budget devoted to personnel costs and the high per unit costs of developing new weapons diminished the force level that the administration could afford. Nixon wanted Laird and Packard to advise him "on the probable long-term strategic implications of rising defense manpower and procurement costs" and on how to minimize their effect on the administration's ability to carry out defense strategy in the years ahead.[65] What level of national security did the United States require? What level of national security could it afford? Addressing these questions and dealing with Vietnam would constitute Laird's main challenges as secretary of defense.

CHAPTER 2

Organizing National Security in a New Administration

MELVIN LAIRD HAD to work within a national security policymaking structure significantly different from that of the preceding Lyndon Johnson administration. President Johnson used his Tuesday luncheon meetings with the secretaries of defense and state, his national security adviser, and on some occasions, the chairman of the Joint Chiefs and the director of central intelligence (DCI) to discuss issues and make decisions. Johnson disliked formal National Security Council sessions for setting policy. Incoming president Richard Nixon prided himself on his expertise in foreign affairs. Before taking the oath of office he had decided to consolidate control of policymaking in the White House. Drawing on his experience as vice president in the Eisenhower administration, he would reinvigorate and make greater use of the NSC, formalizing its procedures for handling national security issues. His assistant for national security affairs, Henry Kissinger, ably furthered the new president's goals and quickly emerged as a key policymaker for Nixon. Like other principals outside the White House, Laird had little opportunity to help shape the new system.[1]

The Nixonian Approach

Shortly after winning the election, Nixon began to assemble his national security team and plan how to organize and employ it. As secretary of state, Nixon chose William P. Rogers, a personal friend who had been attorney general in the Eisenhower administration. In his memoirs, Nixon characterized Rogers as a "strong administrator" and "resourceful negotiator," who would be able to get along with Congress and improve relations between the Senate Foreign Relations Committee and the White House.

President Nixon, Secretary Laird, Assistant to the President for National Security Affairs Henry Kissinger, and JCS Chairman General Earle Wheeler confer at the Pentagon on the occasion of the president's first visit there, 27 January 1969. (OSD Historical Office)

Under the chairmanship of Senator J. William Fulbright (D–AR), that committee had sharply criticized President Johnson's prosecution of the Vietnam War.[2]

Nixon's selection of establishment Republicans like Rogers and Laird for key cabinet posts was hardly surprising. His choice of Kissinger, a Harvard University professor who had long served as foreign policy adviser to Nelson A. Rockefeller, Nixon's main rival for the Republican Party nomination, to be national security adviser was less predictable. Laird and Kissinger had worked well together during the 1964 Republican National Convention, when Laird ran the platform committee and Kissinger was one of the foreign policy advisers. They respected each other. Laird commended Kissinger's tough anticommunism stand; Kissinger esteemed Laird's political pragmatism. Over the years, Laird had kept in touch with Kissinger and deemed him a potential candidate for national security adviser.[3]

Nixon, in contrast, knew Kissinger mainly from his writings, not from personal acquaintance. At a meeting in late November, the president-elect concluded that he and Kissinger shared a common outlook on the world balance of power and the coordination of foreign and defense policy. He confessed that he chose Kissinger in "an uncharacteristically impulsive way," deciding "on the spot that he should be my National Security Adviser."[4]

Nixon changed NSC procedures in the expectation that he would receive a range of genuine options for making policy decisions. In his judgment Presidents John F. Kennedy and Lyndon Johnson had allowed the formal NSC mechanisms and preparation of policy options to atrophy.[5] General Andrew Goodpaster, then deputy to General Creighton W. Abrams, the military commander in Vietnam, worked with Kissinger in redesigning the NSC. Goodpaster was an obvious choice, since he had helped run the NSC system during the Eisenhower administration.[6] Morton H. Halperin, former deputy assistant secretary of defense for international security affairs, drafted a proposed reorganization based on conversations between Kissinger and Goodpaster.[7]

At the end of December 1968 Kissinger brought his proposal for revamping the NSC to Nixon at Key Biscayne, Florida. It called for an NSC review group of senior-level officials from various agencies and departments to examine papers and frame issues prior to consideration by the NSC. Kissinger, not someone from State or Defense, would chair the so-called Senior Review Group.[8] Before Kissinger discussed the reorganization with Laird and Rogers, Nixon had already approved the plan that placed the various subgroups and interdepartmental groups under Kissinger.[9] Nixon's decision diminished the State Department's influence, in particular, representing a significant departure from President Johnson's system of interdepartmental commit-tees. Under Johnson, an undersecretary of state had chaired the Senior Interdepart-mental Group (SIG), which supervised an array of other groups that concentrated on different regions of the world. To continue those procedures, Nixon feared, would give State continued ascendancy over the national security process, so he replaced the SIG with a number of interdepartmental panels chaired by Kissinger.[10] Presented with a presidential decision at the meeting, Laird and Rogers had little room to protest. Both later voiced their objections to Kissinger.[11]

Rather than personally take the lead in objecting to the new system, Rogers let Under Secretary of State-designate Elliot L. Richardson and Under Secretary for Political Affairs-designate U. Alexis Johnson speak on his behalf. They wanted the president to reaffirm the standing of the secretary of state as his principal foreign policy adviser, with authority over other departments as well as his own. State wanted the NSC to serve as a board of appeals to resolve disagreements.[12]

Kissinger and Goodpaster advised Nixon that State's proposal would under-mine the concept of a strong NSC and permit the secretary of state to retain

Clockwise, Secretary Laird, President Nixon, Secretary of State William Rogers, Attorney General John Mitchell, and National Security Adviser Henry Kissinger confer aboard Air Force One during a flight to Florida, 9 November 1969. (Nixon Presidential Library)

control over which papers reached the NSC and which options the president would have to evaluate. In unsparingly critical language Kissinger told Nixon that he feared the department would prove unable to rise above its parochial interests and would instead impose a departmental perspective on papers sent to the NSC. It was hardly surprising that the president reaffirmed his approval of the reorganization plan. Nixon decreed that the new system go into effect on Inauguration Day.[13]

As a secretary holding cabinet rank and exercising immense responsibility, loath to yield any of his authority to the president's ambitious national security adviser, Laird took a different approach in objecting to the reorganization. Unlike Rogers, he directly confronted Kissinger strongly objecting to the new procedures. Kissinger's grab for power was hardly subtle and Laird was not about to acquiesce. He told Kissinger explicitly that he disapproved of the proposal "in its present form," more than suggesting that he would not cooperate unless changes were made. He cited fundamental objections. The NSC could not be revitalized "by aggregating to the NSC and through it to the assistant to the president the major tools that have always been intended to be utilized equally by all of the President's top-level board of advisers in the National Security field." He asserted the authority of the principals making up the NSC to place policy issues on the agenda for discussions and to have a voice in initiating studies. Laird opposed as well the decision to exclude representatives of the intelligence community from NSC meetings and funnel all intelligence information to the president through a single source, Kissinger. Laird saw great danger in designating Kissinger as the gatekeeper for intelligence. Such a procedure could isolate the president from immediate access to information from the intelligence community and even from the secretaries of state and defense. Laird persuaded Nixon to allow the director of central intelligence to attend meetings and NSC principals to propose the initiation of studies.[14]

The reorganized NSC instituted new procedures for formulating policy. The initial step was the request from the president or Kissinger to various departments and agencies to prepare a National Security Study Memorandum (NSSM) on a specific subject. An NSSM might lead to a National Security Decision Memorandum (NSDM), a presidential determination of national security policy. NSSM 1 dealt with setting the administration's policy for the Vietnam War, requesting answers from all agencies and departments to a list of questions about Vietnam policy and the conduct of the war. NSDM 2 put Nixon's NSC procedures in place.[15]

NSSM 3, issued by Kissinger on 20 January, directed the preparation of a far-reaching review of the nation's military posture and the balance of global power. NSSM 3 would be the starting point in developing the Nixon administration's national security policy and help set Defense budget levels for alternative national security strategies in the coming years. Laird and Kissinger sparred over the nature of the request, exposing at the start fault lines between OSD and the NSC staff. Laird had reservations about the broad scope of the review, feeling that NSSM 3 encroached on his department's authority to design force structure and budgets. Kissinger insisted the review concerned policy, not departmental authority. He told Laird that Nixon felt "very strongly" that the NSC should study the policy issues involved.[16]

Kissinger later downplayed Laird's objections and characterized them as an elaborate smoke screen to permit the CIA (Central Intelligence Agency) director to participate in NSC meetings. His explanation underestimated how seriously Laird viewed the matter. Laird sought to preserve the balance of power between the NSC staff and the departments. His comments signaled his unwillingness to permit his department to become subordinate to Kissinger's NSC staff. As Kissinger conceded in his memoirs, Laird proved to be a formidable bureaucratic adversary.[17]

The new National Security Council system would be "the principal forum for consideration of policy issues requiring Presidential determination." Kissinger officially received a new title—assistant to the president for national security affairs—and was responsible for setting the agenda. His predecessors had been termed national security advisers.[18] At the first NSC meeting of his presidency on 21 January, Nixon put his imprimatur on the new system and expressed his desire for free and open discussion. He considered the NSC an advisory and consultative body, not one that made decisions. He wanted to hear all points of view at NSC meetings. Afterward, he said, "I will then deliberate in private and make the decision."[19]

Very early in the administration Col. Al Haig, Kissinger's military assistant, emerged as a key figure in Kissinger's office. Self-confident, ambitious, and hardworking, Haig came to the White House from West Point, where he had served as deputy commandant.[20] He recommended that Kissinger establish himself as the channel for receiving all national security information coming into the White House for the president. He offered to review this information before it went to Kissinger, making him gatekeeper for the national security adviser.[21] In early February he advised Kissinger, who had little managerial experience, to appoint a deputy to help him run the NSC. Haig declared himself "prepared to move, without delay, this weekend," to accept this responsibility.[22] His proposed job description amplified his responsibilities as military assistant to include coordination and liaison with the National Security Council staff. Papers for the review group and the NSC would go through Haig to Kissinger. The military assistant would serve as "the de facto chief of staff for substantive NSC affairs and be the single point of contact to insure final review of NSC papers prior to presentation through the Executive Assistant to you [Kissinger]." Kissinger approved.[23]

Laird had strong grievances about the new system. In May 1969 he complained that sudden changes in NSC schedules and slowness in getting papers to the Senior Review Group and the NSC left insufficient time to study the issues, a criticism shared by the CIA and State Department.[24] Laird desired a more orderly process. Over a year later, in August 1970, still unhappy with the NSC system, he provided Kissinger with his comments and those of the JCS that echoed earlier criticisms. Topics for study needed to be made clear and be more carefully selected to avoid duplication of ongoing studies. Laird wished to minimize the number of high-level ad hoc groups, urging Kissinger to better coordinate within the NSC system the work of the Washington Special Actions Group (WSAG), which had been set up to manage crisis response. Kissinger was unmoved. "When will I get analysis," he scrawled at the top of Laird's paper, in apparent annoyance with the secretary's comments.[25]

Others expressed dissatisfaction. The NSC system continued to irritate the secretary of state, who felt isolated because of the lack of consultation on issuing NSSMs.[26] A number of administration officials complained of the burden of having to produce too many policy study memoranda.[27] Some members of Kissinger's staff also voiced criticism of the new system and Kissinger's management.[28] The new system remained in operation because it suited the president's wishes, providing him with policy options rather than a single course of action.

To help his administration prepare for and handle crises, in March 1969 Nixon issued NSDM 8. It established NSC interdepartmental groups to draft contingency studies on potential crises, aiming at synchronization of political and military actions. Nixon anticipated that these studies would yield timely assessments of U.S. interests and courses of action. The downing of a reconnaissance aircraft off North Korea, the president's first major emergency, sorely tested the new administration. During the crisis Laird and the White House were at odds over how to respond, leaving Nixon and Kissinger frustrated by Laird's ability to outmaneuver them.[29]

An EC–121 Goes Down

On 14 April 1969 North Korean Air Force fighters blew out of the sky an unarmed, unescorted U.S. Navy reconnaissance aircraft (EC–121) over international waters. Part of the Navy's Fleet Air Reconnaissance Squadron One, EC–121s routinely collected information on North Korea's military strength and air defenses. The mission was not considered unduly risky. Between January 1968 and April 1969, 976 reconnaissance flights came within 60 miles of North Korea's east coast without challenge from the North Koreans. Since November 1968, eight planes had flown the same track as the downed plane over the Sea of Japan without provoking a reaction by North Korean fighters. The commander in chief of the Pacific Command (CINCPAC), the Defense Intelligence Agency (DIA), and the JCS conducted the requisite preflight risk assessment of the 14 April flight. Finding no reason to take extra precautions, they evaluated the probability of danger as routine.[30]

An EC–121 aircraft similar to one shot down by North Korean jet fighters in April 1969. (NARA)

The EC–121 took off from Atsugi Naval Air Station near Tokyo on 14 April with a crew of 31 and six tons of electronic eavesdropping equipment. The aircraft was under orders to fly no closer than 50 nautical miles from the North Korean coast. Alerted during the flight to a possible North Korean attack, the aircraft moved farther out over international waters. The EC–121 received three warnings from U.S. monitoring sites that North Korean MiGs were trying to intercept it. The final transmission from the EC–121 acknowledged the third warning. The plane disappeared from radar screens at 11:50 p.m. EST, about a minute after the last warning, crashing into the sea approximately 90 nautical miles from the North Korean coast.[31]

The unexpected loss of the EC–121 shocked the administration. For three weeks in April 1969 the EC–121 incident was the prime concern of the topmost officials of the U.S. government. Laird found himself at odds with Nixon and Kissinger over how to respond. The loss of the plane revealed the contentiousness and difficulties of decision making in resolving crises. In his memoir, Kissinger claims that Nixon's deliberate pace and lack of clear direction made it difficult to take timely action against North Korea. He termed the administration's response as "crisis management in slow motion." Nearly 30 years after the incident, Haig rendered a harsh, hyperbolic verdict: "the biggest mistake of the Nixon presidency; bigger than Watergate."[32]

The EC–121 episode epitomized how the U.S. national security apparatus worked early in the Nixon administration. The focus of much study and debate, crisis management had proved resistant to formulation of general rules because the unique nature of each emergency required different treatment and resolution.

Nixon regarded the destruction of the plane and the death of its crew as an action requiring military reprisal. During the 1968 presidential campaign, he had severely condemned Lyndon Johnson for not taking strong military steps against North Korea after it seized the USS *Pueblo*. Nixon now requested that by the 16 April NSC meeting Laird and the JCS provide him with options for military retaliation and an estimate of needed reinforcements and losses should North Korea attack South Korea. The president wanted to choose a course of action from the JCS options. Before the meeting, he ordered three aircraft carriers to sail from Vietnam to Korea. On 15 April Laird discussed with Nixon the JCS proposal for using aircraft from carriers or land bases to hit targets in North Korea. The JCS offered options for small strikes, anticipating vigorous defensive measures and possible North Korean retaliation.[33]

At the 16 April meeting, Wheeler covered the available military alternatives, conceding that some, such as a show of force, would likely have no effect on the North Koreans. The deliberations ended with allusions to North Korea's defense treaties with the USSR and China but without recommending a specific response.[34]

At the close of the meeting two options remained under consideration: a retaliatory military strike against a North Korean airfield, or resumption of EC–121 flights off North Korea with combat escort, coupled with additional secret bombing raids against North Vietnamese base areas in Cambodia that had started in March. Knowledge of this operation was restricted to a small group of officials. Nixon believed Communist regimes would somehow perceive the linkage between these geographically separated actions. Heavier bombing against base areas in Cambodia would demonstrate, he thought, U.S. resolve to North Vietnam, the Soviet Union, and North Korea and willingness to exert military pressure against Communist forces.[35] Unwilling to risk the loss of another plane, Laird on his own initiative had cancelled all reconnaissance flights in the Yellow Sea, the Sea of Japan, and the Sea of Okhotsk on 15 April. Laird's decision would delay execution of the second option if chosen.[36]

In considering possible options with Kissinger on the phone after the NSC meeting, and following their subsequent discussion with Nixon, Laird expressed caution. He doubted that the United States would get the chance to attack North Korean ships or planes without getting involved in additional combat. Significantly, he did not want to be compelled to pull forces out of Vietnam to deal with a ground attack from North Korea, worrying about how North Vietnam's negotiators in Paris would interpret a sudden withdrawal of American forces. Kissinger agreed: "Yes, you stated the case exactly—that's exactly the problem." Laird responded, "What we're trying to do is get the war in Vietnam over with."[37]

On 16 April Nixon agreed to Kissinger's proposal to set up an informal interagency coordinating committee in Washington to gather information and recommend actions. The group would meet to draft papers and draw on the resources of various agencies. This committee was the prototype for the Washington Special Actions Group.[38]

Nixon pondered his options during a telephone conversation with Kissinger on 17 April. On the one hand, the president believed the situation warranted a bold move and weighed the possible adverse public and press reaction if the loss of 31 American lives went unpunished. On the other, he feared his domestic opponents would accuse him of risking a second ground war in Asia if he retaliated against North Korea. Nixon had asked Laird to check the mood in Congress, and the secretary had detected no congressional pressure to retaliate. Kissinger argued for military action. He saw the risks of retaliation as high in the short term but held that inaction posed an even greater risk over the long term and might force the administration "into an even bolder move a year from now." Nixon mused that failure by the United States to react would encourage "some pipsqueak to do something." Kissinger spoke of the gains to be realized from taking on the North Koreans and facing them down. Despite Nixon's initial instinct to retaliate, he remained reluctant to follow through.[39]

OSD provided the White House with a clearer picture of the military risks of attacking North Korea the next day. On 17 April Col. Robert Pursley forwarded a sobering JCS study on the availability of logistic support for forces in Korea should fighting break out on the peninsula. The study concluded that allied forces in Korea would be unable to sustain a fight against an attack from the North. The U.S. Eighth Army in Korea had significant shortfalls in normal stockage levels of major items of equipment and repair parts, principally in combat vehicles and helicopters. Combining U.S. Army and Republic of Korea (ROK) Army supplies of ground ammunition would support combat for about 28 days. It was not possible to draw items from stocks in the United States or Europe. Equipment and ammunition programmed for Vietnam offered the only readily available source of additional materiel for Korea. Moreover, American forces in Vietnam and Korea and the South Korean army had to draw from the same pool of equipment and ammunition; additional materiel for Korea would mean less for Vietnam. U.S. naval forces in the Korean area would also need to draw ammunition from the Southeast Asia (SEA) pipeline. Air operations could be sustained for 45 days. If war broke out, sufficient stocks of ground ammunition and major equipment items were on hand to meet immediate requirements provided that a major replenishment effort began no later than a week after the start of hostilities. In sum, a war in Korea would weaken the combat effort in Vietnam and the program to modernize South Vietnam's forces. The JCS study made crystal clear how thinly stretched were U.S. resources supporting the war in Vietnam and U.S. commitments to Korea and Europe.[40]

Before choosing a course of action, Nixon ordered the Seventh Fleet on 17 April to assemble in the Sea of Japan a large naval force, designated Task Force (TF) 71, for possible retaliation and to intimidate North Korea. TF 71 gathered ships from the coast of Vietnam and others from Taiwan, adding 20 ships to the three carriers already sailing toward Korea. When assembled in waters south of Korea on 20 April, the entire task force consisted of three attack carrier strike groups, an antisubmarine warfare (ASW) support group, an air defense group, and a surface action group. Assembling the task force strained ongoing naval operations and constituted "an emergency surge effort," according to the JCS. Naval gunfire support ships moved from Southeast Asia to Korea. The number of naval aircraft on Yankee Station, the carrier operating area off North Vietnam, were reduced by a third to deal with the situation in Korea. Nixon's decision to assemble the task force severely strained the available resources of the Seventh Fleet.[41]

Nonetheless, Nixon continued to contemplate retaliation.[42] At his morning press conference on 18 April, he disclosed that he had ordered continuation of the long-standing policy of using reconnaissance flights to protect U.S. forces in South Korea and that the flights would have armed escorts. That morning, behind the scenes, the interagency committee of State, Defense, JCS, and CIA representatives met with Kissinger to discuss retaliation and the resumption of aerial reconnaissance. The group would complete interagency planning to allow the president to carry out either retaliation or armed reconnaissance flights, or both.[43]

As a member of Nixon's cabinet, Laird did not submit views on the crisis to Kissinger's interagency committee, but sent them directly to the president, strongly advising against retaliation. The secretary deemed one-time air strikes against Sondok and Wonsan airfields the best military option under consideration, but he warned that the option risked losing the public and congressional support the administration had garnered for its "present reasoned, calm posture." An attack on North Korea might also weaken political support for the administration's Vietnam policies and the antiballistic missile program to protect the nation against nuclear missiles launched from the Soviet Union or China. Anticipating a close Senate vote on the ABM, Nixon had sent Rogers, Laird, and Kissinger a memorandum on 14 April emphasizing the need for unity and absolute backing of his ABM policy in order to win approval. Laird estimated that only a minority in Congress supported retaliation. A strike might increase public disenchantment with the military and arouse critics of the military's involvement in foreign policy. Moreover, the secretary believed that retaliation would surely raise questions of whether the intelligence value of these reconnaissance flights justified the risks they incurred or the danger of a North Korean counterattack.[44]

Laird opposed reprisal for military reasons as well. Citing the JCS logistics study, Laird doubted that "we have the capability now to handle a major confrontation in Korea." A war in Korea, he believed, would lead Hanoi to suspect the United States would have to withdraw forces from Southeast Asia and slow down the program to improve South Vietnam's armed forces, thus weakening the effort against the North Vietnamese and Viet Cong. For Laird, the hazards of a military operation outweighed "the potential benefits by a substantial margin." He advocated resumption of reconnaissance flights with armed escorts authorized to destroy North Korean planes or ships approaching U.S. planes outside North Korea's territory.[45]

Laird was not the only senior official resisting military action. Secretary Rogers, CIA Director Richard M. Helms, and U.S. Ambassador to South Korea William J. Porter also opposed it. On 18 April Richard L. Sneider, an East Asian specialist on Kissinger's staff, spelled out the difficulty in sustaining public support for military action in Korea that risked a second war in Asia when "U.S. vital national interests" were not at stake. Kissinger remained the principal proponent of military action.[46] Given the opposition within his cabinet, Nixon decided on 19 April not to strike North Korea, but he ordered the carriers to remain in the Sea of Japan until 24 April. He directed the resumption of reconnaissance flights with armed escorts.[47]

Four days after Nixon publicly announced that reconnaissance flights would resume, he was chagrined to learn otherwise. On 22 April Laird informed Nixon that at his direction the JCS had requested CINCPAC Admiral John S. McCain Jr. to prepare for the secretary's approval a plan to resume reconnaissance flights within intercept range of Chinese and North Korean fighters. This plan would estimate the number of flights needed to meet intelligence requirements, how to provide reasonable protection, and the effect on intelligence collection if fewer reconnaissance flights could be protected. Laird mentioned no completion date for reviewing the CINCPAC plan. In addition, he apprised the president that he had initiated an even broader review to weigh the intelligence value of the flights against the risks involved before he would resume them. Despite Nixon's order to resume the flights, Laird ordered all unified or specified commanders, NSA, and DIA to evaluate by 30 April the risks and benefits of worldwide U.S. airborne reconnaissance programs, assessing the necessity of collecting intelligence, the frequency and number of missions, and the amount of protection needed.[48] On 24 April he forwarded to the president General Wheeler's conclusion that having four fighter-escorts accompany each reconnaissance mission "would be beyond the capability of currently assigned PACOM forces" and reduce strength in Vietnam.[49]

Aware that DoD had authorized only one reconnaissance mission between 18 and 24 April, Kissinger repeatedly pushed Laird to restart the flights. On 25 April he sent Laird the formal memorandum of the president's decision to resume scheduled reconnaissance flights along the China coast from the Gulf of Tonkin to the Sea of Okhotsk.[50] Laird, however, decided to delay approving the JCS plan. He wanted to consider alternate methods of collecting intelligence and examine the feasibility of using ships instead of aircraft to collect electronic intelligence, of reducing the requirement for collecting it from North Korea, and of using unmanned or high-flying aircraft to do the job. The secretary would delay resuming reconnaissance flights until the JCS and Defense Research and Engineering finished their examination.[51] Laird's moves, undertaken for plausible reasons, delayed reconnaissance flights for an indefinite period, in effect thwarting Nixon's order. On 28 April Kissinger brought up the China flights in a telephone conversation with the secretary, telling him to resume the China and Soviet Union flights, but to hold off on flights off Korea involving fighter escorts.[52]

Kissinger informed the president of Laird's actions in delaying the reconnaissance strikes in contravention of his stated policy. Kissinger pressed Nixon to call for immediate resumption of reconnaissance flights. The decision to stop the flights, Kissinger feared, had demonstrated to the North Koreans "the efficacy of their attack" and would encourage them to down another aircraft and might even embolden the Chinese to follow North Korea's example. Kissinger believed that standing down flights for more than two weeks "may already have encouraged the North Koreans." Ignoring three presidential orders to restart them signified to Kissinger a direct challenge by the secretary to the president's authority. To neutralize Laird's delaying tactics, Nixon had decided on 28 April that the 303 Committee, an interdepartmental body that reviewed and authorized covert operations, would take over from DoD the review of worldwide reconnaissance operations.[53] Established in 1955, the 303 Committee consisted of the president's assistant for national security affairs, the deputy secretary of defense, the deputy undersecretary of state for political affairs, and the director of central intelligence. The secretary of defense was not a member. Giving the 303 Committee authority to review reconnaissance programs would allow Kissinger as committee head to control the process, hasten the resumption of flights, and, in Haig's words, end the "unilateral action which caused the standdown of reconnaissance activity."[54]

Kissinger's frustration with his inability to curb Laird's independence and to convince Nixon to act more quickly led him to have the president institutionalize the small ad hoc interagency group that Kissinger established to handle the EC–121 crisis. This panel, which Kissinger chaired, became the Washington Special Actions Group and would convene in the future to coordinate the administration's response to crises. Members included Vice Admiral Nels Johnson, CIA Deputy Director for Plans Thomas H. Karamessines, Under Secretary of State Alexis Johnson, and Assistant Secretary of Defense Nutter. Johonson and Nutter thought the WSAG worked well and represented a workable mechanism for dealing with crises.[55]

Decision making in response to North Korea's attack on the EC–121 proceeded slowly and needed improvement, according to Kissinger. The delay stemmed from serious disagreements over policy, the political and military risks involved, and insufficient resources. Laird's unilateral decision to halt reconnaissance flights frustrated Kissinger. Both Laird and Kissinger knew it would be difficult to retaliate militarily without resuming the flights. Behind the scenes the president expressed determination to take action but wound up choosing what he had called in private the "piddly" action of restarting reconnaissance flights. He was checked by the strong opposition of Rogers and Laird, and also by the realization that the nation lacked the military resources to pursue simultaneously wars in Korea and in Vietnam. Moreover, retaliation might jeopardize passage of his legislative agenda, especially the ABM program.[56]

Members of the committee that Kissinger set up to deal with the EC–121 episode quickly became aware of the scarcity of military resources. Karamessines made this point clear: "It is an eye-opener to some of us to learn that a retaliatory strike, if it had been ordered to take place within 24 hours of the shoot down of our plane, would have been practically impossible unless it were to be launched from South Korean-based planes; and political as well as military considerations obviously made this inadvisable." Alexis Johnson reached a similar conclusion, noting that Washington's choice of options in the crisis was "very limited by the absence of a military capability quickly to respond."[57] As the JCS reported, logistic resources in theater were insufficient to simultaneously prosecute the war in Vietnam, modernize the South Vietnamese Army, and prepare for possible conflict in Korea. The shrinking DoD budget and the extent of America's existing military commitments limited the administration's options. How to make the best use of limited and shrinking defense resources remained a problem that vexed the administration and over time continued to strain relations between Kissinger and Laird.

Defense Program Review Committee

In furthering the new system to formulate national security policy, the Nixon administration set up a number of formal groups under Kissinger's direction, among them the Verification Panel for arms control established in July 1969 and the Vietnam Special Studies Group set up in September 1969. The most consequential of these bodies for DoD was the Defense Program Review Committee (DPRC), which operated at the deputy and undersecretary level. Deputy Secretary of Defense Packard, Under Secretary of State Elliot Richardson, CIA Director Helms, Director of the Bureau of the Budget Robert P. Mayo, and JCS Chairman General Wheeler served as permanent members. Kissinger chaired the committee. Laird and Rogers were not members. Kissinger outlined for Nixon a sweeping role for the DPRC: evaluate the "diplomatic, military and political consequences" of changes in the Defense budget and programs, U.S. overseas force deployments, tactical nuclear weapons deployment, and policy and program issues raised by NSSMs. Some of these areas came under Laird's jurisdiction. Nixon approved the establishment of the DPRC on 17 September 1969 (NSDM 26).[58]

From the start, Laird and Kissinger had conflicting views about the role of the committee, which under Kissinger's conception, could in effect place much of the secretary of defense's efforts under Kissinger's review and give him a more intrusive role in formulating and monitoring the Defense budget. Differences between Laird and Kissinger over the role of the DPRC proved difficult to resolve. To provide the president with choices, Laird thought the DPRC should analyze projected DoD budgets and possible trade-offs between defense and other spending. He noted that national security studies failed to analyze the availability of resources to meet requirements. The secretary hoped the DPRC would assess the costs of security commitments; relate government expenditures to the overall level of national resources; and "help to array for the President the various benefits and costs of higher, and lower, National Security budgets."[59]

Kissinger explained his rationale for establishing the DPRC in his memoirs: to prevent Laird from making budget cuts unilaterally. Under pressure from the White House and Congress to cut FY 1970 defense spending by $5 billion, Laird had decided on his own in September 1969, according to Kissinger, to reduce U.S. support of NATO. Kissinger viewed Laird's action as a tactic to forestall deeper congressional DoD cuts and to stimulate greater support from NATO nations.[60] Yet Kissinger seemed to slight the legitimate grounds that Laird had for his move—a real budget problem to which he had alerted Kissinger on 5 September 1969, citing the need to reduce U.S. naval forces committed to NATO and to inform the alliance. Laird also cautioned that further decreases in U.S. commitments to NATO should the FY 1970 budget review, then under way, lead to additional defense spending cuts.[61]

Kissinger consistently viewed the DPRC as a means for his office to influence the Defense budget. When the committee was still under consideration, Laurence E. Lynn Jr., one of Kissinger's analysts who had served as deputy assistant secretary of defense for systems analysis in the Johnson administration, told Kissinger on 10 September that the review committee should establish guidelines to prevent Laird or Budget Director Mayo from taking unilateral action. Having the DPRC exercise control over the DoD program, Lynn acknowledged, "may create real problems with Mel Laird, who stands to lose a great deal of his potential power as Secretary of Defense."[62]

Endorsing Lynn's proposal, Kissinger presented it to Nixon on 17 September as a way to carry out the president's wish "that resolution of major defense strategy and program issues must no longer be the result of 'treaties' negotiated between DOD and BOB [Bureau of the Budget] or compromises struck among the military services." The DPRC represented an alternative to a process that Nixon disliked. In the summer of 1969, DoD and the Budget Bureau argued over how to reduce defense spending for FY 1970, forcing Nixon "to referee disputes over specific line items and dollar amounts without any idea of the implications of his decisions." To "prevent a situation in which inter-service logrolling and compromising among the chiefs was the basis for the defense posture," Nixon wanted to stop the bargaining between DoD and BoB. He preferred the method described in the NSSM 3 study of U.S. military posture and strategies for strategic and general purpose forces. That review disclosed trade-offs between defense and domestic spending for a five-year period, allowing Nixon to decide on a defense strategy and take into account its impact on defense and domestic spending.[63]

At Laird's request, Nixon removed from the final version of the DPRC charter the authority to look at the deployment of tactical nuclear weapons. Invoking his original conception of the DPRC as a group that would look at the interaction of domestic and defense policy, Laird also wanted the committee's efforts broadened to encompass the economic consequences of changes in DoD programs, in addition to diplomatic, political, and military consequences. He requested Paul W. McCracken, chairman of the Council of Economic Advisers, to serve on the committee and help assess the domestic economic impact of the DoD program. Nixon agreed, and on 11 October he signed the revised NSDM 26 setting up the Defense Program Review Committee.[64]

That same day Nixon approved another measure that enhanced DPRC power. NSDM 27, the outgrowth of NSSM 3, specified a significant role for the DPRC in reviewing the Defense budget and program, establishing dollar ceilings on DoD budget outlays for a five-year period, and requiring DoD to submit to the committee every September a Five-Year Force and Program Plan (including overseas deployments) with a rationale for each force category. Nixon directed the DPRC to review proposed changes in the Five-Year Force and Program Plan, due on 15 January 1970, "prior to consideration by the President and the National Security Council." NSDM 27, which Kissinger signed for the president, clearly put consideration of the DoD program and budget within the orbit of the DPRC.[65]

Laird refused to cooperate, telling the service secretaries at the end of October that the DPRC would concentrate on high-level military, political, and economic issues requiring a presidential decision. He insisted that the DPRC was "not established to monitor" DoD internal operations, programs, or budgeting. DoD would continue to develop programs and make decisions through its customary procedures.[66]

Laird's resistance to the DPRC put him on a collision course with the White House. In background papers preparing Kissinger for the first DPRC meeting on 22 October, Lynn laid out an expansive role for the committee. It would consider changes that DoD proposed in its Five-Year Force and Program Plan, examine changes in budgetary planning assumptions and budget level guidelines, and take up subjects such as the role of nuclear weapons in Europe and Asia. To keep Mayo from bringing defense issues directly to the president, Lynn wanted him to come before the DPRC, which would appraise the relative merits of Laird's and Mayo's positions. Kissinger as DPRC chairman would then frame the issues for Nixon. With Kissinger in the chair, the DPRC would constitute a layer between the president on the one hand and Laird and Mayo on the other, sparing the president of having personally to resolve disagreements on specific issues between Defense and the Budget Bureau. At the first meeting of the DPRC in October, Kissinger stressed that point, stating that Nixon did not want to arbitrate budget issues on a line-by-line basis.[67]

Laird continued to stand fast. In November Lynn warned Kissinger that DoD was using delaying tactics to thwart the DPRC. Indeed it was. Packard wanted to wait until December before providing information on key program issues to the DPRC, a holdup that would effectively preclude the DPRC from timely examination of those issues. By the time Packard was ready to address the substance of force program issues in the DPRC, Lynn feared, discussions on the FY 1970 Defense budget would have ended. Laird claimed at the end of November that the department had not yet identified the political, economic, and military issues the DPRC should review and that it was premature to decide on a detailed format for the Five Year Force and Program Plan.[68]

Wrangling over the DPRC went on through the remainder of 1969. Laird continued to contend that the committee should concern itself with major decisions about the allocation of resources and not delve into such traditional DoD business as assessing individual weapon systems or regional force levels. In early December, Laird reiterated his proposal that the DPRC consider DoD spending in the context of the entire federal budget and examine the balance between security commitments and the resources available to carry them out. In projecting outlays for FY 1972, he told Kissinger, the DPRC should be the forum for taking a broader look at revenue and economic projections and the administration's programs than BoB "can provide by itself." Lynn termed Laird's views "a flat rejection of both the spirit and the letter" of the decision to establish the committee. Haig characterized the secretary's guidance as "a stonewall position." He urged Kissinger to settle the dispute, warning of a "complete collapse of our relationships" with DoD. Unless the impasse was resolved, he feared that the DPRC would "remain stillborn."[69]

Kissinger and Laird met on 11 December to discuss the DPRC, but no record of the meeting has been found. Neither man was inclined to compromise. In preparation for the meeting, Lynn advised Kissinger that Laird, still not cooperating with the NSC, was "trying to get the DPRC off his back and divert you to fighting with Mayo, Treasury, and the Council of Economic Advisers over national priorities and the size of the defense budget." Lynn also asserted that the Pentagon's Offices of Systems Analysis and International Security Affairs had failed to comply fully with NSSMs and had failed to cooperate with the DPRC. Moreover, DoD had failed to put forth its best efforts when responding to NSC or interagency requests for studies.[70]

OSD viewed the situation differently. Packard complained that the large number of ongoing NSSMs and requests for country program budgets "heavily overburdened" the department. He had "strong reservations" about the number, timing, and the probable quality of the required studies.[71]

With no resolution in sight, at the end of December Kissinger urged Nixon to tell Laird at the 24 December budget meeting that the DPRC would, in fact, study a number of items such as procurement, the manned strategic bomber, and antisubmarine aircraft carriers. Indeed, force structure issues, such as brigades in Alaska, carrier force levels, and amphibious forces, and how they affected the DoD budget would be on the table, even though these issues clearly fell under the secretary's traditional purview. Kissinger advised Nixon to have Laird and Wheeler comment on the impact of the BoB proposals "for therapeutic and bureaucratic reasons," but defer making decisions until later.[72]

Kissinger made another attempt to put the Defense budget under the DPRC in February 1970, appointing Lynn as chairman of the DPRC Working Group to perform staff work and oversee the preparation of studies for the DPRC. Laird, however, insisted that Assistant Secretary of Defense for Systems Analysis Gardiner Tucker serve as chairman, since DoD would produce most of the studies for the DPRC. Tucker had become assistant secretary on 30 January, replacing the acting director, Ivan Selin. Laird added pointedly that Tucker's appointment as chair was necessary "if the Working Group is to be maintained." Kissinger agreed to have Tucker chair most of the studies done by the working group. Laird again asserted that the DPRC should focus on the allocation of government resources within the economy. It should not be "distracted from this role by lesser issues such as the future role of strategic bombers, requirements for aircraft carriers, and continental air defense." Choosing his words carefully, Laird alluded to his authority as a cabinet officer. "After the President has decided upon strategies and resources for defense, I believe it is my responsibility to provide the forces which implement these decisions."[73] Haig cautioned Kissinger: "I think Laird is more right than we are." Haig reminded Kissinger that Laird highlighted the larger problem of setting priorities for domestic and national security spending and the way in which the growth in domestic spending reduced the funds available for defense.[74]

Kissinger did not back down. At the end of March 1970 he asked Nixon to settle the dispute, arguing that the "DPRC must analyze major DOD policy and program issues well in advance of the final budget review." Endorsing Kissinger's position, the president decided on 2 April that the DPRC should analyze such issues when the DoD program was in its "formative stages, well in advance of the final review" of the budget in December. He wanted the DPRC to prepare a series of studies on the nation's military posture.[75]

Philip A. Odeen, director of the NSC program analysis staff, called this development "a critical first step in our efforts to get better control over the Defense program." However, Nixon's decision did not make OSD or the JCS more cooperative. Although the deputy secretary regularly participated in DPRC meetings, the department waited until February 1972 to present its first five-year program to the DPRC as required by NDSM 27. The Office of Management and Budget (OMB) director, George Shultz, only submitted his office's five-year program information on federal revenues and spending that month. Mayo had previously refused to provide this information to the DPRC because he was unwilling to relinquish control of traditional budget processes to the committee out of concern that it might weaken his prerogatives as director.[76]

With two key agencies resisting the DPRC, it was not surprising that committee meetings did little more than lay out agency positions. The State Department representative, Assistant Secretary for Politico-Military Affairs Ronald I. Spiers, expressed disappointment that the DPRC accomplished little. The working group, which met infrequently, was unproductive. He alleged that DoD's opposition to the DPRC prevented the committee from being an "effective management tool" for the president.[77] He wondered "what the ultimate value of that forum will be," with the "infrequency of the meetings and the resistance of the Pentagon to bringing many major policy issues into the DPRC."[78]

Laird's intransigence and his refusal to cede management of the DoD budget weakened the DPRC. He thought it desirable to know the long-term fiscal impact of incremental increases in domestic programs on DoD programs and the trade-offs between the two. Numerous domestic programs that granted large numbers of citizens benefits from entitlement programs represented spending that was difficult to restrain and constituted a growing claim on the Treasury. In contrast, Congress could control defense spending through legislation or the president could do it by administrative action. Like Haig, Lynn conceded that Laird had raised the important point, lamenting the lack of "widespread recognition of the need to examine systematically and in advance the total problem and the issues that must be resolved in setting priorities and allocating funds."[79]

Trying to Fix Intelligence

In the years since the National Security Act of 1947 had institutionalized intelligence as a function of the federal government, the expanding role of the United States as a global power brought about substantial growth in the number, size, and cost of intelligence entities, particularly in the Department of Defense. With growth came difficulties in coordinating the efforts of the many intelligence organizations operating during the Vietnam War. The passage of time brought innovations and changes. The act had not anticipated the problem of how to manage the collection of intelligence from new technical sources and a multiplicity of agencies. For good reason, intelligence reform engaged the new administration. Nixon, Laird, and Kissinger all weighed in heavily in the sometimes heated debate over how to fix intelligence.[80]

The need for change had been apparent well before the Blue Ribbon Defense Panel convened, leading Laird to assign Assistant Secretary for Administration

Robert Froehlke the additional duty of special assistant for intelligence. Laird tasked him to create a plan to improve the intelligence decision-making process and to facilitate communications on intelligence matters within DoD and between DoD and other agencies. Under the existing arrangement, no high-level official other than the secretary had authority to speak for the whole department when dealing with nondefense agencies. The Pentagon had no central control of intelligence below the secretary. The military services operated their own intelligence agencies and opposed centralized management, insisting that they had to control the collection and analysis of tactical intelligence to conduct successful military operations, and to be sure that they had the information they needed when and where they needed it. NSA and DIA did not control the activities of the service-operated components reporting to them. NSA, for example, could not direct the cryptological activities of the services. Laird's initiative to improve the intelligence decision-making process became part of the larger debate about intelligence reform that culminated with the creation in 1972 of the position of assistant secretary of defense for intelligence.[81]

In July 1970 Nixon expressed to the President's Foreign Intelligence Advisory Board (PFIAB) his dissatisfaction with the intelligence community, citing faulty estimates of the amount of enemy material flowing through the port of Sihanoukville, Cambodia, into South Vietnam and inaccurate estimates of Soviet efforts to build an ABM system.[82] In addition to the high cost of gathering and analyzing intelligence, which Nixon deplored, the organization and management of both civilian and military intelligence agencies needed to be improved, according to the White House. The director of central intelligence, the *de jure* leader of the intelligence community, had difficulty carrying out the overall function because of other responsibilities. He ran the CIA and its collection programs, planned covert operations, and served as intelligence adviser to the president. As an agency head the director competed with other organizations for resources. The secretaries of cabinet-level departments with intelligence programs, such as Defense and State, outranked him.[83]

Eager to overhaul the intelligence system and reduce costs, at the end of November 1970 Nixon told Kissinger he wanted "a good thinning down" of U.S. intelligence activities generally and that Richard Helms could remain as DCI "only on condition that there be a thorough housecleaning at other levels at CIA." In mid-December 1970 Nixon requested a study on how to reshape the process of gathering and analyzing intelligence. Andrew W. Marshall, an analyst at the RAND Corporation, and

President Nixon in the Oval Office with James Schlesinger (center) and Alexander Haig, Kissinger's deputy, January 1972. Schlesinger, author of a study on intelligence reform, held several positions in the Office of Management and Budget and later became secretary of defense. (Nixon Presidential Library)

OMB Assistant Director James R. Schlesinger, a former RAND analyst, directed the study. Nixon's goal was "a real shakeup in C.I.A., not just symbolism."[84]

The OMB report to Nixon in March 1971 presented three organizational options for the president. In the first, a powerful director of national intelligence would control all major collection programs and research and development activities and assume control of many DoD intelligence functions. DoD would remain in charge only of selected tactical collection missions under this option, which required legislative sanction. A director of central intelligence possessing a stronger presidential mandate was the second option. The DCI would be authorized to prepare for OMB review a consolidated intelligence budget but would no longer be obligated to exercise the daily management responsibilities of the CIA. Under this arrangement, the director would have to rely on persuasion and budgetary review rather than a specified grant of authority to eliminate duplicative programs. Option two required no legislation. The third option—a coordinator of national intelligence—would leave essentially unchanged the responsibilities of CIA, Defense, and State.[85] As the entity with the most at stake DoD preferred the status quo and the appointment of an assistant secretary for intelligence to manage defense intelligence resources. State and CIA wanted to boost the DCI's management authority over the intelligence community and strengthen his control of defense resources.[86]

Schlesinger also recommended centralizing DoD's control of intelligence under a director of defense intelligence (DDI), with the authority to allocate resources, including those involving tactical intelligence, and to reorganize the defense collection effort. The ASD(I) would be a staff assistant to the secretary but would exercise no control over defense intelligence collection.[87]

On 5 November 1971 the president announced his decision, choosing the second option—a stronger role for the DCI. His statement took Laird, DCI Helms, and Congress by surprise and caused hard feelings. On 9 November Laird heatedly contended that Kissinger had "pulled a trick" by not informing him of the impending changes. Kissinger said he thought that OMB had discussed them with Laird and Congress. Laird complained that OMB's failure to consult would create problems and cause some legislators to vent their anger when he testified before Congress. "They're so god-damned mad," Laird twice blurted out during the conversation. This dereliction in advising Congress forced Kissinger to call Senators Stuart Symington (D–MO) and William Fulbright to apologize for the foul-up.[88]

Nixon's reforms sought to achieve better intelligence reporting, more efficiency in using resources, and stronger leadership of the entire intelligence community. Selecting Schlesinger's second option, the president wanted the DCI to assume overall leadership of the intelligence community and delegate to his deputy the day-to-day management of the CIA. Under the president's charge, the DCI would lead the planning, reviewing, coordinating, and evaluating of all intelligence programs and activities, and the production of national intelligence. At the heart of Nixon's decision was the grant of authority for the DCI to create a consolidated intelligence program budget that included tactical intelligence. All departments and agencies, including DoD, were to submit information to the DCI, who was required to provide the president an annual detailed review of the needs and performance of the entire intelligence community. In addition, Nixon expected Helms to provide chairmen and staffs for all intelligence advisory boards and committees and reconcile requirements with budgetary constraints.[89]

Nixon's decision involved significant changes in handling and organizing DoD intelligence. No later than 1 January 1972, Laird was to establish a unified national cryptologic command under the director of NSA for conducting both communications and electronic intelligence; a single office of defense investigations; and a consolidated defense cartographic agency that combined the mapping organizations of the services. DIA was to "be fully responsive to tasking" by the JCS in providing intelligence support for military planning and operations.[90]

In November 1971 Laird announced the intelligence reorganization. The position of assistant secretary of defense for administration was redesignated assistant secretary of defense for intelligence (ASD[I]). The new office assumed all functions and personnel previously assigned to the Office of the Deputy Assistant Secretary for Intelligence. The DoD comptroller took over the nonintelligence administrative functions of the assistant secretary for administration. There would be no DDI. Albert C. Hall, a vice president of the Martin Marietta Corporation, became the first ASD(I). In addition, planning would begin to establish a National Cryptologic Command within the National Security Agency.[91]

The specific duties of the ASD(I) were spelled out in January 1972 in DoD Directive 5115.1. The ASD(I) had no authority to control or direct operations, but could issue instructions "for carrying out approved policies and for establishing management procedures" to the military departments through the service secretaries. Among other functions, he could coordinate DoD intelligence activities and coordinate with other government agencies; recommend improvements in the management of intelligence resources; and recommend requirements and priorities for net threat assessments. The assistant secretary could also communicate directly with the military department secretaries, the JCS, the commanders of unified and specified commands, and the directors of defense agencies.[92]

Although the ASD(I) had no control of military intelligence operations or personnel and the services continued to run their own intelligence offices, some officials nonetheless felt the directive centralized too much authority at the top. Air Force Secretary Seamans complained to Laird that the directive seemed "to run counter to the changed environment of delegated authority which you brought to the DoD." He believed the charter would make difficult the "meaningful participation by other members of the DoD intelligence structure."[93]

The president also created within the National Security Council staff a net assessment group to evaluate all intelligence products and produce net appraisals of U.S. capabilities to meet threats to the nation's security. Andrew Marshall headed the new group. Likewise, the Fitzhugh panel had recommended establishing a net assessment office in DoD to make comparative assessments of United States and foreign military capabilities. Laird set up the Office of Net Assessment in November 1971 under Assistant Secretary Hall, and Marshall moved in 1973 from the NSC to the Pentagon to head the office. [94]

The effort to "fix" intelligence, although it brought organizational changes, could not be regarded as fully successful. The sought after cooperation and coordination and clear lines of authority existed more in theory than in practice. The problem continued to plague succeeding administrations for decades. Several months after instituting intelligence reform, Nixon still remained dissatisfied with the intelligence system. During a stressful time for the administration, North Vietnam's Easter Offensive in May 1972, Nixon wrote a mean-spirited, vindictive memorandum to his chief of staff manifesting his disdain for the CIA. He thought the agency needed a "housecleaning" because its "muscle-bound bureaucracy" had "completely paralyzed its brain."[95]

Assistant Secretary of Defense for Intelligence Albert Hall (right), with Secretary Laird and Director of Central Intelligence Richard Helms (center), 9 November 1971. (Department of Defense)

Private Channels

As part of their effort to consolidate policymaking in the White House, Nixon and Kissinger used private communication channels extensively in order to exclude departmental officials, particularly Rogers and Laird at times, from sensitive discussions. Regularly established channels remained in use, but some substantive matters were taken up and resolved in private channels. Kissinger's secret peace negotiations with Le Duc Tho, a senior member of Hanoi's politburo, which began in February 1970, constituted one such channel. While representatives of the United States, South Vietnam, North Vietnam, and the National Liberation Front (Viet Cong) held formal talks on ending the war at a public building in Paris, Kissinger and Le Duc Tho secretly engaged in one-on-one talks in the Parisian suburbs. State Department officials only learned of these sessions, which led to settlement of the war, when Nixon disclosed their existence on 25 January 1972.

In mid-February 1969, at Nixon's behest, Kissinger established a private channel to the Soviet ambassador to the United States, Anatoly Dobrynin. Nixon authorized direct communication between the ambassador and his security adviser. Believing that Dobrynin "might be more forthcoming in strictly private and unpublicized meetings," Nixon arranged for him to arrive at the White House secretly. The president felt that the sessions with Dobrynin, from which Nixon excluded Secretary Rogers, furthered his policy of linkage, tying progress on one issue, such as Soviet assistance in helping reach a Vietnam settlement, with progress on other issues, such as better relations with the Soviets. Kissinger and Dobrynin also came to conduct strategic arms limitation negotiations secretly, without the knowledge of the president's publicly appointed representative at the talks, Gerard C. Smith, director of the Arms Control and Disarmament Agency (ACDA).[96]

Kissinger established similar undisclosed means of communications with the U.S. ambassador to South Vietnam, Ellsworth Bunker, and a related one through Bunker to General Abrams, the U.S. commander in Vietnam. Kissinger, Bunker, and Abrams would use this channel to discuss sensitive aspects of the peace negotiations, Bunker's private meetings with South Vietnam's President Nguyen Van Thieu, planning for some military operations, and information on U.S. troop withdrawals that Nixon or Kissinger did not want to share with Laird or Rogers.[97]

Upon taking office, Laird endeavored to ensure that all communications from the White House and NSC came through his office. He sought to stop the use of private channels between the Pentagon and the president's office, a step his military assistant, Colonel Pursley, reflecting on his experience serving McNamara and Clifford, strongly advised Laird to take.[98] On 22 January 1969 the secretary directed General Wheeler and Nutter to forward all official communications to the NSC or Kissinger through his office. Within OSD, he designated Nutter as the central point of contact for the secretary and the deputy secretary for NSC matters. To help ensure a single DoD position, Laird required the Office of International Security Affairs and the JCS to coordinate a joint talking paper for each item on the NSC agenda.[99] He reiterated his concerns in June 1969 after the president's science adviser, Lee A. DuBridge, directly contacted General Wheeler for assistance. Laird asked that in the future DuBridge make requests to DoD using prescribed procedures. He wrote Wheeler of his misgivings about the White House staff establishing "separate and varied channels to the Department. I believe we both risk losing a measure of control and risk serious misdirection on key matters if such channels get started."[100]

Laird also asked Kissinger to route all official communications to DoD from the NSC and its staff through the Office of the Secretary of Defense. Kissinger agreed in principle, but demurred on the JCS, because it had become customary for the national security adviser to deal directly with the Joint Chiefs on some issues. Their statutory role as military advisers to the president entitled the Chiefs direct access to the White House.[101] Aware of the White House private communications channels, Laird reiterated his policy in September 1969, directing the service secretaries, the JCS chairman, the director of defense research and engineering, the assistant secretaries of defense, the assistants to the secretary, and the directors of defense agencies not to carry out requests or orders from the White House until the secretary or deputy secretary of defense had checked out the order.[102]

Despite Laird's objections, the White House staff directly contacted DoD officials even more frequently, prompting Laird in March 1971 to ask Nixon to reaffirm the president's guidance that the president or Kissinger would communicate directly with him on defense and national security policy matters. A single point of contact in the White House would channel all communications through a single point of contact at the Pentagon, Carl Wallace, Laird's special assistant. Nixon agreed.[103]

Still, the White House wanted to ensure that it heard the military's views on policy issues directly and independently. In December 1969 Nixon and Kissinger discussed in a phone conversation how to get Wheeler more directly and privately involved in policy discussions. Asserting that Laird sometimes delayed sending the chairman's memos for the president to the White House, Kissinger wanted Nixon to have unfiltered access to JCS views, without Laird's knowledge. Kissinger proposed "to work out through Haig that Wheeler will give us copies of memos addressed to P[resident]." Nixon agreed, responding "we should bring him in on these discussions." This procedure contradicted an earlier arrangement between Laird and Kissinger wherein Kissinger agreed to inform Laird whenever the president asked him to call Wheeler.[104] Nixon had no intention of keeping his defense secretary knowledgeable about all of his contacts with the JCS chairman. In November 1971, months after Moorer became chairman, the president told Kissinger "to find an occasion where we can get Moorer in alone with me without Laird to talk about national defense matters." This was not an isolated instance.[105]

THE PATTERNS OF BEHAVIOR that would characterize the Nixon administration were evident at its start. Nixon wanted to hold sway over national security policy, empowering Kissinger in NSDM 2 to do that on his behalf. For his part, Kissinger sought to enhance his power by using the DPRC to oversee the defense program and by setting up other bodies, such as WSAG, to ensure a dominant role for himself in policy formulation. The communication and negotiating channels for the exclusive use of the White House also reflected Nixon's intention to control policymaking and his distrust of the bureaucracy.

Looking back at the NSC system that he helped design, General Goodpaster was critical of its operation, concluding that Kissinger used it to make himself a center of power, an independent source of advice and action. He later observed, "I think that the setup was essentially right under President Nixon, but it served to increase the power and authority of that special assistant to an undue degree."[106]

NSDM 2, the DPRC, and the WSAG were intended in part to restrict the roles of Rogers and Laird in the new administration, but the secretary of defense fought attempts to delimit his responsibilities in setting the DoD budget and program. He persisted in his efforts to ensure that all communications from the White House came through his office, proving adept in keeping the DPRC at arm's length from the DoD budget. A forceful, independent voice during the EC–121 episode, Laird opposed military retaliation and questioned the intelligence value of reconnaissance programs that put the military in harm's way. Over the course of Nixon's first term, the administration would have to deal with major complex national security issues, such as Vietnam, ending the draft, and the ABM. It became evident from these early episodes that Laird intended to play a significant role in shaping national security policy. He would perform cleverly and effectively as the champion of DoD interests.

CHAPTER 3

How Much for Defense?
The FY 1970 Budget

ON ASSUMING OFFICE in January 1969, Laird immediately had to deal with the FY 1970 Department of Defense budget proposal prepared by outgoing Secretary of Defense Clark Clifford. Reflecting the political, economic, and social problems inflicted by the Vietnam War, the budget had to be considered in the context of a host of commanding issues that would persist throughout Laird's tenure as secretary. These larger issues—inflation, balance of payments, strains in the NATO alliance, social unrest, political and popular opposition to the war, the demands of the Great Society for funds—had shaped the projected DoD budget. By 1968 the Southeast Asia conflict, looming ever larger, devoured roughly one-third of Pentagon disbursements.[1]

The battle over the FY 1970 budget constituted the opening engagement of an ongoing fight over the defense program that continued through Laird's tenure. The new secretary would have little time to review or modify Clifford's FY 1970 budget before presenting it to Congress. Economic issues and a political climate less favorable for military spending made it more difficult for Laird to gain the funds he deemed necessary to provide an adequate national defense in the near term and to lay the foundation for a robust military force after the Vietnam War ended.

Laird's Inheritance

On 16 January 1969 President Lyndon Johnson submitted his final economic report to the Senate, lauding his stewardship of the economy. By Johnson's reckoning, the nation's economic output during his presidency had risen nearly 30 percent; over 8.5 million additional workers had found jobs; the overall unemployment rate had fallen to 3.3 percent; and corporate profits, wages, and salaries had climbed by approximately 50 percent each. Johnson took credit for converting a federal budget deficit into an anticipated surplus of $2.3 billion for FY 1969 and an even larger surplus of more than $3 billion for FY 1970. His generally upbeat report refrained from assessing the effect of the Vietnam War on the federal budget or the economy. Johnson blamed inflation on the "excessive and inappropriate stimulus of the Federal budget in late 1967 and the first half of 1968," without mentioning the war.[2]

Before leaving office Johnson sought to reduce defense spending in his proposed FY 1970 budget. The department had set its estimates of FY 1970 expenditures (or outlays) at $79.5 billion, but that remained half a billion dollars above the president's target. Because there was no way to predict them accurately, expenditures had to be estimated. Expenditure ceilings prescribed the total amount of money that DoD could actually spend during the fiscal year from all of its accounts to pay for goods, services, and personnel. FY 1970 expenditures would also include payments for some goods and services contracted for in prior years. Some outlays would be made under budget authority enacted before FY 1970.[3]

Then-BoB Director Charles J. Zwick suggested that Johnson cut spending for a number of weapon and equipment programs (shipbuilding, Poseidon submarine, Sentinel antiballistic missile, and the F–14), military construction, and military personnel. The cuts would result in a cumulative reduction of more than $1.1 billion in expenditures. Zwick also emphasized the savings that would result from a slowdown in the tempo of operations in Vietnam. Consumption of ammunition and supplies would drop and military personnel could return home.[4]

Secretary Clifford, however, had formulated no plans to withdraw U.S. forces from Vietnam in 1969 and opposed Zwick's suggested cuts. In September 1968 he testified before a congressional subcommittee that DoD would continue to build toward the personnel ceiling of 549,500 in South Vietnam. He had "no intention of lowering that level, either by next June or at any time in the foreseeable future."[5] Clifford explicitly assumed "for budget purposes" that combat operations would continue at current levels throughout FY 1970.[6]

JCS Chairman General Earle Wheeler feared Zwick's budget reductions could diminish the military's capability to cope with threats to national security, such as the growing numbers of Soviet land- and sea-based strategic missiles and improved air defenses, especially the increasing deployment of ABMs. The effect of diminished readiness on the ability of U.S. general purpose forces to reinforce NATO adequately or to respond to contingencies also worried him. Of additional concern, the Improvement and Modernization (I&M) Program for South Vietnam's armed forces would divert equipment from U.S. units and thus further lower their readiness.[7] Clifford supported Wheeler and urged the president to keep the projected expenditure level at $79.5 billion for FY 1970, terming the budget "very austere."[8]

Clifford's plea went unheeded. For FY 1970, Johnson set expenditures at $79 billion and New Obligational Authority (NOA) at $80.6 billion. NOA represented the authority to incur obligations in the expenditure account. These were the funds Congress authorized the Treasury to deposit into various accounts such as procurement, operations and maintenance, and personnel for each military service. NOA was the maximum amount that could be drawn upon for spending within an account. NOA would cover the full estimated cost at the start of a project, for example, the development and procurement of a major weapon system, but the actual outlays of money would occur over a period of years until the program reached completion.[9] Johnson's budget (see table 1, page 64), submitted to Congress on 15 January 1969, constituted the starting point for the Nixon administration's efforts to formulate its own FY 1970 DoD budget. For most of 1969 the new president, his national security adviser, budget director, secretary of defense, and other DoD officials would discuss appropriations and expenditures, continually adjusting the numbers. Contrary to Johnson's effusive rhetoric about his economic stewardship, the incoming administration would have to contend with inflation, the falling value of the dollar, and a serious U.S. balance of payments deficit, in addition to a costly and unpopular war.[10]

Economic and Political Realities

Strains in the economy—the growing cost of Lyndon Johnson's Great Society programs and an increasingly expensive war competing for federal spending—shaped the environment for Nixon's policies and the DoD budget. U.S. involvement in the Vietnam War contributed to a growing rate of inflation. From 1958 to 1965, before the United States committed combat units to Vietnam, consumer prices had stayed relatively stable, rising an average of 1.3 percent annually. From 1965 to January 1969, as U.S. participation in the war expanded and spending on social welfare programs grew, the consumer price index shot up more than 14 points. Inflation for March, April, and May 1969 reached an alarming annual rate of 7.2 percent, reducing purchasing power for wage earners and raising costs for new weapons and equipment.[11]

Table 1. Johnson's DoD Budget Request, FY 1970 ($ millions)

Category	Outlays	NOA
Military Personnel	24,164	24,384
Operations & Maintenance (O&M)	21,841	21,941
Procurement	23,435	23,241
RDT&E	7,805	8,174
Military Construction	1,370	1,949
Family Housing	625	618
Civil Defense	72	75
Revolving & Management Funds	(690)	
Military Trust Funds	1	7
Offsetting Receipts	(152)	(152)
Subtotal	78,471	80,237
Military Assistance	529	408
Total	79,000	80,645

Source: BoB, *The Budget of the United States Government, Fiscal Year 1970* (Washington, DC: Government Printing Office, 1969), 73.

The FY 1970 DoD budget took shape not only at a time of economic stress but also at a time of changing public and congressional attitudes and a mounting antiwar political climate. Many expected the new president to extricate the United States from Vietnam. Public opinion, soured by the long conflict, even questioned the value of non-Vietnam defense programs and spending. Four years of costly, inconclusive combat in Vietnam also affected the mood in Congress; the new administration anticipated closer congressional scrutiny of the DoD budget. In March Senator George D. Aiken (R–VT) asserted that DoD "has been running hog wild." Senate Majority Leader Michael J. "Mike" Mansfield (D–MT) stated the country needed "to achieve a balance somehow between external security and internal insecurity," declaring that "the days of the Defense Department asking and receiving are over." Some critics citing the so-called military-industrial complex were certain the Pentagon had become too closely tied to defense industries. Many legislators hoped that the end of the war would free up funds and result in a peace dividend that could be used for social programs. The incoming secretary of defense could not simply invoke the mantra of national security and expect an automatic endorsement of his budget request.[12]

The size of the department's budget (over 40 percent of all federal outlays in FY 1968),[13] the accumulating cost of the war, and the hue and cry to redress social grievances made the military budget the obvious source of additional money for domestic programs and the prime target for cuts. In FY 1968, DoD spending represented about 69 percent of federal outlays other than those of the various entitlement programs mandated by law. Congress could reduce military spending through the normal budget process without having to enact new or repeal old legislation. Domestic programs with open-ended and increasing entitlements had first claim on revenues. Spending on these programs grew more quickly than revenues, raising the specter of chronic deficits and insufficient funding for new programs.[14]

The new administration also faced rising costs for military programs delayed or deferred by the need to finance the ongoing war. Aging ships, tanks, and planes needed replacement. Depleted reserves of bombs, ammunition, communications gear, and other materiel consumed in Vietnam required replenishing. The services also wanted to develop and buy new arms and equipment. *U.S. News & World Report* estimated the total amount of deferred spending on weapon projects at $100 billion, and the *New York Times* reported that the JCS wanted $20 billion–$30 billion more in spending than Secretary Clifford had requested for FY 1970. The new administration also had to keep track of recent developments that could imperil U.S. security: the Soviet strategic missile buildup and the expanding Soviet naval presence in the Mediterranean Sea, Indian Ocean, and Norwegian Sea.[15]

After 1968 rising personnel costs (civilian and military) took a growing proportion of DoD funds. Greater spending on pay and benefits left fewer dollars for R&D and procurement. In 1967 Congress mandated that the pay of federal employees would be made comparable to the pay of civilians holding similar jobs in the private sector and that pay for federal civilian and military personnel would be adjusted at the same rate. The legislation increased DoD personnel costs. Military personnel costs included allowances for food, housing, clothing, and overseas assignments as well as benefits for health care and the G.I. Bill, which granted to veterans a number of benefits such as funds for education and assistance in purchasing a home. In a military retirement system that allowed service personnel to retire on half-pay after 20 years of service, the number of paid retirees expanded from 400,000 in FY 1964 to 625,000 in FY 1968. The base salary on which the benefits were calculated also grew. Military retirement benefits came out of the DoD budget, since no trust fund and no deductions from military pay helped defray retirement disbursements.[16]

Like Congress, Nixon hoped to benefit from a peace dividend as war spending diminished. The new president hoped the extra dollars would help pay for his own domestic and defense agenda, including elimination of the politically unpopular draft. As a candidate, he had announced in October 1968 his intention to move to an all-volunteer force (AVF) after a U.S. withdrawal from Vietnam. Nixon thought the draft was inequitable: "A system of compulsory service that arbitrarily selects some and not others simply cannot be squared with our whole concept of liberty, justice and equality under the law." The change to a volunteer force would require the administration to raise base pay to attract volunteers, which Nixon estimated would likely cost an added $5 billion to $7 billion annually.[17]

In May 1969 Herbert Stein, head of an interagency group on post-Vietnam economic planning, presented his preliminary findings to a cabinet committee on economic policy. He concluded that a peace dividend was unlikely. Scheduled military pay raises and previous commitments to build weapons meant that "net defense spending would decline only $5 billion by fiscal 1973." This finding stood in stark contrast to the Johnson administration's assertion in January that an immediate end to the war would result in a $19 billion decline in defense spending in two and a half years. A $5 billion "dividend" would be insufficient to fund Nixon's initiatives, even if economic growth increased federal revenues during his first term. Existing entitlement programs such as Social Security, Medicare, and Medicaid would quickly consume any peace savings. Stein's group concluded in August that by FY 1974–1975 projected revenues would produce a surplus of $13 billion that would have "to satisfy claims of $100 billion for new spending."[18]

Stein's analysis underscored a major change in the pattern of federal spending that had accelerated with Johnson's Great Society and would continue during Nixon's presidency—the decline in DoD spending relative to domestic spending. Toward the end of the Johnson administration (FY 1968) the department's expenditures constituted 46 percent of all federal spending. In the last fiscal year of Nixon's presidency, 1974, DoD spending represented less than 30 percent of federal outlays.

Over the same period spending for human resources climbed from 33.3 percent to 50.4 percent. Human resources included education, training, employment, social services, health, Medicare, income security, Social Security, and veterans' benefits and services.[19]

Without a peace dividend, Nixon had less room to maneuver. During his first week in office, Nixon set a tone of austerity, admonishing all agency and department heads to review their spending plans and "to achieve all the savings that you can." Cuts in federal spending would likely have the greatest impact on DoD.[20]

Pay Reform

Complicating DoD's response to the president's call for austerity was the matter of pay reform, a potential major claimant of money with ramifications for a projected all-volunteer force. A 1965 law required DoD to review military compensation every four years; the same statute required the president to send Congress the results of the review and his recommendations. Outgoing Assistant Secretary of Defense for Manpower and Reserve Affairs Alfred B. Fitt reported the review's findings to Laird on 21 January 1969. Called the Hubbell Plan after the review's director, Rear Adm. Lester E. Hubbell, it concluded that the existing system of pay and allowances was too complicated and poorly understood, leading service personnel to "undervalue their actual compensation." In Hubbell's view, compensation lagged 5–7 percent below "pay for comparable work elsewhere in the government." The existing pay system left the department with "too few first term re-enlistments, too few men at the mid-career point (10–14 years) and too great an incentive to retire at 20 years." The admiral's study recommended separate pay systems for career and noncareer personnel, putting the career force on salaries linked to civil service pay grades, with deductions for retirement, food, and quarters. Hubbell also proposed a two-tier retirement system, with one amount payable to retirees under age 60 and a higher amount to retirees over that age. Under other provisions, no one on active duty would receive less pay or a lower retirement benefit than under the existing system. The department secretaries and service chiefs, the OSD comptroller, Secretary Clifford, and the Bureau of the Budget supported the Hubbell Plan, but President Johnson omitted it from the FY 1970 budget because of cost.[21]

Fitt urged Laird to support pay reform, which would require legislation. He declared that enactment would be "essentially a no-cost item for FY 1970 surplus (or deficit) purposes" and a "down-payment on President Nixon's pledged effort to move toward an all-volunteer force." Deferring pay reform, according to Fitt, would keep in place a compensation system that frustrated effective force management. Packard estimated the Hubbell proposal would add $1.2 billion to the DoD budget.[22]

Complicating the issue, military pay would increase automatically even without pay reform. Under laws enacted in 1967 calling for comparability of federal and nonfederal civilian pay, salaries of federal civilian employees would

Rear Adm. Lester E. Hubbell, head of the first Quadrennial Review of Military Compensation in 1970, prepared the military pay reform proposal. (NARA)

rise on 1 July 1969 an average of 9.1 percent. Basic pay for the noncareer military force, persons not serving long enough to qualify for retirement benefits, would go up 12.6 percent, significantly above the scheduled civilian pay increase. Packard was concerned about finding the money to cover military pay raises, emphasizing the pressure on the department to cut defense spending or to include the pay raises within the current spending level.[23]

Laird discussed pay reform with Senator John C. Stennis (D–MS), Representative Mendel Rivers, and other congressional leaders. From these sessions, the secretary concluded it would take an "all-out fight" to enact a reform bill by 1 July, the date the 12.6 percent comparability pay increases were scheduled to go into effect. Rivers wanted the 12.6 percent raise without delay. Public sentiment as measured by constituent mail sent to Congress opposed the pay reform proposal. Laird thought that the pay reform measure contained provisions—different treatment for career and noncareer personnel and for married and nonmarried service members—that the Armed Services committees would not tolerate. Concluding that it would require an extraordinary effort by the legislative liaison office to persuade the Hill, he told the OSD staff in March that he believed Congress would not enact pay reform in 1969. The cost of pay reform would not be included in the FY 1970 budget. Rather, Congress would handle the military and civilian pay raises in a separate supplemental bill.[24]

DoD Budget Review

Laird encountered challenges at the very start of DoD's review of the FY 1970 budget. Defense budget cuts were a given, but determining how to trim spending without jeopardizing national security proved most perplexing. During the Johnson presidency, the cost of the Vietnam War forced the department to defer spending on modernization and readiness, a practice that could not continue indefinitely. Reductions in war expenditures during Laird's term would depend on the actual tempo of operations, the size of U.S. forces in theater, and the completion of a negotiated peace settlement. The intensity of the fighting and the peace negotiations lay beyond Laird's control, but they could have an impact on the Defense budget. New initiatives, such as an all-volunteer force, would compete for funding with other pressing requirements. Although not enamored of the budget process that McNamara had put in place, Laird had little choice but to use it for this particular budget given the short amount of time available to conduct a review and prepare for congressional testimony. To compound the problem, McNamara's management practices had strained relations between the Pentagon and Congress and between OSD and the JCS. To maintain a strong defense program Laird had to win the trust of the JCS and Congress.[25]

The DoD budget review began during the first week of the new administration. At the 27 January session of the Armed Forces Policy Council (AFPC), attended by the military department secretaries, service chiefs, and civilian leaders of OSD, Laird placed Packard in charge of reviewing the FY 1970 budget. He hoped that his deputy could carry out this assignment without the preconceptions Laird sensed that he himself might have acquired as a congressman. DoD would submit the changes, likely to be marginal, to the White House and Congress for their consideration.[26]

Packard's guidance to the services and the assistant secretaries on 14 February for reviewing the FY 1970 budget set forth planning assumptions and budget objectives. Spending would be predicated on a scaled-back war effort that balanced current requirements and future reductions. Expecting the cost of the war to decline, he desired to avoid overstocking supplies and ammunition in Southeast Asia and to redistribute excess materiel from the theater elsewhere in order to bring stocks outside the war theater "up to a reasonable level." To handle a possible major enemy offensive in 1969, Packard sought to retain the capability of rapidly expanding ammunition production from a "hot" base. He would review the composition of forces in SEA and try to balance the numbers of attack aircraft sorties and naval gunship actions with the consumption of ordnance. The deputy would consult with the JCS about the items under review before reaching any decisions. Laird asked to see the revised budget by 24 February.[27]

The future cost of the war proved hard to estimate. Ivan Selin, acting assistant secretary of defense for systems analysis, warned Packard in early February that Clifford's estimate of war costs could fall short of actual expenses by $700 million to $1.4 billion, because the former secretary had explicitly assumed that air and ground activity in FY 1970 would remain at the same relatively low level as in the last quarter of calendar year 1968. To reduce costs in FY 1970, Selin believed, would require "a directed reduction in sortie rates or a selective withdrawal of forces." Each U.S. division redeployed from Vietnam, he estimated, would save $750 million to $1 billion annually.[28] Finding an appropriate balance between what General Creighton Abrams, commander of the Military Assistance Command, Vietnam (MACV), needed and what could be safely withdrawn was not easy, since enemy forces tended to control the tempo of the fighting and to initiate most combat actions.[29] To help make up for a possible shortfall in funds for operations, Laird formally proposed on 1 March that Nixon amend the FY 1970 budget sent to Congress by lowering FY 1970 outlays for ground and air munitions by $751 million, in expectation of a decrease in the level of fighting, and for aircraft by $73.6 million, assuming fewer than expected losses.[30]

Packard hoped that the FY 1970 budget review would also help to correct deficiencies in U.S. general purpose forces in Europe and the Mediterranean created by the higher priority of troop deployments and arms shipments to Vietnam. He sought to put the long-term ship modernization program on a financially feasible basis, deferring setting new airlift and sealift requirements until the administration finished its overall policy review. Noting the rapid buildup of Soviet strategic forces and China's ICBM (intercontinental ballistic missile) capability, the deputy desired to reexamine R&D and deployment programs "to ensure that the strategic balance remains favorable to the U.S. over the next five to ten years." In assessing new major weapon systems, Packard aimed for realistic and attainable development and production schedules. To help fund the All-Volunteer Force, he sought to identify areas of greater efficiency in operations and procurement. Cuts in the civilian workforce and overhead costs and the closing of marginal or redundant installations would be on the table.[31]

The department completed the budget review the first week of March 1969 while Laird was in Vietnam. Packard sent Budget Director Robert Mayo a list of proposed budget revisions based on an evaluation by the DoD and BoB staffs. The proposal reduced DoD's budget authority, composed of NOA and loan authority, for FY 1970 by more than $2 billion, cutting President Johnson's request of $80.6 billion to $78.45 billion, and set estimated FY 1970 outlays at $78.5 billion, $500 million less than Johnson's $79 billion. Per Laird's guidance to his staff in March, Packard omitted the $1.2 billion (NOA) in FY 1970 for the proposed pay reform, an amount that would be included in the overall government contingency fund for pay raises. He also advised Mayo that DoD's review had uncovered "several significant cost overruns" possibly requiring further budget adjustments.[32] Laird wanted the budget submission to include "all known cost overruns" so that DoD could start the budget process with a "clean slate."

Mayo received DoD's proposal some two weeks before Laird's first congressional appearance as secretary. Even after this submission, the White House continued its internal review, forcing DoD to make difficult spending choices.[33]

Differences with the White House

Shortly after Packard sent the budget revisions to the White House, Nixon, citing worsening economic conditions, made clear his intention to reduce DoD expenditures even more than the half-billion dollars proposed by the deputy secretary.

Robert Mayo, director of the Bureau of the Budget from January 1969 to July 1970, was a persistent advocate of Defense budget cuts. (Nixon Presidential Library)

During a 14 March press conference, referring to what he called preliminary budget figures, the president said he expected Laird to present a revised Defense budget to Congress that "will be approximately $2½ billion less than that submitted by the previous administration." Later the same month, Nixon warned Congress that inflation, interest payments on the national debt, and higher than expected federal expenditures had shrunk President Johnson's January estimate of a $3.4 billion FY 1970 budget surplus to $1.7 billion by March. To avoid a deficit, Nixon vowed to make budget revisions that reduced FY 1970 expenditures "significantly below the amount recommended in January." He also pushed Congress to extend the income tax surcharge to sustain revenues. Nixon's announcements marked the opening of his campaign to reduce the FY 1970 Defense budget.[34]

Laird's view of the budget differed from the president's. In a press conference in Danang, South Vietnam, on 9 March, he had stated he might have to request a FY 1970 "budget add-on" of about $70 million to cover all the costs of accelerating the program for improving and modernizing South Vietnam's armed forces, an item that the Johnson administration had not included in the budget it submitted to Congress. Laird preferred to fund this effort in full because, as he concluded in his trip report for the president, it could save money. An improved South Vietnamese military would allow the administration to withdraw some 50 thousand to 70 thousand U.S. forces from Southeast Asia by the end of 1969.[35] In his first appearance before the Senate Armed Services Committee on 19 March, Laird conceded that his budget numbers and program changes were "subject to modification" by the president, but he supported Packard's budget submission setting expenditures at $78.5 billion and NOA at $78.45 billion. The committee would consider the budget over the coming weeks.[36]

Taking its cue from Nixon's March announcements, the Bureau of the Budget sought to reduce DoD spending by a greater amount than Laird did. On 18 March James Schlesinger, assistant director of BoB, sent Packard a list of proposed cutbacks that would further reduce outlays by $1.7 billion and budget authority by $4.4 billion. Schlesinger's list would leave Defense budget authority slightly above $74 billion and outlays at $76.8 billion, compared with Laird's $78.5 billion.[37] On 24 March Schlesinger sent Al Haig, Kissinger's chief assistant, a second list (dated 19 March) of even larger cuts for FY 1970. He "suggested" reducing outlays by $1.99 billion and budget authority by $4.9 billion. The largest single cut—$300 million in budget authority and $500 million in outlays—would be achieved by canceling the Manned Orbiting Laboratory (MOL) program in 1970. Other items on Schlesinger's list included reducing R&D and military and family housing, halting production of the F–14A, deferring construction of a nuclear aircraft carrier, and reducing outlays by $387 million and budget authority by $709 million. He advised Haig that there still remained room to negotiate, noting that these "suggestions," in his words, did not "constitute a dictated solution by the BoB."[38]

Alarmed by the size of the proposed BoB cuts, Laird immediately urged the president on 20 March to reject the additional cuts. BoB Director Mayo also wrote directly to Nixon on 21 March, warning him that Laird would argue (erroneously in Mayo's view) that any reduction in outlays in addition to the half-billion already offered by Defense would impair readiness. To preempt Laird, Mayo contended that most items (some $1.3 billion) on the list of cuts were marginal low-priority needs unrelated to military readiness. Other actions, such as deferring construction funds for a second *Nimitz*-class carrier, Mayo conceded, would delay the availability of equipment, but limited production capabilities and development problems would likely cause delays anyway. Nixon was receptive, and penned in the margin of Mayo's memorandum a note to Kissinger: "Henry—He makes a lot of sense."[39]

The BoB director was not the only administration official out to cut the DoD budget. Laird was aware that the Council of Economic Advisers and the secretary of the treasury shared the president's anxiety about inflation, rising interest payments on the national debt, and a possible higher prime discount rate. Although the secretary avowed that Defense could not carry out BoB's budget recommendations "and maintain national security," he was realistic. He told the assistant secretaries and the Joint Chiefs at the 24 March staff meeting that cuts in expenditures were unavoidable. Following up on Laird's statement, Packard declared he would look for ways to make further cuts in spending for personnel and equipment programs.[40]

Invoking Nixon's authority, Mayo continued to press the department, telling Kissinger on 24 March that Laird should produce savings of $1.3 billion in outlays. He offered the White House a three-page list of "belt tightening" budget revisions. Mayo was willing to let Defense proceed with military pay reform if Laird could produce savings of $1.3 billion. Even though it would cost $1.2 billion, Mayo claimed that three-fourths of the costs of pay reform would come back to the government during FY 1970 in the form of tax payments. If Laird could not find savings of

$1.3 billion, Mayo contended that he should agree to a $1.1 billion cut. "A figure any smaller than this," he asserted, "will get me into real problems with all of the civilian agencies."[41]

Laird decided not to pursue pay reform. In a telephone conversation that evening, Kissinger asked Packard if he could accept Mayo's $1.3 billion cut. Although at the secretary's staff meeting that morning Packard had recognized the need to cut expenditures, he responded that it "would be tough to accept Mayo's proposal." Sympathetic, Kissinger told Packard that if he could not "live with Mayo's last decision, we will have to fight for more." The president, according to Kissinger, did not "want to cut national defense in a risky fashion." At Kissinger's urging, Packard agreed to look again at Mayo's proposal.[42] Complicating the budget discussions, as Haig had pointed out to Kissinger, was the uncertainty as to what Nixon had actually approved or what he would accept. At a cabinet meeting, the president seemed to support a reduction of more than $2 billion in the FY 1970 budget, but without making clear whether he meant outlays or budget authority or both.[43]

Mayo had a clear idea of what the president desired. On 24 March Nixon told him to come up with several billions in additional savings and specifically to control spending. Nixon aimed to get the revised FY 1970 expenditure total for the entire federal budget "significantly below the $195.3 billion forecast in the Johnson budget" and warned Mayo that all executive departments and agencies had to "cooperate fully." Mayo passed the president's directive to the departments and agencies.[44]

Armed with the president's guidance, Mayo insisted on additional cuts in defense outlays, notifying Kissinger on 25 March that DoD "should show an absolute minimum further saving of $1.1 billion." Mayo also wanted Packard to consider cutting another $1 billion in outlays. The budget director warned Kissinger he was prepared to ask Nixon personally to order a total cut of $1.6 billion (Packard's $500 million plus BoB's $1.1 billion).[45] However, in a telephone conversation with Packard later that day, Kissinger downplayed Mayo's threat, saying that "he [Kissinger] thinks he has Mayo down to 800 million." Packard believed an $800 million reduction was feasible, with a significant condition, "if we can assume we will be able to plan on 50,000 troops out of Vietnam in FY 1970." Kissinger said "the reason he got Mayo down was that he said he could get a little of the troop reduction money if there was any."[46]

The Army's Cheyenne AH–56A attack helicopter, developed by Lockheed Aircraft Corporation, was canceled after a fatal crash and persistent technical problems. (NARA)

Mayo continued to take a hard line. He sent Laird on 26 March what he called a "secondary list of further possible reductions" that sliced expenditures not by $800 million, as Kissinger reported to Packard, but by $1 billion. Mayo's cuts included reducing procurement of the Cheyenne helicopter and the C–5A, curtailing R&D, slowing the conversion to the Poseidon, inactivating an armored division, reducing two tactical air wings, canceling F–111 procurement (except for the aircraft needed for a two-wing force in the 1970s), and cutting attack carrier forces. Mayo's list seemed carefully crafted to spread the pain of the cutbacks among the services.[47]

OSD yielded. On 27 March, after consultation with the service secretaries, Packard presented Mayo with a list of program reductions of $929 million in budget authority and $613 million in outlays beyond the reductions submitted earlier in March. Total budget authority thus sank more than $3 billion and outlays dropped more than $1.1 billion.[48] These changes to the FY 1970 budget would lower obligational authority to $77.6 billion and outlays to $77.3 billion. On the day that Packard agreed to these reductions, however, Laird indicated his unwillingness to make additional cuts in the DoD budget. In comments to the press, he averred that the $3 billion reduction in expenditures advocated in some reports would make it impossible to "protect the security and safety of our people."[49]

More Defense Cuts

DoD's reductions of late March proved insufficient. Inflation had worsened and the balance of payments surplus of the mid 1960s had vanished, forcing Nixon to take additional belt-tightening measures, specifically a $4 billion cut in spending. On 12 April he proposed a federal spending cap of $192.9 billion in hopes of realizing a budget surplus of nearly $6 billion.[50] On 15 April the president submitted his proposed changes in the FY 1970 Defense budget to Congress, setting NOA at $77.1 billion and outlays at $77.3 billion. Reinforcing Nixon's message of austerity, Mayo warned Laird on 23 April that he would have to stay within the modified budget and be prepared to manage defense programs at even lower limits should Congress make further cuts. Mayo also ruled out supplemental appropriations, affirming that additional requirements for Southeast Asia "should be offset by reductions in non-SEA-related programs."[51] His experience with the Senate Appropriations Committee in May left Mayo with the conviction that Congress was unlikely to exempt unexpected war costs from the ceiling on spending. He pointed out that lawmakers would impose spending limits on all departments for FY 1970 requiring that no new projects or activities be initiated.[52]

Yet Congress itself showed little inclination to control overall spending and that alarmed Nixon. In July, after the start of the 1970 fiscal year, he publicly called on Congress to hold expenditures in check, particularly for such "uncontrollable items as interest on the public debt, Medicare, social security, civil service retirement benefits." The existing aggregate level of expenditures undermined his fiscal goals and compelled him to make additional spending reductions. To meet his spending target of $192.9 billion and restrain inflation, he directed all departments and agencies to slash an additional $3.5 billion in outlays. Most of Nixon's cuts would affect military expenditures.[53]

As a result, the Air Force's MOL program was sacrificed. Nixon wished to stretch out the program, but faced with the need to save money, Packard advised Kissinger that the Pentagon preferred to "kill the whole thing" and transfer the developmental money to other programs.[54] Packard believed that unmanned spacecraft could carry out essential space missions at lower cost and that other programs had greater potential military value than MOL. Initiated in 1965 to learn how humans could work in space, MOL had become redundant. Ending the program was expected to save several hundred million dollars in FY 1970.[55]

Just as the White House continued to extract money from the Defense budget under review in Congress, the legislative branch concentrated on squeezing more money from military spending. In mid-August, Senator Stennis advised Laird of pending amendments to delete funding for the main battle tank MBT–70, a joint U.S.-German project to develop a new battle tank to compete with the next generation of Soviet tanks. Other amendments, Stennis noted, would reduce funding for a number of critical new weapon systems under development. This included the C–5A (a large military transport aircraft with intercontinental range and capable of carrying over-size cargo), the Advanced Manned Strategic Aircraft, or AMSA (initially envisioned as the replacement for the aging B–52 bomber), and the nuclear aircraft carrier. Opposing the amendments, Laird warned Stennis that they would lead to "a gradual erosion of U.S. military capability," involving "risks which I consider imprudent."[56] Also in August, Representative George H. Mahon (D–TX), chairman of the House Appropriations Committee and a respected authority on the military budget, announced his intention to cut at least $5 billion in appropriations from the president's FY 1970 budget request being considered by Congress. He cautioned Laird that he should take immediate steps to cut military programs since the fiscal year was already under way.[57]

The C–5A Galaxy's cost overruns and structural problems nearly led to the cancellation of the cargo plane, which is now a mainstay of the Air Force's air fleet. (NARA)

Laird nonetheless hoped to stave off deeper reductions and to recapture the initiative from Congress in shaping the DoD program. Speaking "slowly and soberly" at his 21 August press conference, according to a *Washington Post* reporter, the secretary announced a spending reduction of an additional $3 billion for FY 1970. This amount represented the preponderance of the $3.5 billion that Nixon wanted to pare from the federal budget. Laird also listed specific cuts of $1.5 billion, the first installment of the $3 billion reduction. Military end strength would fall by more than 100,000 and the number of civilian personnel by more than 50,000. The Army would reduce non-SEA operations, maintenance, and training accounts by $500 million and inactivate the 9th Infantry Division, currently in Vietnam. The Navy would deactivate over a hundred ships, and the Air Force would cut back non-SEA training by 300,000 flying hours. No reductions in NATO combat strength were announced. Although Laird acknowledged that some proposals required consultation with Congress and the NSC, he held that the "$1.5 billion is firm and is the first step in achieving this new $3 billion goal."[58]

Laird sought to dramatize the risks: the $3 billion cut, coming on top of the earlier reduction in spending of $1.1 billion, would lead to "an inevitable weakening of our world-wide military posture." In explaining his decision, he cited the congressionally imposed limitation on expenditures for FY 1970, anticipated cuts by Congress, economic conditions, and congressional delay in passing a budget. Lawmakers would not vote on the FY 1970 DoD budget until midway through the fiscal year, which had begun on 1 July.[59]

It soon became apparent that Laird's attempt at preemption had failed. Senator Thomas F. Eagleton (D–MO) applauded Laird's cuts, but he disputed his contention that they would impair readiness. He warned the secretary that total spending was likely to be cut by an even larger amount when Congress reviewed funding for the C–5A, a third nuclear attack carrier, and the B–1 bomber. In addition, Democratic Senators William Proxmire (WI), Edward M. Kennedy (MA), Edmund S. Muskie (ME), and George S. McGovern (SD), and Republican Senators Mark O. Hatfield (OR) and John Sherman Cooper (KY) expressed their desire to scale back Pentagon spending.[60]

More unwelcome news came when the administration announced officially that the end of the Vietnam War was unlikely to produce much of a "peace dividend." On 26 August Daniel P. Moynihan, executive director of the administration's Urban

Affairs Council, reported that DoD research and existing nonmilitary programs would largely consume the money saved by ending hostilities. DoD Comptroller Robert Moot also noted that continued pay increases (for civilians and military, 23 percent and 34 percent respectively between 1964 and 1969) and rising prices for commodities (15 percent) purchased by DoD would also diminish the revenue available for new domestic programs. Moynihan's disclosure blunted Laird's pre-emptive move and did nothing to pacify congressional opponents of DoD spending. Representative John J. Conyers Jr. (D–MI), for one, asserted that Congress and not Moynihan would determine the nation's spending priorities.[61]

In September and October Laird came up with an additional $1.5 billion reduction in expenditures in the budget under congressional review. He placed ceilings on outlays: Army, $24.7 billion; Navy, $22.3 billion; Air Force, $24.8 billion; OSD, $5 billion; and Civil Defense, $67 million; he informed Mayo that DoD would identify specific program reductions "at the earliest possible date." Laird requested a total outlay ceiling of $77.4 billion, including $556 million for military assistance and a $400 million allowance for pay costs and military retirement.[62]

In October, as part of the $3 billion reduction in military expenditures he announced in August, the secretary approved a list of hundreds of "actions recommended by the Secretaries of the Army, Navy, and Air Force to consolidate, reduce, realign, or close installations and activities in the United States, Puerto Rico and overseas." The military services had passed their recommendations through Assistant Secretary of Defense Barry Shillito, who had the authority to devise the final list in coordination with the service secretaries. Willing to take the political heat for the closures and needing to identify savings, Laird went ahead on his own to eliminate any "horse-trading," realizing he could not "get agreement ahead of time." The proposed changes in domestic bases, located in 42 states, would cause the loss of thousands of jobs in the districts of 84 senators and a majority of representatives. DoD expected these base closings and realignments to lower expenditures by about $609 million and eliminate 37,800 military and 27,000 civilian positions. The 1969 round was the first of several. In four years Laird shutdown more than 400 installations and reduced 1,400 others. In December 1972 he finished his final round, closing or shrinking another 274 bases. Laird's initiative displeased Congress, which later enacted legislation requiring congressional approval for base closures.[63]

Congress Enters the Fray

In September and October, Congress took action on the modified FY 1970 budget it received in mid-April. From Nixon's $75.278 billion request for DoD appropriations, the House cut $5.318 billion, and the Senate, $5.956 billion. The Senate passed an authorization bill on 18 September; the House followed suit on 3 October. A House-Senate conference reconciled the differences early in November. Laird and Wheeler appeared before a subcommittee of the House Appropriations Committee on 17 November to review the FY 1970 budget in final form. In opening the hearing, Representative Mahon stressed the need to restrain defense spending and appropriations in view of continuing inflation and a federal budget deficit, but he pledged to make no reductions that impaired the war effort or Nixon's attempts to end the war.[64]

By design, Laird played different roles in public and private during the appropriation process. Aware that the political mood in the nation and the threat of inflation made defense cuts inescapable, he worked in private with a few congressional leaders—Russell, Mahon, Stennis, and Rivers—to identify in advance of the hearings what reductions could be made without harming national security. Like Laird, they feared that the all-out attacks on the Defense budget could result in the kind of cuts that would prove disastrous to national security. According to the scenario worked out with congressional leaders, Congress would get the political credit for slicing defense appropriations. During his testimony Laird would continue to argue for the president's request for $75.2 billion in appropriations, even though he knew Congress would likely reduce it by $5 billion–$6 billion. Thus the public drama would focus on appropriations to demonstrate that Congress was reining in defense programs.[65]

In his testimony, Laird agreed on the need to curb the DoD budget, but he highlighted the significant reductions the administration had already made in cutting Johnson's proposed FY 1970 Defense budget by $4.1 billion in outlays and $8.6 billion in NOA. The reduction in outlays, the secretary emphasized, was the "greatest cut in an approved budget request to Congress in any single year since 1946." Laird went on to expound his concerns. He would have to finance a funding deficiency stemming from cost overruns of $700 million for FY 1970 through reprogramming. Shortfalls for future years, primarily in shipbuilding and the C–5 and F–111 A/E/D aircraft, totaled over $1 billion. The administration also needed to pay

Senator Richard Russell (D–GA), supporter of a strong national defense, chaired the Senate Armed Services Committee until 1969 when he became chairman of the Senate Appropriations Committee. (U.S. Senate Historical Office)

for cost growth of nearly $16.2 billion from the original contracts for 34 major weapon systems initiated by earlier administrations. Expressing anxiety about the sufficiency of future funding to support the buildup of South Vietnam's military and to allow the withdrawal of U.S. forces, Laird hoped that future authorization and appropriation bills would not reduce money for non-American forces in Vietnam.[66]

Laird found it difficult to deliver the $3 billion spending cut he pledged in August 1969. He had already canceled some programs, for example, the Manned Orbiting Laboratory and the Cheyenne helicopter, but ruled out an across the board 4 percent spending cut. He needed to make major reductions in other areas. Accordingly, Laird decided to phase out all B–58 aircraft by the end of FY 1970 instead of FY 1974 and lowered the B–52 monthly sortie rate for operations in SEA from 1,600 in the January budget to 1,400 in his revised budget. The Navy would phase out 100 ships and announced the inactivation of 111 ships and two antisubmarine warfare carriers. The secretary's budget cuts had a significant impact on military and civilian personnel. One Army division plus two-thirds of a Marine division would be cut. Special Operations Forces were reduced by 15 percent.[67] Table 2 illustrates the effect of congressional budget action on military personnel. Nixon's budget proposal of April cut personnel levels by only 3,200 from Johnson's budget, but to reduce spending Laird would have to remove 216,800 military personnel from the April budget level.

Table 2. Personnel Strengths for End of FY 1970

	Johnson's Budget (Jan)	Nixon's Budget (Apr)	Laird's Budget (Nov)
Army	1,507,900	1,509,300	1,435,400
Navy	771,500	766,900	694,300
Air Force	861,200	861,200	811,200
Marines	314,500	314,500	294,200
Total	3,455,100	3,451,900	3,235,100

Source: House Subcommittee on Appropriations, *Hearings: Department of Defense Appropriations for 1970*, 91st Cong., 1st sess., 17 November 1969, table, 367.

In the November revisions, the proposed number of DoD full-time permanent civilians decreased by 69,000 from 1.235 million in January to 1.166 million.[68]

Laird used his testimony to make a larger point about defense spending and national security: The DoD budget had to be sufficient to carry out the national strategy. Contending that previous military budgets had not provided sufficient funds to implement the current strategy of waging two major wars and one minor war at the same time, he stressed the need to devise an overarching strategy that the DoD budget could actually support. The secretary reminded the House committee that in 1968 the JCS had sent a Joint Strategic Objectives Plan to Secretary Clifford with a price tag of $111 billion for FY 1970 to support the 2½-war concept, a figure significantly higher than the $80 billion that President Johnson decided the nation could devote to defense. In Laird's view, Johnson's budget would not allow the United States "to handle two major wars and one minor war." For FY 1971, Laird said he would determine the kind of force and strategy that "can be financed with the resources available for defense programs." His fiscal guidance to the Joint Chiefs of Staff and military departments would estimate the resources needed to carry out the strategy.[69]

Laird's candor won praise from several representatives but no additional funds. On 8 December the full House took up and passed the DoD FY 1970 appropriation bill of $69.9 billion in NOA, $5.3 billion less than Nixon's revised budget. This reduction in NOA even exceeded the $5 billion that Mahon had pledged in August to remove from the budget. The House budget supported a force of 17 Army and 3⅓ Marine divisions, 11 Army brigades, an active fleet of 770 ships and 23 carrier air groups, 3 Marine air wings, 66 Air Force combat air wings, and 118 Air Force support squadrons. The principal reduction in operating funds would be derived from troop withdrawals

from Vietnam and Thailand, cutbacks in operations elsewhere, cuts
in end strength, and base closures.
Cancellation of the November and
December 1969 draft calls helped
reduce end strength by 50,000. Military assistance, construction, housing, civil defense, and pay raises
came under separate legislation. The
House planned a $2.1 billion supple-
mental bill to cover the pay increase
for the military and all civilians in
government.[70]

The message from Congress
was crystal clear. In time of war the
appropriations committee, consisting of long serving members who
normally supported the budget
requests of the Pentagon, approved
cuts deeper than at any time since
the end of the Korean War. House members let it be known that their discontent
derived from more than the expense of the war and cost overruns on programs such
as the C–5A cargo aircraft. Representative James H. Scheuer (D–NY) declared: "The
need for reduced military spending is glaring. Our Nation's internal problems are
clamoring for treatment and funds. The air we breathe in our cities is endangering
our health. Our cities' schools are becoming market places, not of ideas, but of crime
and narcotics. Inflation is hurting the middle class as well as the poor." Sharply
reducing NOA gave unambiguous expression of the country's changing political
climate, recognized by both the press and many representatives.[71]

On 9 December Laird appeared before the Senate Appropriations Subcommittee on Defense, appealing for restoration of about $429 million of the $5.3 billion
(NOA) cut by the House. He sought $129 million to purchase additional copies of
the new Navy fighter, the F–14, to ensure the service had enough to carry out tests
of the craft, and restoration of funds to purchase reconnaissance aircraft, modify

Representative George Mahon (D–TX),
chairman of the House Appropriations Committee and traditional advocate of national defense,
sought to curb Pentagon spending. (NASA)

various Navy and Air Force aircraft, develop the Navy's MK–48 torpedo, and procure the Short-Range Attack Missile (SRAM).[72] Wheeler, who accompanied Laird, expressed wariness about the reduced budget. With the latest reductions, he warned, "the Joint Chiefs of Staff believe that we have reached the limits of prudent risk in the present circumstances."[73]

Table 3. New Obligational Authority (NOA), FY 1970 ($ millions)

		Change
Title I, Military Personnel	20,835	(807)
Title II, Retired Military	2,735	
Title III, O&M	20,860	(932)
Title IV, Procurement	17,842	(3,045)
Title V, RDT&E	7,369	(854)
Total	69,641	(5,638)
Army	22,134	(1,821)
Navy	20,802	(2,002)
Air Force	22,269	(1,691)
Defense Agencies	1,701	(124)
Retired Military	2,735	
Total	69,641	(5,638)

Source: OASD(C), "Department of Defense Appropriation Act P.L. 91-171, 29 December 1969," column 8 in Financial Accounting Document (FAD) 666, 17 September 1970, tab FY 1970, binder Fiscal Tables 1970, box 819, Subject Files, OSD Historical Office.

When the Senate took up DoD appropriations, it soon became apparent that Laird and Wheeler had changed few minds. The Appropriations Committee had recommended cutting more deeply than the House, limiting NOA to $69.3 billion. It advocated an appropriation more than $5.9 billion below Nixon's revised budget of April and more than $5 billion less than the total appropriations provided for fiscal year 1969.[74] The Senate passed the appropriation bill on 15 December. The Senate and House conference report roughly split the difference between the two Houses, setting NOA at $69.64 billion. The bill cut the Title I budget estimate for military personnel by $3.32 billion. Title I covered the pay and allowances of officers and enlisted personnel on active duty and their moving and travel expenses when reassigned to a different duty station. However, $2.74 billion was transferred from Title I, "military personnel," to a newly created Title II, "retired military," to cover the costs of the military retirement system. Because retired pay had become such a substantial expenditure, the House Appropriations Committee recommended the creation of this separate title for retirement pay. Title III encompassed the costs of operations and maintenance; Title IV, the purchase, manufacture, and modification of weapons and equipment; and Title V, the expenses for research, development, and test and evaluation. Table 3, page 84, shows the breakdown of FY 1970 NOA by title and service and compares both to the changes from Nixon's revised April budget. The FY 1970 DoD appropriation bill, P.L. 91-171, was enacted on 29 December 1969.[75]

FY 1970 outlays are shown in table 4 below. The total of around $77 billion was slightly below Laird's goal of $77.4 billion as stated in his September letter to Budget Director Mayo.

Table 4. Outlays, FY 1970 ($ millions)

Title I, Military Personnel	23,031
Title II, Retired Military	2,849
Title III, O&M	21,609
Title IV, Procurement	21,583
Title V, RDT&E	7,166
Military Construction	1,168
Special Foreign Currency Program	
Housing	613
Offsetting Receipts	(949)
Total	77,071
Army	24,724
Navy	22,501
Air Force	24,865
Defense Agencies/OSD	4,981
Total	77,071

Source: OASD(C), FAD 633, 23 October 1970, tab FY 1970 Expenditures, binder Fiscal Tables 1970, box 819, Subject Files, OSD Historical Office.

The FY 1970 reductions seemed to be just the first round of austerity. Citing public interest in spending more for domestic needs, Mahon expressed his readiness to cut the DoD budget for FY 1971 and succeeding years as well. In his judgment, Americans wanted to spend less on defense and more on improving the environment, health, and education. He believed the changed political climate and the errors of experts about the Vietnam War made Congress more skeptical of spending for defense and more confident that it could reduce spending without endangering national security. He predicted that in coming years the Pentagon would have to reduce the size of the armed forces and restructure the military to get money to modernize the Air Force and Navy.[76]

The administration would have more time and latitude to shape the budgets of later fiscal years. To help it do so Nixon requested a study, NSSM 3, of the balance of power and the nation's military posture. He specifically desired an analysis of the budgetary implications of various strategies and levels of force structure. An interagency study group under Packard prepared options for defense spending, national security strategy, and the size and composition of general purpose forces and strategic forces.[77] That review led to the promulgation in October of a new strategy, NSDM 27—preparing the armed forces to fight one major and one minor war. Laird thought the new concept more realistic, reflecting the kind of strategy that DoD could actually carry out. But the new strategy entailed additional DoD cuts over succeeding fiscal years. NSDM 27 specified alternative budget guidelines between FY 1971 and FY 1975 under two different scenarios. The first scenario assumed U.S. combat in Vietnam would cease after 1 July 1970 and defense outlays would fall to $71 billion in FY 1972. Under the second, U.S. troop strength in Vietnam would drop to 260,000 at the end of FY 1971, with combat continuing through 30 June 1973. DoD outlays would then come to $76 billion for each of FY 1971 and 1972.[78] Both expenditure targets fell below the FY 1970 ceiling of $77.4 billion that Laird had advocated in his September 1969 letter to the budget director. NSDM 27 was not the only evidence that the administration wanted additional reductions. Just before Christmas 1969, Mayo prepared for Nixon's review a list of $793 million in spending cuts from the FY 1971 DoD budget.[79]

THE FY 1970 BUDGET formulation process was a new experience for Laird. For many years he had examined the DoD budget and criticized it from a congressional perspective. Now he was witnessing first hand from the administration's vantage point the central and dominant role of the budget and its interlocking relationship with the economy and strategy in conceiving and implementing national security policy. At the beginning of a period of winding down the Vietnam War, Laird had to take into account the threatening growth of Soviet military power and the ever-increasing cost and complexity of weapons. In this environment he had to lead the reshaping of the U.S. military establishment while holding down the cost of national defense. And most particularly, he had to defend his department's budget and interests against a president determined to reduce defense spending.

Laird did not have sufficient time before his initial congressional testimony to make significant changes in the program prepared by Secretary Clifford. Nor did he have sufficient time to institute in full new procedures for reviewing the budget within DoD. Laird perforce used the system that McNamara had established, requiring that he and Packard fight a holding action to defend the budget from critics in Congress and the White House. In subsequent fiscal years, Laird would set in place his own program and his own procedures for formulating the budget.

During the administration's review of FY 1970 DoD spending, Laird and Mayo vied for the president's support, forcing him to decide on specific line items. Nixon disliked this procedure and wanted the Defense Program Review Committee under Kissinger to arbitrate line item disputes between the budget office and DoD when considering future budgets. Mayo prevailed in the first battles over DoD expenditures, in part because the president saw reductions in defense spending as the primary way to help him achieve a budget surplus and fight inflation. Laird continued during his tenure to resist Kissinger's pressure, leading the NSC staff to complain about the lack of cooperation from DoD on fiscal matters.

In his effort to sustain the defense program, Laird found himself swimming against a tide of advocates for greater funding for domestic needs. To stint on domestic spending when Congress, administration critics, and public opinion sought more was hardly a realistic political option for the administration. For DoD the unfortunate truth was that entitlement spending on domestic programs, such as Medicare and Social Security, grew faster than defense spending in the latter half of the 1960s despite a costly ongoing war. Between FY 1964 and FY 1970, DoD outlays increased by $28 billion, while spending for social programs, welfare, education and training, low and moderate income housing, and community development rose by more than $37 billion.[80] Thereafter, entitlement spending exceeded defense spending by ever larger amounts.

Vietnam was the subtext of the FY 1970 budget battles, consuming nearly a third of the DoD budget and growing increasingly unpopular. Mounting opposition to the war and high defense spending, coupled with inflation and the possibility of deficits, fueled actions in the White House and Congress to cut military outlays. Not surprisingly, during Laird's tenure reductions in defense money would eventually affect U.S. troop levels and the air war in Vietnam. In subsequent fiscal years, Laird would deftly use the limits imposed on spending to control the pace of Vietnamization and foreclose the options of slowing or reversing the program.

─── CHAPTER 4 ───

The Predicament of Vietnam

THE WAR IN SOUTHEAST ASIA inherited from President Lyndon Johnson presented no easy path to a settlement. For most of Johnson's elected term the United States had been engaged in air, ground, and naval combat in Vietnam. Yet a military victory or a negotiated settlement seemed no closer in 1968 than it had been in 1965, when Johnson began sending large numbers of U.S. combat troops there. In March 1968 Johnson announced that he would not seek reelection, hoping that his withdrawal would hasten a settlement. The opening of talks with the North Vietnamese and the pause in the American bombing of North Vietnam had not brought the conflict nearer to resolution when Johnson left office in January 1969. U.S. combat deaths averaged 180 per week in 1967. By December 1968 they exceeded that weekly average for every month that year except October and November. Relative to the number of troops deployed in Vietnam, U.S. combat deaths consistently exceeded those of South Vietnam's forces, stark evidence that the Americans had taken over the burden of fighting from their Vietnamese allies.[1] In helping to preserve South Vietnam as a noncommunist, independent nation, more than 30,000 Americans had lost their lives by the end of the Johnson administration. In January 1969 over 536,000 U.S. military remained in theater, and the cumulative cost of the conflict to the United States had climbed to more than $52 billion.[2]

Finding what Nixon called an honorable end to the war had been a major theme of his presidential campaign. Speaking to the Republican Party's platform committee in August 1968, he called for greater emphasis on engaging in small-unit actions, uprooting the Viet Cong infrastructure, and enhancing the training as well as the equipment of the Republic of Vietnam Armed Forces (RVNAF). The American combat role was unlikely to diminish until larger, better led, better armed, and better organized South Vietnamese units were able to assume a greater share of the fighting.[3]

Even before January 1969 the Nixon administration-in-waiting pondered a U.S. withdrawal. On 13 January former chairman of the JCS retired General Maxwell D. Taylor assessed for Kissinger some alternatives for pulling out forces. A few days later Air Force Brig. Gen. Robert N. Ginsburgh, military assistant on the NSC staff to national security adviser Walt W. Rostow, raised the issue with Kissinger. Ginsburgh expected that Nixon would soon have to decide "what posture to take on the issue of reducing U.S. troops in Vietnam," because of reports that President Nguyen Van Thieu would propose a reduction, statements by Army Chief of Staff General William Westmoreland and others that some U.S. forces could be withdrawn, and the expectation that Saigon could shoulder more of the combat.[4] U.S. officials in Saigon also discussed the possibility of withdrawing troops. On 17 January Ambassador Ellsworth Bunker and MACV Commander General Creighton Abrams met with President Thieu to hold their first discussion on the subject. Abrams told Thieu that he contemplated recommending the redeployment of the U.S. 9th Infantry Division in July 1969. In forwarding the Abrams suggestion to Laird on 25 January, Paul Warnke, still serving as assistant secretary of defense for international security affairs, urged that Laird have the JCS commence planning for the unit's withdrawal.[5]

From 22 January 1969, the day Melvin Laird entered office as secretary of defense, his objective was to extricate U.S. forces from Vietnam, and by doing so lessen and repair the war-caused damage to the nation's social and economic fabric. In Vietnam War policy, Laird was, like Nixon, a politician at heart, but he was less affected by personal political considerations than were the president and Kissinger. The three shared the same goal of ending the war, but disagreed over how to get there. Laird proved successful in exercising the means to reach the desired end. Eventually, circumstances and Laird's skillful manipulation of the levers of power (the budget, Congress, draft calls, military strategy and operations, rate of withdrawal of forces from Vietnam) forced Nixon and Kissinger to grudgingly accept Laird's position on troop withdrawals. It seems clear in hindsight that Laird was convinced that there could be no detours or slowdowns in seeking to end U.S. combat in Vietnam.

Before the exploratory discussions about redeploying U.S. units came the ongoing "T-Day" planning, for termination of hostilities. T-Day Plans, predicated on a cease-fire agreement with the enemy that would require some form of U.S. withdrawal, were at the time independent of plans to improve and modernize South Vietnam's forces. The Pentagon began T-Day planning in May 1966. In December 1968 the JCS submitted a withdrawal plan and worked on programs for pulling U.S. forces out of Vietnam subsequent to the cessation of hostilities.[6]

Under the Manila communiqué issued jointly by Presidents Johnson and Thieu in October 1966, the incoming administration also had to be prepared to redeploy all U.S. forces from Vietnam within a six-month period. The Americans and their allies agreed in Manila to leave South Vietnam if North Vietnam withdrew its forces and discontinued its support of the Viet Cong, thus lowering the level of violence. Acting Assistant Secretary for Systems Analysis Ivan Selin reported to Laird in March 1969 that a total withdrawal under the terms of the communiqué, while feasible, would place an added burden on the DoD logistics system and cost an additional $3.5 to $5.8 billion according to information supplied by MACV. By the end of April 1969 CINCPAC was expected to complete a detailed six-month redeployment plan.[7]

If the domestic political situation, the change of administration, and the inconclusive nature of the unpopular war pushed the United States to explore a new path, the North Vietnamese leadership also felt pressure to change. The Communist regime, hurt by battlefield losses throughout 1968, could ill afford, in the view of some U.S. analysts, to continue the 1968 military strategy of large nationwide offensives. In 1968, the year of the enemy's Tet and follow-on offensives, official DoD statistics claimed that Communist forces (Viet Cong and North Vietnamese Army [NVA]) suffered 181,000 combat deaths in South Vietnam, more than 60 percent of their forces fighting in the south that year.[8] North Vietnam and the United States began to talk in May 1968 about settling the war, but these meetings soon deadlocked. Following suspension of the U.S. bombing of North Vietnam in November, expanded peace talks included representatives of the National Liberation Front (NLF), known as Viet Cong, and the Republic of Vietnam (South Vietnam) but these sessions soon mired in procedural wrangling.

By the beginning of 1969 South Vietnamese and American forces had recovered from the 1968 Tet offensive, which primarily struck South Vietnam's cities. The Accelerated Pacification Campaign, which concluded at the end of January 1969, expanded the government's presence in over a thousand previously contested villages and hamlets, and Saigon's cadres and paramilitary forces seemed poised to make further gains during 1969 in securing the countryside and its people. The Regional and Popular Forces (RF/PF), paramilitary units providing security to the rural populace, the police forces, and government cadre teams had grown in size and benefited from better training and equipment. The U.S. embassy and MACV were guardedly optimistic about the situation in Vietnam and future prospects.[9]

Paradoxically, Nixon inherited an improving military and political situation in South Vietnam but waning political support for the war in the United States. This unusual combination of military advance and domestic retreat formed the backdrop of his administration's efforts to develop policy. Shaping Vietnam policy became the prime concern of Nixon's two principal advisers on Vietnam, Laird and Kissinger, whose often opposing views contributed to the president's difficulties in making military and policy decisions. Laird, who had sensitive political antennae and acute awareness of growing domestic discontent, focused on the need to withdraw U.S. forces. Kissinger, though not insensitive to domestic politics, still hoped to achieve an outcome favorable to Washington and Saigon through a combination of military pressure in Southeast Asia and hard negotiating in Paris.

As a congressman Laird had frequently spoken about the war. Some of his public commentary was a partisan expression of his growing prominence after the 1964 election as a leading member of the opposition party. But he also voiced fundamental disagreements with the Johnson administration's conduct of the war. He supported the Tonkin Gulf resolution in August 1964, but at the same time saw the need to develop a war policy and questioned whether the country had the will and capacity to win in Southeast Asia. Without the determination to win, the United States should pull out, he said. In November 1965 he attacked Johnson's lack of candor for not providing information about plans and for "drifting dangerously close to a major ground war." In 1967 he wanted the administration to use U.S. air and sea power more effectively by bombing significant targets in North Vietnam and the port of Haiphong and to de-escalate the ground war. Yet, he feared that withdrawing U.S. forces at that point would lead to a Communist takeover. He did not "believe that the South Vietnamese are ready today, or will be ready within the short space of a year or so, to act successfully against a rejuvenated Viet Cong unhampered by American involvement."[10] In June 1967 Laird criticized the Johnson administration for misleading the public by underestimating the cost of the war by

$15 billion in FY 1966, and by $13 billion in FY 1967. He projected that the gap in FY 1968 between actual costs and funds requested would reach $5.5 billion.[11] At that time, he posited "only two realistic choices . . . reaffirm our original objective and proceed from there; or pull out of Vietnam before another drop of American blood is needlessly shed."[12] In September Laird expressed his deepening dissatisfaction with Johnson's inconclusive policy. In an address to the American Mining Convention, a disenchanted Laird came to the conclusion that if the Communists were likely to win sometime in the future, then it would be better to abandon the war now "to prevent further American casualties." Not all Republican leaders supported his break with the administration, but with a presidential election less than a year away, Laird thought the Republican Party should develop a position on Vietnam that did not simply parrot Johnson's. In the interest of ending the fighting, Laird even came to advocate direct negotiations with the Viet Cong, a position Johnson opposed. Before he became secretary it was clear that Laird was neither hawk nor dove. As a member of the World War II generation he was willing to fight, but the goal needed to be clear and attainable. He found abhorrent the notion of sacrificing lives and treasure in an unwinnable struggle.[13]

The Nixon Administration's Opening Moves

Shortly after being elected in November 1968, Nixon began to formulate his administration's Vietnam policy, initiating a comprehensive review of the war based on input from all agencies and departments. Prepared in December under the auspices of the RAND Corporation by Daniel Ellsberg and Fred C. Ikle, the review revealed fundamental divisions among government agencies regarding the outcome of the war and South Vietnam's prospects. Hoping to better understand these disagreements, Nixon had Kissinger initiate a second review.[14] On 21 January 1969 the questionnaire known as NSSM 1, or the "29 Questions," went to the secretaries of state and defense, director of central intelligence, Bunker, JCS, and MACV. These questions were intended to elicit a broad spectrum of official views from U.S. agencies and departments in Saigon and Washington on South Vietnam's capacity to fight and govern on its own. Nixon hoped NSSM 1 would "develop an agreed evaluation of the situation in Vietnam as a basis for making policy decisions."[15] The president requested all responses by 10 February, but it took a month just to complete the formidable task of sifting through and analyzing the lengthy detailed responses. By mid-March Kissinger's staff completed its analysis of the answers and circulated it to the NSC Review Group.[16]

With public patience growing thin, the new administration knew it could ill afford to postpone consideration of Vietnam policy pending the outcome of NSSM 1. On 25 January the NSC met to review the Vietnam dilemma and explore policy options. Instead of rehashing old arguments, Nixon asked for new approaches. "Seek ways in which we can change the game."[17] The four alternative outcomes presented—retention of U.S. forces in Vietnam to assure Government of Vietnam (GVN) control, mutual withdrawal of forces, political accommodation and mutual withdrawal, and territorial accommodation—were found to be deficient even before the meeting. William Bundy, a Johnson administration holdover in the post of assistant secretary of state for East Asian and Pacific affairs, noted that the options drafted for the NSC neglected to consider adequately the reactions of the North Vietnamese and Viet Cong, the irreversible continuing decline in U.S. domestic support for the war, and the questionable capabilities of South Vietnamese forces. The International Security Affairs office and the JCS warned Laird that the options omitted consideration of Vietnam in the context of other U.S. national interests and believed that the war should be related to the larger context of East-West relations and the containment of China and the Soviet Union.[18]

In addition to the four outcomes, the 25 January NSC session heard a range of military strategies. The first, escalation, included expanded military operations, possibly in Cambodia, Laos, and North Vietnam. A second strategy continued the current levels of forces and operations. A third called for a substantial reduction in the U.S. presence to a sustainable level less costly in money and personnel, allowing the United States to remain as long as necessary.[19] The JCS advocated a different alternative. The Chiefs wanted to build up the RVNAF without withdrawing U.S. forces, a policy likely to increase dollar and personnel costs of the war. They believed the current program for modernizing South Vietnam's armed forces could not go any faster, estimating it would take two to three years to prepare them just to be able to cope with the internal Viet Cong threat. The JCS emphasized that the program was "not intended to build an RVNAF capable of dealing with an external (NVA) threat."[20]

When the long 25 January discussion ended, Nixon selected none of the outcomes or strategies. He ruled out the goal of assured South Vietnamese control, which called for U.S. forces to remain until the North Vietnamese Army withdrew and the Viet Cong were eliminated, because it would be too difficult and costly. From the start, the administration realized it would have to accede to a settlement that involved the departure of American forces in some manner. The president did outline a short-term Vietnam policy blending continued military pressure and a willingness to pursue negotiations in the hope of gaining a breathing spell from critics. He stated at the meeting that "the mix of actions should be something like this. We talk hard in private but with an obvious peaceful public stance, seeking to gain time, initially giving the South Vietnamese a chance to strengthen the regime and add to the pacification effort while punishing the Viet Cong." He also raised the possibility of bringing home a few U.S. troops unilaterally within a few months to appease critics while seeking a military settlement at the peace talks. The stick of military pressure to coerce the enemy and the carrot of troop withdrawals to placate domestic critics would form the basis of Nixon's Vietnam policy over the long term.[21]

Regarding the negotiations, Nixon laid down an uncompromising line. The United States would not introduce at Paris the issue of de-escalation or a cease-fire, nor propose a unilateral troop withdrawal. However, the administration would continue to discuss with the Saigon government on a close-hold basis the issues of selected U.S. troop reductions and improvement of Saigon's military capability. To obtain a better idea of the Saigon government's long-term viability, Nixon asked JCS Chairman General Earle Wheeler to report on programs for improving internal security and police forces in Vietnam. The president also wanted continued pressure on the government in Saigon to replace incompetent ARVN (Army of the Republic of Vietnam) leaders. Finally, he wanted no public mention of the topics discussed on 25 January.[22]

Deliberations continued on 30 January when Kissinger met with Laird and Wheeler at the Pentagon. The topic, how to intensify military operations, flowed from Nixon's admonition at the 25 January NSC meeting about continuing to punish the enemy. Kissinger asked what military pressure could be applied against enemy forces in South Vietnam so that North Vietnam would know there was "a new firm hand at the helm." Wheeler offered no new ideas. He saw little chance of stepping up operations within South Vietnam because U.S. forces there were already fully engaged; exceeding the current level of 60 B–52 sorties per day would lead to fatigue and a loss in efficiency. The JCS chairman thought that carrying out previously drafted JCS plans for operations in the Demilitarized Zone (DMZ) and air attacks in North Vietnam could signal the new firmness in U.S. leadership.

Operations in Laos or Cambodia, or short duration ground forays against North Vietnamese base areas or sanctuaries, might also transmit that message, Wheeler believed. Laird opposed increased military action in Vietnam on political grounds, reminding Kissinger that since the start of the Paris talks sentiment in the United States was moving in the direction of de-escalation. The secretary warned that additional operations in Cambodia would create political problems.[23]

After the meeting Laird forwarded to Kissinger a JCS contingency plan for attacks on targets in North Vietnam south of the 19th parallel. Reviewing the plan for Kissinger, his military assistant Al Haig thought the contemplated actions fell short of what the president wanted. Haig tried to elicit a stronger set of options from the Pentagon, drafting a memorandum of the 30 January meeting signed by Kissinger that reiterated the main points of discussion and stipulated actions for Laird to undertake.[24] According to Haig's memorandum, the JCS would prepare plans for operations within South Vietnam that would signal the administration's intention to increase pressure on the enemy during the initial negotiations in Paris.[25]

The president considered it "vitally important" to keep pressing the enemy in Vietnam. He directed Kissinger to convey this message to Wheeler and to advise him to find ways to ratchet up the military pressure that did not risk breaking the negotiations.[26] Kissinger talked with Wheeler on 1 February; then on 5 February he explained the president's request to Laird, who wanted Kissinger to assure the president that MACV was doing everything possible to keep pressure on the enemy. Laird questioned the wisdom of military operations that would likely increase American casualties, attributing the recent rise in losses to intensified efforts to make contact with major enemy units, an initiative, he wrote, that "cannot be expected to produce any significant change in the military situation over any short run period of time."[27] Laird's answer failed to satisfy Kissinger, who believed that DoD could take additional measures to escalate without U.S. domestic repercussions. To step up operations without arousing a public outcry seemed almost wishful thinking at a time when support for the war was waning. Most likely it could only be done by keeping some military operations out of the public view.[28]

The White House continued its quest for military operations that would pressure Hanoi to be more forthcoming at the Paris talks in February and March. On 21 February Laird sent Kissinger preliminary JCS plans for "actual or feigned airborne/amphibious operations" against North Vietnam, "an actual or feigned airborne/airmobile expedition in force" against enemy lines of communication in Laos and Cambodia, and "actual or feigned renewed and expanded air and naval operations" against North Vietnam. Both Kissinger and Laird were wary of implementing them. Kissinger deemed the risks unacceptable and hoped the JCS could develop plans for more subtle actions that would have little serious repercussions at home.[29] Laird remained cautious about intensifying military operations, contending that General Abrams was already applying maximum military pressure. To reinforce that point, Laird informed Nixon that the combined consumption of air and ground munitions was higher in January 1969 than in January 1968, and that battalion days of operations had risen from 1,270 in January 1968 to 2,136 in January 1969. He suggested moving naval gunfire support ships or a carrier task force into the Gulf of Tonkin, believing that Hanoi might construe these steps as potential preparations for a strike against North Vietnam. On 7 March the president decided to move some naval units closer to North Vietnam and to increase air reconnaissance for a week.[30]

At Kissinger's request, planning for feint operations against North Vietnam continued in April. With the approval of Chief of Naval Operations Admiral Thomas Moorer, the Navy developed a proposal for a mining feint of Haiphong harbor, North Vietnam's main port, without informing Laird. Wheeler sent the finished plan to Laird. In forwarding it to Kissinger on 11 April, the secretary stated his serious misgivings. Making it clear that he knew that he had not been involved from the outset, Laird cagily noted that "I understand you and some of your staff have been working on [it] with the Navy." Kissinger informed him on 12 April that the president had approved the first step of the Navy plan to make a mining feint to create fear in Hanoi about intended U.S. military actions. The ruse included transferring mines to ships operating in the South China Sea, a move Hanoi would notice and thus infer that the allies were planning to mine Haiphong harbor. Kissinger stated the Navy plan "does not visualize actual mining operations," but intended to transmit "low-risk intelligence indicators to Hanoi." Succeeding phases would be initiated only after further consultations. Each military action taken would have a deniable cover story for the government. The program would end 25 April.[31]

Adding to Laird's concern about the risks of stronger military pressure was his distress at being excluded from operational planning. The episode of the Navy's

April plan was not the first or only time Laird was bypassed in the initial stages of planning. Nor would it be the last. Kissinger asked Wheeler in early February for ideas on additional operations before informing Laird. In September Wheeler called the White House to say that he feared his weekly attendance at high-level review group meetings "would certainly become known with accompanying problems," a likely reference to his superior, Laird. The chairman expressed his willingness to comment on "any products which can be fed to him via the Robinson route," an allusion to then-Capt. Rembrandt Robinson, a naval officer who headed the White House liaison office with the Pentagon. Believing that the office was used deliberately to bypass him, Laird had tried unsuccessfully to close it. On other occasions, Laird had asked Kissinger to route communications from the NSC to the JCS through the secretary of defense's immediate office first, but Kissinger never pledged to comply fully.[32]

From the early days of the administration, Laird disagreed with Kissinger and to some extent the president over the conduct of the war. Nixon and Kissinger expected that increased battlefield pressure would lead to a negotiated settlement and urged the military to find a way to do that without alienating the public. And the JCS agreed, contending that increased military pressure would not inevitably multiply U.S. casualties. Laird, ever sensitive to domestic reaction, believed strongly that the public expected the war to wind down, not heighten in intensity. In his view, more aggressive conduct of the ground war would lead to more American casualties and a loss of political support. Consequently, Laird urged the president to defer a final decision on the proposed JCS military response to minor enemy attacks on population centers until he and Secretary Rogers could review it. Fundamental differences had surfaced about how to proceed in Vietnam. To use Kissinger's words, it was a "conceptual stalemate."[33]

Laird Goes to Vietnam

And a stalemate is where matters stood when President Nixon embarked on an eight-day official visit to Western Europe in late February 1969. Ironically, one purpose of the trip, as Nixon later wrote, was "to show the world" that he was "not completely obsessed with Vietnam."[34] Vietnam remained very much on his mind, however. Before his departure, he met with Laird to discuss the secretary's forthcoming trip to Vietnam, 5–12 March. Nixon wanted Laird to look first hand

Laird with his trusted military assistant, Col. Robert Pursley, during a trip to Vietnam in March 1969. Pursley helped draft Laird's trip report for the president and memoranda on many subjects. (NARA)

at the military situation.[35] To help him in Vietnam, Laird brought along Wheeler; Assistant Secretaries of Defense Robert Froehlke, Daniel Henkin, and Paul Warnke; and his military assistant, Col. Robert Pursley.[36]

In Vietnam, Laird discussed with Bunker and Abrams what the U.S. military could do to increase pressure on the enemy, but he focused on changing strategy and tactics in order to decrease the war's cost should negotiations bog down. He did not believe that the United States should escalate to break the military stalemate and force Hanoi to capitulate. In sessions with U.S. military leaders, Laird also sought to temper any unrealistic expectations they might have about obtaining more resources. He communicated his basic message that the American people expected Nixon to conclude the war and to most Americans that meant "the eventual disengagement of American men from combat." He instructed Abrams to speed up the programs that gave more responsibility to South Vietnamese forces.[37]

In sessions on 8 March with South Vietnam's leaders, President Thieu, Prime Minister Tran Van Huong, and Minister of Defense Nguyen Van Vy, Laird broached the topic of U.S. disengagement. He set forth the proposition that withdrawals would depend on the ability of South Vietnamese forces to take over the responsibilities of American forces and pledged to coordinate closely with South Vietnamese officials. A key point for Laird and the Vietnamese concerned the provision of additional funds to accelerate the modernization of South Vietnam's forces. Thieu, who had previously discussed a troop reduction with his cabinet, agreed with the general concept of bolstering his forces so that U.S. units could redeploy. Laird emphasized to Vietnamese officials that the new administration had a grace period with the American public of 6 to 12 months to resolve Vietnam issues.[38]

On the return trip to Washington, Laird, Warnke, Henkin, and Pursley stayed at a military compound on Oahu long enough to draft a lengthy report for the president that would greatly influence the administration's Vietnam policy. Meeting with Nixon on 13 March to discuss his trip, the secretary made a strong case, based on his report, for improving South Vietnam's forces so they could replace U.S. forces. In his judgment, the United States could ill afford to station indefinitely a substantial number of its military in Vietnam. Disappointed at the slow rate of progress in improving the capability of South Vietnam's forces to assume more of the fighting, Laird recommended that Nixon accelerate plans to improve South Vietnam's armed forces "to achieve full modernization" for their regular, paramilitary, and police forces. He considered the Phase II Improvement and Modernization Plan unsatisfactory on two grounds. First, it did not allow the administration to make meaningful reductions in U.S. forces in South Vietnam. Second, and more significant, it prepared the RVNAF to cope with only Viet Cong insurgents, not NVA regulars. Laird urged Nixon to approve a study that would find the best way to replace U.S. combatants with South Vietnamese. Despite the disappointing rate of improvement of South Vietnam's forces, Laird concluded that the United States could redeploy 50,000 to 70,000 troops during the remainder of 1969 without jeopardizing U.S. and allied troops remaining in Vietnam. Viewing the situation politically, he believed such a course "necessary to retain U.S. public support for our continued efforts in South Vietnam."[39]

Although troop withdrawals were under consideration, Nixon was not yet sold on the idea. Wary about the potential adverse impact of withdrawal on the peace

Secretary Laird presents his Vietnam trip report to the president on 13 March 1969. (Nixon Presidential Library)

talks and exasperated by the enemy's stepped up military operations, he publicly discounted the notion. At his 14 March press conference, the president declared that the current enemy offensive ended the "prospect for a reduction of American forces in the foreseeable future."[40]

Shortly after Laird's return from Vietnam, Kissinger disseminated to the NSC a summary of the responses to NSSM 1, the assessment of the situation in Vietnam. The findings lent encouragement to Laird's proposal that the ARVN take over the fighting from departing U.S. units. A consensus that the allied position in Vietnam had improved was offset by a shared recognition that the RVNAF on its own would be unable in the foreseeable future to withstand Viet Cong and North Vietnamese forces. MACV bluntly asserted that without U.S. ground and support forces the South Vietnamese military could not handle North Vietnam's army. Nor did MACV envision that much could be done to improve the South Vietnamese, believing that the current modernization plan was the most that could be carried out. Saigon's forces were deemed incapable of becoming self-sufficient and of attaining military superiority over the Viet Cong and North Vietnamese. Respondents generally agreed that the Saigon government remained weak in rural areas and might not survive a peacetime political competition with the Communists. They also agreed that the enemy retained sufficient military strength to continue to pursue his objectives. By choosing when and where to fight, North Vietnam controlled the casualty rates of both sides. There was also general acknowledgment that Hanoi agreed to start negotiations not out of desperation but out of the need to pursue its objectives at a lower cost.[41]

NSSM 1 uncovered basic disagreements. The embassy staff in Saigon, JCS, CINCPAC, and MACV tended to be hopeful about the future course of the war. They believed that recent gains on the battlefield and in securing the countryside through the Accelerated Pacification Campaign were likely to last. In their view, allied military pressure caused the enemy to reduce his operations; continued interdiction of supply routes in Vietnam, Laos, and Cambodia could cut off enough supplies to induce Hanoi to yield. The State Department, OSD, and CIA found less reason for optimism. In their assessment, the battlefield stalemate continued, with little likelihood of defeating the enemy. Organizational and leadership weaknesses persisted in South Vietnam's forces; pacification gains were inflated and fragile; and political support for the Saigon government was questionable. They attributed the reduction in enemy military operations to changes in his motives and tactics. NSSM 1 highlighted the persistence of disagreements within the administration. Consequently, it provided no blueprint for future policy and strategy.[42]

The disagreements over NSSM 1 mirrored the differences between Kissinger and Laird. Kissinger sought to crack the foe with increased force that would then lead to progress in the peace talks. But State, OSD, and the CIA had little confidence in the success of a strong military option. Laird wanted to focus on the buildup of the RVNAF and the redeployment of American forces. NSSM 1 made clear, however, that at that time no one, including Laird, believed the existing program to modernize South Vietnam's forces was adequate.

Laird's trip had a significant effect, helping to stimulate continued examination of withdrawals. Consideration of U.S. troop withdrawals, discussed during the presidential campaign and at the January NSC meetings, generated its own momentum and assumed a higher place on the administration's agenda. Wheeler informed Abrams on 14 March of the withdrawal figures that Laird recommended to the president. A week later, Abrams discussed a possible reduction in forces with his deputy General Andrew Goodpaster, who was then at the so-called "western White House" in San Clemente, California, with the president. On 23 March Abrams gave his conditional assent to the notion of U.S. withdrawals, telling Goodpaster that he directed the staff to prepare tentative plans to redeploy up to 50,000 soldiers in 1969 under certain conditions. Abrams believed withdrawals were feasible but only if pacification continued to make progress; if the RVNAF continued to improve at the current pace; if the enemy did not increase his strength or infiltration rate or logistics system; and if the current levels of B–52 sorties, tactical air, and artillery support were maintained. Abrams wanted the 3rd Marine Division redeployed first, but only to Okinawa so it could be available as a reaction force. He warned that premature public commitment to reductions could harm morale and possibly lead Hanoi to misinterpret U.S. intentions. Understandably wary about troop withdrawals, at the end of March Abrams reiterated to Wheeler his opposition to a unilateral and unconditional pullout of forces.[43]

Vietnamization

The NSC met again on 28 March to discuss Vietnam. Troop withdrawals were the focus of discussion. Should the United States maintain residual combat forces in South Vietnam after a mutual withdrawal? How quickly should withdrawal occur? At this meeting, the administration took additional significant steps in formulating policy.[44]

Bunker presented President Thieu's views. Thieu realized that the United States would not support South Vietnam indefinitely, but he stated that his government was growing stronger and could take on a greater share of the fighting. Nixon framed the issue more broadly, asking how the United States could "de-Americanize" the war to hasten a settlement, understanding that de-Americanization depended on improvements in the RVNAF. Laird pointed out that the American people would be skeptical of claims that South Vietnam's forces had improved. Only a "couple of divisions . . . are worth anything," he observed, and several had not improved at all. Goodpaster disagreed. He contended that the ARVN had made substantial headway since the Tet offensive of 1968, but even he conceded that South Vietnam's military could not yet replace American forces. Nixon wanted a plan that imparted a sense of urgency in training and improving the RVNAF, believing his administration had only a six to eight months grace period before it would lose political support. During this discussion Laird stated that "Vietnamization" was a more suitable term to emphasize what the administration wanted to do, namely build up Vietnamese forces to assume greater responsibility for the war. The term Vietnamization had already gained public currency after Laird used it during his appearance on NBC's *Meet the Press* on 23 March. Nixon agreed and thenceforth the term was commonly used within administration councils.[45]

The discussion turned naturally to the question of how and when to begin withdrawals. Goodpaster asserted that the United States should formulate plans to withdraw a first increment, but pull out ground forces only under favorable conditions: progress in pacification and improvements in the ARVN. He opposed a withdrawal during the enemy's expected May offensive. Noting it would take U.S. forces three months to prepare for withdrawal, he believed July would be the right time for the first increment. Goodpaster related withdrawals to completing the second phase of the I&M Plan in FY 1973. He estimated it would take two years of preparation before the South Vietnamese could take over the defense of their country from the Americans.[46]

Nixon stated that American withdrawals would be contingent on the other side's actions and would not be unilateral, a position that became a formal decision (NSDM 9) after the meeting. The United States would keep residual forces in Vietnam either by negotiating an agreement that permitted them to stay or by specifying stringent conditions for withdrawal, "which we know won't be met." Nixon stressed "that the conditions of withdrawal were the operative portions of any agreement." He intended to keep U.S. forces in Vietnam "for some time." This was also the president's position at the January NSC meeting.[47]

At the March meeting Nixon moved forward in developing Vietnam policy, requesting further study of phased withdrawals accomplished either by a mutual withdrawal of forces or by Vietnamization. Nixon designated "Vietnamization"— gradually turning over the American combat role to South Vietnamese forces—as an alternative to mutual withdrawal.[48] In pursuing mutual withdrawals and in maintaining military pressure on the enemy, Nixon continued the Johnson administration's policy. What differed was Nixon's determination "that the time was right to begin reducing the U.S. involvement in Vietnam regardless of progress in negotiations." He later called this decision "another turning point in my administration's

Vietnam strategy," crediting Laird's "enthusiastic advocacy" of Vietnamization as the basis for his decision.[49]

On 1 April the president issued NSDM 9 to implement his decisions of 28 March. He wanted no reduction in military pressure. Washington would initiate no proposals for de-escalation at the Paris talks and would discuss it only in the context of mutual withdrawals. Nixon formulated stringent conditions for a U.S. withdrawal, expecting Hanoi to reject them. The United States would agree to pull all combat forces from Vietnam if Hanoi agreed to a verifiable and supervised withdrawal of its forces from South Vietnam, Laos, and Cambodia, and provided guarantees that it would honor the agreement. His administration would finish its redeployment within six months of Hanoi's complete withdrawal. Nixon wanted to be "in a position to control the timing of the completion of our withdrawal, since we can determine if Hanoi has fully met the conditions of the mutual withdrawal agreement. The key point will not be the timetable but rather getting Hanoi to comply with the conditions for withdrawal." Nixon's formulation of his withdrawal terms manifested his underlying belief that by being tough he could outwait Hanoi and force it to make concessions. In other words, Hanoi would not stay the course, but Washington would. His optimism that the United States could control the terms of its withdrawal from Vietnam would be sorely tested in the years ahead.[50]

On 10 April Nixon took the first step toward implementing his policy. He approved NSSM 36, directing Laird to plan for the Vietnamization of all aspects (military, civilian, and paramilitary) of American involvement in Vietnam—including combat and combat support forces, advisers, and equipment—in coordination with the secretary of state and director of central intelligence. Laird was to prepare timetables for transferring the U.S. combat role to the South Vietnamese with four alternative completion dates—31 December 1970, 30 June 1971, 31 December 1971, and 31 December 1972. He was to assess the effect of each alternative on combat capability, the budget, and the balance of payments. For planning purposes, withdrawals would begin 1 July 1969. When completed, the U.S. military presence in Vietnam would shrink to a support and advisory mission. The president wanted an outline of planned actions on 1 June.[51] Significantly, NSSM 36 assumed the war would continue and that North Vietnamese Army and Viet Cong military units would remain in South Vietnam as the Americans redeployed. NSSM 37 issued on 10 April reinforced that point, stating the South Vietnamese would progressively take over the combat role "in the absence of reciprocal enemy withdrawals." In apparent conflict with NSDM 9, which stipulated the mutual withdrawal of U.S. and North Vietnamese forces, the two new papers envisioned unilateral U.S. withdrawals.[52]

Unable to decide on new military measures to demonstrate toughness, the administration was still of two minds on withdrawals, considering conflicting paths for disengaging from Vietnam—mutual withdrawal and limited unilateral American withdrawal. In spite of Wheeler's and Abrams' reservations about pulling out U.S. troops, the president approved Vietnamization. Contrary to the restrictive conditions Nixon placed on mutual withdrawals and his professed but implausible hope of forcing North Vietnam to consent to an American timetable, he accepted Vietnamization and its implicit embrace of unilateral withdrawal. Like Laird, Nixon knew the United States had to leave Vietnam, and Vietnamization represented an exit strategy in case negotiations with North Vietnam led only to endless wrangling and stalemate.

Knowing the likelihood that public pressure for withdrawal would grow over time, the president hoped to avoid fueling public speculation about U.S. troop withdrawals. However, Thieu's public comment in January 1969 that his forces were capable of replacing "a sizable number" and that U.S. withdrawals would shortly start made it difficult for Nixon to avoid the issue. At his 6 February press conference, he said that he would make no troop announcements. On 4 March, in response to a reporter's question, Nixon conceded that he was reviewing troop levels and the improvement of South Vietnam's forces, but stated that "there are no plans to withdraw any troops at this time or in the near future." He repeated that position during a press conference on 14 March. To ensure that his top officials did not contribute to public conjecture about U.S. redeployments, the president admonished Rogers; Laird; Bunker; Henry Cabot Lodge, the U.S. negotiator at the Paris peace talks; and Kissinger in mid-April to adhere to the position he laid down in his press conferences and not deviate from it in public. The president reiterated to his top advisers that U.S. troop withdrawals were contingent on progress in the peace talks, the ability of the South Vietnamese to defend themselves, and the level of offensive action by enemy forces, but not at all on enemy troop withdrawals.[53]

Although the administration wanted to employ the new NSC procedures in developing Vietnam policy systematically, some officials worried that a methodical approach would prove too slow for impatient critics and the public. In addition, they feared that the policy might be based on overly optimistic assumptions about Hanoi's behavior. Dean Moor, a member of the NSC staff, thought the administration "ought to come to grips with the issue of where we go and what we do if our beautiful strategy gets nowhere and the public starts to holler," adding that "domestic criticism and flack from capitol hill is mounting a lot faster than I expected. . . . The other side may stonewall for discussion of political issues, inclusion of the NLF, and a change in the Saigon government."[54]

Maxwell Taylor feared that public pressure would prove irresistible and compel unilateral withdrawal. Late in March, he told Kissinger, "I am afraid that over-eagerness here in Washington to bring back some American forces will result in unilateral action and thereby will nullify efforts to obtain reciprocal action from the other side. This will be a regrettable outcome in its own right and, in addition, will adversely affect the conduct of the subsequent negotiations." He concluded, "We should not overlook the possibility of creating a popular furor to 'bring the boys home' which can get out of control."[55]

Without committing to a timetable, Nixon in his press conferences and his televised 14 May speech on Vietnam acknowledged only that withdrawal of U.S. forces was under consideration, but discussions within the administration were much more concrete than the president's public comments suggested. In May MACV submitted a draft plan to withdraw two U.S. divisions over six months. Ivan Selin of Systems Analysis warned Laird that the plan would leave in Vietnam virtually all of their combat support, logistics, and headquarters personnel—integral parts of the division—and redeploy a few tactical aircraft from Vietnam and Thailand. Agreeing with Selin, Laird requested a more balanced withdrawal plan that included support and aviation units, not just ground combat units.[56]

At the end of May the JCS sent Laird a plan for Vietnamization based on input from MACV, the Pacific Command, the State Department, CIA, and the embassy in Saigon. Absent a reduction in the enemy threat, the JCS did not believe that the RVNAF would be able to fill the void left by departing U.S. combat forces. Moreover, they argued that a faster withdrawal pace brought increased risks. The Joint Chiefs saw advantages to Vietnamization: fewer U.S. casualties, a better negotiating climate, an improved likelihood of mutual withdrawals, and a shot in the arm for South Vietnam's forces. The JCS plan presented five withdrawal alternatives for

1969, each to include support units as well as ground combat units. Three called for redeploying 50,000 troops in various combinations; the fourth, for withdrawing 85,000; and the final one, for withdrawing 100,000. In forwarding the alternatives, Laird urged the president to limit the initial withdrawal to 20,000–25,000 and to pull out a total of no more than 50,000 troops in 1969 in light of South Vietnam's disappointing progress to date in taking on more of the fighting. Laird had concerns about the RVNAF's ability in the short run to "stand alone against the current North Vietnamese and Viet Cong force levels," even with additional training, improved equipment, and better combat support. He recommended that Nixon make an early announcement of a modest withdrawal (20,000–25,000) and evaluate the situation before taking a second step. In Laird's thinking, the initial withdrawal would show the South Vietnamese government that the United States was serious about Vietnamizing the war and leaving the allied military position strong enough to counter an enemy offensive. Withdrawals would play well with some segments of the American public, although Laird admitted they would not placate the most vocal opponents of the war. At this time, he saw risks in moving too quickly: "To withdraw much faster (such as by the end of 1970), in the absence of some North Vietnamese withdrawals, could result in serious setbacks to the pacification program, a significant decline in allied military capability, and the possibility of a GVN collapse."[57]

A few days after Nixon's 14 May speech, in which he proposed the mutual withdrawal of U.S. and North Vietnamese troops within a year of signing a peace agreement, came news of a costly ground assault by elements of the 101st Division against well-entrenched North Vietnamese units on Hill 937 in the A Shau valley. Between 11 and 20 May, friendly forces fought to capture the hill at a cost of 61 killed and 441 wounded only to abandon it a few days later. The action became infamously known as "Hamburger Hill" because U.S. forces suffered heavy casualties in repeated attempts to seize it. Kissinger's deputy, Al Haig, saw Hamburger Hill as a military fiasco, "an inexcusable squandering of U.S. lives for a piece of real estate, which . . . could have been neutralized by overwhelming fire superiority available to every U.S. commander." Maj. Gen. Melvin Zais, commander of the 101st, and General Abrams vigorously defended the assault as a valid military operation, because the hill overlooked the main enemy supply route through the Laotian panhandle.[58]

The battle took on political as well as military significance, arousing critics and adding to the political pressure on Nixon to disengage from Vietnam. On 20 May Senator Edward Kennedy condemned the military's costly tactics at Hamburger Hill and denounced the administration's policies on the Senate floor. He was "disappointed that Nixon had not ordered a significant cutback in military operations in Vietnam and troop levels when he spoke to the nation." Kennedy's speech opened public debate on U.S. tactics and the cost of the war and garnered editorial support from numerous newspapers.[59]

The administration feared the uproar over the fight for Hill 937 could weaken support for its Vietnam policies. Nixon regarded Senator Kennedy as a political rival with enormous public influence and a possible presidential contender in 1972. Kennedy's speech and the ensuing debate in the Senate, according to Haig, gave "the doves on the Hill who were badly split and disorganized as a result of the President's [14 May] speech . . . a rallying cause." Haig opined that Hamburger Hill "in a political sense could not have been more costly to the President in our current efforts to sustain public support to go the route in Vietnam." Laird in private expressed again his doubts to Nixon that Abrams' practice of exerting maximum pressure on the enemy actually minimized U.S. casualties. He told Nixon he was considering issuing new guidance to the field. Contentious public argument lasted for weeks; for critics of Vietnam, the engagement came to symbolize the futility of the war.[60]

The Midway Conference and Troop Withdrawals

Just before the clamor over Hamburger Hill broke out, the White House announced on 20 May, the day of Senator Kennedy's speech, that Nixon would travel to Midway Island in the Pacific Ocean to meet Thieu on 8 June. In the interest of garnering favorable publicity, Nixon would stop in California and Hawaii on the way to Midway. Especially sensitive about his image at this time, he wanted his receptions in those states "to show public support."[61] Intending to announce the initial troop withdrawals at Midway, Nixon wanted to avoid creating the impression that the withdrawals would weaken South Vietnam politically or militarily. Thieu knew about the withdrawals in general. Rogers told him in mid-May that unilateral withdrawals were likely during the summer, but would not endanger South Vietnam's security. Laird, Abrams, and Bunker also discussed the issue with Thieu.[62]

High-level military and civilian leaders meet in Honolulu to discuss the first U.S. troop withdrawals from Vietnam, June 1969. Left to right: Commander in Chief Pacific Admiral John McCain, Wheeler, Laird, Nixon, Rogers, U.S. ambassador to the Paris peace talks Henry Cabot Lodge, U.S. ambassador to South Vietnam Ellsworth Bunker, and Kissinger. (Nixon Presidential Library)

Nixon thrashed out his final decision on the actual size of the initial withdrawal in a conclave on 7 June in Honolulu with Rogers, Laird, Wheeler, Lodge, Bunker, Abrams, CINCPAC Admiral John McCain, and Kissinger. On the table were the options for withdrawing U.S. troops in 1969 that Laird had presented to the president in his 2 June memorandum. The following day, Nixon met privately with Thieu on Midway Island. According to Kissinger's memorandum of the meeting, Thieu broached the topic of American withdrawal. Recognizing the political pressure on Nixon to disengage from Vietnam, Thieu believed that by 15 July the United States could phase out part of the 3rd Marine Division and six battalions in the Mekong Delta.[63]

Immediately following the session, Nixon announced his decision to withdraw 25,000 Americans by August in accordance with the recommendations of Thieu and Abrams. Future U.S. withdrawals, Nixon stated, depended on making headway in training and equipping the RVNAF, progress in the Paris talks, and the level of enemy activity. By characterizing the withdrawals as conditional, the administration hoped to convince the public and Hanoi that it would take forces out of Vietnam only when its ally was capable of coping with the adversary.[64]

To help carry out Vietnamization, Laird took a number of steps immediately after Midway. He sent several members of his staff, including Assistant Secretary for Public Affairs Daniel Henkin, to assist CINCPAC in planning the redeployment of 25,000 troops from Vietnam in July and August. He approved the Army's plan to relocate about 7,400 soldiers from Vietnam to Hawaii and another 8,000 to the continental United States (CONUS) for demobilization. About 8,000 Marines would transfer to Okinawa and 400 to Japan. Some 1,200 Navy personnel would redeploy to the Pacific Fleet and locations in CONUS. He also appointed Assistant Secretary of Defense (ISA) Warren Nutter on 17 June to head a DoD task force to review the progress in managing Vietnamization. The group would study redeployment planning and improvements in Vietnamese forces. The U.S. military services and commands would still bear responsibility for planning and executing the redeployments of their units. Nutter's group, which met daily starting on 18 June, contained representatives from key OSD offices. The effect of withdrawals on the negotiations, the Defense budget, and the conduct of the war would become clearer in the coming months.[65]

On 8 June Nixon's off-the-cuff comments undermined his carefully orchestrated public withdrawal plan. Former Defense Secretary Clifford in the June issue of *Foreign Affairs* called on the administration to withdraw 100,000 U.S. ground troops by the end of 1969 and all U.S. ground troops by the end of 1970. In his 19 June press conference the president first disparaged Clifford's suggestion, noting that the former secretary had not withdrawn any U.S. forces. Then he concluded with an unscripted flourish, stating he hoped to "beat Mr. Clifford's timetable."[66] Kissinger, discouraged by this impromptu statement, thought Nixon had given the impression that he had decided to pull out of Vietnam. He saw Nixon's statement as impetuous, rendering implausible the administration's insistence on mutual withdrawals. Haldeman believed the president simply overplayed his hand rhetorically in trying to one-up Clifford, but the impact of the pronouncement was not easy to dismiss. Concerns expressed by nations contributing troops to South Vietnam's defense—Australia, Thailand, Korea, New Zealand, and the Philippines—forced the White House to try to clarify the president's position. The State Department sent a cable on 21 June to these nations, stressing that the pullout of American forces remained contingent, as always, on the improvement of the RVNAF, progress in the Paris talks, and reduced combat levels in South Vietnam.[67]

Nixon's comments disquieted Thieu, apprehensive about withdrawals in 1969 that might exceed the levels he discussed with Nixon at Midway. After meeting with South Vietnam's president in July, Wheeler concluded that a failure to confer with South Vietnamese officials regarding the number of troops withdrawn in 1970 "would impose severe psychological and political handicaps" on the Thieu government. Wheeler did not believe that the United States could complete the pullout of all troops by the end of June 1971, expecting that it would have to keep a residual force in Vietnam "for some years to come" unless and until the North Vietnamese withdrew.[68]

Nixon found it necessary to personally reassure Thieu on future withdrawals. During his round-the-world trip the president made an unscheduled stop in Vietnam on 30 July to visit U.S. troops and consult with Thieu, who told him that it was important to develop a plan for further reductions in 1970 and coordinate it with the South Vietnamese government. Thieu stressed that "it was important that the reductions should not appear to be sudden improvisations." Nixon agreed to follow a plan for withdrawing troops, but he added that it should be kept secret and not disclosed publicly to avoid revealing to Hanoi "what we propose to do."[69]

Unlike Kissinger, Laird was not discouraged by Nixon's 19 June impromptu remarks. He regarded them as a reason to speed the rate of withdrawals and to revise MACV's mission. With the policy of withdrawals already in place, he believed the existing mission of seeking to defeat Communist forces in South Vietnam no longer conformed to the president's new objectives. In requesting the JCS to review the mission, Laird cited Nixon's 14 May speech that had "ruled out attempting to impose a purely military solution on the battlefield," and his 19 June statement about withdrawing 100,000 (instead of 50,000) service personnel from Vietnam in 1969. Accordingly, Laird considered it compulsory to reassess military strategy and the employment of U.S. forces in Southeast Asia.[70]

Disagreeing with Laird, Kissinger saw pitfalls in accelerating the rate of Vietnamization. Removing troops too quickly, Kissinger told Nixon, would weaken Thieu's confidence and increase the pressure on him to reach a political settlement. Kissinger believed that faster withdrawals would lead to a U.S. "cop out" by the summer of 1970. He urged intensified military pressure in hopes of forcing Hanoi to seek a settlement within six months.[71]

The president attempted to resolve the differences between Laird and Kissinger at what Haldeman termed a "big meeting" with his top advisers on the presidential yacht *Sequoia* on 7 July. The meeting grew out of a Rogers proposal that Nixon establish a Vietnam policy level group comprising Rogers, Laird, Wheeler, and Kissinger, over which the president would preside. Nixon agreed with the proposition and added Attorney General John N. Mitchell as a member. He wanted to meet with the group only "as the need arises in lieu of the full NSC." Present on 7 July were Rogers, Laird, Kissinger, Wheeler, Mitchell, and Lt. Gen. Robert Cushman, the deputy CIA director.[72]

Kissinger carefully laid out for Nixon the issues likely to arise at the meeting. At the top of his list was how to respond to the drop in the fighting first noted in May. From 1 April to 9 May, American units reported a total of 633 enemy attacks, a number that fell to 254 for the period 10–26 May. The decline in enemy activity continued into June. Some North Vietnamese units returned to North Vietnam, and Hanoi had not sent reinforcements south. The infiltration pipeline was empty. Given the drop-off in enemy activity, Kissinger advised that the United States remain firmly on course—adhere to its negotiating position in Paris and not ease up militarily in Vietnam. He recommended delaying until August a decision on the number of additional U.S. troops to pull out in 1969, warning that "a too-rapid withdrawal might seriously shake the Thieu government" and "create excessive optimism in the United States and make the withdrawal irreversible."[73]

The meeting's participants, with the exception of Wheeler and Kissinger, expressed their views that the administration should respond to the enemy by slowing down operations and accelerating the withdrawals, discounting Kissinger's counsel. Increasing the pace of U.S. operations during the lull, they feared, would demonstrate disinterest in pursuing a negotiated settlement and place the onus for the continuing casualties on the administration. Following this discussion, Nixon asked Wheeler to review General Abrams' mission statement, which dated from the Johnson administration, to determine if it could be changed, a step that Laird supported. Wheeler opposed any change that would lessen the intensity of operations. He later told McCain and Abrams that he wanted the allies to apply maximum pressure on the enemy.[74]

Laird overrode Wheeler, directing that U.S. objectives be changed to conform to the tenets of Nixon's 14 May speech. He wanted to make the preparation of the RVNAF to take over responsibility for the war the primary goal. He expressed his position to Assistant Secretary Nutter, who was advising him on Vietnam: "If our objectives in Southeast Asia are to be secured, the RVNAF modernization and improvement program *must* succeed. It is as simple as that." The secretary also wanted General Abrams to understand that minimizing American casualties was "a specific part of U.S. policy." Laird decreed that the second increment of withdrawals in 1969 should exceed 25,000, a significant change from his earlier position.[75]

In July Wheeler conferred with McCain in Hawaii and Abrams in Vietnam. On his return to Washington, Wheeler reported that the United States could withdraw up to 25,000 more troops in 1969 if battlefield conditions warranted, but he considered a higher number to be infeasible. For future redeployments, Wheeler, Abrams, and McCain urged a "cut-and-try approach" based on progress in building up the RVNAF and the actions of the enemy. Wheeler continued to defend the current Abrams strategy of maintaining contact with and preempting the movement of large enemy formations against cities and towns, asserting that the MACV commander's use of mobility and massive firepower was frustrating the enemy's actions at the lowest level of friendly casualties. Wheeler and Abrams were convinced that lessening the pressure on enemy units would allow them to move more freely and lead to higher friendly losses. Constant pressure on large enemy formations kept them away from population centers. The two generals found it mistaken to conclude that offensive operations automatically led to more American dead and wounded.[76]

Laird persisted despite Wheeler's opposition to changing the mission statement, but he did coordinate closely with the JCS on the revisions. His military assistant, Colonel Pursley, suggested some new language for the revised statement. On 7 August the secretary informed Nixon that he had changed the mission statement to reflect "your policy guidance much more accurately than does the current mission statement" and to describe more exactly what U.S. forces were actually doing. Instead of calling for military force to halt Communist efforts to defeat the Saigon government, the new statement called upon the United States to assist in training and equipping the RVNAF, continue military support to pacification, reduce the flow of materiel and personnel support for enemy forces, and revise directives for employing U.S. forces in accordance with the change of mission. In Laird's view, the revision put the focus properly on building up South Vietnam's forces and government, interdicting enemy supply lines, and reducing the American ground combat role. Laird wanted the JCS to issue the updated statement in a low-key manner without making any public announcement. Kissinger later claimed that Nixon at the last minute decided not to issue the new mission statement, but was thwarted because Laird had already issued the new instructions to the JCS, which went into effect on 15 August. In his account, Kissinger, however, gave no reason for Nixon's alleged change of heart or why the president simply did not countermand Laird's action, but clearly the secretary had outmaneuvered the presidential assistant. The August statement made Vietnamization the primary focus. The need to improve and modernize South Vietnam's forces took on fresh importance.[77]

Improvement and Modernization Plans

Efforts to strengthen the RVNAF went back to the Truman administration and had always been among Washington's objectives, although after 1965 such programs were clearly secondary to the U.S. combat role. The appointment of Abrams as Westmoreland's deputy and selection of Robert W. Komer to run U.S. support of pacification under the MACV commander in May 1967 signaled renewed interest in strengthening South Vietnam's forces. Walt W. Rostow, Johnson's national security adviser, expected Abrams to remold the ARVN into a first-class counter-guerrilla force. Komer, who was Lyndon Johnson's special presidential assistant for overseeing pacification support, was to increase U.S. military support of Vietnamese pacification efforts and to enhance South Vietnam's paramilitary forces providing rural security.[78]

In November 1967 Westmoreland gained Pentagon approval to increase the size of South Vietnam's armed forces to 801,215 in 1970 from the earlier planning figure of 777,884. Although Secretary Clifford made no plans to withdraw troops in 1969, he shared the sense of urgency about strengthening South Vietnamese armed forces. At Deputy Secretary of Defense Paul Nitze's direction, the JCS prepared a two-phase Improvement and Modernization Plan based on the existing Vietnamese force structure. The goal was to build a balanced, self-sufficient force by the end of FY 1974 that could handle the VC insurgents only, not the North Vietnamese Army. In December 1968 Nitze questioned whether the plan's emphasis on conventional combat units was appropriate for the kind of political-military struggle that he expected would follow a reduction in hostilities. Reflecting the Johnson administration's policy, Nitze wanted the RVNAF to be capable of dealing with VC insurgents after American and North Vietnamese forces withdrew. On 4 January 1969 the JCS submitted to Clifford an accelerated I&M Plan with a FY 1972 completion date, earmarking additional U.S. equipment for the RVNAF.[79]

The Johnson administration had planned to build up the South Vietnamese military but not to withdraw U.S. forces. Nixon intended to do both. Vietnamization made the Improvement and Modernization Plans a central part of the new president's policy. Not wanting to pull out unconditionally and thus abandon South Vietnam, Nixon tied withdrawals to the ability of South Vietnam's forces to replace departing U.S. units and to be capable of standing on their own. This required a larger, more capable, and better equipped military that could handle both the insurgents and the North Vietnamese Army.

Secretary of the Army Stanley Resor warned Laird in mid-March 1969 of the problems an accelerated I&M plan would create for the U.S. Army. He pointed out that the diversion of U.S. equipment would result in "further reducing the readiness of major U.S. Army commands outside Southeast Asia and of the Reserve Components." To carry out the accelerated plan using FY 1969 and FY 1970 funds, Resor observed, would defer meeting the equipment requirements of the active Army and reserves for 12 to 18 months. Additional funding and procurement authority was necessary "to preclude the further decline of the already inadequate level of readiness of forces outside of Southeast Asia," Resor asserted. A month later he highlighted the impact of I&M on an already stretched Army aviation program. Providing UH–1 Iroquois helicopters to the Vietnamese air force "will delay distribution to U.S. Army commands in Europe and Korea and will require those commands to retain less modern helicopters as first line aircraft."[80]

Deputy Secretary of Defense David Packard approved the accelerated plan on 28 April 1969, despite its impact on the U.S. Army. He observed that "Vietnamizing the war should have the highest priority" and that equipment provided to the RVNAF should include the requisite training and logistic support. To Vietnamize the war, the administration had little choice but to draw equipment from American units if it wanted the South Vietnamese military to stand on its own against both VC and North Vietnamese forces. Packard authorized the selective turnover of equipment from U.S. units and was willing to accept some impact on the readiness of Army units not in the war theater. The accelerated plan raised the RVNAF force structure to 875,750.[81]

The size of South Vietnam's armed forces required continued review. At the Midway Island meeting in June, Thieu had requested additional air, armor, and artillery units for the RVNAF that would raise the force structure above one million. Abrams considered these new units unnecessary given the current level of U.S. support and deemed them too complex for the Vietnamese to handle on their own. The JCS agreed, citing leadership deficiencies and the limited technical expertise of Vietnamese forces. Abrams and the JCS deemed the current modernization plan adequate and congruent with Vietnamese capabilities. The Joint Chiefs also resisted the idea of pulling out all U.S. forces and strengthening South Vietnam's forces to handle the VC and North Vietnamese Army. Like Abrams, the service chiefs assumed U.S. forces would need to remain in-country. Laird had a different view. On 12 August he approved an increase of 77,883 in the RVNAF force structure and directed the U.S. military departments to provide the requisite supplies and equipment. The total approved RVNAF force structure would reach 953,673 by the end of FY 1970 and 992,837 by the close of FY 1971.[82]

Most significantly, Laird's August decision changed the purpose of the Improvement and Modernization Plans. No longer were the Joint Chiefs to prepare the RVNAF to handle only an insurgency, Laird decreed. Henceforth they were to "transfer progressively to the Republic of Vietnam greatly increased responsibility for all aspects of the war" and develop armed forces "with the capability to cope successfully with the combined Viet Cong–North Vietnamese Army threat." The additional FY 1970 costs of Vietnamization would be met by reprogramming or transfers between appropriations. Increases for FY 1971 would stay within Packard's fiscal guidance of July 1969.[83]

Vietnamization Triumphant

Laird's determination to make South Vietnam capable of taking over the entire ground war from withdrawing U.S. forces, coupled with North Vietnam's refusal to discuss mutual withdrawal at the Paris talks, brought Vietnamization to the verge of irreversible unilateral withdrawal. This outcome occurred much to Kissinger's dismay and in spite of the president's fervent insistence during the winter and spring of 1969 that the withdrawal of forces would be mutual. Kissinger brought his forebodings to Nixon on 10 September. Basing his comments on a memorandum drafted by one of his assistants, Anthony Lake, Kissinger feared that time was moving more quickly against Washington than it was against Hanoi. Kissinger did not believe that current plans would achieve a U.S. victory in two years. Troop withdrawals were unlikely to reduce public pressure on the administration to end the war. Moreover, this pressure would highlight for Hanoi the internal divisions in the United States and the weakness of Nixon's political support. The "withdrawal of U.S. troops will become like salted peanuts to the American public: The more U.S. troops come home, the more will be demanded." Nor was Kissinger confident that the RVNAF could take over more of the fighting. He concluded, "There is not therefore enough of a prospect of progress in Vietnam to persuade Hanoi to make real concessions in Paris. Their intransigence is also based on their estimate of growing U.S. domestic opposition to our Vietnam policies. It looks as though they are prepared to try to wait us out. . . . I do not believe we can make enough evident progress in Vietnam to hold the line within the U.S."[84]

Two days later, on 12 September, with Bunker and Abrams present, the NSC met to discuss Vietnam policy and additional troop pullouts. The meeting lasted all morning. Nixon held an additional session with Bunker and military commanders in the afternoon. Much of the NSC meeting dealt with the withdrawal of U.S. troops, about which, Kissinger noted, there was no debate. Nixon wanted no public comments on this issue and no disclosure prior to the next redeployment announcement. At the end of the meeting, a frustrated Kissinger remarked tersely that the administration needed "a plan to end the war, not only to withdraw troops. This is what is on peoples' minds."[85]

On 16 September Nixon announced that he would lower the authorized U.S. troop ceiling in Vietnam of 549,500 in effect at the start of his administration to 484,000 by 15 December. This reduction included the 25,000 personnel cut (Phase I) of June and the 40,500 reduction (Phase II) of September. Phase II would reduce Army personnel by 14,263; the Navy, by 5,239; the Air Force, by 2,541; and the Marine Corps, by 18,457. Nixon decided to withdraw more troops than he had announced at Midway, but he made no mention of future withdrawals. In discussing the president's decision with the press, Laird acknowledged the reductions exceeded the JCS recommendation. According to a news account, Laird overruled the JCS based on his conviction that "only sharper cuts will persuade Thieu we are leaving and take the heat off the Administration on the college campuses this fall." The Phase II redeployments would also inactivate 20,000 spaces, predominantly Army, also part of Laird's effort to cut defense expenditures. Laird's measures would shrink the overall size of the armed forces by more than 150,000 in 1969.[86]

The lower Vietnam troop ceiling also cut back the number of men that the government needed to draft. On 19 September Nixon announced the cancellation of the November (32,000) and December (18,000) draft calls. The October call-up of 29,000 would be spread over the last three months of 1969. The number of future draftees would depend on progress in Vietnamization. Reductions in overall military strength allowed DoD to lower the January call to 12,500.[87]

Uneasy about the president's decision to proceed with redeployments, Kissinger late in October brought to Nixon's attention once again his "serious doubts about the assumptions underlying our reliance on Vietnamization." Among the faulty assumptions that Kissinger cited were the belief that Vietnamization would slow the growth of opposition to the administration's policies, confidence in the ability of the South Vietnamese to assume a greater combat role, and optimism about the effect of the enemy's losses on his political strength and will to continue the struggle. He believed that Hanoi's current strategy of protracted war, using "low-cost tactics" while waiting for a U.S. domestic collapse, was the same used against the French. "In the long run, Vietnamization will become unilateral withdrawal," he correctly predicted. Kissinger implored Nixon to change the policy of Vietnamization because he believed it played to Hanoi's advantages and would lead to failure. Kissinger failed to sway Nixon. Politics remained a powerful force pushing Vietnamization inexorably forward.[88]

The Military Option: Duck Hook

Although Nixon was committed to withdrawing American forces, he still wished to mount a punishing military operation that would cause Hanoi to reduce its military effort and become more cooperative at the Paris talks. Earlier, in February and March 1969, the White House had directed the JCS to prepare military plans for carrying out feigned operations, such as mining Haiphong harbor. When the issue of employing military force to coerce Hanoi came up again in May, Laird, ever sensitive to the political aspects, voiced concern that escalation would inflame the administration's critics. The JCS, however, wanted real action, fearing that threats and feints without military follow-through would have little effect on Hanoi, leading it to conclude that the United States was only bluffing.[89] In the fall, planning for a military operation against Hanoi began in earnest. Nixon had decided in July to "go for broke" and attempt to end the war through negotiations or by an increased use of force. He set 1 November, the anniversary of President Johnson's bombing pause, "as the deadline for what would in effect be an ultimatum to North Vietnam." Kissinger set up a military planning group in September and October to explore military options. Duck Hook, the name given to this campaign, would begin on 1 November.[90]

On 7 October the JCS forwarded to Laird their plan for concentrated air and naval operations against North Vietnam "to achieve maximum practicable psychological and military impact." In the first phase of the plan, U.S. forces would neutralize North Vietnam's air force, close the country's ports, and destroy important logistical facilities. Allowing for bad weather, this phase would last 9 to 21 days, according to JCS estimates. The second phase would target Hanoi's will and ability to continue the war by striking port facilities and coastal vessels and by interdicting the northeast railroad line from China. According to planners, the combined effect of both phases would reduce the flow of imports to North Vietnam and erode Hanoi's ability to wage war and support the insurgency in South Vietnam. Laird opposed the plan because he thought its risks and costs outweighed its benefits. He further undermined the plan by insinuating that the JCS had reservations, writing the president that even the Chiefs did not claim it would lead to "decisive results."[91]

Kissinger reached a similar conclusion, finding the plan inadequate. Noting the lack of unanimity within the administration, he urged Nixon to defer the Duck Hook plan, because it could not attain the quick, decisive military action he thought was necessary. The plan would not achieve the goal of developing a military operation (mining and bombing) that would exacerbate the economic strains and convince North Vietnam that it faced "the prospect of increasing economic and industrial deprivation if they do not come to a settlement." Kissinger urged the president to encourage the Chiefs to develop a plan that better fit his objectives, an operation consisting of "short, sharp military blows of increasing severity" to ensure that the destruction achieved "a lasting military and economic effect." Kissinger's concept would warn North Vietnam it would bear even higher costs should it fail to come to terms. His doubts about Vietnamization were unshakeable. In his mind the program would founder on the intractable problem of having to battle North Vietnam and domestic critics at the same time.[92]

In weighing Duck Hook, Nixon also took into consideration ongoing campus protests and the forthcoming 15 October Moratorium, a nationwide demonstration against the war. In an attempt at preemption, Nixon announced on 13 October that he would make a major speech on Vietnam on 3 November. Hanoi sought to exploit the demonstration, releasing a letter on 14 October encouraging antiwar protesters to demand that Nixon end his war of aggression. Although Nixon felt he needed to take action to maintain his credibility, he avoided military escalation for a number of reasons. U.S. casualty figures were falling; a new operation would cause them to rise. The death of North Vietnam's leader Ho Chi Minh in September 1969 might present a new opening for negotiation. Duck Hook would do nothing to improve the ability of South Vietnamese forces, upon which continued withdrawals depended. With antiwar protests looming in early November, with Kissinger, a strong proponent of military action dissatisfied with the military planning, and with Laird opposed, in the final analysis it was no wonder that Duck Hook was put aside. The operation's goal, to punish North Vietnam with military strikes, would surely energize U.S. antiwar sentiment. Carrying out as harsh a plan as Kissinger wanted would be a great difficulty; achieving decisive military results seemed well-nigh impossible.

Nixon's televised 3 November speech related his administration's efforts to reach an agreement and reduce the number of American combatants. Appealing to what he called the silent majority of Americans supporting his policy, the president said he would keep his commitments in Vietnam to fight and negotiate and to build up the RVNAF to reach an honorable settlement of the war. He stated his opposition to the unilateral exodus of U.S. troops from Vietnam. The schedule and size of future withdrawals, Nixon declared, would remain contingent on progress in Paris, on improving the capability of South Vietnam's forces, and on the level of violence in Vietnam. Wanting no public speculation about additional redeployments, Nixon enjoined Laird and Rogers not to discuss the topic. After the speech the president's approval rating rose to 68 percent, and the House of Representatives passed a resolution supporting his policy. His speech and its reception strengthened his negotiating position at the Paris talks.[93]

Nonetheless, the administration's withdrawal planning continued unabated. On 15 November Nixon scheduled a meeting with Rogers, Laird, Kissinger, and Mitchell to consider the timing and size of the next redeployment increment, Phase III, and the long-term withdrawal program. This was the same day as a massive antiwar demonstration in Washington, the so called New Mobilization, which Haldeman estimated attracted some 325,000 protesters. Three options for the next withdrawal increment were under review: 50,000 over three months; 60,000 over 4½ months; or 100,000 over 6½ months. Kissinger urged the president to pull out fewer troops to confirm that he was not yielding to the protests. Rogers supported a predetermined schedule for the withdrawal program, while Laird and Mitchell favored flexibility. Nixon did not want to be hemmed in by a rigid timetable, believing that a flexible approach to withdrawals would moderate pressures to withdraw larger numbers faster.[94]

Abrams also weighed the withdrawal options, but he did not consider it "militarily sound to redeploy any more U.S. troops at this time." He strongly opposed the withdrawal of 100,000 by July or August 1970 and warned that the even higher figures being discussed, up to 235,000, would materially compromise the Vietnamization program. Abrams did not believe that South Vietnamese forces could compensate for the reduction in U.S. forces. The JCS recommended deferring the next troop withdrawal (Phase III), fearing the enemy could initiate a major offensive on short notice and that the ability of allied forces to respond would be seriously reduced by the redeployment of American combat brigades. If the president thought he had to announce additional redeployments, the JCS recommended that he pull out no more than 35,000 troops, and no earlier than March or April 1970.[95]

In forwarding to Kissinger the JCS recommendations on 12 December, Laird expressed his disagreement with their position. The secretary contended that the evidence the JCS adduced weakened the conclusions they reached. The JCS believed the enemy could not sustain an attack for a long period, citing an increase in enemy combat losses and defectors and continued progress in Vietnamization and pacification. To Laird these were reasons to carry out, not defer, the third increment. Believing that "progress in Vietnamization begets further progress," Laird asserted that halting or impeding the momentum of Vietnamization "could readily beget further delays or impediments to progress."[96]

Nixon announced his decision on 15 December. He reminded the radio and television audiences of his criteria for continued withdrawals: progress in the peace talks, no escalation of enemy military activity, and success in training South Vietnam's forces. He acknowledged the absence of any progress in the negotiations since November and the substantial increase in enemy infiltration, but the improvement of South Vietnam's forces encouraged him enough to be cautiously optimistic. Accordingly, he had decided to reduce the U.S. troop ceiling by another 50,000 by 15 April 1970, reflecting a cut of 115,500 since 20 January 1969. As he had in other speeches, the president warned that he would not hesitate to take "strong and effective measures" should enemy moves jeopardize the American forces remaining in Vietnam.[97]

Behind the debate over troop withdrawals lurked a fundamental issue: the Vietnam force level that the FY 1971 budget could support. Based on the decisions of NSDM 27, defense planners, working with data from the comptroller and Systems Analysis office, assumed that projected FY 1971 spending levels required a total reduction of 190,000 troops by the end of the fiscal year (30 June 1971). Under current planning assumptions, the in-theater force level at the end of June 1971 could be no higher than 260,000.[98] On 20 December Laird brought this to Nixon's attention, recommending that the administration "base the budget on the 260,000 figure." The secretary also pointed out that the administration needed to present the FY 1971 budget to the public and Congress without disclosing the administration's plans for Vietnamization or the year-end strengths of U.S. forces in Vietnam, information of real significance for North Vietnam's leaders. Nixon agreed and directed "that efforts to surface these figures . . . be strenuously deflected."[99] More important, the president approved Laird's memorandum and its FY 1971 budget strategy for Vietnam, which set the maximum U.S. force level for 30 June 1971 at 260,000. Because of budget limits, the administration had to meet that figure, whether or not the president's criteria for continued withdrawal were met. Adjusting the pace of the withdrawals to reach that target offered the only flexibility the administration would have between December 1969 and June 1971. In accepting Laird's figures and his arguments, Nixon effectively undercut any future arguments against the cuts that Kissinger might make. For better or worse, this made Secretary Laird a key figure in winding down the war.

IN 1969 NIXON DISPLAYED frequent ambivalence in making war policy. Bending to domestic political realities, he agreed to withdraw, but still wanted to press Hanoi with military power to force a settlement. He displayed firmness in private in adhering to conditional and mutual withdrawal, but in public he offered to negotiate. Hoping to retain political support, he announced his decision to withdraw American units from Vietnam even in the absence of concessions by Hanoi. His impromptu, unguarded response to Clark Clifford's proposal undermined his carefully crafted façade, revealing his vulnerability to political pressure. His instinct to escalate the fighting and to conduct military actions outside Vietnam reflected his deep-seated belief that a leader should take bold decisive steps. Nixon said he decided in July 1969 to attempt to end the war through negotiations or the increased use of force, yet he abandoned Duck Hook, the plan for escalation, that Laird had opposed. Through 1969, the Nixon administration wavered, talking of mutual withdrawals and military action but eschewing both in favor of a policy of unilateral withdrawals and reliance on negotiations.

The president's chief advisers, Laird and Kissinger, differed strongly in their positions on war policy. So that American combatants could leave Vietnam, Laird changed the purpose of the Improvement and Modernization Plans. The RVNAF was to be prepared to cope with the Viet Cong insurgency and the North Vietnamese Army. He also changed MACV's mission statement to reflect the policy of preparing South Vietnam to fight the entire war on its own. Laird viewed himself as a pragmatic political adviser convinced of the need to set the United States on the path to disengagement and to reduce casualties. He pushed for a quicker disengagement than Kissinger, who advocated military pressure to wrest concessions from the North Vietnamese. Fearing the ramifications of Laird's pressure to withdraw, Kissinger was frustrated by the secretary's success in pushing through Vietnamization and by his own inability to persuade Nixon to intensify military operations against North Vietnam. Laird, the politician, and Wheeler and Abrams, the military experts, disagreed on the relationship of the intensity of operations to the number of casualties, but that issue had less import once Laird had given clear instructions to reduce the tempo of ground operations.

During the debate over Vietnamization, Nixon had sidestepped the strong measures of Duck Hook, but he sought other ways to increase military pressure on Hanoi. In 1969 he began a secret bombing campaign against enemy base areas in Cambodia and followed that in 1970 with a cross-border assault to clean out the sanctuaries. The president, abhorring the thought of seeing the United States lose a war, kept the nation engaged in Vietnam until the start of his second term.

—— CHAPTER 5 ——

The Battle over Troop Withdrawals

WHEN EVALUATING POLICY CHOICES early in 1970, the Nixon administration faced multiple uncertainties—among them the depth of domestic political support for its Vietnam policy, the true capabilities of South Vietnam's armed forces, and the military risks of continuing U.S. withdrawals—that complicated its decision making. Laird and Kissinger reached different conclusions on how to handle these uncertainties. Convinced above all else of the need to get out of Vietnam, Laird became the architect and main proponent of Vietnamization. A hard-nosed Kissinger reluctantly accepted the need to withdraw forces but continued to press for strong military operations as a way to facilitate negotiations to end the war. With Vietnamization underway, how many troops to withdraw and how quickly became the central, contentious questions for which Kissinger and Laird found differing answers.

With his background in politics, Laird was convinced of the necessity of withdrawing U.S. forces from Vietnam, and he wanted it done as quickly as possible without undue risk to the effort in Vietnam. It was his conviction that a slow, incomplete withdrawal would have adverse political consequences for the president. To Laird, U.S. withdrawals and the transition from a conscripted to an all-volunteer force were tightly linked: Both furthered the common goal of bolstering political support for the administration. Kissinger favored a slower pace of withdrawals than Laird primarily to sustain military pressure on the enemy and maintain morale in South Vietnam. The battle over the speed of redeployments began in earnest after Laird's February 1970 trip to Vietnam. The secretary eventually won the fight over the size and timing of the fourth tranche of troop reductions through a mix of bureaucratic skill, consideration of the Defense budget, and reductions in the size

Right to left: Secretary Laird; General Creighton Abrams, commander of the U.S. Military Assistance Command, Vietnam; and JCS Chairman General Wheeler listen to a briefing in Vietnam, February 1970. (NARA)

of the draft calls. Before he took that trip, Laird had already won the president's approval for a U.S. troop ceiling at the end of FY 1971 and used this ceiling to drive the pace of withdrawals.

Complicating these Washington-based bureaucratic battles were the capabilities and goals of the enemy. The undeniable, hard truth was that Hanoi had no intention of giving up or compromising its goal of uniting all of Vietnam under its flag. Viet Cong and North Vietnamese forces located in South Vietnam continued to mount operations. Enemy forces also remained stationed in sanctuaries across the border inside the officially neutral nation of Cambodia and could easily enter South Vietnam, launch an attack, and retreat across the border. Under the Johnson administration's rules of engagement, U.S. and South Vietnamese forces were not allowed to undertake large-scale offensive operations against these cross-border bases. Infiltration of troops and supplies into the South primarily through Laos and Cambodia along the Ho Chi Minh Trail continued unabated to fuel the war.

Cost and Pace of Withdrawal

Laird and Wheeler visited Vietnam, 10–14 February 1970, to consult with Bunker, Abrams, and President Thieu. The secretary and the JCS chairman sought answers to the difficult policy questions facing the administration. Foremost was whether U.S. programs could meet the objective of building a South Vietnamese military force and government able to function on their own. On his return, Laird sent a lengthy, generally upbeat report to the president, characterizing the view of top U.S. and Vietnamese officials as one of "cautious optimism." These leaders thought that the Americans and South Vietnamese had sufficient fighting strength to prevent the enemy from achieving victory and that the South Vietnamese were "making satisfactory progress in Vietnamization, especially on the military front." To sustain Vietnamization and national self-determination, Laird argued, the United States would also have to do more to assist the South Vietnamese in developing a self-sufficient economy, a position Nixon supported.[1]

Laird concluded and so informed Nixon that fiscal and political constraints made necessary continued U.S. withdrawals under Vietnamization. In the current austere economic environment, diminished funds for national security would narrow the latitude for U.S. operations. To sustain domestic support, something that could not be taken for granted, and operate within available resources, Laird considered it essential to shift the burden of military combat to South Vietnam. In his view, the fiscal situation provided "an incentive and reinforcement to the Vietnamization policy." Referring to cuts in the FY 1970 Defense budget and the proposed reductions in the FY 1971 budget, Laird alerted Nixon to a shortfall of $1 billion in the total cost of MACV and Vietnamese proposals to build up the Republic of Vietnam Armed Forces. He believed that the shortfall left him with two choices: using available assets more efficiently or increasing the rate of U.S. redeployments. He foresaw no possibility of getting an FY 1971 supplemental appropriation from Congress.[2]

The secretary perceived a larger issue as well. He and Wheeler agreed that the department could no longer "consider Vietnam outlays separately from our world-wide defense needs." During his years in Congress, Laird bemoaned, leaders in Washington had paid insufficient attention "to the fact that Vietnam war costs have such a direct relationship to our total national defense needs, or that difficult tradeoffs are involved."[3]

The secretary's report to Nixon conveyed points that Laird had also brought before American and South Vietnamese leaders. He argued not just for continuing Vietnamization but for quickening its tempo. Laird had to take into account the unrelenting pressure to cut his budget. A Bureau of the Budget analysis prepared in March 1970 of the FY 1971 Defense budget concluded that even if DoD kept its outlays at the low end of the fiscal guidance of NSDM 27 ($73 billion vice $76 billion) it would confront "very serious problems in the near-term." Accordingly, BoB lowered projected Defense budget guidance to $72.6 billion in outlays.[4]

Unsurprisingly, MACV Commander General Abrams differed with Laird, expressing to the secretary when he was in Vietnam his misgivings about quickening the pace of withdrawals. Above all Abrams wanted to have the necessary forces and equipment on hand to cope with the military situation, and he told Laird that he doubted whether it was possible to devise military procedures that could save money and accomplish the mission. The MACV commander believed the coming fourth redeployment increment would be difficult—the "crunch" increment he called it—citing weak leadership in the RVNAF, logistical difficulties in executing the withdrawals, and possible severe psychological impact on the South Vietnamese. Wheeler sided with Abrams, warning that hastening the rate of withdrawals would put Vietnamization at risk if the enemy threat increased. Laird did not budge, telling Wheeler and Abrams at the 11 February briefing at MACV headquarters that "the number one national priority is to make Vietnamization work."[5] And that meant the withdrawals had to continue as scheduled.

Laird's report to Nixon downplayed the difficulties that Abrams expressed in Saigon. He reminded the president that the MACV commander believed the enemy lacked the ability to mount widespread, sustained or decisive offensives in the near future. Alluding to the Abrams report, Laird concluded that enemy action was unlikely to put Vietnamization at risk. He indicated that OSD was working to resolve the logistical problems of Vietnamization and downplayed the military leadership weaknesses that Abrams had identified. Laird noted that South Vietnam's leaders expressed confidence that their forces could fill in for the departing Americans, but U.S military leaders did not embrace this view. This was a significant difference of judgment. Nixon termed Laird's account "an excellent report" and made numerous handwritten notations in the margins for Kissinger to take follow-up actions.[6]

Haig erupted when he read Laird's arguments for faster withdrawals. He had traveled to Vietnam in mid-January at the president's direction to look at the effectiveness of the Army of the Republic of Vietnam. Kissinger had recommended Haig's trip to Nixon because, as he observed, the ARVN "suffers from rather serious problems." During his two-week visit Haig found not cautious optimism but concern that the ARVN had not significantly improved under the Vietnamization program to date. Moreover, even the rate of improvement had slowed at the end of 1969. He condemned Laird's view of the coming "crunch" withdrawal as "naïve, misinformed and indicative of his failure to understand or his unwillingness to carefully assess the existing military situation in Vietnam." Haig expressed shock that the president in reading the secretary's report had glossed over what he called Laird's whitewashing of the situation, even seeming unconcerned over the $1 billion shortfall that Laird noted. To Haig, the requirement for those funds was valid, deriving from the military commanders' assessments of what they needed to build an effective military. Calling Laird's report an "optimistically glossed propaganda ploy," a rationalization for getting out of Vietnam as quickly as possible, Haig feared it would be the basis of future decisions on withdrawals and the shape of South Vietnam's armed forces. Although infused with inflammatory language, Haig's comments were nonetheless a realistic, sobering commentary on the military situation in Vietnam.[7]

Like Abrams and Haig, Kissinger opposed an accelerated rate of withdrawal, fearing it could demoralize South Vietnamese leaders and result in a loss of territorial security and popular support for the Saigon government. With the Paris negotiations stalemated, Kissinger told Nixon in January that he saw no reason to expect the North Vietnamese to give up their 25-year struggle to take over the South. He warned the president to be skeptical of the sanguine reports about Vietnamization emanating from Vietnam, asserting there was a lack of "proof that ARVN has really improved." Kissinger thought there might be "too much pressure from the top for optimistic reporting."[8]

Kissinger also took issue with Laird over the viability of Vietnamization, choosing to focus on what South Vietnam's forces could actually accomplish. Laird's withdrawal scheme could succeed, only "if ARVN performance, GVN [Government of South Vietnam] territorial force performance, and GVN government effectiveness improve as planned" and if the enemy threat continued to decline. Kissinger emphasized to the president that such improvements were "far from certain," seeing instead the likelihood of reverses because the enemy had neither given up nor been defeated. He derided the notion that the Saigon government could overcome its deficiencies according to a schedule and that the enemy would follow the U.S. plan. On the contrary, Kissinger highlighted issues of serious concern: the intensive enemy logistic buildup in Laos, faltering pacification gains, shortcomings in the ARVN and the territorial forces, and continuing government corruption and ineffectiveness.[9]

Haig looked at the situation in Vietnam from the perspective of a career Army officer, who saw serious deficiencies in Vietnam's forces as reason to slow the rate of the withdrawals. Kissinger, also conscious of the ARVN's weakness, viewed the situation as a strategist, who saw faster, scheduled withdrawals as weakening the negotiating efforts. Although Laird was certainly aware of the ARVN's limited capabilities, he viewed the quickening pace of withdrawals largely from a political perspective, believing it would yield domestic benefits and budget savings.

Rather than debate Kissinger on the accomplishments of Vietnamization and the capabilities of the ARVN, Laird instead focused on the implications of a smaller FY 1971 budget. Writing to the president shortly after returning from Victnam, Laird emphasized the decline in the budget would influence the rate of withdrawal despite the misgivings of MACV and the White House. With Total Obligational Authority (TOA) funding for the war dropping from $14.7 billion in FY 1970 to $10.5 billion in FY 1971, mounting a larger number of military ground operations would depend on the availability of funds. The reduction in money would also affect air operations, forcing a cut back in tactical and bomber sortie rates. Most significant, in Laird's analysis lower budget levels would force the administration to keep withdrawing forces from the war theater. Fewer troops in Vietnam would obviously reduce expenditures. Laird pointed to an inexorable logic of a tightly linked chain of circumstances: Vietnamization would result in diminished U.S. combat operations, which in turn would require fewer funds, imposing further restrictions on forces and combat operations in Vietnam. To reinforce his case, Laird made clear that increasing the activity level in Vietnam would require additional reductions elsewhere and affect "readiness levels necessary to support NATO and other non-Southeast Asia commitments."[10]

Kissinger faulted Laird's reliance on budget ceilings to set the pace of withdrawals. This course of action would force other military programs to compete with

Vietnamization, requiring the JCS to make trade-offs between programs. Budget ceilings could even compel field commanders to operate cautiously in order to avoid incurring large expenses. Laird's budgetary restrictions, Kissinger asserted, would make it impossible for Nixon to follow through on his threats to take drastic military steps against Communist forces. As a result, the president could expect resistance to funding any operation undertaken to sustain his warnings.[11]

Kissinger believed that Nixon needed stronger control of the withdrawal process and a better understanding of the actual capabilities of South Vietnam's forces, lamenting the absence of a sound analytical framework to evaluate the effectiveness of the RVNAF. Agreeing, Nixon established an interagency task force under the Vietnam Special Studies Group that prepared quarterly reports with detailed information on Vietnamization and special assessments of the situation in the countryside and in specific provinces. At Kissinger's prompting, the group also devised a composite index based on available data on rural security to measure enemy or governmental control of Vietnam's hamlets and villages.[12]

The Fourth Tranche

Differences over the pace of Vietnamization came to a head in March 1970, when Nixon considered how many troops to withdraw in the fourth or next phase, termed critical by Abrams. Haig used the term "tranche," a slice or cut, to describe the phase. Aware of the conflicting positions, the chief executive heard the views of his key advisers on Vietnam (Laird, Kissinger, Abrams, and Wheeler), but he closely held his own deliberations. In making his decision, the president could not finesse the limitations of the Defense budget.

On 11 March Nixon opened the discussion by asking Wheeler for his views on the next withdrawal phase. The president did this privately to avoid having Wheeler's conclusions filtered or interpreted by the defense secretary. Nixon asked whether Wheeler preferred two small reductions—one between 15 April and 15 June 1970, and a second between 15 June and 15 August 1970—or a single sizable one between April and August. On 17 March Wheeler replied to the president in an unsigned, undated single-page memorandum through Captain Robinson, his liaison officer in the White House, to avoid informing Laird. Wheeler preferred one large reduction, because it would allow greater flexibility in the selection of forces to redeploy, be easier to handle logistically, and permit retention of key units in Vietnam until late in the withdrawal period. He believed the overall situation did not warrant further redeployment and recommended delaying the fourth slice pending another assessment.[13]

In a 13 March cable to Wheeler expressing similar views, Abrams warned that budget cuts in FY 1971 would reduce U.S. forces in Thailand and fix U.S. withdrawals "without regard to the requirements imposed by the enemy situation or the pace of Vietnamization." He claimed that the reductions would also undermine the president's ability to carry out his pledge to take strong measures if enemy actions jeopardized remaining American forces in Vietnam. Abrams urged postponement of further withdrawals because South Vietnam's forces had not improved sufficiently and lacked a sufficient number of capable leaders for expansion.[14]

Wheeler endorsed Abrams' views and recommended deferring a decision on the next withdrawals until 15 June. The JCS chairman concluded that the increase in the effectiveness of Vietnamese forces thus far "barely compensated" for the decrease in the number of U.S. battalions. Further reductions would increase the chances that the enemy could make fresh gains. Laird did not treat Abrams' 13 March message with urgency, waiting until 7 April to forward it to the White House, telling Kissinger somewhat disingenuously that he did not want to "burden" the president with the "full compendium" of JCS and MACV views.[15]

Despite pleas in April from Abrams and Wheeler to defer the next redeployment, the White House nonetheless proceeded to plan for additional withdrawals, deferring to political realities. On 6 April Kissinger informed Bunker that "any announcement which is substantially less than the pattern set heretofore could be the source of major problems with domestic critics." Kissinger's statement acknowledged that the administration did not fully control the withdrawal process. Nixon contemplated pulling out a minimum of 150,000 troops over the next year, with a possible token withdrawal over the short term. This approach, Kissinger wrote to Bunker in early April, would permit the military situation to dictate the rate of withdrawals and provide Abrams more flexibility. Kissinger asked Bunker whether he and Abrams preferred the large cut of 150,000 over a 12-month period or the redeployment of 40,000 between 15 April and 15 August, which Laird had proposed. Bunker and Abrams favored the large cut and believed Thieu would accept it. They preferred it because they could slow down the rate of withdrawal during the rest of 1970 and thus provide more troops in-country. Bunker assumed the reduction would lower U.S. troop levels in Vietnam to 284,000 by 30 June 1971, apparently unaware that his figure was 24,000 higher than the 260,000 maximum that Laird told Nixon the budget would support.[16]

For his part, Laird wanted no easing of redeployments. On 7 April he informed the president that he desired to remove 40,000 soldiers from Vietnam between mid-April and mid-August. In his mind, the dividends of withdrawal were significant: reduction of American combat deaths, greater Vietnamese efforts to attain self-suffi-ciency, lower costs to the United States, and diminished opposition to the war. From Laird's perspective, the steady reduction of U.S. forces offered the main incentive for the Saigon government to keep improving its forces and to strive to stand on its own. Crucial for retaining public and congressional support for Vietnamization, redeployments would help make the domestic economic burden tolerable.[17]

Ostensibly to discuss the fourth redeployment increment, the president sched-uled a meeting with Laird, Wheeler, Rogers, and Kissinger for 13 April. Kissinger wanted Nixon to give Laird and Wheeler the impression that he was thinking of withdrawing 35,000 to 40,000 soldiers between April and August 1970, offering them an opportunity that day to express their views. The session would be a cha-rade, for Nixon had already resolved to withdraw 150,000 troops over the next year. To prevent leaks, he intended to keep this decision from members of his cabinet and the bureaucracy, informing cabinet members of the size of the withdrawal shortly before making it public.[18]

On 20 April the president announced from California that he would pull out an additional 150,000 troops by spring 1971, saying the military and diplomatic situa-tion would set the timing and pace. The authorized force remaining in Vietnam at the end of FY 1971 would fall to around 259,000, a level that the DoD budget could support. Spreading a large withdrawal over a full year, Nixon concluded, would permit him to keep the bulk of U.S. combat troops in-country until the fall of 1970.[19]

Laird expressed reservations to Kissinger the same day. The secretary was upset that Nixon had abandoned "all of the arguments for regular announce-ments," apparently referring to Nixon's oft-stated policy of linking withdrawals to the level of enemy activity, progress at the peace talks, and the degree of progress in improving Vietnamese forces. Laird wanted to set classified target dates for the withdrawals to keep Vietnamization on track. In addition, he wanted to pull out 50,000 soldiers by 15 August to allow him to stay within DoD's budget, believing he could still meet his budget ceiling even with a withdrawal of 40,000 troops by that date. Kissinger responded that Nixon wanted a slower rate of withdrawal and believed that taking out even 40,000 by mid-August would be too fast. Laird objected, insisting that he had no choice but to lower authorized troop strength in Vietnam to 260,000 by the end of June 1971. "I have to make it," he told Kissinger, "because it's all the money I have."[20]

Before Nixon decided the exact timing and rate of the 150,000 troop withdrawal, he again in April consulted with Abrams and Laird. Abrams wanted to redeploy about 20,000 by 1 September and another 30,000 by 1 January. Laird wanted to press ahead with U.S. reductions because Abrams would have more forces in Vietnam in August than the budget would support. On 22 April Nixon decreed that no more than 60,000 soldiers would be withdrawn in 1970. He directed the secretary not to schedule withdrawals until he reviewed a plan to that effect. The president wanted the flexibility to base the redeployments primarily on progress in Vietnamization and the option of accelerating or delaying the withdrawals, depending on progress in the talks and the level of enemy activity.[21]

Laird nonetheless pressed to speed up the withdrawal. On 24 April he asked Wheeler to prepare a redeployment plan to pull out at least 50,000 troops by 15 October (a higher figure than Abrams desired by that date), but not more than 60,000 by the end of December. Laird used a figure of 284,000 for a 1 May 1971 ceiling, emphasizing to Wheeler the need to make trade-offs to keep within the budget.[22]

At the end of May, Laird informed the president again of DoD's fiscal problems. He anticipated that Congress would reduce the FY 1971 budget by another $1 billion and that revised budget planning levels would be lowered over the next few years, forcing him to make drastic cuts in the conduct of the war and U.S. commitments and capabilities elsewhere. Spelling out dire consequences, he asserted the reduced FY 1971 budget would compel him to retire 3 or 4 attack aircraft carriers and all 4 antisubmarine warfare carriers; inactivate 2 Army divisions, including one from Korea; eliminate 4 Air Force fighter/attack wings and 130 of the oldest B–52 bombers; reduce continental air defense forces; cut military and civilian personnel by about 800,000; and cancel some major procurement programs. Laird contended that he could hold the cuts to these illustrative levels "only if we meet our current budget planning assumptions" for SEA deployments and sortie levels. Specifically, that meant reducing the number of troops in Vietnam to 260,000 by the end of

FY 1971 (30 June) and to 152,000 by the end of FY 1972. Monthly fighter and bomber sorties would have to be severely curtailed during those two years. Laird clearly indicated that the budget would determine the future withdrawal rate. He intended to use these budget planning assumptions, "unless," he wrote Nixon on 30 May, "I hear from you to the contrary." Nixon told Laird to hold off. He wanted the Defense Program Review Committee to examine DoD's budget in mid-July before Laird made decisions on programs, sortie rates, and troop withdrawals. Laird raised no objection but advised Nixon that JCS planning would employ the assumptions of his December 1969 memorandum that Nixon had previously approved. At the end of 1969, the president had approved Laird's budget strategy for Vietnam, setting the maximum U.S. force level for 30 June 1971 at 260,000.[23]

The budget complicated troop withdrawal planning, especially for the Army, which had the largest personnel contingent in Vietnam and created pressure to speed up redeployments. Laird's goal of pulling 50,000 troops from Vietnam by mid-October instead of mid-August, and the planned withdrawal of some Marine Corps rather than Army units, meant that the Army would keep more forces in Vietnam for a longer time and incur estimated additional costs in FY 1971 of $460 million. The reason was that troops were more expensive to maintain in Vietnam than in the United States. Slower withdrawals would cost the Marine Corps an extra $24 million.[24]

As an added difficulty, the January to March draft calls (50,500) fell short, affecting the Army's personnel and training pool. The result, Secretary of the Army Stanley Resor warned Laird at the end of April, would be a temporary shortfall of around 40,000 in Army strength for the remainder of 1970 that could affect the readiness of units in the strategic reserve. Moreover, the Army and the Marine Corps argued that the FY 1971 budget underfunded them by $500 million. Other pressing budget demands included the additional $1 billion cost of tactical air and B–52 sorties desired by MACV and CINPAC and the extra $500 million for the most recent refinements of the RVNAF Improvement and Modernization Plan. To meet these requests for higher outlays Laird had to find savings. Accordingly, on 15 May he requested that Wheeler draw up a second withdrawal plan accelerating U.S. redeployments from Vietnam.[25]

In consultation with Abrams and McCain, the Joint Chiefs in June formulated two alternatives for withdrawing 150,000 troops. Alternative A would reduce U.S.

manpower in Vietnam by 60,000 between 1 July and the end of 1970 and by 90,000 by 30 April 1971. Alternative B, based on DoD budget constraints, accelerated the withdrawal schedule, redeploying 60,000 by 15 October, an additional 40,000 by 31 December 1970, and another 50,000 by 1 May 1971. Wheeler, McCain, and Abrams opposed the latter alternative, warning Laird that pulling out 100,000 soldiers by the end of 1970 would be risky and allow little flexibility to slow deployments should the military situation make that necessary. They recommended alternative A, which accorded with Nixon's policy and their estimate of the military situation.[26] The Army dissented from the JCS recommendation. In July Secretary Resor informed Laird that the Army lacked the funds to support alternative A and could not produce sufficient replacements to sustain the larger Vietnam force required by alternative A in January and February 1971. Resor believed that the Army could maintain the Vietnam troop level of alternative B.[27]

During his trip to Vietnam from 26 June to 11 July, Resor tried to make MACV leaders aware of the budget pressures driving the withdrawal rate. Meeting with the MACV command group on 29 June, Resor told them, "You've got a limited amount of dollars to spend on the war here, and if you need them in one area—say to slip your deployment schedule—you'll have to watch immediately the dollar cost of that and be ready to fund it yourself out of a saving of some other program." Resor's comments met with dismay. General William B. Rosson, Abrams' deputy, protested that MACV withdrawal planning should be guided by the number that could be redeployed without undue military risk, not by budget considerations, and that military channels in Washington had supported that approach. Resor's response was blunt: "I think the JCS really ought to send you the [budget] numbers, because I think from now on one has to really manage it [the war] out here with the resources in mind." On his return, Resor alerted Laird that he "received the impression that General Abrams and the MACV staff currently believe that they have substantially greater flexibility in determining the rate of redeployment and the level of air sorties than is in fact the case. If this is true, it could lead to serious misunderstanding." On the basis of his trip, the Army secretary concluded that Abrams should be made aware of the FY 1971 and FY 1972 program constraints.[28]

In July Resor expressed the hope that the upcoming DPRC session would focus on near-term issues and highlight for the NSC and the president the Army's manpower and budget problems. Kissinger, who thought Laird based his May memorandum on unsupported fiscal generalizations, gave the DPRC a different focus. He directed the group to examine the trade-offs between defense and non-defense spending and the impact of various spending levels on U.S. capabilities, not withdrawal schedules or the Army's manpower problems.[29]

Kissinger further entreated Nixon to adhere to current bombing and withdrawal levels at least through July and not consider any redeployments beyond those announced in April, citing the September negotiations and a possible enemy offensive before the U.S. fall elections. To keep the defense secretary from taking new initiatives, Kissinger asked Nixon near the end of July to discourage Laird from telegraphing "either through in-house planning or by public statement that the U.S. may expedite already announced withdrawal schedules."[30] Undeterred, Laird wanted the momentum of redeployments to continue through 1970 and took steps to that end. Citing the Army's manpower problems and the infeasibility of a budget supplemental, on 30 July he requested the JCS to review withdrawal plans, taking into account currently planned FY 1971 funding and the Army's manpower constraints. The secretary wanted the plan by 5 August.[31]

To its frustration, the White House saw no way to break the link between the DoD budget deficiency and U.S. troop levels in Vietnam. On 9 August Haig ruefully complained to Kissinger that Laird's "management chicanery," underfunding the Army and establishing draft quotas of 10,000 a month, had "painted the President into a corner." In July Laird had set the monthly draft calls for August to December at roughly 10,000, attributing the decrease to progress in Vietnamization and a subsequent decline in strength. "The insidious way in which Laird reduced draft calls," Haig concluded, "has made it totally impossible for the Army to maintain approved force levels in Vietnam even if Laird had provided the money." Kissinger informed Nixon on 17 August that Laird's budget and his scheduling of draft calls made it necessary to accelerate the president's withdrawal plan of 20 April. This speedup would occur even though the JCS thought a faster redeployment schedule posed imprudent risks to U.S. objectives and Vietnamization. To Kissinger, Laird's approach of allowing the budget to dictate the troop ceiling in Vietnam meant the administration had sacrificed its "biggest bargaining chip"—its ability to time the withdrawals.[32]

The White House's unease became palpable after Laird sent Kissinger on 20 August 1970 the JCS recommendation, which took into account the Army's budget shortfall. The Chiefs insisted that only alternative A (their previous recommendation) met the force requirements of the field commanders and incurred no undue military risk, but they had to concede that the Army's fiscal and manpower constraints precluded its adoption. That left alternative C (a slightly modified alternative B)—pulling out 50,000 by 15 October, another 40,000 by 31 December, and another 60,000 by April 1971—as their preference. Deciding that it was prudent and affordable to accommodate the JCS, Laird accepted the recommendation, even though the resulting mid-October 1970 troop ceiling (384,000) exceeded the level submitted to Congress (367,000). He believed DoD could manage its spending to pay for the additional troops. Laird also told Kissinger that the Office of Management and Budget wanted to reduce outlays $1.2 billion below the FY 1971 request and that a budget supplemental was unlikely.[33]

Frustrated by Laird's actions, the White House reacted harshly to what he had done. Haig characterized Laird's approach as "patently dishonest," because the secretary had forced the Joint Chiefs to make recommendations within monetary and manpower constraints. Robinson, the JCS liaison officer in the White House, asserted that Admiral Moorer, who took over as JCS chairman on 2 July 1970, had not seen Laird's memorandum to Kissinger, an action that without irony he called "devious." He noted that Laird neglected to assess the risks of the quicker pullout. In an "eyes only" communication on 21 August, Robinson privately informed Moorer of the contents of Laird's memorandum. According to Robinson, Laird heatedly told Kissinger and Haig in private that the president had accepted the stepped up withdrawal pace. Kissinger replied that the issue remained unresolved. On 27 August Kissinger brought Laird's memorandum to Nixon's attention, pointing out that the secretary had required the JCS to make choices within strict fiscal guidance and assume the greater risk of withdrawing troops more quickly. He highlighted the personnel turbulence of a faster pace and reminded Nixon of his decision to withdraw no more than 50,000 troops by December 1970. A slower pullout would leave in Vietnam a higher residual U.S. combat strength that would help discourage a Tet offensive in 1971 and provide maximum bargaining leverage. Whatever his reason, Nixon requested no action or change and merely placed a check mark on the document. Apparently the president had accepted faster withdrawals. Even though Kissinger failed to persuade Nixon to oppose Laird's acceleration of the April withdrawal plan, he followed Haig's recommendation and sent Laird a memorandum stating that the

As a captain, Rear Adm. Rembrandt Robinson was assigned in 1969 to the office of the Joint Chiefs of Staff and headed the JCS Liaison Office at the White House. In that capacity he worked with Kissinger and Chairman Thomas Moorer. He was killed in a helicopter crash in 1972 while serving in Vietnam. (U.S. Navy)

president requested his views and those of the JCS, MACV, and CINCPAC on the risks of faster redeployment.[34]

Laird stood by his 20 August recommendations, seeing no "significant difference in the risk associated with the slower schedule" and the one he proposed. Optimistically viewing progress on the fighting front, in pacification, and in reducing the enemy threat as more favorable than he had anticipated a year before, Laird believed his recommendations represented "the best balance between military requirements and manpower and budgetary constraints." A slower pace would cost an added $400 million. Laird also reaffirmed his recommendation to redeploy 40,000 troops between 15 October and 31 December, because available funds and manpower could support that schedule. "The added risk of such a schedule is minimal," Laird asserted, "particularly when viewed in context of the progress of pacification and Vietnamization."[35]

On 24 September Wayne Smith, an analyst on Kissinger's staff, after reviewing the redeployment issue, warned Kissinger emphatically that the scarcity of military manpower "*all but precludes manning a force in South Vietnam larger than that he [Laird] recommends.*" Low draft calls and low enlistments and reenlistments meant that DoD could attain the JCS desired troop level in Vietnam only by drawing forces from NATO and other theaters. He decried Laird's budget argument as "full of holes" but stated that the secretary's decisions on draft calls and manpower had "all but ruled out any option other than Laird's." With no viable alternative to Laird's recommendation, it was hardly surprising that Nixon in a terse public statement on 12 October announced that he had authorized Laird to withdraw an additional 40,000 from Vietnam by Christmas.[36]

Looking back, Laird had outmaneuvered Kissinger on the pace of withdrawals. Deciding the size of the critical fourth withdrawal increment proved long and complicated, but Laird's shrewd, calculating use of the limits of DoD's budget and the availability of manpower trumped the military's desire to keep a larger force in Vietnam for a longer time and the White House's wish for flexibility. During the discussions, Laird repeatedly emphasized to the White House and JCS that the budget would determine the maximum U.S. troop level in Vietnam. Kissinger, Haig, and Robinson, hardly innocent of intrigue, characterized Laird's approach as a devious and dishonest way to speed up the withdrawals. In Laird's defense, how could he not consider his budget when planning troop withdrawals? How could the defense secretary not request the JCS to take costs into account when formulating redeployment options? Laird accomplished his goal by foreclosing any other real alternative to his course of action, but his successful maneuvers exasperated, even angered, White House officials.[37]

Shortly after the president's October announcement, Resor presented Laird with additional information on the Army budget that served to further validate Laird's position on Vietnam withdrawals. Given current budget levels, reduced monthly draft calls, and shortfalls in trained personnel, the Army could support a force of only about 192,000 in Vietnam at the end of FY 1971 and might be forced to draw down forces elsewhere. By contrast, the MACV commander planned a year-end Army strength of 203,000 for Vietnam. Resor believed that Abrams, although aware of the 192,000 figure, had not been formally notified of the final decision. A lower Army manpower ceiling meant a loss of flexibility in planning the U.S. withdrawals from Vietnam in FY 1972 and later, raising the possibility of unplanned withdrawals from NATO and Korea in FYs 1972 and 1973. Resor reported that the Army would have difficulty in carrying out Laird's request to reduce overall Army manpower to 915,000 by the end of FY 1972 and to 838,000 by the end of FY 1973 without having to withdraw additional Army combat and support forces from Vietnam. For perspective, the Army projected it could maintain at the end of FY 1971 a worldwide force of 1.08 million, about 158,000 fewer than provided for in the FY 1971 budget.[38]

At the DPRC meeting on 24 November to discuss the Army's manpower situation, Deputy Defense Secretary Packard reported that the Army faced serious shortfalls in units in Europe and Korea because monthly draft calls were capped at 10,000 for the rest of 1970. Raising draft calls in 1971 to alleviate manpower shortages could create domestic political problems. There was no debate at the meeting about the sobering reality of the Army's problem and the hard choices facing the president. If he desired more U.S. soldiers in Vietnam, he would have to raise 1971 monthly draft calls above 15,000 or change personnel policies. If he wanted to keep monthly draft calls at 10,000, he would have to reduce the Army's Vietnam strength below planned deployment levels or change established personnel policies such as the 12-month tour in Vietnam. Kissinger's summary was glum: "It is obvious from today's briefing that we have been operating on two totally inconsistent tracks. On the one hand we have the Presidential directive that there are to be no further withdrawals from Europe, Vietnam, or Korea beyond those he has approved for FY 71. On the other hand we have manpower policies that force the President to make changes which make it impossible to carry out planned deployments. The President has to address this problem immediately."[39]

Afterward, Packard presented Kissinger with alternatives for handling the situation. First, if the president decided to hold Army draft calls to 10,000 and to maintain the 260,000 force level in Vietnam for FY 1971, then in the event of a crisis the administration could alleviate the overall strength shortage of 50,000 to 60,000 for much of FY 1972 by extending terms of service for men completing their tours of duty. Second, if Nixon raised the draft calls in early 1971 to 15,000 or more and kept total Vietnam strength at 260,000, it would reduce worldwide shortfalls and provide flexibility to slow or stop redeployments from Vietnam during the Tet holiday of 1972. This alternative would come with an increased budget cost of $75 million in FY 1971 and $170 million in FY 1972. The final alternative would reduce the 30 June Vietnam end strength to 250,000 and draft 14,000 to 17,000 men per month. This option would shrink the Army manpower shortfall to 20,000 or less and provide greater flexibility in redeployment planning in FY 1972 at a relatively lower cost. The most sensitive alternatives—extending terms of service and increasing draft calls—had obvious political costs.[40]

The JCS resisted Resor's proposed reductions. They recognized that the Army would be unable to support more than 192,500 in Vietnam without reducing forces elsewhere, but nonetheless argued in favor of CINCPAC's assessment that total U.S. manpower in Vietnam not go below 255,000 (198,000 Army). The JCS believed that an end strength below 198,000 would threaten the gains of Vietnamization and elevate the risk of an enemy offensive that could increase U.S. casualties. The Chiefs also proposed that the Army retain 152,000 soldiers in Vietnam until the end of

FY 1972, but the service remained opposed, arguing it could sustain no more than 115,000 in Vietnam. General Westmoreland warned that the JCS recommendations would cause "serious degradation of force levels elsewhere, including NATO." At the end of December 1970 DoD supported the Army, setting its end FY 1972 Vietnam force level at 115,000. The Army's manpower shortfall, the product of the tighter Defense budget and limited draft calls, would continue to affect the pace of American withdrawals from Vietnam.[41]

CHAPTER 6

Taking the Fight into Cambodia

PRESIDENT NIXON'S EMBRACE of the Vietnamization program in 1969 and reliance on bombing and ground operations to pressure the enemy to make concessions in Paris did not create a quick path to disengagement from the war. A major obstacle on that path was North Vietnam's use of Cambodia as a sanctuary, a supply route, and a launching pad for operations against South Vietnam. Before settling on the Vietnamization policy, the Nixon administration had embarked on a politically sensitive covert bombing operation against North Vietnamese bases in Cambodia for 14 months. The objective was to stem the flow of North Vietnamese combat and support units and supplies entering South Vietnam through the DMZ and through Cambodia and Laos, both officially neutral countries. The weak kingdom of Cambodia under Prince Norodom Sihanouk did not publicly protest the presence of North Vietnamese and Viet Cong forces inside its territory along South Vietnam's border.[1]

Long before Laird became secretary, the enemy's Cambodian base areas, within striking distance of Saigon, posed a critical problem for U.S. and South Vietnamese forces. In 1964 the JCS had sought permission for U.S. and South Vietnamese units to pursue enemy forces retreating into these cross-border sanctuary areas. President Johnson had prohibited ground operations but had authorized air reconnaissance and covert insertions of small U.S. Special Forces teams into Cambodia to gather intelligence. Nixon continued these limited ground operations (renamed Salem House in 1969). After the 1968 Tet offensive weakened the Viet Cong inside South Vietnam, Cambodia played a more significant part in Hanoi's military strategy. Following a course of protracted warfare to help rebuild its guerrilla forces and strengthen its political arm, North Vietnam moved additional NVA forces into

Cambodia, staged raids from bases there into South Vietnam, and supported the infrastructure and guerrilla forces remaining in South Vietnam.[2]

Nixon was receptive to new approaches in dealing with Cambodia. Before assuming the presidency he had voiced dissatisfaction with Johnson's limited response to the Cambodian sanctuaries. In early January 1969 he requested information on the enemy's presence in Cambodia and on what the United States was doing "to destroy the build-up there. I think a very definite change of policy toward Cambodia probably should be one of the first orders of business when we get in." Enemy strength in Cambodia included 11 known base areas, 3 divisions, and perhaps 5 to 7 regiments along the Cambodia-Vietnam border from Laos to the Mekong Delta.[3]

President Nixon first tried diplomacy, seeking to reopen U.S.-Cambodian relations. On 5 February 1969 Secretary Rogers urged Nixon to probe the Cambodian government's interest in resuming diplomatic ties, which had been severed in May 1965, anticipating better communication with the Cambodians and increased intelligence information. He expected no improvement in the military situation in light of Cambodia's cooperation with the North Vietnamese Army and Viet Cong. Kissinger also believed it important to improve relations before considering military activity against the North Vietnamese in Cambodia. The Joint Staff and OSD, concerned by the enemy's growing use of Cambodian sanctuaries, were leery of a rapprochement that might inhibit an expansion of the military's limited operating authorities.[4] Seeing little risk, Nixon wrote to Sihanouk about restoring relations. After the U.S. pledged in mid-April 1969 to respect Cambodia's sovereignty, neutrality, and territory, Sihanouk declared his readiness to begin talks. In July 1969 the two countries announced they would exchange chargés d'affaires.[5]

Pursuing Military Options

Concurrently with diplomatic overtures Nixon considered military action. Early in February 1969, MACV Commander General Creighton Abrams renewed his request for authority to conduct a short-duration, concentrated B–52 attack against Cambodian sanctuaries. He saw an opportunity to strike the Central Office for South Vietnam (COSVN), the enemy headquarters directing the war in the southern part of South Vietnam, reportedly located in the Fishhook area of Cambodia just across the border. Abrams contended that bombing the area would disrupt enemy

Secretary Laird enters the U.S. Embassy in Saigon with Ambassador Ellsworth Bunker, 12 February 1970. (NARA)

plans for an offensive in South Vietnam.[6] Ambassador Bunker concurred, but his cable to Nixon alarmed the president, who feared public disclosure and resistance by State Department officials should they learn that a bombing strike against targets in Cambodia was under consideration. Nixon, who wanted the matter "held as closely as possible in all channels and in all agencies," put into place elaborate precautions to keep the discussion of Abrams' request exclusively within military channels. Following explicit White House instructions, Rogers told Bunker that the president wanted to drop the bombing matter in view of his upcoming trip to Europe. The White House also instructed Abrams to have no further discussions with Bunker or embassy personnel on the issue. That message to Abrams, however, was intended only to keep the State Department in the dark. On an extremely close-hold basis Nixon continued to explore options for Cambodia and asked Abrams to send covertly to Washington a small military team to discuss a bombing operation.[7]

On 18 February two officers from MACV briefed Laird, Packard, Kissinger, Wheeler, Haig, and Pursley on a possible B–52 strike on the Central Office for South Vietnam. The session took place during breakfast in Secretary Laird's dining room, allowing Pursley in his notes to dub the conclave "the breakfast group." No State Department representative was present. The group considered two options—an overt deliberate strike on the enemy base and "a covert strike officially categorized as a mistake"—that Kissinger later presented to Nixon. An overt raid against COSVN absent enemy provocation had numerous advantages: It would display public candor and honesty, avoid credibility problems, and demonstrate the administration's willingness to escalate to achieve a settlement. Comparative ease in planning and executing also made the raid an attractive choice. On the other hand, this option contained considerable political risks, exposing the president to the charge of expanding the war against "neutral" Cambodia, possibly provoking a Soviet reaction, and forcing Sihanouk to denounce the United States publicly. Kissinger preferred to launch a covert strike against COSVN that could be characterized as accidental. Such an operation would show "the Soviets that we are serious about the war, without forcing them to take a public stance against our attack."[8]

Bunker's earlier endorsement of the Abrams request to bomb Cambodia narrowed the administration's options. It took away the possibility of a covert accidental strike because of the possibility that State personnel would claim deception and create credibility problems for the administration. A covert strike would pose no political risk as long as it remained concealed, but it would require extraordinary steps to preserve secrecy. Kissinger recommended that Abrams be allowed to bomb right up to the border in the Fishhook and prepare for a covert strike in Cambodia "on a contingency basis," in the event of enemy action in that area. Should the enemy make no move, Kissinger wanted the president to reconsider the proposal at the end of March 1969. Nixon approved and Kissinger informed Laird of the decision.[9]

Wheeler sent Abrams two separate messages on 22 February 1969: a routine cable authorizing him to bomb right up to the Cambodian border on the South Vietnamese side of the Fishhook and a backchannel "eyes only" communication advising him to continue planning for strikes on Cambodian sanctuaries on a contingency basis. In the backchannel message, Wheeler disclosed that the front-channel message was "for cosmetic effect only and is part of a cover plan now unfolding which may lead to an authorization to conduct a B–52 attack on the COSVN HQ facilities. We are attempting now to lay the groundwork for use of a rationale later that a mistake had been made due to ground radar or off-set bombing error." As requested by Kissinger, Wheeler prepared three "cover stories for B–52 strikes resulting from error." He warned Kissinger that none of the "stories will stand up, at least at this time, in view of Bunker's message to State," but could be used later in conjunction with an actual enemy attack across the border.[10]

To the administration, hitting the sanctuaries offered the possibility of strategic gains, and destroying COSVN headquarters would provide a tactical win. The strikes would signal to North Vietnam and the Viet Cong, as well as to the Soviet Union and China, that the United States would hold firm in pursuit of an honorable peace. Bombing Cambodia in conjunction with ongoing ground and air attacks in South Vietnam and Laos, constant reconnaissance of North Vietnam, and stepped-up B–52 raids in Laos would demonstrate to Communist powers Nixon's readiness to escalate.[11]

North Vietnam's 22 February offensive throughout South Vietnam increased U.S. casualties and set in motion further consideration of the secret bombing plan. Nixon regarded the attacks as a deliberate test designed to take his measure, as well as a rebuff to his overtures to North Vietnam during the transition to work on an honorable settlement. Kissinger described Nixon as "seething." The next day Nixon left for Europe. Haig and Col. Ray B. Sitton, a U.S. Air Force officer with B–52 expertise then serving on the Joint Staff, flew to Brussels, where Sitton briefed Haldeman, Nixon's chief of staff, and Kissinger on 24 February while Air Force One was on the ground. Nixon did not attend the very secret briefing fearing his presence would attract attention. Rogers and Bunker were admonished to ensure that knowledge of the plan went "no farther in Department of State channels." Kissinger alerted Laird to be ready to execute the attack with minimum notice.[12]

Nixon, however, waited until his return to Washington before proceeding with the bombing. On Saturday, 15 March, after a rocket attack on Saigon, the president ordered Laird to launch a B–52 strike against base area 353 in the Fishhook section of Cambodia on 17 March. Immediately after issuing the order, he wrote a memorandum for the record explaining his decision.[13] Having publicly warned that he would respond to additional North Vietnamese attacks, Nixon believed his credibility was at stake and the only way to jump-start the stalled negotiations was through military action—the kind of forceful step the North Vietnamese would appreciate. Under the president's 15 March order, the State Department and Ambassador Bunker were to be notified "only after the point of no return in the implementation of the Plan." Nixon would brook no appeal from his order to commence bombing. No officials were to comment on the attack without his permission. Remarking on his decision, Nixon boasted to Kissinger that this "will let them know who is boss around here."[14] Rogers was consulted about the bombing only after the decision had been made. Laird and Wheeler helped persuade Rogers to support the strike. It was important, Laird and Kissinger thought, "to keep the team together" and retain State Department support.[15]

The secret bombing, codename "Breakfast," was kept from the public and President Thieu. Nixon authorized Bunker to inform the South Vietnamese leader as soon as the operation actually began that the attacks were in response to enemy actions in III Corps. There would be "absolutely no reference" to "Breakfast" in press guidance. Kissinger prepared a public relations scenario to handle a possible disclosure. If the Cambodian government protested, only then would the administration apologize.[16]

Keeping the bombing surreptitious, Nixon hoped, would allow Sihanouk to remain silent. The president believed the Cambodian leader objected to the presence of North Vietnamese troops in his country but dared not protest because he was too weak to force them to leave. By the administration's reasoning, if the bombing became publicly known, Sihanouk would be forced to make an outcry. North Vietnam would not object because it had officially denied the presence of troops or installations in Cambodia, making it politically infeasible for Hanoi to disclose casualties or damage there. Thus the administration felt confident it could bomb without adverse international or domestic reaction.[17]

Laird was fully involved in planning the Breakfast bombing but disagreed with Nixon and Kissinger about doing it clandestinely. He later explained, "I told Nixon you couldn't keep the bombing in Cambodia secret. . . . It was going to come out anyway and it would build distrust. . . . I was all for hitting those targets in Cambodia, but I wanted it public, because I could justify before Congress and the American people that these were occupied territories of the North Vietnamese, no longer Cambodian territory. I could have made that case, but they [Nixon and Kissinger] thought it was important to keep it secret."[18]

The initial solitary Breakfast strike on 17 March 1969 started a secret 14-month-long nighttime bombing campaign, known as Operation Menu, which repeatedly attacked six base areas in Cambodia close to the border until 26 May 1970. To maintain secrecy, MACV and the Pentagon employed an elaborate dual reporting system for subsequent B–52 attacks on Cambodia. The JCS history of this period described how the system worked. Abrams would submit a limited-distribution backchannel message to the JCS requesting approval to bomb a target in Cambodia. The JCS then passed the request to Laird for approval. At the same time Abrams would make a separate routine request to bomb "a target in South Vietnam as cover for the Menu strike. Both strikes were approved, but normally only the Menu strike was carried out." The B–52s flew past the targets in South Vietnam and dropped their bombs in Cambodia. Of the B–52 crewmembers, only the pilots and navigators knew their aircraft were being directed by ground control sites to release ordnance in Cambodia. Target coordinates were hand-carried to the control sites just before the strikes occurred. "Routine reports were filed as though the strikes had been carried out on Vietnamese targets; separate reports, on a strict need-to-know basis, were submitted by special channel for the MENU strikes." The Menu sorties appeared in the overall statistical tallies but were in no way linked to Cambodia. During the course of the operation B–52s dropped 108,823 tons of ordnance and flew 3,875 sorties (see table 5). Laird noted that between March 1969 and March 1970 the Menu bombing amounted to "nearly one-fifth the tonnage dropped by U.S. forces in the Pacific theater during all of World War II."[19]

Table 5. Menu Sorties

Base Area	Sorties	Tons
350	706	20,157
351	885	25,336
352	817	23,391
353	228	6,529
609	992	26,630
704	247	6,780
Total	3,875	108,823

Source: "DoD Report on Selected Air and Ground Operations in Cambodia and Laos," 10 September 1973, folder Cambodia, box D17, Melvin Laird Papers, Gerald R. Ford Library.

The White House informed a small group of legislators. At Nixon's direction, Kissinger briefed Senators John Stennis and Richard B. Russell Jr. (D–GA) on 11 June 1969, emphasizing the absence of complaints from Sihanouk about the bombing. The administration justified the secrecy as enabling the United States to demonstrate its "resolve in a manner which has completely befuddled Hanoi" and allowing the U.S. to retaliate for Communist offensives without generating the domestic or international backlash that overt retaliation might have caused. Senate minority leader Everett M. Dirksen (R–IL) and Representatives Gerald Ford and Mendel Rivers were among the small group of legislators whom Nixon and Kissinger briefed on the Menu operation. In addition, Laird informed key members of the Appropriations and Armed Services committees of both houses. Nixon saw no need to consult the full Congress, claiming he was following accepted briefing practices for classified operations.[20]

The dual reporting system remained secret until its disclosure during the Watergate scandal. A DoD report in September 1973 put the reporting system in context, explaining that information on Menu sorties was blended into less highly classified material in the database on air operations. As a result, Menu sorties were included in the overall statistical totals but identified with Cambodia only in special security channels of which few officials knew. Thus decision makers with access to the special channels received accurate and complete data on all Menu sorties. Those without a need to know were unaware that some sorties targeted Cambodia. Information furnished to Congress about air strikes inadvertently provided erroneous statistics about the country-by-country location of the bombing.[21]

Once embarked on a course of secret bombing, the need to maintain secrecy became all-consuming for the White House. On 9 May 1969 *New York Times* reporter William M. Beecher published a story about the Cambodian bombing. His report provoked no public outcry, but the administration feared the security breach would lead to full disclosure of the Menu campaign. The administration took drastic measures to discover Beecher's source. On the day Beecher's article appeared, Kissinger urgently requested the director of the Federal Bureau of Investigation (FBI), J. Edgar Hoover, to assist in finding the informant. Two days later Haig, on behalf of Kissinger, requested FBI wiretaps on several high-level officials, among them Morton Halperin of the NSC staff and Laird's military assistant, Colonel Pursley.[22] Laird also came under suspicion because of his opposition to the secrecy. He later recalled that Kissinger phoned him on the golf course to say that the president was mad at him, accusing him of leaking the story to the *Times*. Laird said he told Kissinger "to go kiss off" and went back to the links.[23] In preparing for an interview with ABC television in 1980, Beecher acknowledged that neither Laird nor anyone close to him was responsible for the leak. ABC chose not to air Beecher's comments, and he refused later to reiterate when Pursley pressed him to go on the record. "I make it a practice," Beecher responded, "not to talk about sources or non-sources. In a weak moment I bent my own rule. But thanks to ABC, the world will never know."[24]

At the end of September 1969, six and a half months after the start of Menu, Laird wanted assurances that the results of the secret bombing justified the associated risks. He asked if the military could achieve the same impact with fewer strikes. The acting chairman, Admiral Thomas Moorer, contended that the strikes inflicted more damage on the enemy than recent B–52 (Arc Light) missions in South Vietnam. The strikes had opened up the border area to more extensive reconnaissance, giving the JCS and MACV a clearer picture of the enemy's infrastructure in Cambodia. The Chiefs deemed the military risks minimal; likewise, the political risk, as long as the bombing harmed no Cambodians. The Chiefs had little to say about the political and diplomatic damage that exposure of the Menu operation would inflict on the administration. Pursley believed that such a revelation would have a detrimental impact on the administration's efforts to elicit support for U.S. policies in the region. To keep the bombing secret required continued precautions. When a strike possibly harmed some Cambodians, Laird asked Abrams to have "Menu-cleared people" conduct the investigation. To maintain secrecy, he did not want the State Department involved.[25]

The possibility of public disclosure worried Nixon. Early in March 1970 he asked Laird to assess whether the results outweighed the political hazards of continuing the raids. Laird reported that the Joint Chiefs and Abrams strongly affirmed the value of the Menu strikes in contributing to the overall interdiction of supplies and soldiers. Abrams described the extensive damage to facilities, the large number of secondary explosions, and the numerous cave-ins as significant. Moreover, the strikes weakened the enemy's ability to mount a major offensive, thus permitting continued U.S. withdrawal of its forces. Suspending the strikes would allow the enemy to reestablish his sanctuaries and possibly outstrip the capabilities of Vietnamese defenses. Abrams concluded that the Menu bombings, in conjunction with small forays along the Cambodian border, reduced the enemy's flexibility and restrained Hanoi's forces from going "deeper into Cambodia." He speculated that the Menu strikes contributed to the deteriorating relations between Cambodia and North Vietnam, allowing Phnom Penh to acknowledge publicly that the North Vietnamese Army and Viet Cong occupied parts of Cambodia. "Cambodian Government policy appears to have gradually shifted from one of cooperation to one of applying graduated pressure against VC/NVA troops" in hopes of forcing their eventual withdrawal, Abrams concluded. Although Laird remained apprehensive about the political risks, he concurred with the military's judgment that the operations were effective at an acceptable level of risk. Abrams and Bunker considered Menu "one of the most telling operations in the entire war." However effective the JCS and Abrams declared the bombing, by itself it could not end the threat of border sanctuaries to the security of South Vietnam. In fact, Abrams conceded in his 12 March 1970 evaluation that the enemy remained in the target areas and continued to rehabilitate and reestablish his bases.[26]

Striking the Sanctuaries

Harboring doubts about the enemy's ability to win the war, Sihanouk in February 1970 made public the presence of North Vietnamese forces in Cambodia and worked through diplomatic channels for their departure. Prime Minister General Lon Nol advocated an even tougher stance against Cambodia's historic adversary. This split between the country's leaders over the threat to its sovereignty occurred at a time of economic crisis. Falling rice exports, a chief source of income, undermined the weak unindustrialized economy. The continued presence of outside military forces and the economic downturn threatened to destabilize the government.[27]

While Sihanouk was in France on an extended stay, anticommunist demonstrations broke out in Svay Rieng Province on 8 March 1970. Instead of returning to Phnom Penh, Sihanouk flew from Paris to Moscow five days later. On 18 March the Cambodian National Assembly in secret session voted 92–0 to remove Sihanouk as chief of state. Lon Nol and Deputy Prime Minister Sirik Matak assumed control of the government in a bloodless coup. Following the change of government, NVA and Viet Cong forces seized a number of Cambodian outposts, and the now exiled Sihanouk, with the backing of Hanoi and Beijing, proclaimed from China the establishment of a Cambodian liberation army to restore him to power. The North Vietnamese Army and Viet Cong pledged military support.[28]

Believing that Lon Nol's regime would be unable to survive on its own, Nixon directed Laird on 25 March 1970 to prepare plans for possible attacks against the border sanctuaries. Laird endorsed the idea, seeing an opportunity to deal with a serious threat and also to highlight the enhanced capabilities of the Army of the Republic of Vietnam under Vietnamization. When he sent the president's request to JCS Chairman Wheeler, Laird termed it a request for a contingency plan for use if the Communists attacked Phnom Penh. The plan was to examine three alternatives: an offensive by an all-South Vietnamese force, a combined attack by American and Vietnamese units, and an exclusively U.S. assault. Laird assigned top priority to an ARVN-only operation. MACV had already been planning for a possible cross-border ground attack by U.S. and South Vietnamese troops, so they sent their plan immediately to Laird on 26 March. In forwarding the plan to Nixon, Laird complained it was "more a concept or proposal than a detailed outline for action." The secretary asked the JCS for additional information on the number of troops needed, the risks and benefits of the plan, and the cost of the planned operation. He also was looking for an assessment of its impact on Vietnamization.[29]

The Cambodian coup and the possibility of U.S. military intervention alarmed some senators. Majority leader Mike Mansfield, lamenting the overthrow of Sihanouk, who had kept his country out of the fighting, urged the Nixon administration at the end of March not to get involved militarily in Cambodia. Senator Hugh D. Scott Jr. (R–PA), the minority leader, agreed, and in April two other senators, John Sherman Cooper and Frank F. Church (D–ID), submitted an amendment to the defense appropriations bill prohibiting the entry of U.S. ground forces into Cambodia.[30]

Shortly after the coup, the administration established relations on "a temporary basis" with the new Lon Nol government, publicly stating it would respect Cambodia's neutrality.[31] But Nixon also saw the necessity of helping the new regime battle the Communists. Bunker warned that Sihanouk's return to power or a Communist victory would be regarded as an American defeat, make the Paris negotiations more difficult, discourage the South Vietnamese, and slow down the Vietnamization program. The president wanted to explore what military assistance the United States could provide to Lon Nol in secret. On 26 March he requested detailed plans for combined U.S.–South Vietnamese ground operations against Communist bases (see map, page 154). The State Department was kept ignorant of the planning. Abrams was authorized to consult with Bunker on condition that the ambassador would not inform his superiors in the department.[32]

In coordination with Cambodian officials, on 30 March MACV and South Vietnam's general staff prepared plans for attacking two different sets of base areas. Abrams sent the plans to Washington for review. The first option envisioned a combined multi-division assault by U.S. and South Vietnamese Army units against COSVN headquarters (base areas 352/353) with follow-on attacks. The second proposal, favored by the South Vietnamese, would use the ARVN alone to attack base areas 704 and 367/706, thought to be storage areas and transshipment points for men and supplies. Abrams, however, thought the first option would be more effective and result in fewer civilian casualties but higher American and Vietnamese

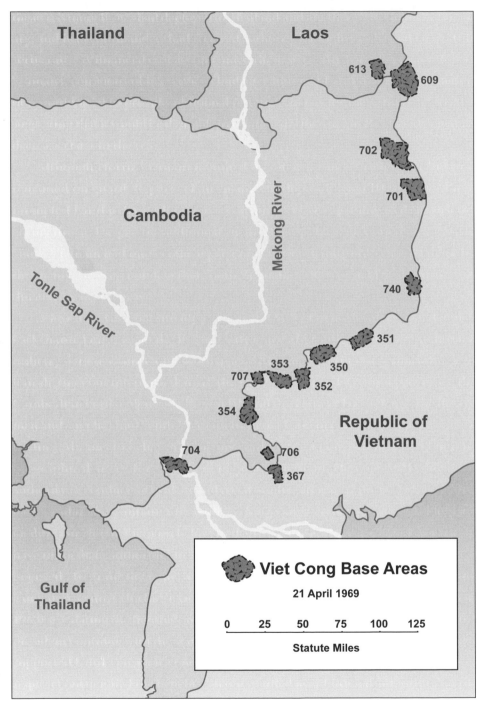

Source: Folder 37, box 3, Records from SecDef Vault, Acc 330-74-142, WNRC.

battle losses. He recommended the combined operation if intelligence indicated a high probability of an enemy move against Phnom Penh.[33]

Laird hoped to preserve Cambodia's neutrality and to provide military assistance to Lon Nol's government, but he understood "there may be no way to control events" in Cambodia. Unlike Abrams, he wanted to do so without American combatants. Meeting with Nixon on 31 March, he protested the suspension of the small South Vietnamese cross-border operations, persuading Nixon to reauthorize them "very quietly, providing they were purely ARVN." The State Department had instructed Bunker to ask Thieu to respect Cambodia's neutrality and to suspend small-scale ARVN cross-border actions. In discussing the issue with Thieu in late March, Bunker "thought we should not think about how to carry the war into Cambodia but rather how to strengthen the government there." Laird was reluctant to use American troops inside Cambodia and told Nixon that the U.S. military thought the ARVN could conduct large-scale operations single-handedly against base areas 704, 706, and 709. Kissinger, on vacation at the time, later reacted angrily to Laird's meeting and to his proposal. On Haig's account of the president's session with Laird, Kissinger scribbled, "When the hell did all this happen?" Particularly skeptical of the South Vietnamese Army mounting major cross-border operations on its own, Kissinger wrote, "I don't believe it," adding, "I think US forces should participate if only to get out again."[34]

While the White House considered military operations and assistance, Rogers sought to avert American military involvement in Cambodia altogether. Regarding the long-term survival of the Lon Nol government as doubtful, he cautioned the president on 30 March that it was not in the nation's interest to acquire "another client state in Southeast Asia." He preferred to publicize North Vietnam's continuing violation of Cambodia's territory in hopes of making it increasingly uncomfortable for Hanoi to maintain the secrecy of its bases. Rogers believed that a large-scale military action against the sanctuaries "would push the VC/NVA deeper into Cambodia," encourage them to take over the whole country, and detract from Lon Nol's efforts to maintain neutrality.[35]

Despite Laird's opposition to U.S. ground operations in Cambodia, and Rogers' fear that an attack against the sanctuaries would further threaten Cambodia's survival in the long term, the White House continued to examine options for U.S. military missions in Cambodia. Bunker and Abrams provided Kissinger a cautious endorsement of cross-border operations. In a message labeled for "White House eyes only" sent to Kissinger on 8 April, Bunker conceded such activity could cause problems for the United States but stated that he and Abrams endorsed the idea of a few limited operations against enemy bases and supply lines in unpopulated areas. These actions would "induce uncertainty and worry in the enemy that we may take advantage of his exposed position if he commits himself too deeply into Cambodia." These steps would also demonstrate that Washington would not ignore pressure against Lon Nol and would provide tangible support for his government. Neither Laird nor Rogers saw Bunker's backchannel message addressed to Kissinger. On record as opposing U.S. ground forces in Cambodia, Laird and Rogers found themselves isolated.[36]

In April Viet Cong and North Vietnamese Army forces overran a number of Cambodian border outposts and soon dominated a 10–15-kilometer-wide corridor along the Cambodia/South Vietnam border from the Fishhook to the Gulf of Siam (Thailand) and Mekong River. Cambodia's small, poorly-equipped and incompetent armed forces—an army of possibly 40,000, an air force of 1,750, and a navy of 1,400—was no match for trained and battle-hardened VC and NVA units. The new government made several urgent requests for U.S. military assistance. In remarks to a few congressional leaders after the start of the incursion, Kissinger explained that the White House feared Communist forces would create "a contiguous belt of sanctuaries along the South Vietnamese border," from which they could launch guerrilla attacks against South Vietnam. Should the border become one large enemy base, it would also increase the threat to the Vietnamization program. In assessing the situation for Nixon, Kissinger argued the necessity of keeping Cambodia out of Communist hands. Its fall would cause psychological shock in South Vietnam, surround the country with hostile armed forces, ensure that enemy supply lines into South Vietnam remained open, and make Vietnamization impossible to carry out. In short, South Vietnam "could not preserve itself against pressure from all sides without a very large continuing presence of U.S. forces." In making his case, Kissinger obviously intended to strengthen his position against a rapid withdrawal of U.S. troops from South Vietnam, in contrast to Laird's plan to redeploy troops at a faster pace.[37]

The Washington Special Actions Group, which included DoD and JCS officials, took up the issue of military aid for Cambodia on 14 and 15 April. It adopted a modest package that it thought would be sufficient to give the government confidence, but not so big as to provoke a reaction from the North Vietnamese Army and the Viet Cong. The United States would provide Phnom Penh with captured AK–47 rifles (initially 1,500) and find out what else the government needed. Not wanting to side overtly with Lon Nol or to be perceived as expanding the war into Cambodia, the administration did not wish to have Americans deliver the equipment. The enemy's consolidation of control of Cambodian territory along the border made ground transport too risky. Nixon decided that the South Vietnamese Air Force should make the first delivery. By the end of April more than 4,000 AK–47 rifles had reached the capital. Washington also approved the shipment of equipment packages (M2 carbines, pistols, light machine guns, submachine guns, rocket launchers, and mortars). Each package would equip a force of 1,000 troops.[38]

As April wore on, Viet Cong and North Vietnamese forces cut virtually all the major roads and waterways leading from the border to Phnom Penh, with the exception of some roads to the west. By 22 April enemy units were within 15 miles of Phnom Penh, causing the administration to label the presence of NVA and VC troops a foreign invasion. General William Westmoreland, Army chief of staff and acting JCS chairman, told Laird the situation had become so serious that the provision of aid to Lon Nol "will no longer be enough to stem the enemy advance."[39]

Meanwhile, Abrams continued to refine the plans for cross-border operations. He reported to CINCPAC Admiral John McCain and Wheeler that the South Vietnamese were willing to attack base areas 706/367 in the Parrot's Beak without U.S. forces and had consulted with the chief of Cambodia's Svay Rieng Province. Laird endorsed the idea of coordinated South Vietnamese–Cambodian operations but emphasized to Abrams that "US participation be restricted to South Vietnamese territory." The secretary later recalled, "I wanted to test the South Vietnamese to the maximum at that particular time, and didn't think we should take over and be the primary movers."[40]

As he watched the situation in Cambodia deteriorate, Nixon discarded without internal debate the policy of neutrality and minimal aid. He decided to take steps on his own. Meeting with Kissinger on 20 April, the president told Haldeman and Kissinger that he would "personally take over responsibility for war in Cambodia" and decide what to do without Rogers. Nixon wanted to bypass Laird too and "set up a back channel to issue orders to military not through Secretary of Defense," expecting him to object to military action. Nixon wanted to hit the sanctuaries and to have Haldeman tell Laird and Rogers that the president could not "bug out." In a live radio and television speech on 20 April, Nixon detailed his efforts to negotiate a settlement and bring home U.S. soldiers and warned Hanoi's leaders that they would be taking "grave risks" should they jeopardize the security of American forces by "increased military action in Vietnam, in Cambodia, or in Laos." The president proclaimed he would "not hesitate to take strong and effective measures to deal with that situation."[41]

Early in the morning of 22 April, the president pondered how to help Lon Nol. Writing a memorandum to Kissinger at 5:00 a.m., Nixon regretted that his administration had been "taken in with the line that by helping him [Lon Nol] we would destroy his 'neutrality' and give the North Vietnamese an excuse to come in. . . . We fail to learn that the Communists never need an excuse to come in. . . . They are romping in there and the only government in Cambodia in the last 25 years that had the guts to take a pro-Western and pro-American stand is ready to fall." He thought the United States had to do "something symbolic to help him [Lon Nol] survive."[42]

At the 22 April NSC meeting, Nixon ended the policy of minimalism and neutrality. He directed that the U.S. immediately increase its military assistance to Cambodia, using third-country channels where possible and ordered State to make the utmost efforts to obtain support from other nations. He authorized attacks against Cambodian base areas by a division-size ARVN force with cross-border American artillery support. No American units or advisers would cross the border. Laird could authorize U.S. tactical air support after consultation with Abrams, should the need arise. Abrams would develop an attack plan in coordination with the South Vietnamese Joint General Staff. As Haldeman observed, Nixon realized the difficulties of getting involved openly in Cambodia and knew he would need a virtuoso communications performance to hold public support. He expected strong criticism in Congress. Haldeman believed the president was willing to take risks because he thought that intervention might be decisive: "He still feels he can get it wound up this year if we keep enough pressure on and don't crumble at home. K[issinger] agrees."[43]

Nixon envisioned the ARVN cross-border operation as only the first phase of his plan to deal with the sanctuaries. On 24 April he met with Kissinger, CIA Director Richard Helms, Admiral Moorer (sitting in for Wheeler), and Marine Corps General Robert Cushman. Per Nixon's 20 April decision to issue orders directly to the military, Laird was excluded from the session. The president ordered going ahead with the planning for the second phase, a combined U.S. and South Vietnamese operation—although still without U.S. troops—against base areas 352/353.[44] In consultation with the Joint Staff, MACV refined this operational plan without Laird's participation. The plan now included U.S. ground troops and aimed to destroy COSVN headquarters and the complex of logistics facilities, ammunition storage sites, hospitals, and POW camps believed to be situated in the targeted areas. The combined cross-border operation, involving elements of the U.S. 1st Cavalry Division and 11th Armored Cavalry Regiment and a brigade of the ARVN Airborne Division, was expected to last three to four weeks. Kissinger thought the start of the combined operation should begin right after the ARVN launched its solo attack in the Parrot's Beak.

Nixon scheduled a meeting with Rogers, Laird, Helms, Wheeler, Kissinger, and Attorney General John Mitchell on the afternoon of 26 April in his private hideaway in the Executive Office Building to inform Laird and Rogers about what the White House and JCS were considering. Kissinger reminded the president that "care should be exercised at today's meeting not to surface the fact that General Wheeler has been conducting intensified planning to implement the attacks on base areas 352/353 without the full knowledge of the Secretary of Defense." Kissinger further noted that Laird was unaware of the likelihood of the plan being approved and expected Laird and Rogers to oppose it.[45]

Not surprisingly Laird was discomfited at the 26 April meeting. Afterward he lamented to Nixon and Kissinger that he felt unprepared to discuss the military options under consideration. He did not realize that *both* the Parrot's Beak and base area 352/353 operations would be discussed and did not know "the decision on the operations had already been made by the time of our meeting this morning," emphasizing to the president his knowledge of being excluded from the planning. In summarizing the secretary's views for Nixon, Kissinger merely noted Laird's distress, not the reasons for it. The concealment from Laird of the true status of the plan to invest base areas 352/353 had succeeded very well. It manifested Kissinger's continuing effort to diminish Laird's role and influence in making Vietnam policy.[46]

Throughout the deliberations on Cambodia, Laird opposed the involvement of U.S. forces in large-scale ground operations. In his view, the intervention would not be decisive militarily, nor would it induce Hanoi to negotiate seriously. He thought it might have the opposite effect. If American entry into Cambodia aroused public and congressional disapproval, Hanoi would have no reason to make concessions but would wait for popular discontent to undermine the administration's political support. Laird told Nixon that repeated forays into Cambodia would further strain the Defense budget, possibly increase the number of U.S. combat deaths, and "put at risk the support of the American people for our operations in Southeast Asia."[47]

On 27 April Rogers, Laird, Mitchell, and Helms met with Nixon to discuss the president's decision to authorize ground operations by combined U.S. and South Vietnamese forces against base areas 352/353 and the Fishhook up to 30 kilometers inside Cambodia to protect U.S. forces in South Vietnam. U.S. tactical air, helicopter, and artillery support was permitted in Cambodia up to a depth of 30 kilometers from the border. Nixon would approve additional operations against other base areas on a case-by-case basis. U.S. forces would be in charge of the combined operation, a notion that Laird had opposed. The same day Nixon called Wheeler to admonish him that the operation in Cambodia was "not business as usual. . . . The military is really on the spot, and if they blow this you've had it."[48]

Laird objected to the wording of Nixon's directive, NSDM 57, because it granted implementing authority for the Cambodian operation to Kissinger's WSAG. After all, it was Laird's responsibility as secretary to handle the military operation. In NSDM 58, the president agreed with Laird, changing the role of WSAG to coordinating rather than implementing operations.[49]

Laird and Kissinger also clashed over whether Abrams actually opposed or advocated the operation in the Fishhook. Their disagreement delayed the Cambodian operation for 24 hours so Nixon could get the "unvarnished" views of Bunker and Abrams. On 27 April the president asked them if the attack on base areas 352/353 was their first choice based on merit or "because [Abrams] assumes it represents my wishes?" In reply, Bunker and Abrams strongly endorsed assaulting base areas 352/353, stating an attack on no other base "would have as great an effect on the overall security posture of our forces in South-Viet-Nam." Striking the base area would also boost the ARVN's morale and unsettle the enemy. They recommended that operations begin as soon as possible in light of the approaching rainy season. On 28 April Nixon authorized a combined U.S.–South Vietnamese operation against COSVN.[50]

Nixon determined that the operation would protect U.S. forces engaged in South Vietnam, "sustain the continuation of the Vietnamization Program," and possibly help efforts to negotiate peace. He informed Rogers and Laird that he had considered their opposition to American troops on the ground in Cambodia and the "fact that Dr. Kissinger was leaning against the recommendation of such use." Nixon also said he was mindful of the "probable adverse reaction in some Congressional circles and some segments of the public."[51] "Probable adverse reaction" grossly understated the tumultuous public outcry against what the administration termed the Cambodian incursion.

The first phase began on 29 April (Saigon time), when the ARVN infantry and armored battalions moved with American military advisers and logistical support against the Parrot's Beak. The Pentagon announced that the ARVN operation was intended to save U.S. lives and strengthen the Vietnamization program by destroying a complex of enemy bases and depots in Cambodia. The foray drew sharp criticism from Senators Cooper, Church, and Mansfield, which surprised the administration and did not augur well for public reaction for Nixon's next step, the U.S. incursion. The combined U.S. and Vietnamese engagement began 1 May (Saigon time) as 15,000 American and South Vietnamese troops broke into the Fishhook area from the south, east, and north.[52]

At 9:00 p.m. on 30 April, ninety minutes after the second phase began, Nixon went before television cameras to announce the operation. He did not regard his move as an invasion, declaring, "The areas in which these attacks will be launched are completely occupied and controlled by North Vietnamese forces" and had been for five years in blatant violation of Cambodia's neutrality. "We will not allow American men by the thousands to be killed by an enemy from privileged sanctuaries." When American and South Vietnamese forces drove enemy forces from their sanctuaries and destroyed their supplies, Nixon stated, U.S. forces would withdraw, having no intention of occupying Cambodian territory. Destruction of COSVN, the enemy's headquarters for Communist operations in South Vietnam, was a major objective. Heeding Cambodia's request for U.S. assistance, Nixon said he also agreed to provide limited aid to the Phnom Penh government to enable it to defend itself. Nixon presented his action as a limited response to a long-term, grave threat to American soldiers and to his ability to continue withdrawing them from Vietnam. Nixon asserted that dealing with North Vietnam's forces in Cambodia was the right step even if it cost him reelection in 1972.[53]

President Nixon, declaring that America would not act like a "pitiful, helpless giant," announces on television the start of U.S. ground operations inside Cambodia, 30 April 1970. The speech and the military incursion inflamed war critics. (Nixon Presidential Library)

Reaction to the incursion disclosed just how divisive the Vietnam War had become. Although Nixon retained the backing of his strongest allies in Congress, such as Senate Minority Leader Hugh Scott, other Republican senators, such as George Aiken (VT) and Robert Dole (KS), joined the bipartisan opposition. Within days of the president's announcement the Cooper-Church amendment moved closer to passage in the Senate. This amendment to the Foreign Military Sales Act, which covered sales to countries other than South Vietnam, would prohibit U.S. assistance to Cambodia. It was intended to preclude U.S. involvement in a wider war in Indochina and to hasten the withdrawal of American forces from Vietnam.[54]

Domestic political upheaval quickly overshadowed the military operation and put the administration on the defensive. A Gallup poll in May found that 58 percent of those Americans surveyed disapproved of dispatching U.S. troops into Cambodia. Many worried that these troops would get bogged down in a new war. The incursion energized war protesters. On the weekend of 9–10 May an antiwar rally drew a crowd estimated at 75,000 to 100,000 to the nation's capital. Students in many colleges and universities demonstrated. By 10 May protests, some violent, had spread to 448 campuses. Fires were set at Ohio State University and Case Western Reserve University. The University of Wisconsin in Madison was the scene of 20 fire-bombing incidents and the arrest of 83 students. At Kent State University in Ohio, four students were killed on 4 May by Army national guardsmen sent by Ohio governor James Rhodes to restore order. Ronald Reagan, governor of California, closed the state's university system early in May to quell student demonstrations.[55]

On 3 June Nixon addressed the nation, declaring the Cambodian operation the "most successful operation of this long and very difficult war." He reported that the large amount of food, supplies, weapons, and ammunition captured by the Americans and South Vietnamese in Cambodia during May nearly equaled what was captured in Vietnam for all of 1969. It would take the enemy months to rebuild his damaged installations and replace destroyed or captured equipment. South Vietnam's forces acquitted themselves well in the fighting, bolstering their confidence and morale. The president concluded that the incursion's success allowed the withdrawals to continue and granted additional time for South Vietnam to prepare to shoulder its national defense burden. In August General William Rosson, the MACV deputy, reported the enemy would need to replace lost supplies before mounting large-scale military operations. The invasion disrupted the enemy's supply lines and complicated Viet Cong efforts to control the population of South Vietnam.[56]

But the offensive failed to capture or destroy COSVN headquarters, which moved west before the assault began and functioned without serious interruption. Security in the Cambodian countryside failed to improve in May 1970 because enemy forces continued to encircle the capital. Abrams and Haig, concerned enough then by the situation in Cambodia, recommended slowing the pace of U.S. withdrawals. By October the enemy was developing a new system of base areas along the Mekong River to the west of the previous sanctuaries, and some units returned to their old base areas after U.S. forces left Cambodia at the end of June. The Communists were ensuring the security of their logistics routes from southern Laos, building an insurgency in Cambodia, isolating the capital, interdicting government supply lines, and putting Cambodia's armed forces on the defensive. To keep Lon Nol's government from defeat, the administration set up a small military equipment delivery team based in MACV headquarters to provide arms and committed itself to a policy of helping develop Cambodian forces capable of establishing government control of the countryside.[57]

THE ASSAULT INTO CAMBODIA by a president who had promised to end the war and to bring U.S. troops home underscored the fundamental weakness of the administration's Vietnam policy, especially at a time of declining public support. Increased military pressure could only be short-lived and ineffective when political sentiment, as measured by congressional actions and campus and public unrest, was moving toward reducing the U.S. combat role. Continuing to believe that military pressure would force its adversary to negotiate, the administration recognized that politically necessary withdrawals constituted a disincentive for the other side to compromise its long-term objective of taking over South Vietnam. The incursion had the effect of weakening support for Nixon's Vietnam policy and creating more pressure to withdraw U.S. troops. Ironically the incursion strengthened Laird's position of speeding up the redeployment rate.

Of all Nixon's advisers, Laird proved the most consistent in trying to shape Vietnam policy in accord with the domestic political situation. He pushed hard for Vietnamization, but by Nixon's design had no real voice in the decision to send ground forces into Cambodia. Apparently determined on making a bold decisive move, the president isolated Laird and Rogers from deliberations and planning. The move into Cambodia, although it disrupted the enemy's logistics, would prove troublesome in the long run. Lon Nol's government showed itself unable to handle the Communist military threat. After U.S. troops departed Cambodia, Communist forces returned to the sanctuaries and continued infiltrating men and supplies to Vietnam through routes in southern Laos, further threatening Vietnamization. The situation would push the administration to turn to Laos in 1971.

CHAPTER 7

The War in Laos

IN THE 1960s LAOS REMAINED CRITICAL for the U.S. struggle to prevent domination of Indochina by the North Vietnamese Communist regime. The dysfunctional Laotian government had permitted North Vietnam to maintain bases there and establish a conduit for resupplying the Viet Cong in the South. Even more than Cambodia, Laos served Hanoi's logistical needs. North Vietnam's powerful presence in Laos created further instability in a small, weak nation already racked by a struggle for control between contending factions, including a Communist insurgency assisted by Hanoi. U.S. efforts to prop up the officially neutral Royal Laotian government by providing military aid served to draw the Kennedy and Johnson administrations further into the Laotian imbroglio. Hanoi's presence in Laos and its use of the country as a main supply route presented the U.S. government with a perilous military threat to its position in South Vietnam. The continually threatening circumstances culminated during February-March 1971 in a U.S. inspired large-scale attack on North Vietnamese forces and bases in Laos by the Army of the Republic of Vietnam supported by U.S. air and logistical resources.[1]

In 1962 the United States, Soviet Union, North Vietnam, South Vietnam, Laos, and other nations signed an agreement in Geneva according Laos neutral country status under a coalition government. Hanoi and Washington agreed to withdraw their forces. The United States removed its military personnel through international checkpoints and disestablished its Laotian Military Assistance Advisory Group (MAAG), but Hanoi left more than 5,000 soldiers in-country. After the coalition government collapsed in 1963, Hanoi took over the southern part of Laos, expanding the Ho Chi Minh Trail into a labyrinth of roads, jungle paths, and waterways that carried an increasing flow of men and supplies from North

Vietnam through southern Laos into South Vietnam and Cambodia. From base area 604 near Tchepone, a Laotian town about 40 kilometers west of South Vietnam's border along Route 9, the North Vietnamese moved materiel and fighters further south to other large depots before bringing them into Cambodia or South Vietnam. The trail assumed greater significance for North Vietnam after 1970 because allied military action reduced the effectiveness of other major infiltration routes. The naval blockade of South Vietnam's coast significantly reduced the flow of supplies from the sea, and the government of Lon Nol shut down the port of Sihanoukville, Cambodia, closing that supply route.[2]

In the mid-1960s the Johnson administration assisted the neutralist leader, Premier Souvanna Phouma, by providing funds for the Royal Lao Army and the irregular, largely tribal forces led by senior Laotian commander General Vang Pao, as well as Thai "volunteers" (recruited and trained by the United States) battling Pathet Lao and North Vietnamese forces. The press reported this assistance from time to time, but Washington officials, attempting to preserve the appearance of neutrality, did not formally acknowledge it "to avoid giving Hanoi a pretext" to conquer all of Laos.[3] President Johnson also authorized tactical air strikes and B–52 sorties along the trail. The number of B–52 sorties in Laos grew from 18 in December 1965, when they started, to 647 in 1966 to over 3,300 in 1968. The Laotian government tacitly permitted the United States to bomb the Ho Chi Minh Trail in Laos provided Washington did not publicly admit it and avoided killing Lao civilians.[4]

JCS Chairman General Earle Wheeler and Assistant Secretary of Defense Paul Warnke both conceded that the United States could not prevent the Pathet Lao and North Vietnamese from overrunning the country if they decided to do so. By the same token, the Johnson administration believed that Hanoi had refrained from overthrowing the fragile Lao government because it too wanted to preserve the façade of neutrality and not provoke a more massive U.S. effort to interdict the movement of men and equipment.[5]

The Administration Takes on Laos

Nixon continued Johnson's cautious policy, but in mid-1969 he sought recommendations on what else the United States could do to counteract a North Vietnamese offensive in north central Laos. Deputy Assistant Secretary of State for East Asian and Pacific Affairs William H. Sullivan, former ambassador to Laos (December 1964–March 1969), thought the United States could only supplement ongoing efforts. Like Warnke and Wheeler, he believed additional U.S. assistance to Lao forces would prove insufficient to stop Communist forces if they decided to overrun the country. And introducing American ground forces into the Laotian panhandle would create political problems. Air operations there had already reached the saturation point with about 400 tactical air sorties and 20–30 B–52 sorties per day. To increase the air effort in direct support of troops in north central Laos would require better communications, air control, and targeting capabilities, he pointed out. Given the uneasy equilibrium in Laos, the limited American objectives in that nation, and the meager capabilities of the Lao military, Sullivan recommended in June 1969 minimal measures: providing the regular armed forces with additional M16 rifles, AC–47 aircraft to defend outposts, and T–41 training airplanes.[6]

Also under consideration was a July 1969 proposal from the ambassador to Laos, G. McMurtrie Godley, and Pacific Commander Admiral John McCain for B–52 strikes in northern Laos, an area into which strategic bombers had not yet ventured. The American ambassador as the senior government official had responsibility for U.S. military activities, including all air operations. No U.S. general in Laos advised him. MACV Commander General Creighton Abrams, in charge of carrying out air operations in southern Laos, delegated responsibility to the Seventh Air Force commander, but the ambassador ultimately approved or disapproved the selection of targets.[7]

Laird, who questioned what B–52 strikes could accomplish in northern Laos, concluded that they could not prevent the North Vietnamese from taking over Laos. Hanoi had the strength to do that whenever it chose. U.S. air strikes in the north might cause the enemy to intensify his efforts in other areas of the country. Wheeler thought it would be difficult to identify suitable targets for B–52s. According to Al Haig, Kissinger's military assistant, Laird and Wheeler were also "highly irritated by the tendency of local military officials to make proposals to you [Kissinger] and the President without prior clearance from Washington." Nixon had discussed the B–52 strikes in Laos with Abrams and Thai officials during his visit to Asia in July 1969. Interested in the strikes "for their political and psychological impact in Thailand," the president ordered the Seventh Air Force to have RB–52Bs conduct radar reconnaissance missions in northern Laos to obtain information about possible bombing targets, beginning no later than 4 August.[8]

Laird and the JCS raised objections. They believed MiG aircraft stationed in nearby North Vietnam posed a serious threat to the bombers. The secretary indicated that other aircraft would have to identify and fix on targets before any decision was made on whether to use B–52s to carry out specific reconnaissance missions. State and Defense also viewed "the use of B–52s in northern Laos as unwarranted escalation, which could provoke further NVA ground attacks to which the Lao and the U.S. would not be able adequately to respond."[9]

In turn, Kissinger requested that Defense, State, and CIA analyze possible military options in support of the Laotian government. On 19 August Laird submitted their conclusions. All three agencies recommended against extending B–52 reconnaissance and bombing operations to "the northern and heretofore restricted areas of Laos," fearing that North Vietnam might respond with ground attacks. Moreover, bombing previously restricted areas might interfere with diplomatic efforts to calm the situation. Laird also claimed that "the requirement for B–52 strikes" in South Vietnam and southern Laos far exceeded availability "by a ratio of 5:1." At a time of reduced resources, it was better to use military power directly to support South Vietnam. In any event, the stark reality was that additional bombing missions and other military measures, such as more equipment for Lao forces, could not stop Hanoi from conquering Laos.[10]

The White House found the analysis unsatisfactory. Anthony Lake, one of Kissinger's assistants, termed it "shoddy." Kissinger characterized the analysis of military options as "surprisingly negative and unhelpful." Disregarding Laird's submission that incorporated the views of Defense, State, and the CIA, Kissinger recommended that the president provide M16 rifles, additional fixed-wing aircraft, and helicopters to Lao forces; transfer T–28 aircraft from Thailand to Laos; improve logistic and ammunition support to the Lao; increase artillery support; and improve reconnaissance and radar capability in the north. He also advocated retaliation should Communist forces attack another key site in Laos. On 15 September Nixon directed Laird to carry out these recommendations. He also requested State, Defense, the CIA, and the U.S. Information Agency to draft contingency plans for retaliatory operations and initiate a public relations campaign to prepare public sentiment for the possibility of U.S. action in Laos.[11]

The administration's deliberations on providing additional military assistance to Laos occurred even as the Senate turned its attention there. Senator Stuart

Symington, chairman of the Foreign Relations Committee's Subcommittee on U.S. Security Agreements and Commitments Abroad, opened hearings in the fall of 1969 on what he called the "secret war" in Laos and Nixon's plans to enlarge it. His avowed aim was to let "the American people know more of the facts" about the long-standing U.S. involvement that he alleged was veiled from the public. U.S. actions were hardly a secret. As former Assistant Secretary of State for East Asian and Pacific Affairs William Bundy later noted, the Johnson and Nixon administrations frequently explained U.S. military operations in Laos to congressional committees and to

Senator Stuart Symington (D–MO), a subcommittee chairman of the Senate Foreign Relations Committee, held hearings critical of what he called the "secret war on Laos." (U.S. Senate Historical Office)

senators and representatives visiting Laos or Thailand. Kennedy, Johnson, and Nixon administration officials had refrained from making public announcements about these operations "partly to keep alive Laos's façade of neutrality." On visits to Laos, Symington had received briefings about the war from the ambassador, CIA officials, and Laotian General Vang Pao. Accounts of the fighting had also appeared in the media, allowing Bundy to reasonably conclude that "any careful news reader or member of Congress knew basically what was going on."[12]

Expected to run for a year or more, the hearings, Kissinger warned Nixon on 25 September, represented "the opening move in an effort to seize for the Senate a new role in formulating and implementing United States foreign and defense policies." The subject was not just Laos, but also defense treaties with 42 countries as well as U.S. military installations worldwide.[13] The Symington committee and other senators registered concern that Nixon might expand the U.S. role in Laos and send in ground troops or advisers as the previous administration had done in Vietnam.

To prevent that move, on 12 August Senator John Sherman Cooper had submitted an amendment to the FY 1970 military procurement bill prohibiting the use of funds for combat support of U.S. forces in Laos. He pledged to submit amendments to other appropriations bills on the grounds that Congress first had to approve such support.[14] The final appropriations bill agreed to by the House and Senate in December 1969 proved more restrictive, barring the expenditure of any money for U.S. combat troops in Laos. Chairman of the House Appropriations Defense Subcommittee George Mahon reluctantly agreed to the ban because the president had endorsed it, having no intention to deploy

Senator John Sherman Cooper (R–KY) in 1970 authored the amendment prohibiting the use of funds for U.S. forces in Laos. (Library of Congress)

military units there. With the amendment, Congress had taken a significant step, invoking its power of the purse to control operations by legislation.[15]

While the administration continued to examine military options other than the deployment of ground troops in Laos, Laird urged caution, seeing no chance for a military solution. What would the United States gain, he asked Kissinger, if additional American involvement failed to prevent the North Vietnamese and Pathet Lao from conquering the country? But a "restive" president, to use Kissinger's term, wanted ideas on how to handle Laos, linking conditions there to the negotiations in Paris, and the security of Thailand, which also faced a Communist insurgency. At a Washington Special Action Group meeting on 29 September 1969, Kissinger urged the members to come up with tougher political and military options, including the possibility of B–52 strikes.[16]

On 6 October Laird sent the president a lengthy review of U.S. military support in Laos, urging him to examine carefully the current U.S. political environment and the effectiveness of additional support to Lao forces before taking new steps. The secretary pointed out the growing cost of the U.S. effort in Southeast Asia. Attack sorties by the U.S. and Lao Air Forces had more than doubled from 6,560 in 1968 to 13,769 during the seven-month period January through July 1969. The incremental cost to the U.S. Treasury of these air operations amounted to about 95 percent of the cost of the war in Laos, reaching nearly $2 billion per annum. U.S. escalation in Laos seemed a dead-end option to Laird, since North Vietnam could introduce more sophisticated weapons and equipment to compensate for increased U.S. pressure. Hanoi possessed the combat reserves not only to sustain losses but also to increase the number of fighters in Laos. Before proceeding, the secretary wanted to understand better the risks and costs of having U.S. personnel provide military assistance and training for the Lao forces.

The White House was dismissive of the secretary's concerns. Haig termed Laird's use of statistics "specious." John Holdridge of Kissinger's staff complained that Laird had given no thought to actions that might be required if the existing military balance were upset and Communist forces moved to take over the country. Kissinger believed Laird had ignored the political and military implications of a likely enemy offensive during the dry season and resorted to a delaying tactic of setting up an ad hoc interagency group to coordinate planning and operations in Laos. Chaired by Deputy Assistant Secretary of State for East Asian and Pacific Affairs Jonathan Moore, this group would meet weekly but would leave policy questions for the National Security Council. The group got off to a rough start when Defense representatives were excluded from some early private sessions between CIA and State officials that dealt with the Agency's proposals.[17]

In Laos the situation continued to deteriorate. The North Vietnamese Army stocked supplies and massed 15,000 soldiers on the Plain of Jars in January 1970 for an offensive that ended in late February, when Hanoi's forces drove Vang Pao's Meo tribal forces from the plain. While the fighting heated up, pressure from Symington and Fulbright to disclose U.S. policy and actions in Laos grew more intense.[18]

On 3 February Symington warned Rogers that the administration risked a serious credibility problem about Laos. If the White House contemplated an increase in combat assistance to counteract a new Communist offensive, it needed to inform the American people, the senator argued. Fulbright directly questioned the administration's credibility, noting that Laird had publicly evaded answering questions about the use of B–52s after the *Washington Post* reported that they had struck the Plain of Jars. "I believe we have come to a sorry state," Fulbright said, "when the Secretary of Defense, in order to support an ill-conceived policy of secrecy, is forced over national television to maintain the dignity of such a policy by openly evading a direct question on United States military activities."[19]

The NSC met on 27 February to decide how to respond to the sensitive problem of demands for public explanation of the U.S. role in Laos. As an aide to Assistant Secretary of Defense Warren Nutter framed

Senator William Fulbright (D–AK), chairman of the Senate Foreign Relations Committee, 20 February 1969. Fulbright was a prominent critic of the war in Vietnam. (Nixon Presidential Library)

the issue: Was it in the national interest to acknowledge in public a violation of the Geneva accords; disclose the role of the CIA; provide operational details that might jeopardize the safety of Americans in Laos; and embarrass the Thai government by disclosing its activities, which the United States had agreed to keep secret?[20] Bryce Harlow, counselor to the president, cautioned that Symington would continue to pursue the issue because he was up for reelection and sought "a confrontation with the President." Rogers, warning that Congress was looking for a major clash with the administration, saw in Laos a repetition of Vietnam, "a replay in escalation." In words reminiscent of Laird's opposition to the Cambodian secret bombing, he supported disclosure of the administration's actions, asking pointedly: "How about the air sorties? How can I defend keeping this secret?" Kissinger argued for continued involvement. To him, a North Vietnamese takeover of Laos would undermine the U.S. negotiating position. Even an increase in Communist military pressure could conceivably force Souvanna to "refuse to permit" aerial interdiction of the Ho Chi Minh Trail, "catastrophically" damaging U.S. military operations in South Vietnam. He did not want to release the testimony of the Senate subcommittee's executive sessions but realized the administration needed a way to inform the public. Laird agreed that the administration faced "a major issue of credibility." Following the suggestion of Col. Robert Pursley, his military assistant, and Daniel Henkin, his public affairs adviser, Laird recommended that the president issue a new public statement as a way to quiet critics.[21] Nixon agreed to put the policy on the public record to avoid the impression that the White House was "withholding something," but he did not want to expose the role of the CIA or Thai forces in Laos.[22]

Assistant Secretary of Defense for Public Affairs Daniel Henkin urged the adoption of a new presidential public policy statement for Laos. (NARA)

On 6 March the president presented his public statement on Laos, depicting his efforts as a continuation of the policies of previous administrations, which, like his, wanted to prevent a Communist conquest of Laos, return to the 1962 agreements, and obtain the withdrawal of North Vietnamese troops so that the Lao people could settle their differences. The president would continue U.S. air interdiction of the Ho Chi Minh Trail, reconnaissance flights in northern Laos, and combat support missions for Lao forces. American aid, according to Nixon, was limited: "It is requested. It is supportive and defensive. It continues the purposes and operations of two previous administrations."[23]

The administration took other measures to inform Congress. On 17 March Kissinger briefed congressional leaders on U.S. operations in Laos, including classified information omitted from the public statement. The administration withheld nothing from the Symington subcommittee, not even top secret military operational plans, and declassified the entire transcript of the executive session, except information that might endanger the lives of U.S. personnel or pertaining to Thai operations in Laos (at the urging of the Thai government), sortie rates, and exact statistics on casualties and aircraft losses from the Johnson administration.[24]

Nixon had no intention of curtailing the bombing, even though he had "the feeling that a lot of bombs are dropped on barren territory.[25] The president also brushed aside Laird's concern about costs. Laird warned that future sortie rates might be affected by the cuts planned in the FY 1971 budget. He also informed the president in March that the September 1969 directive to provide additional support to improve Royal Lao forces would affect funds programmed for other defense programs and likely necessitate supplemental funding.[26]

The White House contemplated further steps in Laos. In March 1970 Haig drafted two memoranda for Kissinger to send to Nixon advocating stronger U.S. action.[27] Meeting twice on 19 March to discuss Laos, the WSAG recommended a number of limited measures that the president approved. By June 1970 Lao irregular forces also received significantly increased support. Deputy Secretary of Defense David Packard noted that in June 1970 the Air Force flew nearly four times as many sorties in support of Lao government forces in northern Laos as it did in January 1969, and the sortie rate ran a third higher than the 1969 average. In addition, the United States made qualitative improvements in tactical aircraft, including the AC–130 and AC–119 gunships and a B–57 squadron with night sensors. Packard thought that the improvements would allow DoD to reduce sortie levels (and save funds in FY 1971) without creating an imbalance between Lao government and Communist forces.[28]

As U.S. assistance grew in 1970 so did the enemy's forces. CIA Director Richard Helms reported a significant increase in North Vietnamese and Pathet Lao forces from May to November. Most of the 40,000 North Vietnamese in combat units were deployed in southern Laos to protect the infiltration routes. Allied incursions into Cambodia in May and June 1970, the loss of the Sihanoukville supply route, and the fear of large-scale interdiction induced Hanoi to give priority to keeping open the existing supply route through Laos and to expand the infiltration system in southern Laos and Cambodia with a new route west of the existing arteries.[29] With the enemy making greater use of the trail, the notion of blocking it with ground forces, discussed and rejected by the Johnson administration, had fresh appeal. Reducing the flow of enemy supplies and personnel into South Vietnam would lessen the likelihood of a major enemy offensive there, allowing the administration to keep the pace of troop withdrawals on track. Meeting with Laird, Packard, Wheeler, Chief of Naval Operations Admiral Thomas Moorer, Admiral McCain,

General Abrams, and Kissinger at the end of May 1970, the president told Abrams to prepare plans for an offensive in Laos, without specifying, however, who would conduct the operation. The administration could not afford to wait, for the steady withdrawal of military personnel would make U.S. support of an offensive operation less feasible as time went on.[30]

Origin of Lam Son 719

Consideration of a ground assault into Laos to cut the Ho Chi Minh Trail had a long history. Westmoreland had proposed a large-scale strike to seal off infiltration routes in the Laotian panhandle many times during his tenure as MACV commander (1964–1968), but President Johnson never approved such a plan despite the endorsement of Ambassadors Lodge and Bunker. The Cooper-Church amendment of January 1971 prohibited U.S. ground combat troops from entering Laos and Cambodia. Consequently, it would be left to the South Vietnamese Army to carry out a cross-border thrust.[31]

The Cambodian incursion of 1970 served as precedent for White House plans to use ARVN units to strike enemy supply routes and bases in Laos. On 30 November Laird informed Kissinger of the presence of about three enemy divisions in the Laotian panhandle, clear evidence of Hanoi's intention of controlling the area. Laird believed one South Vietnamese division could be deployed into the eastern portion of Laos for a short-term operation to disrupt enemy lines of communication.[32] In response to a request from Moorer (now the JCS chairman), McCain provided an operational plan to prevent consolidation of enemy control of the Laotian panhandle.[33] On 4 December Vice President Spiro T. Agnew discussed with McCain a ground campaign against the Ho Chi Minh Trail. Moorer wanted all knowledge of these sensitive deliberations kept strictly within the JCS. Early in December Moorer told McCain of the White House's interest in a campaign to disrupt enemy plans for an offensive. Under consideration were ARVN ground operations in Cambodia and Laos as well as covert strikes against North Vietnam. Moorer noted that Abrams would examine the feasibility of committing the ARVN to the campaign and MACV's capability to take over for the ARVN units while they were fighting in Laos and Cambodia. Laird was excluded from these early White House and JCS discussions.[34]

On 5 December Rear Adm. Rembrandt Robinson, the JCS liaison officer in the White House, met with Kissinger and Haig to review the planning for a three-part campaign that included a spoiling operation in Cambodia, a covert strike into North Vietnam, and a drive into the Laotian panhandle. The operation in Laos envisioned one to three ARVN divisions—with extensive U.S. air support—entering the panhandle to disrupt enemy operations, destroy stockpiles, and ease pressure on U.S. and allied forces in South Vietnam. Kissinger indicated "such a plan should be ready for execution in early 1971, possibly using the earlier thrust into Cambodia as a cover." To garner support for an offensive in Laos, Haig would travel to South Vietnam and meet with Abrams to assess MACV's plans and the likelihood of the ARVN's participation. If Abrams deemed such operations feasible, then Haig and Abrams would seek President Thieu's endorsement of the three-part offensive and overcome any reluctance to commit his forces. Haig was "prepared to use the full leverage of the President's office on Thieu."[35] In a phone conversation on 9 December, Kissinger assured the president that Haig would make certain "Abrams will know that you want him to launch spoiling operations." Nixon directed that Kissinger send Abrams a message from the president, not from Laird or Moorer, stressing the importance the chief executive attached to the contemplated operations and that he had asked Haig to discuss them. Nixon also expressed interest in having ARVN forces strike the growing North Vietnamese contingent near the rubber plantation at Chup in Cambodia, located in the Fishhook area.[36] Laird's absence from these deliberations was conspicuous.

In mid-December Abrams was enthusiastic about a ground operation in Laos because of his "growing faith in the capabilities" of the South Vietnamese. He advocated a coordinated air and ground attack to sever the enemy's logistic corridor at Tchepone in Laos, with a multi-regimental task force of South Vietnamese soldiers seizing the town and destroying enemy stockpiles, forces, pipelines, and facilities in the area. The South Vietnamese task force was to hold Tchepone and its airfield long enough to allow ARVN engineers to upgrade it for C–123 and possibly C–130 aerial resupply. ARVN units would maintain security on Route 9 from Tchepone to the Vietnamese border. In the final phase of the operation, guerrilla and stay-behind forces would be inserted in the target area before ARVN forces withdrew. McCain urged approval of the plan, but Moorer wanted to compare Abrams' concept with a proposal by General Westmoreland. The chairman hoped to keep discussions within military channels, especially to avoid tipping off the State Department. On 11 December, however, Westmoreland presented his views on operating in Laos to the WSAG, much to Kissinger's surprise and Moorer's dismay. Westmoreland recommended a series of hit and run raids by South Vietnam airmobile units instead of the frontal assault and lengthy stay inside Laos envisioned by Abrams. By 18 December Moorer had ruled out Westmoreland's plan, affirming that as far as he was concerned "we are going to do the Laotian operation . . . exactly like GEN ABRAMS wants to do it and *no other way.*"[37]

Laird still knew nothing about the planning for the operation. The chairman realized his predicament, confiding in his diary that the secretary had "to be pulled into this thing" before he and Laird went to Southeast Asia in January. Moorer's great fear was that Laird might learn of the plans inadvertently or through a leak, creating a potentially disastrous situation for the chairman. Robinson advised Moorer to wait until Haig returned from Vietnam before asking Kissinger to inform Laird. Aware of the problem that secrecy created, Kissinger warned Nixon on 19 December that if Laird learned about the operation during his trip to Vietnam "he'll try to kill it." It verged on the bizarre that the chairman and his White House liaison officer discussed privately how to inform the secretary of defense, their superior, about an operation deliberately concealed from him that would require his support. But they kept the information from Laird at the direction of the White House. Fearing trouble in gaining Laird's endorsement, Moorer pressed Abrams for more information on U.S. air support and reassured Abrams of his backing: "I am already sold on the Plan and   [need] additional ammunition to sell it to higher authority."[38]

Haig came back to Washington bursting with optimism, telling Kissinger that "we are within an eyelash of victory" in Vietnam. He stressed Thieu's willingness to move forces into Cambodia and Laos on condition of having "maximum US air support—including airlift and gunships." Speaking with Nixon on 19 December, Kissinger relayed Haig's view that the operation might have a decisive impact and "do in the northern two Corps what the other operation [the Cambodian incursion] did in the southern two." The president said, "[I]t's about time to rip them up, finish them off. . . . Sell the whole thing in terms of accelerating the withdrawals." Like Haig, Kissinger was optimistic, telling Nixon, "I've looked at this concept and it really looks good." With such optimism in the White House and enthusiasm for the operation in Laos, Nixon could no longer risk keeping his secretary of defense in the dark. Laird's involvement was needed. Nixon decided to inform Laird about the operation before the secretary went to Asia and to insist that he not inform Rogers. Nixon would apprise Rogers after Laird returned and expected Laird to help sell the idea.[39]

Abrams' concept of a Laotian operation had four phases. In the first, a U.S. brigade would establish a forward operating base and airfield inside South Vietnam close to the Laotian border. In the second phase, South Vietnamese units would cross the border and move toward the key road junction of Tchepone in Laos. Following intensive bombing of the airfield there, South Vietnam's forces would seize it. In the third phase, Vietnamese engineers would upgrade the airfield, and the ARVN would establish blocking positions to the north to allow their units to destroy enemy stockpiles near base area 604. The fourth phase would see Lao guerrillas and South Vietnamese units "inserted into or remain[ing] in the objective area." Abrams selected Tchepone because of its many lucrative targets. At a 22 December meeting with Haig and Moorer, Kissinger hoped the operation would have an early start. Moorer thought it could begin in early February. Moorer and Haig emphasized that Abrams would "need authority to use the full range of US air support, to include tactical and strategic bombing, airlift and gunships." Kissinger vowed to get the authority and advised military planners to continue working on the assumption that approval would be granted.[40]

After reviewing the Abrams plan, Moorer, Haig, and Kissinger agreed on a detailed scenario for informing the secretary of defense. As Moorer described it, during a meeting with Laird "the President will be asked to raise the issue of future operations within the context of HAIG's recent trip. Specifically, he would say that he had asked HAIG to look into the various options available, and he had found an interesting plan involving the insertion of ARVN troops into the Tchepone area." Because the concept was promising, the president would say he decided to proceed with detailed planning.[41]

Haig briefed the president on 22 December. Nixon's initial reaction was to allow maximum U.S. tactical air support, the use of gunships, and the airlift of supplies, but he refused to involve the United States in crossing the border or moving assault forces to Tchepone. He would not "authorize any airlift other than that which can be portrayed as administrative in nature and limited to the transportation of supplies." He did not wish to endanger the Defense budget supplemental by flouting the Cooper-Church amendment prohibiting use of U.S. ground forces and advisers in both Cambodia and Laos. A disappointed Haig privately hoped Nixon could be persuaded later to allow a U.S. airlift of Vietnamese forces into Tchepone or to employ U.S. helicopters with their "markings replaced with those of the RVN." The president would inform Laird of the proposed operation at the following day's meeting and ask him and the chairman to carry out the necessary planning for an ARVN attack on Tchepone.[42]

At the 23 December 1970 meeting with Nixon, Laird was finally included in the planning.[43] Essentially for Laird's benefit, Haig briefed the president, Laird, Kissinger, and Moorer on his discussions with Abrams, citing the ARVN's more confident attitude as a reason for carrying out the operation. Lamenting that the previous administration had refrained from taking "bold action three years ago," Nixon expressed his preference to take preemptive measures, believing that cross-border operations would help bolster South Vietnam over the long run. He approved the ARVN operation against the Chup plantation in Cambodia but asked for further study of the Tchepone plan to block the transport of supplies and destroy enemy stockpiles in that area before approving it. Laird supported the move against Tchepone.[44]

Just before their January trip to Vietnam, Moorer sent Laird the Abrams plan of 15 December that envisioned a two-division ARVN force and supporting troops seizing Tchepone and its airfield then upgrading the facility for air resupply. Moorer expected the operation to last two to three months and urged Laird to approve it. According to an estimate by the Defense Intelligence Agency, enemy strength in the Tchepone area numbered 25,000 to 30,000 troops, of which 15,000 to 18,000 were in combat units.[45]

During his Vietnam visit Laird discussed the operation with Thieu and Abrams. Afterwards, he informed the president on 16 January that Abrams was enthusiastic about continuing the extensive air interdiction in southern Laos and having the South Vietnamese Army launch a major thrust into the Tchepone area with U.S. logistics and air support. Laird also reported major improvements in South Vietnam's armed forces as well as a "growing resolve by the leaders and the people to help themselves" and to enhance their security. MACV's commander judged that the ARVN had improved over the past six months. In Abrams' view, the proposed operations "had the possibility of affecting the war *at least* as much as the Cambodian operations had last year." Abrams asserted that the "Laotian panhandle and the northern provinces of South Vietnam comprised the key to the military situation in early to mid-1971." Plans for taking Tchepone were prepared on a close-hold basis. To ensure security, Abrams sent to Washington on 18 January 1971 a briefing team with the finalized Tchepone plan. MACV would transmit no messages detailing the plan. Laird wanted no B–52 strikes north of the DMZ and no U.S. personnel in Cambodia or Laos.[46]

President Thieu needed little persuading when Laird recommended that the United States and South Vietnam plan for the strike against the Ho Chi Minh Trail. He was convinced that operations in Laos would have a more desirable effect than the 1970 incursion into Cambodia and "would shorten the war." In Thieu's judgment, "operations into the Laotian panhandle could and would succeed."[47]

On 18 January 1971 Rogers and CIA Director Helms met with Nixon, who informed them for the first time of the possible operation into Tchepone. After obtaining the secretary of state's support, the president agreed to the first phase of the Tchepone operation, moving troops and supplies close to the border with Laos. On 19 January Laird authorized Abrams to provide U.S. support for the operation with important restrictions: no forward bases outside Vietnam with U.S. personnel and no B–52 strikes in the DMZ or in North Vietnam. U.S. airlift could transport troops, supplies, and the wounded between Laos and South Vietnam "as necessary when beyond the capability" of South Vietnam's Air Force. Each U.S. air movement of Vietnamese troops was to include if possible some shipment of supplies. This "execute" message, prepared by the JCS, deliberately omitted at Moorer's request any reference to planning messages prior to 19 December in order not to divulge to Laird "the fact that we were working on the Tchepone operation prior to Al HAIG's trip to Southeast Asia."[48]

The administration discussed the Tchepone operation in a series of meetings, making more officials aware of the plan. At the 19 January WSAG session, however, Under Secretary of State Alexis Johnson raised objections. He feared that the ARVN offensive would disrupt the military balance in Laos, cause Souvanna to lose political support, and possibly open the door for a North Vietnamese attack in the north and a strike by the Chinese Communist forces building a road in the northern part of the country. Packard, Moorer, and Helms favored it. Underscoring Johnson's concerns, the State Department expressed its unease about violating the Geneva accords, provoking Congress and the press, prompting an unfavorable reaction from Souvanna, and risking adverse effects on Vietnamization or on Thieu's reelection prospects in 1971 should the operation fail.[49]

Left to right, Helms, Kissinger, Rogers, Nixon, Laird, and Moorer meet in the Oval Office to discuss the military operation in Laos, 18 January 1971. (Nixon Presidential Library)

An unwelcome complication for the military was the discovery that the planned operation was no longer secret. The advantage of surprise was gone. The administration learned in late January 1971 that the French government had asked Souvanna about the operation. Moorer observed that the enemy seemed to be expecting an offensive. "For the first time the North Vietnamese are prepared to stand and fight," Moorer noted, relishing the opportunity to strike hard while enemy forces were massed. Nixon wanted to proceed with phase one, moving troops to the border, and to decide later whether to begin phase two, moving the South Vietnamese units into Laos. The WSAG agreed on a public rationale for the first phase—the need to reinforce Military Region I as a defensive measure to counter the enemy buildup across the border.[50]

A large-scale troop deployment to the Laotian border would be hard to conceal, so Abrams imposed on 29 January a press embargo on all stories related to U.S. and Vietnamese units in Military Region I. Depending on progress in prepositioning forces and in clearing Route 9, phase one was expected to be completed by 5 February. The logistical effort required to equip and move ARVN troops proved impossible to conceal, making it obvious to the press and the enemy that a major attack was likely. Despite McCain's argument that the press embargo would only alienate reporters, and Moorer's suggestion that Abrams lift the embargo on reporting U.S. troop movements, Abrams held firm. If Nixon approved phase two, it would begin around 6 February with the entry of ARVN forces into Laos along Route 9.[51]

Souvanna agreed to support the Tchepone plan as long as there was no public acknowledgement of prior U.S. consultation with him, but the top echelon of the Nixon administration remained divided. In a January memorandum to Kissinger, Haig summarized the operation's benefits and risks. On the positive side, the operation could disrupt the enemy's land route for supplies and men just as the Cambodian incursion had closed the sea supply route through Sihanoukville, setting back a major enemy offensive in South Vietnam by possibly a year. The operation could enhance the ARVN's confidence and capability to survive, represent a psychological blow to Hanoi, and be carried out with limited U.S. casualties. Haig saw a significant strategic gain in seizing Tchepone, "the single most decisive option available to the Free World forces to successfully conclude U.S. involvement in the war and to convince Hanoi that negotiations are the preferable course." The risks were considerable. Haig recorded the prediction of Secretary Rogers that the operation would likely fail because the enemy knew about the plans. Moreover, the United States wanted South Vietnam to conduct an operation that Washington had repeatedly refrained from conducting with its own forces. Rogers, who foresaw difficulty in extricating ARVN units if they ran into trouble in Laos, expected congressional opposition and public criticism about expanding the ground war. The operation might upset Souvanna's political position within Laos. A setback in Laos could undermine Thieu's political support and the ARVN's confidence in its ability to replace American forces. Thus the operation also risked a setback in the Vietnamization process. Kissinger provided Rogers, Laird, and Helms Haig's list of the pros and cons prior to their meeting with the president on 2 February. Nixon made no decision that day.[52]

With phase two still under review, the enemy's awareness of a possible invasion worried the administration, but not enough to halt the planning for it. CIA reports in early February noted that North Vietnam was moving additional troops toward Tchepone and rearranging their defenses in expectation of a cross-border offensive.[53] The loss of secrecy troubled Laird, who feared heavy losses of ARVN troops and U.S.

helicopters, but he wanted to go ahead as did Moorer. As a precaution he requested intelligence information about how many troops Hanoi could move to the Tchepone area and how long it would take.

Ending all discussion, Nixon directed Laird on 3 February to prepare an "execute" message. The secretary's 4 February order authorized Abrams to provide U.S. support for the initial and subsequent phases of the Tchepone operation from 8 February through 5 April, allowing for an extension beyond 5 April. Laird's message cautioned that "continued support in various quarters in Washington may be contingent on limiting the operation to the 6 to 8 weeks which has been postulated in initial planning." Kissinger, however, wanted no termination date attached to the operation, commenting that if it went well the Vietnamese would stay, but if "we get a bloody nose, we will get out early." On 3 February Abrams lifted the press embargo on phase one. On 8 February Thieu announced the start of the operation. From then on the military and press called it by its Vietnamese name, Lam Son 719, after the site of a historic battle in northern Vietnam where the Vietnamese defeated the Chinese. Thieu stated Lam Son 719 would be limited in duration and in how far Saigon's forces went into Laos. Upon completion, he pledged, Saigon's forces would withdraw totally from Laos.[54]

Operation Lam Son 719

Launched with high expectations, Lam Son 719 began promisingly. Laird, already making a case for the success of Vietnamization and the continuation of withdrawals, gave an optimistic background briefing for the Pentagon press on 10 February. He highlighted the ability of Saigon's forces to execute a major military offensive, advancing as evidence that the Vietnamese had planned Lam Son 719 on their own. Abrams took exception, criticizing Laird's presentation as misleading and too optimistic. He reminded McCain that MACV had planned the operation, claimed the Vietnamese had only assisted in working out some of the details, and warned that the enemy could inflict heavy personnel and helicopter losses as the ARVN advanced into Laos. "If the public is misled in believing losses are unexpected," Abrams told McCain, "the conclusion could be made that the operation is not proceeding according to plan."[55] Abrams's comments were prescient.

Indeed, the operation stalled after a few days. In the face of enemy resistance ARVN units found it difficult to move along Route 9, a narrow, deeply rutted, single-lane passage that required the work of military engineers to make it traffi-cable. North Vietnamese forces put up a stiff fight and brought in reinforcements the deeper South Vietnam's forces moved into Laos. By 10 February the South Vietnamese had progressed 18 kilometers, reaching the town of Ban Dong, but they were reluctant to push ahead. On 11 February the advance came to a halt, although the operational plans had called for rapid movement toward Tchepone while the North Vietnamese were presumably off-balance and before they could reinforce. By 13 February the normally cautious Thieu had become concerned about the enemy's growing and more rapid than expected counterattack. He ordered General Hoang Xuan Lam, the ARVN corps commander, to halt his forces at Ban Dong. General Cao Van Vien, chief of South Vietnam's Joint General Staff, assured Abrams that the delay would last only three to five days. In turn, the MACV commander told Moorer that the offensive would resume after the ARVN established security, but he omitted mention of Thieu's order to General Lam. On 19 February the enemy launched a major assault against Lam's northern flank, forcing a South Vietnamese Ranger battalion to abandon its firebase. Respond-ing to White House queries about the delay, Moorer reassured Kissinger that the ARVN was being careful and establishing strong points before venturing further into the panhandle. He told Kissinger on 20 February that the ARVN task force would resume the offensive after it established logistics bases (see map, page 185).[56]

The delay in moving forward, in part attributable to high helicopter losses, alarmed the White House. After the first two weeks of the operation only 25 of the 88 AH–1G and 8 of the 44 UH–1C U.S. helicopters assigned to Lam Son were flyable, forcing temporary curtailment of resupply, medical evacuation, and combat assault missions. Replacement aircraft from South Vietnam arrived slowly, diminishing com-bat effectiveness. On 22 February a "nervous" Kissinger called Moorer, complaining that he did not understand what Abrams was doing. Criticizing ARVN operations south of Route 9 as unaggressive, he feared that the units north of Route 9 had settled down in static positions, which the North Vietnamese Army could exploit. A cable to Moorer from Abrams informing him that the ARVN would move into Tchepone in the next few days and then pull out disturbed Kissinger. The plan for Lam Son 719 had called for South Vietnamese units to stay in Tchepone long enough to upgrade the airfield. Kissinger told Moorer that he kept his doubts and concerns to himself: "I tell the President everything is great." He also wondered why South Vietnam had

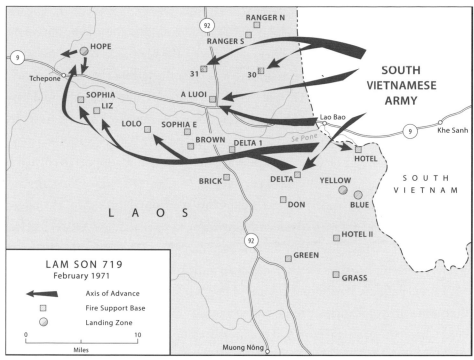

(Courtesy U.S. Army Center of Military History)

not committed any reserves to the battle, warning, "If we get our pants beaten off here I tell you we have had it in Vietnam for psychological reasons." He asserted that the Vietnamese had to remain in Laos until April and disrupt the enemy's supply system. Admitting problems, a still optimistic Moorer averred that once the ARVN established its logistics base Kissinger would see action. About three hours later the chairman also assured Nixon that the Vietnamese would move against Tchepone in the next two or three days with two brigades of the airborne division after establishing firm logistics and fire support bases. "Actually, I think the operations are going exactly as we expected them to," Moorer confidently assured the president.[57]

Moorer's certainty failed to assuage Kissinger, who was dissatisfied with the military briefings on the operation because they did not "hang together." Seeking another perspective, on 23 February Kissinger asked Westmoreland to critique Lam Son 719. Although reluctant to second-guess his successor, General Abrams, Westmoreland had to respond and communicated his skepticism regarding the operational concept and the ability of South Vietnamese commander General Lam to run it. Moorer had not served in Vietnam, but he had a higher opinion of Lam than did

Westmoreland, who as the former MACV commander had observed the general firsthand. Afterward, Westmoreland told Moorer about his discussion and on the following day briefed the Joint Chiefs at length on the high risks of the operation. Tchepone, its objective, was too ambitious a goal for the number of ARVN soldiers committed to the operation. He told the Chiefs that the United States should have considered alternatives, such as quick-hitting airmobile raids by Vietnamese forces to cut the Ho Chi Minh Trail at various points. The elite ARVN airborne troops operating in Laos had neither the experience nor the organic support to engage in sustained combat and would take heavy losses. Lt. Gen. Du Quoc Dong, the airborne division commander, was no "fighter" in Westmoreland's view. He judged further that the operation had not gone according to plan, that the ARVN had lost the benefit of surprise, and that its slow pace had given the enemy the chance to react. As a result, resistance was greater than anticipated, creating doubts about the ARVN's capability, Westmoreland feared that a major setback might cause South Vietnam's army to collapse, as he had seen it do "many times." He reminded the Joint Chiefs that General Lam had not measured up in 1964 as commander of the 1st ARVN Division, making it necessary at the time for the MACV commander to send American advisers to take over.[58]

Although Kissinger downplayed Westmoreland's comments when he discussed the matter with Moorer, they were obviously a slap at Abrams, Moorer, and the Joint Staff. Laird and Moorer were especially perturbed. They regarded his criticism as tantamount to casting doubt on the commander on-scene. Laird pointedly reminded Kissinger that Moorer was "closer in touch with this operation and Abrams than anyone else," and he had to trust his judgment more than that of the former MACV commander. This was not one of Laird's more astute observations. Kissinger tartly remarked, "If you look at the military history it isn't field commanders who are always right." Westmoreland's criticism touched a raw nerve. Nixon had become "uptight" and Kissinger as "jumpy as a cat," to use Laird's terms, about the course of the operation.[59]

On 24 February Laird held a press briefing to put the conduct of Lam Son 719 in the best light and to dispel the notion that the ARVN was bogged down and the operation was in trouble. With Lt. Gen. John W. Vogt, director of the Joint Staff, at his side, the secretary echoed Vogt's comments that Tchepone "has never been an objective [of] this operation." The objective, Laird stated to the media, was to disrupt the enemy's logistic system and the flow of supplies. That statement was certainly true, but it was not the whole truth and did not reflect the importance that the Abrams' plan had attached to holding the key road junctions at Tchepone. Laird was trying to lower expectations of what the operation would accomplish.[60]

Moorer defended Lam at a meeting with the president on 25 February, reporting that Abrams supported his moves and considered the Vietnamese general to be a solid but cautious leader. At the NSC meeting on the following day, however, Moorer had to report unfavorable developments. First, thanks in part to the ARVN's halting conduct of the offensive, the enemy had massed twice as many soldiers (28,000) against South Vietnam's forces as originally estimated. Given this unexpected disparity, the Saigon government had to bring in additional units to bolster its original contingent of 10,000 troops. Second, the chairman passed on Abrams' belief that South Vietnam's airborne unit needed better leadership. Moorer also disclosed that bad weather in the rainy season would force ARVN units to leave Laos around the beginning of May.[61]

Despite Moorer's continued assurances, events in Laos roiled Nixon and Kissinger. On 1 March Kissinger sent an "exclusively eyes only" cable to Bunker, calling it "a personal communication with no official status" that expressed profound concern about the evolving events in Laos. He wanted Bunker to meet privately with Abrams to assess what was happening. Reminding the ambassador that Nixon had agreed to support Lam Son 719 in the expectation that it would disrupt the enemy's supply network and lessen his ability to mount an offensive, Kissinger stated, "I am beginning to wonder what if anything has been achieved in this regard." He found troubling the discrepancy between the plan's milestones and actual events. Informed that the ARVN would seize Tchepone four to five days after the operation's start, Nixon learned a week after the operation began that weather, road conditions, and enemy resistance would delay attaining that objective for another eight to ten days. Then he was informed that Tchepone was not that important, because the routes through Tchepone were being severed southeast of the town. Most troubling to Kissinger (as it had been to Westmoreland) was the limited ARVN strength involved in Lam Son 719—against which, he noted, the enemy was fully committing all resources. ARVN numbers, insufficient to achieve the operation's goals, made defeat a possibility. The argument that the enemy's losses exceeded South Vietnam's would carry little weight in Washington.[62]

Notwithstanding Kissinger's elaborate disclaimer, his exceptionally blunt message to Bunker bore the president's imprimatur. In forwarding Bunker's reply to Nixon, Kissinger cited his so-called unofficial backchannel to the ambassador. Bunker's response, coordinated with Abrams, provided reassurance: If the administration held steady Lam Son 719 would have the "impact on the enemy's activities in South Vietnam and our troop withdrawals which we originally contemplated." Moorer also remained consistently upbeat. In a phone call on 3 March he assured the president that the ARVN could operate in southern Laos for another month and that no change from that goal was contemplated. Abrams believed that in general South Vietnam's forces were fighting well and not panicking. In an overly optimistic assessment, Moorer emphasized that the South Vietnamese would reap an important psychological benefit by remaining longer in Laos and showing that "they can hold their own with the best of the North Vietnamese."[63]

Despite Moorer's sanguine expectations, Nixon's doubts persisted. Like Laird, the president wished to moderate public expectations about the operation. On 6 March he told Moorer that the administration should make clear that the allied aim was not to capture Tchepone and "stay there for an indefinite period. . . . The point I'm trying to make is that we're there to disrupt the supplies and we will be moving out later." This represented a decided change from the initial plan. In terms of public relations, Nixon feared creating the impression that the ARVN was forced to withdraw. Before the ARVN reached Tchepone, the president wanted Kissinger to inform the press on a background basis that the South Vietnamese had no intention of holding that town, in contradiction of Abrams' original plan. Agreeing with the president, Moorer said Tchepone had "no military significance whatsoever," flatly contradicting his original view and the original plan.[64]

In private, the administration lowered its expectations about the operation, emphasizing now that the core goal of Lam Son 719 was to provide time for U.S. withdrawals to continue. Kissinger commented to Nixon on 3 March that even with the best military outcome for the South Vietnamese in Laos, North Vietnam's forces would be able to refit themselves in two to three years, "but then we will be out," that is, no longer have troops in Vietnam.[65]

Nonetheless, Nixon wanted ARVN units to remain in Laos as long as they could, as close to 1 May as possible, a point which Kissinger stressed to Laird and Moorer. At Moorer's suggestion, Kissinger instructed Bunker and Abrams on

9 March to "put some starch" in Thieu to ensure that South Vietnamese forces remained in Laos and to assure him that the United States would provide military support for the operation beyond 5 April. Laird's authorization message had set that date as a cutoff for U.S. support (including air operating authorities) of the ARVN's move into Laos. On 11 March Laird explicitly waived the 5 April termination date, not wanting to deprive Vietnamese forces of support or risk having the South Vietnamese government claim that the United States had forced a reluctant ally to undertake Lam Son 719.[66]

Moorer believed that the South Vietnamese should persist and fully exploit what they had achieved. Alarmed by signs that they might be easing up, however, he stressed to Abrams that Lam Son 719 was the last opportunity for the Vietnamese to achieve long-range benefits from an offensive. "They are not going to get another chance like this. We just won't be around." Abrams warned that the South Vietnamese had their own ideas and planned to begin withdrawing forces in roughly two weeks, which Abrams and Moorer thought was too soon. "Admiral," Abrams said to Moorer, "you can rest assured that I have been giving them [the South Vietnamese] pep talks, hand-holding and whatever the situation called for and I will continue to do that, but in the end, they are running it."[67]

Abrams had read the situation correctly, for indeed President Thieu had implemented his own concept of the operation. After meeting with General Lam on 28 February, Thieu decided to lift ARVN units by helicopter to Tchepone. On 7 March elements of the 1st Division reached Tchepone and on the following day began a southerly withdrawal from the town. On 9 March Lam flew to Saigon to consult with Thieu on withdrawing ARVN forces from Laos.[68]

Thieu's decisions aggravated the frustration of a White House counting on the South Vietnam leader to continue the operation. On 9 March Kissinger urged Bunker to impress upon Thieu that the 5 April termination date would be lifted, and the current operation would be the last time the ARVN would receive assistance on the scale currently provided. Lam Son represented the final opportunity for South Vietnam to mount a offensive while the U.S. military still had an effective combat presence in-country. Kissinger hoped Bunker could persuade Thieu to continue Lam Son 719 well into April and schedule his withdrawal for the period just before the end of the dry season in May.[69] Bunker's response on 10 March was not reassuring. Thieu's latest plan would extend the operation for only another 14 days to be followed by a move into base area 611 and the A Shau valley. These messages, exchanged exclusively through the private Kissinger-Bunker channel, bypassed Laird and Moorer, but as usual the chairman covertly received copies from his NSC liaison officer, who advised him to hold them closely.[70]

At a White House briefing on 11 March, Kissinger angrily reacted to Thieu's new timetable: "Then they are really bugging out in the next ten days, those sons of bitches. It's their country and we can't save it for them if they don't want to. We would never have approved the plan if we thought they were only going to stay for a short time, six to eight weeks." On 14 March General Lam hyperbolically told the press that his forces had accomplished the mission that Thieu had given them: "We have cut the main portions of the Ho Chi Minh Trail and destroyed the enemy's supplies. We have badly hurt at least four North Vietnamese regiments and cut half of Hanoi's supply flow to the south."[71]

News reports confirmed that some South Vietnamese units were pulling back but concluded that they were forced to do so under heavy enemy pressure. On 13 March South Vietnamese troops withdrew from firebase Sophia, three miles southeast of Tchepone, under threat of attack by a rapidly growing North Vietnamese force. Saigon's troops reportedly departed in haste, spiking several 105mm artillery pieces as they left the firebase. On 17 March U.S. pilots reported that ARVN forces had retreated some 15 miles under enemy pressure and had abandoned two of four firebases south of Route 9. The South Vietnamese pronounced the moves tactical, but the administration was skeptical. Reacting to television and radio accounts, Rogers remarked to Kissinger on 17 March, "It looks like we are getting clobbered."[72]

That morning Nixon asked Moorer if the ARVN had been driven out of two bases. As usual, Moorer tried to reassure the president, not directly answering the question, only saying that the ARVN had to keep moving and was executing its phase three plan, which Moorer thought would take several weeks. About two hours later Kissinger called the chairman to find out how long the ARVN would remain in the strategically important area of Route 914. Moorer relayed his latest information from Abrams, who described General Lam's new concept for Lam Son 719. It envisioned completing a phase three and starting a phase four on 15 April. The revised phase four plan would concentrate on base area 611. Moorer cautioned that a "premature or hasty withdrawal" opened the door for the North Vietnamese to advance "exaggerated claims of a South Vietnamese defeat."[73]

Lam's plan was short-lived. By 18 March Thieu had scrapped it, and the first withdrawal of ARVN units had already begun. Abrams reported the process as orderly but admitted he did not know why Thieu had decided to withdraw. Moorer concluded that Thieu was "bobtailing this operation and going to move to the east. The concept has been drastically altered in the last 24 hours." Finally alarmed, Moorer warned Abrams that the redeployment of South Vietnam's forces "could add fuel to the current pessimistic press reports claiming a rout of Vietnamese units from Laos." Kissinger also worried about public relations problems for Nixon and Thieu if press accounts gave the impression that the ARVN withdrawal was in fact a rout. The security adviser vented his frustration to Moorer, "I have been telling Senators that we are moving out of Tchepone to hold [Route] 914. Now they [the South Vietnamese] are not moving near 914. I think they are bugging out." He could not understand why the ARVN was avoiding Route 914, which was south of Route 9 and led to base area 611. Kissinger had expected Thieu to slowly withdraw his forces through base area 611, southeast of Tchepone, and remain there long enough to destroy enemy weapons and supply caches. He complained to Bunker on 18 March that the administration had received no advance warning of Thieu's change of plan. "It would be hard to exaggerate the mystification and confusion caused here by the ARVN's latest scheme of maneuver which envisages a rapid pull-out from Laos."[74]

In mid-March the White House, nervous about gloomy news stories and Thieu's intentions, sent Haig to Vietnam to observe Lam Son 719 and to urge South Vietnam's leader to keep the ARVN in Laos as long into April as possible. Nixon and Kissinger had wanted Haig to go to Vietnam in late February, but Laird had adamantly opposed a visit at that time and got the president to delay it for two weeks. Fearing that Abrams would consider an early visit as meddlesome and resent it, Laird insisted to Kissinger that the administration had "to rely on Abe. Whether we like it or not. He's the best man we could possibly have in this particular job at this time."[75]

Ironically, Laird defended Abrams on the same day that Kissinger heard Westmoreland's criticism of the operation. Haig's trip in March evidently ruffled no feathers in Saigon, but his findings added to the consternation in Washington. President Thieu told him that the combination of the enemy's strength, "which exceeded all expectations," the unanticipated "degree to which the enemy would reinforce his defenses," the difficult terrain, poor weather, and unexpectedly heavy casualties made it necessary to modify the operation. After visiting Military Region I, Haig concluded the problem was no longer trying to keep the ARVN in Laos: South Vietnamese commanders wanted to end Lam Son 719 as soon as possible. As he put it in his message to Kissinger, "ARVN has lost its stomach for further operations in Laos." For Abrams, the main concern was "not getting ARVN to stay but rather to influence them to pull out in an orderly fashion." Haig expected the enemy to make a strong effort against withdrawing units, "seeming to sense waning ARVN aggressiveness." Despite the problems, he surprisingly thought Lam Son 719 had accomplished most of what the administration wanted.[76]

Kissinger reached a different conclusion. He believed that Thieu pulled out ARVN forces because he needed the ARVN 1st Division in Saigon "for his election and he doesn't want them to have a lot of casualties." Although abruptly shortened, Kissinger opined to Nixon that the operation "was the best possible thing that could conceivably have been done at this period" and conceded it was "better for them to pull out than to take a shellacking." While the operation had not realized its full potential, he told the president on 20 March, "I have no doubt that the enemy is on the verge of cracking on Laos. He has thrown in everything and it's a pity the SVN can't put in another division." This view of the enemy did not accord with his talk about the ARVN taking a "shellacking." As a result of the pullout, Nixon and Kissinger realized the administration would have to adopt a new public posture— the ARVN had accomplished its major objectives and then left Laos. They sought to rebut any suggestion that South Vietnam's forces had been pushed out.[77]

On 21 March Laird and Kissinger discussed the South Vietnamese withdrawal. The secretary reminded Kissinger that from the beginning Thieu wanted to limit the Lam Son operation to a five- to eight-week period and that Laird tried to get that point into the operational order. Laird believed Thieu was following his plan. Kissinger countered that the administration had not really understood that point as well as Laird did, implying that the Pentagon was at fault and that the ARVN's seemingly unexpected withdrawal had made the president uneasy. As recently as 17 March, Kissinger said, he was told that the last phase of the operation would not start until 15 April, only to learn the following day that the ARVN was getting out before the end of March. "This is what got the President so concerned whether there was a rout." Laird insisted that the withdrawal was not a rout. The South Vietnamese decided to withdraw, he told Kissinger, but faced "tough fighting" under heavy contact with the enemy. Other writers rendered harsher verdicts, citing serious squabbling among South Vietnamese generals and the near collapse of the ARVN forces. The last ARVN contingent left Laos around 23 March pursued by a North Vietnamese force of around 40,000 soldiers.[78]

While acknowledging losses and shortcomings, Abrams, like Kissinger and Laird, found reason to judge Lam Son 719 an overall success. He thought the ARVN's ability to mount two cross-border operations (Cambodian and Laos) consecutively testified to the success of Vietnamization and a dramatic change of thinking on the part of Thieu's government. The MACV commander claimed Lam Son achieved its primary objective of fighting the enemy in his sanctuary and disrupting his lines of communication. The plan's original objective of holding Tchepone long enough to upgrade its airfield was omitted from his evaluation. As a consequence of the operation, Abrams noted, the Saigon government had additional time to strengthen its armed forces, and the United States could continue to withdraw troops. Swallowing his disappointment, Kissinger thought that the operation, though not as successful as anticipated, bought time. As a result of Lam Son, he told Nixon, he did not expect the enemy to launch a major offensive before May or June 1972, which meant the administration could speed up the redeployments. The rate of withdrawal, he acknowledged, had become moot in any event, because by May and June the United States would no longer have enough troops in Vietnam to constitute an effective combat force. Kissinger thought the president "should give an impression of confidence and serenity" about the operation.[79]

Indeed, the administration spoke optimistically in public. On 7 April Nixon reported on Lam Son 719, telling the nation, "Vietnamization has succeeded. . . . The South Vietnamese demonstrated that without American advisers they could fight effectively against the very best troops North Vietnam could put in the field." The president claimed that South Vietnam's forces had inflicted more enemy casualties than they had suffered and the disruption of enemy supply lines and North Vietnam's consumption of arms and ammunition to defend the trail proved even more damaging to its capabilities than the earlier operation in Cambodia. As a consequence of the Laotian operation, the success of the Cambodian incursion, and the demonstrated strength of South Vietnam's forces, Nixon would bring home 100,000 additional U.S. troops between 1 May and 1 December 1971.[80]

In private the administration was much less sanguine. Haig wrote another lengthy assessment of Lam Son 719 for Kissinger that clearly indicated a change of mind since the March report. Evincing less certainty about South Vietnam's military capabilities, he noted, "[W]e badly underestimated the enemy's ability and obvious willingness to reinforce as he did." South Vietnam's leadership was "obviously reluctant to commit the necessary forces to wrest the initiative from the enemy" or to move forces in a manner that preempted the enemy from concentrating his ground and artillery forces against the ARVN. Haig viewed this reluctance as "a crisis of confidence between US and ARVN commanders." He argued that Thieu's personal intervention slowed the pace of the operation and allowed the enemy time to regroup, reinforce, and resupply his forces.[81]

Regretting that the operation fell short of the administration's ambitious goals, Kissinger laid the fault at the feet of the U.S. commander. He criticized Abrams for taking leave during the operation, for not better coordinating ground and tactical air support, and for not always providing satisfactory information. In a phone call to Westmoreland on 12 April, Kissinger brought up Westmoreland's alternative plan for Lam Son 719. "I have thought with nostalgia and regret of our conversation here many weeks ago. You were right." Referring to the Army chief's analysis of South Vietnam's forces and leaders, Kissinger ruefully concluded, "Your briefing at the end of Feb. was very clairvoyant."[82]

Another member of the Joint Chiefs, Air Force Chief of Staff General John Ryan, noted a significant misreading of communications between Washington and Saigon. He believed Abrams failed to perceive Washington's apprehensions about the operation and left too much of the conduct of Lam Son 719 to the U.S. command in Region I.[83] Removed from Washington, Abrams did not fully appreciate White House anxieties despite the frequency and urgency of messages from Kissinger, which were filtered through Moorer or Bunker. From the military's perspective, given the number of calls Nixon and Kissinger made to Moorer, White House oversight of the operation approached meddling. Laird and Moorer proved more even tempered and less emotional than Kissinger. While anxious at times, Nixon was chiefly concerned that the operation not be perceived as a rout or a defeat of South Vietnam's forces so he could claim that Lam Son had a positive outcome.

Despite Nixon's public assertion of the ARVN's prowess, he realized Vietnam's armed forces would need continued American military assistance. He told Kissinger on 25 March that the South Vietnamese could not "hack it" unless the United States continued to provide adequate support. "They should have everything they need. I don't care about budgets and inventories."[84] The clear implication was that the president would consider increases in the DoD budget. Nixon's position made it necessary to reexamine the Improvement and Modernization Plans to make certain Saigon's armed forces could defend their nation in the future without the presence of American combatants. Nixon's order amounted to an admission that Lam Son offered little reassurance about the ability of South Vietnamese forces to engage the North Vietnamese Army on their own. During the operation an unnamed high administration official was quoted as saying, "If they [South Vietnam's forces] can't do the job with the kind of air and firepower they'll have in Laos, then they'll never be able to do the job, and we might as well know that now, rather than later."[85] Before the operation the administration viewed Lam Son as a test of whether the South Vietnamese could take over the entire ground war; after the operation the administration realized it would need to do more to prepare South Vietnam's forces for their next trial by fire.

On 23 March, shortly before the last South Vietnamese units actually left Laos, the WSAG met to evaluate Lam Son. Consistent in his defense of the operation, Moorer asserted that Lam Son had prevented the enemy from mounting a major attack in Military Region I. Kissinger contended that South Vietnam's forces had done well in the face of serious handicaps. Much of the discussion focused on how the operation sapped the morale of some ARVN units. Moorer reported Abrams' belief that morale would improve and the force would be stronger as a result of Lam Son, prompting Kissinger to ask, "Why do you think they [RVNAF] will draw the conclusion that they won? Won't it look to them as though they have been routed?" In the discussion that followed, General Vogt argued that the operation made South Vietnam's ground forces more conscious of their heavy dependence on U.S. air support. To which Kissinger responded, "What worries me is that the ARVN will draw the conclusion that even with our support they weren't successful." Vogt wondered about the implications of that conclusion for the ARVN's morale and willingness to fight when U.S. support was no longer available. He believed that "the confidence of some of the ARVN units has been shaken as a result of Lam Son. They have been somewhat sobered about their capability against first-line enemy units. . . . It is fair to say that RVNAF confidence in their ability to carry out the plans originally contemplated was shaken."[86]

Over the course of Lam Son 719 the White House became more defensive. Not questioning the notion of a cross-border invasion, Nixon and Kissinger found fault with General Abrams. Before the operation Nixon was full of praise, commending Abrams for "instilling his drive into the South Vietnamese. He is in the mold of Patton. . . ."[87] That high opinion did not endure. Frustrated and dissatisfied with the conduct of Lam Son, Kissinger ordered a review of the operation. One finding of the report compiled by Commander Jonathan Howe, a naval officer on Kissinger's staff, was that the assurances and evaluations from various officials, even Abrams, seldom corresponded with the reality of the battlefield. Abrams was faulted for his slow pace in both reporting and correcting problems and for his failure to appreciate the need to keep Washington abreast of developments. Kissinger took up his misgivings about the MACV commander with the president on 23 March. According to Haldeman, who attended the session, Nixon and Kissinger felt "they were misled by Abrams on the original evaluation" of what Lam Son might accomplish and "that Abrams went ahead with his plan even though it was clear that it wasn't working." Kissinger believed that they should have followed Westmoreland's advice. Nixon and Kissinger "concluded that they should pull Abrams out, but then the P[resident] made the point that this is the end of the military operations anyway, so what difference does it make."[88] Moreover, relieving Abrams would have reinforced the impression that Lam Son had been a failure.

Abrams found himself in hot water in mid-September 1971 after he met with Senator George McGovern in Vietnam. Nixon and Kissinger were agitated by comments that McGovern attributed to Abrams that there would be no residual U.S. force in Vietnam. Laird and Moorer assured Kissinger that Abrams had been misquoted. Not assuaged, the president again raised the issue of removing his Vietnam commander. Kissinger advised against actually doing it at that time, because "it will look like the last days of the Johnson administration," when Johnson replaced Westmoreland as MACV commander after the Tet offensive of 1968. Nixon agreed and told Kissinger, "Get someone second in command that will keep him [Abrams] from drinking too much and talking too much."[89] Despite White House dissatisfaction, of which Laird was aware, the defense secretary remained a steadfast supporter, telling Kissinger, "I'll defend Abrams any day in the week."[90] Laird had no intention of bowing to White House pressure to replace Abrams, a stalwart of the secretary's Vietnamization plans.

LIKE HIS PREDECESSORS, Nixon could not ignore the war in Laos. Unlike them, he decided to support a cross-border strike into Laos. Unfortunately for Laird, his caution about the consequences of greater U.S. involvement in Laos with U.S. air strikes and other military support put him at odds with a White House that had grown wary of his efforts to restrain the administration from undertaking what it considered were bold new military initiatives. Accordingly, Nixon used elaborate procedures to keep Laird uninformed about the planning for the cross-border operation into Laos for as long as possible. Ironically, when Laird was told, he raised no objections and even defended the operation vigorously when the South Vietnamese offensive ground to a halt, suggesting that White House scheming was unnecessary.

Laird's Vietnamization efforts helped make Lam Son feasible. Without it the operation would not have been considered. The president endorsed a South Vietnamese ground assault into Laos, expecting it to succeed thanks to progress in improving and modernizing the RVNAF. The Vietnamization program remained a central element of Nixon's policy, but the president thought it necessary to intervene with ground troops in Cambodia and Laos to help Vietnamization by weakening the enemy and showcasing the improvements of South Vietnam's forces. Attracted to grand plans and dramatic moves, the president saw bold military action as essential and Laird as a potential obstacle.[91]

Justifications for Lam Son 719 held that South Vietnam's army had become capable enough to carry it out and that cutting the Ho Chi Minh Trail even for a while would preclude an enemy offensive and buy more time for Vietnamization to take root. As the operation stalled and ARVN units departed from Tchepone in seeming haste, the administration tried to scale back expectations for the operation and redefined its objective to avoid the conclusion that the ARVN had retreated in the face of a superior fighting force. Lam Son raised basic questions about the accomplishments and durability of Vietnamization as well as the competence of the Thieu government to wage war on its own. As a consequence, the administration had to take a more critical look at plans to modernize South Vietnam's armed forces.

Laird publicly defended the performance of the army, but with his high-level staff he was equivocal. At the 29 March 1971 staff meeting, which covered public affairs problems, Laird said that DoD needed to get into a "posture that evaluation of the operations will come in September or October," that is, when the furor had died down. Moreover, according to Laird, the forthcoming presidential announcement of an unchanged monthly withdrawal rate should not be "interpreted as proof of failure of LAMSON 719."[92]

In the aftermath of the operation, the secretary found himself further separated from the White House over the prosecution of the war. Nixon complained about Laird's execution of the Improvement and Modernization Plans. In the future he would not inform the secretary about withdrawals in advance.[93] Abrams also fell from favor. Laird, who depended on the MACV commander to carry out Vietnamization, remained his primary and apparently sole defender. In the coming year, to the discomfort of Nixon and Kissinger, he vigorously advocated Abrams' candidacy for the post of Army chief of staff. The rift between the White House and Laird would only widen during the enemy's Easter Offensive of 1972. Nixon would then demonstrate greater confidence in exercising his authority as commander in chief.

CHAPTER 8

Preparing South Vietnam
to Stand Alone

LAM SON 719 GRANTED the Nixon administration no reprieve from the political pressure to pull out of Vietnam. Given the schedule for continued withdrawals and the ARVN's mixed performance in Laos, Defense Secretary Laird and the White House wanted to do everything possible to prepare South Vietnam's armed forces to take over the defense of their country after all U.S. combatants withdrew. A major issue was finding the right balance of resources in expanding South Vietnam's force structure and in improving its leadership. In his exchanges with U.S. officials Thieu argued for additional military assistance because his forces had taken on extra responsibilities in mounting the ground offensives in Cambodia and Laos—a major change, as the South Vietnamese leader pointed out. When Vietnamization began in 1969 the United States had not anticipated that the ARVN would undertake offensive operations outside South Vietnam's borders.

Troop Withdrawals: How Fast?

The rate of troop withdrawals remained the central issue—how quickly could Saigon's forces assume combat responsibility from the Americans should negotiations fail to end the fighting. Laird was the chief advocate of faster withdrawals, but he and other officials realized that Vietnamization incurred greater military risks with each withdrawal. By the spring of 1970, with fewer U.S. troops in Vietnam, General Creighton Abrams, the MACV commander, was "no longer in a position to be able to meet all threats everywhere," as Kissinger's deputy Al Haig expressed it.[1] Worried about withdrawing too quickly, Abrams favored a temporary pause. In April 1970 he advised Washington that U.S. redeployments to date had "stretched the South

Vietnamese ability to take over new areas of tactical responsibility and maintain adequate general reserves." President Nixon's assistant for national security, Henry Kissinger, had his own concerns about the withdrawals, fearing that budget issues, so important to Laird, would drive the administration's withdrawal decisions and limit air operations. As a consequence, South Vietnam's ground forces would have less air support when the more robust U.S. units left.[2]

Seeking to control the withdrawal rate, Kissinger advised Ambassador Ellsworth Bunker and Abrams (before Laird and JCS Chairman Admiral Thomas Moorer arrived in Vietnam in January 1971) to make no commitments to a firm schedule should the secretary pressure President Thieu. Although Laird did not discuss specific timetables with Thieu, the secretary expected U.S. troop levels overall would decline to 255,000 by 1 July 1971 and would be in the range of 50,000 to 75,000 by the fall of 1972.[3] Abrams wanted flexibility in redeployments to allow him to deal with contingencies. Laird, with an eye on the budget and domestic politics, sought to carry out the scheduled withdrawals. In his report to Nixon, the secretary remarked that he had told Abrams, "We are working against time in that a *de facto withdrawal timetable has been established relative to 1972*," a veiled reference to the upcoming U.S. presidential elections. In Laird's view, that timetable required the United States to have by 1972 only a military assistance advisory group in Vietnam.[4]

The JCS, less inclined than Laird to accept the risks of a speedier departure, preferred an in-country strength of about 200,000 by the end of FY 1972, of which 152,800 would be Army personnel. Admiral Moorer arranged for Rear Admiral Robinson, his White House liaison officer, to provide Kissinger the latest JCS planning figures for U.S. strength in Vietnam while the chairman and Laird were overseas. The JCS figures, higher than Laird's, were unrealistic, because the Army's budget (see chapter 5) could support a force level of only 115,000 in Vietnam at the end of FY 1972.[5]

On his return to Washington, Laird continued to push for withdrawals, assuring Nixon that his "pledge to have the U.S. out of military operations in Southeast Asia by 1972 can and will be met." South Vietnamese officials briefed Laird about the status of their forces, serving to reaffirm his position on continuing scheduled withdrawals. The White House, however, remained skeptical, because it had received two intelligence reports asserting that South Vietnamese officials "made a deliberate effort to present an optimistic picture of the situation to Secretary

Laird," and that South Vietnam's Joint General Staff had deleted from the briefing all references to the ARVN's operational and logistical problems and requirements for added military aid. Not taken in by the slanted briefings, Laird continued to report on South Vietnamese military deficiencies, especially leadership and morale problems, which were less easily remedied than equipment shortages.[6]

Moorer took exception to the secretary's findings, reminding Laird that Abrams wanted a sufficient number of American forces in Vietnam to maintain security, especially while the RVNAF conducted cross-border operations. As Moorer noted, Abrams and his deputy, General Frederick C. Weyand, objected to reducing the U.S. presence in Vietnam to only a military assistance group by 1972 because it entailed a major security risk. The secretary and the JCS had a serious disagreement over U.S. troop levels. Laird desired a ceiling of 75,000 on all U.S. forces by the end of FY 1972; the JCS, CINCPAC, and MACV recommended about 200,000. In fact, the budgets could support slightly over 150,000 U.S. personnel.[7]

The conflicting advice from Moorer and Laird only complicated the president's deliberations. He faced unrelenting political pressure to announce another withdrawal, but the ambiguous outcome of Lam Son 719 argued for slowing down the withdrawals and increasing assistance to South Vietnam's forces. Kissinger perceived the Laotian foray as placing "the President under increasing political pressure here," making the retention of public support imperative. With tensions building, Nixon decided in March 1971 not to inform Laird, Moorer, and Abrams of the exact size of the next withdrawal until just before he announced it publicly.[8] According to Kissinger, the president contemplated a withdrawal of around 100,000, a figure higher than Abrams' recommendation.[9]

Unaware that Nixon had resolved not to consult with him about the size and timing of the next pullout, Laird sent the president on 3 April three withdrawal options, comparing the department's Vietnam requirements with its global responsibilities. The secretary judged the available defense resources for FYs 1969–1971, after deducting the incremental costs of the war, as "substantially below those needed to maintain the base-line capability" and "one of the major reasons the Soviet Union has been able to make such marked military strides relative to the United States during the past few years." As he had stated on many occasions, the costs of the Vietnam War diminished the administration's ability to support its national security policies elsewhere. Nixon never saw Laird's memorandum.

Respecting Nixon's plan to move ahead with the next round of troop cuts without consulting the secretary, Kissinger did not forward Laird's proposal.[10]

On 7 April Nixon announced a sizable redeployment shortly after Lam Son 719 to bolster assertions that the operation was a success. The president declared he would accelerate the rate of troop withdrawals and send home an additional 100,000 troops between 1 May and 1 December 1971. In November 1971 and January 1972 Nixon announced additional reductions that would lower the U.S. troop ceiling to 69,000 by 1 May 1972.[11] This number fell within the 50,000 to 75,000 range that Laird advocated but was far below the JCS recommendation of 200,000 for the end of FY 1972. In short, by the spring of 1972 the United States would have a severely limited combat capability in Vietnam.[12]

Secretary Laird briefs the press corps at the Pentagon on Vietnamization, 11 October 1972. The chart displays the decline in U.S. troop strength from its peak in early 1969 to the projected low in December 1972. (OSD Historical Office)

A Growing South Vietnamese Force, 1970–1971

While pressing for U.S. withdrawals, Laird sought larger and stronger armed forces for South Vietnam. The Defense Department had expanded its Improvement and Modernization Plans before South Vietnam carried out the Cambodian incursion of May 1970. Prompted by Laird the JCS prepared the Phase III Plan in January 1970, raising the authorized strength of the RVNAF to 1,061,505 by the end of FY 1973 and creating new support units to replace departing U.S. forces. A U.S. residual MAAG would remain in Vietnam to support, train, and advise the South Vietnamese after American combat units departed. Thieu's February 1970 request for additional American support led to a modified plan, known as the Consolidated RVNAF Improvement and Modernization Plan (CRIMP). It raised the force structure ceiling to 1.1 million, provided better equipment and combat support, and enhanced logistic capabilities for South Vietnam's military. Most significant, the plan did not alter the RVNAF's defensive mission or deployment. South Vietnamese Army divisions were largely immobile, rarely venturing far from the areas in which they were stationed. The revised Improvement and Modernization Plan of March 1970 was not intended to prepare or equip Saigon's forces for the ground offensives in Cambodia or Laos that occurred.[13]

Nor did CRIMP include a South Vietnamese aerial interdiction capability to stem the southward flow of enemy troops and supplies along the Ho Chi Minh Trail, a role mainly carried out by U.S. aircraft. U.S. Air Force planners contemplated a South Vietnamese air force that could support only ground operations. As early as December 1969, Leonard Sullivan, deputy director of defense research and engineering for Southeast Asia, pointed out the need for better border security, because the U.S. aerial interdiction campaign, Commando Hunt, would not go on indefinitely. DDR&E John Foster made Sullivan responsible for carrying out research and development on an emergency basis to support the war in Southeast Asia. Although he focused on using technology to develop new weapons, Sullivan perceived a major flaw in Vietnamization, concluding it could not succeed without some way to impede infiltration from North Vietnam. Unfortunately, the creation of a Vietnamese interdiction capability would not occur until 1971.[14]

In June 1970 Laird approved the FYs 1971–1972 modest increases in South Vietnam's army and air force recommended by the JCS (see table 6, page 204), noting that all necessary funding would have to come from anticipated DoD funds. He advised then-JCS Chairman General Earle Wheeler that if estimated costs for FYs 1972–1973 exceeded his fiscal guidance, funds would have to come from reductions in Vietnam or trade-offs elsewhere. Laird was concerned that setting up a large military establishment would be too costly for the South Vietnamese government and economy to support. Accordingly, he approved the FY 1973 force structure for planning purposes only, instructing Abrams to draft plans for a force structure of no more than one million personnel for that year. At least half of this number consisted of localized Regional and Popular Forces (RF/PF). Laird noted the FY 1972 approvals were subject to further review in light of the Defense budget and economic conditions in South Vietnam.[15]

Table 6. South Vietnamese Force Structure

	FY 1971	FY 1972	FY 1973
Army	434,019	441,829	447,456
Navy	39,611	39,611	39,611
Air Force	38,780	44,712	46,998
Marine Corps	13,462	13,462	13,462
Regional Forces	294,446	294,446	294,446
Popular Forces	258,027	258,027	258,027
Total	1,078,345	1,092,087	1,100,000

Source: Willard J. Webb, *The Joint Chiefs of Staff and the War in Vietnam, 1969–1970* (Washington, DC: Office of Joint History, Office of the JCS, 2002), 240.

In March 1971 Laird informed Nixon that the RVNAF was close to attaining its force structure targets for ground combat, combat support, and artillery units. He noted progress in turning over naval craft to the Vietnamese and in expanding the aircraft inventory as well as the number of air squadrons. The drive to bolster the Vietnamese air effort was lagging, with an inadequate number of helicopters and a projected decline in combined U.S. and Vietnamese air force sorties. Desiring to do more to improve the RVNAF, Nixon asked Laird, Kissinger, and Wheeler to take a detailed look at expanding ground forces above 1.1 million and modernizing Vietnam's military.[16]

Enlarging the South Vietnamese military structure had strategic implications. In June 1970 Laird sought to attain four goals: successful Vietnamization, reduction of U.S. casualties and costs, continuation and possible acceleration of troop withdrawals, and stimulation of meaningful negotiations. Envisioning the end of

U.S. ground combat operations, he told Wheeler following the Cambodian incursion, "US combat operations are to be steadily decreased, commensurate with the increasing capability of RVNAF to assume combat and support responsibilities, and commensurate with the security of remaining US forces." The secretary took a dim view of military escalation because of its cost and what he considered its ineffectiveness in pressuring the enemy to negotiate.[17]

The administration was preparing not only for the possible expansion of South Vietnam's armed forces but also for the end of U.S. combat. In August Nixon issued NSSM 99, a request for a study of strategic alternatives for 1970–1975. Seven months later, in late March 1971, the study had settled on two options. The first was to increase South Vietnam's force structure to 1.2 million by the end of FY 1972, an alternative that raised questions about the availability of Vietnamese troops and higher costs. The second was to geographically redistribute existing forces within the current ceiling of 1.1 million by shifting more forces to Military Regions I and II in the northern part of the country.[18] Laird took Nixon's request as an opportunity to refine his thinking. He viewed Vietnamization as a test case for the Nixon Doctrine, which called for the United States to provide military assistance (not troops) to allies in the third world. As usual, Laird's immediate objectives were to keep within budget guidelines, reduce U.S. casualties, and continue to withdraw U.S. military forces. His focus was on bolstering Vietnamese forces and winding down U.S. involvement in Vietnam.[19]

In January 1971 Laird said publicly the administration would be "in a position in the course of this year" to end the American ground combat role, the fighting that caused the most U.S. casualties. That statement caused the White House to ask him to refrain from bringing up the subject. It did not disagree with the policy to end direct American combat but wanted to avoid press speculation about a termination date. With fewer and fewer U.S. military troops in-country, the combat role and capability of U.S. forces in Vietnam would inexorably wane. The contemplated end of the combat role lent urgency to plans and programs to improve and modernize South Vietnam's armed forces.[20]

Improvement and Modernization

After the Cambodian assault, Laird saw the need to accelerate the Vietnamese modernization program "in every possible way." In his hopeful view the incursion demonstrated that South Vietnam could take on "much greater responsibility for conduct of the war by the end of FY 1971. The new RVNAF confidence born in the recent cross-border operations [in Cambodia] must now be translated into specific and definable milestones." Speeding up modernization would allow Laird to hasten U.S. withdrawals. He saw an urgent need to control the cost of Vietnamization, noting that political and economic conditions in the United States ruled out a request for supplemental funds.[21]

To the secretary, growing expenses tended to preclude further expansion of Vietnamese forces. In April 1971 he advised Kissinger that the United States and South Vietnam should focus on qualitative improvements, such as reducing desertions and upgrading the caliber of leaders "within acceptable dollar, piaster [South Vietnam's currency] and manpower limitations." "The problems facing RVNAF are not soluble by increasing strength levels beyond the 1.1 million currently programmed."[22] Earlier in February, he told the service secretaries and JCS Chairman Admiral Moorer, "We cannot give the Government of Vietnam all the capabilities US forces now have in Southeast Asia. Even if we chose to try, the economy of the Republic of Vietnam could not support such a force structure."[23]

South Vietnamese officials thought otherwise. They wanted a more mechanized and heavier force to enhance the capability of their military to defend the nation without the presence of U.S. combatants. After evaluating the ARVN's performance in Lam Son 719, General Cao Van Vien, chief of South Vietnam's Joint General Staff, asked MACV for more firepower, seeking in April 1971 heavier tanks, antitank missiles in place of recoilless rifles, and additional tank, artillery, and armored infantry battalions. Agreeing with Laird, Abrams considered most of these items nonessential.[24]

In February 1971 Laird turned his attention to developing a South Vietnamese interdiction capability, some combination of means to constrain future North Vietnamese infiltration. Leonard Sullivan, the deputy DDR&E, had pointed out this deficiency in late 1969. Now, with the administration contemplating the eventual departure of the U.S. Air Force units conducting aerial interdiction of the Ho Chi Minh Trail, this requirement could no longer be ignored. Reducing the U.S. interdiction campaign in FY 1972, Moorer cautioned Laird, would allow the enemy to concentrate his efforts in Cambodia and increase the danger for U.S. forces in Vietnam. The secretary believed South Vietnam needed some capability, on a smaller scale than the U.S. program, to reduce the North's infiltration of men and supplies after the American air role ended. In February 1971 he was thinking in terms of South Vietnamese strikes against nearby cross-border base areas and passageways where the Ho Chi Minh Trail entered South Vietnam.[25]

Laird and Deputy Secretary David Packard pressed the issue in the spring of 1971, asking for simple, inexpensive solutions. In April Sullivan provided an interdiction plan that employed ground radars and sensors operated by the South Vietnamese to improve border surveillance and control. He also advocated short-duration airborne strikes and ground attacks by small Vietnamese raiding parties into Laos to disrupt North Vietnamese forces and provide reconnaissance. By mid-June DoD came up with a plan to improve equipment for cross-border patrols, provide more advanced sensors for surveillance, and increase Vietnamese firepower.[26]

Laird gave interdiction a high priority. In July he asked the Joint Staff to prepare a combined campaign plan for FY 1972 that would bolster participation of South Vietnamese air, ground, and naval forces resulting in their assuming total responsibility for the interdiction effort. "The fate of our national Vietnamization policy," Laird asserted, "rests in part on the evolution of a credible RVNAF interdiction capability at the earliest possible time."[27] Admiral John McCain, the PACOM commander, sounded a note of caution, pointing out that such a Vietnamese capability needed to "avoid sophisticated systems which place unmanageable burdens" on the South Vietnamese forces that suffered from a shortage of personnel with the requisite technical and management skills to handle complex equipment. Laird disagreed. On 8 October 1971 he told Moorer that he intended "to accelerate all programs" and not to "underestimate the RVNAF ability to operate and maintain limited amounts of additional equipments." If South Vietnam needed additional materiel to reduce reliance on U.S. forces, then Laird wanted immediate action to transfer the equipment to the RVNAF. Because "US interdiction cannot continue indefinitely," Laird set a goal of "achieving an optimal RVNAF interdiction capability by the fall of 1972 which could, if necessary, be self-sustaining with no more than limited US advisory effort."[28] In FY 1972 the South Vietnamese Air Force was to be incorporated into Commando Hunt plans for aerial interdiction of the Ho Chi Minh Trail and given CBU–55 bombs and other air munitions. The service was also to receive aircraft to give it a limited maritime air patrol capability. For future campaigns the secretary wanted South Vietnam's enhanced forces to plan, execute, and evaluate the interdiction campaign "to the extreme limits of their capability," using their own resources whenever possible.[29]

Laird, in sum, continued to push Vietnamization and eventual self-sufficiency for South Vietnam, but he was mindful of how much support the DoD budget would allow and how much aid, military equipment, and technology the Thieu government could realistically absorb. At the same time, the United States had to help prepare South Vietnam to handle a range of enemy actions from guerrilla raids to an all-out conventional invasion.

Planning for the Enemy Threat

Throughout much of 1971 the president and his top advisers devoted attention to preparing the RVNAF for an anticipated large-scale enemy offensive. They continually balanced the pace of RVNAF improvement and modernization against the U.S. level of combat and logistic support that would be available in such an attack. Given the rate of U.S. troop withdrawal, the buildup of South Vietnamese forces took on increasing urgency for the administration's leadership during the year.

NSSM 99 had prepared two options for bolstering South Vietnam's military: expand the force structure to 1.2 million or assign more forces to the northern provinces and central highlands. To provide the South Vietnam Armed Forces with all the equipment, weapons, and supplies they needed, in March 1971 Nixon asked Laird for a thorough analysis of their capabilities and requirements.[30] Laird told the president on 18 May 1971 that the RVNAF had the potential to cope with the projected threat from North Vietnamese and Viet Cong forces as long as they improved qualitatively and mustered sufficient will, leadership, and morale—a formidable caveat, indeed. The secretary held that the RVNAF had the troop numbers to meet the anticipated enemy threat nationwide. In his view a further military expansion would strain the local economy and lead to the "ultimate reduction of the force structure."[31]

The White House disputed Laird's assessment. Wayne Smith, one of Kissinger's assistants, concluded that friendly forces were not optimally distributed within South Vietnam, particularly in the northern part of the country, Military Region I, the most threatened sector, where, according to Laird's figures, a shortfall of about 26,000 troops existed. Smith concluded that South Vietnamese forces could not stop a major enemy offensive unless more combat units were added or existing ones redeployed to threatened areas. The withdrawal of American troops added urgency to the deliberations. Abrams estimated that by 1 December 1971 the U.S. ground combat force (Army and Marines) would comprise only five infantry brigades and two armored cavalry squadrons. Ready or not, in Abrams' view, the South Vietnamese would have to take over.[32]

The NSC Senior Review Group, which synthesized issues before they were presented to the National Security Council, took up the topic of South Vietnam's ability to handle a 1972 enemy offensive. On 24 May 1971 the JCS provided an assessment of enemy strategies, emphasizing the effect of U.S. redeployments on the balance of enemy and friendly forces in each military region. The Joint Staff considered Region I the most likely site of an enemy offensive and foresaw a growing shortfall in friendly capabilities as more U.S. forces left that area. The JCS believed South Vietnam's forces could cope with the enemy threat in 1972 with its available reserves as long as 150,000 U.S. troops remained in-country. If U.S. troop levels declined to 100,000, then the Saigon government would have to permanently strengthen its forces in Military Regions I and II. If only 50,000 U.S. soldiers remained in-country, the enemy threat represented a still manageable risk. The JCS did not consider simultaneous enemy offensives in Regions I and II militarily decisive even at lower American troop levels. Uncomfortable with the JCS evaluation, Kissinger complained that Laird and the services were "increasingly willing to accept greater risks during withdrawal," an incontrovertible observation.[33]

The Vietnam Special Studies Group (VSSG) also laid out the perils of an enemy offensive. With fewer U.S. forces, Hanoi could engage the ARVN in South Vietnam without fear of a strong response from the U.S. Army. Moreover, the North Vietnamese Army had also gained confidence in fighting the ARVN in Lam Son 719. The 1972 U.S. presidential election would provide Hanoi an opportunity to gain politically if they launched a dramatic military effort. According to the VSSG, the South's critical problem lay in preparing for the enemy's estimated ability to support simultaneous offensives in Military Regions I and II, where South Vietnamese units could find themselves outnumbered.[34]

In July Nixon decided the United States would support qualitative improvements in the RVNAF and augment the number of ARVN combat units in Regions I and II. NSDM 118 directed DoD and the U.S. Mission in South Vietnam to take special measures to implement new training and promotion programs to improve morale, urge the removal of incompetent Vietnamese military leaders, and provide incentive pay to RVNAF units in isolated areas. DoD and the U.S. Mission were to negotiate with the South Vietnamese government the strengthening of Vietnamese forces in Regions I and II, specifically increased manning levels in combat units to 90 percent, an additional combat division to Region I, and a division headquarters to Region II. Nixon also held out the possibility of supporting an increase in the RVNAF force structure should the transfer of units from Regions III and IV jeopardize security there. Laird was instructed to accelerate shipments of ammunition, fuel, and equipment so that the RVNAF would have on hand sufficient amounts, including the M48 tanks that General Vien and General Abrams had requested, by the end of September 1971.[35]

To hamper the North's capability to launch a major offensive in Regions I and II, Moorer wanted the RVNAF to conduct preemptive operations in Cambodia and in Laos and to develop detailed plans for shifting forces from Region III to Regions I and II. Moorer also asked Laird for additional operating authorities to strike airfields, MiG aircraft, missile-launching sites, radar sites, and transshipment points in North Vietnam below 18 degrees north. Although Laird appreciated the seriousness of the enemy threat, at the end of June he reaffirmed his position on the adequacy of existing operating authorities, recognizing that at some point South Vietnam's forces had to prove themselves. Doggedly contending that the RVNAF had the size and strength to handle even the most severe threat, Laird reiterated his belief that "*the most important issue . . . is the South Vietnamese will and desire to persevere in their own defense.*"[36] In July he wanted Moorer and Abrams to concentrate U.S. efforts on specific measures to bolster RVNAF morale and leadership so as to achieve the greatest possible improvement in the shortest time.[37]

Abrams and Moorer responded in August without enthusiasm, claiming with more than a little justification that leadership problems were too complex for a solution "on an expedited basis." They nonetheless contended that leadership was improving at a satisfactory rate. Laird found this response too vague, especially in light of South Vietnam's dilatory record in carrying out reforms. He detected no South Vietnamese commitment to overhaul personnel practices or to attain the 90 percent manning level in combat units. Again he urged Moorer and Abrams to tackle leadership problems, reminding them that South Vietnam's military reform efforts had been going on for years without accomplishing real change.[38]

In September Laird updated Nixon on the status of South Vietnam's forces. Although MACV reported some improvement in training, in removing incompetent commanders, and in promoting officers and noncommissioned officers on merit, Laird remained concerned about the quality of South Vietnam's military leadership and the government's slowness in eliminating incompetence and corruption. Even though the Vietnamese had bolstered their forces in Regions I and II, the secretary believed moving a division to Region I would not get serious attention before the October election in which President Thieu was running for reelection.[39] Laird continued to argue that South Vietnam's military had as much materiel as they could absorb. The accelerated logistics buildup had provided the South Vietnamese in two months what DoD had previously planned for the next 11 months. Expecting the manning level of South Vietnamese combat units to reach 90 percent by 1 January 1972, Laird told Nixon, "I don't see how we can deliver more on our program or get the South Vietnamese to assimilate more equipment."[40]

Leonard Sullivan's report on his October 1971 trip to Vietnam, in stark contrast, evinced no optimism. Its conclusion—not endorsed by the JCS, CINCPAC, or MACV—gave the South Vietnamese under the current Vietnamization program only "a reasonable chance" to fight "indefinitely and indecisively." Some kind of interdiction capability was essential, he argued. If the RVNAF simply tried to protect the populated areas without slowing infiltration, security would eventually deteriorate and Vietnamization would fail. Improving its interdiction capability would slightly boost chances of long-term survival, but he characterized the recent attempt to do so as a case of too little too late. Sullivan was discouraged by MACV's failure to recognize the urgency of transferring the interdiction function to the South Vietnamese.[41] Unappreciated in DoD, Sullivan's unsparing appraisal was not far off the mark.

In November Nixon sent Laird and Moorer to Vietnam to assess the war for the second time in 1971. Both returned optimistic. Moorer found the overall military situation encouraging, the leadership good, and believed that the South Vietnamese were making excellent progress. He reported that Abrams considered the Vietnamese regional commanders outstanding; only the 22nd Division commander needed to be replaced. Laird's dominant impression of his meetings with key American and Vietnamese officials, as he reported to the president, was "one of success."[42] His optimism about the ARVN was clearly at odds with Sullivan's sober assessment, which seemed to undercut the ostensible rationale for U.S. withdrawal—the continuing, steady improvement of the ARVN.

U.S. and South Vietnamese military and civilian leaders were indeed upbeat. They believed "that we now have and can maintain sufficient military strength to preclude the enemy from achieving any kind of military verdict in South Vietnam. A dynamism is at work leading to increased RVN self-reliance." The secretary noted that no U.S. or South Vietnamese leader believed Hanoi could make a decisive military move during 1972. General Abrams was convinced the Vietnamese had more than enough troops in Regions III and IV to meet the expected enemy threat there. Recommending "no radical changes in the programmed force levels or composition," Laird counseled the continuation of U.S. withdrawals and a U.S. force of 50,000–60,000 in-country by the end of June 1972. Thieu, less confident than Laird, asked the United States to offset the redeployments by supporting an increase of 30,000–50,000 in his forces and additional armor, artillery, and helicopter support.[43]

Laird adhered to his view that Vietnamization was an overall success, writing the president in December 1971 that "it was hard not to be over-optimistic about the progress of Vietnamization." A newly activated ARVN division would deploy to Region I by April 1972, and Bunker would aggressively push the Saigon government to ensure a 90 percent manning level for Vietnamese combat units by January 1972. While maintaining that leadership was improving "satisfactorily," he inserted a note of caution, advising Nixon that it was "premature to state flatly that all necessary progress has been made in improving RVNAF leadership." That unproven leadership could be tested only in a time of struggle.[44]

No longer swayed by Laird's repeated assurances that South Vietnam would be able to meet any threat from North Vietnam, a wary and doubting president wanted a more robust force. When he met with Laird on 13 January 1972, Nixon expressed dissatisfaction "with the level and types of equipment being provided under the Vietnamization program." He sought to increase the mobility of ground units by providing extra helicopters and even questioned whether the ARVN had enough conventional units to contend with North Vietnam. He doubted that the South Vietnamese Air Force "was being adequately equipped" to handle a North Vietnamese offensive once U.S. air units withdrew. Laird pledged to review modernization requirements in detail, but he was under the impression that President Thieu did not want additional conventional force units. Haig, present at the meeting, disagreed, asserting that Thieu wanted another division in Region I and possibly another division as a strategic reserve. Nixon opposed Laird and directed him to examine the Improvement and Modernization Plan, making certain that the United States was "not withdrawing at a rate and equipping South Vietnamese forces at a rate which would leave them vulnerable to a major North Vietnamese attack following our withdrawal." Nixon firmly intended to ensure the long-term viability of the South Vietnamese armed forces and questioned Laird's Vietnamization efforts.[45]

At the start of 1972 most high-level officials in the administration thought the military situation in Vietnam was favorable. South Vietnamese ground force units that suffered heavy casualties in Lam Son 719 had returned to full strength, and Saigon's regular and territorial forces had more than a million under arms. The newly created 3rd Infantry Division deployed along the DMZ to increase the number of combat troops in Region I. South Vietnam's military had amassed a formidable arsenal of 844,000 individual and crew-served weapons, including 1,880 tanks and artillery pieces, much heavy engineering equipment, 44,000 radios, and 778 helicopters and fixed-wing aircraft. South Vietnam's pacification program appeared to be doing well with the continued expansion of local security forces (RF/PF), the sweeping land reform legislation of 1970, and an ever increasing number of government-controlled villages with locally elected officials. Maj. Gen. Williams E. Potts, the MACV director of intelligence, estimated the total strength of the Viet Cong guerrilla forces in South Vietnam had fallen from 77,000 in January 1968 to 25,000 in May 1972. The Viet Cong control apparatus or infrastructure that exercised political and military dominance in Communist-held villages similarly declined from an estimated 84,000 in January 1968 to 56,000 in February 1972.[46] It seemed that while the South Vietnamese military had improved and increased in size, the enemy had been weakened.

North Vietnam Prepares for an Offensive

The politburo in Hanoi had discussed the possibility of mounting a large-scale offensive prior to Lam Son 719, but it considered the idea in earnest only after the South Vietnamese operation ended. The weaknesses of Saigon's forces operating in Laos—their lack of mobility and shortage of reserves—helped convince North Vietnam's leaders that they could defeat their foe after American combat units pulled out. They also believed that the U.S. political environment would keep Nixon from deploying new combat troops or support forces to Vietnam and that Nixon himself would not risk jeopardizing détente with the Soviet Union by escalating the war. Observing the U.S. troop withdrawal, Hanoi's leaders calculated that fewer than 65,000 U.S. troops would remain in South Vietnam by April 1972. Since this number included headquarters and combat support troops, North Vietnam considered the remaining force militarily insignificant. The chance to defeat South Vietnam in a major offensive, to wound Nixon politically in an election year, and to demonstrate that Vietnamization had failed proved irresistible to Hanoi in calculating options for 1972. The continued expansion of security in the countryside, thanks to the pacification program and the ongoing buildup of South Vietnamese armed forces, further persuaded the North that they could not afford to wait too long to take action. In June 1971 the party central committee decided to mount an offensive in 1972, hoping to end Vietnamization and force the United States to negotiate a settlement from a weak position. To prepare for the attack, the North Vietnamese requested large quantities of modern weapons from the Soviet Union and China, receiving MiG-21 jets, T–54 tanks, surface-to-air missiles (SAMs) , large mortars, antiaircraft guns, and heat-seeking SA–7 antiaircraft missiles. In addition they stockpiled spare parts, ammunition, and fuel.[47]

These preparations in the North did not go unnoticed. How to deal with the expected offensive absorbed the attention of policymakers in Washington and Saigon in the early months of 1972. The civilian and military officials in both countries often reached different conclusions about what to do. Laird found himself at odds with the White House. Citing the enemy buildup in the central highlands in Military Region II, he asked Moorer on 6 January 1972 for an updated assessment of the South's capability to handle the threat in Region II and a list of prudent actions to take to ensure a successful response. Moorer believed that friendly forces could handle the situation with U.S. air support, provided the Saigon government improved and utilized the mobility of its forces—a routine caveat.[48]

Mindful of the enemy's growing capability, DoD continued to measure enemy resources against the number of U.S. troops remaining in Vietnam. In early January an OSD and JCS task force believed the Communists might undertake an offensive in Region II in the first three months of 1972, but thought it unlikely that they could significantly set back pacification or threaten the "viability" of the government before 30 June. After that date, with only 60,000 U.S. troops remaining in-country, the risk for South Vietnam would increase.[49]

Bunker and Abrams, less sanguine than officials in Washington, explicitly warned the White House on 17 January of a countrywide offensive: "It has become more and more evident that this year the enemy is planning a large scale and sustained offensive in which it looks as if they mean to commit all but one of their reserve divisions in the north, which they have only done twice before—in Tet 1968 and in the Lam Son 719 counter-offensive." The prime targets would be northern Military Region I (including the DMZ), the central highlands of Region II, and limited activity in Regions III and IV, where the enemy had much less capability. This message would prove to be accurate.[50]

On 20 January Abrams urgently requested a range of additional authorities to counter the "impending enemy offensive," which he thought would occur in late January or early February. Believing Hanoi was prepared to commit four of its five reserve divisions then in North Vietnam to an offensive, he wanted to be able to protect U.S. forces prior to an enemy attack. "I must have the necessary authority," he insisted, "to deal with those [enemy] forces from the outset. There will not be time for reassessment of the need for additional authorities as in the past." He sought permission to strike targets in North Vietnam: aircraft on three airfields at 19 degrees latitude and southward; ground control intercept radars south of 20 degrees; occupied SAM sites within 19 miles of the DMZ; and enemy logistic facilities below 18 degrees. He also intended to plant sensors in the northern half of the DMZ and to provide air support for cross-border operations into Cambodia and Laos. Given the gravity of the Abrams message, Laird sent it quickly to the White House.[51]

Moorer believed Laird had another concern about the enemy's impending offensive: the possibility of a setback. According to the admiral, the secretary had "advocated the [troop] reduction to 70,000 spaces and said we could take certain risks and now he wants to justify the position when the thing goes sour." Alluding to his superior's strained ties with the Oval Office, Moorer also insinuated that Laird wanted to meet with Abrams to avoid consulting with the White House.[52]

A skeptical White House discounted Abrams' arguments and "the likelihood of a major enemy push in MR I." One of Kissinger's analysts, Phillip Odeen, recommended against additional authorities, citing a Pentagon systems analysis study that concluded South Vietnam's forces "should be able to handle the threat this year with only limited U.S. help. . . . There is no reason for panic."[53]

Laird reacted differently and granted most of Abrams' requests for standby operating authorities. He informed Kissinger on 26 January that to help prepare for an enemy assault in Regions I and II, he had authorized the MACV commander to emplace sensors throughout the DMZ to provide intelligence for friendly forces. He also granted authority for fixed- and rotary-wing aircraft, logistic troop lift, and support of RVNAF cross-border operations against enemy bases. The secretary allowed MACV to engage enemy aircraft below the 18th parallel and to use anti-radiation missiles against ground control intercept radar sites outside the Hanoi-Haiphong area when MiGs were airborne. Although the Saigon government had deployed an armored cavalry unit to Region II, had formed an additional division in Region I, and had alerted elements of the reserve for movement to Region II, Laird was still concerned over the low manning level of South Vietnam's combat battalions.[54]

Kissinger informed the president of Laird's actions, calling them a "dangerous precedent." In Kissinger's eyes, Laird had usurped the chief executive's prerogative by granting operating authorities without prior presidential approval. Only the president, Kissinger pointed out, could weigh operational requirements against domestic and international concerns. At this point, however, Nixon could only in effect ratify the authorities Laird had already granted Abrams, but he decided to rein in the defense secretary. The president told Laird on 1 February that in the future "any modifications to or extension of existing approved authorities or any new authorities to be granted should be submitted for my approval prior to being conveyed to Commanders in the field."[55]

The National Security Council met on 2 February to consider additional measures to improve U.S. and South Vietnamese capabilities to halt an enemy offensive that some expected as early as mid-February. There was cause for concern. Infiltration of enemy personnel had climbed 20 percent higher than 1971 levels; at least three North Vietnamese divisions stood in position to attack; and the movement of supplies into Laos had accelerated. Especially worrisome were the ARVN combat units with only about 60 percent of authorized strength and the weak leadership at the division level. Abrams still deemed the 22nd Division commander incompetent. These developments, however, failed to shake Kissinger's confidence. He told Nixon that U.S. and South Vietnamese forces should be able to handle a *"major NVA offensive against South Vietnam without a major setback."*[56]

At the meeting Laird, optimistic like Kissinger, saw no need for more resources or added authorities. South Vietnam had not suffered a defeat, he observed, and its military leaders appeared confident of handling an enemy offensive. Bringing in reinforcements "would indicate that we do not have much confidence in the Vietnamization Program." The president rejected Laird's recommendation. Determined to leave little to chance in an election year, Nixon decided to reinforce the capability of Saigon's forces to withstand an enemy offensive. He ordered Laird to add another aircraft carrier to the three already in the Southeast Asia theater; to deploy additional B–52s to allow a sustained monthly sortie rate of 1,500; and to remove "all existing sortie restrictions for both B–52 and tactical air missions during the current dry season in South Vietnam." Wanting Abrams to have freedom to deal with the surface-to-air missile threat, Nixon authorized fighters to strike occupied SAM sites in North Vietnam located within 19 nautical miles of the provisional military demarcation line (PMDL) dividing the two Vietnams, and within 19 nautical miles of the Laotian border as far north as 19 nautical miles north of the Mu Gia Pass. This authority would become effective with the start of an enemy offensive and could be exercised "only after final clearance with the President." This NSC meeting demonstrated Nixon's interest in assuming a stronger, more direct role as commander in chief, particularly in light of Laird's reluctance to employ additional resources.[57]

The president emphasized to Moorer that South Vietnam should have all the air support it needed to avoid defeat. On his historic arrival in Beijing during the last week of February 1972, Nixon did not want to be embarrassed to find that a North Vietnamese offensive had forced South Vietnam's military to retreat. According to Moorer, "the President said to hell with the budget, he wants to have plenty of resources there in the dry season." It was more important to have B–52s assigned to Vietnam than to the Single Integrated Operation Plan (SIOP). Nixon could not "stand to have anything to go wrong while he is in China." Moorer told Chief of Naval Operations Admiral Elmo Zumwalt of his discussions with Nixon, prompting Zumwalt to comment that "it looks like the back channel is still open," referring to Moorer's ability to bypass Laird in talking with the president.[58]

Following the 2 February NSC meeting, at Laird's request the JCS prepared plans for tactical air attacks on logistic targets and ground control intercept radars in the panhandle of North Vietnam as well as a contingency plan for handling a major assault across the DMZ. Early in March, the additional carrier had arrived in theater; 8 more B–52s had deployed to Thailand and another 29 to Guam in February; and field commanders had received authority for higher B–52 and tactical air sortie rates. A financial cost accompanied these steps. Air Force Secretary Robert Seamans, conscious of his service's budget, cautioned Laird that the administration would need to provide additional resources to pay for the extra B–52 strikes, suggesting that it would be desirable to balance any increase in B–52 sorties against decreases later in the year.[59]

Although North Vietnam mounted no offensive in February, Washington remained on guard. Reports of an enemy buildup in Region III in early March prompted Laird to have Moorer assess again RVNAF capability to deal with the enemy threat. Despite the additional enemy forces, Moorer reported on 7 March, South Vietnam had more combat personnel in the vicinity of Region III than did the enemy. He was confident that South Vietnamese forces could deal with a coordinated enemy offensive.[60]

A few days later the situation changed. On 8 March Abrams sent a detailed backchannel message to the JCS urgently requesting authority to take additional military action against a likely offensive. Abrams identified a serious threat in four distinct but interrelated areas: the DMZ, Pleiku and Kontum provinces, the Cambodian border alongside Region III, and the Plain of Jars in Laos. The flow of men and supplies into South Vietnam from the Laotian panhandle had increased, leading Abrams to believe the enemy could mount concurrent attacks in four geographical areas, three of them in South Vietnam. He requested additional authority to conduct tactical air and naval gunfire attacks against SAM sites, MiG bases, radar sites, antiaircraft artillery, long-range artillery, tanks, and logistic facilities in North Vietnam below 18 degrees north. Moorer wanted Abrams to have immediate authorities to strike the enemy north of the DMZ, but Laird was opposed. To grant the request would be tantamount to resuming the bombing campaign against North Vietnam (which the United States had agreed to halt in 1968), escalating the fighting, and enraging war critics. He recommended that the president continue with the status quo for the time being. On 18 March Kissinger supported Laird's position, concluding that the costs and political risks of Abrams' requests outweighed the benefits. Nixon granted no additional authorities on the 18th, but he stated that he would reassess his decision "should the anticipated major enemy assault begin."[61]

On 22 March Laird told Moorer that all existing authorities would remain in effect until 1 May. Moreover, he would approve no additional authority for bombing or naval gunfire. In accordance with Nixon's position, Laird would reconsider new authorities if a major enemy offensive occurred, but he remained confident that the existing ones and "the firm RVNAF posture have, from all reports, disrupted the enemy's offensive plans."[62]

Although intelligence predictions about an offensive in January and then in February proved wrong, little doubt existed in the mind of any high official in Washington or Saigon that the enemy intended to mount a major assault. There was less confidence that the ARVN could deal with it. Near the end of March an NSC staff report, based on the views of the DIA, CIA, National Security Agency (NSA), and State Department analysts, concluded that an enemy main force offensive could begin as early as 1 April because the units designated for an offensive in the highlands were at or near their attack positions. The analysts anticipated that ARVN units in the central highlands of Region II, outnumbered nearly two to one by the enemy, would face a difficult test. Moreover, the presence of three North Vietnamese Army divisions in Cambodia across the border from Region III would probably preclude the movement of ARVN reserves from Region III to the central highlands. The concentration of enemy forces in Regions I and II would make it difficult to obtain reserve forces from these areas to meet the anticipated offensive. The unprecedented presence of heavy enemy mortars, the analysts believed, could imperil ARVN bases with heavy bombardments. They were less certain of the enemy's intentions in Regions I and II.[63]

The senior U.S. adviser in Region II, John Paul Vann, told Abrams on 27 March of his concern about South Vietnamese preparation for an enemy assault in Region II, which would "probably commence within the next seven days." He noted that neither the South Vietnamese regional commander, Lt. Gen. Ngo Dzu, nor the 22nd ARVN Division commander, Col. Le Duc Dat, had "displayed a willingness to properly deploy or use available forces to preempt the enemy's plans when he is located."[64]

Intelligence about an impending enemy offensive in the central highlands of Region II did not dissuade key U.S. officials from leaving Vietnam. General Abrams went to Thailand on leave at the end of March and was scheduled to return to Vietnam on 3 April. At the same time Ambassador Bunker was in Nepal visiting the U.S. ambassador there—his wife. The assault began while Abrams and Bunker were away.[65]

The opening attacks of the Easter Offensive occurred in Region I on 30 March 1972. The politburo in Hanoi had decided to mount an all-out offensive to transform the battlefield and the negotiating environment. North Vietnam intended that its military campaign would expose the ARVN's weakness and the failure of Vietnamization, roll back gains in pacification, and reestablish the North's control of the countryside. Despite the administration's significant efforts in 1971 and early 1972 to strengthen Saigon's forces so that they could engage the North Vietnamese on their own, South Vietnam would be pushed to the brink of defeat by the enemy's offensive on three fronts.

CHAPTER 9

A Time of Trial: The Easter Offensive and Vietnamization

THE REPUBLIC OF VIETNAM Armed Forces were severely tested when Hanoi launched a massive invasion of South Vietnam at the end of March 1972. With few U.S. combatants in country, Saigon's forces, supported by U.S. airpower, felt the full fury of the all-out ground attacks. Hanoi called the offensive the Nguyen Hue campaign in honor of the birth name of the Vietnamese emperor Quang Trung, a national hero who had defeated a Chinese occupation force in the eighteenth century and liberated Vietnam from foreign rule. Washington referred to the invasion as the "Easter Offensive," because it began the Thursday before Easter.

General Vo Nguyen Giap, North Vietnam's defense minister, envisioned an invasion of simultaneous assaults by North Vietnamese Army divisions in three widely separated areas. Attacking on three fronts would make it difficult to shift reserves to reinforce a threatened area, keeping South Vietnam's forces off balance. Any of the enemy's thrusts could seriously damage South Vietnam. The attack in Region I could lead to the loss of the northernmost provinces; the thrust in the central highlands of Region II could sever South Vietnam in two; and the strike in Region III could endanger Saigon. As it turned out, the North Vietnamese Army proved unable to invade on three fronts at the same time: In Region I the first strike hit South Vietnam's northernmost province, Quang Tri, on 30 March; the second began in Region III on 4 April; and the third, the attack on Kontum Province in the central highlands of Region II, started on 11 April (see map, page 222).[1]

When the offensive began, fewer than 70,000 U.S. military personnel were in-country, and nearly all combat forces had withdrawn. With the redeployment of advisers as well, relatively few U.S. Army advisers remained attached to ARVN units. According to statements by the Nixon administration, South Vietnam's

(Courtesy U.S. Army Center of Military History)

forces, which had grown in size and firepower, had improved sufficiently to allow the United States to withdraw combatants. Laird was the most vocal proponent of this argument. The South Vietnamese Army would by and large have to stand on its own.[2]

The offensive also exposed schisms in Washington. With his belief in the efficacy of Vietnamization, Laird saw little reason to resort to extreme measures in responding to the enemy invasion. Nixon, however, demanded that DoD take extraordinary measures to prevent Saigon's defeat. By this time Nixon had lost confidence in Laird, who was largely relegated to the sidelines, and Laird knew it. Nixon felt he had wrongly allowed himself in the past to forego retaliation, especially for the 1969 downing of the EC–121 reconnaissance plane by the North Koreans.[3] To stem the offensive, Nixon tried to maximize the use of U.S. air and naval power to punish the enemy. The president consciously endeavored to act more vigorously and more effectively than the Johnson administration had, and for geopolitical reasons he was determined to show his resolve to the Communist regimes in Moscow and Beijing. In battling the enemy assault, Nixon and Kissinger at times seemed also to be waging war on other members of the administration.[4]

The timing of the offensive at the end of March also complicated Nixon's diplomatic efforts. Before the offensive, the United States and Soviet Union had agreed to hold a summit in Moscow in May to sign a strategic arms agreement. Could Nixon afford to sign an agreement with North Vietnam's major supplier of arms and equipment? Would a strong counteroffensive scuttle the summit?[5]

The Invasion Begins

On 30 March an intensive artillery bombardment on the 3rd ARVN Division positions along the DMZ announced the start of the long-expected invasion. Maj. Gen. Frederick J. Kroesen Jr., the deputy commanding general of XXIV Corps, located in Military Region I, reported the invasion extended "south from the DMZ, southeast from the road network in the western DMZ," and east from Route 9. The attacks blatantly violated the Johnson administration's 1968 "understanding" that Hanoi would not conduct operations in the DMZ in exchange for a U.S. bombing halt in North Vietnam. The understanding included an agreement to begin serious peace talks and an acknowledgment that the bombing cessation was contingent on respect for the DMZ and no attacks on South Vietnamese cities.[6]

Word of the DMZ attack reached Washington on the morning of 30 March. Nixon and Kissinger learned the enemy assaulted eight firebases along the DMZ.[7] If the attack along this broad front continued, the president wanted a plan for bombing the enemy on 2 or 3 April. On 31 March Laird and Moorer informed Kissinger of heavy continuing attacks. Laird characterized the assault on Quang Tri Province as a major enemy offensive.[8] Kissinger saw no need for high-level decisions on the basis of these reports because South Vietnam's fire support bases seemed to be holding. In his memoir, Kissinger treated these attacks "as a major enemy probe." On 3 April, when the magnitude of the offensive became clear, he complained to Moorer about the reporting. The media realized the offensive had begun 12 hours before the White House did, Kissinger later conceded.[9]

On 2 April Laird and Moorer learned from Abrams, who had returned from leave, that the situation was "very serious." North Vietnam's invading forces drove ARVN units south of the Cua Viet River and Route 9, capturing Camp Carroll, a defensive strong point south of Route 9. Lt. Gen. Hoang Xuan Lam, who had performed poorly in Lam Son 719, remained in charge in Region I. Failing to take warnings of an offensive seriously, his forces were unprepared. The relatively inexperienced 3rd ARVN Division, which had recently been moved to Region I along the DMZ, bore the brunt of the enemy assault. The 1st ARVN Division, widely regarded as South Vietnam's best, protected the western approaches to the city of Hue but was not engaged in the early battle.[10]

In early April the White House faced a complicated choice in reacting to the offensive. Retaliation could have political repercussions domestically and internationally. With declining public support for the war, striking North Vietnam could affect Nixon's reelection chances. U.S. response in the form of renewed bombing against North Vietnam might lead to cancellation of the Moscow summit scheduled for May. Nixon had recently traveled to China, and attacking North Vietnam might jeopardize his effort to improve relations with the Chinese.[11]

Those Communist nations provided the war materiel to North Vietnam that made the invasion possible, and the president perceived grave risks and loss of credibility if he failed to respond. He had repeatedly warned in public statements that he would react if the enemy attacked. If the United States took no action, and the ARVN was defeated, then he would be blamed for losing the war, for allowing Vietnamization to fail, and for risking the lives of the remaining American soldiers, most of whom at that point were support troops. A defeat in Vietnam would in turn weaken the U.S. strategic position around the world. As Nixon later wrote, "The U.S. will not have a credible foreign policy if we fail, and I will have to assume the responsibility for that development." Nor could Nixon abide the idea of being the first American president to lose a war. Moreover, he had already pledged to grant additional operating authorities for Abrams in the event of an offensive, although not all that Abrams had requested. Nixon concluded he had to halt the offensive and assume the political risks of taking the war to North Vietnam in an election year. The massive invasion of South Vietnam gave him an opportunity to pin down Hanoi's troops, most of which were now in South Vietnam, and unleash a devastating offensive against the North. With few American ground combat units in theater, airpower and naval bombardment were perforce the only means of U.S. military retaliation.[12]

On 2 April Nixon authorized strikes against military forces in North Vietnam, allowing tactical air, artillery and naval gunfire on military targets in North Vietnam as far north as 25 nautical miles above the DMZ and B–52 strikes throughout the DMZ. Abrams also received presidential authority for a 48-hour air strike in North Vietnam below 19 degrees north. Kissinger criticized Laird's slowness in issuing the bombing order, but bad weather and low visibility had scratched the 48-hour operation. On 4 April the president enlarged the target area to 18 degrees north with allowance for protective reaction strikes even further north. Freedom Train was the name given to these operations. Fearing political fallout, Laird proved less enthusiastic than the White House about a stepped-up bombing campaign, regarding the invasion as a test to see if South Vietnam's armed forces could stand on their own. Some civilian officials in the Defense and State departments tended to agree with him.[13]

Command and Leadership

The severity of the invasion exacerbated tensions within the administration, heightening the atmosphere of distrust that seemed to emanate from the Oval Office. Nixon was convinced that Laird withheld information on the situation in Vietnam. Even though the JCS chairman assured Nixon on 3 April that Laird had already issued an order mandating that all information be passed to the president, Nixon directed Laird to transfer all reports from Abrams immediately to the White House.

Nixon was also upset that Laird had opposed Abrams' mid-March request for additional bombing authorities, an episode that provoked him to denigrate his defense secretary in Moorer's presence. Nixon, Moorer wrote afterward, "reiterated what he told me before—he was an elected official and the SECDEF was appointed and, as he put it, was only a 'procurement officer.'" Nixon stressed that as the commander in chief he, not Laird, would issue orders.[14]

In lashing out at Laird, Nixon forgot that he and Kissinger had supported the secretary's 18 March recommendation to deny Abrams request for additional bombing authorities. After the 3 April meeting, Haig reminded Kissinger of his error, and Kissinger phoned Laird to apologize later that day. During the call Laird expressed his willingness to absorb criticism in order to deflect it from the president and even to take the blame for turning down the request if it helped Nixon, but the secretary expressed dismay at the lack of trust in him by Nixon and Kissinger.[15] Despite his apology, Kissinger seemed not to fully convey Laird's anguish to the president. In a telephone call on the evening of 3 April, Kissinger told Nixon that "Laird has been crying all day. He wants to come over." In his meeting, Laird assured Nixon that he had withheld no information.[16]

Because he distrusted Laird, Nixon wanted direct contact with Moorer and Abrams and bypassed Laird. Moorer assured Kissinger that he would immediately carry out any order that came directly from the president, without clearing it with the secretary. To go around Laird, the president also used Bunker as a conduit for passing guidance to Abrams. Later, after General Fred Weyand, the deputy MACV commander, replaced Abrams in July 1972, the White House continued to bypass Laird. Kissinger reminded Haig, who was then in Saigon, to be certain that "General Weyand understands from what source he will receive the clearest presidential instructions."[17] Still, the White House even felt uneasy about Moorer, suspecting that he would inform Laird of his sessions with the president in order "to protect his flank," as Haig put it.[18]

If Moorer did not always fully inform Laird about the president's intentions, he failed to see the irony of his complaints that Laird did not consult him. The chairman was convinced that Laird sent recommendations to the White House without informing him and delayed White House requests to issue new bombing authorities, of which the White House had informed him. He grumbled to new Deputy Secretary of Defense Kenneth Rush that he was unable to act sometimes because he received one set of instructions from Laird and another from Kissinger. Moorer also chafed at Laird's January 1972 memorandum, issued after Yeoman Charles Radford was caught in December spying for the JCS chairman, which required all contacts with the White House to go through the secretary. Moorer also complained to Rush that this procedure created a bottleneck and an opportunity for Robert Pursley, Laird's military aide, to stonewall actions and assume too much authority.[19] Moorer remained convinced that Pursley deliberately kept information from the White House and was disturbed that "an assistant, such as MG Pursley, can dominate his boss in such a way."[20]

Moorer quietly reestablished the private liaison channel between the White House and the JCS, which Laird had closed in the wake of the Radford affair. In February 1972 he justified the continuation of this direct channel on the grounds that the president wanted to see him frequently for updates on the war. Nixon had ended the Radford matter quickly, avoiding a public confrontation with the JCS chairman and preventing Laird from taking action against Moorer. (See chapter 20 for more on the Radford episode.) On 5 May Moorer named admiral-designate Kinnaird R. McKee as his liaison with the White House, to assume the post previously held by Rear Admirals Robinson and Robert O. Welander. Haig informed Kissinger of this appointment. Given the uproar occasioned by Radford's spying, Moorer was sensitive to the risk of having McKee's role exposed. If Laird learned of the new liaison arrangement, Moorer's position would be in jeopardy.[21]

Relations between the White House and the MACV commander also became strained. Nixon wanted Abrams to maximize the number of air attacks and expected him to carry out the air offensive continuously, imaginatively, and aggressively. Having no intention of losing, Nixon stated he would lift restraints on military action and grant still more extensive operational authority to Abrams even if it cost him the election. The president expected Abrams to do whatever was necessary to defeat the enemy.[22] Faced with heavy enemy pressure on the battlefield, Abrams resented being told from afar how to conduct the war. He was especially angered by the prospect of White House instructions directing him to employ all B–52 sorties in Region I. On 5 April he called Moorer (shortly after midnight in Saigon), while the chairman was in Kissinger's office, saying he would resign if he actually received such an order. Abrams said he was fed up with people in Washington, who did not understand the situation, trying to direct the tactical effort.[23]

In addition to mistrust and intrigues at the top levels of the administration, the White House and Laird faced a serious command problem in Vietnam just before the invasion began. On 23 March 1972 Seventh Air Force Commander General John D. Lavelle was recalled to Washington amid congressional inquiries about his conduct of the air war. As General Abrams' deputy for the air war, he was responsible for carrying out much of the bombing campaign in Vietnam. The Air Force inspector general went to Vietnam and confirmed allegations that Lavelle had violated the rules of engagement for bombing North Vietnam. Lavelle was charged with carrying out 17 preplanned air strikes between December 1971 and March 1972 against North Vietnam without permission from higher authority and for false reporting. Given the charges, on 30 March Laird relieved Lavelle of command pending completion of the inquiries.[24]

With the onset of the North Vietnamese invasion, the president quickly found "a smart aggressive man" to replace Lavelle. On recommendations from Laird and Moorer, Nixon personally selected Lt. Gen. John Vogt, director of the Joint Staff, after meeting him on 5 April. The president used Vogt's appointment to reiterate his intention for strong action, expecting him to improve the Air Force's bombing of North Vietnam. Nixon also advised him to bypass Abrams. The president no longer regarded Abrams as the bold commander of the 1970 Cambodian incursion, and he was also upset that Abrams left Vietnam during Lam Son 719 and was not in Vietnam at the start of the Easter Offensive. Vogt understood the president's meaning.[25] He and Moorer envisioned a difficult relationship with Abrams. Given the strains between the White House and the MACV commander,

General John Vogt, commander of the Seventh Air Force, directed a stepped-up bombing campaign against North Vietnam during the Easter Offensive. (U.S. Air Force)

Moorer feared that Abrams might regard Vogt as an administration spy. With Vogt's appointment, Nixon sought stronger control of the air campaign, pushing Laird and Abrams further to the sidelines.[26]

The Offensive Intensifies

On 4 April Hanoi opened a second and separate front, storming into Region III. U.S. intelligence reports had concluded that an enemy offensive in the region was unlikely, but elements of two NVA divisions crossed the Cambodian border into Binh Long Province. After capturing the district capital, Loc Ninh, on 7 April, the enemy pushed south, laying siege to the provincial capital, An Loc, astride the main highway to Saigon. President Thieu ordered his forces to defend An Loc to the death. OSD had doubts about the ARVN carrying out that directive, because South Vietnam's forces no longer had much of a numerical advantage over their foe after the enemy moved his main forces into Region III from Cambodia. In Region I, the strength of government forces amounted to about 91 percent of the strength of VC guerrillas and NVA units. In Region II, the government had a slight force ratio advantage of 1.3 to 1. The full commitment of VC and NVA forces severely eroded the ability of South Vietnamese forces to maneuver.[27]

The JCS drafted two plans for contingency operations to satisfy the president's desire to strike North Vietnam: a onetime air attack against military targets in the Haiphong area, and the mining of Haiphong harbor, the North's major port. Moorer asked Vogt, who would soon leave for Vietnam, to have the Joint Staff update the contingency plans to mine Haiphong.[28]

On 6 April Laird assessed both plans for Kissinger, but in so doing he revealed how sharply his thinking differed from the president's. Laird saw only limited military gains in an aerial interdiction of enemy supply lines, which could be rebuilt, and minimal political value in bombing North Vietnam's industrial base. Once the country's base of economic growth was destroyed, the secretary believed, Hanoi would have little further to lose from continued bombing. For the United States, however, continued bombing would come at a political cost and stir up the war critics. Laird doubted a onetime strike on the Haiphong area would make the political threat to Hanoi more credible. In a handwritten note, Laird concluded: "The political impact of these plans may be what is wanted by the president—the military impact would be minor and the impact on present battle would be even less. If the Russians want an excuse to stop their present major (80% supplies) contribution to North Viet Nam, mining might have that political impact but I would doubt it." Laird and Kissinger discussed the secretary's views on the phone, but Kissinger was unpersuaded. At that moment he was considering even more extensive military operations, having greater faith in the effectiveness of bombing than Laird.[29]

The White House and Abrams also held conflicting views on bombing. The White House wanted the B–52s to bomb North Vietnam "as soon as possible" to have a political impact on North Vietnam and the Soviets, a move that would undo President Johnson's 1968 bombing suspension of North Vietnam. Kissinger wanted to strike further north despite the added political and military risks because the more valuable targets, such as oil tanks farms, rail yards, and Haiphong harbor, were there, but Abrams disagreed. He preferred to employ the bombers to halt the enemy offensive inside South Vietnam. He opposed unleashing B–52s against North Vietnam for the purpose of making political statements to Moscow, Beijing, and Hanoi when the military requirement was obviously so pressing elsewhere. The enemy had already completed his force and logistical deployments to South Vietnam where the critical battle was being waged.[30]

The president remained determined to bomb hard after North Vietnamese missile defenses had been pounded. He ordered additional B–52s to stand by for possible strikes. To Nixon, North Vietnam's blatant invasion had gained him the support of American public opinion to retaliate. As he told Kissinger on 8 April, "From the standpoint of American domestic psychology right now they want us to do something we haven't done before. They want the enemy to be outraged. From the standpoint of the NVN [North Vietnamese] we have got to do something to let them know we aren't screwing around."[31] Nixon authorized air and naval gunfire support against North Vietnam south of the 19th parallel and permission to strike all MiGs up to the 20th parallel with air and ship missiles.

In his message to McCain and Abrams, the JCS chairman tried to transmit the president's anger at what he perceived as a lack of intensity (some of that anger had been directed at Moorer) and his fervent desire "to give the North Vietnamese as well as the Soviets a clear message that he [Nixon] intends to use whatever force is necessary." Moorer underlined Nixon's direct role: "I cannot impress upon you too strongly how intensely involved the president is in this operation, how determined he is that the enemy does not succeed in their objectives, and how forthcoming he is when presented with requests for authorities and additional resources—however, he does expect immediate action and forceful response."[32]

Reacting to White House moves to employ additional U.S. firepower to support the South Vietnamese, Laird urged restraint. He continued to express confidence that South Vietnam's armed forces could withstand the invasion, assuring Kissinger on 8 April that they would not collapse: "I don't want everybody to think we are in a panic state, because this thing will work out. This fighting is going to go on for some time. . . . The South Vietnamese are going to come through all right."[33]

Three days later Laird's optimism was put to the test. On 11 April the third prong of the Easter Offensive began in Region II. Although U.S. intelligence reports had by and large ruled out the likelihood of an invasion on three fronts, Communist forces crossed South Vietnam's border and swept through the central highlands, attempting to cut off the strategic cities of Pleiku and Kontum from the rest of the country. The invading force, three NVA divisions supported by artillery and 400 tanks, attacked several fire support bases. On 23 April, after capturing two district capitals in Binh Dinh Province on South Vietnam's coast, the enemy struck the 22nd ARVN Division in full force, capturing the command post with little opposition. The 22nd was no longer a cohesive combat unit; its commander, Col. Le Duc Dat, was relieved. By the end of April the North Vietnamese Army controlled most of Binh Dinh. Hanoi had pulled out all the stops with its invasion of South Vietnam across three separate fronts. Thirteen NVA divisions, nearly 200,000 soldiers equipped with Soviet tanks, armored personnel carriers, and long-range artillery, were on the attack inside South Vietnam's borders. This force constituted virtually all of North Vietnam's army; one infantry division remained in reserve in North Vietnam.[34]

Faced with the real possibility of defeat, Nixon did not share Laird's confidence in South Vietnam's forces and was unwilling to let them fight the tremendous enemy invasion alone. To prove his resolve to the Communist powers, the president decided to mount a heavy B–52 and tactical air attack against Haiphong on 16 or 17 April. Abrams balked. On 14 April he said he wanted to postpone the Haiphong bombing until 21 or 22 April to give priority to air strikes in South Vietnam, particularly in An Loc where the enemy had massed over three divisions against the besieged town. Laird, however, supported the president's decision.[35] Air Force and

Navy planes carried out the attacks on the Haiphong area on 16 April, striking petroleum storage and SAM sites.[36]

Nixon was in Canada when he received Abrams' petition to delay the Haiphong strikes, and it "drove the president up the bulkhead," according to Moorer. Even though Laird opposed Abrams' request and told Kissinger on 15 April that Abrams would carry out the strikes (even though they occurred on 16 April), Nixon remained convinced that the defense secretary was sending Abrams instructions that contravened his and that Abrams was maneuvering to ensure that Nixon would absorb the blame if the enemy offensive succeeded. The president could not understand why Abrams wanted to use all available air sorties in South Vietnam. Having given the MACV commander more firepower than he had requested, Nixon thought Abrams could spare planes to bomb North Vietnam. He dispatched Haig to Vietnam "to get across to Abrams what the president really wants."[37]

Kissinger also lost all patience with Abrams. On 15 April he asked Laird to submit by 17 April the names of two possible replacements for the general, but Laird ignored Kissinger, having no intention of abandoning the MACV commander. To the contrary, he wanted Abrams to become the next Army chief of staff.[38]

Abrams had served continuously in Vietnam since May 1967, first as Westmoreland's deputy and then from July 1968 as MACV commander. Under a demanding and suspicious Nixon, he had the thankless assignment of balancing the functions of waging war and withdrawing forces simultaneously. Given Nixon's bitter disappointment with Abrams, it had been clear for some time that his tenure as commander was nearing its end. Abrams' sinking stature with the White House failed to deter Laird. As early as August 1971 Laird had mentioned Abrams as a possible replacement for General Westmoreland when his term as Army chief of staff expired in June 1972. At the end of 1971 the very junior Haig was also under consideration to become Army chief of staff.[39]

Laird prevailed despite Nixon's reservations. In March 1972, before the enemy offensive began, Laird and the president had agreed that Abrams would become chief of staff of the Army after Westmoreland. To obtain the appointment Laird played his trump card. In 1968 Laird had agreed to serve as secretary on the condition that he could select personnel. However, Nixon attached a contingency to the Abrams appointment. On 17 March Kissinger told Laird that Nixon would appoint Abrams if the secretary got "a firm commitment from him that he will retire in two

General Creighton Abrams, with Secretary Laird and Army Secretary Robert Froehlke, on the reviewing stand at his swearing in as Army chief of staff, 16 October 1972. Laird secured Abrams' appointment despite the president's objections. A close friend of Laird's, Froehlke also served as assistant secretary of defense for administration. (NARA)

years." Laird accepted this arrangement and also assented to the president's desire to have Haig, at that time a recently promoted major general, become Army vice chief of staff, a 2-star position.[40]

Abrams was not a unanimous choice for chief of staff. Secretary of the Army Froehlke deemed Abrams too old and too closely linked to the war to lead a post-Vietnam army. Laird stood by the MACV commander who faithfully executed the Vietnamization program. On 21 March he telephoned Abrams, informing him that he would serve as chief of staff "for no longer than two years—though we would not divulge such criteria as part of any assignment provisions." Abrams "said he would be willing to take the position, if nominated and confirmed, for a two-year period."[41]

The president announced the Abrams nomination on 20 June. Haig assumed the position of Army vice chief of staff in January 1973.[42]

Augmenting U.S. Power

The first quarter of 1972 saw a vast increase in U.S. air and naval forces in Vietnam as the administration prepared for the expected North Vietnamese offensive. Even after North Vietnamese troops crossed into South Vietnam, Laird was expressing his concerns to Kissinger about the expansion. On 21 April he argued that the U.S. buildup exceeded "that which is needed for military purposes." On national security and financial grounds the secretary questioned how long the United States could sustain a major force surge in the Vietnam theater. Aircraft deployments had reached "saturation point" in terms of available aircraft ramp space, security, and safety standards in-theater. He advised keeping some U.S. forces in reserve to cope with enemy attacks or crises elsewhere in the world and cautioned that the deployments might affect the retention and motivation of military personnel. The secretary also worried about the department's ability to pay for the new air and naval deployments and the increased operational tempo. Despite the secretary's worries about funding, Nixon wanted these naval and air forces to remain in-theater for at least six months and placed no ceiling on air sorties, the expenditure of munitions, or naval gunfire.[43]

In April, after the invasion began, Nixon further increased the number of U.S. forces committed to the war. Determined to stop the offensive, he was unwilling to test Laird's assertion that South Vietnam could weather an enemy invasion essentially with the forces and equipment on hand. At the beginning of 1972, U.S. Air Force assets in-theater comprised 247 fighter planes (F–4s and F–105s), 14 electronic warfare aircraft (EB–66s), 55 B–52 bombers, and 69 KC–135 tankers. At that time, the U.S. Navy had two aircraft carriers with 121 tactical fighters, one cruiser, and 15 destroyers on station. Between 1 January and 30 April the number of B–52 bombers assigned to operations in Southeast Asia jumped from 55 to 139. Over the same period the Navy added four aircraft carriers to the two already off the coast of Vietnam (see tables 7 and 8). The additional Air Force and Navy personnel needed to operate the new ships and planes in-theater did not count against the troop ceiling under the Vietnamization program.

Table 7. USAF Aircraft in Southeast Asia, 1972

	1-Jan	Added Jan-Mar	Total 30-Mar	Added Apr	Total Added	Total Force
B–52s	55	29	84	55	84	139
KC–135s	69	10	79	16	26	95
F–4s	229	18	247	54	72	301
F–105s	18	0	18	12	12	30
EB–66s	14	0	14	8	8	22

Table 8. U.S. Navy Forces in Southeast Asia, 1972

	1-Jan	Added Jan-Mar	Total 30-Mar	Added Apr	Total Added	Total Force
F–4s	22	20	42	71	91	113
F–8s	25		25			25
A–4s	45		45			45
A–6s	8	12	20	30	42	50
A–7s	21	20	41	72	92	113
USMC F–4s				39	39	39
Carriers	2	1	3	3	4	6
Cruisers	1	1	2	3	4	5
Destroyers	15	6	21	21	27	42

Source: Memo, Laird for Kissinger, 21 Apr 11 1972, folder 1, box 39, Melvin R. Laird Papers, Gerald R. Ford Presidential Library, Ann Arbor, MI.

At the end of April Nixon affirmed to the American people his determination to continue air and naval attacks on military targets in North Vietnam. To the president, a loss in Vietnam had global consequences. If North Vietnam's invasion was successful, "the risk of war in other parts of the world would be enormously increased. But if . . . Communist aggression fails in Vietnam, it will be discouraged elsewhere, and the chance for peace will be increased." Nixon also announced that he would bring out another 20,000 American troops by 1 July. At this point withdrawals carried more political than military significance because the president wanted fewer troops in Vietnam before the July Democratic Party convention. U.S. troops remaining in-theater were largely support units, and their departure would have little effect on the fighting.[44]

Nixon's resolve imposed a considerable financial cost on DoD. The additional planes and ships assigned to the war theater and the heightened operational tempo strained the budgets of the U.S. Navy and U.S. Air Force. Secretary of the Navy John Chafee estimated the incremental buildup costs for the Navy and Marine Corps to be $450 million for FY 1972, ending on 30 June 1972, and $466 million for the first quarter (July-September) of FY 1973. Chafee believed the Navy could maintain the projected force level through September but would have to transfer additional personnel from the Sixth and Atlantic fleets and shore units, an action that could adversely affect recruitment and reenlistment. The longer the augmentation lasted the more it would deplete ammunition and aircraft inventories. Secretary of the Air Force Robert Seamans estimated the incremental cost of the augmented air units at $201 million in FY 1972 and $290 million for FY 1973. He proposed paying the additional costs through reprogramming. The U.S. Army bore the cost of supporting and replacing the equipment for the ARVN and the Regional and Popular Forces.[45]

Hoping for better control of the budget problem, Laird tried to slow the U.S. buildup. At the end of April, before another deployment, he asked the JCS to evaluate "carefully the incremental benefit of further augmentations versus the incremental costs" and determine the effects of additional deployments on the DoD budget, the logistics system, the availability of personnel, the move towards an all-volunteer force, and the ability to meet another NVA attack or a major crisis elsewhere in 1972. How to pay for the costs of responding to the invasion was a constant worry for Laird. On 28 April he warned Kissinger, "I am really in a bind. There is not [a] chance in hell of getting a supplement out of Congress for Vietnam."[46]

At the beginning of May Laird brought his financial concerns to the president, advising him that the additional war-related expenses threatened DoD's ability to support the administration's overall foreign policy in FY 1973. First, the logistics buildup of the fall of 1971 exceeded the FY 1972 budget by $100 million. Laird had financed this buildup (which was not included in the FY 1972 budget) by deferring other programs until FY 1973. Second, he now estimated that the cost of augmenting naval and airpower in Vietnam would reach $350 million–$400 million in FY 1972 and $600 million–$750 million in FY 1973. The secretary feared DoD would have to absorb those costs, which were not included in the FY 1972 budget or the FY 1973 budget request. Moreover, additional requirements for ammunition and spare parts for Vietnam would further reduce the stocks available for CONUS and NATO forces. What made DoD's situation more complicated and precarious was the determination of Senate majority leader Mike Mansfield and other Democratic senators to cut the FY 1973 Defense budget by $3.5 billion. Laird believed their effort had a good chance of succeeding in the next budget go-around, thus limiting the president's program and policy options in Vietnam more so than earlier attempts to enact antiwar legislation. Laird planned to meet with congressional leaders, hoping to minimize the impact of any cuts, but he cautioned Nixon that even if Congress granted flexibility in making reductions, the months ahead would lead to "critical problems." Nixon agreed to meet personally with key legislative leaders to support Laird's efforts. As a matter of prudence, however, the president expected Laird to work with the National Security Council and the Office of Management and Budget to find ways to absorb the extra costs of Vietnam and minimize the effects on his Vietnam policies and force readiness should the secretary fail to persuade Congress.[47]

In a bind, Laird had little choice but to request a supplemental to pay for the increased costs of combat. On 13 May he asked OMB to support supplemental funding of $648 million in FY 1972 to cover procurement of munitions, increased operations and maintenance costs, and added personnel expenditures (hostile-fire pay, combat rations, and moving expenses). Laird told OMB Director George Shultz that he had already moved some costs from FY 1972 to FY 1973 to minimize the size of the request. The secretary also requested that the White House submit to Congress a budget amendment for more than $1.9 billion for FY 1973 to cover operations and procurement because DoD could not absorb the extra costs in its FY 1973 budget.[48]

Kissinger and Shultz decided to defer Laird's request until after the Moscow summit, scheduled to begin on 22 May. But after the summit ended Shultz and his deputy, Caspar W. Weinberger, ruled out any requests for additional funds until after the presidential election. They feared a petition for more defense funds without spending cuts elsewhere would ultimately require raising taxes. OMB wanted the administration to work out a budget strategy before Laird informed Congress of the excess expenditures. Facing a shortage of funds to pay department expenses, Laird ignored the stricture. He told his staff that he would notify Congress, "even without OMB or presidential approval," that the department had exceeded the FY 1972 authorization of $2.5 billion in FY 1972 for support of allied forces in Southeast

Asia.[49] As Al Haig noted, the secretary was required by law to inform Congress of the overspending. Laird also needed money to pay for the additional operating costs in Vietnam before the fiscal year ended on 30 June.[50] Kissinger advised Nixon that ruling out the DoD supplemental risked degrading the readiness of forces in the United States and Europe and might narrow options in Southeast Asia regarding bombing and support for allies. Without a supplemental, the Navy might have to retire some vessels; the Army, to thin out the manning of some divisions; and the Air Force, to cut back the staffing of some tactical wings. Shultz pressed the countervailing case. The OMB director wanted spending cuts to offset the supplemental in the belief that the president had to realize the political consequences of a move that might lead to a tax increase.[51]

In testimony before the House Appropriations Committee on 5 June, Laird discussed the impact of war on the FY 1972 and FY 1973 Defense budgets. His presentation disturbed Richard K. Cook, deputy assistant to the president for congressional relations, who thought that Laird's assertion of increased costs of U.S. military activity would help war critics and erode moderate and conservative support for the president's Vietnam policy. Laird also informed the committee that spending in support of Vietnamese forces would shortly exceed the congressional authorization of $2.5 billion and asked that the FY 1972 authorization for support be increased to $2.7 billion. He would submit a request for funds to cover Navy and Air Force operations later.[52]

On 9 June Laird submitted to OMB a revised FY 1973 budget amendment for nearly $3.6 billion. In arguing for more funds, Laird outlined the stringent actions he had taken to meet FY 1972 requirements. He urged Acting Director Weinberger to transmit quickly the requested amendment to Congress, but the secretary confided to his staff that he expected OMB to resist.[53]

Laird also enlisted Kissinger's help in getting OMB to submit the amendment to Congress "immediately. There is neither time nor reason for debate. The Defense Department just cannot swallow these SEA costs along with anticipated Congressional cuts in our FY 73 budget." Without action on the amendment, Laird would have to halt the Enhance project to resupply South Vietnam's forces. The president approved Laird's request at the end of June, on the assumptions that the intense combat in Vietnam would last until the end of September and that ground combat was unlikely to continue at April's high rate. Weinberger agreed to support the budget amendment, but he believed that DoD should make offsetting cuts in low priority programs. Kissinger disagreed, pointing out to Nixon the unfairness of making DoD absorb the added war costs forced on the department by the White House. In a significant victory for Laird, Nixon decided to drop the offsets, but he expected the defense secretary to "submit a list of those cuts which he would consider least damaging to our security. We must have these ready on a confidential basis—since Congressional action on our budget may *require* this." But this supplemental quickly proved insufficient. Before the end of September Laird requested an additional supplemental of $1.5 billion to continue the heightened operations through December to stem the enemy offensive. Kissinger and Weinberger supported Laird's additional request.[54]

Striking North Vietnam

At the beginning of May the enemy's assault intensified, and South Vietnam's plight seemed desperate. The offensive indeed tested South Vietnam's forces as Laird expected, but early results were troublesome. Quang Tri city, the northernmost provincial capital, and most of Quang Tri Province fell to Communist forces by 1 May. The ARVN 3rd Division, which had defended the city, totally collapsed. On 1 May Abrams issued a dire report on the performance of South Vietnam's forces, questioning their "resolve and will to fight." He worried that the serious problems in Quang Tri "may be beyond correction." South's defeat was a real possibility.[55] Abrams concluded that the effectiveness of field commanders would determine the outcome.[56] The next day Laird used Abrams' warnings as an opportunity to reiterate to Nixon his own conviction that better leadership, not more equipment, was the key to victory or defeat: "More than tanks or artillery or other equipment, the South Vietnamese principal need now is backbone."[57]

How to improve the South Vietnamese leadership during a crisis was a question that Laird could not answer. But Nixon had already taken immediate, practical steps to shore up the South Vietnamese by sending a high-level team of logisticians to Vietnam to assess what equipment was needed for South Vietnam's defenses. Led by Assistant Secretary of Defense for Installations and Logistics Barry Shillito, the team departed for Vietnam on 3 May with the intention of reassuring the South Vietnamese government and military that the United States would continue to support them.[58]

Although Laird supported Shillito's visit, he pressed his case for better leadership. He told Kissinger that the South Vietnamese did not "need equipment, what they need right now is just a kick in the ass." To support his point, Laird referred to the abandoning of all the heavy T–48 tanks in Region I during the enemy advance. He complained: "I think it's inexcusable the way they [South Vietnamese] handled those tanks up there. They left them, Henry. . . . They got them over to a place where they couldn't get them back, 'cause there was no bridge. . . . We've got a couple hundred million dollars in that one damn thing." When Kissinger said the president wanted to send more B–52s to Vietnam, Laird responded that it was "just crazy" and suggested sending F–4s instead. Two F–4s carried as much of a bomb load as a B–52 and would be more effective than a B–52 in Laird's view. Finding places to park the B–52s already in-theater was a problem. U-Tapao Air Base in Thailand had reached its maximum number, and the Pentagon wondered how it could squeeze onto Guam the extra B–52s Nixon ordered. Believing that sufficient airpower was already on hand, Laird declaimed, "Jeez, you gotta win this damn thing on the ground. You can't win the damn thing just with airpower."[59]

Unmoved, Nixon would not wait to see if South Vietnam could survive the enemy onslaught. He told Kissinger he wanted to "belt the hell out of them [North Vietnam's forces]." Believing Hanoi would not negotiate until its offensive was halted, the president was ready to bring the war to North Vietnam's capital. In mid-April he had raised with Kissinger the possibility of blockading the shipping channel into Haiphong harbor, which had been part of the planning for Duck Hook in 1969.[60] At the end of April Nixon wrote Kissinger that he wanted to launch a three-day strike using a minimum of 100 B–52s to bomb the Hanoi-Haiphong area during the coming week. A date any later would put the bombing too close to the upcoming Moscow summit. In forwarding the president's order, Kissinger advised Moorer to expect only an oral order, not a written one, to lessen the likelihood of a leak. On Monday, 1 May, Moorer told McCain to prepare plans for air strikes, code-named Frame Glory.[61]

Abrams continued to oppose a strike in North Vietnam. He believed it imperative that he "have the authority and flexibility to employ all available air assets to deal decisively with major threat areas in-country as a matter of first priority over requirements in areas outside the battle zone." On 4 May Abrams wrote Moorer that additional enemy divisions had moved into the DMZ and were expected to attack Kontum city, making it impossible to divert air sorties for a strike on the Hanoi-Haiphong area. Admiral McCain endorsed Abrams' view, forcing the president, who was reluctant to overrule the commander on the scene, to stop the strikes scheduled for 6–7 May.[62]

Abrams' cable brought an angry response from Kissinger who warned Bunker that "the president is nearing the end of his patience with General Abrams on the issue of air action against North Vietnam." Kissinger, involved in intense negotiations with Moscow on a number of issues and with Hanoi on ending the war, could not understand the general's failure to comprehend the geopolitical significance Nixon attached to bombing North Vietnam, especially after Haig made this clear to him during his April visit. Nor could Kissinger fathom why Abrams could not divert some aircraft to bomb the North since Nixon had provided the MACV commander with more airplanes than he had requested. Kissinger instructed Bunker to tell Abrams "in the frankest terms" the president's concerns. To ensure that Abrams would pay less attention to guidance from Laird, Kissinger wrote: "There is some suspicion here that confusing signals from sources in Washington may be contributing to the problem. General Abrams must understand that henceforth the president's thinking on questions of this import will come to him only through you [Bunker] and that any contrary signals, no matter what the source, are inaccurate."[63] Nixon still intended to bomb the Hanoi-Haiphong area regardless of the consequences.[64]

Meeting with his chief of staff, H. R. Haldeman, and Kissinger on 4 May, Nixon reflected on his mistakes in prosecuting the war. He felt he should have followed his instincts and bombed North Vietnam during the Cambodian incursion and during Lam Son 719. Now he believed he had no choice but to hit North Vietnam even if the bombing cost him the summit. In his mind he could afford to lose the Moscow summit but not the war. Kissinger recommended a blockade of Haiphong, asserting that interdiction of the sea lanes would constitute a stronger political move than symbolic and sporadic bombing in the North. A blockade would also allow the B–52s to concentrate on bombing in the South for the time being. Nixon accepted the idea of a blockade as long as a sustained bombing campaign followed.[65]

Shortly before 5:00 p.m. on 4 May, Kissinger called Moorer to the White House for secret discussions with the president. As usual, the reason was to exclude Laird and Rogers, who might raise objections to the "possible blockage and mining of

Haiphong and other North Vietnamese ports." That evening, Moorer instructed CNO Admiral Zumwalt to set up a small select task force to develop a plan "on a very close hold basis" for mining Haiphong harbor. At 11:00 p.m. Moorer met with Deputy Secretary of Defense Kenneth Rush and Zumwalt to review the planning. Rush had succeeded Packard, who left the Pentagon in December 1971. Kissinger regarded the new deputy secretary, who had served as Nixon's ambassador to West Germany, as totally loyal to the White House. Zumwalt's group worked through the night so Moorer could brief Nixon and Kissinger on 5 May. That afternoon Moorer informed the Joint Chiefs of the mining plan. Laird remained in the dark. Kissinger and Moorer agreed that Kissinger would inform the secretary about the mining plan on 6 May but would not mention the chairman's prior involvement.[66]

At Moorer's direction, the JCS drafted a message to begin the mining at 9:00 a.m. on 9 May (Saigon time), but Laird had to approve the message before Moorer could dispatch it. At 8:30 a.m. Kissinger and Moorer briefed Laird on the plan. Recounting the meeting for Rush, Moorer told the deputy secretary, "I played it cool like I had never heard of it." Although Laird reacted negatively at first, according to the chairman, after further discussion with Kissinger he supported the mining operation. The president seemed surprised that Laird gave his support, but he nevertheless continued to criticize his defense secretary, asserting that he had restrained Abrams from being imaginative. Nixon complained that Laird was doing "everything by the numbers" and was thinking only about the effect of Vietnam on the presidential election, while the president was concerned about the consequences of defeat if South Vietnamese forces failed to win the war on their own. Nixon also suspected that Laird would write a memorandum for the record on the mining decision and told Kissinger not to forward such a document to him. For his part, Laird was conscious of his distance from the president, lamenting to Kissinger, "he doesn't have any confidence in me."[67]

Although Nixon had already decided to mine Haiphong, he reviewed the issue in a morning NSC meeting on 8 May with Vice President Spiro Agnew, Rogers, Laird, Secretary of the Treasury John B. Connally, Helms, General George A. Lincoln, and Kissinger. As he had done at other meetings, Nixon tried to create the impression that he was soliciting advice. The discussion concentrated less on the effect of a blockade on Hanoi and more on its effect on the South Vietnamese as well as the geopolitical consequences for the United States of South Vietnam's defeat. In the president's view, each available option—doing nothing, only bombing the North, only blockading, or mining and bombing—would put the Moscow summit at risk. To do nothing and wait out the situation was tempting, allowing the administration to place the onus of a failure on the South Vietnamese. He ruled out this choice, which was Laird's position, believing "our ability to conduct a credible foreign policy could be imperiled." He later added, "The bug-out choice is a good political one but I am not sure what this office would be worth after doing that." He ruled out a bombing-only campaign against the North, citing Abrams' requirement for airpower to stem the enemy's ground offensive in the South. That left the option of cutting off the sea and rail shipment of supplies to Hanoi by mining Haiphong harbor and bombing the rail system, power plants, and POL (petroleum, oil, and lubricants) storage sites. The very real risk of defeat led the president to think that "there is a better than even chance that if we do nothing we will fail."[68]

Contending that the administration had enjoyed a longer than expected grace period to build up the South's armed forces, Laird reminded the group that the current crisis was not caused by a lack of equipment. "The problem facing South Vietnam is whether they are willing to stand and fight." He remained convinced that South Vietnam would not win unless it improved the leadership of its armed forces. The blockade and mining would have an effect on the Hanoi regime in four to six months, but in his view would not deter North Vietnam from pursuing its goals especially with the approaching 1972 presidential election. The secretary feared that putting additional resources into Vietnam would compromise U.S. defenses in Europe and reduce the nation's leverage with the Soviet Union and China. Nonetheless, Laird believed the South Vietnamese would prevail.[69]

Laird's arguments evoked pointed questioning from Nixon. He asked if Laird was not saying the administration should resign itself to South Vietnam's possible fall. Seeming to sidestep the question, Laird said he believed the South Vietnamese could prevail. "Your point," Nixon said, "is South Vietnam can make it without either the strikes or sea interdiction," but if Vietnam falls, the president asked, what does the administration do? Laird again asserted that if the South Vietnamese did not find the will to fight, "then all the equipment in the world won't save them." Others attending the meeting rejected Laird's argument that the cost of air and sea interdiction was too great, and in any event they did not think the decision should be made on that basis. Some attendees believed a U.S. defeat would provide an opportunity for the Soviets to make gains in the Middle East and the Indian Ocean and open wars of national liberation elsewhere in the world. Vice President Agnew, who supported interdiction, proclaimed, "By not doing anything more we would be giving testimony to our weakness." Laird's dissent was not well received. Nixon was allegedly upset when it was reported in the press, but the secretary asserted that he should be able to raise questions in meetings without fear of being quoted in public.[70]

The president announced his decision in a television and radio broadcast at 9:00 p.m. on 8 May. Reminding his audience that Hanoi had spurned his negotiating offers over the past three years and now threatened to defeat South Vietnam, Nixon explained he had to act to protect that nation and the American troops still there. The situation called for decisive military action. The United States could no longer exercise restraint in waging war when North Vietnam's entire army threatened South Vietnam's existence. The United States would mine all entrances to North Vietnamese ports to prevent access to them and shut down North Vietnamese naval operations. U.S. forces would interdict the delivery of supplies "within the internal and claimed territorial waters of North Vietnam," cut rail and communications links, and continue air and naval strikes against military targets in North Vietnam. At the time the president spoke on television, Navy aircraft dropped the first mines in the shipping channel to Haiphong. The mines would not be activated for three days to allow foreign ships in Haiphong harbor the opportunity to leave.[71] Nixon warned Moorer on 9 May not to flub the operation. "There is no damned excuse now. You have what the military claimed it never had before. You've got the authority to do it."[72]

The mining of North Vietnam's ports apparently surprised General Abrams. Before the president's pronouncement, Abrams was hosting a dinner in his quarters with Assistant Secretary of Defense Shillito during which he complained that the U.S. Navy had suddenly and without notice pulled ships from a naval gunfire support mission. At that point it dawned on Shillito that no one had informed the MACV commander of the impending mining, which was why the ships in question had been moved. Shillito called Laird, who confirmed the omission and later apologized to Abrams. The alleged oversight could be taken as yet another indication of the president's loss of confidence in the MACV commander.[73]

The mining did not lead to cancellation of the Moscow summit, even though Hanoi requested that the Soviets scrub the summit and send a naval task force to Haiphong harbor to challenge the U.S. Navy. Any hesitation to go ahead with the summit gave way to the Soviets' expectations that they would gain an arms control agreement, improve trade relations, and earn international prestige from a successful summit meeting. Moreover, cancellation would affect Brezhnev's status as a leader. The Soviet pursuit of détente with the United States took priority over support of a Communist ally in this instance.[74]

Given Moscow's acquiescence, Nixon took the next step in the campaign against the North: heavy bombing of military targets in hopes of pressuring Hanoi to negotiate seriously. Linebacker I, the name of the bombing campaign against North Vietnam, quickly followed the mining of Haiphong. He instructed Kissinger and Haig that he expected a minimum of 1,200 Air Force and Navy sorties each day, up to 1,300 if another carrier, the *Saratoga*, arrived on station, and a minimum of 200 sorties daily in the Hanoi-Haiphong area. The military were to launch the maximum number while he was at the summit meeting in Moscow, unless he directly ordered a change, "so that there can be no implication at all to the effect that we are letting up because of our trip to Moscow." The president restricted bombing near the Chinese border and in the area immediately around Hanoi to avoid risking civilian casualties while he was in Moscow. U.S. Air Force and Navy fighters flew most of the sorties, but B–52s were also employed.[75] Moorer concluded that Linebacker I and the mining forced North Vietnam to rely on a land supply route that stretched 400 miles from the Chinese border to South Vietnam. The destruction of key rail facilities and bridges forced the enemy to shuttle supplies in a time-consuming and inefficient manner.[76]

By June the enemy's offensive in the South began to falter, a result of heavy aerial punishment; problems in supplying large conventional forces scattered along three fronts; faulty coordination of armor, artillery, and infantry units; and not least, the dogged resistance of ARVN forces especially at An Loc in Region III. The North Vietnamese, perhaps in the belief that Nixon was too crippled politically to strike as hard as he did, underestimated the effectiveness and scale of U.S. airpower. Without airpower and the presence of U.S. advisers, who coordinated the U.S. firepower and logistic support that helped keep South Vietnamese units intact, it is possible that the invasion would have had a much different outcome. Backed by massive U.S. support, the South Vietnamese proved good enough to avoid defeat. As one historian assessed the outcome, "The South Vietnamese had survived the 1972 NVA [North Vietnamese Army] invasion, but they owed much of their success to the United States and not to their own ability to defeat the NVA on the battlefield."[77]

The administration recognized the shortcomings of the South Vietnamese military sufficiently to embark on additional large-scale efforts, Enhance and Enhance Plus, to better prepare the South Vietnamese to defend their country. The Enhance program, beginning in May 1972, supplied equipment for new South Vietnamese armor, air, and artillery units, supplementing the ongoing effort to replace weapons, artillery pieces, vehicles, and communications equipment lost in combat during the Easter Offensive. Nixon asked DoD to study additional steps to ensure that the South Vietnamese could meet the current enemy threat. Although Laird's response covered familiar ground, arguing the need "not to delude the GVN and RVNAF that hardware can in some way substitute for backbone," he prepared a number of extensive equipment packages to sustain South Vietnamese forces. The secretary advised Nixon that the additional equipment under consideration was unfunded and unprogrammed in the FY 1972 and FY 1973 budgets. On 19 May Nixon approved Laird's recommendations for additional helicopters, aircraft (gunships, fighters, and reconnaissance planes), mortars, antitank weapons, an additional M48 tank battalion, a composite field artillery battalion, and 64 Vulcan antiaircraft weapons. Providing the added equipment to South Vietnam entailed a short-term reduction in U.S. antitank capabilities in NATO. Some of the more sophisticated equipment and weapons required training the South Vietnamese units that would use them.[78]

Laird subsequently pledged to Nixon that he would get the additional equipment to the South Vietnamese as quickly as possible. The equipment costs coupled with the higher operational tempo through December 1972 would roughly total $1.35 billion. The secretary took the opportunity to reiterate the fundamental leadership problem among South Vietnamese forces. The setbacks suffered "were not due to shortcomings in weapons or organization, but rather were caused by deficiencies in leadership and will." The inability of the army to reach the goal of a 90 percent manning level for combat units especially worried Laird. He told the president that ARVN combat battalions stood at roughly 69 percent of strength when the Easter Offensive began.[79]

Despite Laird's compliant response to Nixon's latest call for more equipment for South Vietnam's armed forces, not to mention the long-term buildup of the RVNAF under Improvement and Modernization Plans over several years, the president felt his orders had been ignored. In an eyes-only memorandum for Kissinger and Haig on 19 May, the same day that he had approved Laird's recommendations, Nixon complained, "I have ordered, on occasion after occasion, an increase in the quantity and quality of weapons made available to the South Vietnamese. All that we have gotten from the Pentagon is the run around and a sometimes deliberate sabotage of the orders that I have given."[80]

In October Laird initiated Enhance Plus to expedite the delivery of weapons and equipment from previous requests and to provide as quickly as possible additional materiel for South Vietnam before a possible cease-fire. The goal was to maximize the amount of materiel in South Vietnamese hands by 20 November 1972. On 17 November Laird informed the president that all Enhance Plus items were either in-country or en route by surface transportation. Between 23 October and 12 December a massive airlift and sealift provided South Vietnam with more than 105,000 pieces of equipment.[81]

The impressive buildup of weapons and equipment during and after the offensive did not eliminate questions about South Vietnam's military capabilities, especially in Laird's mind. Modern equipment and weapons failed to improve the underlying RVNAF leadership problems. The deployment of ARVN units remained geographically fixed. Desertions continued at a high rate in 1972, creating personnel shortfalls that required additional recruiting and training. Despite these issues and an apparent need for American advisers, as evidenced in part by their actions in holding together some ARVN units during the Easter Offensive, Laird requested that the JCS review the U.S. advisory effort with an eye toward further cuts. The review led to the elimination of 1,700 advisers in Vietnam and reduced the number of division advisory teams from 36 to 15. This drastic cut in American advisory support came at an inopportune moment, depriving the RVNAF of the kind of technical and moral support that might have helped them rebuild after the enemy offensive.[82]

Intense negotiations in Paris during the fall and winter led to the signing of a cease-fire agreement in January 1973. It called for the withdrawal of all American forces and advisers and the termination of all U.S. military supporting actions, in effect ending Vietnamization. South Vietnam's armed forces would have to meet their next battlefield test without the benefit of U.S. air support or advisers. In March 1973 General Weyand, the last MACV commander, assessed the capability of Saigon's forces. According to his estimates, the RVNAF could defend their country from any threat save a massive enemy offensive. What concerned him, however, was South Vietnam's inadequate maintenance program to keep helicopters and other equipment operating as well as the lack of trained personnel to provide the maintenance support. Ineffective leadership, poor discipline, and the fixed territorial deployment of units, which prevented the concentration of combat power for conventional fighting, also worried him. The official U.S. Army history concluded that Saigon's ground forces in 1973 "were no more mobile than they had been in 1965 and were thus vulnerable to the military and psychological disabilities of fighting a static defensive war."[83] Although Laird had been instrumental in getting U.S. forces out of South Vietnam, it was far from certain that the enhanced RVNAF could survive in the long run.

OVER THE COURSE OF THE EASTER INVASION, Laird's influence ebbed further. In contrast to the president's attitude toward Laird in early 1969, by 1972 Nixon was less willing to listen to his secretary's frequently cautionary advice. Nixon asserted himself as commander in chief, pushing the civilian and military leadership to maximize military pressure against North Vietnam, insisting on beefing up U.S. air and naval forces, and improving the quality and quantity of RVNAF equipment. In overruling his civilian and military advisers, he occasionally accused them, especially Laird and Abrams, of not fully supporting him. The president's growing assertiveness merged with his paranoia that opponents, within and without the administration, were attempting to derail his efforts.

The Easter Offensive brought out Nixon's mean-spirited side, manifested by an atmosphere of distrust in the White House. Although much of the distrust contributed to Laird's diminished status, the president's scorn also fell heavily on the military. During the invasion Nixon envisioned himself as a bold, imaginative leader, frustrated by the military's performance. He vented his displeasure in harsh language. He wrote Kissinger on 15 May 1972 that the military men were "notorious for the plodding mediocrity of their strategy and tactics," and should know that "the president is the Commander-in-Chief." Four days later Nixon told Kissinger he was "thoroughly disgusted" with the military's failure to carry out orders during his presidency and especially during the enemy invasion. Placing most of the blame on the Pentagon, the president lamented, "We left too many of the McNamara people around in high places and they are constantly sabotaging everything we are trying to do."[84]

Although Laird was successful in getting additional funds from Congress to pay for the heightened operational tempo and ensuring additional arms and equipment reached the RVNAF, the period of the 1972 invasion evinced Laird's declining influence. Laird knew it and was distraught by Nixon questioning his loyalty. Laird may have maneuvered around the White House but believed nonetheless that he acted in the president's best interests. Nixon continued to bypass Laird in making decisions, expressing annoyance with the secretary and his dissenting views.

Throughout most of Nixon's first term, Laird was a voice of moderation. During the internal deliberations on the war, he attempted to weigh military actions in light of their domestic, political, and budgetary consequences. Nixon had grown more confident and assertive after his diplomatic successes in China and his signing of an arms agreement with Moscow. But he still resented Laird's political maneuvering during the EC–121 crisis, for example, that had made it virtually impossible for Nixon to launch a strong military response. The high likelihood of a reelection also boosted Nixon's confidence. From his perspective, he would face a weak Democratic opponent for president, Senator George McGovern, whose positions on the war and the military were outside the mainstream. Nixon realized he could expect to return to the White House despite an unpopular war and the efforts of those he perceived as his enemies in the government, media, and Congress to thwart the election. This frame of mind made it easier to discount the counsel of his defense secretary.

Despite his waning influence, Laird remained a central figure in shaping the administration's policy toward Vietnam. The troop withdrawals that he initiated against the resistance of Kissinger and the military were instrumental in winding down U.S. participation in the war and lowering U.S. casualties. Vietnamization certainly enhanced Nixon's reelection prospects by reducing U.S. military forces in Vietnam from over a half-million in 1969 to less than 30,000 by the end of 1972. The president gave Laird little credit for helping minimize Vietnam as a campaign issue. Laird's prime objective was essentially political: to extract the United States from the Vietnam morass. As president, Nixon fervently desired to pull out; as commander in chief, he wanted to win the war, or at least appear not to have lost it.

CHAPTER 10

Looking Beyond Vietnam:
The FY 1971 Budget

BESET BY COMPETING DOMESTIC and war-related demands for money, rising inflation, a budget out of balance, the possibility of higher taxes, and scarce funds for social policy initiatives, President Nixon had little choice but to cut defense spending. It was the largest source of non-entitlement funds. In 1969 he could point to recent strategic and military developments that made DoD cuts feasible: plans to wind down the Vietnam War by troop withdrawals and a negotiated settlement with the North, and efforts to secure an agreement with the Soviets limiting the number of strategic nuclear weapons. The Sino-Soviet rivalry also represented a diplomatic and military opportunity for the United States to leverage the tensions between the two Communist superpowers, thus lowering the possibility of having to wage war against Russia and China at the same time. Like Defense Secretary Laird, the president endeavored to have America's NATO allies contribute more toward their mutual defense. The so-called Nixon Doctrine of July 1969 called for America's Asian allies to do more and the United States to do less in defeating local insurgencies. Friendly nations could no longer expect a repeat of the expensive large-scale U.S. military intervention in Vietnam. Successful relations and partnerships with allies would permit the United States to remain strong even as the Defense budget shrank. As the Pentagon began building its FY 1971 budget early in 1969, Nixon initiated National Security Study Memorandum 3, a fundamental review that would have profound consequences for the DoD budget.

A New Budget Process

As they had done when they shaped the FY 1970 budget, Laird and Deputy Defense Secretary David Packard prepared the FY 1971 budget under constraints imposed by unrelenting presidential cost-cutting imperatives. Early in 1969 Laird and Packard reviewed the FY 1971 DoD program and budget guidelines issued in 1968 by the Johnson administration. The FY 1971 budget, the first Nixon-originated budget, emerged from a new process within the Pentagon. When his tenure began, Laird introduced what he called "participatory management," in which the Joint Chiefs of Staff became more heavily involved in budget formulation than they had during the McNamara years. The secretary not only gave the JCS a greater voice but also modified the budget process so that it concentrated on identifying what was actually affordable in the current fiscal environment. The FY 1971 budget looked ahead, laying out a blueprint to meet the nation's security requirements in the post-Vietnam era. It would be the first to embody the new administration's priorities and the first crafted under DoD's revised Planning, Programming, and Budgeting System, or PPBS, introduced by Secretary Robert McNamara to provide more comprehensive DoD management.[1]

For most of the 1960s DoD had been "planning and budgeting on an unconstrained 'requirements basis,'" in the words of Comptroller Robert Moot, determining requirements without regard to resources at hand. Under McNamara, each service stated generously the resources it believed necessary to carry out its role in fighting simultaneously two large wars and one small one. Systems analysts then prepared Major Program Memoranda (MPMs) that routinely slashed the service budget requests to a feasible level. Given the continuing expense of Vietnam, the budget could no longer support these expansive requirements. In coordination with the services and the JCS, Laird and Packard made four major changes to this PPBS process in 1969 to align budget numbers more closely with available resources, and to enhance the role of the military services in shaping the budget. First, the altered system required the military services at the start of the budget process to advocate programs that could reasonably be funded. The second change kept the JCS involved in the budget process longer, an important manifestation of Laird's notion of participatory management, using their priorities and risks as critical elements in developing the Five-Year Defense Program, or FYDP. Third, the new PPBS cycle was extended four months, allowing more time for discussion among the services, JCS, and OSD. The fourth change made the services responsible for budget analysis, requiring them to assess alternatives to current and planned programs. In a new basic budget document, the Program Objective Memorandum (POM), each service would review, analyze, and justify its overall program. Unable to use the full 15-month cycle in preparing the FY 1971 budget for submission to Congress in January 1970, DoD employed a shortened version of the revised PPBS.[2]

Laird found unacceptable a White House change in budget procedures, which granted the Bureau of the Budget a significant increase in power. Under Johnson, the bureau had to get White House approval before it could change McNamara's budget submission. Under Nixon, BoB exercised greater control over department and agency budgets, including the DoD budget, requiring Laird to defend funding requests against the bureau's cuts and to contend with BoB Director Robert Mayo's assertive efforts to restrict departmental authority.

In May 1969 Mayo presented his plan for formulating the FY 1971 budget to the president, proposing to "mark up" each agency's budget requests, adjudicating disagreements with department and agency heads, and then briefing the president (not the principals) on his recommendations. In effect he would speak on behalf of the departments and agencies and decide what was important enough for the chief executive to hear. The White House informed Laird of Mayo's plan on 28 May.[3]

Laird objected, viewing the BoB procedure as tantamount to setting a formal FY 1971 budget mark without consulting him. The secretary did not oppose a joint BoB/OSD review of the Defense budget, but he wanted to be fully engaged. "National security is such a key goal that any determination of a Defense budget target without Department of Defense participation would be" Laird wrote Mayo, "a serious error." He wanted to present his views directly to the president prior to a final decision. At the end of October, Mayo set forth procedures for appealing BoB's budget decisions to the president; they remained unchanged in substance from his May proposal. Mayo informed Laird that BoB would "communicate to your staff the president's decision on your 1971 allowance." The director believed that Nixon would change his initial budget determination only in exceptional cases, leaving Laird with less latitude and authority in budget decisions than McNamara had enjoyed.[4]

Major Program Memoranda

During Laird's long-running dispute with Mayo, the Pentagon prepared the FY 1971 budget for submission to the White House. In the spring of 1969 Packard sent a series of draft MPMs to the military services and defense agencies for review and comment. Analysts in various staff sections of OSD prepared the MPMs, which separately addressed each major force element: land, naval, air, and personnel. Some MPMs requested proposals for restructuring forces; and others, for a list of priorities in weapons acquisition. Packard advised the services that they might have to revise the program guidance once the study on strategy and forces (NSSM 3) was released. For planning purposes, the armed forces could assume that the Vietnam War would continue through the end of the fiscal year.[5] Packard's fiscal guidance of July reduced total obligational authority, or TOA, from the $88.9 billion of the FYDP to a ceiling of $84.8 billion, but that figure included funds for the July 1969 pay raise. Although DoD initially planned to authorize 3,402,300 military and 1,352,200 civilian personnel for the services and defense agencies in FY 1971, Packard warned the services to plan for reductions.[6]

The Major Program Memorandum in May on ground forces left the number of Army and Marine Corps (active and reserve) divisions at $32^2/_3$ for FY 1971. Army personnel would total 1.917 million; and the Marines, 275,000. For the post-Vietnam period, OSD envisioned cutting the ground force to $16^1/_3$ Active and 8 reserve Army divisions plus 3 active and 1 reserve Marine Corps divisions. It also contemplated changing the Army's force structure and manning concepts to improve the readiness of reserve forces.[7] In June, relatively early in the process, Packard sliced the FY 1971 TOA for the Army and Marines to $20.6 billion from the $29.4 billion that the secretary had recommended only a month earlier.[8]

Naval forces received similar scrutiny. Noting that the Navy's FY 1971 program of $10.4 billion exceeded the president's FY 1970 figure by nearly $3 billion, Packard advised Navy Secretary John Chafee to develop the FY 1971 program at an overall cost of $8 billion or less. During the review process Packard reduced the FY 1971 TOA for naval forces from $9.5 billion (a figure based on the FYDP) to $8 billion.[9]

Laird envisioned changes for the naval forces. He urged the Navy to revise the type and quantity of the currently programmed fleet air defense systems. He wanted to reduce spending for antisubmarine warfare. The secretary believed that previous budgets had neglected naval support forces in favor of combat forces, leaving behind an old and inefficient support fleet of tankers and transports. He intended to accelerate the program to build support ships and to retire ships contributing "little additional capability."[10]

Looking to the needs of a postwar military, Laird focused on strategic mobility—the ability of U.S. forces to deploy overseas with their equipment in a future crisis. To carry out the national strategy of waging 2 1/2 wars simultaneously, DoD needed the capability to deploy forces simultaneously to Europe and Asia as well as to transport a small force within a 10-day period to handle a minor crisis in the Western Hemisphere. The MPM on mobility forces assumed that a strategic airlift force of C–141s and C–5As would be sufficient to meet deployment requirements and provide a cushion for unanticipated needs. Unfortunately, cost overruns and serious engineering problems plagued the C–5A program.[11]

In reviewing service programs, Packard also found shortcomings in the Navy's sealift program for transporting troops, supplies, and equipment overseas during war. The department lacked a "sealift force which is especially designed and managed as part of an integrated rapid deployment system." Without "a responsive and controlled sealift force," DoD would have trouble deploying the forces and equipment to carry out the 2 1/2-war strategy. Packard wanted to retain the current program of 15 Fast Deployment Logistics (FDL) ships and 19 Forward Floating Depot ships. Expecting that Congress would not appropriate funds for the FDL ships, he approved a plan to charter 10 new privately owned cargo ships for the Military Sea Transportation Service to operate.[12]

Packard used the review not just to formulate the budget but to evaluate the process for acquisition, particularly procedures for scrutinizing weapons and equipment with developmental problems. He singled out several Army weapon systems, among them the M551 Sheridan vehicle, the Shillelagh gun system for the M60 tank, and the Cheyenne (AH–56A) helicopter. Packard concluded that both the Sheridan and the Shillelagh had gone into production without adequate testing. The Sheridan would require extensive retrofits to make it effective, and the Shillelagh might have to be scrapped because it had proved more expensive and less effective than the system it was designed to replace. Packard faulted the Johnson administration for approving the limited production and procurement of 375 Cheyennes without first demonstrating the helicopter's effectiveness. The per unit production cost had risen much higher than estimates and the production schedule was in danger of slipping, leading Packard to believe that the system was doubtful. As a matter of policy, he refused to approve full production of a new system until operational tests simulating combat conditions demonstrated its effectiveness. He would approve limited production if the sub-systems passed all critical tests and if circumstances warranted an exception. Packard aimed to adhere to these principles as much as possible in reviewing new programs already in the production phase.[13]

The deputy secretary advised the JCS, the Navy, the Air Force, and the director of defense research and engineering to be realistic about the development and acquisition of new technically sophisticated aircraft and ships. Packard stated the issue bluntly. If DoD introduced new aircraft, such as the F–14, F–15, F–111, and E–2C, and nuclear-powered ships at current spending levels, then it would have to cut the Air Force from 23 to 15 wings; the Navy from 15 to 12 attack carriers and from 12 to 10 air wings; and shrink each Marine Corps wing from 139 to 103 aircraft. Less expensive and less complex fighters would free up sufficient funds for the Air Force to build up to 30 wings, the Navy to 15, and the Marines to 192 aircraft per wing. Packard left it up to the services to "recommend a larger quantity of inexpensive aircraft or a smaller quantity of more expensive aircraft." He estimated that replacing older aircraft and ships on a one-for-one basis with more costly planes and ships would increase the cost of the tactical air program by 64 percent between FY 1970 ($10.6 billion) and FY 1975 ($17.4 billion).[14]

Developed under Packard's supervision, the MPMs reflected Laird's intent to put the defense program on a sound fiscal basis in shaping a new force structure to carry out national strategy and meet post-Vietnam security requirements. Embedded in the MPM review was the goal of establishing more rigorous and timely testing of weapon systems before building them. Likewise, the altered PPBS imposed tighter fiscal discipline on the services. Service budget requests based on rigorous analysis of requirements would be more credible and a step in the right direction. Better service analyses of budget issues would strengthen their justification and help erase suspicion that the military routinely inflated budget requests to make it more likely that the armed forces would receive more of the funds requested. The altered PPBS attempted to make a complicated, inexact budget process more realistic by seeking a balance between a prudent estimate of the requirements, tolerable risk, and affordability.

The MPM review occurred at the same time that Packard was undertaking for the president a fundamental reassessment of U.S. strategy, NSSM 3. Started in January 1969 and completed in September, NSSM 3 led to a major change in strategy. It complemented what Laird and Packard tried to accomplish with the MPMs and their budget guidelines and procedures, explicitly linking the choice of a national strategy to the forces and funds needed to execute that strategy.

NSSM 3: Rethinking the Budget and National Strategy

Nixon selected Packard to head the steering group that would prepare over the spring and summer of 1969 NSSM 3, a comprehensive study of national security strategy and its cost. The group, which included presidential assistant Henry Kissinger and representatives of State, Treasury, JCS, CIA, and BoB, examined alternative military strategies and the force structure and funds required to execute them. Divided into two parts—general purpose forces and strategic nuclear forces—the study assessed the military risks and likely political and diplomatic effects of each. General purpose forces, accounting for more than 60 percent of defense spending, had a much greater impact on the budget than the 25 percent allotted to strategic nuclear forces.[15]

A major issue on the table concerned whether the United States, as current policy dictated, needed to maintain sufficient forces to meet simultaneous attacks by the Warsaw Pact in Europe and the Chinese in Asia. Growing tensions between the Soviet Union and China seemed to render that possibility less likely, creating a chance to consider fresh approaches to national security.

National Intelligence Estimate (NIE) 11-69 of 27 February 1969 observed that the Soviets, concerned about preserving their position as the leading Communist power, sought to contain China as an ideological and great power competitor. In March 1969 a series of armed clashes occurred between Soviet and Chinese forces along their common border.[16] According to the 17 July 1969 Special National Intelligence Estimate (SNIE), Soviet leaders viewed "China as their most pressing international problem" and contemplated a form of collective security to contain their Communist rival. Nixon viewed this split between the two powers as an opportunity for Washington.[17] The time was right for the NSSM 3 steering group to assess the likelihood and cost of fighting two Communist countries at the same time and to define a new context for strategic planning and future budgets.[18]

On 10 September 1969 the National Security Council reviewed the NSSM 3 paper on general purpose forces—Army and Marine divisions, carrier-based and land-based tactical air forces, antisubmarine forces, airlift and sealift forces, and tactical nuclear weapons.[19] The meeting was critical to future strategy and force structure planning. Like Laird and Packard, Kissinger wanted change, fearing that "the JCS and Services will continue to design weapon systems and establish requirements which are not disciplined by budgetary considerations." Kissinger supported Laird's and Packard's decisions to impose fiscal discipline within DoD on budget formulation, but he still urged the president to authorize the Defense Program Review Committee to exercise direction of the budget and defense strategy. Like Robert Mayo, Kissinger envisioned a reduced role for DoD: "I do not believe major strategy, force and budget issues should continue to be resolved in bilateral negotiations between the Budget Bureau and the Defense Department."[20]

The heart of NSSM 3 consisted of its analysis of five alternative military strategies for employing general purpose forces, explicitly linking the size of general purpose forces to DoD outlays. Most of the forces stationed in the United States were earmarked for deployment to Europe or Asia during an emergency. NSSM 3 numbered the strategies for general purpose forces 1 through 5 (see table 9), but each strategy assumed an end to the Vietnam conflict and a substantial reduction in personnel.

Of the five, Strategy 1 made the fewest demands on the U.S. military. It called for an initial defense in Europe lasting no more than 90 days, based on the assumption that there would be either a cease-fire or an escalation to full nuclear war. It also called for the United States to simultaneously provide materiel assistance to its allies in Asia in the event of an attack from an adversary other than China. This was essentially a one-war strategy. Strategy 2 called for enough active forces to conduct an initial NATO defense of Europe *or* a joint defense of either Korea or other Southeast Asia allies against a Chinese attack. The force structure under this strategy was sufficient to conduct major operations only in one theater at a time, allowing the United States to wage one large-scale war and a small one, but not at the same time. Strategy 3 envisioned the initial defense in Europe *and* assistance against a Chinese attack in Korea or Southeast Asia— essentially two major wars. Strategy 4 provided for a sustained NATO defense and a holding action in Asia, or the initial defense of NATO and the joint defense of Asia. This strategy provided the capability to mount a sustained defense of Europe while creating additional forces for a counteroffensive. Strategy 5, the most costly and comprehensive, required total defense of NATO and joint defense of Korea and SEA.[21] Table 9 presents the manpower for general purpose forces and the annual expense implied by each strategy.

Table 9. NSSM 3 Alternative Strategies

	Manpower (millions)	Implied Outlays ($ billions annually)
Strategy 1	1.94	72
Strategy 2	2.08	76
Strategy 3	2.30	81
Strategy 4	2.58	93
Strategy 5	2.86	102

Source: NSSM 3, General Purpose Forces Section, 5 September 1969, folder NSSM 1–4, box NSSM (1969) 1–49, OSD Historical Office.

The White House and DoD Hammer Out a Budget

Following the September NSC meeting, at which Nixon made no decision, Laird requested that the president meet with the Joint Chiefs to hear their concerns about the effect of budget cuts on national security before selecting a new national strategy. In August BoB's budget guidance had set FY 1971 defense outlays at $72.5 billion, an amount the Chiefs not unexpectedly judged would significantly diminish the nation's military capabilities. The Vietnam War was a major expense. From FY 1964 to FY 1970 the budgets of the military services had absorbed about 40 percent of the costs related to Vietnam, compelling the armed forces to reduce spending on other programs, especially research and development and programs to improve existing weapons. The erosion in non-Southeast Asia spending, JCS Chairman Earle Wheeler believed, would allow the Soviets to narrow the qualitative advantage of U.S. general purpose and strategic forces. He highlighted the growth in Soviet nuclear missile submarines and improvements in the SS–9 missile and strategic defenses. The FY 1970 DoD budget calculated in FY 1964 dollars, he pointed out, came to less than $42 billion, "after adjustments for inflation and costs of war." The chairman advocated a spending figure that would compensate for the budget decline in real terms since 1964 and restore a degree of the deterrent capability lost to the Soviets.[22]

Wheeler's plea met with unyielding resistance from BoB and the president. To help carry out Nixon's new domestic initiatives and economic policies, Mayo wanted to lower FY 1971 DoD expenditures even further to $71 billion. The 2½-war strategy, for which the JCS sought money, was too costly. Thus the president adopted a less expensive strategy after reviewing NSSM 3. Linking national strategy with associated costs, NSSM 3 made affordability the critical issue in selecting a strategy for general purpose forces and setting the size of the Defense budget. The implied expenditure of $81 billion for fighting two wars under Strategy 3 would be far too expensive, especially when BoB sought to limit outlays to $71 billion, cut the overall budget, and fund Nixon's new domestic initiatives.[23] Strategies 4 and 5 were prohibitively costly. Strategies 1 and 2 were affordable, but the JCS protested that Strategy 1 was too risky. Hardly surprising, Nixon selected Strategy 2 when he issued NSDM 27 on 11 October 1969. That strategy, preparing the military services to fight 1½ wars, called for FY 1971 outlays of $76 billion on the assumption that U.S. forces would remain in combat in Vietnam through 30 June 1973. Should the United States end its involvement in Vietnam before June 1973, but after 1 July 1970, budget outlays would fall to $73 billion. Nixon directed DoD to use these budget figures for planning purposes and develop a five-year program consistent with the approved strategy and budget guidelines. Notwithstanding NSDM 27, BoB's August expenditure target of $72.5 billion remained in force. Packard acknowledged that DoD's FY 1971 budget decisions would take NSDM 27 into account, but he advised Kissinger that the redesign of the force structure required additional study, which could not be completed before he submitted the budget.[24]

Strategy 2 represented a fundamental change from the previous national strategy, a change driven in large part by economic and budgetary constraints, but not without political and military considerations. The new strategy reflected a more clear-sighted view of capabilities. As Kissinger noted, "We had never generated the forces our two-and-one-half-war doctrine required; the gap between our declaratory and our actual policy was bound to create confusion in the minds of potential aggressors and to raise grave risks if we attempted to apply it. There was no realistic prospect that the Chinese and the Soviets would move against us at the same time."[25]

At the 13 November DPRC meeting to review the FY 1971 budget, DoD and the Budget Bureau clashed over defense expenditures at a time when inflation, rising unemployment, and increased Medicare costs were pushing up nondefense outlays. Government revenues might drop because of lower tax revenue and a business slowdown in FY 1971. At the time of the meeting, DoD proposed a budget of $74.7 billion in outlays. Packard contended that the outlays could not fall lower than BoB's expenditure target of $72.5 billion. The department would have to cut $2.2 billion from the force structure of all services to meet BoB's goal, but for the Navy and Air Force, reductions would also encompass equipment (ships and aircraft). James Schlesinger, BoB's representative, countered that the administration would "have to stick with $72.5 billion or lower for defense."[26]

The DPRC discussion concentrated on the relationship between budget outlays and the forces that would remain in the Vietnam theater at the end of the fiscal year (30 June 1971). The department's ability to meet the administration's expenditure goal depended primarily on the timing of withdrawals from Vietnam (see chapter 4). Packard presented four alternatives that started from DoD's proposed expenditure of $74.7 billion. The first posited a withdrawal period of 24 months (1 July 1969 to 30 June 1971), leaving a force of 260,000 in Vietnam and reducing outlays an estimated $1.2 billion. The second assumed a withdrawal period of 18 months, reaching the 260,000 troop level in January 1971. This alternative would lower expenditures by $1.6 billion. Alternative three would leave 180,000 troops in Vietnam at the end of June 1971, saving $1.9 billion. The final alternative would reach the 180,000 troop level by January 1971, saving $2.3 billion. Depending on the alternative, DoD expenditures then would fall within a range of $72.4 billion to $73.5 billion. As Packard emphasized, overall end strength was the critical variable because it affected programs worldwide. End strength targets could be achieved by withdrawing from Vietnam or by reducing forces and readiness in the United States, which in turn would affect DoD's ability to carry out national strategy. Slowing withdrawals from Vietnam would weaken NATO readiness, Packard pointed out.[27]

The DPRC convened again on 9 December to further consider the Defense budget. During discussions DoD estimated FY 1971 expenditures at $72.5 billion in conformity with the BoB target, on the assumption that 260,000 military personnel (all services) would remain in Vietnam at the end of June 1971. According to estimates, Vietnam redeployments (190,000) would help pare $1.5 billion in expenditures. To meet the expenditure level of $72.5 billion, the department would have to make additional cuts of $700 million, resulting in the overall reduction of more than 200,000 in end strength of the armed forces—from 3,159,000 at the end of June 1970 to 2,942,000 at the end of June 1971. By the end of FY 1971, the number of active Army divisions would fall from 17²/₃ to 14²/₃ and the Marine Corps would lose an active division and 2 fighter squadrons, leaving it with 3 divisions and 13 fighter squadrons. Naval carrier air wings would be cut from 14 to 13. The

Air Force would suffer no personnel losses, but C–5A production would halt at 81 aircraft; F–111 production would cease after the purchase of 38 aircraft; and procurement of the A–7D and the F–4E would be curtailed. DoD would slow the hardening of Minuteman missile silos and reduce the number of missiles by 34. Outlays for research, development, and test and evaluation were set at $7.5 billion. Some reductions would affect the readiness of NATO forces. The committee also expressed interest in exploring the possibility of saving funds by removing a U.S. division from Korea in FY 1971.[28]

Compared with the Navy and Air Force, the Army took a disproportionate share of the cuts because of the necessity to pull ground forces from Vietnam, reduce end strength, and make funds available for the Army's non-Vietnam programs. If no additional withdrawals occurred in FY 1971, if 205,000 Army personnel remained in-country, and if the strength of all services in-country remained at 260,000, then the Army might need an additional $1.9 billion in obligational authority for non-Vietnam programs. The worst case, a deficit of $2.4 billion in non-Vietnam obligational authority, would arise if the large redeployments assumed in the FY 1970 budget (147,000 soldiers in Vietnam) did not actually occur in FY 1971.[29]

On 19 December a BoB proposal to eliminate another $2.952 billion in TOA and $1.87 billion in outlays provoked an immediate objection from Laird. Since January 1969, the FY 1971 budget had fallen by $10 billion in TOA and $9 billion in expenditures. Laird emphasized that the service secretaries and the Joint Chiefs had already rejected with few exceptions the cuts that BoB advocated. He cautioned Kissinger that the "further major reductions proposed by BoB would be so disruptive as to severely impact on essential military readiness." Wheeler vigorously agreed, believing "that the imposition of these further reductions would cause a degradation in our military forces and readiness beyond the range of acceptable and prudent risks." Among BoB's more controversial proposals were cuts to the aircraft carrier force (from 15 to 12) and cancellation of a new nuclear carrier.[30]

Before the president could meet with Mayo on 22 December to review the FY 1971 budget, Laird made a preemptive move. In a memorandum on 20 December, the secretary asked Nixon to base the FY 1971 budget on the assumption that 260,000 troops would remain in Vietnam at the end of June 1971.[31] This proposal would help the Army avoid a budget shortfall. On 27 December Nixon approved Laird's "budget strategy as it pertains to Vietnam," providing the secretary with leverage in carrying out Vietnamization.[32] The FY 1971 budget allowed the secretary to retain no more than 260,000 troops in Vietnam, but he absolutely had to withdraw troops to meet that goal. There could be no stopping or going back to higher troop levels without having to increase the DoD budget. Laird thus gained a real measure of control over the size and cost of the U.S. force in Vietnam, but his budget remained a target for further cuts.

On the day Nixon approved Laird's budget strategy, he directed DoD to reduce outlays an additional $335 million. The president stipulated that $75 million of the reduction include "an accelerated phase out of marginal naval forces," and he placed restrictions on the development of the B–1 bomber and a third *Nimitz*-class nuclear carrier (CVAN 70). Before committing funds to the B–1, the president wanted DPRC to verify that the aircraft design best fulfilled the requirement for a new strategic bomber. For the Navy, Nixon agreed to include funds for the long lead-time components of the nuclear carrier on condition that none of the funds would be committed or expended until the Senate and NSC completed their studies on the carrier. On 29 December Packard informed Nixon that he would slash the $72.5 billion figure by $375 million to a total of $72.13 billion.[33]

The directive to reduce naval forces by $75 million upset Packard. On 30 December he warned Kissinger that DoD needed leeway to meet this requirement or else it would be "in a hell of a mess." Packard believed the new requirement would force the department to cut 63 more ships when the Navy was already scheduled to lose 36 ships and an air wing in FY 1971, with about 44,000 people leaving the service. The deputy secretary could reduce the Navy's budget by $75 million by making cuts elsewhere and including some of the ships already earmarked for elimination, thereby limiting further cuts to another 13–15 ships. Kissinger thought Packard's proposal was reasonable.[34]

Nixon, however, insisted on more cuts. According to Kissinger, the president sought an additional reduction in DoD civilian personnel for political reasons, not solely to save money. Nixon wanted to demonstrate that he had reduced the size of the government in 1970 by cutting the civilian workforce. Laird was on the golf course on 30 December when Kissinger relayed to him the president's endorsement of the BoB proposal to cut another 30,000 DoD civilians from the payroll. Taken aback, Laird reminded Kissinger that the department had already programmed a reduction of 130,000 civilians; this latest cut would force the closing of 10 additional bases and a couple of shipyards. With one day left in 1970 to meet the president's arbitrary deadline, Laird had virtually no time to figure out how to make additional reductions.[35]

Instead of trying to hastily prepare a new list of positions to cut, Laird, Packard, and DoD Comptroller Robert Moot compiled overnight a summary of previous civilian personnel cuts, illustrating the consequences of past and pending workforce reductions, and sent it to Kissinger on 31 December. Between 30 June 1969 and 30 June 1971, Laird pointed out, DoD would eliminate 127,000 full-time permanent civilians. Cutting an additional 30,000 civilians would prove costly and impractical, compelling the department to replace civil servants with contractors to meet already validated work requirements. Between the end of FY 1968 and the end of FY 1971, the secretary noted, BoB wanted to eliminate 80,000 civilians from the DoD payroll, lowering full-time permanent employment to 1.086 million. Laird believed that BoB's proposal was not supported by an analysis of DoD's workload or personnel requirements. Confronted with Laird's strong and cogent objections, Nixon decided against additional civilian cuts.[36]

Yet the president was still looking to extract more funds from the DoD budget, so Packard, Haig, and Kissinger met in mid-January 1970 to find another $500 million–$600 million in reductions. Packard hoped they would be able to limit the reductions to $200 million–$300 million. Seeing the danger in further reductions, Kissinger supported Packard. By eliminating $500 million, Kissinger warned the president, "You could easily find yourself in a situation two to three years from now where you just don't have the forces for an emergency." Kissinger believed that Wheeler would not support a reduction of $500 million, because it could jeopardize the nation's security.[37]

Aware of the difficulty in pulling $500 million more out of the DoD budget, Nixon still continued to push for that amount. Laird held firm, considering any amount beyond $300 million too excessive and warned that he would have to slow down the Poseidon submarine conversions and stretch out the deployment of Safeguard missiles to meet the president's goal. In the end his pleas were in vain. Nixon's quest for a balanced budget without a tax increase forced Laird to accede at a 15 January 1970 cabinet meeting to pruning $500 million from the FY 1971 expenditure level of $72.5 billion.[38]

The cumulative budget cuts from November 1969 ($74.7 billion in outlays) to January 1970 ($72 billion in outlays) would lead to large personnel reductions. In

FY 1970 and FY 1971, the armed forces would shrink by 551,000; the civilian work-force, by about 130,000; and employment in defense-related industries, by some 640,000. The total reduction came to more than 1.3 million personnel, representing about 1.6 percent of the American labor force.[39]

On 2 February Nixon presented his FY 1971 budget to Congress, describing it as an anti-inflationary one that met his pledge to produce a balanced budget. The president stressed that he cut estimated outlays more than $5.8 billion compared with FY 1970. With estimated revenues at $202.1 billion and outlays at $200.8 billion, he claimed a budget surplus of $1.3 billion. Nixon boasted that his budget was the first in two decades to spend more on education, health, income security, and veterans benefits, that is, human resources (41 percent of outlays), than on defense (37 percent of outlays). The chief executive had good reason to urge Congress to exercise fiscal restraint during FY 1971 to keep inflation in check and the budget in balance.[40] His revenue estimates assumed that the economy would exhibit healthy growth. If the economy stalled, revenues could fall $1 billion below estimates, according to BoB calculations.[41]

Despite reductions in defense spending, Nixon expressed confidence that the United States would remain strong enough to deter aggressors. He contended that his administration could devote less to national defense for a number of reasons. His efforts to negotiate an end to the Vietnam War and withdraw U.S. forces would reduce costs. The start of strategic arms limitation talks (SALT) with the Soviets could possibly result in an agreement allowing reductions in strategic weapons. Renunciation of biological weapons and initiatives to dispose of them could also lead to savings. The Nixon Doctrine, which declared that the United States would no longer fight limited wars on behalf of its allies, anticipated that these nations would assume more responsibility for their own defense, thus allowing the United States to meet its own security needs with fewer resources.[42]

The FY 1971 DoD budget submitted to Congress in February 1970 set outlays at $71.79 billion, total obligational authority at $72.94 billion, and new obligational authority at $71.25 billion.[43] Table 10 lists the budget submission by category.[44] The planned number of direct-hire civilians at the end of FY 1971 stood at 1.103 million.[45]

Table 10. DoD Budget Estimate, FY 1971 ($ millions)

Military Personnel (Active & Reserve)	21,033
Retired Pay	3,194
O&M	19,512
Procurement	18,649
RDT&E	7,346
Combat Readiness, SVN Forces	300
Special Foreign Currency Program	8
Military Construction	1,424
Family Housing	737
Civil Defense	74
Military Assistance	664
TOA	$72,941
Financing Adjustments	(1,690)
NOA	$71,251
Total Outlays	$71,791

Source: HCA, *Department of Defense Appropriations for 1971: Hearings*, 91st Cong., 2nd sess., 25 February 1970, 298.

Table 11. Estimated Active-Duty Military Personnel for End of FY 1971

Army	1,240,000
Navy	644,000
Marine Corps	241,000
Air Force	783,000
Total	2,908,000

Source: SCAS, *Military Authorizations and Defense Appropriations for Fiscal Year 1971: Hearings*, 91st Cong., 2nd sess., 20 February 1970, 57.

Table 12. Ready and Standby Reserves

Army	2,005,000
Navy	402,000
Marine Corps	308,000
Air Force	409,000
Total	3,124,000

Source: SCAS, *Military Authorizations and Defense Appropriations for Fiscal Year 1971: Hearings*, 91st Cong., 2nd sess., 20 February 1970, 94–95.

Laird Testifies

The president's budget cuts failed to assuage Senate Democrats critical of military spending. In addition to reductions, they wanted to reorder national priorities: more funds for anticrime, antipoverty, and environmental programs. Not surprisingly, Senator William Proxmire, a longtime critic of DoD spending, found Nixon's cuts insufficient. In a further sign of the changing political tide, even a longtime Pentagon ally and supporter of DoD programs, Senator Scoop Jackson, wanted more funds for environmental programs.[46]

Amid growing congressional and public opposition to the Vietnam War and a steady drumbeat for austerity in defense spending, Laird testified before the Senate Armed Services Committee authorization hearings in February 1970. His budget presentation incorporated Nixon's views for achieving lasting peace through partnership with allies, a strong defense, and a willingness to negotiate.[47] He presented the FY 1971 budget as transitional, "designed to move the Nation's defenses in a safe and orderly way from the national security policies of the 1960's to those deemed more appropriate to the 1970's," a shift from an era of war and confrontation to one of negotiation. Nixon's review had pared the FY 1971 submission to "a rock bottom budget," according to Laird.[48] He estimated that the incremental costs of Vietnam would fall more than $4 billion from FY 1970 to FY 1971, owing mostly to lower personnel and operations and maintenance expenses. Laird expected that further reductions in deployments and combat would be feasible, but he warned that slowing down troop withdrawals would increase the cost of the war and render estimates about DoD spending unreliable.[49]

Laird's testimony was a balancing act. On the one hand, he asserted that the president's budget provided sufficient resources to allow the armed forces to cope with a full range of threats from nuclear war to limited conflicts and preserve the U.S. strategic position, even in the absence of progress at the strategic arms limitation talks with the Soviets. On the other hand, he argued that the international situation remained too dangerous to risk additional cuts to Nixon's budget submission. Laird noted with dismay that the Soviet Union had not reduced its defense budget, was rapidly deploying strategic offensive weapons, and continued to upgrade many of its missiles with multiple warheads and larger payloads. Should SALT break down, in the secretary's judgment, it was imperative to continue work on the ABM program without interruption or delay. He cited other reasons for concern. The Warsaw Pact could assemble a 1.3-million-man force in NATO's central region, and the Soviet submarine fleet continued to expand. Laird argued for keeping R&D spending at a reasonable rate in light of a stronger USSR seeking a global military presence and the emergence of Communist China as a nuclear power. The secretary emphasized that he had already reduced spending from the Johnson administration's original figure of $81.6 billion by $4.6 billion in FY 1970 and now by an additional $5.2 billion for FY 1971.[50]

To Laird, the president's budget manifested a change in national priorities because it allocated less of the nation's economic resources to defense. Estimated FY 1971 outlays ($71.8 billion) represented 7 percent of GNP and 34.6 percent of the federal budget—the lowest percentages since 1950, when the corresponding figures came in at 4.5 percent and 27.7 percent respectively. Spending levels were higher even for the last pre-Vietnam War budget (FY 1964), when expenditures came to 8.3 percent of GNP and 41.8 percent of the entire federal budget. Actual FY 1964 outlays amounted to $50.8 billion. Estimated FY 1971 outlays came to $54.6 billion in 1964 dollars. Defense spending, Laird concluded, had increased relatively little in real terms. For FY 1971 Laird had to fund a war and run DoD with a budget smaller relative to GNP than the last peacetime budget.[51]

Alluding to McNamara's practice of sometimes ignoring JCS views, Georgia Senator Richard Russell questioned Laird on the role of the JCS: What programs did they want and what role did they play in shaping the budget? Russell feared that Laird or a representative would dictate to the Chiefs what the secretary wanted, and the Senate would not "even know what the Joint Chiefs want to emphasize or what they want to give first priority to." Alleging that the "Joint Chiefs can't make any independent recommendations," Russell wanted to hear JCS views so he could compare their priorities and the secretary's when examining the budget. Laird denied imposing his views on the JCS and asked Wheeler to tell the committee of their differences.[52] Some did seem significant. The Chiefs wanted full-scale development and deployment of the B-1 bomber; Laird favored only a limited engineering development ($100 million). The JCS wanted to continue the current program for producing and procuring the C–5A; Laird reduced the FY 1970 purchase and decided to end further procurement. Laird also cut the procurement estimates of the services: the Army, by $676 million; the Navy, by $857 million; the Marine Corps, by $283 million; and the Air Force, by $679 million.[53]

The secretary also had to fend off skeptical Republican senators who, like their Democrat counterparts, were inclined to reduce the budget. Senator Margaret Chase Smith of Maine thought Laird's budget request should be smaller in light of the administration's less ambitious security strategy of preparing to fight one war and one contingency. Laird countered that the current budget was designed to finance the new strategy; an additional $20 billion would be required to carry out the 2½-war strategy.[54] Senator Edward W. Brooke III (R–MA) believed that the budget should shrink because of ongoing SALT negotiations and Nixon's policy of detente. Laird asserted that his department needed the funds should negotiations or détente fail.[55]

House Hearings

Laird faced another interrogation in the House. He first appeared before Chairman George Mahon's House Appropriations Subcommittee from 25 to 27 February 1970, and then for several days in March and April before the House Armed Services Committee chaired by Mendel Rivers. Laird tried to persuade members of both committees that the administration had already cut its submission to the bone, but Rivers pressed the secretary to identify what programs might be eliminated because of the tight budget. Laird cited the F–111 and the third nuclear aircraft carrier. The development of the F–111, still being studied for structural problems by a scientific review board, had reached a critical point: Laird would have to decide whether to complete the fourth wing. Like the C–5A's, the F–111's costs outstripped the original estimates. Even if he decided to staff fewer than four wings of the aircraft, the Air Force would still need those funds.[56] Should Congress authorize and appropriate additional money, Laird assured Rivers, he would spend $435 million on shipbuilding, $200 million on R&D, $30 million on tank modernization, and $144 million on Air Force aircraft modernization.[57]

Laird noted that he would not proceed with a third nuclear carrier (CVAN 70), until Congress and the White House completed their reviews. Nevertheless, "to avoid delays should the carrier be approved," he wanted Congress to support a line item of $152 million in advance procurement funds for CVAN 70, as requested by the Navy to keep open the *Nimitz*-class nuclear component production lines building two other nuclear carriers (CVAN 68 and CVAN 69). Congress had authorized and funded these carriers under construction on a multiyear contract.

The costs, budgeted at $536 million (CVAN 68) and $510 million (CVAN 69), were expected to rise. If Congress approved the FY 1971 budget request for CVAN 70 and funded the carrier in FY 1972, it could be completed in 1977 at a final cost of around $640 million.[58] In the meantime, Laird intended "to make an all-out fight for every dollar in this bill."[59]

Laird and Wheeler also addressed the maritime requirements for moving equipment and supplies. The JCS wanted 30 fast deployment logistics ships. Laird had decided on 15, but he did not include funds for them in the FY 1971 budget because Congress in the past had shown reluctance to fund these ships. Moreover, he had an alternative in mind. The secretary viewed privately built cargo ships on charter, a plan previously approved by Packard, as a viable substitute for the FDL ships to fulfill the requirement for rapid sealift deployment. Procurement of the C–5A cargo plane would provide airlift capability of troops and equipment.[60]

Much of the secretary's testimony concentrated on strategic mobility, specifically the C–5A cargo plane, a huge and expensive program whose development had encountered serious delays, escalating costs, and problems with the wing, avionics, and airframe. In his judgment and that of the JCS, the jumbo cargo plane was necessary to transport large and bulky equipment such as tanks, helicopters, and artillery. For FY 1970, the C–5A purchase program was reduced from 33 to 23 planes. These 23 along with the 58 on order would provide a four-squadron force. In effect, Laird confirmed the 16 January 1969 decision of his predecessor, Clark Clifford, who in exercising the contract option with Lockheed, decided to purchase only an additional 23 C–5As. Clifford reserved the government's right to decide later whether it would authorize expenditures for the fifth and sixth squadrons. Laird thought 4 C–5A squadrons, along with 14 squadrons of C–141s on hand and the 450 four-engine jets in the Civil Reserve Air Fleet (CRAF), would meet inter-theater airlift requirements. He set aside $200 million to cover contingencies. Wheeler testified that the JCS wanted to buy a total of 120 C–5As (the entire current program), but Laird contended that spending on the cargo planes would inevitably mean cuts elsewhere.[61]

The C–5A program exemplified the problems encountered in developing weapon systems and the powerful effect of a single system on the DoD budget. Lockheed Aircraft Corporation, ranked first among defense contractors in FY 1969, built the C–5A and other aircraft, ships, missiles, and helicopters for DoD.[62] The

Air Force and OSD paid close attention when the firm disclosed in March 1970 its difficulty in fulfilling the contractual terms of developing and producing critical weapon systems, not only the C–5A contracted in October 1965, but also the short-range attack missile, or SRAM, contracted in November 1966 and the Cheyenne helicopter contracted in March 1966.

Lockheed's problems in developing and building the C–5A were widely known before Laird took office. The Lockheed contract was the first awarded under the Total Package Procurement (TPP) concept, a single contract with a fixed price and performance guarantees for the life of the project. TPP encompassed the aircraft, training equipment, ground equipment, and aircraft spares for testing. Under a fixed-price incentive contract, Lockheed originally agreed in 1965 to build 115 C–5A aircraft at a cost of more than $1.9 billion. By July 1969 the estimated cost had grown to $3.2 billion, causing the Air Force to worry about the firm's ability to meet delivery schedules.[63]

In February 1970 Lockheed asked the Air Force for permission to slow the monthly production rate, citing the need to strengthen the aircraft's wings. Cracks in the wings had caused a temporary grounding of the aircraft and made necessary a redesign of the production process. Troubles with avionics and the airframe contributed to delays and increased costs. Lockheed needed an additional $435 million to $500 million more than the contract specified to cover the cost of building 81 C–5As in 1971 and 1972.[64]

In the midst of the March congressional hearings, Lockheed asked for financial help. In a letter to Packard on 2 March 1970, Lockheed chairman D. J. Haughton detailed the firm's financial plight. (Laird provided this letter to Congress.) The company could not afford to continue work on a number of large defense contracts—C–5A, shipbuilding, AH–56A (Cheyenne), and SRAM—unless it received additional funds from DoD immediately. Lockheed asserted that so much money was in dispute that it could not afford to comply with the contracts, especially if it had to await resolution of the issues under litigation before receiving further funds. Lockheed attributed its financial plight in part to the total package procurement procedure of the mid-1960s, acknowledging retrospectively that it erred in competing under a flawed system: "We believe that the hindsight of today shows us that the procurement procedure utilized for these programs was imprudent and adverse to our respective interests."[65]

The Pentagon could ill afford to ignore a plea from a company as large and important to weapon systems programs as Lockheed. Stopping C–5A production would produce a widespread adverse economic reaction that could put nearly 20,000 employees out of work at Lockheed plants in Tennessee, Pennsylvania, Ohio, South Carolina, and West Virginia, and affect an estimated 20,000 subcontractor jobs in 42 states. Over 2,300 firms provided parts and supplies for the aircraft. General Electric Corporation, the prime contractor for building the engines, employed 6,500 people for this purpose.[66] Given the importance of the aircraft for strategic airlift and the large number of jobs that would be lost in many states, it seemed unlikely that Congress would risk incurring the political fallout from cancelling the C–5A.

Packard testified before the House Armed Services Committee in early March on Lockheed's plight. The latest Air Force estimate put the cost of the C–5A at $3.164 billion for 81 aircraft and Lockheed's estimated losses at more than $640 million. Packard saw two solutions: either cancel the program and absorb outstanding costs, or restructure the contract so that the government obtained the 81 aircraft that the Air Force deemed necessary.[67]

The C–5A program would continue because it was too big and too essential. Packard renegotiated the contract, and on 9 August 1971 the president signed legislation approving a $250-million loan guarantee for Lockheed, enabling it to ward off bankruptcy.[68] The House FY 1971 appropriations bill included $544.4 million for the C–5A, including $200 million as a contingency for use when the contract issues with Lockheed were resolved. The Senate Armed Services Committee approved a total of $623 million.[69] Over time, the C–5A proved much more expensive than anticipated even in 1970. The Air Force ultimately received only 77 C–5As at a total cost of $4.5 billion, or nearly $60 million per aircraft, compared with the original estimate of $2.6 billion for 115 planes at $23 million per plane. The Air Force incurred even more costs after Laird left office, spending an additional $1 billion over ten years to strengthen the plane's wings.[70]

The Army terminated a smaller but still costly Lockheed program, the Cheyenne AH–56A, in May 1969 for contract default. In its defense, Lockheed claimed that neither it nor the Defense Department appreciated the difficulties involved in starting production of the Cheyenne before solving its developmental problems. Speaking for DoD, Packard faulted Lockheed's management of the project for not resolving serious engineering problems before going ahead with production.

He hoped the recently instituted procurement procedures would help ensure that technical problems were fixed before new systems like the Cheyenne underwent engineering development. The Senate Armed Services Committee included no funds for the Army's Cheyenne.[71]

Congress Decides

Congress remained implacable about defense cuts. The only question was how much. At the end of May 1970, Laird warned Nixon to expect that Congress would reduce the defense bill by another billion dollars. Given congressional pressures, he also believed that the projections of DoD spending outlined in September 1969 in NSDM 27 would have to be scaled back.[72] Despite his close contacts with Congress, Laird had underestimated what the legislative body would do. In July 1970 the Senate Armed Services Committee cut the Pentagon's budget request by $1.3 billion. Even that reduction in authorization was insufficient for an alliance of 28 senators and 70 representatives going after $10 billion by slashing outlays for weapons and personnel and returning some troops from Europe and Korea. Moreover, big differences remained between the budget bills of the two chambers. The Senate scaled down the ABM program to four sites and reduced funds for shipbuilding. The House wanted the full ABM program of 12 sites and more money for ship construction.[73]

The White House was upset with congressional handling of the budget. In February 1970 Nixon had submitted a budget with an estimated surplus, but in July he feared that Congress would enact one with a deficit. In his view, Congress increased expenditures for nondefense programs but was reluctant to provide additional revenue to cover interest on the national debt, extra spending for public assistance, and pay raises for federal employees. Furthermore, Congress seemed in no hurry to pass a DoD appropriations bill. The legislature would take up 13 other appropriation bills before the House acted on the DoD bill after the November elections, forcing the Defense Department to go through much of FY 1971 without an approved budget.[74]

Uncertainty about the size and actual date of passage of the FY 1971 budget made it more difficult to manage defense spending. DoD Comptroller Moot warned that even if the department received all requested funds it still faced a potential shortfall of $3 billion stemming from war-related costs—the Army's withdrawal plan, a pay raise, the current bombing sortie rate, improvements for the South Vietnamese Air Force, and economic assistance to South Vietnam. The only way to make up the shortfall, according to Moot, was to cut back on procurement or operations in Southeast Asia. Reducing procurement would mean stretching out major programs.[75]

Under siege from congressional critics, Laird also had to contend with opposition from the Office of Management and Budget. Deputy Director James Schlesinger, a firm advocate of a balanced budget, disagreed with DoD's practice of heavily cutting personnel instead of tactical aircraft and expensive weapon systems. Laird saw no other way. Given the unrelenting pressure to cut quickly, Laird contended that "manpower is the place where you save dollars the fastest."[76] OMB Director George Shultz complained in October that Laird had not suggested specific additional savings, a charge that drew an angry response from the secretary, who was "both shocked and disappointed" by the director's apparent unawareness that since Nixon took office DoD had made "massive cuts." Laird contended that the "rock-bottom, bare-bones" budget had to be increased to help the president gain his overall objectives. He informed Shultz that he would make a strong reclama to the Senate regarding the additional reductions made by the House: "We are going to do everything we can to restore most of these cuts."[77]

Laird was so upset that he complained to Kissinger and sent him a copy of his reply to Shultz. In a phone conversation Laird told the national security adviser that "I hope you won't think it sounds like a snide reply but I can't reduce anymore." The White House and OMB were "trying to make me into a Louie Johnson," a reference to President Truman's Secretary of Defense who slashed the DoD budget shortly before the outbreak of the Korean War in 1950. "I won't cut unless I am ordered to do it." Kissinger agreed with Laird: The Defense budget should go no lower.[78]

Laird did not content himself with defending his budget from cuts. He was on the hunt for more procurement and R&D funds. In September he sent Chairman Rivers of the House Armed Services Committee a request that the House cancel its reduction of defense appropriations, seeking $80 million for RDT&E. The secretary also sought restitution of $957.8 million in appropriations cuts made by the Senate, including $152 million for CVAN 70 and $352.1 million for RDT&E.[79] At the same time, Laird asked Representative Mahon to push the budget process forward, requesting that Mahon proceed with a markup of the appropriations bill as soon as possible. Mahon proved reluctant.[80]

Laird's plea for restitution went nowhere. In October the House Appropriations Committee cut $2.1 billion from the request, including $343.5 million from military personnel, citing the reduction in draft calls; $298.4 million from O&M to reduce what it viewed as overstaffing at the Pentagon; $390.9 million for research and development; and $1.11 billion for procurement. The committee added $417.5 million for shipbuilding at the request of Mendel Rivers and $58.5 million for Vietnamization. Laird planned to ask the Senate to restore some of the eliminations made by the House. Laird was swimming against the tide of public opinion. A Gallup poll claimed 49 percent of the public favored additional military decreases and 34 percent supported the size of the current outlays.[81]

In November Laird appealed to Senator Russell for restoration of more than a billion dollars of the appropriation cuts the House had made to the Defense budget and close to $355 million to cover requirements that emerged after he had submitted budget estimates in February. He requested an overall $68.2 billion from the Senate, an increase of $1.4 billion from the $66.8 billion in the House Appropriations Bill (H.R. 19590).[82] His plea went unheeded. Nine months after the president submitted his budget request, and more than four months after the start of the fiscal year, Laird had not averted deep slashes to his original "rock-bottom" request of $68.7 billion.[83] The Senate appropriation fell nearly $2.329 billion below Laird's original submission.

On 8 December 1970 Laird made another effort to obtain additional money. In identical letters to Russell and Mahon he asserted that DoD required a minimum appropriation of $67.209 billion. He sought more funds for military personnel, operations and maintenance, RDT&E, and procurement, but to no avail. The FY 1971 House DoD appropriation remained at $66.807 billion; the Senate appropriation at $66.417 billion. The conference report on H.R. 19590, approved on 16 December 1970, set NOA at $66.596 billion (see table 13, page 276), more than $6 billion below the FY 1970 appropriation and more than $2 billion less than the final FY 1971 budget estimate.[84]

In a public statement Laird declared that congressional action in reducing his rock-bottom submission of $68.7 billion by $2.1 billion to a final total of $66.6 billion would force him to slash expenditures by $800 million in the remaining six months of the fiscal year. The cuts would compel him to make additional military and civilian personnel reductions, close bases, and remove additional ships from the fleet. He especially chided Congress for its slow pace: "It has been most difficult for us to run the Defense Department in an orderly, economic manner for six months without having Congressional action on our budget."[85]

Table 13. Defense Appropriations (NOA), FY 1971 ($ millions)

Personnel	20,735
Retired Pay	3,194
O&M	19,360
Procurement	16,029
RDT&E	6,976
Combat Readiness, SVN Forces	300
Special Foreign Currency Program	2,621
Total	66,596

Source: OASD(C), "Appropriations Provided," column 10 in FAD 673, 1 June 1971, tab FY 1971, binder Fiscal Tables 1971, box 820, Subject Files, OSD Historical Office.

The administration contended not just with congressional cuts but also with legislative attempts to shut off spending in Cambodia and Laos. Nixon wanted no restrictions on U.S. funds for South Vietnamese forces operating in the two countries and sought also to provide money for Thai and Laotian defense forces.[86] The appropriation bill passed on 11 January 1971 forbade the use of funds for Vietnamese forces and other Free World forces to provide military support and assistance to the governments of Cambodia and Laos. However, the bill's language provided leeway for the president. Section 838 stated that "nothing contained in this section shall be construed to prohibit support of actions required to insure the safe and orderly withdrawal or disengagement of U.S. Forces from Southeast Asia, or to aid in the release of Americans held as prisoners of war."[87]

THE FY 1971 BUDGET OUTCOME complicated DoD's efforts to deal with its myriad money, force structure, and weapons problems. The department could not withstand the unwavering determination of the administration and Congress to cut spending and appropriations for defense. The president and legislators slashed with a seeming vengeance what Laird repeatedly called a rock-bottom, bare-bones budget. In the midst of the budget deliberations, the disclosure of Lockheed's financial plight jeopardized production of the C–5A cargo plane needed to deploy heavy equipment to a war theater. Cost overruns on several Lockheed contracts and problems in developing new weapons and equipment confirmed the suspicions of defense critics that DoD spending was not only out of control and but also producing flawed weapon systems. Spending for R&D and procurement in the

FY 1971 budget, critical to the post-Vietnam force was reduced. Military and civilian personnel strength suffered severe reductions. Yet some positive signs emerged as measures to reform procurement offered the promise of some improvement. The newly adopted 1¹/₂-war strategy of NSDM 27 offered a more realistic match of plans, capabilities, and finances than the previous strategy. The department's newly revised PPBS system gave the JCS a more meaningful role in the budget process, helping to ensure closer cooperation with the military as DoD shaped the post-Vietnam armed forces. Although Laird lost numerous appeals to reinstate congressional cuts, he did convince the White House and Congress that the DoD budget had been cut as much as prudence allowed, a significant accomplishment. For the first time since FY 1969, an appropriations budget (FY 1972) showed an increase over the previous year.[88]

CHAPTER 11

A Turning Point:
The FY 1972 Budget

IN ASSEMBLING THE 1972 Defense budget, Secretary Laird faced familiar constraints. Inflation fears, budget deficits, and fluctuating federal revenue levels complicated budget formulation and created enormous pressure to cut federal spending. The Bureau of the Budget and its successor, the Office of Management and Budget, sought to exact the lion's share of federal spending reductions from the Department of Defense whose budget contained the largest amount of discretionary spending. The steady, built-in growth of nondefense entitlement programs such as Social Security and Medicare, as well as the need to address a host of domestic problems, further intensified the calls to cut defense spending. As with previous budget fights, Laird battled on two fronts: one with a White House that wanted a strong defense structure at a lower cost and a direct role in shaping the DoD program, and the other with the Joint Chiefs of Staff who, as usual, judged defense spending as already low enough to imperil national security. Economic and political pressures had caused spending to drop significantly in FYs 1970 and 1971 from the Johnson administration highs. At the same time inflation diluted purchasing power. Looking to the future, Laird was concerned with rebuilding and reshaping U.S. armed forces at a time when the Soviet Union was pumping up its strategic and conventional military might. The secretary faced the difficult challenge of protecting outlays from additional cuts while continuing to withdraw the U.S. military from Vietnam.

The FY 1972 budget was the first to employ the full 15-month cycle of Laird's revised Planning, Programming, and Budgeting System, with its multilevel review. The secretary had two basic goals—first, to set the size and structure of the armed forces as realistically as possible within fiscal limitations; and second, to involve the JCS in the budget process to a greater degree than afforded by the previous administration. Under the altered PPBS procedures, DoD fiscal guidance would become a rough gauge of affordability and would directly impact military strategy.

Fiscal Guidance

In early December 1969 the JCS submitted volume one of the Joint Strategic Objectives Plan (JSOP), the starting point for discussions on the FY 1972 budget, to Deputy Secretary David Packard who was leading the DoD budget process. Based on intelligence estimates and NSC policy determinations, JSOP 72-79 presented the national security objectives and strategy for employing military forces under the new 1½-war strategy of National Security Decision Memorandum 27.[1] This strategy called on DoD to provide sufficient armed forces to reinforce Europe and assist NATO against an offensive, *or* to reinforce Asia for a sustained defense against aggression in Korea or Southeast Asia. In addition, U.S. armed forces were to be capable of simultaneously providing limited assistance to one nation confronting non-Soviet or non-Chinese attacks. NSDM 27 could require shifting U.S. forces in wartime from Asia to Europe.[2]

In mid-January 1970 Packard issued tentative FY 1972 fiscal guidance of $76 billion (total obligational authority). The deputy admonished the service secretaries and the JCS chairman to stay within the overall total, cautioning it would be "unrealistic to plan on higher levels of funding."[3] Packard assumed that the department could make significant reductions in general support costs, which included base support, training, headquarters, and logistics, or "we will be forced to make deeper cuts in forces." Regarding the war, Packard's guidance reduced the number of Army maneuver battalions in Vietnam from 27 at the end of FY 1971 to 15 by the end of FY 1972. For that same period, it cut the number of monthly naval tactical sorties, B–52 sorties, and Air Force tactical sorties in half and reduced overall U.S. military strength in Vietnam from 260,000 to 145,200 personnel.[4]

Packard's strategy guidance issued at the end of January 1970 was also based on NSDM 27 and took into account the Nixon Doctrine expectation that Asian allies would supply the combat forces for their own conventional defense. With the reduction in the number of U.S. overseas bases and curtailment of operating rights, the Military Assistance Program would provide technical assistance and support economic development when requested. The program would help allies expand their capabilities to meet security threats from nonnuclear powers.[5] The guidance also incorporated the Nixon administration's June 1969 policy of strategic sufficiency (NSDM 16), which emerged from the NSSM 3 review of strategic forces necessary to deter a nuclear attack on the United States.[6] With strategic sufficiency, the president hoped to provide a high degree of confidence that the Soviet Union would neither be tempted to attack the United States nor be able to prevent Washington from launching a counterattack.[7]

The JCS expressed reservations about the size of the forces specified by NSDM 27. Doubting NATO's ability to prolong a conventional defense of Europe for longer than 90 days, they questioned the feasibility of Packard's "swing" concept, under which the United States would curtail military operations in Asia and transfer forces to fight in Europe. The Chiefs tried to make the deputy secretary aware of the enormous logistical difficulties and risks in transferring units, equipment, and supplies between theaters, warning that such a transfer might tempt the Soviets, who after all were a Pacific as well as an Atlantic power, to threaten U.S. interests in the Pacific Ocean. The JCS argued for a more expansive (and expensive) strategy of defending Europe after mobilization that would allow the United States to assist allies, continue forward deployments in Europe, and move forces from Asia to Europe.[8]

The debate within DoD was about more than spending levels. Conflicting approaches to the budget centered on a perennial question: Should the basic criterion for budget formulation be a spending level affordable under current economic conditions or an amount sufficient to prepare the nation to respond to national security threats at minimal risk? For the JCS, the security threat and the nation's treaty obligations were the primary considerations in formulating a strategy and paying for it. They objected to Packard's $76 billion TOA fiscal guidance because it failed "to provide adequate funding levels for sufficient forces" to meet foreign policy commitments and handle the security threat. They wanted sufficient funding levels to allow flexibility in responding to crises and modernizing to hedge against technological obsolescence. The costs of the Vietnam War had already forced program cuts to the point where JCS Chairman Admiral Thomas Moorer felt that "other program areas can no longer absorb reductions." Additional resources were needed "to replace aging and obsolescent equipment and to round out and modernize war reserve stocks. . . . We must also provide for the procurement programs necessary to improve the readiness of Reserve forces, which were virtually stripped of equipment to meet more urgent operational needs" in Southeast Asia. Moorer offered seven program options that ranged as high as $80.5 billion.[9]

Packard upheld the guidance. In March he responded to the secretaries of the military departments, the directors of the defense agencies, and Moorer, who had argued that the strategy guidance could not "be followed within the fiscal guidance." His response was unequivocal. The fiscal guidance "must be followed, and the strategy guidance followed *to the extent possible*." Packard reaffirmed that the budget should reflect what the nation could afford; the level of spending would in turn determine national strategy and force structure.[10]

Laurence Lynn of the NSC staff in April 1970 sharply criticized Packard's decision, claiming he enforced rigid budget ceilings "regardless of their strategic implications," thereby placing responsibility for strategic risks on the president. Instead, Lynn thought DoD should seek to balance strategic and budgetary requirements within presidential guidelines. Yet the White House allowed Defense little room, because it continued to press for cuts in outlays as a way to cope with economic conditions. The president called on each federal agency in May 1970 to cut spending for FY 1972. In June BoB suggested reducing the DoD fiscal guidance by another $3 billion or more. The president's budget director advised the chief executive to keep defense expenditures no higher than $72 billion, reminding him, perhaps unnecessarily, that "*two-thirds* of all controllable outlays in the budget are Defense outlays." Nixon and Mayo emphasized cutting outlays because they wanted to make an immediate economic impact.[11]

Battling the Defense Program Review Committee

The DPRC reviewed the Defense budget on 17 July 1970, seeking to determine how much money the department needed to implement its strategic objectives. The session took place at a time of worsening economic conditions—inflation and unemployment stood higher than in the fall of 1969 when NSDM 27 was issued. The budget surplus projected then had already evaporated. Now, the DPRC had another factor to consider—a likely overall federal deficit in the range of $20 billion to $26 billion that would require cutting projected outlays. OMB Director George Shultz reminded everyone that President Nixon believed that spending curbs would help avoid the kind of "substantial deficits that we can't live with." Nixon's aversion to deficits would mean lower spending on defense. As happened before, DoD outlays became the prime target for budget cutters attempting to reach an overall federal spending level of $225 billion–$230 billion. The defense spending cutbacks, as high as $6 billion on the table, presented stark choices for the policymakers.[12]

Packard staunchly defended the DoD program he helped to develop, objecting to spending decreases that compromised DoD's ability to carry out the president's policy. He said it would be "disastrous" to cut Defense by $6 billion just to bring total federal expenditures in FY 1972 below $230 billion. Moorer criticized the notion, "if we can't afford our present strategy, we should get one we can afford," as the wrong approach. The unprecedented (in his view) Soviet buildup of strategic and general purpose forces should in some ways "determine the strategy we have to follow. . . . We are moving into a situation where the President will have no options in a confrontation with the Soviets."[13]

Packard stood firm against efforts to go to $76 billion in outlays and justified an even higher figure at the meeting. The projected FY 1972 spending ($79 billion) was the "lowest practicable figure" and was based on earlier guidance: $76 billion in outlays of NSDM 27, plus $2 billion for the All-Volunteer Force and $1 billion to cover inflation. Spending less than $79 billion, a $3 billion cut in strategic forces (one option under discussion), would reduce the size of the bomber force as well as the number of Safeguard (ABM) missile sites from 12 to 7. It would also leave less money for improving the survivability of missile sites and for air defense (interceptors and SAMs), forcing the department to rely to a greater extent on sea-launched ballistic missiles (SLBMs).

Another option, a $6 billion cut from the $79 billion expenditure level, would bring the number of Army divisions down to pre-Korean War levels and pare the number of ships to 514 from 794, seriously degrading the Navy's ability to maintain control of the seas in a confrontation with the Soviets. To Packard, the impact of such a large reduction was "just too great to be seriously considered." By reallocating funds, he thought DoD could take a maximum cut of $3 billion in strategic and general purpose forces from his desired $79 billion spending level. His preference was to cut military personnel (primarily Army) but maintain Air Force and Navy strength. Accelerating Vietnam withdrawals and reducing the number of tactical air sorties could mitigate the effect of personnel reductions.[14]

Significantly, Packard was not the only person at the DPRC meeting concerned about the effect of budget cuts. National Security Adviser Henry Kissinger viewed the DoD budget under review as insufficient to carry out national security objectives, even before the additional reductions were taken. Alexis Johnson of the State Department worried that cuts in general purpose forces would cause the administration in a crisis to rely more on the massive use of nuclear weapons at a time when the Soviets had strategic parity with the United States. Chairman of the Council of Economic Advisers Paul McCracken thought it unwise "to take all budget cuts out of defense funds."[15] McCracken's comment reflected the DPRC's awareness of the security risks in using Defense budget cuts to avoid a federal budget deficit. It was a significant meeting, during which the Pentagon seemed to be winning its case against severe spending cuts.

Nixon appreciated the gravity of the DoD position and postponed issuing a revised fiscal guidance until he could review additional information. The president had concerns about the effects of a cut on air defense and strategic bombing, tactical air capability, antisubmarine warfare, and the size of land forces in general as well as their ability to support NATO. Once he weighed the risks, he would revisit the issue of cuts at the August NSC meeting.[16]

DoD budget reductions were a given, but how much could defense spending be cut without affecting the president's commitment to an all-volunteer force? Eliminating the ABM might save the administration over $1 billion, but this move might undermine the U.S. negotiating position at SALT and an arms agreement. In July 1970 the DPRC had deemed it unwise to cut general purpose forces by as much as $5 billion, but Kissinger thought that reductions of $2.4 billion to $3 billion incurred a manageable risk. Lowering Army strength to around 830,000 would save money but raise questions about the U.S. commitment to NATO; pruning general purpose forces too much would invite exploitation of perceived U.S. weakness.[17]

The August NSC meeting focused on the difficulties of providing a credible defense force at a time of budget cutting. As Nixon stated at the session, "We want a defense policy which makes it possible for us to have a foreign policy. We need the confidence of others. We think there is some question abroad about that confidence. Budget cutting may then raise questions about our role in the world." Looking forward to the post–Vietnam War period, he added, "We must have a new concept for a national defense program—one which can be sold around the world—one which will be supported by the American people and one which does not destroy the morale of the Services." Kissinger saw practical and symbolic reasons to limit cuts in general purpose forces—they projected "credible power abroad in a situation where general nuclear war is no longer a likely or reasonable alternative."[18]

Squeezed between demands to balance the budget or to fund a strong military, Nixon made a major shift in spending. His new FY 1972 guidance (NSDM 84) lowered the NSDM 27 spending targets to $74.5 billion, but increased the spending levels for subsequent years. He affirmed his commitment to outlays of $1.3 billion for an all-volunteer force and adhered to the current funding levels for strategic programs pending the outcome of SALT. However, he wanted to spend less on air defenses and on operational uses of the strategic bombers. General purpose forces would not be spared, particularly tactical air, antisubmarine warfare, escort ships, and amphibious task forces. DoD was to maintain no fewer than 16⅓ active Army and Marine divisions, the number the JCS believed necessary to support NATO requirements and also provide a strategic reserve.[19]

Seeking flexibility, Laird petitioned Nixon to allow trade-offs to maintain 16⅓ divisions. Admiral Moorer complained to Kissinger that the president's cuts in general purpose forces fell too heavily on the Navy and Air Force and would create imbalances in the overall force structure. With fewer ships and planes, he wondered, how ground forces would get to battle. He feared arriving troops would find insufficient equipment on hand. Kissinger persuaded Nixon to revise NSDM 84 in September, providing DoD some latitude. The revised NSDM stated that the "force level reduction priorities are illustrative only" and that the president would review alternative force reduction options.[20]

The NSDM 84 spending level of $74.5 billion approximated the amount that Laird initially requested. His initial $79.1 billion budget guidance to DoD included money for inflation and the All-Volunteer Force. Administration reviews had pared that amount by $4.7 billion, according to Defense Comptroller Robert Moot's calculations, leaving Laird with around $74.4 billion in requested outlays. The NSDM 84 guideline, a little higher than Laird's request, convinced Moot that the secretary "was fighting for the maximum amount that we could justify for FY 1972." Moot took a sanguine view of NSDM 84 because it did not require sharp DoD cuts.[21]

Laird resisted additional spending cuts beyond NSDM 84. He responded testily to OMB Director Shultz's charge that DoD had failed to heed the president's request to identify savings. He told Shultz that OMB failed to realize that the defense program was already cut "to the bone." "As to the Fiscal 1972 budget," Laird continued, "we are working day and night trying to squeeze our minimal requirements from current estimated outlays of $77.4 billion into the $74.5 billion fiscal guidance we were given in NSDM 84. . . . All the scrubbing in the world of so-called ineffective or low priority programs will not result in a net decrease without jeopardizing national security." The secretary warned that additional cuts were also likely to put more people out of work. In the past two years alone reductions had added around two million people—military, civilians, and workers in defense-related industries—to the unemployment rolls.[22]

Packard, Moorer, Moot, Assistant Secretary of Defense for Systems Analysis Gardiner Tucker, and other Pentagon officials worked hard to resolve the $2.9 billion expenditures gap between the $77.4 billion budget submissions of the military services and NSDM 84 guidance of $74.5 billion. Spending for Vietnam had deferred the procurement of new weapons; thus the armed services had included funds for weapons and equipment needed by the postwar military. The Air Force requested money for the B–1 bomber, the F–15 fighter, and the Airborne Warning and Control System (AWACS). The Navy wanted funds to build 30 modern destroyers, a fourth nuclear-powered carrier, and nuclear-powered submarines armed with the Undersea Long-Range Missile System (ULMS). The Army hoped to keep alive the Cheyenne attack helicopter and continue to develop the MBT–70 tank (even though the Germans withdrew their support in 1969 and the project was over budget). Started in the 1960s as a joint U.S.-German endeavor, the MBT–70 was designed to be more advanced than Soviet tanks and compensate for the Warsaw Pact's numerical superiority in armor.[23] Moot thought that Congress might reduce the gap in expenditures by as much as $1 billion, and the department would save about a half-billion by holding down ABM outlays. The comptroller estimated that the department would need to identify a total of about $1.5 billion in additional expenditure cuts in the military services.[24]

For the November 1970 DPRC session, Laird decided that Packard should stand firm on expenditures, leave NATO commitments unchanged, and keep planned Vietnam redeployments from Vietnam on schedule. In papers prepared for the meeting, DoD sought more than $77 billion, a large increase over the $74.5 billion in NSDM 84.[25] A skeptical and unswayed OMB analyst thought Laird was just making a tactical move to protect the department's $74.5 billion budget request from additional cuts. The budget office thought it made little sense on economic

The MBT–70 tank began as a joint U.S.-German project in the 1960s. The U.S. Army fought to keep the program alive after the Germans ended their support, undated. (NARA)

grounds to increase defense spending while the nation was transitioning from wartime to a peacetime economy.[26]

When the DPRC convened on 9 November, Kissinger anticipated that the committee would be able to assess alternate force packages that could accommodate the president's guidance. He believed additional analyses of different force mixes and deployments could help evaluate the trade-offs between deployments and readiness on the one hand and the existing force structure and modernization on the other. But Kissinger was thwarted. The Pentagon submitted a single revised program of strategic and general purpose forces that complied with the NSDM 84 target of $74.5 billion but offered no alternatives. As he had in the past, Kissinger wanted the DPRC to help shape the spending program, but the committee could not do so without having alternate force packages to examine. Packard defended DoD's submission at length, insisting that he could make no further reductions in forces beyond the serious cuts already made. Packard's stance stymied Kissinger. Without the comparative force packages, he had less influence on shaping the program. Afterward, Moorer termed the meeting "non-productive." The session perhaps was nonproductive in that no spending figure was decided upon, but it was significant because DoD went on record as insisting that NSDM 84 failed to provide an acceptable level of national security. The session also signaled again that Laird and Packard were not about to cede control over the defense program to the DPRC.[27]

After the November meeting Packard continued to press Kissinger for FY 1972 spending levels of at least $75.7 billion. To maintain current levels of readiness and pay for modernization, he sought specifically an additional $600 million in outlays. To increase aid to allies through the military assistance program, Military Assistance Service Funded, and credit sales, DoD sought another $800 million. Packard insisted that the program presented at the DPRC meeting prescribed "the minimum acceptable for national security." Wayne Smith of the NSC advised Kissinger to ignore Packard's request because he offered no convincing justification for even a $75.7 billion program and no persuasive rationale to justify this spending level to the Congress and to the public. Smith did not take Packard's proposal seriously, dismissing it as a political move to convince the JCS that he was still trying to get them more money. In the immediate aftermath of the November DPRC meeting, the administration's FY 1972 defense program remained a matter of contention between the NSC staff and DoD.[28]

The Pentagon's resistance to spending reductions paid off. Later in November the president changed his position, expressing a willingness to increase expenditures. He regarded the recent Soviet buildup in the Middle East (see chapter 17), its military construction at Cienfuegos, Cuba, and its actions at the strategic arms talks as inconsistent with the pursuit of détente. Nixon was firmly convinced that effective U.S. military strength was required to influence Soviet decision making. At the 23 November OSD staff meeting, Moorer reported that Shultz was now receptive to the DoD position. At the same session Moot hinted that he expected to get more funds than the fiscal guidance had allocated when he met with OMB officials. At the end of November, Kissinger privately suggested to Moorer that Nixon might even consider a level of more than $79 billion, "provided he is given a clear concept of just what we would buy and how such increases would affect his policy options."[29] Kissinger discussed a smaller increase in a 14 December phone conversation with Laird, informing the secretary that the president wanted "to start loosening the strings a bit on the Defense budget" and was willing to push spending as high as $77 billion. He suggested that Laird prepare three separate spending requests for $75 billion, $76 billion, and $77 billion.[30]

Laird quickly took advantage of the new opportunity to boost the budget. On 18 December he told Moorer that he would submit to the president alternative spending packages requesting the addition of between $500 million and $2 billion to the FY 1972 budget. Moorer advocated the highest amount asserting it would give the president the most flexibility in exercising his options, and Congress would in any event trim the president's request. Laird decided on a lesser increase, believing that the $2 billion request would not receive serious consideration. He asked the president to raise the fiscal guidance and budget request to a total of $76 billion in outlays.[31]

After the DoD and OMB staffs had jointly reviewed the FY 1972 budget, Laird sent Kissinger on 23 December two spending alternatives of $76 billion and $75.5 billion. The higher alternative requested $1.5 billion in additional outlays for the war, readiness, and modernization; the smaller, $1 billion. Neither alternative included money for MAP or cost of living increases for military retirees. Laird renewed his recommendation for a $76 billion budget request (outlays) and flatly ruled out as "not acceptable" the decreases proposed by OMB. He wanted the new money (outlays) to go first for readiness and then for modernization. He also submitted to Kissinger a list of additional force readiness enhancements to meet the preparedness level recommended by the JCS. With understandable satisfaction, the secretary remarked to his staff this was the first time in 25 years that the comptroller could report at this stage of the budget preparation that the numbers were going up instead of down. Laird's and Packard's resistance paid off.[32]

Nixon's 29 January 1971 budget message to Congress laid out a FY 1972 DoD spending program that was higher than the previous fiscal year. Nonetheless, defense outlays would constitute a smaller percentage of total federal spending in FY 1972 (34 percent) than in FY 1971 (36 percent). The president asked Congress for $77.5 billion in defense expenditures. When the money for atomic energy, defense-related activities, and deductions for offsetting receipts was subtracted, requested defense outlays came to $76 billion. To justify the higher outlays, Nixon identified the need to improve readiness and support for NATO. The rising costs of U.S. military equipment and personnel during a period of inflation meant that earlier levels of defense expenditure could no longer match Soviet outlays on powerful nuclear and conventional forces. Nixon's request for higher defense spending seemed remarkable in view of his adoption of "a 'full employment' budget in which spending does not exceed the revenues the economy could generate under the existing tax system at the time of full employment," and his new proposal to establish a formula for sharing federal revenues with states and local communities. Revenue sharing would reduce the dollars for Washington to spend; the full employment budget policy announced in July 1970 had set a cap on federal spending.[33]

Compared with FY 1971, the FY 1972 budget asked for $1.8 billion (TOA) less in FY 1972 for military personnel, but increased retired pay by $357 million, in part to cover cost-of-living increases. Although overall military strength and civilian personnel would fall by the end of the fiscal year, the budget included more than $1.5 billion in additional TOA for a military and civilian pay increase. Personnel cuts would help offset the mounting costs for the military and civilian payrolls, retirement benefits, and the transition to an all-volunteer force. The administration sought more than $1.7 billion over FY 1971 in additional TOA for procurement of new ships, naval aircraft, Air Force missiles, and enhancements for Army readiness as well as an increase of $779 million for research, development, and test and evaluation in FY 1972. Overall, FY 1972 TOA totaled $79.2 billion; NOA came to $78.7 billion.[34] The hikes in the funds requested for procurement and RDT&E would help serve Laird's efforts in shaping the post-Vietnam force.

Tables 14 and 15 present the president's FY 1972 NOA and outlays requests.

Table 14. President's DoD Budget Request (NOA), FY 1972 ($ millions)

Military Personnel	20,164
Retired Military	3,744
O&M	20,270
Procurement	19,570
RDT&E	7,888
Military Construction	1,479
Allowances	4,548
Subtotal	77,663
Military Assistance	1,080
Total	78,743

Source: OASD(C), Table 11 accompanying DoD News Release 72-71, 29 January 1971, binder Fiscal Tables 1972, box 820, Subject Files, OSD Historical Office.

Table 15. President's DoD Budget Request (Outlays), FY 1972 ($ millions)

Military Personnel	20,105
Retired Military	3,744
O&M	20,234
Procurement	17,936
RDT&E	7,504
Military Construction	2,019
Allowances	3,580
Military Assistance	1,025
Subtotal	76,147
Offsetting receipts	(147)
Total	76,000

Source: Executive Office of the President, Office of Management and Budget, *The U.S. Budget in Brief, Fiscal Year 1972* (Washington, DC: Government Printing Office, 1971), 30.

Laird Confronts Congress

The secretary's initial congressional testimony on the FY 1972 budget on 4–5 March 1971 before the Department of Defense subcommittee of the House Appropriations Committee was reprised ten days later for the Senate Armed Services Committee. Laird's formal statement laid out the rationale of the Nixon administration's first Five-Year Defense Program based on a so-called strategy of realistic deterrence. The strategy sought to prevent conventional and nuclear war through a combination of national strength, partnership with allies, and negotiations. Laird termed the strategy realistic because it took into account "the multiple threats to peace" and was based on U.S. and allied military capabilities as well as fiscal and political realities. The way he looked at it, the strategy took "a prudent middle course between two policy extremes—world policeman or new isolationism." Modified DoD management practices that fostered decentralization in procurement, and new acquisition policies that called for testing equipment before purchasing it, would ultimately yield savings. Defense expenditures were now lower than federal expenditures on nondefense programs, a historic shift as Laird pointed out. To provide for its security in a period of tightened defense spending, the United States would call on its allies to a greater extent and would utilize military assistance during the 1970s more than it had in the past. Realistic deterrence represented a strategy that necessarily glossed over the shrinkage in the budget.[35]

Laird presented the FY 1972 budget in the context of a shift from a wartime footing to an era of meaningful negotiation. He alluded to the decreasing number of American combatants, casualties, and combat sorties in Southeast Asia and the transition to a post-Vietnam military. As part of the passage, Laird highlighted a new entry in the financial summary—over $1 billion for the All-Volunteer Force.[36]

The secretary was not only working toward an AVF and an end to the draft but also planning for greater reliance on the combat and combat support units of the reserve components and the National Guard. Utilizing these forces would help compensate for rising personnel costs. In August 1970 Laird directed the service secretaries to provide in the FY 1972 and future budgets "the necessary resources to permit the appropriate balance in the development of Active, Guard and Reserve Forces." He looked for the most advantageous mix of components of what he called the "total force," so that guard and reserve units would be "prepared to be the initial and primary source" for augmenting active forces in any future contingency requiring rapid and substantial mobilization. The new policy would allow a larger total force for a given budget or the same size force for a smaller budget since guard and reserve units incurred lower costs in peacetime than active units did.[37]

Table 16 summarizes the president's FY 1972 budget request by component. The rounded total would be $76 billion.

Table 16. President's DoD Budget Request, FY 1972 ($ millions)

Component	Outlays
Army	21,025
Navy	21,275
Air Force	22,855
Defense Agencies	1,597
Defense Wide	4,564
Civil Defense	77
Pay Increase	2,430
Volunteer Armed Force	1,150
Military Assistance	1,025
Total	75,998

Source: OASD(C), Table 11 accompanying DoD News Release 72-71, 29 January 1971, binder Fiscal Tables 1972, box 820, Subject Files, OSD Historical Office.

The FY 1972 budget request reduced general purpose forces and equipment from FY 1971 levels. There were fewer Navy carriers and ships and fewer Air Force squadrons. The Army would drop to 13⅓ divisions at the end of FY 1972, a loss of three divisions from FY 1971. However, the number of Marine Corps divisions and aircraft wings remained unchanged at three each respectively and are omitted from Table 17.

Table 17. General Purpose Forces

	End FY 1971	End FY 1972
Army Divisions	13.6	13.3
Carriers	18	16
Carrier Air Wings	16	15
Air Force Tactical Squadrons	112	105
Airlift Squadrons	45	38
Commissioned Ships	710	658
Fixed-Wing Aircraft	20,724	19,850
Helicopters	11,542	11,229

Source: Chart 4 accompanying DoD News Release 72-71, 29 January 1971, binder Fiscal Tables 1972, box 820, Subject Files, OSD Historical Office.

The cost of developing and buying new weapon systems received much attention during the hearings. The president requested more than $17.9 billion in outlays for procurement and $7.5 billion for RDT&E. Critics in Congress alleged that DoD was funding duplicative and unnecessary weapon systems. Representative Robert L. Sikes (D–FL), a longtime influential member of the House Appropriations Committee, questioned the wisdom of developing two separate jet fighter aircraft—the F–14 for the Navy and the F–15 for the Air Force—with similar characteristics. The F–14, a two-man, swing-wing fighter, was designed to operate from aircraft carriers or austere airfields. The Navy wanted to purchase about 700 F–14s at an estimated cost of $11.5 million per aircraft. The F–15 was a fixed-wing aircraft designed to replace the F–4E as the fighter plane for the 1975–1985 period. The Air Force sought some 700 F–15s, at a price of about $10 million each. The new planes cost three to four times more than the different versions of the F–4 that the Navy, Marine Corps, and Air Force utilized. DoD never made a comparative study of the two new planes, Sikes alleged, and the committee's own investigation had not established the superiority of either plane over the other. Sikes complained that the expense of building two different planes with similar performance capabilities would exceed $15 billion. The high price would restrict the number purchased, given the economic and political pressure to cut spending. Why not, he asked Laird, begin work on an even more advanced aircraft superior to the F–14 and the F–15? Sikes wondered, with the F–15 unable to meet the mission requirements of the F–14 and lagging about 1.5 years behind it in development, why not build only the F–14, as it represented a major increase in capability over the existing F–4?[38]

Over this discussion hovered memories of the costly experience of the TFX (or F–111 fighter-bomber), the abortive attempt by Secretary Robert McNamara to force the Air Force and the Navy, services with different operational requirements, to develop jointly and buy the same basic plane. The original total cost for 1,726 planes was $4.8 billion. When the F–111 went into production, the Navy found it unsuitable, and Congress appropriated no funds for the Navy version. The Air Force purchased approximately 500 planes at a cost of $7.6 billion. The Air Force found the plane too small as a bomber and too big as a fighter. It made only limited use of the aircraft in Vietnam and frequently grounded the planes. The TFX proved to

Laird frequently consulted with members of the House Committee on Appropriations. On this occasion he met with (left to right) George Mahon (D–TX), William Minshall (R–OH), and Robert Sikes (D–FL). Sikes questioned the need to develop separate, expensive jet fighters for the Air Force (F–15) and the Navy (F–14) instead of one aircraft. (NARA)

F–15 with wheels down during its first flight, 1973. (NARA)

be a financial loss for the services and the DoD budget.[39] With this fiasco still fresh in everyone's mind, it was not surprising that the services and Laird resisted the idea of developing the F–14 for use by both services. The Air Force, contending that the F–14 could not be used to achieve the Air Force mission requirement, success-fully categorized the F–15 as the "most cost effective system for the air superiority mission." In this role, the Air Force averred, the F–15 enjoyed a clear performance advantage in being able to "out climb, out accelerate, and out turn the F–14."[40]

Sikes also focused on another instance of weapon system duplication, the development of three different aircraft—the Army Cheyenne helicopter gunship, the Marine Corps Harrier jet, and the Air Force AX (Attack Experimental) aircraft, later designated A–10—for the same mission, close air support of ground forces. Several months earlier, the chairman of the House Appropriations Committee, Texas Democrat George Mahon, had expressed similar doubts during hearings about the wisdom of supporting three new systems with the same mission. In October 1970 Mahon expected that after a hard-nosed analysis of alternatives the Pentagon would recommend the best aircraft for the task. But DoD was still work-ing on this recommendation when Laird testified in March 1971 that his staff under David Packard would issue a report in June. In July 1970 the Senate Armed Services Committee had eliminated funds for the Cheyenne and backed the AX, suggesting that Laird initiate a formal review of the roles and missions assigned to the Air Force and the Army as a way to eliminate duplication. Lurking in the shadows was the

Three F-14A Tomcat prototypes 1972, showing the different wing configurations that were available. (National Naval Aviation Museum)

precarious financial health of the Lockheed Corporation, the manufacturer of the Cheyenne and the troubled C–5A. Some in Congress suspected that the Pentagon was trying to keep the firm in business.[41]

Mahon also raised a fundamental question about the realism of the budget request: In light of the planned reductions in military personnel would there be enough forces to attain Nixon's goal of strategic sufficiency? Military personnel strength was expected to drop to 2.5 million by the end of FY 1972, and Laird planned to end the draft by mid-1973. The secretary expected improvements in firepower and mobility and greater reliance on strategic deterrence to compensate for the decline in the number of people in uniform. Would those improvements and the existing stockpile of nuclear weapons be sufficient?

In their appearance before the committee, Laird and Moorer tried to reassure Mahon, citing important programs under development intended to strengthen the strategic arsenal, such as the Multiple Independently Targetable Reentry Vehicle (MIRV), the B–1 bomber, and the Undersea Long-Range Missile System for use in ballistic missile submarines, as well as upgrades to the B–52 bombers. The MIRV, with multiple nuclear warheads, would increase the number of targets existing missiles could reach. The B–1 would replace the aging B–52 bomber in the late 1970s and become part of the nation's nuclear deterrent force. The ULMS—a large, submarine-launched missile in development—was designed to upgrade the ballistic submarine fleet (SSBN) and to counter improvements in Soviet antisubmarine warfare capability. The most likely component of the U.S. nuclear triad to survive a Soviet strike, submarine-launched missiles had a strategic deterrence mission. The new ULMS would be installed in an improved nuclear submarine. In convincing Congress that his budget struck a workable balance between financial prudence and military preparedness, Laird explained that the FY 1972 budget request funded the B–1 and ULMS "at the maximum rate consistent with good management." Monies for the B–1 would increase from $75 million in FY 1971 to $370 million in FY 1972 to cover system and engine design engineering. Over the same period, support for ULMS would jump from $45 million to $110 million to pay for design work on the submarine, missile, and propulsion system.[42] For a number of House and Senate legislators, the B–1's high cost remained a concern. They preferred that DoD develop a less expensive aircraft to replace the B–52.[43]

For the White House, Pentagon, and Congress, the underlying question was whether the rising costs of new weapons and personnel (salaries and retirement benefits) might make it too expensive for DoD to field a military force capable of carrying out even the 1½-war strategy. The Nixon administration had already scaled back the previous administration's strategy of preparing to wage 2½ wars simultaneously, in part because it was unaffordable. It was possible that rising weapon and personnel costs could render even Nixon's less ambitious strategy too expensive. In May 1971 Kissinger brought to the president his concerns about the increasing cost of military personnel and the growing per unit costs of building and maintaining ever more sophisticated military equipment. Upward spiraling costs had already led to a reduction in the size and readiness of the active forces; additional personnel cuts would make it harder for the United States to compete militarily and diplomatically with the Soviets. In Kissinger's judgment escalating costs would also make it difficult to carry out national strategy and deal with the Soviet threat unless the nation could "begin to master the problem of procuring adequate numbers of less expensive but effective equipment for our forces." Nixon told Laird he wanted the DPRC to address the issues Kissinger raised, or "we may find ourselves priced out of the strategies we have adopted." Senator John Stennis, chairman of the Senate Armed Services Committee and an advocate of a strong national defense, had reached the same conclusion: Runaway spending on new weapons threatened to undermine the ability of the nation to protect itself. He warned that "if the geometric cost increase for weapons systems is not sharply reversed," then even greater spending would not assure the forces needed for national security. If spending remained at current levels or fell, Stennis concluded, "it will thus soon become clear that our present system cannot provide sufficient forces to protect our security."[44]

Defense would also face increasingly stiff competition for funds from domestic programs in the coming years. According to a Brookings Institution study, over the next five years the growth in nondefense expenditures would absorb all expected *additional* government revenues. The result, according to this analysis, would leave no funds available for the president's new initiatives unless he raised tax rates, reduced domestic programs, or lowered defense spending below FY 1972 levels. The growth of domestic spending and higher DoD personnel and procurement costs threatened to undermine the viability of the current national security strategy. Without "fresh thinking in our management of defense resources," Wayne Smith warned Kissinger, "force levels and readiness are sacrificed in order to meet short term budgetary constraints and the net result is an overall loss in capability." He saw no need to remind Kissinger that force levels had already been reduced by 25 percent over the past three years. The danger was that a budget which funded smaller and more expensive general purpose forces would lead to a greater reliance on strategic weapons for deterrence. A balance between preparedness and fiscal prudence was needed.[45]

Although roughly half of the DoD budget covered personnel costs, Congress in general showed little interest in further slashing the size of the armed forces, scheduled to be smaller at the end of FY 1972 than they had been before the start of the Vietnam War. In an election year, legislators, sensitive to the issue of discharged service personnel joining the ranks of the unemployed, were unlikely to advocate closing redundant military installations. However, Congress questioned the necessity for the high ratio of administrative, combat support, and combat service support positions relative to the number of personnel assigned to combat units. The large numbers in overhead and support positions in the eyes of critics represented a wasteful expense analogous to cost overruns in weapons development.[46] In addition, like the military itself, Congress worried about growing morale and disciplinary problems in the armed forces—racial tensions, increasing AWOL (absent without leave) and desertion rates, illegal drug use, and low reenlistment rates.[47]

Some liberal, antiwar senators nonetheless believed that sharp DoD budget cuts were in order. On behalf of several other senators, Wisconsin Democrat William

Proxmire submitted on 4 June an amendment (the Proxmire-Mathias proposal) to the military authorization bill, placing a ceiling of $68 billion on FY 1972 defense spending. The amendment addressed funds in three bills: military appropriations, military construction, and civil defense, all covered by separate legislation. The proposed ceiling roughly equaled the amount that Congress had appropriated the previous year. With a continuing decline in the costs of the war and a reduction in military and civilian personnel, Proxmire contended that the budget should go down, not up, even when inflation and pay raises were considered. In his mind, the only way to reorder priorities and provide more funds for domestic programs was to cut defense spending, especially research money for development of "weapons systems which too often turn out to be obsolescent, redundant, or cost-ineffective."[48] In a lengthy rebuttal, Laird charged that Proxmire based his amendment on erroneous premises and faulty information. The consequences of cutting $7 billion out of what Laird deemed a rock-bottom Defense budget "would be so extreme as to provoke a crisis in national security."[49]

Although the secretary felt confident that Proxmire's amendment would be defeated because it cut spending too drastically, he warned Pentagon leaders in June that the Senate was also considering an amendment by Senator Gordon L. Allott (R–CO) to cut expenditures $2 billion below the DoD submission. In addition, Senator Stennis wanted to limit expenditures to $75 billion. In the existing political environment, the services had no choice but to stay within their fiscal guidance.[50]

From the administration's perspective, amendments to cut spending were not the only threat to the DoD budget request. Other influential factors were the state of the national economy and the pace of congressional action. OMB Director Shultz noted at the end of April that although Congress had barely begun work on the FY 1972 budget, it had already increased overall federal spending. He anticipated a possible budget deficit of more than $15 billion. Shultz understood how difficult it was to cut domestic spending and feared the White House would not know until June or later what spending level the House or Senate would recommend. Reluctant to propose a tax increase to shrink the deficit, the administration faced a Hobson's choice of cutting defense or tolerating a larger budget deficit.[51]

In August Nixon expressed to Laird, Packard, and the military chiefs his pessimism about congressional willingness to increase DoD spending or to support the administration's rock-bottom request. Laird was more sanguine. While Packard had been concentrating for several months on reviewing the program requests of the services, Laird was testifying and privately visiting key congressional members, seeking their support for the president's budget request. Based on his discussions with legislators and his previous experience as a member of the House of Representatives, Laird expected Congress to cut the administration's defense request by only 1.5 percent.[52] Yet Congress proceeded at its own deliberate pace. Nixon and Laird had to wait until 11 November, more than four months into the fiscal year, for final action on the FY 1972 budget request.[53]

Congress Decides

Congress had limited choices in cutting defense appropriations (NOA). It could not drastically reduce operating and maintenance funds, which included essential items such as petroleum, oil, lubricants (POL) needed to maintain operational readiness. Sharp reductions could ultimately curtail air, land, and sea operations and training exercises. Congress cut the president's request for O&M funds by $348.6 million from $20.6 billion, a reduction of 1.6 percent. Personnel costs—salaries, wages, and retirement benefits—all fixed by law, were trimmed by $267.4 million, or 1.2 percent, requiring personnel reductions. Congress had more leeway to cut appropriations for RDT&E and procurement, the very functions that Nixon and Laird wanted to increase. Procurement was reduced by over $1.9 billion, or 9.6 percent. The RDT&E appropriation was lowered by $430.4 million or 5.4 percent from $7.9 billion to $7.5 billion. Overall, the president's request of $73.5 billion fared better in the House than in the Senate. The House passed an appropriations bill of more than $71 billion; the Senate approved an appropriation of $70.8 billion. In conference, appropriations were sliced even further, to a total of $70.5 billion. Table 18 compares the president's budget request with the amount appropriated in thousands of dollars.

Table 18. Congressional Action (NOA) on DoD Budget, FY 1972 ($ thousands)

	President's Request	Appropriations	Difference
Active Personnel	21,291,969	21,024,574	267,395
Retired Personnel	3,777,134	3,777,134	–
O&M	20,647,834	20,299,231	348,603
Procurement	19,681,660	17,776,892	1,904,768
RDT&E	7,949,362	7,519,062	430,300
Spec Foreign Currency Prog	12,655	12,000	300
ABM Construction	183,570	109,570	74,000
Total	73,544,184	70,518,463	3,025,366

Source: OASD(C), "Congressional Action on FY 1972 Budget Request by Appropriation Title and Item," FAD 698, 15 December 1971, tab FY 1972, binder Fiscal Tables 1972, box 820, Subject Files, OSD Historical Office.

Congress appropriated funds for active and reserve forces and the National Guard at levels below the amount the president requested.

Table 19. Military Personnel ($ thousands)

Appropriation	President's Request	Conference Action
Army	7,483,137	7,315,637
Navy	4,594,111	4,558,571
Marine Corps	1,343,810	1,332,550
Air Force	6,521,413	6,470,283
Army Reserve	386,139	385,084
Navy Reserve	183,011	182,791
Marine Corps Reserve	57,448	57,368
Air Force Reserve	101,756	101,716
Army National Guard	486,444	485,954
Air National Guard	134,700	134,620
Total	21,291,969	21,024,574

Source: OASD(C), "Congressional Action on FY 1972 Budget Request by Appropriation Title and Item," FAD 698, 15 December 1971, tab FY 1972, binder Fiscal Tables 1972, box 820, Subject Files, OSD Historical Office.

In cutting funds for R&D and the procurement of weapon systems, Congress limited ABM (Safeguard) construction to the two missile sites already being built at Grand Forks, North Dakota, and Malmstrom Air Force Base in Montana. The

House-Senate conference approved funds for the Marine Corps' Harrier and the B–1, but it cut procurement funds for the F–14, C–5A, and shipbuilding. Congress appropriated no funds for purchasing the Cheyenne helicopter or the MBT–70 tank, although it provided more RDT&E funds for developing a new tank than the president requested and included some $9 million for development of the Cheyenne.[54]

Table 20. Weapon Systems (NOA), FY 1972 ($ thousands)

	President's Request	Appropriations
Procurement		
Cheyenne	13,200	0
Safeguard	329,400	294,400
MBT–70	59,100	0
F–14	806,100	801,600
Shipbuilding	3,327,900	3,005,200
C–5A	412,400	340,200
RDT&E		
Safeguard	0	0
Tank Development	27,500	40,000
Cheyenne	0	9,300
C–5A	26,000	22,400
ULMS	109,500	103,000

Source: OASD(C), "Congressional Action on FY 1972 Budget Request by Appropriation Title and Item," FAD 698, 15 December 1971; OASD(C), "Congressional Action on FY 1972 Authorization Request for Procurement & RDT&E," FAD 691, 21 January 1972: both in tab FY 1972, binder Fiscal Tables 1972, box 820, Subject Files, OSD Historical Office.

Despite FY 1972 reductions of more than $2.3 billion in procurement and RDT&E funds, DoD protected its weapons programs from serious long-term cuts by exploiting the distinction between outlays and the budget authority granted by Congress in the form of appropriations to incur obligations. Outlays represented the sum of budget authority remaining from previous fiscal years and the monies authorized for spending in the current year. Congress concentrated its cuts on accounts such as R&D, where much of the money would not necessarily be used during the fiscal year. Unspent budget authority money could be used in succeeding fiscal years. Between FY 1970 and FY 1975 Congress reduced procurement *authority* by almost 13 percent and R&D *authority* by more than 7 percent. Yet during that period *outlays* were scaled back by much smaller percentages—procurement by 5.4 percent and R&D by 2.6 percent. Likewise, Congress reduced the amounts authorized for a number of weapons. Still, a good deal of the R&D and procurement monies were designated for the future, not the current year. Laird persuaded Congress to restore much of the budget authority (NOA) in the out-years of the budget cycle to help offset reductions taken in the current one, so the Pentagon eventually received full funding for such programs as the F–14 and F–15. Deftly taking advantage of this distinction between budget authority and expenditures, Laird shielded Pentagon programs from drastic permanent cuts, justifying his boast that he never lost a budget roll-call vote as secretary.[55]

THE FY 1972 DEFENSE BUDGET marked a significant turning point, the beginning of yearly increases during the remainder of Laird's time as secretary. The change in TOA was striking. In FY 1971 the budget had fallen to its nadir with a TOA of $72.49 billion. For FY 1972 TOA climbed rather dramatically to $76.467 billion. Thanks in good measure to Laird's determined resistance to cuts from the White House, the budget continued to rise in subsequent years.[56] Laird and Packard also kept control of the details of the Defense budget, thwarting Kissinger's efforts to give the DPRC a substantive and, from Laird's perspective, intrusive role in reviewing the DoD program. The FY 1972 budget, the first formulated by the Nixon administration and the first to utilize Laird's revision of the PPBS, represented the outcome of a lengthy and contentious process of trying to match resources and strategy to ensure that national security was affordable, doable, and sufficient to protect U.S. interests. The FY 1972 budget also had significance for the future design of the armed forces, helping ensure the continued development of new weapon systems such as ULMS and the C–5A that would prove well-nigh indispensable after the Vietnam War. With Laird's strong support, the budget also initiated funding for an all-volunteer military that would fundamentally change the nature and organization of the armed forces.

The budget also had significance for U.S. alliances in the coming post-Vietnam period, raising concerns about the level of U.S. support for NATO. The Pentagon's requirement to fight in Vietnam and build up South Vietnam's military forces had diminished its support for NATO and gave the Soviet Union an opportunity to build up its conventional and strategic forces. Faced with strong Warsaw Pact forces, Nixon and Laird sought to improve U.S. support and NATO readiness, and prodded European allies to take on more of the common defense burden.

CHAPTER 12

The Enduring Commitment to NATO

IN APRIL 1969, A FEW MONTHS after Melvin Laird became secretary of defense, the North Atlantic Treaty Organization (NATO) celebrated its twentieth anniversary as a military and political alliance. In the North Atlantic Treaty of 1949, the 12 signatory nations had agreed "that an attack against one or more of them in Europe or North America shall be considered an attack against them all," and each pledged to assist the nation or nations under assault with necessary measures, "including the use of armed force, to restore and maintain the security of the North Atlantic area." During the European postwar reconstruction in NATO's early years, alliance members perforce relied on the United States to carry the main responsibility for defense of the continent.[1]

However, the alliance, which Laird and the administration regarded as indispensable to American security, was showing the strains that had built up over the years. As Western Europe recovered from the war, it enjoyed greater affluence and political stability. Yet, from Washington's perspective, alliance members had failed to increase their military spending commensurate with their new prosperity despite repeated American appeals and growing Soviet might. Laird viewed the buildup of the Soviet arsenal in the 1960s, including its naval power, as threatening to neutralize the U.S. advantage in strategic weapons. The sizable Warsaw Pact conventional forces stationed along NATO's central front constituted a serious threat. Soviet strength was especially worrisome to the secretary when over a half-million Americans were fighting in Vietnam. West Europeans, however, viewed the situation differently. With the years of security and prosperity, the American military presence on the continent, and the hope of a détente with the Soviet Union, Western European nations regarded a Warsaw Pact attack as unlikely, despite the brutal

Soviet invasion of Czechoslovakia in August 1968 that abruptly quashed indigenous liberalization measures.[2] Sustaining a viable U.S. partnership with NATO while the defense budget was shrinking and the Soviet threat was growing would prove challenging for Laird.

Deep-Seated Troubles

From his extensive experience in foreign affairs, Nixon understood the challenges of retaining solidarity with Western Europe. "The new economic independence of European countries and the lack of fear of Soviet aggression," he had said in 1967, "have contributed to a situation where it is not possible to keep the old alliance together on its former basis."[3] Having inherited a strained relationship with NATO, Nixon took every opportunity to assure member nations that the American government remained committed to the defense of Europe. On his first presidential overseas trip, an eight-day visit to Europe to demonstrate U.S. support, Nixon pledged to consult with NATO allies before undertaking negotiations with potential adversaries and to maintain the current level of U.S. troops in Europe.[4]

Pressure to reexamine the U.S. role in NATO came also from Congress, likewise mindful of Western Europe's growing affluence, the balance of payments deficit, the mounting costs of the Vietnam War, and the desire to reassert its authority in foreign policy. While Laird was a member of Congress, Democratic Senator Mike Mansfield from Montana submitted his first resolution for a NATO troop reduction in August 1966, contending that the United States could substantially reduce its forces permanently stationed in Europe without abandoning or affecting its ability to fulfill its North Atlantic Treaty obligations. When Mansfield introduced a similar resolution in December 1969 to ease the balance of payments deficit and cut the expense of stationing U.S. troops overseas, Laird would have to deal with the consequences if U.S. forces in Europe were sharply cut. If Europeans did not do more to support NATO, Congress might force the United States to do less.[5] Secretary Laird recognized Mansfield's concerns, but would handle them without resorting to the extreme measures the senator advocated. Laird fully appreciated how economic issues and a shrinking defense budget further complicated NATO relations.

Laird's predecessor Clark Clifford launched the Reduction of Costs in Europe (REDCOSTE) program in March 1968 to preempt congressional action to reduce

U.S. forces and to help alleviate balance of payments and budget shortfalls.[6] In May he urged NATO allies to provide more resources for Europe's defense. In June he directed the U.S. services to come up with significant reductions in personnel and facilities in Europe ($300 million–$500 million) to meet the expected balance of payments deficit in 1969. The Johnson administration withdrew some 33,000 soldiers from Europe in 1968, reducing yearend authorized U.S. strength to 319,000 personnel.[7]

The shadow of the Vietnam War fell on Europe. Coming into office Laird immediately confronted the war's harmful effect on relations with NATO allies, many of whom opposed the Johnson administration's war policies. Defense Secretary Robert McNamara had partially paid for the Vietnam buildup by shortchanging U.S. forces in Western Europe, weakening the alliance to the chagrin of many Europeans.[8]

During the 1960s the United States repeatedly called for increased Western European military contributions in large measure to compensate for the U.S. military involvement in Vietnam. At first McNamara tried to support the war without drawing down units in NATO, but the growing magnitude of the U.S. commitment in Vietnam soon changed his policy. By mid-1967 an estimated one-half to two-thirds of Air Force reconnaissance aircraft earmarked for NATO went to Vietnam; 30,000 soldiers with specialized skills departed from Europe. Some Army units assigned to NATO were understrength and lacked a full complement of combat support personnel. High personnel turnover and a shortage of experienced noncommissioned officers (NCOs) and officers in leadership positions eroded the effectiveness of U.S. forces in Europe. McNamara lowered supply levels in Europe to help meet Vietnam requirements, and before leaving office early in 1968, he finalized plans "to withdraw tens of thousands of U.S. troops from Europe" that same year. The diversion of troops and funds from Europe to Vietnam raised questions about the U.S. commitment to defending Western Europe. McNamara's repeated requests for alliance members to increase their spending and forces even as he was pulling U.S. troops out of Europe caused resentment and skepticism among NATO allies and eroded Washington's credibility.[9] At the end of Johnson's term the United States still had in Europe $4^1/_3$ divisions, 2 armored cavalry regiments, and 32 air squadrons, along with supporting and logistical units. The U.S. Sixth Fleet defending NATO's southern flank deployed 25 fighting ships and associated support vessels.[10] U.S. analysts feared the growing Soviet presence could neutralize the Sixth Fleet, but Europeans viewed the Soviet naval buildup in the Mediterranean "more as a problem of political rivalry than as a direct military threat to NATO's southern flank."[11]

Many NATO allies believed they could never afford to build conventional forces capable of standing up to those of the Eastern Bloc. Moreover, they believed that relying on conventional forces risked turning Europe into a battleground, with the kind of bloodletting seen in two world wars. Unwilling to increase their financial and military commitment to NATO, European nations had come to rely on the American nuclear shield for protection and maintained that no additional commitments on their part were necessary. They judged the threat of the early use of nuclear weapons as a better deterrent to the Warsaw Pact than conventional forces. Secretary McNamara conceded in 1968 that despite years of effort NATO lacked the capability to deal successfully with a nonnuclear attack without recourse to U.S. nuclear weapons.[12]

Even the Soviet invasion of Czechoslovakia with 275,000 troops failed to sway European members from the belief that "the danger of an all-out Soviet assault remains low." The invasion neither kept them from seeking better ties with the Soviet Union nor curtailed efforts to expand trade and economic relations with the Communist nations of Eastern Europe. The United States Information Agency (USIA) observed that European public opinion supporting NATO rose during the invasion of Czechoslovakia, but by the end of 1968 it had "returned almost to the normal rather apathetic level." The invasion had little effect on European military support of the alliance. West Germany increased its annual defense budget by roughly $150 million, but none of that money would help reduce the U.S. balance of payments deficit. Norway added $14 million to its defense budget for the next five years; and Denmark, $62 million over the next two.[13]

As the second largest NATO member in population and economic power, West Germany commanded close U.S. attention. The United States had long contended that the Federal Republic of Germany's defense effort was not commensurate with its capability. Shortly after Laird became secretary, Assistant Secretary of Defense for International Security Affairs Paul Warnke warned him that West German armed forces fell below NATO standards for manning M-Day (day of mobilization) units and faced a shortage of officers, NCOs, and skilled specialists. West German war reserve stocks, logistical support, reserve training, and mobilization programs were also deemed inadequate. Warnke termed the balance of payments issue "the most important unresolved problem" in U.S.-German relations. After deducting expected German military purchases, he estimated that the net U.S. balance of payments deficit on military spending in Germany would average $700 million annually from 1970 to 1974. No long-term solution was on the horizon for covering the net deficit. To Warnke, a shift of the military and economic burden was overdue, and he expected Washington to ask for and receive substantial relief. Laird needed little convincing that European complacency had to end.[14]

At the end of January 1969 Laird took up West Germany's contribution with his German counterpart Gerhard Schroeder. The secretary assured Schroeder of Nixon's strong and continuing commitment to NATO but argued that Germany should do more, especially when Congress was dissatisfied with the relative levels of European and American defense spending in relation to GNP. Compared with U.S. defense spending, which exceeded 10 percent of GNP and 42 percent of the federal budget, the West Germans devoted about 4.5 percent of GNP and 23 percent of their national budget to defense.[15]

Laird meets with Minister of Defense Gerhard Schroeder of Germany. The secretary urged the Germans to increase their NATO contribution, undated. (OSD Historical Office)

The dollar costs of stationing U.S. troops in Germany and having the Federal Republic of Germany offset those costs were major issues for Nixon and Laird. The Johnson administration had ratcheted up the pressure on Germany to purchase military equipment and U.S. Treasury bonds, and to pay for a large part of annual U.S. purchases in Germany. Nixon pushed ahead with the offset talks. The German cabinet offered a two-year package offsetting about $700 million, or about 75 percent of the nearly $1 billion annual American military expenditures in Germany. The agreement reached in July 1969 set the total amount of the offset at $1.5 billion for FYs 1970 and 1971 and stipulated that half of it would come from German military purchases in the United States, compared with 10–15 percent in the previous two agreements. The remainder would be in the form of West German loans to the United States for 8 to 10 years at an annual interest rate of 3.5 percent to 4 percent, compared with the 6 percent rate of previous loans.[16]

Conventional Forces: A Credible Deterrent?

NATO's conventional military forces, the bedrock of the flexible response strategy, were intended to deter a major attack on Western Europe and to be capable of stopping a Warsaw Pact offensive. Along the central front, which extended through Germany from the North Sea to the Alps, NATO forces numbered around 725,000, including 400,000 in combat units. The Warsaw Pact had about 700,000 troops, of which 450,000 were in combat units. NATO had more armored personnel carriers, antitank weapons, and vehicles, but the Soviet side had twice as many tanks. The Warsaw Pact could mobilize 700,000 soldiers from divisions in the western Soviet Union and reinforce its frontline forces in two to three weeks. NATO would need 90 days (M+90) or more to mobilize 600,000–700,000 troops from the United States and Europe and to get them into fighting positions. As of December 1968, the U.S. reserve force committed to NATO amounted to one mechanized infantry division and two airborne brigades to be in Europe by M+30, plus one airborne, one infantry, and one mechanized brigade in Europe by M+60.[17]

On the eve of Nixon's European trip in February 1969, military and civilian officials in the administration remained at odds over NATO's capability, disagreeing as to whether NATO's conventional forces could stop an attack. Laird saw no decisive military superiority on the part of the Warsaw Pact and believed that increased expenditures by Western European nations would improve NATO forces enough to attain a true balance. In contrast, the JCS perceived an unstable situation, believing Warsaw Pact forces had an overall edge "in conventional capability which could be decisive unless our Allies increase their conventional forces, and unless the US maintains and improves its own forces now in Europe." The Chiefs believed NATO "failed to provide adequate forces" to support flexible response, citing NATO units manned at 70 percent or less of their M-Day requirement and NATO divisions missing entire companies, battalions, and brigades.[18] General Lyman L. Lemnitzer, the supreme allied commander, Europe (SACEUR), was even more pessimistic than the JCS, when he asserted that NATO forces were "not equal to the opposing Warsaw Pact forces, and . . . not capable of engaging in sustained combat."[19]

Although Laird had a higher regard than the JCS for NATO's conventional capability, he agreed with the military chiefs that European governments ought to provide greater support and conveyed that message to NATO allies. In March 1969 he expressed concern that the military situation would "progressively shift against NATO unless substantial improvements are made in NATO forces, above all ground forces." He deemed that NATO had to make a rapid and substantial improvement in mobilizing forces and had to spend more on defense.[20]

Sensitive not only to military reasons to enhance NATO, Laird was also keenly aware of the domestic political reasons for pressing the Europeans to strengthen their support. Because the alliance had to be perceived as a credible conventional adversary to the Warsaw Pact armies, Laird believed that the president should in no way even intimate that European defense efforts sufficed or that his administration had deviated from its insistence on improving NATO conventional forces. A perception of NATO military weakness, the secretary feared, would intensify congressional and domestic pressure to pull forces out of the alliance. As Laird explained, "It would be said that if the whole conventional effort is pointless anyway, we might as well withdraw some of our expensive conventional forces from Europe and rely more on nuclear weapons."[21] When Canada announced on 3 April its intention to withdraw many of its 10,000 troops from Europe, administration officials feared that congressional demands to cut the number of U.S. forces stationed on the continent would intensify.[22]

Nuclear Weapons

The U.S. emphasis on the role of conventional forces under flexible response heightened sensitivity within the NATO alliance to the possible use of nuclear weapons on European territory. Member nations were acutely aware that initiating the use of tactical nuclear weapons, as part of flexible response, risked crossing the threshold to all-out nuclear war. "Nuclear weapons for use on European battlefields are 'tactical' to us," stated Secretary of State William Rogers, but "strategic to the Europeans." Smaller member-nations of NATO's Nuclear Planning Group (NPG) desired to establish policy guidelines for using nuclear weapons, an idea that the United States resisted, fearing that inflexible procedures might tie the hands of the U.S. president in a crisis.[23]

Like President Johnson before him, Nixon carefully consulted with NATO on this sensitive topic. In early May 1969 Laird and Rogers approached Nixon to discuss changing U.S. policy on the use of nuclear weapons in Europe. Both secretaries wanted to replace the Athens guidelines, articulated by McNamara in 1962, which governed the use of nuclear weapons in NATO, with a new statement more responsive to the concerns of nonnuclear allied nations such as the Netherlands. The Athens guidelines sought to assure NATO that U.S. nuclear protection extended to Europe as well as North America, but also recognized the limited likelihood of consultation in the event of an attack. Under the Laird and Rogers proposal, major NATO commanders would notify governments, if time and circumstances permitted, of their request to use nuclear weapons. The allies could then express their views to the nuclear powers (France and the United Kingdom). Laird and Rogers had several goals in mind: ensure that consultation would not weaken the credibility of the nuclear deterrent; avoid exposing friendly forces to the risk of destruction from a preemptive enemy attack; and preserve the president's freedom to act during war. Laird saw no point in adopting formal and fixed procedures that might prove unworkable during a crisis and wanted to be sure that America's allies fully understood the limits of a U.S. consultation with them.[24]

National Security Adviser Kissinger supported Laird's initiative, praising it because the procedures were simple and flexible and could be used appropriately and expeditiously in war. He emphasized the main condition of consultation: "Any suggestion of a veto or absolute inhibition on nuclear release is unacceptable." Nixon authorized Laird to inform NATO ministers of his endorsement.[25]

At the request of Defense Minister Paul W. Segers of Belgium, European defense ministers at the NPG meeting on 29–30 May discussed the U.S. proposal. Segers sought modifications permitting a government or a military commander to notify other governments of a request to release nuclear weapons, and to convey their views through the council or by other means. Nixon agreed to these changes, supported by Laird, Rogers, and Kissinger, but the president still wanted to keep open the possibility of additional discussions. Laird informed Segers on 24 July 1969 that Nixon had approved his amendments and in the spirit of greater consultation invited further comments.[26]

Developing NATO Policy

In April 1969 the administration began a formal review of overall NATO policy for a number of reasons. The prospect of talks with the Soviets on strategic arms limitations and the mutual reduction of forces in Europe would directly affect NATO. Nixon's decision in March to go forward with deployment of an ABM system (see chapter 15), along with the ongoing review of the nation's force posture (NSSM 3), had implications for relations with NATO. The initial review by the National Security Council on 8 April 1969 concentrated on reduction of costs in Europe (REDCOSTE), consultations with NATO, burden sharing, and the offset agreement with Germany.[27]

Laird reassured NATO allies, telling the Defense Planning Committee in Brussels on 28 May 1969 that the United States would continue to regard its own security as inseparable from that of Europe. The secretary also employed strong language in discussing the need to substantially improve the posture and combat effectiveness of NATO conventional forces. It would be easier to retain domestic support for a robust U.S. commitment to NATO if the European allies carried out a determined program to build forces comparable to those of the United States in terms of capability and staying power. This was a high standard and difficult to reach.[28]

The possibility of reducing U.S. forces assigned to NATO greatly worried European leaders. A member of Kissinger's staff noted that the allies would regard a drawdown as evidence of a wavering U.S. commitment and a signal that Washington had downgraded the Soviet threat. A pullback could in turn lead to reduced European support for NATO. One cynical U.S. official theorized that Europeans viewed "their defense requirements primarily in terms of what they need to provide to keep the Americans committed."[29]

The administration's policy review continued in July 1969 with the issuance of NSSM 65. DoD conducted a formal assessment of U.S. nuclear and conventional forces capability to deter and counter nuclear and conventional attacks on NATO, drawing on the findings of the ongoing NSSM 3 exercise, a fundamental review of force levels and strategy. To keep his options open, Nixon deferred any decision on the number of U.S. troops in Europe until NSSM 3 was completed.[30]

As part of the NSSM 3 overall strategy review, on 23 October 1969 the Joint Chiefs submitted to Laird their NSSM 65 study, which presented an even bleaker picture of U.S. military capabilities than did their February evaluation. The Americans no longer had a lead over the Soviets in strategic nuclear weapon capability. The emergence of strategic parity between the two nations had diminished the deterrent value of the U.S. nuclear arsenal and, according to the JCS, would result in less flexibility for NATO in responding to an attack. The Chiefs had little confidence that NATO was prepared to counter a full-scale nuclear attack and considered SACEUR's nuclear program inflexible and flawed because it relied on strikes deep into Soviet territory to affect the outcome of a conflict in Western Europe. The JCS also doubted whether NATO could conduct "a successful forward defense against a determined Pact conventional attack." Packard sent the study to the White House in January 1970, expressing his and ISA's view that the JCS had misjudged the relative capabilities of Warsaw Pact and NATO forces, but by then the study had been overtaken by NSDM 27, the new directive that Nixon had issued on 11 October.[31]

Based on NSSM 3, the directive limited U.S. defense strategy to fighting 1½ wars and changed the forces that would be used to defend Europe. Calling for an initial defense of Western Europe, the directive posited that 90 days after the start of a conventional Warsaw Pact attack a political settlement would be reached; that the Soviet conventional offensive would have run its course; or that the fighting would have escalated to a nuclear exchange. Nixon's change of strategy also prompted him to request in November 1969 a second assessment (NSSM 84) of the number and the cost of troops needed to carry out the new strategy.

Packard's guidance issued on 28 January 1970, which "stipulated that our peacetime NATO forces and their logistical support need not be able to sustain a defense against a major attack for longer than about 90 days," raised troubling questions and ambiguities.[32] Did the 90-day period apply only to resource allocation and logistics planning? Or did it establish for planning purposes the maximum length of a future conventional war? Under Secretary of the Army Thaddeus R. Beal protested that the 90-day limitation, "if applied to force design as well as to logistics guidance," represented a significant change in the capabilities required to carry out flexible response. Based on a review of earlier guidance, Beal concluded that flexible response required "a capability for indefinite conventional combat." He saw no advantage in limiting U.S. options after 90 days of conventional combat to either surrendering or escalating to a nuclear response. Beal urged Packard to apply the 90-day limit "only to logistic guidance and not to strategy or force planning." The issues raised by Packard's guidance would not be resolved until the Senior Review Group met in August.[33]

Budget Constraints

As usual, early on in the review process, budget issues surrounding U.S. troop levels for NATO were integral to the deliberations. In the summer of 1969 reductions in the FY 1970 Defense budget had made it necessary for Laird to trim naval forces earmarked for NATO. The need for cutbacks had become apparent during the preparation of the NATO Defense Planning Questionnaire (DPQ) required of each troop-contributing NATO member. Submitted annually, a DPQ estimated a nation's force commitments for the following calendar year and updated its commitments for the current year. The Pentagon had missed the 1 August deadline for completing the questionnaire. On 20 August Helmut Sonnenfeldt of the NSC staff raised two warning flags with Kissinger. First, the reduction of FY 1970 defense outlays would force the Navy to announce on 22 August that it would retire over 100 ships, some of them designated for NATO. The Navy claimed that it cost $1 million a day to keep the ships on the active rolls. The second concern was credibility. He thought NATO allies deserved candid and accurate data on the U.S. defense commitment in contrast to what he called "past phony information on our NATO-earmarked forces," a not too veiled criticism of the Johnson administration's reporting practices. Sonnenfeldt specifically cited the example of mothballed U.S. destroyers listed in the DPQ that would not be ready for battle 90 days after the start of mobilization as specified by NATO plans.[34]

Laird duly informed Kissinger in September 1969 that he would be obligated to inform NATO of a reduction in the number of ships committed to the alliance (he had in mind eliminating one attack carrier, 6 ASW carriers, and 48 destroyers), and of the reduced readiness of Army strategic reserve units and dual-based contingents of the 24th Infantry Division. The secretary underscored the likelihood of political problems if the administration's ongoing review of the FY 1970 budget required additional reductions in NATO commitments beyond those already under consideration.[35] Concerned about the eroding credibility of the U.S. commitment, Sonnenfeldt feared that Laird's announcement would be interpreted "in NATO against a background of other indicators that the US is actually cutting back on its commitments in Europe." He added another issue: "The fact that these reductions in effectiveness and readiness have already occurred, of course, raises the further question of consultation."[36]

In light of the president's pledge to maintain a substantial conventional force in Europe, explaining the cuts became a ticklish problem for the administration. Growing Soviet naval activity in the Mediterranean made it impossible to justify a decrease in U.S. naval forces for military reasons. Yet Laird realized it was essential to apprise NATO candidly and immediately of the reductions, as well as likely cuts in Army forces devoted to NATO, if redeployments from Vietnam did not meet the tight budget forecasts.[37] Nixon agreed, but in informing NATO he wanted to emphasize the enduring U.S. ties to the alliance. He told the permanent representative to NATO, Ambassador Robert Ellsworth, specifically to assure NATO allies that the reductions would not affect the American commitment to maintain the quality of U.S. forces and that the president personally would review any additional reductions in the readiness of Army units. Nixon reiterated that he would consult with NATO allies in advance of making decisions.[38] Despite the president's reassurance, he had to consider additional reductions that could complicate relations within NATO and asked the Defense Program Review Committee to prepare recommendations for further cutbacks.[39]

Even though the administration internally debated for budgetary reasons about whether to reduce the size of its NATO commitment, in public, for political reasons, it argued strongly the need to maintain U.S. forces in Europe, highlighting the risks of drawing down forces. The White House, State Department, and Pentagon warily eyed anti-NATO sentiment in the Senate. On 1 December 1969 Senator Mansfield introduced Resolution 292 expressing the Senate view that "a substantial reduction of United States forces permanently stationed in Europe can be made without adversely affecting either our resolve or ability to meet our commitment under the North Atlantic Treaty." The resolution offered no specific number for withdrawal. On behalf of the administration, Rogers made a strong argument against the resolution. He warned Senator Fulbright, chairman of the Senate Committee on Foreign Relations, that troops hastily returned to Europe in the midst of a crisis would be less effective and less of a deterrent than forces already in Europe. Troops traveling to Europe would need time to establish liaison with counterparts and gain familiarity with the terrain and the threat. The requirements to transport supplies and equipment and pre-position them in Europe would strain the transportation capability and the capacity of storage areas in Europe. SACEUR regarded the conventional forces on hand as barely sufficient to respond to an attack. Moreover, the likely cost of bringing the troops home would be greater than the potential balance of payments savings. In addition, withdrawing troops would politically destabilize the alliance. Rogers concluded "that passage of the Resolution would create uncertainty about US intentions to maintain its commitment to a strong and successful NATO just at a time when there may be a prospect for advantageous negotiations with the countries of the Warsaw Pact." Despite this vigorous defense of the NATO troop commitment, Europeans came to realize that pressure from the Senate to cut U.S. forces was unlikely to abate.[40]

Senator Mike Mansfield (D–MT), the majority leader, submitted several resolutions to scale back the U.S. commitment to NATO, undated. (U.S. Senate Historical Office)

Indeed, the pressure to shrink spending was unrelenting and gave Laird little room to maneuver. After the 15 January 1970 DPRC meeting, he advised Nixon that planned spending levels would require further reductions in naval forces support- ing NATO. The secretary had already warned the NATO defense ministers at the December 1969 meeting in Brussels of necessary reductions in FYs 1970 and 1971. OSD and the JCS proposed eliminating three destroyers, nine maritime patrol air- craft, and one submarine from the forces (category "A") designated as immediately available to NATO. Twelve destroyers and one destroyer escort in category "B," that is, vessels scheduled to be available at a later date, would also be stricken from NATO rolls. In making these proposals Laird cited not only financial necessity but also the need to shift some naval forces to the Pacific Ocean to counter the presence of Soviet submarines there. In the event of war with the Soviet Union, the U.S. Navy would have to fight in both the Atlantic and Pacific oceans. Just as he had warned the NATO ministers, Laird cautioned Nixon that if the FY 1971 and later DoD budgets contin- ued to fall "still more reductions in our NATO-committed forces may be required." The State Department opposed cutting back category "A" naval forces, fearing such a move would lead to the piecemeal erosion of military capability and U.S. credibil- ity within the alliance.[41] Siding with Laird, Nixon authorized him in March 1970 to discuss the reductions with NATO, but the president wanted to keep open the possibility of a compromise if consultations with NATO allies proved contentious.[42]

In April ISA cautioned Laird that simply maintaining the present U.S. force commitment to NATO through December 1971 would be problematic. The current fiscal guidance, probable personnel pay increases, and possible congressional action to control inflation militated against such a commitment.[43] Not unexpectedly, Laird encountered resistance to the cuts he wanted. The supreme allied commander of NATO's Atlantic naval forces (SACLANT) warned in August that reductions would affect his antisubmarine warfare capability and his ability to control the Atlantic sea lanes of communication given the large and improving Soviet submarine force. Despite SACLANT's warning, Laird instructed the JCS and the Navy in August 1970 to carry out the reductions, citing the absence of political resistance during consultations with NATO.[44] ISA reiterated its concern to the secretary in September, noting the over optimism within the executive branch about the administration's ability to maintain the current levels of forces in Europe and withstand congressio- nal pressure to cut American forces. Acknowledging the serious budget problem,

Packard believed it necessary to contemplate even more rapid personnel reductions at any budget level.[45]

Secretary Rogers thought otherwise. Prior to Nixon's trip to Europe in September 1970, he advised the president that it was an inopportune time to cut forces in light of the "delicate and fluid political situation." Rogers noted that Soviet military capability remained strong, but that the new German policy of *Ostpolitik*, seeking a political modus vivendi with Eastern Europe, made possible the reordering of relations with the Soviets. Negotiations about mutual force reductions were possible especially if the Strategic Arms Limitation Talks met with success. And finally, he was hopeful that the Europeans might consider new burden-sharing arrangements. Rogers considered that maintenance of U.S. military strength at current levels was necessary to give NATO allies a sense of confidence in dealing with European security issues in the future and provide a foundation for realistic negotiations with the Soviets on force reductions.[46]

Nixon agreed with his secretary of state. Meeting in Naples with NATO Secretary General Manlio Brosio at the end of September 1970, the president made a clear commitment not to reduce U.S. forces unilaterally. Recounting that session for the press, he said, "I stated categorically to the NATO Commanders . . . that the United States

The longtime NATO secretary general Manlio Brosio meets with the new secretary of defense in the Pentagon in February 1969 to discuss the state of the alliance. (OSD Historical Office)

will, under no circumstances, reduce, unilaterally, its commitment to NATO. Any reduction in NATO forces, if it occurs, will only take place on a multilateral basis." Most important, cuts would be made in the context of mutual force reductions. His position represented a direct challenge to congressional critics and reassurance to NATO allies that he would oppose legislative efforts to reduce U.S. forces in Europe.[47]

During his trip to Europe in late September and early October, the president raised the issue of burden sharing but did not press the Europeans for it. At this point he preferred that they spend more for their own defense rather than resort once again to special financing arrangements to repay the United States for the cost of stationing its soldiers overseas. Keeping an eye on congressional critics, Nixon concluded greater European expenditures "would be quite decisive in firming up U.S. support for making our present contribution to the Alliance."[48]

The president's decision to delay asking the West Europeans outright for additional funds to offset U.S. costs put Laird in a bind. He needed these payments to avoid cutting additional forces. At a NATO Defense Planning Committee meeting in June 1970, he warned that without financial assistance the United States would have to reduce forces. Laird expected the West Germans to help pay for the presence of American troops in their country.[49] Adding to Laird's discomfort was the president's decision in September to reduce defense outlays by $1.5 billion to $74.5 billion for FY 1972, the third consecutive fiscal year of cuts. This amount was below the $76 billion in outlays that NSDM 27 had set in October 1969.[50]

Faced with a constricting budget and Nixon's decision to eschew burden sharing, Laird saw no choice but to advocate reducing U.S. forces in Europe. Collective European defense, Laird stressed to the president, should not be a commitment to maintain a fixed U.S. force level. He sought a more equitable NATO defense posture, but with a smaller, yet substantial U.S. presence in Western Europe. Moderate reductions in U.S. support forces and overhead in FY 1972 were needed not only to save money but to demonstrate the U.S. intention to shift the burden and economize in the long run. He believed his approach would garner public and congressional support and reassure the Europeans about the continued U.S. presence and commitment to European security.[51]

Kissinger's assistant Al Haig dismissed Laird's views as "pure rationalization" and "wishful thinking" to believe the United States could "shock the Europeans into a sounder philosophic attitude by more withdrawals." In his mind, additional cuts would further loosen U.S. ties with European nations and perhaps even give them an incentive to negotiate with the Soviets. Fearing that Laird might initiate unilateral reductions in Europe and elsewhere, Kissinger and Haig wanted the president to prohibit Laird from reducing U.S. forces pending completion of interdepartmental studies on NATO. Haig also thought that the DPRC, which Kissinger chaired, should review the studies before any cuts were made.[52] At the end of October, Nixon decided that no U.S. forces or personnel for NATO were to be withdrawn from Europe during FYs 1971–1976. He instructed the DPRC to review all proposed redeployment plans for FYs 1972–1976 and then submit alternatives for his examination. Nixon's guidance would remain in effect until the DPRC completed its review.[53]

The Battle over U.S. Forces in NATO

The review of U.S. strategy and forces for NATO (NSSM 84) that began in November 1969 proceeded along a rocky path. The key question was to determine what NATO needed to defend Europe. The initial draft of May 1970 pleased no one. Prepared by an interagency steering group under John Morse, the deputy assistant secretary in ISA for European and NATO affairs, the draft study concluded that the United States could reduce its NATO forces by 30,000 without "a major effect on our deterrent posture or war-fighting capabilities." The JCS viewed this finding with dismay and incredulity. To cut what they considered a minimal combat force to defend NATO would increase the risk of nuclear war and weaken the deterrent effect of U.S. conventional forces stationed mainly in Germany. A reduction of U.S. forces without a Soviet quid pro quo would compound the folly. Fearing a hollowing out of the armed forces, the JCS also wanted units withdrawn from Europe to remain in the active force.[54] The NSC objected to the May draft as well as the revised version of June 1970, terming the latter a disjointed set of proposals for cutting conventional forces, not a systematic strategic review. The NSC assigned Assistant Secretary of Defense (ISA) Warren Nutter, with assistance from Laurence Lynn of the NSC staff, to redo the study, establishing criteria for assessing military force redeployment options and providing information on how long American forces could operate in Europe with the supplies on hand.[55]

Before the NSC convened again on 19 November to consider the latest iteration of NSSM 84, the president had decided to lower FY 1972 DoD expenditures to $74.5 billion and to keep the authorized FY 1971 force level in Europe at 319,000.

Nixon would also make no unilateral cuts of U.S. forces nor seek European financial support to offset the costs of stationing U.S. forces in Europe.[56] The combination of a budget cut without a reduction in forces in Europe squeezed DoD. Insisting that $74.5 billion was insufficient to preserve national security at reasonable risk levels, the department sought an additional $800 million. From Laird's perspective, paring U.S. forces in Europe was the only solution to ease the pressure on the budget. The day before the NSC meeting Moorer warned Laird that even with the most optimistic FY 1972 DoD budget projections the Navy would have to retire 34 ships currently in category "A" (available to NATO within 48 hours of an attack). If the budget came in lower than the projections the reductions might be greater.[57]

Kissinger opposed the cuts in U.S. forces. Even with the lower budget guidelines, Kissinger contended, the absolute necessity for a strong conventional deterrent force ruled out U.S. reductions until NATO allies had improved their armed forces to the point where the United States could redeploy units and equipment without risk to the alliance. The JCS and the State Department also opposed Laird's suggested downsizing.[58]

At the November NSC meeting, which considered NATO issues only, Laird favored large cuts in Europe over a period of years. Kissinger concluded that the flexible response strategy made U.S. forces essential in Europe, a position ruling out U.S. withdrawals. Unilateral reductions, Rogers warned, would cause NATO allies to make deals with the Soviets that could harm U.S. interests. Laird tried to shift the discussion to budget issues. He too wanted a conventional force to serve as a major deterrent, but he pressed for reductions, raising the issue of what DoD could actually afford, given "the manpower, fiscal and political problems that we face in the United States." His main thrust was to make the Europeans more capable. Nixon's paramount concern was to have "a credible conventional force that can hold for 90 days or more" to preempt a Russian attempt to strike. As was his custom, Nixon made no decisions at the meeting.[59]

After the meeting Nutter summed up for Laird the status of defense planning by NATO allies in the most recent DPQ. Nutter provided no comfort to those hoping that European nations would improve their military forces. Their defense spending plans were sketchy and reflected no growth; expenditures would even decline as a percent of GNP in Denmark, Norway, Portugal, and Turkey. Nutter's report found no evidence that European allies would actually contribute more to NATO. Without an increase in expenditure levels, DoD would be in a bind.[60]

On 25 November Nixon issued his decision on strategy and troop levels (NSDM 95). To withstand a full-scale conventional attack by the Warsaw Pact, he wanted to upgrade the combat capability of U.S. and allied forces; the size and structure of all U.S. forces supporting NATO were to be capable of providing a conventional defense of 90 days. Most significant for the DoD budget, the authorized end FY 1971 U.S. force level would remain at 319,000, and actual strength would be as close as possible to that figure. The president also called for improvements in NATO armor and anti-armor capabilities, aircraft and logistics, war reserve stocks, and mobilization and reinforcement capabilities.[61]

On 27 November Laird made a last attempt to pare U.S. forces earmarked for NATO. He told Nixon that he was planning to reduce the Navy's commitment to NATO by 34 category "A" ships as soon as possible, taking reductions from the Atlantic Fleet, not from naval forces stationed in Europe, to meet DoD's budget guidance to the Navy. Laird argued that the reductions would impress on NATO allies the need for burden sharing. Fiscal restraints impelled him to seek presidential approval to consult with NATO about the reduction during the scheduled December meeting in Brussels. Nixon did not approve Laird's proposal at this time, but it would become part of the next review of NATO; Laird was not to inform NATO authorities about possible future naval reductions in December.[62]

Nixon's paramount concern was maintaining U.S. force levels to provide a credible conventional defense for Western Europe and to demonstrate a steadfast commitment that would help NATO allies resist political overtures from the Soviet Union and Eastern Europe. Reducing force levels, even if justified on budgetary grounds, risked weakening NATO politically and militarily. Kissinger's quip at the Senior Review Group meeting in August, calling U.S. forces in Europe hostages whose presence on the continent kept the alliance together, was a basic political truth.[63]

Despite continual congressional pressure to scale back the U.S. military presence in Europe, the administration took pains to reassure NATO of its intention to remain fully engaged. Laird informed reporters before he left for the 2–4 December NATO ministerial meeting in Belgium that the United States would make no cuts in U.S. forces committed to NATO at least until the end of June 1972.[64] With no troop cuts imminent, the Brussels meeting focused on burden sharing and greater

European military support of the alliance. European members of NATO dutifully pledged to increase their military contribution to NATO and affirmed the need to preserve the military strength of the alliance. The members also pronounced that a strong collective defense posture was a prerequisite for détente and negotiations of mutual force reductions with the Warsaw Pact.[65]

Mutual and Balanced Force Reductions

The Soviet invasion of Czechoslovakia in 1968 had shelved consideration of mutual and balanced force reductions (MBFR), but continued European interest made the Nixon administration aware of the possibility of resuming MBFR talks with the Warsaw Pact. Still, despite a willingness by NATO and Warsaw Pact ministers to consider discussions of reductions in central Europe, neither the civilian nor the military leaders in the administration were in a rush to reach an agreement.[66]

When the subject of balanced force reductions came up at the September 1969 meeting of NATO political advisers, the U.S. delegation agreed to prepare studies on the topic. For his part, in February 1970 Laird advised moving cautiously, to take no action pending completion of ongoing defense studies, and only then decide how to proceed. Packard handled MBFR for DoD; Under Secretary of State John N. Irwin II was the State Department's lead official on this issue. The lack of adequate comparative data on military forces made it difficult for Packard to assess the capabilities of opposing military forces and to construct models of how to reduce forces. Aware of these difficulties, he nonetheless recognized that OSD and the JCS had to consider the feasibility of MBFR.[67]

The interest in MBFR increased after Nixon met with German Chancellor Willy Brandt in April 1970. Brandt, engaged in making diplomatic overtures to the Soviet bloc, pressed Nixon to signal to Warsaw Pact nations his interest in balanced force reductions. Following the meeting, Nixon requested a comprehensive study (NSSM 92) from the Verification Panel, which had been established for SALT and MBFR negotiations between NATO and the Warsaw Pact. The panel covered the extent and nature of possible reductions, verification issues, potential savings for the United States, and the effect of reductions on the military capabilities of NATO and the Pact.[68]

Its study disclosed that the administration remained divided over how to cut forces under MBFR. The JCS insisted that force reductions not weaken deterrence or worsen the imbalance in military forces that already favored the Warsaw Pact, that any reductions be verified, and that allied and U.S. forces continue their presence in Germany. Concerned that NATO was at a military disadvantage, the JCS believed that equal percentage reductions would inequitably diminish NATO's ability to defend against an offensive. Warsaw Pact forces would be able to mass for an offensive and reinforce quickly, while fewer NATO forces would have to protect the same defensive lines and would be unable to reinforce as easily. To balance opposing military capabilities, the Chiefs favored asymmetrical reductions, cutting opposing forces more than NATO, an option unlikely to appeal to the Warsaw Pact.[69]

In contrast, the Arms Control and Disarmament Agency, at that time a separate agency, was ready to begin MBFR talks, contending that balanced reductions would not appreciably alter the military balance between NATO and Pact forces. State and ACDA wanted to decide on a negotiating position by December, although they accepted the notion of conducting additional studies first. As Wayne Smith of Kissinger's staff noted, NATO allies expressed conditional interest in initiating MBFR talks as a political gesture to avoid confrontations and to limit or postpone "what they think are almost inevitable unilateral U.S. force cuts."[70]

The interagency Verification Panel met on 31 August 1970 to review the administration's position on MBFR, initially to sort out procedural issues for any negotiations. The Pentagon believed it necessary before starting MBFR negotiations to settle such questions as troop levels in Europe, burden sharing, imbalances in weaponry such as tanks, and whether to include the topic of nuclear weapons. No tangible advantages of mutual reductions for the United States appeared obvious. No easy formulas existed for reducing forces that would improve the current military situation. The underlying concern was that proportionate reductions might weaken rather than enhance NATO. The panel decided on further study, directing its working group to refine its approach, breaking the overall NATO force into component parts and tailoring approaches to specific military issues, such as the number and balance of tanks and tactical aircraft and the size of personnel cuts. The panel also wanted an analysis of the role of tactical nuclear weapons and the impact of reductions on mobilization and reinforcement capability.[71]

Meetings of the Verification Panel on 28 October and on 23 November brought no resolution of these issues and no agreed negotiating position. In October the group settled on the need for more study of war reserve stocks, the employment of nuclear weapons, the advantages and disadvantages of different approaches to MBFR, and verification procedures. At the brief November session Kissinger agreed with DoD's inclination to proceed slowly on MBFR talks. It served the interests of the administration and the West Europeans to express a willingness to talk but to move deliberately. The mere prospect of talks, the administration believed, would make it harder for Congress to mandate unilateral U.S. reductions. At the same time, NATO allies believed that MBFR talks would preclude American reductions until a negotiated agreement was reached to cut NATO and Warsaw Pact forces.[72]

After the 19 November NSC meeting and the North Atlantic Council's decision in December to increase its support of NATO's infrastructure, the president reaffirmed his earlier decision to maintain the U.S. troop commitment at its existing level and to improve forces in Europe. He would not reduce U.S. forces except in the event of a mutual reduction. Soviet leader Leonid Brezhnev's declaration in May 1971 of his country's willingness to negotiate mutual reductions proved to be a boon for the administration's efforts to prevent passage of the Mansfield amendment requiring cuts to U.S. forces stationed in Europe. Supporters and opponents of the amendment found common ground. Both concluded the likelihood of mutual force negotiations made unilateral withdrawal unwise at the moment. Nixon believed that Brezhnev made his offer because he saw MBFR talks as a way to slow down or undercut U.S. efforts to improve the quality of NATO troops.[73]

After Brezhnev's offer, Nixon promulgated his policy on MBFR on 21 May 1971. The epitome of delay, the policy laid out a convoluted negotiating plan that could only be carried out at a snail's pace. The United States would first work with its allies to analyze issues. Then it would consult with NATO to reach a consensus on the issues and the negotiating procedures. The initial phase of these discussions with the alliance would focus on "diplomatic explorations" to identify Soviet objectives. Following these explorations, the initial formal negotiations would begin to determine whether the allies could develop "a substantive foundation for concrete proposals." Only after these consultations were completed would the administration begin talks with the USSR or the Warsaw Pact. Throughout the process, Nixon pledged to consult closely with European allies. Serious talks on mutual reductions would not occur until the Vietnam War ended.[74]

LAIRD FACED NATO ISSUES that differed little from those besetting McNamara and Clifford. The perceived disparity in military capability between NATO and Warsaw Pact forces, and the differences between the Americans and West Europeans regarding the military threat and their respective financial and military contributions to NATO, framed the policymaking of Presidents Johnson and Nixon. Both administrations attempted to get European nations to contribute more to NATO through burden sharing or higher defense spending. However, Laird dealt with a new element: the military and economic consequences of the previous administration's Vietnam policy that had eroded U.S. military strength in Europe. With the continued expense of the Vietnam War, a weak domestic economy, and pressure to cut military spending, Laird had no choice but to try to shrink the Defense budget, a reality that caused him to advocate cutting the U.S. commitment to NATO and seek greater European support.

Nixon accepted the reality of reduced defense outlays but would not accept cuts that might undermine the alliance. Maintaining NATO unity was paramount to the president. He prevented Laird from reducing U.S. NATO forces and directed him to improve the U.S. military in Europe, a decision that added to DoD's costs and forced Laird to find savings elsewhere in the budget. Unwilling to incur the risk of a militarily weakened NATO, or having allies question the firmness of the U.S. commitment to Europe's defense, Nixon acted to ensure that NATO remained viable. At a time of growing Soviet military strength and U.S. efforts to reach an agreement on strategic weapons, the president would not risk undermining relations with NATO allies. However, Nixon's decision later provided an opening for Laird when he sought to raise the expenditure level of the FY 1972 budget. The painful cuts to the FY 1970 and FY 1971 budgets enabled Laird to argue that DoD spending could be reduced no further. It had to be increased.

Nixon's policy in Europe proved an exception to the Nixon Doctrine that expected U.S. allies in Asia to provide more resources for their defense. In dealing with Asian allies, the administration faced issues similar to the ones it wrestled with in Europe. Laird and Nixon pushed an increasingly affluent Japan to spend more on defense to help ease the burden on the United States. Laird argued strongly for reduction of American forces stationed in South Korea just as he had with U.S. forces in Europe.

CHAPTER 13

Change in East Asia

.

AFTER WORLD WAR II, Japan and South Korea were vital U.S. allies in containing communism in the East Asian Pacific rim. When Laird became secretary of defense in 1969, economic and political changes underway in Asia, similar to those in Europe, would alter foreign relations with the United States. Growing prosperity and stability after the war inspired in Asian allies a greater assertiveness in dealing with the United States. The Nixon Doctrine of July 1969 set forth a new relationship with U.S. allies envisaging a larger role for them in regional defense. In a similar way, under the 1½-war strategy approved in September 1969, the United States scaled back its force estimates for national security requirements in Asia and Europe, concluding that the nation needed to prepare to fight one major war and one small war.[1]

A number of issues strained U.S. ties with Japan. The Vietnam War was unpopular with Japanese political groups on the left. The presence of U.S. bases in Japan and Okinawa, on which the United States relied to help wage war against North Vietnam, exacerbated the antiwar protests. Official and public sentiment to end U.S. control of Okinawa was strong and virtually universal in Japan. Under the Nixon Doctrine the administration sought to reduce U.S. forces in Asia, but found it difficult to get a more prosperous Japan to increase defense spending to compensate for a lower U.S. profile. Laird hoped that South Korea's growing strength since the end of the Korean War would allow DoD to withdraw some ground forces. Yet the Republic of Korea continued to depend on U.S. economic and military aid, taking for granted the continued presence of two U.S. Army combat divisions on its territory.

Nixon's trip to China in 1972, clearly a transformative event, portended a possible progression to more normal relations with the Communist nation. His diplomatic overture also had the potential to change U.S. relations with its traditional Asian allies—Japan, South Korea, and Taiwan—that had been based in large measure on the need to keep China and its growing nuclear arsenal in check.[2]

Policy Review

When Nixon took office, he could ill afford to defer a review of nuclear weapons policy in Asia, especially with the growth of China's nuclear weapons arsenal and the likely reversion to Japan of Okinawa, a storage site for U.S. weapons. Moreover, DoD was formulating new plans in accord with the Nixon Doctrine for the eventual replacement of U.S. forces by Asian ground forces and increased reliance on U.S. tactical nuclear weapons for deterrence. In July 1969 the administration began a policy review of nuclear weapons and conventional forces for Asia (NSSM 69) within the larger context of overall U.S. policy for the region.[3] The draft completed in July 1970 revealed intractable differences within the administration over the role and use of nuclear weapons and their value as a means to deter China's strengthening military power.[4]

Six months later, the Senior Review Group under Henry Kissinger took another look at the NSSM 69 in March 1971, seeking to clarify the administration's options in dealing with China as a strategic threat over the next five to ten years. Recognizing a need to evaluate nuclear strategy in conjunction with the use of U.S. general purpose forces, the SRG expanded the scope of NSSM 69 to encompass planning for both conventional and nuclear forces to counter Chinese threats.[5]

When the administration further considered NSSM 69 at the July 1971 Defense Program Review Committee session, the OSD Systems Analysis office proposed reducing conventional U.S. forces and increasing reliance on tactical nuclear weapons. There was no support outside OSD for this position. The JCS opposed using the presence of nuclear weapons as a reason to reduce U.S. ground force requirements. The State Department and the Arms Control and Disarmament Agency resisted making improvements in strategic forces or using tactical nuclear weapons.[6]

Frustrated by the stalemate over NSSM 69, Secretary of State William Rogers sent Secretary Laird in December 1971 a proposal to maintain ground deployments through June 1973. Rogers believed it imperative to reassure America's Asian allies that force reductions did not signify U.S. disengagement.[7] His initiative resulted in a joint formal proposal on forces that he and Laird submitted to Nixon on 9 February 1972. Based on recommendations from the JCS and the military services, the two secretaries asked the president to approve a deployment schedule for U.S. forces in Asia (excluding those in Vietnam) for FY 1973. Ground forces would comprise an Army division in Korea and two-thirds of a Marine division on Okinawa; tactical air capability included three Air Force wings, one each in Korea, Okinawa, and the Philippines/Thailand, and two-thirds of a Marine wing in Okinawa. Two airlift squadrons would remain on Taiwan and one on Okinawa. Naval forces would come to 3 attack carriers, 18–24 cruisers and destroyers, 7 attack submarines, and 3 antisubmarine warfare squadrons. A strategic force would consist of one B–52 squadron on Guam and six ballistic missile submarines. Laird assured Nixon that these force levels would provide adequate capability in the area. Rogers advised the president that the deployment plan would support the State Department's political and diplomatic objectives in Asia and alleviate any unease among Asian governments about U.S. intentions in the area.[8]

Kissinger, outraged by the very notion of the State-Defense initiative, deemed it an infringement on his responsibilities. But the lengthy deliberations by Kissinger's SRG and DPRC had failed to reach a policy consensus. Rogers was correct about the immediacy of reassuring American allies about U.S. deployments, even if the more difficult underlying strategic weapons issues remained unresolved. Nixon approved the deployment schedule.[9] The DPRC continued to review NSSM 69 in 1972, but its deliberations resulted in no change in policy, perhaps because of the difficulty of reconciling conflicting agency views. In the absence of a NSDM on strategic weapons and forces for Asia, the Rogers-Laird agreement provided an informal framework for U.S. policy.[10]

An Assertive Japan

In the years after its defeat in World War II, Japan had transformed itself from a devastated, destitute nation into an economic powerhouse. This remarkable postwar growth rekindled national pride, helped Japan regain political influence regionally and internationally, and brought a new self-confidence that had the potential to disrupt a relationship that constituted the bedrock of U.S. security policy in the Far East. Key to sustaining the relationship was how to deal with Japan's desire to regain control of the Ryukyu Islands. Article 3 of the peace treaty ending WWII with Japan gave the United States "the right to exercise all and any powers of administration, legislation and jurisdiction," but it imposed no obligation on the

United States to cede control. Eisenhower's Secretary of State John Foster Dulles had acknowledged Japan's residual sovereignty over the islands, a position reaffirmed by later U.S. presidents.[11]

At the very start of his administration, President Nixon directed preparation of an interagency study (NSSM 5) to examine all aspects of U.S.-Japanese relations, especially Okinawa reversion, U.S. bases in Japan, the security treaty, and economic policy. These issues also encompassed the sensitive matters of nuclear weapons storage, U.S. bases on Okinawa, the financial arrangements for reversion, and Japan's role in Asia.[12]

The Japanese government had serious security concerns of its own: the growth of Soviet and Communist Chinese military power and Soviet unwillingness to give back islands claimed by Japan. However the Japanese constitution and the U.S.-Japan Mutual Security Treaty complicated efforts to get the government to bolster its defenses. Article 9 essentially prohibited Japan from developing offensive weapons or dispatching forces overseas, circumscribing the role of Japan's postwar armed force of 231,000 and leaving Japan largely dependent on the United States for homeland defense. Article 10 made termination optional but not mandatory after ten years.[13]

The insistent Japanese demand for reversion of control of Okinawa recalled for Laird the sacrifice of the many Americans killed or wounded in the battle for the island, the bloodiest in U.S. naval history. As a U.S Navy officer on active duty in World War II he had participated in the pre-invasion bombardment of the island in 1945. As secretary of defense Laird wanted to ensure reversion did not seriously compromise U.S. national security. The JCS regarded Okinawa, the most important of the Ryukyus and the location of U.S. military installations, as essential to security in the Pacific and indispensable in providing logistic support and air bases for the U.S. war effort in Vietnam.[14]

Pro-reversion sentiment building in Japan over the years could not be ignored. During two meetings in November 1967 with Prime Minister Eisaku Sato, Secretary of State Dean Rusk had acknowledged that the Ryukyus would at some point return to Japan, but with a condition. He insisted that "Japan must permit the U.S. to operate militarily in the Ryukyus in ways which might ultimately involve operations requiring nuclear weapons to be placed there and combat operations to be conducted from there." The United States could ill afford any move that appeared

President Nixon greets Japan's Prime Minister Eisaku Sato on the south lawn of the White House. Sato was in Washington to open consultations about the reversion of Okiniwa to Japan, 19 November 1969. (NARA)

to weaken its war effort in Vietnam. Sato, who enjoyed strong political support in Japan for advocating reversion, argued that both governments take up the matters of nuclear weapons and military bases only after agreeing on how and when reversion would come about.[15] If the United States resisted handing over Okinawa it would inflame opposition by leftist and nationalist Japanese political elements to the U.S.-Japan security treaty and to the continued presence of U.S. military bases on Japanese soil.[16]

Okinawa's proximity to potential theaters of military operations—less than 1,000 miles from most of China, Japan, Korea, and Taiwan—offered U.S. bases there a unique strategic value. Okinawa served not only as a critical staging area for troops and supplies for the Vietnam War, but also as a storage depot for nuclear and chemical weapons. In 1969 the 79,000 Americans stationed there included military personnel and dependents, civilian employees, and contractors. U.S. forces directly used about 28 percent of the island's acreage, obviously a sensitive issue with Okinawans.[17]

Reversion entailed military risks cautioned chairman of the Joint Chiefs General Earle Wheeler. Basing forward-deployed military forces on the island was indispensable to U.S. strategy in the Pacific. He warned Laird in March 1969 of a hasty settlement that failed "to provide adequate safeguards for our military requirements." The existing arrangement provided irreplaceable strategic benefits for the United States: "unrestricted access and freedom of action in the use of our Okinawa bases, including B–52 operations, nuclear ship visits, and the storage of nuclear weapons." "Denial of storage rights on Okinawa," Wheeler asserted, "would reduce the US nuclear capability in the forward area, with a lessening of credibility in overall nuclear deterrence in the PACOM [Pacific Command] region." A loss of nuclear weapon rights would mean relocating those weapons and constructing new storage facilities elsewhere, most likely resulting in longer reaction times to launch operations. Wheeler, who advocated an agreement with Japan to ensure the continued unimpaired use of existing facilities until U.S. interests in Asia were no longer threatened, wanted Laird to espouse this position at the next National Security Council meeting.[18] Other observers, however, warned that the United States could be forced to choose between the status quo on Okinawa or close ties with Japan, but not both.[19]

Laird asked Wheeler to assess the importance of the nuclear armament stored on the island for U.S. forces and military plans and to provide cost estimates for developing nuclear storage sites and support installations in Guam and the Trust Territories (the Caroline, Marshall, and Mariana—except Guam—islands). Policy options included continuation of the status quo, permission for interim storage, emergency storage rights, and transit rights through Okinawa.[20] In Wheeler's judgment, nuclear weapon storage on Okinawa was "an essential element of effective [military] capability." In any event, the removal of nuclear weapons would have to await the funding and construction of replacement facilities.[21]

Nixon set forth his policy toward Japan (NSDM 13) at the end of May, just before Japanese Foreign Minister Kiichi Aichi visited Washington. Seeking improved relations and a larger Japanese role in Asia, the president remained open to gradual modifications to the system of U.S. bases in Japan in order "to reduce major irritants while retaining essential base functions." On the development of Japan's defense posture, he would encourage "moderate increases and qualitative improvements," but apply no "pressure on her to develop substantially larger forces or to play a larger regional security role." Nixon would accept Okinawa's reversion in 1972 "provided there is agreement in 1969 on the essential elements governing U.S. military use and provided detailed negotiations are completed at that time." Laird had insisted on including this condition. He also wanted a senior military representative on the U.S. negotiating team on Okinawa. The president's objective was "maximum free conventional use of the military bases, particularly with respect to Korea, Taiwan and Vietnam." The United States wished to retain nuclear weapons on Okinawa, but as the negotiations proceeded Nixon would consider their withdrawal, "while retaining emergency storage and transit rights." The president would not insist on nuclear storage rights if other elements of the agreement were satisfactory.[22] Aichi's visit resulted in a tentative schedule: Negotiations would start in July and end in late November with Prime Minister Sato's visit to Washington.[23]

To the president's dismay, the substance of NSDM 13 appeared in the *New York Times* on 3 June. An article that presidential Chief of Staff H. R. Haldeman called "complete and accurate" detailed Nixon's Okinawa decisions and negotiating strategy. Nixon complained bitterly that its "premature revelation seriously undermined our bargaining position." Kissinger, Under Secretary of State Elliot Richardson, and Alexis Johnson, also of the State Department, thought the revelations could jeopardize the talks with Japan and complicate discussions with Aichi. Nixon asked Haldeman to identify the officials in the Pentagon, State Department, and CIA who had access to NSDM 13 and who might have leaked it. Although Nixon's memoir is evasive on whether wiretaps were actually instituted at this time, Haldeman stated that he set up a program for wiretaps but did not carry it out until later. Haldeman called on Laird several times to launch an investigation in the Pentagon. Laird denied leaking the document.[24]

Wheeler attempted to slow the process of reversion, alleging the U.S. government was "rushing precipitously to meet deadlines and commitments largely set by the Japanese" and had already made many concessions "in the interest of building them up to a position of Free World strength in Asia." He asked Deputy Secretary David Packard on 24 July 1969 for a review of the negotiating timetable in hopes of maximizing the concessions Washington might gain from the Japanese. As soon as the United States committed itself to a reversion date of 1972, Wheeler feared, it would lose bargaining leverage. He believed a prolonged negotiating schedule was in Washington's interest.[25]

Slowing the process seemed unlikely given the attitude of Japanese officials. Based on his trip to Okinawa, Navy Secretary John Chafee considered reversion a certainty. After meeting with Japanese foreign ministry and defense officials, Assistant Secretary Warren Nutter advised Laird that "Japanese officials seem to take it for granted that Okinawa will revert on schedule and on Japanese terms. . . . Japanese officialdom appears confident that it will get its way without tying its hands in any specific way." Like many others, Nutter regarded the bases on Okinawa as irreplaceable: America's "military posture in the Pacific will suffer a serious blow when we lose free use of Okinawa." A meeting with Japanese Foreign Minister Aichi at the end of July led Secretary Rogers to believe that talks on the continued military use of Okinawa might be difficult.[26]

Moreover, the Japanese seemed unlikely to budge on the issue of storing nuclear weapons on Okinawa. In the view of Richard L. Sneider, the State Department's country director for Japan, the Sato government would more likely break off talks on reversion than compromise on the storage issue. Yet, if the United States gave up nuclear storage rights on Okinawa, the Japanese government would probably accept a settlement that met "the substance of other U.S. military requirements." Sneider concluded that the key issue involved what concessions to seek from Japan if the United States conceded on the nuclear issue. Al Haig disagreed with Sneider's argument and advised Kissinger to take a harder line.[27]

Odyssey of Chemical Weapons

The unexpected disclosure of a U.S. arsenal of chemical munitions on Okinawa, a closely held secret, further complicated the Okinawa reversion talks. Resolving the matter to satisfy the Japanese and Okinawans on the one hand and U.S. security needs and U.S. public on the other proved to be a complex and prolonged process involving powerful political, environmental, and public pressures that required Laird's direct involvement.

Stockpiled for possible use in a Pacific war, most likely on the Korean Peninsula, were mustard gas (HD) and nerve gases (GB or sarin and VX). Almost a decade earlier, in January 1961, the JCS had authorized the head of the Pacific Command (CINCPAC) to store up to 16,000 tons of these chemicals, but no one had thought to inform the Japanese government because the United States then controlled the island. In 1969, 11,000 tons of chemical weapons, shipped to the island in 1963, were stored at the Chibana Army Ammunition Depot near the air approach to Kadena Air Force Base, the key U.S. military facility on the island. The Army planned to ship the balance of 5,000 tons to Okinawa in the summer or fall. Fearing a possible accident at Kadena, the assistant secretary of defense for installations and logistics had requested in 1967 that the Army relocate the weapons elsewhere on the island. As of mid-1969 the Army had not submitted a plan to OSD but was working on a proposal to construct storage facilities on Guam, estimated to take two years to complete.[28]

The presence of chemical munitions on Okinawa was no longer a secret after 8 July 1969. On that day during routine maintenance GB leaked from a 500-pound bomb stored in the Army depot. To avoid an adverse public reaction, the Pentagon at first kept the incident quiet and dispatched a team of specialists to detoxify the defective munitions. Laird and Deputy Assistant Secretary of Defense for International Security Affairs Dennis J. Doolin said that DoD notified the White House immediately, forwarding on 9 July the initial message about the leak from the U.S. commander in Okinawa. However, Kissinger was not informed. When the story was about to appear in print more than a week later, Kissinger told Laird that he was "trying to assemble the facts so the President could be informed." Laird had Doolin send Haig at the NSC a second notice on 17 July, with a warning that the Japanese government had not been notified of the leak, nor was Tokyo even "aware of the storage of such weapons on Okinawa."[29]

The incident came to public notice after the *Wall Street Journal* published a story on 18 July. The discharge of GB and the revelation of the presence of deadly chemicals on Okinawa angered Japanese officials and island residents.[30] Four days after the newspaper account Laird issued a detailed public announcement, stating that a U.S. Army civilian employee and 23 American soldiers were briefly exposed to GB during routine maintenance. No Okinawans or non-U.S. citizens were affected. DoD would carry out Nixon's order to "accelerate the previously planned removal of lethal chemical agents from Okinawa." The secretary's pledge helped minimize the harmful public impact of the leak. Laird hoped to begin the removal operation and have "a general timetable for its completion" before Sato's visit with Nixon in November.[31]

Nixon's order to remove the chemical munitions, more than a conciliatory gesture, accorded with the administration's ongoing examination of the chemical biological warfare (CBW) policy initiated in part by Laird. Concerned about the potentially damaging political and public relations ramifications of U.S. chemical and biological warfare programs, he had asked Kissinger in April 1969 for a comprehensive NSC review to include an assessment of the military utility of CBW. Existing policy required DoD to maintain a "defensive and retaliatory capability," until other nations, including the Soviet Union, eliminated their chemical and biological programs. To that end, the department funded an R&D program and defensive measures against the effects of chemical and biological weapons. It also maintained a minimal offensive capability to deter the use of chemical or biological weapons against the United States.[32]

The question of what to do about the chemical weapons on Okinawa figured prominently in the policy review. Laird feared increasing pressure from the public and Congress who, because of recent stories involving chemical weapons, had become more conscious of their dangers. A public outcry forced the Army to scrap its plan to keep dumping surplus and defective chemical weapons into the Atlantic Ocean. The accidental death of thousands of sheep in March 1968 near the U.S. Army's Dugway, Utah Proving Ground, a facility for storing and testing chemical and biological agents, underscored the risks of the CBW program. The deaths coincided with open-air tests of the nerve agent V X, lethal in small doses. Between 1951 and 1969, hundreds or perhaps thousands of open-air tests of chemical agents were conducted at the Dugway site. The Army initially denied responsibility, but it quietly reached a legal settlement with the affected ranchers, paying damages for the loss of livestock.[33]

As part of the policy review DoD had to evaluate whether it needed to stockpile chemical agents in the Pacific and, if so, in what quantities. The JCS, contending that U.S. chemical weapons were essential to deter the Soviets and that the chemical stocks currently positioned overseas were too small to pose a credible retaliatory threat, advocated an immediate expansion of stocks and improvements in storage. The JCS saw no easing of the danger from Soviet forces, whose training and doctrine had prepared them to use chemical weapons. In the Chiefs' view, "an enemy's advantage in initiating chemical operations would be enhanced if the overseas commands [in Europe and the Pacific] were forced to wait for movement of munitions from CONUS before retaliating." The JCS wanted the chemical stocks on Okinawa relocated to Guam, which they considered the only feasible alternative site in the Pacific. They urged that suitable facilities be built there on an expedited basis using military construction units and contingency funds.[34]

In contrast to the JCS, the Systems Analysis office saw only political problems and additional costs in expanding the storage capacity for CBW agents. In its assessment, the Chinese Communist government lacked the capability to use chemical weapons offensively and the Soviet Union was unlikely to use them. Accordingly, SA concluded that the United States probably had no need "to maintain a chemical deterrent in the Pacific."[35]

Systems Analysis prevailed. On 24 October Laird informed Wheeler that a chemical warfare deterrent "should be based on stockpiles maintained in CONUS rather than regional stockpiles." The secretary considered it highly unlikely that the Soviets or the Chinese would use chemical weapons on the Korean Peninsula because of the inherent risk of escalating a conflict to the nuclear level. Citing political and budgetary reasons for not moving the chemical weapons to Guam, he ordered the Army to transfer the munitions on Okinawa to the continental United States, or to Alaska, and to review alternative storage sites for chemical weapons. Relocation criteria called for minimal additional construction costs, no new acquisition of land, availability of disposal facilities for World War I–type munitions (mustard gas), and minimal "adverse public reaction." Laird wanted the Army to start moving chemical munitions from Okinawa to the selected site by 15 November, with the final shipment "scheduled for departure from Okinawa no later than 1 March 1970."[36]

When safety and environmental issues complicated the move, the administration feared that delays in carrying out the president's directive might undermine relations with Japan and the credibility of the Defense Department.[37] Under Secretary of the Army Thaddeus Beal advised Laird on 6 November that of the four sites under consideration he ruled out two in Alaska, in part because of the unknown effect of the cold climate on the munitions. Of the two remaining locations—the Umatilla Army Depot in Oregon and the Bangor Naval Ammunition Depot at Bremerton, Washington—Beal thought the naval depot the better choice, even though he conceded the Navy lacked experience in handling and storing chemical munitions. The McIntyre/Philbin amendment added to the military procurement authorization bill, which Beal expected to become law, made site selection more difficult. The amendment required prior notification to the Department of Health, Education, and Welfare (HEW) of the movement of chemical munitions. In addition, ten days before shipment to a CONUS military facility, DoD would also have

to notify the President of the Senate
and Speaker of the House as well as
the governors of any states through
which the chemicals would travel.
The amendment in effect nulli-
fied Laird's tight deadline, so Beal
offered a two-phase plan. The first
would involve a token shipment
of munitions from Okinawa by
15 November. The second would
begin later and complete the transfer before 1 March 1970.[38]

OSD's Installation and Logistics (I&L) directorate overrode the
Army's selection of the Washington site, concluding that the Army's
long and unique experience in
storing chemical munitions made
Umatilla, in a remote area of central Oregon near the Columbia

Under Secretary of the Army Thaddeus Beal
was involved in the difficult and controversial
removal of chemical munitions from Okinawa.
(NARA)

River, a better choice. Local people were "accustomed to the storage of these types
of munitions at this location," acting ASD (I&L) Glenn V. Gibson wrote, inferring
that a docile populace would be unlikely to protest. The plan to ship GB munitions
by air from Okinawa to McChord Air Force Base in Washington and then move
them by rail to Umatilla proved impossible to carry out expeditiously. The McIn-
tyre/Philbin amendment did not allow enough time for advance notification of
HEW officials, key congressional leaders, and the governors of Washington and
Oregon. In light of these requirements Beal recommended waiting until after Prime
Minister Sato's visit before notifying Congress, HEW, and the two governors. This
delay would avoid embarrassing the Japanese leader by raising such a sensitive issue
while he was in Washington.[39]

Given the difficulties in selecting a site, Nixon could not even allude to a token
shipment during Sato's visit, but he did announce a new national policy on chemical and biological weapons, the outcome of the review that Laird had initiated.

The president's policy, renouncing the first use of lethal chemical weapons and the first use of incapacitating chemicals, underscored the point that the United States would use these weapons only in self-defense. The United States also relinquished "the use of lethal biological agents and weapons, and all other methods of biological warfare," and would restrict its biological research to defensive measures. Nixon also requested DoD recommendations for "the disposal of existing stocks of bacteriological weapons." The announcement served to reaffirm the U.S. commitment to remove chemical weapons from Okinawa.[40]

This effort encountered numerous roadblocks.[41] A still-growing petition had allegedly obtained the signatures of one million Oregonians against the plan. On 5 December 1969 Oregon's Republican governor Tom L. McCall, who had campaigned for office as an environmentalist, wrote Nixon that he had learned only recently "that the Army already had [dangerous] chemicals . . . stored at the Umatilla installation" and questioned why they were too dangerous for Okinawa but not too dangerous for Oregon.[42] He wanted no munitions transferred to Oregon and requested that the chemicals at Umatilla be detoxified and removed. McCall's opposition alarmed Army Under Secretary Beal, who advised Laird not of the environmental risks but of the danger of a restrictive precedent. Failure to complete the relocation, Beal wrote, would "seriously threaten all future transportation within the United States of chemical munitions and agents." Laird supported Beal's position, urging the president to send a letter to McCall that would provide "the strongest support to his political problems."[43]

McCall desired a direct response from the president. With chemical weapons such a sensitive issue in Oregon, he hoped a personal letter from Nixon explaining the necessity of the transfer and the safety measures taken to minimize risks would "take him off the hook" and help protect him from the critical attacks of his political opponents.[44] Nixon ignored the issue. On 30 December 1969, weeks after the White House had received McCall's letter, Haig had to ask Laird or Packard to prepare and sign a response. Laird's letter of 8 January to Governor McCall argued that national security required DoD to maintain limited stockpiles of chemical weapons to serve as a deterrent. They "presented no unusual danger to the citizens of Okinawa" and were being removed only because of the reversion process. Laird's reply failed to provide sufficient reassurance or political cover. Mounting political opposition and a lawsuit filed in federal court by the governors of Washington and Oregon on 21 April 1970 blocked any shipment.[45]

With domestic critics up in arms, Nixon and Laird agreed to delay shipment of the chemicals to Oregon until after the November 1970 election, but they feared that such a lengthy postponement might lead the Tokyo government to conclude that the administration was edging away from its commitment to remove the munitions. Local authorities on Okinawa as well as Japanese officials expressed dismay over the delay in removing the poison gas. On 19 May the Okinawa legislature unanimously approved a resolution requiring the immediate removal of poisonous munitions. At the same time, the Japanese government, facing protests from opposition parties and leftist groups complaining about the holdup, pressed the administration for information on its shipping plans.[46]

With legal and political resistance mounting in an election year, the president decided in May 1970 to scrap the Oregon site and to consider moving the munitions to Kodiak Island, Alaska. But that alternative fared no better. The governor and representatives from that state were also vehemently opposed. The president and Laird eventually settled on Johnston Island, a small coral atoll 700 miles southwest of Honolulu, as the destination for the chemical weapons on Okinawa. Johnston Island was used for testing nuclear weapons in the 1950s and 1960s; storage sites and detoxification facilities would have to be built there.[47]

Despite the difficulty of finding a new location for the chemicals, Nixon and Kissinger remained convinced that DoD had to remove some chemicals from Okinawa quickly in order to demonstrate the administration's good intentions. In early June, Laird was told to begin moving some weapons as soon as it was feasible and after the legal requirements were met. In addition, Nixon asked the secretary to determine whether the chemical stocks on Okinawa were actually needed to carry out the strategy of fighting 1½ wars (NSDM 27). If they were not essential "would it be to the Administration's advantage to announce plans to detoxify the munitions in Guam, Alaska or elsewhere?" Before Laird finished his review, however, the Senate added another complication, passing an amendment at the end of June banning the use of any funds to transport chemical munitions to the United States and its territories and authorizing money for the destruction or detoxification of the munitions, but not on U.S. soil.[48]

On 1 July Packard recommended that the president authorize destruction of all chemical munitions on Okinawa because they were not essential to U.S. security. Destroying them outside the continental United States would provide a public relations boost at home. The Army and Admiral Thomas Moorer, who became JCS chairman that month, strenuously objected, claiming the weapons were needed for retaliation against a chemical attack. Moorer feared that Packard's proposal would eliminate the U.S. deterrent to other nations from using chemical weapons. Getting rid of these munitions without an offsetting concession from the Soviets would indicate weakness and indecision. Moorer wanted to proceed with the transfer to Johnston Island, but to defer the decision on whether to destroy the chemical weapons. In any event, the munitions could not be detoxified without construction of new facilities. At the end of July Packard agreed to wait until completion of another review.[49]

In August, however, the White House decided to delay once more the initial shipment. With an environmental impact statement not yet completed, the Surgeon General's Scientific Advisory Committee in late August imposed additional requirements before it would approve the transfer to Johnston Island. Among those requirements, chemicals could not be stored on the island as long as Air Micronesia flights landed there; no missile tests could be conducted while munitions were stored on the island; and rockets with chemical munitions would have to be stored in earth-covered igloos. Aware of the sensitive political questions, Laird ruled out a September date for the token initial shipment. To reassure the public that it would keep its commitment, in mid-September DoD issued a vague statement of intent to remove the chemical munitions sometime in late 1970 or early 1971.[50]

Nixon waited until December to instruct Laird to ship the chemicals, telling him to give priority to constructing the necessary facilities so that all munitions would leave Okinawa by 1 July 1971. Laird then approved the expenditure of more than $6 million in contingency funds to accelerate construction on Johnston Island.[51] The token initial shipment, one percent of the chemical munitions on Okinawa, occurred in January 1971. The final shipment left Okinawa on 11 September for storage on Johnston Island in the middle of the Pacific.[52]

The Reversion Agreement

Nixon and Sato issued a joint communiqué in Washington on 21 November 1969 establishing a framework for the reversion of Okinawa. The two leaders affirmed the Treaty of Mutual Cooperation and Security, concluding that reversion of Okinawa to Japanese administration could be accomplished in a manner that accommodated the interests of both nations. Japan would seek to expand its security responsibilities and the United States would continue to have its bases. The central point of the communiqué was the joint decision to enter into talks immediately to accomplish the reversion of Okinawa. Nixon and Sato "agreed to expedite the consultations with a view to accomplishing the reversion during 1972 subject to the conclusion of these specific arrangements with the necessary legislative support."[53]

Fortunately for the administration, the delays in removing chemical weapons from Okinawa had no appreciable effect on the negotiations over reversion, but other important issues, such as defense of the Ryukus and disposition of U.S. facilities, needed to be settled. Expecting Japan to assume responsibility for defending the islands after the turnover, the JCS wanted reassurances that the Japanese could deploy Self-Defense Force units to protect Okinawa and that U.S. forces would still be able to implement their military plans and support the Vietnam War. DoD agreed in April 1971 to release some land and military facilities—White Beach, Naha Wheel, and Naha Air Base—to the Japanese government upon reversion so that Japan could assume responsibility for Okinawa's defense.[54]

On 17 June 1971 the Japanese and U.S. governments signed the agreement returning the Ryukyus to Japan. Formal Japanese control would not begin until 1 July 1972, allowing time for ratification of the agreement in both countries and for conclusion of all administrative and financial arrangements. Under Article 7 of the reversion agreement, Japan agreed to pay the United States $320 million in compensation for the U.S. facilities it would take over and for the cost of relocating nuclear weapons. Although the agreement itself did not explicitly mention nuclear armaments, Article 7 further stated that the United States would carry out reversion "in a manner consistent with" Japanese policy banning the presence of nuclear weapons on Japanese soil as expressed in the 1969 Nixon-Sato communiqué. The United States would remove the weapons but retained the right to reintroduce them in time of crisis. Washington would also keep most of its military installations and personnel on Okinawa. A number of bases would close and the land they occupied would return to the Okinawans, but most importantly for DoD the agreement gave the United States the indefinite, continued use of 54 major installations on Okinawa, including Kadena Air Base.[55]

A separate U.S-Japan agreement transferring responsibility for the defense of Okinawa was ratified in Tokyo on 29 June 1971 by U.S. and Japanese officials.

Under the terms of the transfer, the mutual security treaty and the status of forces agreement would apply in Okinawa as well as in Japan. The United States would continue to maintain essential military forces on Okinawa and consult with the government of Japan prior to major changes in U.S. deployments, equipment, and the usage of bases. Thus the United States would be able to carry out its security obligations. DoD would still have more than a hundred installations, storage, range, and training areas. The Japanese would purchase in-place surface-to-air missiles and assume responsibility for the close-in air, sea, and land defense of Okinawa in one year, saving DoD about $35 million annually. The United States would relinquish those installations related to the immediate defense of Okinawa, 33 excess facilities, and Naha airport for use as a civilian airport. The Japanese agreed to pay the U.S. Treasury $175 million for civil assets and $200 million for DoD costs related to reversion and the residual value of military facilities. DoD would pay $25 million to relocate naval aviation units from Naha and to construct new facilities for storing nuclear weapons.[56] Laird viewed the $200 million as a real budgetary savings for DoD, with the entire sum to be spent on normal items in the DoD budget so that it represented a "net financial benefit" to the U.S. government.[57]

Early in July 1971 Laird traveled to Japan to meet with Prime Minister Sato and top officials of the Japanese Defense Agency. He had several goals: confirm the mutual security treaty; encourage Japan to improve the quality and effectiveness of its defense force; and solicit the Tokyo government to play a larger role in Asian affairs, especially by increasing its economic assistance to free nations in Asia needing support. Laird stressed to the Japanese that Congress was also pressing the administration to have America's allies in Europe and Asia raise their defense spending, believing that they were not contributing their fair share. He focused on the need for the Japanese to replace obsolete equipment with modern weapons, flesh out their forces, and participate in regional joint training exercises. The prime minister acknowledged that Japan needed to improve its forces.

Outgoing Defense Minister Yasuhiro Nakasone pressed Laird on nuclear weapons, seeking a verification plan for their removal from Okinawa after reversion. For internal political reasons the Japanese wanted to be able to state with assurance that the nuclear arms had been removed. Laird urged Nixon not to go along; in his judgment the word of an American president should constitute sufficient assurance for the Japanese government.[58] Although Japan wanted no nuclear

Minister of Defense Yasuhiro Nakasone of Japan visits the Pentagon on 9 September 1970 to hold meetings with Laird and other top U.S. officials on Japan's defense program. (OSD Historical Office)

weapons on Okinawa or its home islands, it nonetheless desired the protection of the U.S. nuclear umbrella against a possible attack by the Soviets or Communist China. To enjoy that protection Tokyo was willing to let the United States retain its military bases.[59]

When reversion took place on 15 May 1972, the Ryukyu Islands became a prefecture of Japan, and the United States preserved its political-military alliance with Japan. The successful exercise in diplomacy satisfied the basic interests of both countries. The restoration of territory and the removal of nuclear and chemical munitions helped quell Japanese domestic opposition to continuing the security alliance with the United States. In turn, the United States obtained renewal of the security treaty and continued use of essential bases in Japan and Okinawa, and retained the right to mount operations from those bases. At Laird's insistence the Japanese government agreed to increase its share of the costs of keeping U.S. military units in Japan and to pay for the costs of relinquished facilities and their relocation. Although trade conflicts (specifically the importation of Japanese textiles) and competition for markets continued to be irritants between the two nations, Nixon attained his security objective of keeping Japan closely allied to the United States.[60]

South Korea

Along with Japan, South Korea stood strong as a vital U.S. ally in eastern Asia. Since the 1950s, when the Korean Peninsula had been a battleground with North Korea and its ally China, U.S. national security policy called for using military strength in the Pacific to deter another conflict with the two Communist nations. As with NATO, Laird encouraged a more prosperous South Korea to strengthen its military so he could reduce U.S. forces needed to defend against a possible attack from North Korea. Under the Nixon Doctrine, the United States remained committed to South Korea's defense, but Nixon and Laird believed relative stability could be accomplished with a smaller U.S. presence.

A Japanese possession from 1910 to the end of World War II, Korea became a Cold War battleground. Above the 38th parallel, North Korea emerged as a full-fledged Communist state under the aegis of the Soviet Union and Communist China. To the south, the United States supported the democratic Republic of South Korea. As part of the World War II demobilization, President Harry Truman withdrew the last U.S. forces from South Korea in 1949 and established a military advisory group to build up the ROK armed forces. The armistice agreement of 1953 that ended the Korean War left the peninsula divided into two even more hostile armed camps than before the war and Communist China and the United States as adversaries.[61]

To keep South Korea secure and independent, the United States had signed a formal defense treaty with the Seoul government. From 1953 to 1969 the United States provided South Korea $4 billion in economic aid and nearly $2.5 billion in military assistance. At an annual cost of about $800 million, two combat-ready U.S. Army divisions designated exclusively for the defense of South Korea kept station along the Demilitarized Zone, the likely invasion corridor.[62]

Over the years, South Korea's armed forces had grown in size and capability, but the country still lacked the strength to defend itself without outside assistance.[63] During a time of retrenchment in U.S. spending, Laird had to determine how large a force the United States needed to keep in South Korea to defeat another invasion, how many troops it could withdraw, and what military assistance programs would strengthen and modernize the capabilities of South Korea's conventional forces over the next few years. The Johnson administration had examined those questions in its September 1968 interagency review of U.S. policy toward South Korea. Nixon decided in February 1969 to complete the study (NSSM 27), predicated on the continuation of U.S. policy goals and the security commitment to South Korea.[64]

The downing of an American EC–121 reconnaissance aircraft by North Korean fighter-jets in April 1969 was a reminder of the Pyongyang regime's continued hostility (see chapter 2). It spurred Nixon to establish the Washington Special Actions Group under Kissinger. Over the course of several months the WSAG examined contingency plans for another Korean crisis similar to the EC-121 episode. The action group, which included Assistant Secretary Nutter, Director of the Joint Staff Vice Admiral Nels Johnson, and representatives from the State Department and CIA, produced several political-military scenarios for handling various levels of aggression from North Korea. These scenarios were reviewed and updated periodically.[65]

The South Korean government used the EC–121 episode to seek additional U.S. defensive measures to deter North Korea. Minister of National Defense Im Chung Sik sought to persuade Laird that the current U.S. military assistance program did not adequately prepare ROK forces for a surprise attack.[66] During his visit to Washington in the spring of 1969, Deputy Prime Minister Park Choong Hoon pressed Nixon to build up U.S. airpower in South Korea and help strengthen Seoul's forces, especially its air force. Nixon told Park to discuss the issue with Laird.[67]

Citing North Korea's aggressiveness and military buildup, in May 1969 Laird sought a supplemental FY 1969 appropriation of $108 million to demonstrate U.S. support of South Korea. Nixon initially backed the request that would provide materials and equipment to enhance airfields from air attack, but State and Bureau of the Budget were opposed. Without strong, unified support from the administration Laird concluded that Congress would not pass it. Rather than risk having Congress reject the supplemental, the president decided to withdraw it. "Laird may have to fight more important battles," he informed Kissinger. Nonetheless, Nixon wanted to be certain that NSSM 27 policy review carefully examined South Korea's military assistance requirements.[68]

NSSM 27: Shaping a New Policy

The first NSC session on NSSM 27 on 14 August 1969 came shortly after the unveiling in July 1969 of the Nixon Doctrine, calling for America's Asian allies to assume a greater share of their defense burden. In contrast to South Korean officials, the administration believed their ally could do more. Improving conditions in South Korea—a strengthening economy, strong leadership, and more effective military forces—made feasible the NSSM 27 goal of limiting "US budgetary and balance of payments costs to reasonable levels."[69] Deciding how many U.S. troops to keep in Korea proved contentious. The State Department wanted to reduce the number of U.S. bases and troops and shift the U.S. Army's 2nd Infantry Division away from the DMZ, asserting the shift would not impair U.S. military capability. Moving the division would presumably make it less vulnerable in an offensive and perhaps ease tensions along the DMZ. General Wheeler objected, citing CINCPAC Admiral John McCain's opposition to the relocation. McCain feared that North Korea might interpret the relocation of the 2nd Division as a weakening of the U.S. commitment. The presence of U.S. troops at the DMZ, he pointed out, also served to restrain the ROK Army from taking rash action and allow U.S. forces in the area (where the armistice commission met at Panmunjom) to remain under United Nations rather than South Korean control. Laird forwarded McCain's views without endorsing them.[70]

Thinking about more than relocating a single division, Nixon told Kissinger in late November 1969, seven months after the EC–121 crisis, that before the end of 1969 he expected to see a plan that cut in half the number of Americans stationed in Korea. He would brook no delays. The president wanted to retain an air and sea presence on the peninsula sufficient to carry out "the kind of retaliatory strike which we have planned," alluding to the contingency plans of the WSAG. President Park Chung Hee resisted, fearing a substantial pullout of U.S. troops would make war with North Korea inevitable, but Nixon was not swayed. On 6 December he pointedly reminded Kissinger, "I want a plan developed *now* to bring about the ROK take over. U.S. to provide a trip wire and air and sea support only."[71]

With the drafting of NSSM 27 underway, at Kissinger's urging Nixon decided to postpone consideration of a withdrawal plan until the policy study was completed in December. NSSM 27 was needed to provide the framework for carrying out the president's decision on cutting American troops in Korea. The study could lay out policy alternatives on U.S. force levels, military and economic assistance, and burden sharing of military and economic responsibilities by the Americans and Koreans. Seeing the NSSM 27 process to completion would keep State, Defense, and the JCS engaged in policy formulation with the optimistic aim of reaching a unified approach to the Koreans. State and Defense were already working on withdrawal issues.[72]

The NSSM 27 draft of December 1969 argued for withdrawing some U.S. forces on the grounds that another North Korean invasion was "improbable." The study pointed out that in 1950 North Korea's army had been twice as large as South Korea's and that the U.S. pullout before the invasion probably created the impression that Americans would not defend its ally. In 1969, however, the United States had a formal treaty obligation to defend South Korea, whose army was now much larger than its enemy's. NSSM 27 concluded that a South Korean force of 386,000 to 419,000, with current equipment and U.S. air and naval support, could repel an all-out attack by North Korea alone with no additional ground combat assistance. A larger ROK force (600,000) with U.S. support could stop even a combined Chinese/North Korean attack north of Seoul for 30 to 60 days. Moreover, 16 to 18 modernized ROK divisions would have the same fighting capability as 23 divisions with their current equipment. It would cost an estimated $4 billion to modernize 16 ROK divisions for FYs 1970 to 1974.[73]

Not unexpectedly, NSSM 27 spawned disagreements. The JCS insisted that 21 combat divisions were needed in Korea: 19 ROK and 2 U.S. ISA argued for 16 active-duty and 5 ready reserve ROK divisions, plus one U.S. division with adequate support. Deeply involved in DoD budget preparation, Packard hoped to cut U.S. Army personnel in South Korea by 20,000 to 25,000, that is, by more than a division.[74] High-level South Korean military and civilian officials exhorted U.S. Eighth Army commander in Korea General John H. Michaelis and U.S. Ambassador William Porter not to withdraw U.S. forces in the near future.[75]

NSSM 27 also brought basic questions to the surface. If the South Koreans could in fact stem an enemy offensive largely by themselves, then how much U.S. support was necessary? How many U.S. combat forces needed to remain in Korea while ROK forces were modernized?[76] What would modernization of Korean forces cost the United States? The administration assumed that the South Korean government could not take on a significant share of the cost of modernizing its forces without harming its future economic growth and foreign exchange earnings.[77] Modernization plans concentrated on improving ROK ground forces, but the JCS also asked for a substantial increase in American support for ROK air and naval forces.[78]

The revised NSSM 27 study of late February concluded that withdrawing one U.S. division and keeping 18 or 19 divisions in the ROK Army "involves no military risks of any significance." The study also contended that the United States "need not 'modernize' the entire ROK 18 or 19 division force structure to enable them to defend themselves against the present or likely future North Korea force structure."[79] All U.S. force reductions contemplated under NSSM 27 supposed improved ROK Army readiness and equipment modernization, but the FYs 1970 and 1971 congressional Military Assistance Program authorizations were well below the level assumed for all NSSM 27 alternatives under consideration. A supplemental appropriation was crucial to modernization and withdrawal plans.[80]

At the 4 March NSC session Secretary Rogers advanced a two-phased withdrawal plan: an immediate reduction of forces and further cuts in U.S. strength after the return of two ROK divisions from Vietnam. The State Department believed 16 modernized ROK divisions were sufficient, arguing that the first withdrawal of U.S. forces should be 20,000 soldiers rather than an entire division to "keep as much muscle in Korea as possible." OSD proposed withdrawing at least 20,000 U.S. personnel—including an entire U.S. Army division. The JCS wanted a minimum force of one and a third U.S. divisions, 18 modernized ROK divisions, as well as modernized Korean air and naval forces, and no cuts in U.S. air and naval strength. Deputy Secretary Packard appreciated the Chiefs' desire to proceed cautiously, but he feared that Congress would not approve funds for modernizing ROK forces unless U.S. forces, "in the order of magnitude of 20,000" were withdrawn. Packard knew that the Army wanted to stay within its FY 1972 budget guidelines. That would require a withdrawal of 18,000 soldiers by the end of FY 1971 and an additional 15,000 by the end of FY 1973.[81]

Nixon intended to withdraw U.S. forces from Korea, but not to weaken the U.S. commitment to defend the peninsula. He supported pursuing modernization of ROK forces and seeking Korean support for a scaled-back U.S. force. The president viewed withdrawals as a prerequisite for congressional backing of a long-term U.S. military commitment in Korea. "We are faced," Nixon noted, "with increasing emphasis on domestic spending here at home. Thus, we have to find a way to continue playing a role [in South Korea] by drawing down our strength somewhat or else the Congress will refuse to support anything."[82]

On 20 March 1970 Nixon issued his decision (NSDM 48) to withdraw 20,000 U.S. military personnel from Korea by the end of FY 1971. He hoped that the ROK government would support the reduction in light of its own military strength and additional U.S. military assistance. The president's program for modernizing ROK forces amounted to $200 million per year in grant military assistance and excess equipment over a five-year period (FYs 1971–1975), a total package of $1 billion, plus economic assistance of $50 million per year.[83] Under the president's order DoD would pull out and deactivate one U.S. Army division and its supporting units, turning over unneeded property and equipment to ROK forces. The JCS withdrawal plan called for replacing a U.S. corps headquarters, artillery units, and the 2nd Division on the DMZ with South Korean units. U.S. forces would, however, retain control of the DMZ at Panmunjom. Nixon approved the redeployment by the end of FY 1971 of 18,400 soldiers and 1,600 Air Force personnel.[84]

The South Korean government resisted. President Park and other high-level Korean officials pressed for a delay and for modernization funding. Prime Minister Chung Il Kwon insisted that force upgrades had to come prior to a U.S. pullout, threatening to resign along with his entire cabinet if the United States went ahead with its planned withdrawal. The South Koreans also intimated that they might bring home some or all of their soldiers serving in South Vietnam if the United States cut the number of troops stationed in South Korea. None of this deterred the administration. Packard reaffirmed the decision to carry out the planned withdrawal, still hoping it could be accomplished with Seoul's support.[85]

The South Korean government made it difficult to carry out the withdrawals. DoD could not redeploy the U.S. 2nd Division as an entity because the Koreans did not replace departing American forces with ROK units along the DMZ. The Korean failure to cooperate had forced the U.S. Army to transfer personnel from the 7th Infantry Division in Korea to the 2nd Infantry to replace departing soldiers and to maintain combat-ready units on the DMZ. The 7th Division was being hollowed out; some of its units were not even manned. In August 1970 U.S. Army forces in Korea were already 10,000 below target strength of 52,000. In October Packard let Kissinger and Alexis Johnson of the State Department know that South Korean intransigence was thwarting President Nixon's plan.[86]

Laird stands in a foxhole during a visit to South Korea troops, undated. (OSD Historical Office)

Not only did the Seoul government hamper the U.S. withdrawal, it pressed for more military aid, seeking $2.5 billion in addition to the $1 billion that Nixon had already proffered for operational requirements and for replacing outmoded equipment over the next five years. U.S. officials dismissed the request as "excessive" in view of planned budget reductions in FY 1972 and the possibility of additional U.S. withdrawals from Korea in FY 1972 and FY 1973. The NSC Undersecretaries Committee recommended increasing the five-year Korean $1 billion military assistance package by $500 million, including a supplemental FY 1971 appropriation of $150 million as the initial increment of that package. The additional $500 million would allow "some modernization of air and naval as well as ground forces" and offset the "planned world-wide reductions in U.S. air and naval forces [that] will affect our reinforcement capabilities in Korea." It would also permit U.S. planning for additional redeployments. At the urging of Laird and the JCS, Nixon approved the five-year $1.5 billion military assistance program.[87]

Washington and Seoul reached formal agreement in February 1971 on the $1.5 billion modernization program and the withdrawal of 20,000 U.S. troops. The United States reaffirmed its commitment to defend South Korea from armed attack under the 1954 Mutual Defense Treaty. At the time of the formal signing, Congress had already approved $150 million in supplemental funds for the program. The withdrawal of 20,000 U.S. troops was scheduled for completion by the end of June 1971.[88]

Laird, however, planned to redeploy even more U.S. forces from South Korea by linking their departure to the return of South Korean forces from South Vietnam. Two ROK divisions, the Capital and the 9th, and a brigade of Korean marines, underwritten by U.S. funds, fought alongside U.S. and South Vietnamese forces. Laird estimated the annual cost of U.S. support for ROK units in Vietnam at $250 million–$300 million, a figure that included funds for modernizing the firepower, communications, and mobility of these Korean units.

The secretary advocated the withdrawal of ROK forces from Vietnam not just to facilitate the pullout of U.S. soldiers from Korea. Like American commander General Creighton Abrams and others, Laird expressed doubts about the military value of the Korean units in Vietnam. The Johnson administration had urged South Korea to deploy forces to Vietnam and had provided generous assistance to enable them to do so, but Korean forces added disproportionately little to the war effort in South Vietnam. In the judgment of a State Department report, "They have appeared reluctant to undertake offensive operations and have been useful for guarding only a small sector of the populated area." South Vietnamese territorial forces, although lacking the organic heavy equipment and firepower of ROK divisions, operated as a buffer between the Korean units and the North Vietnamese Army. Corruption on the part of the Koreans was endemic, well organized, and well known. Investigations "revealed that substantial amounts of US funds and property have been diverted from their intended purposes by the ROKFV [Korean forces in Vietnam]." To persuade the Koreans to take a more active combat role, the U.S. mission in Saigon estimated, would come with a high price on top of the nearly $244 million in direct costs borne by the U.S. Treasury in FY 1972. The United States had limited leverage. American pressure on the Koreans to remain in Vietnam in strength would reinforce their insistence that existing U.S. force levels remain in Korea.[89]

Nixon decided at the end of June 1971 to continue U.S. support for the two ROK divisions in Vietnam through December 1972 and to review the issue in 1972. U.S. negotiators were instructed to press the Korean forces for better performance but to offer no increase in U.S. support. He wanted no linkage between possible additional U.S. withdrawals from Korea and having Korean forces remain in Vietnam.[90] Laird objected, seeing little chance of improving the performance of ROK forces, and favored withdrawing them from Vietnam. The money saved would be more productively spent on building up South Vietnam's forces instead. He urged the president to proceed with talks on South Korean redeployments from Vietnam beginning in December 1971.

Laird's proposal went nowhere. Kissinger reminded the president that the Koreans wanted to keep a large military contingent in South Vietnam. Their combat units would be needed in Vietnam, Kissinger argued, should North Vietnam and the Viet Cong shift from their current protracted guerrilla war strategy to one of conventional warfare. The Senior Review Group agreed with Kissinger. According to its assessment, the SRG expected a major enemy assault in 1972. ROK forces, representing a third of allied main force strength in South Vietnam's Military Region II, would provide extra combat power to help repulse an offensive. Moreover, South Vietnam's President Thieu wanted South Korean units to remain through December 1972, claiming that his forces lacked the personnel or capability to fill in for them. In July 1971 Nixon reaffirmed his decision to support two ROK divisions in Vietnam through the end of 1972. South Korean forces did not completely leave South Vietnam until March 1973, after the Paris peace agreement was signed.[91]

Reopening the Door to China

Nixon's brief announcement on 15 July 1971 that he would visit the People's Republic of China (PRC) in 1972 "to seek the normalization of relations between the two countries" was the fruit of painstaking behind-the-scenes diplomacy by the White House and State Department. Although the Pentagon was not a primary player in this transformative diplomatic process of engaging China, it affected defense policy. Nixon's visit to Beijing in February 1972 had major implications for U.S. relations with its military allies, especially Taiwan.[92]

In 1969 the United States had no diplomatic relations with the government in Beijing, but, in keeping with its Cold War objective of containing Communist expansion, it supported the noncommunist, nationalist Chinese government of Taiwan (Republic of China, or GRC) with military assistance. Consequently, military ties between the two countries remained strong with the United States reaffirming its defense commitment to the Taiwan government after budget cuts forced Washington in September 1969 to announce the end of the U.S. Navy's routine Taiwan Strait Patrol. The Seventh Fleet would continue to transit the strait and call at Taiwan ports. In the summer of 1970 the GRC under U.S. auspices undertook a review of the modernization and organization of its forces.[93]

Although Laird wanted to continue to provide military assistance to Taiwan, he realized that normalizing relations with mainland China might eventually jeopardize the retention of U.S. installations on Taiwan. Others shared his concern. Packard saw the need to assess Taiwan's role in America's Asian policy. Army Chief of Staff General William Westmoreland warned that reducing or removing the U. S. military presence from Taiwan might require some backtracking in the U.S. retrenchment in Japan and Okinawa. Admiral Moorer foresaw a severe impact to the island if the U.S. military left Taiwan, citing the financial cost and a reduced tactical and strategic military posture.[94]

Decades of antagonism and mistrust stood in the way of improved ties with the PRC. The United States and China had been adversaries since the ouster of Chiang Kai-shek and his forces from mainland China in 1949. Communist China's sponsorship of insurgencies in Asia and Africa, so-called wars of national liberation, and its provision of advisers, military aid, and equipment to North Vietnam kept the two nations at odds. Indeed, one reason (among many) that Washington had advanced in the early 1960s for its intervention in Vietnam was to prevent the expansion of Chinese Communist influence in Asia. Although U.S. military strategy assumed that China's large, defense-oriented army posed only a limited military threat, Beijing in the 1960s developed nuclear and strategic weapons, including medium-range bombers and missiles. The Nixon administration rationalized its ABM program in part as a defense against a Chinese missile strike on the United States. China's nuclear weapons program also induced the U.S. government to maintain nuclear forces in the Far East large enough to serve as a credible deterrent.[95]

Nixon, who had gained political renown in the 1950s as a hard-line anticommunist, came to doubt the policy of isolating China over the long term. As part of an overall national security review early in February 1969, he planned to reassess

U.S. relations with Communist China and Taiwan. The review (NSSM 14) examined three basic policy options: continue the military and diplomatic status quo;
intensify China's isolation and pressure its leadership to adopt more moderate policies; and lessen the areas of conflict and China's isolation within the international
community. The JCS wanted to continue the current policy, expecting no benefit
from easing it. Assistant Secretary Nutter believed an alternative policy would not
have helped any more than the current policy in moderating Chinese behavior.
Kissinger and his staff favored moving toward an approach that lowered tensions
with China, a position that State and Secretary Rogers favored.[96]

Nixon's meeting with French President Charles de Gaulle at the end of February
1969 reinforced his inclination to change position. It might be wise for the United
States, he suggested to de Gaulle, to develop lines of communication with both the
Soviets and Chinese since it would be detrimental to long-term U.S. interests "for it
to appear that the West was ganging up with the Soviet Union against China." De
Gaulle thought the United States should recognize China before its growing power
made diplomatic recognition obligatory.[97]

Still, not everyone in the administration agreed with Nixon's thinking. A special
national intelligence estimate expected no major changes in China's stance toward
the United States or the Soviet Union as long as Mao was in power. Beijing would
continue to aspire to political dominance in Asia and support wars of national liberation. Another NIE concluded that the Chinese would deploy medium- and long-
range nuclear missiles in the future. Looking at China's policies and armed forces,
the JCS and ISA did not see enough evidence for Washington to justify a change in
approach to China.[98] Nixon pressed ahead, asking Kissinger what the United States
could do to indicate its readiness for a "possible opening toward China."[99]

Skirmishes between Russian and Chinese forces along the Sino-Soviet border
in March 1969, which heightened tensions between the Communist countries,
provided an opening. A national intelligence estimate at the end of February 1969
concluded that the Soviets regarded Beijing as a competitor and feared losing their
position as the leading Communist power. Nixon looked to exploit the rift, theoriz-
ing that Soviet nervousness about its Communist rival might provide a diplomatic
opportunity for the United States. Assessing an intensified Sino-Soviet rivalry and
the possibility of war, a review of U.S. policy options (NSSM 63) concluded that
U.S. overtures to China might induce the Soviets to expand détente with the west.[100]

After two years of thought, study, and debate, the opening to China began to take shape. Nixon's forthcoming visit to Beijing prompted Laird to prepare DoD for possible changes in U.S. relations with Taiwan, but he warned his staff not to expect too much from the initial meeting. He connected the China initiative to the underlying principles of the Nixon Doctrine, which he defined as strength, partnership, and negotiation. From DoD's perspective the pending visit was only one move in the overall effort to negotiate an era of peace, and it was essential to maintain strength during this period.[101]

Laird supported the president's initiative, but in August 1971 he reminded Kissinger that as secretary he needed to be involved in the planning as it related to politico-military matters. He had concern about the effect that closer ties with mainland China could have on the size and presence of U.S. forces on Taiwan, the military assistance program for Taiwan, and relations with allies such as Japan. The secretary also requested the JCS to assess how the removal of U.S. forces and installations from Taiwan would affect American security interests. Laird thought it imperative not to let an emerging relationship with Beijing make the Japanese, essential U.S. allies in the Pacific, feel they were being relegated to a lower status. Maintaining trust and cooperation with Japan "is of the utmost importance, requiring full, frank, and timely discussions on a continuing basis. The possible removal of the US military presence from Taiwan makes our Japanese bases, especially on Okinawa, almost indispensable."[102]

Admiral Moorer warned of adverse effects in a future withdrawal of U.S. military forces from Taiwan: slower responsiveness during a crisis as well as the possible perception that the United States was less willing to meet its defense commitments under the 1954 Mutual Defense Treaty and was losing the resolve to meet other defense treaty commitments. Curtailing or ending military assistance to Taiwan would degrade the effectiveness of its military forces. Relocation of U.S. personnel and installations from the island would require identification of new military sites, transfer of U.S. intelligence capabilities, new communications systems, and revision of the Single Integrated Operational Plan target coverage.[103]

Nixon wanted better ties with the PRC but not at the cost of discarding long-term allies. The Shanghai communiqué of 27 February 1972 issued by the United States and China at the end of Nixon's visit ensured continuity of policy toward Taiwan in the near term. Yet the document also portended future policy changes and established a framework for the future. The two nations agreed to move toward normal diplomatic relations and to reduce the danger of international military conflict. They separately agreed not to seek hegemony in the Asia-Pacific region and not to enter into agreements directed at other states. At the same time, the United States reaffirmed its existing regional commitments. It would maintain close ties with and support for South Korea and continue to develop close bonds with Japan. On the status of Taiwan the two nations stated their differences. China identified Taiwan as a central obstacle to normalization of relations with the United States; it demanded the return of Taiwan, which it considered a province of mainland China, to the motherland and U.S. withdrawal of all forces and military installations from the island. The United States acknowledged that Taiwan was part of China but insisted on a peaceful resolution of the issue by the Chinese themselves. It defined the withdrawal of U.S. forces and installations as an ultimate objective and pledged to "progressively reduce its forces and military installations on Taiwan as the tension in the area diminishes." Yet it was Nixon's judgment that the China summit and communiqué had no immediate effect on the maintenance of U.S. defense commitments. As Kissinger explained to James C. H. Shen, Taiwan's ambassador to the United States, Nixon had made no commitment to PRC leaders to withdraw or reduce forces from U.S. military installations on Taiwan.[104]

Laird continued to advocate military aid for Taiwan, believing it inadvisable to back away from the military assistance program for Taiwan. He believed that about 2,400 U.S. personnel, primarily advisers, intelligence analysts, and maintenance workers, were still needed there to help defend the island. Laird supported the Taiwanese government's request to replace older jets (F–100As and F–5As), ships, and tanks with newer versions. In July 1972 Taiwan asked DoD for F–5Bs and F–5Es, replacement destroyers, and two submarines with SAMs; M48 tanks to replace WWII and Korean War models; and TOW (Tube-launched, Optically-tracked, Wire-guided) Missile System and Red Eye missiles. In addition, Taiwan's defense minister sought MAP support to upgrade communications and electronic countermeasure capabilities.[105] Kissinger backed Laird's position but insisted on discretion to avoid alienating Beijing. Thus the administration approved the transfer of the F–5Es, but the financing and public relations were to be handled in a way that minimized the political effects on the evolving relationship with China. In October 1972 the State Department notified the Taiwan government that it hoped to supply the

F–5Es in FY 1974. The request for the two submarines was also approved but with the stipulation that they were to be used only for antisubmarine warfare training.[106]

Events in Vietnam affected the request for newer jets. In October 1972 the State Department requested the transfer of all F–5As in Taiwan's air force to South Vietnam. Under the Enhance Plus program, the administration wanted to build up Saigon's defenses and place South Vietnam in the strongest possible military posture in its struggle against North Vietnam. South Vietnam's air force was trained to fly this type of aircraft. The State Department stated that Washington would credit Taiwan for the value of the aircraft and work out a method for replacements. In the meantime, the U.S. was prepared to discuss the deployment of U.S. F–4s and U.S. pilots to Taiwan to fill any gaps in the nation's defenses and hoped to deploy the aircraft with U.S. pilots within 90 days.[107]

LAIRD'S TENURE AS SECRETARY coincided with a transition in relations with two key Asian allies, Japan and South Korea. His measures to lessen their dependence on U.S. military assistance were analogous to his efforts to have America's NATO allies assume a greater share of the defense burden in Europe. Greater involvement by the Japanese and Koreans would also ease somewhat the pressure on DoD to cut back U.S. defense spending. Nixon withdrew some U.S. forces from Korea, but not as many as the secretary had advised. The basic question of NSSM 69—to what extent tactical nuclear weapons could substitute for American ground forces fighting alongside their allies—was never resolved. The reversion of Okinawa, a major accomplishment, served to strengthen the alliance with Japan without diminishing American military might or presence in the Pacific. The United States retained its bases on Okinawa. Moreover, Laird obtained pledges from the Japanese to provide more resources for defense. Nor did the removal of chemical weapons from Okinawa, which occurred when Nixon changed U.S. policy on chemical and biological weapons, weaken U.S. defenses in Laird's view, but the episode forced Laird and the administration to resolve a host of unanticipated political and environmental problems that would also confront other defense secretaries. The full consequences of the transition in relations with China and Taiwan would be felt only after Laird was long out of office, but the near term required the administration to engage in a balancing act to support Taiwan without harming the emerging relationship with Beijing. It was important that the United States retained military bases on Taiwan.

For a defense secretary concerned about national security after Vietnam and above all matching U.S. defense strategy with the likelihood of diminishing resources, it made sense to begin the process of engaging China. A friendlier China would make the Nixon Doctrine, expecting Asian allies to provide a greater share of their defense, more feasible. Amid change in East Asia, the United States continued its strong relations with critical allies—Japan, South Korea, and Taiwan.

CHAPTER 14

The All-Volunteer Force

WHEN LAIRD CAME INTO OFFICE, the administration envisioned fundamentally changing the way the nation obtained military personnel by ending the draft and creating an all-volunteer force. This transformation would represent a signal accomplishment for Laird as secretary of defense. For most of its history the United States relied on volunteers to serve in its armed forces, resorting to conscription during the last two years of the Civil War. The World War I Selective Service System began operating in May 1917, shortly after the United States became a belligerent. In September 1940, more than a year before the United States entered World War II, the nation instituted its first peacetime draft that eventually filled the ranks of the military services during the war. The long-term peacetime draft began in 1948, early in the Cold War to supply the armed forces, especially the Army, with a steady and sufficient number of recruits at low cost in salaries and benefits. Functioning during peacetime and wartime, the draft had become an accepted part of American life—until the U.S. became involved in Vietnam. Without fanfare or controversy, in March 1963 President Kennedy signed legislation extending the draft for four years.[1]

The operation of the Selective Service System during the Vietnam War exposed the glaring inequities of the system. The U.S. troop buildup in Vietnam increased draft calls, but relatively few in the post–World War II baby boom generation were called up and a variety of deferments exempted many others. As opposition to the Vietnam War grew so did antagonism to the draft. Disapproval came from opponents of the war: libertarians, who saw conscription as an infringement on individual liberty; reformers, who found the selective service system unfair and in need of major overhaul; and free-market economists, who advocated a system of voluntary service that would compensate military personnel more fairly. This powerful and near-irresistible dissatisfaction brought about a willingness to end conscription and institute an all-volunteer force.

Draft Reform and Vietnam

The Pentagon completed in June 1965 a comprehensive review of the draft system requested by President Johnson. The DoD study recommended moving to a force composed totally of volunteers, just as the Vietnam buildup began. The need to obtain troops to fight the war, however, derailed draft reform. It would be virtually impossible to obtain enough volunteers to meet the expanding war's demand for personnel. Hence, Johnson continued to rely on conscription to supply manpower for the war, a step that allowed him also to avoid the politically sensitive step of mobilizing the reserves for service in Vietnam.[2]

The swelling number of Vietnam-bound draftees increased public sensitivity to serious flaws in the induction system. A number of local draft boards, unrepresentative of the population of their districts, inconsistently classified draftees and granted deferments. Critics pointed out that the draft had the effect of discriminating against minorities and the less well-off. Draftees tended to be less educated, members of minorities, and from blue-collar families. Educational deferments allowed college students or those planning a higher education to avoid military service. Moreover, the casualty rate for Vietnam draftees rose because so many were trained for combat assignments. Volunteers on the other hand could frequently select their specialties and choose technical or administrative positions. Criticism of the draft corresponded with the dramatic increase in the number of men called to service. Out of nearly 340,000 inducted during the first year of U.S. involvement in Vietnam, 317,500 went to the Army, 19,600 to the Marine Corps, and 2,600 to the Navy.[3]

As the antidraft movement quickly gathered strength during the Vietnam War escalation, Selective Service had to deal with draft resisters, draft card burners, and court challenges. Morale problems—drug usage, desertion, and AWOL rates—began to increase as the war dragged on. A few well-publicized draftees even refused to deploy to Vietnam.[4]

With opposition to the war rising and congressional reauthorization of the draft pending, in July 1966 President Johnson had created the Presidential Advisory Committee on Selective Service headed by Burke Marshall, his former assistant attorney general for civil rights. The commission rejected the concept of an all-volunteer force as too expensive but proposed ending most occupational and educational deferments and adopting a national lottery. In reauthorizing conscription, Congress enacted no reforms of the selective service system. But even opponents of a volunteer force suspected the current system could not long endure. Democratic congressman Mendel Rivers, whose House Committee on Armed Services opposed a force of only volunteers, nonetheless recognized the continued great public interest in the idea. In September 1968 he asked DoD to keep him informed about ongoing studies and new departmental incentives to increase the number of enlistees. Assistant Secretary of Defense for Manpower and Reserve Affairs Alfred Fitt told Rivers in mid-October that he planned to initiate an assessment of how "to reduce or eliminate the need for inductions in the post-Vietnam period." He named the study Project Volunteer and asked Harold Wool, his director of procurement policy, to begin work in November 1968. Army Chief of Staff General William Westmoreland, who anticipated the possibility of a new military personnel procurement system, directed the Army in 1968 to study the effects of ending the draft and shifting to a volunteer force.[5]

The prospect of an all-volunteer force emerged as an issue in the 1968 presidential campaign. As a candidate for the Republican nomination, Richard Nixon read with close attention the memoranda on the AVF by his research director, Martin Anderson, an associate professor of business at Columbia University. His analysis encouraged Nixon in October 1968 to endorse the idea of phasing out the existing conscription system and shifting toward an AVF after the Vietnam War ended. The Democratic candidate, Vice President Hubert H. Humphrey, supported a lottery to replace the existing selective service system.[6]

Martin Anderson, member of the White House staff, and influential proponent of the All-Volunteer Force. (Nixon Presidential Library)

A New Administration Acts

Shortly after the inauguration Nixon made clear his determination to carry out his campaign pledge. He wanted to replace Lt. Gen. Lewis B. Hershey as director of the Selective Service System. In charge of the organization since July 1941, Hershey by the 1960s had become an unpopular and controversial figure, the public symbol of an inequitable system. On 29 January, Nixon directed Laird to begin planning right away to set up a special commission that would develop "a detailed plan of action for ending the draft." The president expected Laird's findings and recommendations by 1 May 1969.[7]

Although Laird had seen the need for a commission even before inauguration, he was just settling into his new position and wanted to move slowly. DoD was already studying the draft issue (Project Volunteer), so it seemed inadvisable to establish a separate special commission for the same reason. He advanced other arguments for proceeding with deliberation, contending that military pay reform had to be implemented prior to shifting to a volunteer force and that the establishment of a new commission would only delay pay reform. He believed that Fitt's ongoing study would serve as a suitable alternative to a special commission and promised to complete a comprehensive study in about one year. Although Nixon encouraged Laird to press ahead with Project Volunteer, the president wanted more. Strongly convinced "that the time has come to develop a detailed plan of action for ending the draft once expenditures on Vietnam are reduced substantially" and intolerant of delay, he told Laird on 6 February to come up with a list of suggested members for a special commission by the end of the week.[8] The following day Laird sent 29 names to the president, suggesting that the commission have no more than 15 members.[9]

On 25 March the White House provided Laird 15 names for the commission that would bear the name of its first chairman, former Secretary of Defense Thomas S. Gates. Other members included former DoD and high ranking government officials, retired generals (Alfred Gruenther and Lauris Norstad), manpower and labor relations experts, educators, executives from private industry, economists (Milton Friedman, Alan Greenspan, and W. Allen Wallis), and physicians. Jeanne L. Noble, a professor at New York University, was the only woman. Of the 15 members, only 5 came from the list submitted by Laird. Government funded research organizations—Center for Naval Analyses, Institute for Defense Analysis, and

RAND Corporation—were tapped to provide support to the commission. It also received help from the assistant secretaries for systems analysis and manpower and reserve affairs.[10] By design, commission members spanned a broad spectrum of opinion to meet Nixon's desire to have all viewpoints taken into account. Some members, including Gates himself, were known to oppose an all-volunteer force; others, particularly the economists, were known proponents.[11]

The impediments to achieving the AVF loomed obvious and significant, especially the cost of attracting volunteers. Alexander Haig, no supporter of a volunteer force in 1969, voiced skepticism about its economic feasibility. He believed that "a Republican budget could not sustain the simple economics of such a force, even if the Vietnam conflict were settled tomorrow." Another obstacle—the magnitude of the recruiting problem—received attention at Laird's staff meeting of 10 February 1969. Harold Wool's research revealed that the majority of those entering military service under voluntary programs did so only because the draft existed. The draft motivated 70 percent of the enlistments into the reserves. According to Wool, "the current voluntary recruitment gap, including both draftees and draft motivated volunteers, is about 750,000." No reputable study had "suggested that this current gap could be filled on an all-volunteer basis."[12]

Nixon's insistence on a commission to study the AVF narrowed Laird's room for maneuver. By linking the end of the draft with lower spending on Vietnam the president afforded Laird another reason, in addition to growing public antagonism, to scale back U.S. involvement in Vietnam and reduce the armed forces. A smaller force would cost less and require fewer volunteers. With the strength of the armed forces anticipated to fall to around two million after the end of the Vietnam War, OSD's Systems Analysis office estimated that the military would need only 150,000 to 200,000 men per year in new accessions and be able to attract volunteers from a larger cohort of males ages 17 to 20 in the 1970s and 1980s.[13]

Project Volunteer

Prodded by the president, Laird accelerated DoD's Project Volunteer. In April he designated Assistant Secretary for Manpower and Reserve Affairs Roger Kelley chairman of the Project Volunteer committee to oversee development of an action program for establishing a volunteer force. He also appointed civilian and military leaders of the services to the committee to involve them in developing the plan that they would have to carry out. Serving under Kelley were the assistant secretary for systems analysis, the military department assistant secretaries for manpower and reserve affairs, the military personnel directors of the four services, and the JCS. The group would prepare a wide range of studies on recruiting, military compensation, morale and job satisfaction, qualifications, and personnel staffing policies. Project Volunteer would also examine military personnel requirements and availability, cost-effectiveness, reserves, and the socio-economic implications of an AVF, including racial composition. Wool, the secretary and staff director, regarded Project Volunteer as a counterweight to the work of the Gates Commission, whose objectivity he questioned.[14] Kelley made each service responsible for analyzing its requirements and building its program. He stressed that the services should regard the project as "a major redirection of our total efforts rather than a separate and new layer of work activity," assessing manpower actions in terms of their contribution to the realization of an AVF.[15]

The services reacted in different ways to Kelley's charge. The Navy made its assistant chief of plans of the bureau of naval personnel responsible for Project Volunteer, deeming it essentially just another personnel action to be handled through normal processes. The Marine Corps assigned the deputy chief of staff for manpower to oversee the effort. The Air Force initially treated AVF as a routine issue to be handled by a staff section within the personnel directorate, but later it embarked on an internal study called Saber Volunteer.[16]

With the most at stake, the Army moved ahead more quickly and more comprehensively than the other services. Well before the formal start of Project Volunteer, General Westmoreland, after he became Army chief of staff in the summer of 1968, had directed the Army staff to do a feasibility study of the AVF. After learning of Nixon's January 1969 directive to Laird, Westmoreland organized in February another study group, Project Provide under Lt. Col. Jack R. Butler, to work with OSD. Deputy Chief of Staff for Personnel Lt. Gen. Walter T. Kerwin Jr. and Assistant Secretary for Manpower and Reserve Affairs William K. Brehm worked closely together, enabling the Army to take the initiative on the Project Volunteer Committee.[17] With a positive approach early on, Westmoreland and his top staff recognized the link between manpower procurement and the Army's social problems, understanding that the end of conscription was in the institution's best interest. As the Army's study of the AVF concluded, "If the dissent, undiscipline, and drug and alcohol abuse were indeed imports from society, . . . reduced reliance on the draft and unwilling draft-motivated volunteers might offer a way for the Army to solve some of its own social problems." With a smaller, post-Vietnam AVF, the Army could raise standards and weed out malcontents and misfits.[18]

Special Assistant for the Modern Volunteer Army Lt. Gen. George Forsythe Jr. (NARA)

In October 1970 the Army established the position of special assistant for the modern volunteer army within the office of the chief of staff to carry out its commitment to a zero-draft force. For the position Westmoreland personally selected Lt. Gen. George I. Forsythe Jr., whose experience in Vietnam handling complicated issues of civil-military coordination made him the first choice. In 1967 Forsythe had served in Vietnam as deputy to Ambassador Robert Komer in Civil Operations and Revolutionary Development Support (CORDS), a unique organization made up of civilian and military officials operating within MACV headquarters. Forsythe accepted the new position with the understanding that he would be more than a recruiter and have a role in reforming the Army to make military service more attractive to volunteers. He had authority to set objectives and priorities for the Army staff and Army commands, review staff and command actions, and coordinate troop and public information programs related to the Army's transition to a volunteer force.[19]

In January 1971 Forsythe initiated a series of experimental reforms, known as VOLAR, for Volunteer Army, at Fort Benning, Georgia; Fort Bragg, North Carolina; Fort Carson, Colorado; and Fort Ord, California. Post commanders had authority to try out ideas for improving living conditions and dealing with disciplinary problems such as racial conflict, drug use, and violence. At Fort Carson, for example, commander Maj. Gen. Bernard Rogers allowed soldiers to decorate their barracks as they saw fit, put up partitions for privacy, and drink beer in their quarters. Topless go-go girls entertained soldiers at the noncommissioned officers club. Although some changes proved controversial, Forsythe supported the experimentation. He appointed as his deputy Col. (later Brig. Gen.) Robert M. Montague Jr., commander of the 5th Division Artillery at Fort Carson. The garrison experiments had convinced Forsythe that changes in life style were indispensable for improving morale even with a conscripted force and could make the Army more appealing to volunteers. Laird, who had visited General Rogers in October 1969, was influenced by and supported his efforts to transform the post. He thought the Rogers initiatives could serve as a test case for the AVF and advised Westmoreland to follow closely what was being tried at Fort Carson. Systems Analysis believed that the Army needed those new selling points if it hoped to increase enlistments.[20]

To reduce the number of draftees, who by law were males, one idea under consideration was to expand the role and numbers of women in the military. Butler's Project Provide study had concluded that the pool of women was large enough "to provide an almost limitless source" of volunteers for the Army. His study recommended increasing the enlisted strength of the Women's Army Corps (WAC) by 22,400 over five years and converting more positions classified as male only to "male or female" status. Butler suggested further research might sanction an even larger expansion. Although the Gates Commission remained silent on the question of recruiting women to reduce the need for men, DoD endorsed the idea.

The Army developed plans to increase the size of the WAC by around 50 percent in two phases beginning in FY 1973. In mid-1972, when congressional reductions would compel the Army to eliminate one or more divisions, an Army study on how to reduce the service's dependence on male personnel found that adding 5,000 trained WACs by the end of FY 1973 might help the Army keep a 13 division force. This expansion would require funds for constructing barracks and training facilities for women as well as the opening of more military jobs to females.

Officials soon considered a larger, more rapid expansion. The Central All-Volunteer Task Force set up by Kelley and managed by General Montague asked the services in February 1972 to analyze the feasibility of doubling the number of women on active duty by 1977. On the basis of this study, the Army concluded that only 48 of the 482 military occupational specialties (MOS) needed to be restricted to males only. In August 1972 Secretary Robert Froehlke and Brig. Gen. Mildred C. Bailey, chief of the WAC, announced the expansion. Between 1972 and 1978 the

WAC would increase from 12,400 to 23,500. They also announced that, excepting positions associated with combat and combat support, hazardous duty, and strenuous physical demands, most military occupations would be opened to women. Thus the need to find sufficient numbers of volunteers for the Army had also expanded opportunities for women.[21]

Seeking Fairness: The Draft Lottery

Before the Gates Commission and Project Volunteer began their work, Laird believed something needed to be done right away to make conscription more equitable. On 3 February 1969 he raised the issue of selective service reform with the president, pointing out flaws and procedures that needed immediate fixing. The armed forces required only about half the number of men who reached the age of 19 each year, yet all men remained vulnerable to the draft until age 26. Selective Service procedures also required that the oldest members of a specified age group in a calendar year be selected first. That meant all men born in January would certainly be drafted, while those with December birthdays would certainly not be. He sought to have the Selective Service Act amended to permit establishment of an impartial, random system for determining who would serve.[22] In a February press briefing on manpower issues he proposed instituting a lottery before the war ended as an interim draft reform measure to eliminate the unfairness of the current system. The administration would send a draft reform bill to Congress "to do away with the inequities that presently exist in our Selective Service Act." Deputy Secretary of Defense David Packard, present at the briefing, ventured that it would also be necessary to change the military compensation system before progress could be made in reducing the draft. He viewed higher salaries as a motivational tool to attract volunteers in lieu of conscripts.[23]

Some White House officials, among them Martin Anderson, were unenthusiastic about a lottery, terming it a cosmetic change. Anderson thought a lottery might conflict with and detract from the work of the Gates Commission in addressing the fundamental issue of replacing the draft with the AVF. Undeterred, Laird sent the Bureau of the Budget a legislative proposal on 4 March for a lottery; a cabinet meeting at the end of April adopted Laird's proposal.[24]

On 13 May Nixon presented Congress with a draft reform package to amend the Selective Service Act of 1967, giving him authority to modify call-up procedures.

Since some form of conscription would be needed for the foreseeable future, the president wanted to make the system as fair as possible and to minimize disrupting young lives. He proposed selecting draftees through a lottery based on randomly selected birthdays so that men born in January or December would incur the same chance of being picked for military service. Nixon also reduced the period of prime draft eligibility to one year, continued undergraduate student deferments, and allowed graduate students to complete the full academic year. These short-term measures would make the draft fairer, but the president's ultimate goal remained to end the draft. Nixon pursued draft reform not merely to make the system more palatable but as part of his policy to disentangle his administration from Vietnam and dampen domestic antiwar protests. It was no coincidence that the day after his draft reform announcement he went on national television to outline a comprehensive peace proposal involving the withdrawal of all foreign troops from South Vietnam—both U.S. and North Vietnamese.[25]

Congress, lacking Nixon's enthusiasm for draft reform, did not plan to consider the issue until 1970, when it expected to take up renewal of the Selective Service Act, due to expire on 30 June 1971. House Armed Services Committee chairman Mendel Rivers opposed a lottery; Senate Armed Services Committee chairman John Stennis was cool to the idea. In June Laird approached both men, but they proved noncommittal about when hearings might start. Unwilling to wait for Congress, Nixon decided in August (1969) that he would put reforms in place by executive order, except for selection by lottery, which required legislative authorization. Laird supported the president's initiative and suggested as a possible alternative to a lottery a complex procedure that would not require new legislation should Congress fail to act. Laird lobbied hard to secure passage of the draft reform measure. The House passed it 382 to 12 at the end of October, but the Senate delayed passage.[26]

The secretary coupled his advice to the president with a recommendation to cut draft calls for October, November, and December 1969. Laird justified the smaller call-up by citing progress in Vietnamization and plans to cut the armed forces by 150,000 by July 1970. Henry Kissinger, no fan of an AVF, warned Nixon that Laird's draft call reductions would only increase the pressure to withdraw U.S. troops from Vietnam, but the president supported his defense secretary, approving the elimination of the November and December draft calls, a total of 50,000 men. Those selected in October would be called up over a three-month period. Also in October, the president

Nixon and Laird announce on 19 September 1969 the cancellation of draft calls for November (32,000) and December (18,000) 1969. (NARA)

announced that after almost 30 years, the 77-year-old General Hershey, who had resisted calls for his resignation, would leave his post as Selective Service director to become the president's adviser on manpower mobilization, a job with vague responsibilities, effective 16 February 1970. The administration hoped that troop withdrawals, lower draft calls, and Hershey's reassignment would help dampen campus protests against the war and conscription.[27]

At the beginning of November the draft reform proposal was still languishing in the Senate, despite the president's exhortation that congressional inaction would only add to the disillusionment of the young. Senate minority leader Hugh Scott of Pennsylvania had made a similar appeal, warning that delay on draft reform risked renewed outbreaks of campus demonstrations, "because of the deep-rooted and just concerns of the young people over the present draft system."[28] The president's message and Scott's admonition had little discernible effect on the Senate, but the testimony of Yale University president Kingman Brewster in early November before the Senate Armed Services Committee did influence the members. His blunt warning that a delay in taking up draft reform would cost the Democrats the political support of the young imparted a sense of urgency to the reform effort: "This bright, cynical generation of students is not going to appreciate it if this opportunity for meaningful reform falls by the wayside because of a desire to do more than realistically can be done in this session of Congress." Brewster's testimony, coupled with his suggestion that the Senate handle draft reform in two phases, prompted Congress to act. On 10 November the committee voted unanimously in favor of a bill amending the Selective Service Act of 1967. Senate passage by voice vote followed. On 26 November Nixon signed the bill allowing him to establish a random system of selection. The first lottery drawing was held five days later, 1 December 1969.[29]

Setting up a lottery was not just a step toward eliminating the draft. The lottery also helped weaken the antiwar movement. Laird claimed that the combination of troop withdrawals, lower casualties, smaller draft calls, and more equitable conscription meant that dissent and unrest in the country would diminish. Laird biographer Dale Van Atta summarized the lottery's effect: "No longer was an entire generation subject to the draft. The two-thirds not likely to go to Vietnam had no vested interest in protests." According to a contemporary Harris poll, Americans overwhelmingly approved of the lottery, which went into operation before the Gates Commission issued its final report. The lottery helped the administration politically and neither diminished the work of the Gates Commission nor slowed the transition to an AVF.[30]

Toward Consensus

As the Gates Commission got down to work, in May 1969, the executive director solicited the views of the military services and OSD on how to overcome the obstacles of moving to an AVF. Although this represented an opportunity for the services to bring their concerns directly to the commission, they did so with some wariness. The Army focused on the service's dependence on the draft and how the strains of the Vietnam War made it much harder to retain personnel. Already developing its own ideas on establishing an AVF at General Westmoreland's behest, the Army did not share them with the Gates Commission because it needed the draft to fill its manpower requirements and feared any disruption to the status quo. Sharing the belief held by many in OSD that the Gates Commission would not objectively consider the draft issue, since it was tasked with developing a plan for an AVF, the Army developed its own approach.[31]

Within Army channels, Assistant Secretary Brehm's pragmatic and prescriptive submission to Project Volunteer posited a two-pronged approach: minimize active force requirements, and find dramatic and innovative ways to make active and reserve duty more attractive. He wanted to enhance the public image of the armed services as offering a "respected and attractive career." To this end he recommended a tenfold increase in the Recruiting Command's advertising budget to convey the positive attributes of an Army career. To change the Army's "Beetle Bailey" image, he proposed eliminating kitchen police (KP) duty, trash collecting, and latrine cleaning, the kind of activities that did not contribute to a soldier's training and development. "Young men are not going to be persuaded that we consider their time and talents valuable if we squander them on janitorial or custodial duties," he stressed. Among his remedies were comprehensive educational development programs to enhance career mobility and raise self-esteem and improvements in the quality of family housing and barracks. Brehm's proposals required additional funds and legislation for implementation.[32] In OSD, Roger Kelley and his deputy, Paul Wollstadt, agreed with Brehm, believing that military pay across the board needed to be competitive with nonmilitary careers to sustain the AVF over the long term. Endorsing Brehm's recommendations, Kelley informed Laird late in December that they "must be major parts of our formula for attaining the All-Volunteer Force."[33]

Before reaching its decision, the Gates Commission wrestled with the conceptual basis of a volunteer force, divided over whether it was justified in considering military service a commodity, an economic problem resolved by better pay and benefits to attract volunteers. Crawford H. Greenewalt, former president of the DuPont Corporation, objected to reducing military service to a matter of supply and demand. He, for one, doubted that additional pay would attract a sufficient number of volunteers in time of war, and at a deeper level he expressed "serious philosophical reservations about paying people to die for their country." Economist Milton Friedman, a free market advocate, advanced economic and social reasons in favor of the AVF, arguing that "it was far worse to use the draft to force young men to sell their lives cheaply and that it would be infinitely preferable to pay those risking their lives a decent wage." In the course of the commission's deliberations Greenewalt's general arguments proved no match for the statistical, analytical studies of the panel's economists that supported the feasibility of an AVF.[34]

In December 1969 and January 1970 the commission staff briefed the services and OSD on its draft findings. It did not surprise DoD that the Gates Commission endorsed the AVF concept, which after all was its charter, but its unexpected recommendation to end the draft by 30 June 1971 evoked skepticism. Gus Lee, Kelley's director of manpower utilization, was quoted as saying, "Virtually everyone in the Department who had worked on the problem thought that the Commission had underestimated the difficulties of achieving a volunteer force."[35] Laird's public remarks questioning the feasibility of Gates' deadline for ending the draft disturbed the White House because they seemed to undercut the commission even before its findings were officially released.[36]

On 9 January 1970 Army Secretary Stanley Resor met with Gates and the commission. He spelled out the Army's concerns, especially the use of financial incentives to attract volunteers on the assumption that higher pay was the best way to acquire manpower. In his judgment, to rely exclusively on pay would likely attract recruits with limited civilian prospects. Army surveys had concluded that more volunteers would be drawn to service by enhanced educational and training benefits. The Army needed people whose talents were also attractive to civilian employers. Conscription inclined some of those to volunteer. But without the draft, Resor observed, "the potential loss of volunteers would be greatest among those individuals with above-average educational qualifications and with specialized skills and aptitudes." Those persons had the ability and qualifications to become radar and missile repairmen, intelligence analysts, and communications specialists, skills desperately needed by the service. The question for the Army was "whether we can get the kind of force we need, for a price we are willing to pay." Pay set so low would leave the Army "recruiting the person whose prospects in civilian life are relatively meager. This meagerness is likely to be a function of limited talent." Resor's presentation evoked resistance from Friedman and the commission's staff director, William Meckling, who vigorously defended the draft report. Although Resor may have failed to sway the commission, his arguments were incorporated into the NSC review of the Gates Commission's final report.[37]

As expected the report, submitted to President Nixon on 20 February 1970, endorsed the AVF. On behalf of a unanimous panel, Gates wrote "that the nation's interests will be better served by an all-volunteer force, supported by an effective standby draft, than by a mixed force of volunteers and conscripts." The commission

President Nixon meets in Oval Office with economist Milton Friedman and OMB Director George Shultz, 24 September 1971. Friedman developed economic arguments against continuation of the draft. Shultz favored cuts to the Defense budget. (Nixon Presidential Library)

estimated that the Defense budget would need an additional $3.24 billion to cover increased base pay and other recruiting incentives to achieve an AVF by 1 July 1971. Nixon appointed Martin Anderson to review the report in coordination with the NSC and DoD.[38]

Pending official comment from the president and Laird, DoD officials initially took a cautious approach. Kelley assured Anderson that DoD supported the commission's basic conclusion. The Project Volunteer Committee would incorporate as appropriate the commission's recommendations into DoD plans. At the same time Kelley expressed reservations about the availability of sufficient funds to attain an AVF and the effect of the changing attitude of young people toward enlistments and reenlistments for military service (the result of antiwar opposition and cultural changes). In his estimation, a high-quality AVF would require "the restoration of the sense of 'duty-honor-country' which should symbolize the uniform and the man in it." The range and availability of civilian jobs and new alternative career opportunities might lessen the appeal of military service. What especially mattered to Kelley and Resor, long-term retention of personnel, would require increased pay and nonmonetary incentives, such as education, training, and better housing. Reflecting the views of the armed services personnel chiefs, Kelley called attainment of an AVF by July 1971 "unlikely" and deemed it essential that the draft authority be extended beyond July 1971, when the present law expired.[39]

For Laird also, timing was critical. The draft remained necessary as long as the United States had troops in Vietnam. He considered the DoD budget to be "rock-bottom" and knew that ending conscription would only increase personnel costs. Therefore he was reluctant in February 1970 to establish a starting date for the AVF. Appearing on *Meet the Press* on 22 February, Laird rejected the Gates Commission's deadline: "I do not want to give a fixed timetable as far as July 1, 1971, because I do not believe that our force structure will necessarily be at the 2.5 million figure that is projected in this report." Although presidential chief of staff H. R. Haldeman grumbled that Laird's comments undermined the commission's work, there was no uncertainty regarding Laird's support of the AVF concept. Like Haig, he feared that pushing a volunteer force too hard too fast would jeopardize the passage of legislation extending the draft. Resor endorsed Laird's position, emphasizing, "We must not allow expectations of a totally draft-free environment to grow when we are certain that the draft will be necessary beyond June 1971."[40]

Laird's wish for an extension of draft authority beyond June 1971 also drew a sharp response from Gates Commission member Milton Friedman, who criticized the secretary's approach as "both highly undesirable on its merits and not feasible politically." Friedman asserted the commission's report demonstrated that a volunteer force was feasible for any force level between two and three million. In reply, Laird reiterated his support for the AVF believing it feasible, given existing financial restraints, when force levels had fallen closer to two million. The tight FY 1971 budget ruled out achieving the AVF by the end of June 1971. Laird wanted an AVF, but under the right conditions including affordability.[41]

The secretary sent his formal evaluation of the Gates Commission report to Nixon on 11 March, incorporating the concerns of Kelley and Resor and advocating phasing out the draft, but only "when assured of the capability to attract and retain an Armed Force of the required size and quality through voluntary means." Laird recommended that the administration emphasize reducing draft calls prior to instituting the AVF: "It will be easier to reach your objective by focusing public attention on eliminating the draft rather than stirring those who object to the concept of an All-Volunteer Force." The secretary called for a phase-out of occupational and paternity deferments, legislation to ensure that local draft boards would employ uniform procedures in calling up individuals, and congressional extension of draft authority for two years beyond 30 June 1971. He observed that the drawing power of higher pay was still unknown, particularly in view of changing attitudes of young people toward military service and the allure of alternative careers. Nonetheless, Laird called for a 20 percent pay increase, effective 1 January 1971, for enlisted personnel with less than two years of service; better on-base housing; increased housing allowances; and improved conditions of service through expanded in-service educational programs and more ROTC scholarships. Other quality of life measures advocated by the secretary included liberal payments for moving expenses, reduction of KP and other extra duty chores, and greater assistance in making the transition from military service to civilian life.[42]

Martin Anderson and Peter Flanigan of the White House staff chaired an interagency group that prepared options and timetables for the NSC to consider in establishing the AVF. Anderson's group included representatives from the Departments of Commerce; Health, Education, and Welfare; and Labor; the Bureau of the Budget; and the JCS. Paul Wollstadt, Vice Admiral William P. Mack, and William Brehm represented DoD.[43] The group tackled a number of thorny issues. Winding down of the Vietnam War increased the pressure for draft abolition, but ending conscription would make it harder to maintain an armed force large enough to carry out international security commitments. Rising antidraft sentiment could make it difficult to gain an extension of induction authority. Achieving the AVF with a high payroll too early would add to the difficulty of incorporating the extra costs in the Defense budget. DoD could not absorb the added costs of an accelerated elimination of the draft through budget cuts or force reductions. Increased spending in FY 1971 would worsen inflation and budget deficits and result in higher taxes. Budget Director Robert Mayo warned that internal DoD FY 1972 targets allowed no room for pay increases at the level suggested by the Gates Commission without significant and unacceptable cuts in the Defense budget. To avoid a tax increase or budget deficit in FY 1972, DoD's budget would have to be reduced below the FY 1971 level. Mayo's dire conclusion: "Major pay costs . . . would further endanger the force structure implied in NSDM 27." That decision memorandum of October 1969 had set guidelines for defense spending for FY 1971 through FY 1975.[44]

The 24 March NSC meeting discussed the strategy for achieving the AVF and the desirability of reforming the draft system while it remained in operation. Nixon immediately ruled out the Gates Commission recommendation of ending draft calls by 1 July 1971. The draft extension beyond July 1971 was imperative for an orderly, safe transition to the AVF: "The effect on foreign policy of having no draft at all will be terrible." Alluding to the need for congressional approval, Nixon averred, "This is a must vote, just like ABM. Otherwise our credibility goes down the drain."[45]

Laird agreed with the need to extend the draft beyond FY 1971. Although he conceded the point that an extension might give the impression that the administration was moving too slowly, in his judgment a faster end to the draft could threaten Vietnamization by pulling too many U.S. troops out of Vietnam too soon. The secretary recognized the difficulty of getting draft extension legislation through Congress but believed it doable. He preferred to phase out conscription, advocating the elimination of draft calls between mid-1972 and 1973 and a 20 percent pay increase for first term enlistees. The projected costs for this option were $2 billion in FY 1972 and $3.5 billion in FY 1973. Agreeing with Laird that the emphasis to Congress and the public should be on reducing draft calls to zero, Nixon insisted on moving toward the AVF, but only by setting a timetable with attainable goals.[46]

In considering how abolition of the draft and establishment of an AVF would affect national security, Nixon decided to weigh the reaction of NATO allies. Secretary of State Rogers, who analyzed the issue for Nixon, saw reason for alarm. He questioned whether the projections on actually attaining the AVF were realistic. The grave danger in failing to meet a target, he feard, would tie the president's hands in foreign policy. A congressional refusal to extend the draft law would be seen as reflecting public and congressional disenchantment with overseas commitments, an expression of isolationism, and dislike of the military that would further erode collective security. Rogers worried that defeat of a draft extension might be seen as a precursor of losses on other legislation, such as the maintenance of U.S. force levels in Europe. NATO would also react negatively if the United States established an AVF but then failed to provide U.S. NATO-assigned forces with sufficient combat capability. The alliance would be better able to resist domestic pressure to reduce conscription numbers if the United States retained the draft while it gradually moved toward an AVF. These conclusions provided backing for the president's intended direction.[47]

Nixon's 23 April 1970 message to Congress set forth his decision on how the United States should raise its military forces in the future and how to reform the existing recruiting system. Agreeing with the Gates Commission's basic recommendation, the president stated that his policy was "to reduce draft calls to zero, subject to the overriding considerations of national security." To assure maintenance of a strong defense during the transition, the draft would be phased out rather than prematurely ended. He requested an extension of induction authority beyond 1 July 1971 and the establishment of a standby draft for use in emergencies. To facilitate the transition and attract volunteers, Nixon proposed an additional 20 percent pay increase, effective 1 January 1971, for enlisted personnel with less than two years of service. The raise would cost $250 million for FY 1971. The president also requested an additional $2 billion in added pay and benefits for FY 1972; the economic case for a pay increase was strong. The annual starting enlisted pay of around $1,500 was not even half the minimum wage in the private sector. To reform the draft, Nixon issued an executive order ending future deferments for employment and paternity. He also sought legislation granting him authority to end undergraduate student deferments and to institute uniformity in the operation of the lottery, using a national call by lottery sequence numbers to eliminate the variations in the practices of local draft boards.[48]

To a large degree, phasing out the draft depended on the success of Vietnamization, the rate of U.S. troop withdrawals, and reductions in the overall size of the nation's armed forces. A week prior to his April 1970 draft reform decision, Nixon had declared that 150,000 troops would be withdrawn from Vietnam in 1971. His message to Congress and the draft reform initiative generally met with favor from the media and public and calmed critics, but that positive reaction evaporated a week later when Nixon sent U.S. ground forces into Cambodia to dismantle enemy operating and supply bases, a foray the administration characterized as necessary so that U.S. withdrawals could continue. The war-widening incursion sparked widespread antiwar protests, especially on college campuses, and undid the positive public and congressional reactions to the announced troop pullout and the decision to phase out conscription. Carrying out troop withdrawals and escalating military operations, while trying to gradually end the draft and reduce the size of the armed forces, revealed the vexing contradictions in Nixon's complex war policy. These issues added to Laird's already difficult juggling act. Funds for establishing the AVF were expected to come in part from savings generated by scaling back combat operations and lowering troop strength in Vietnam.[49]

Enacting the Decision

With the president's announcement, the administration's effort shifted to carrying out his policy, but some aides advocated that Nixon end the draft before 1973. In Martin Anderson's view, public unrest and the difficulty in sustaining the conscription system (because of the vociferous and sometimes violent outbreaks of college campus protest after the Cambodian operation) made it necessary to reduce draft calls to zero as soon as possible. He reported that passive resistance to the draft was increasing at a significant rate across the nation. More and more young men simply failed to appear when their draft boards called them, many believing that the government was "almost powerless to apprehend and prosecute them." Moreover, passage of legislation extending the draft faced trouble. Senator Peter H. Dominick (R–CO), a member of the Armed Services Committee, warned in July 1970 that the Senate would not act on the matter in the current session and that the administration would have to push both houses of Congress to pass it in the first six months of 1971. He doubted that extension of the draft would win approval from the Senate Armed Services Committee. Some senators sought to hasten the demise of conscription. Senator Mark Hatfield (R–OR) had submitted a bill cosponsored by ten other senators to eliminate draft calls by 1 July 1971. Characterizing the draft as a "discriminatory tax-in-kind upon those persons required to serve," a phrase that echoed the language of the Gates Commission, the bill asserted that military manpower requirements could be met through a voluntary system. Since draft calls had dropped to an average of about 10,000 men a month in 1970 and were estimated to stay at that level through the end of June 1971, Anderson feared people would conclude that smaller draft calls had made it easier to eliminate conscription entirely. He thought a speedy end to the draft would also help dispel the impression that Nixon was "procrastinating on his pledge to eliminate the draft as soon as possible."[50] The question was whether DoD could obtain sufficient manpower without conscription.

The president opposed the bill, arguing that there could be no certainty that greater pay and other incentives would actually attract enough volunteers to allow cancellation of the draft at the end of June 1971. Moreover, higher pay and new incentives would add billions in unanticipated costs to the FY 1971 budget. Laird advanced other reasons for opposing the amendment, foremost that to ensure national security the draft had to be phased out, not eliminated in one stroke. Inducements for attracting volunteers and procedures for standby emergency induction authority had to be put in place. Ending the draft, Laird advised Senator Stennis in August, "even before the Congress has appropriated funds for pay increases and other incentive programs designed to increase the number of volunteers, would seriously impair the Services' ability to meet their military manpower requirements. Funding for such legislation is not provided in the FY 71 budget."[51] In addition, Laird relied on the draft to help carry out Vietnamization as planned. Without a draft, it was doubtful that enough men would volunteer to serve in Vietnam. Laurence Lynn of the NSC staff estimated that if only volunteers went to Vietnam the administration could sustain a force there of 160,000 men (120,000 Army troops) at most, a force level that would be reached in about two years under current plans.[52]

Laird stayed on course to reach the AVF. He informed top DoD officials in October of his policy to shift to the AVF, eliminating draft calls at the end of FY 1973. Getting congressional action on the 20 percent pay raise and the increase in combat pay had top priority. He wanted the services to identify the requisite measures they needed to take before phasing out the draft at the end of June 1973 and to work with Roger Kelley and the Project Volunteer Committee. The secretary directed the services and the JCS chairman to give this issue their "urgent personal attention, and action plans should proceed without delay." For a smooth transition and for national security reasons, he assumed out of necessity that Congress would recognize it had to extend the draft for another two years. To be prepared he could not wait until Congress made a decision. He also expected that the services would make plans for a standby draft system that could be used in an emergency.[53]

As in the previous year, Congress was in no rush. The Senate Armed Services Committee did not plan to hold meetings until early February 1971. Yet Laird got the agreement of House Armed Services Committee chairman F. Edward Hébert (D–LA) to help move draft renewal legislation through the House in return for Laird's help in pushing the establishment of a military medical school, the Uniformed Services University of the Health Sciences (USUHS), which Nixon opposed. Laird had supported the idea from his days in Congress. Now with the end of the draft in view, Laird made the case for it in testimony, even though the White House had discouraged him. The school, it was hoped, would help solve a fundamental problem for DoD. Only one in four physicians in the armed forces intended to make a career of military medicine. Most doctors were drafted and did not reenlist after their first term. Without a medical draft the armed forces might not have enough doctors to care for military personnel. A military medical university that provided scholarships and in-house specialized education could help alleviate the shortfall of medical personnel. The school might also foster loyalty and a long-term commitment to the military from doctors. Laird directly lobbied Health, Education and Welfare Secretary Elliot Richardson, who opposed the idea of a government-run university. Deputy Assistant Secretary of Defense for Health and Environment Louis Rousselot prepared an assessment, which eventually went to Martin Anderson in the White House, rebutting Richardson's arguments. The effort was successful and the school was established, enrolling its first students in 1976. After he left office, Laird continued to defend USUHS from budget cuts or elimination. From his early days in Congress to his service as secretary of defense, health care remained a high priority for Laird.[54]

Obtaining money for the unfunded AVF program was difficult. The Five-Year Defense Plan of 1970 contained no line item for an AVF. The president's FY 1971 budget request then before Congress included no outlays for it. The planning cycle for the FY 1972 budget, the first to request money for the AVF, began in May 1970. Wollstadt's Project Volunteer committee, in collaboration with the OSD comptroller, estimated the cost of DoD programs in Project Volunteer at $2.5 billion plus, almost $600 million more than Nixon wanted to spend. Resor warned Laird that without an additional $71 million in FY 1971 and more than $523 million extra in FY 1972 the Army could not eliminate draft calls by the end of June 1973. He needed money for a long bill of particulars: expansion of the Army's recruiting command, incentives (proficiency pay) for retaining junior enlisted men and junior officers in the combat arms, more extensive advertising to include prime time spots on television and radio, improvements in living standards for soldiers, restoration of operations and maintenance funds to free soldiers from support duties that were tacked onto their normal responsibilities, and support for experimental programs to remove irritants to service life. The Army regarded better living conditions as essential selling points to help recruiters attract a sufficient number of volunteers.[55]

The administration presented its case for the AVF on 28 January 1971. Just before the Senate hearings opened, Nixon sent Congress a special message laying out his proposal for a pay raise and a two-year extension of induction authority to 1 July 1973. He pledged to reduce draft calls to zero by then, "subject to the overriding considerations of national security."[56] During the hearings, Laird requested FY 1972 DoD outlays of $1.4 billion and $1.52 billion in new obligational authority to cover recruiting and advertising, ROTC, medical scholarships, barracks improvements, enhanced quality of life, and selective pay increases. The Army's portion of these expenditures, $651.5 million, well above Resor's request, gave an indication of the administration's strong support of the AVF. Pay raises for all services ($865 million) accounted for over two-thirds of the total. The Army's share of the pay increases came to $419 million. The effect of these measures, Packard estimated, would allow reduction of draft calls in FY 1972 to about 80,000, or fewer than 7,000 monthly, a number based on OSD analyses.[57]

Whether the armed forces, in particular the Army, could actually meet manpower goals remained the key question. As Brig. Gen. Robert Pursley, Laird's military assistant, noted, there was no roadmap, nor did the United States have any experience it could draw on to manage the shift to an AVF. DoD had never

At a Pentagon press conference, Laird announces plans for a zero draft call by the end of FY 1973. (NARA)

structured a large modern force on a volunteer basis. Moreover, it would have to do so at a time when capital and manpower costs, especially the latter, were rising.[58]

Even under normal conditions DoD manpower requirements were difficult to estimate. But now, at the beginning of 1971, manpower planners in the services and OSD had to include additional variables in their calculations, making the task infinitely more difficult. DoD pursued a number of conflicting policies simultaneously: fight a war, withdraw forces from Vietnam, reduce the size of the armed forces, cut its budget, and reduce draft calls, but with no corresponding diminution of national security responsibilities. The extension of draft authority was essential for DoD to maintain a steady and sufficient supply of manpower until the transition was complete, but the Army's personnel situation had deteriorated seriously by December 1970. Worldwide, Army combat units had 45,000 fewer trained men than required. Overseas deployments in Europe, Korea, and Vietnam had also dropped below planned levels. An increase in draft calls in November 1970 would eliminate the shortfall by June 1971 and return manpower strength to authorized levels.[59]

The House passed the administration's manpower request, including an additional $1.2 billion in expenditures for pay increases, but it approved the two-year extension of the draft by only two votes. The Senate, which had under consideration a one-year draft extension and a 50 percent cut in U.S. forces in Europe, presented more trouble for the administration. A reduction of this magnitude, Kissinger feared, would weaken U.S. ability to mount a conventional defense of Europe against a Warsaw Pact offensive and also lessen the capability to assist Asian allies.[60]

In addition, the Senate Armed Services Committee proposed for FY 1972 a 56,000-man-year reduction in the armed forces, of which 50,000 man-years would come from the Army. This cut equated to an end strength 82,000 lower than the president's budget request and would shrink the Army's force structure to $12\frac{1}{3}$ or fewer divisions. Nixon had asked for an active force of $13\frac{1}{3}$ divisions.[61] The Army protested the 50,000 man-year strength reduction as excessive and warned that combined with the expiration of existing draft authority at the end of June 1971 it would impair the capability of land forces. The Senate's proposal to curtail Army man-years, combined with Laird's decision to cut monthly draft calls from May 1971 until achievement of the AVF, would significantly reduce the size and capability of U.S. ground forces. Smaller draft calls were consistent, however, with Laird's accelerated rate of withdrawals from Vietnam that would leave only a residual force there by the end of FY 1972.[62]

As of mid-September 1971, Congress had not passed an extension of the draft authority. It was even possible that the measure would expire in conference. Senator Gordon Allott (R–CO) wanted to table it. Knowing well that the absence of the draft would lead to manpower shortages and degraded readiness, Nixon met briefly with Allott, urging him not to table the conference report on the draft extension bill because it would in effect kill the bill. Although Allott was unmoved, the administration's lobbying proved successful. At the end of the month Congress passed the bill, which extended the draft through 30 June 1973 and raised military pay. On signing the act into law on 28 September 1971, Nixon hoped it would be the last time a chief executive would have to extend draft authority. He also expected the reforms, especially improved military living conditions and more generous pay scales, to help make the AVF a reality. As an example, he noted that a single soldier living on base and earning $149 a month would receive $299 under the new law.[63]

In December Laird asked Kelley to formulate a manpower program that would allow DoD to attain its goals and also to request additional funds if needed. The White House had cut the FY 1973 outlay level of $3.5 billion for the AVF by $350 million, adding to the challenge of putting together a comprehensive and attractive

Nixon signs the bill extending the draft, 28 September 1971. Behind the president are Senator John Stennis (D–MS), Laird, Representative Leslie Arends (R–IL), Senator Gordon Allott (R–CO), and Representative Edward Hébert (D–LA). Laird worked hard in support of this bill. (Nixon Presidential Library)

manpower program.[64] Kelley's office coordinated the plans and programs of OSD and the services. To carry out Laird's directive, Kelley established a small AVF staff consisting of representatives of each of the services, the reserve components, the comptroller, Systems Analysis, and Manpower and Reserve Affairs (MRA).[65]

At the end of July 1972 Laird reported to the president substantial progress in ending the draft. By 1 September U.S. troop levels in Vietnam would drop to 39,000 compared with a high of 549,000 at the start of Nixon's presidency. Over the same three and a half years of Nixon's first term, draft calls would have fallen from 300,000 to 50,000 annually. But the secretary was not entirely sanguine. By the end of FY 1974 the Army could face a possible shortfall of 40,000 personnel; and the Navy, a shortage of 15,000. There also loomed prospective scarcities in the critical areas of medical and nuclear-trained personnel. Guard and reserve forces at the end of FY 1972 were 49,000 below authorized strengths, a significant shortfall, because under the total force policy of 1970 the guard and reserve forces were expected to assume additional peacetime missions with a significant overall savings in money and manpower and to constitute the primary source for augmenting the active force in time of war or emergency.[66]

With the end of the draft less than a year away, recruiting efforts would have to become more effective to sustain a 2.3-million active peacetime military force and reserve and guard forces of one million that Laird advocated. To reduce the requirements for male soldiers, DoD explored ways to utilitze additional military women and civilians as well as to improve the accessioning and screening of volunteers. The department fought for passage of legislation for enlistment and reenlistment bonuses and other pay incentives for the guard and reserve forces, but a draft OSD report noted lingering uncertainty over how successful pay incentives might be in helping to attain an end to the draft by July 1973. Failure to eliminate the gap between the required number of volunteers and the number actually joining (estimated to be 15,000 to 85,000) could compel the Army to reduce some divisions and support unit forces by one-third in FY 1974. The wide range in estimates related to uncertainty regarding force levels, reenlistment rates, the number of spaces that actually could be filled by women or civilians, the supply of true volunteers, and the quality standards used to screen enlistees. Between November 1971 and March 1972 the services had raised recruiting qualifications, increasing the number of high school graduates accepted and decreasing the percentage of low mental category enlistees.[67]

Given the uncertainty involved, Philip Odeen, one of Kissinger's assistants, felt it imperative that the administration assess the prospects of reaching FY 1974 manpower requirements in the face of possible cuts in funding and the absence of conscription. He thought a combination of lower entrance standards, more women in the armed forces, and additional monetary incentives ($170 million for the Army only) would have the best chance of meeting manpower goals without the draft. OMB, however, recommended in November lowering FY 1974 expenditures set aside for pay raises and other initiatives to pursue the AVF by $400 million from the total programmed funds of $3.1 billion.[68]

OSD divided over how much additional money was needed. Agreeing with Odeen, Systems Analysis recommended providing $170 million in new incentives to the Army, but Assistant Secretary Kelley sought $400 million. In December 1972 Deputy Defense Secretary Kenneth Rush settled the dispute and approved the expenditure of $205 million for programs to improve accession and retention of service personnel. As evidence that DoD was getting closer to attaining the AVF, Rush directed that in future budgets the requirements for the AVF would be contained within the basic budget rather than broken out separately.[69]

At the end of August 1972 manpower statistics seemed to indicate that the draft would be needed well into 1973. With the Army 25,000 below authorized strength level and the Navy 9,000 under strength, the two services obviously needed the draft to help them reach their strength goals. The 1971 congressional cut of 50,000 man-years had caused the Army's shortfall. The Army hoped to draft 20,000 men during the remainder of 1972 and another 25,000 in the first half of 1973, bringing its strength to 830,000 by June 1973, but that was 10,000 below target. The Navy's problem related to the demands of the Vietnam War and a drop in reenlistments. To gain congressional support for pay and bonus legislation needed for the AVF, Laird had to engage in a balancing act. Too much pessimism about the manpower situation would cast doubt on the feasibility of the AVF. Too much optimism might cause Congress to seek to terminate the draft before enacting an extension of conscription authority. By the end of September higher recruiting numbers for July, August, and September encouraged Laird, but he believed that passage of the legislation on enlistment bonuses and pay incentives was necessary to end the draft by July 1973. The Special Pay Act in 1972 gave the Army and Marine Corps authorization to provide bonuses of $1,500 for men who enlisted in the combat arms for four years. Between June 1972 and May 1973, over 35,000 joined the Army's combat arms; more than 23,000 signed up for four years and received the bonus.[70]

Improved recruiting through the end of 1972 made officials in OSD optimistic about prospects for the AVF. They decided that no draft calls would be needed between January and July 1973, a judgment dependent on sustained success in recruiting volunteers, the timing of a settlement in Vietnam, and the lower manpower levels for the armed forces set by the president. Since fewer men were needed, the annual draft call fell from 98,000 in 1971 to 50,000 in 1972. The proportion of true volunteers, as opposed to draft-motivated volunteers, rose from 40 percent in 1968 to more than 75 percent in 1972. Measured by the Armed Forces Qualification Tests, as a group the men and women enlisting in the military exceeded the minimum quality requirements for enrollment in the various service training courses. Greater numbers of high school graduates were enlisting, a development that gratified manpower officials because high school graduates tended to perform better in their military assignments and had fewer disciplinary problems than nongraduates.

Analysts in MRA attributed the better quality and higher numbers of volunteers to the pay raises enacted in November 1971 and January 1972 that brought military pay more in line with civilian salaries. Improvements in service life, better training, and an emphasis on professionalism also attracted volunteers. More careful selection and training of recruiting cadres and an increase in advertising had rejuvenated the military recruiting services. Highly motivated recruiters received a boost from an Army advertising budget of around $67.5 million for active components in FY 1973. Additional advertising money became available for reserve forces. Barring the unforeseen, Kelley's office had confidence that manpower requirements for FY 1974 and beyond could be fulfilled without conscription.[71]

Buoyed by the favorable trends, Laird decided to announce the end of conscription. On 27 January 1973, two days before his tenure as secretary came to an end, he issued a news release: "With the signing of the peace agreement in Paris today, and after receiving a report from the Secretary of the Army that he foresees no need for further inductions, I wish to inform you that the Armed Forces henceforth will depend exclusively on volunteer soldiers, sailors, airmen and Marines." Laird was fully justified when he boasted that DoD had beaten Nixon's objective of no draft calls by five months. The Paris Peace accords provided for a cease-fire and the withdrawal of remaining U.S. forces from South Vietnam. It was no coincidence that the draft and the active U.S. military role in the Vietnam War ended on the same day, for the two were closely interwoven in Laird's policies. On taking office he had set for himself two top goals: withdraw U.S. troops from Vietnam and end the draft. He had attained both. Although news of the peace agreement overshadowed the announcement of a new system for raising military forces, the AVF represented a momentous change in national security policy.[72]

Laird's successor, Elliot Richardson, who assumed the duties of secretary on 30 January 1973, endorsed the new policy. The following month he recommended that Nixon officially advise Congress that it would be unnecessary to extend induction authority beyond 1 July. Speaking at the Air Force Academy on 21 March, Richardson announced on behalf of the administration that he had informed Congress "it will *not* be necessary to extend the draft induction authority beyond its expiration date of July 1. . . . Our recruiting and retention progress toward an all-volunteer force now convinces us that there is no reason to ask Congress to extend the induction authority." He pledged to make the AVF "a working reality."[73]

The first six months of 1973 provided the initial test of the AVF, with the services relying exclusively on voluntary enlistments. At the end of July, the armed services reported they were 1.1 percent, or 19,000, below planned strength. The Air Force and Marine Corps each fell short by 1,000. The Navy was 9,000 under planned strength. The Army was 14,000 or 1.7 percent lower than its targeted end strength. The Army had come very close to meeting its recruiting goals even with the higher qualitative standards in place from January to June 1973. DoD concluded that the armed services could have met their targets under the prior, less demanding qualitative standards.[74]

LAIRD BELIEVED THAT ENDING THE DRAFT represented his most important accomplishment as secretary, after Vietnamization. President Gerald Ford later agreed with this assessment, noting that although the public failed to appreciate the significance of Laird's action at the time, it was "a major accomplishment." Others such as Richard Holbrooke rightly labeled the end of conscription an important social change.[75] Laird deserved much of the credit. Bernard Rostker, author of an exhaustive study of the AVF, praised Laird's work with Congress at critical moments and his intercessions to gain the support of former legislative colleagues, some of whom agreed only reluctantly to the volunteer military. In Rostker's judgment,

Laird not only got the military services to back the AVF, but did it on his terms, keeping Kissinger and the NSC at arm's length during the transition. Martin Anderson in the White House complemented Laird's efforts in the Pentagon. If Anderson operated behind the scenes to advance the cause, Laird presented the public face of the AVF and was the right person to announce the end of conscription.[76]

The unpopularity of the Vietnam War and selective service, combined with the changing demographics of the draft age population, had made the start of the Nixon administration an appropriate time to change the conscription system. Ever sensitive to the political climate, Nixon and Laird understood well that ending the war and the draft would greatly benefit the administration, especially in gaining greater public support.

In this political and social milieu, the economic arguments attacking the unfairness of the draft had a critical role. As Rostker explained, "They presented a totally new paradigm for evaluating military organizations. . . . They addressed all the issues of demand and supply, attrition and retention, and the mix of career and noncareer members in the context of management efficiency and personal equity. As a result, the proponents of an all-volunteer force were able to muster persuasive arguments at a time when the need for change was strongly felt and the demographics made change feasible."[77]

Another study of the AVF, which went further, offered the view that antiwar protestors and the discontent of those subject to the draft had less influence than the analyses of free market economists and libertarians. The novel economic arguments trumped politics: "Instead of framing the debate about the AVF around notions of citizenship and obligation, or around concerns about the shared burden of service and social equality, they [the economists] offered plans based on conservative or libertarian doctrines of market economies."[78] The economists constructed a cogent argument, which in essence provided empirical evidence of the AVF's feasibility.

Manpower costs were, of course, an important consideration. In evaluating the AVF after he left public service, Laird stated that his preference would have been universal service, but an all-volunteer service seemed the cheaper alternative, and he pushed for it. He believed manpower costs would have risen under the draft anyway because draftees were not sufficiently paid: "I was in a position where I was taking the military services down by a million men, so it was easier to do it [end the draft] at that particular time."[79]

Should military service be regarded as a commodity, as the economists believed, or did an individual have an obligation to one's country that transcended economic considerations? The end of the draft raised profound issues about freedom and the obligations of citizenship: Young Americans now had the freedom once again to choose not to serve and to plan their lives without fear of being drafted. The nation would have to wage war with volunteers. With no shared obligation for military service from the larger society, the military henceforth would be a force of professionals, who alone would bear the physical and emotional costs of fighting. Persons outside the military would be spared from most of the hardships and consequences of war, and as a result might have less personal interest in opposing or protesting an unpopular or unjust conflict. The issues that arose when conscription ended in 1973 had also been debated in 1917 when the World War I draft went into effect. President Woodrow Wilson justified the draft conceptually as a universal obligation to serve. Others at the time protested that conscription would erode the traditional American ideals of individual freedom and volunteerism. This lesser engagement of the public in initiating and conducting war conferred on the nation's leaders— particularly the president—greater discretion in making decisions about war and peace. With the end of conscription in 1973, the AVF would constitute a test of whether the needs of national security during the Cold War could be met without recourse to conscription.[80]

CHAPTER 15

Strategic Defense: ABM and SALT

FROM THE TIME THE SOVIETS exploded their first atomic bomb in 1949 through the 1960s, the strategic arms competition between the United States and the Soviet Union raised the horrifying prospect of nuclear war, giving urgency to the pursuit of a mutual accommodation. During the 1968 presidential election campaign, Nixon had argued for U.S. nuclear superiority over the Soviet Union to allow for a retaliatory strike, but early in his administration he warmed to a less ambitious concept—sufficiency—a nuclear weapons capability that would provide an adequate defense of U.S. interests and maintenance of security.[1] Once in office the president informed both Secretary of Defense Laird and Secretary of State Rogers that he hoped to change the character of U.S. relations with the Soviet Union "from confrontation to negotiation," and at the optimum time to hold talks on strategic weapons. He viewed curbs on these weapons as essential to improved relations with the Soviet Union and as a way to reduce Cold War frictions.

In its first year the administration embarked on two major strategic arms initiatives: deployment of an antiballistic missile system and strategic arms limitation talks. Nixon linked the two, believing a viable missile defense system would strengthen his hand in negotiating limits on strategic arms. As in his efforts to end the Vietnam War, Nixon sought to pursue an arms agreement from a position of strength and supported the development of the ABM.[2] He and Laird considered approval of the ABM an indispensable preliminary to serious strategic arms limitation talks.

Laird's standing in Congress helped the administration win a bitterly contested Senate battle to obtain funds for a defensive system against missiles that the secretary fully realized would be sacrificed later in order to achieve a strategic arms agreement with the Soviets. The debate over the ABM had begun well before Nixon took office and intensified after his inauguration. Before the Senate approved the ABM in August 1969 the issue had unleashed nearly as much passionate debate as the Vietnam War.[3]

Evolution of Ballistic Missile Defense

In the years following the Cuban missile showdown of 1962, the Soviet Union and the United States had reached different conclusions about their nuclear weapon requirements and had carried out different policies. The Soviets embarked on an ambitious program of building large land-based offensive strategic missiles, achieving parity in intercontinental ballistic missiles, or ICBMs, with the United States relatively quickly by the late 1960s. In 1965 the Soviets had approximately 220 ICBMs and more than 100 submarine launched ballistic missiles (SLBMs). By the end of 1969, as Laird testified, they possessed over 1,100 operational ICBMs and were capable of building 35–40 Y-class submarines, similar to the Polaris submarine, by 1974–1975, adding to their fleet of smaller, older ballistic missile submarines. The Soviets had also begun deploying a defensive missile system code-named *Galosh* to defend Moscow from ballistic missile attack. Another worry for U.S. military leaders was the large SS–9 missile, which could possibly carry a multiple reentry vehicle (MRV) warhead that posed an offensive threat to U.S. ICBM missile sites.[4]

In contrast, the United States had decided after 1962 to accept eventual parity in numbers of strategic offensive weapons but to seek an assured second-strike capability comprising accurate land- and sea-based missiles. After attaining a missile arsenal with this capability, the United States stopped its intercontinental missile building program, closing production lines in 1966. In 1969, the U.S. nuclear armament triad consisted of 1,054 land-based ICBMs (550 Minuteman I and 450 Minuteman II missiles plus 54 Titans); 656 sea-based SLBMs; and 450 B–52 bombers. The United States planned to replace the Minuteman I with the more powerful and accurate Minuteman III, capable of carrying MIRV warheads. The Poseidon SLBM (submarine-launched ballistic missile), which could be equipped with MIRVs, was scheduled to replace the Polaris missile. The growing number of Soviet offensive missiles increased concerns about the ability of the U.S. strategic missile force to withstand a nuclear attack.[5]

Events in the Soviet Union and China during 1966 forced the Johnson administration to focus on missile defense. That year China set off a nuclear explosion and launched a test missile with a nuclear tip. These revelations, together with the *Galosh* missile and continued expansion of the Soviet strategic weapon forces, intensified congressional and JCS pressure on the Johnson administration to build an ABM system comparable to the *Galosh*. In September 1967 McNamara announced his support for a limited ABM system, known as Sentinel, for protecting key U.S. cities against missile strikes. At the same time McNamara had Deputy Secretary of Defense Paul Nitze prepare an initial negotiating position for possible strategic arms talks with the Soviets.[6]

Nixon Reviews the ABM

Well before Nixon was sworn in as president the sentinel program had become controversial. Of the 15 proposed Sentinel sites, 8 were close to population centers of a million or more. Citizens in Seattle, Chicago, and Detroit feared that nearby missile sites would put them at considerable risk from an accident and make them likely targets for incoming missiles. Taking their cue from scientists opposed to ballistic missile defense, numerous representatives and senators opposed Sentinel, deeming it too expensive, of dubious technical feasibility, incapable of providing sufficient defense, and likely to intensify the nuclear arms race. With controversy increasing, Nixon wanted the National Security Council in early March to examine alternatives to Sentinel within the framework of the FY 1970 budget.[7]

Even before Nixon's instructions to the NSC, Laird initiated a review of the Sentinel program, relating it to Soviet capabilities and Communist China's development of missiles. Greatly concerned about the magnitude of the Soviet effort, he placed Deputy Secretary David Packard in charge of a review panel that included representatives of other agencies and received input from OSD and the JCS. With his science and engineering background, Packard was well suited to lead the review. While outspending the Americans on antimissile defenses by a ratio of almost 4 to 1, during the past 24 months the Soviets had also stepped up the pace of offensive missile building. The JCS considered the expanding Soviet strategic offensive missile program to be "the most serious threat to the security of the United States."[8] Before reaching a decision on the configuration of the ABM system, Laird also consulted with key congressional leaders—Senators Richard Russell and John Stennis and Representatives Mendel Rivers and Leslie Arends.[9]

With the review still in progress, the defense secretary assumed an active public role. Possibly to deflect congressional criticism, he directed the Army temporarily to stop acquiring new ABM sites and to halt site construction, but at the same time to continue research and development and procurement. He more than hinted that the ABM program would resume. In the face of sharp questioning during his 9 February 1969 appearance on the CBS television show *Face the Nation*, he fervently argued that missile defense was essential in light of the threat from the Soviet Union and China. Laird strongly denied a reporter's assertion that the administration would cancel the Sentinel program because of congressional opposition. Moreover, he averred that a defensive missile program would allow the United States to enter strategic arms talks in a strong position.[10]

During the ABM review Packard met nearly every day with Director of Research and Engineering John Foster, acting ASD(SA) Ivan Selin, and Laurence Lynn of the NSC. Lynn played devil's advocate, devising arguments to invalidate all deployment options under consideration.[11] The group developed four alternatives, with varying capabilities. The first, essentially an enhanced version of Sentinel as originally conceived, limited damage to U.S. urban and industrial centers and provided an area defense against Chinese missiles and accidental launches. The second, more modest option, provided area defense against Chinese ICBMs and some protection for Minuteman sites. The third choice, a modified version of Sentinel, protected Minuteman installations, SAC bomber bases, and the national capital area from a Soviet strike. It would also defend some heavily populated areas from the emerging Chinese missile threat and provide protection against accidental launches. The final alternative continued the R&D effort but not the building of a missile defense system. Laird and the JCS preferred the third option, the modified Sentinel, and Kissinger urged the president to approve it.[12]

The modified system, built in stages, would change President Johnson's Sentinel program from defense of cities to protection of military bases. The first phase would see construction of only two sites, one at Malmstrom Air Force Base (AFB) in Montana and the other at Grand Forks AFB in North Dakota, with possible expansion in later phases to 12 sites. The modified system would eliminate three sites from the interior of the United States plus one each from Alaska and Hawaii. This option would also move radars and missile batteries away from large cities; eliminate coverage for Alaska and Hawaii; add Perimeter Acquisition Radar (PAR) in California and Florida; add Sprint missiles at each radar site to enhance defenses against SLBMs; and construct a site in the Washington, D.C. area. The modified program would have roughly the same number of missiles and the same total investment as the Sentinel program (about $6 billion), but it would lower FY 1970 spending by about $300 million. The first site was expected to be operational near the end of 1973, with full deployment completed by early 1975.[13]

Gerard Smith, head of the Arms Control and Disarmament Agency, working with Packard on the Sentinel review, argued that the group's ABM recommendation should be conditional, which indicated that the United States had not made a "final point-of-no-return decision" and would wait until more became known about the scope of possible SALT talks before making an irreversible decision. Packard disagreed, fearing that Smith's approach would complicate relations with Congress and jeopardize support for the ABM: "Any delay in explanation, any fuzziness, or even an indication that we would proceed with SENTINEL only under certain contingencies could raise serious doubts in Congress as to our requirements for the funds and authorizations in question." Immediately after the president made his decision, Packard stressed, DoD would have to justify its budget figures to Congress.[14]

At its 5 March 1969 meeting the NSC examined the modified Sentinel proposal, taking into account the expanding Soviet and Chinese missile programs and the political and fiscal pressure to cut the FY 1970 budget. The Soviets had continued to build SS–9 missiles, had test-launched the SS–9 with multiple warheads, and had put into production the Y-class submarine capable of carrying SLBMs. In addition, the Chinese had tested a three megaton warhead and expanded their testing facilities. Apprehensive about the Sentinel program's expense during a time of overall belt-tightening, Budget Director Robert Mayo wondered where the administration would make offsetting cuts if it approved the modified ABM program. He noted dryly that "other agencies aren't taking budget stringency that seriously." Nevertheless, Packard urged moving ahead with the modified defense system, arguing that the United States could not deter adversaries if it relied only on offensive missiles and bombers. Further, building additional offensive missiles would be destabilizing and "encourage continuation of the arms race. It would be more provocative."[15]

Nixon, who had recently returned from a European tour, ostensibly wanted more time to decide, but he had already settled the issue behind closed doors. On specific instructions from the president, Kissinger informed Soviet ambassador Anatoly Dobrynin at a private lunch on 3 March at the White House that Nixon had concluded that the United States needed an ABM system to protect the launch sites of its offensive missiles. Kissinger gave Dobrynin a full explanation of the president's thinking and emphasized that the ABM was not intended to threaten the USSR. By protecting missile sites the United States would seek to prevent a first strike against it and retain the potential for a counterstrike.[16]

Funding the ABM would be difficult. The Sentinel ballistic missile defense system had aroused public anxiety in cities where deployments were planned. Many scientists and engineers doubted the feasibility of missile defense, and there was widespread conviction that costs would escalate out of control. Senators Hubert H. Humphrey Jr. (D–MN) and Edward Kennedy spoke out in opposition, and the chairman of the Senate Foreign Relations Committee's Subcommittee on Disarmament, Senator Albert Gore, began hearings on the ABM in March 1969. A number of distinguished scientists—Hans Bethe, Herbert York, George Kistiakowsky, James Killian, Wolfgang Panofsky, and George Rathjens—testified before Gore's panel, condemning the ABM as too complex and unreliable to achieve its purpose. Carl Kaysen, former White House deputy assistant for national security affairs under President Kennedy, testified that the ABM would not enhance U.S. security, but would divert funds from other projects. Democratic senators opposed to the ABM echoed those views. Early in 1969 Senator Kennedy sponsored the publication of a book marshalling an array of political, technical, military, and economic arguments against the ABM.[17]

Opposition in part manifested the nationwide antimilitary mood that grew out of frustration with the ongoing war in Vietnam. The Pentagon presented a large, conspicuous target for those in Congress worried about military domination of foreign policy, militarization of American society, and out-of-control defense spending. Senator Scoop Jackson charged that the congressional anti-ABM campaign offered a rationale "to ransack the Defense Department." The continued invocation of the dangers of the "military-industrial complex," *Life* magazine opined, was converting that phrase into a cliché used by the left akin to the right's charge of "communist conspiracy." Kissinger found the changed political atmosphere ironic. With a Republican administration now in power, Democrats no longer had to mute their criticism of the antimissile defense program that the Johnson administration had begun in "the mid-1960s when Congress virtually forced ABM appropriations on McNamara."[18]

Despite widespread opposition and controversy, on 14 March Nixon announced his decision to proceed with a modified ABM system, renaming it Safeguard to emphasize its role in protecting the United States. Safeguard would be sufficiently robust, according to the president, to provide defense from a Chinese missile attack for 10 years; protect the U.S. deterrent, providing a shield against any small irrational or accidental attack from the Soviet Union; and adequately defend offensive missile locations so that the United States would be able to mount a retaliatory second strike "of such magnitude that the enemy would think twice before launching a first strike." In sum, Safeguard could not completely stop an all-out Soviet missile assault or defend cities, but it could help ensure that the United States mounted a credible retaliatory strike. Because Safeguard was a defensive system only, Nixon did not regard it as an impediment to the start of arms talks on limiting strategic offensive weapons.[19] Although the ABM would be hard to sell in the United States, Nixon was convinced that it was a necessary bargaining chip in talks with the Soviets. Testifying before a congressional committee in March 1969 in support of the president's decision, Laird asserted that the Soviet strategic forces buildup aimed to eliminate U.S. defenses in one strike. The Russian press treated Nixon's ABM announcement in a low-key manner, viewing the issue as an internal U.S. matter and not an obstacle to arms talks.[20]

A major advance in missile technology, the Multiple Independently Targetable Reentry Vehicle, complicated the debate over the ABM because it greatly improved first-strike capability. The multiple warheads in the nose cone of a MIRV missile could strike separate, widely dispersed targets simultaneously, increasing the chances of penetrating Soviet missile defenses. MIRV technology had become feasible after the creation of the Minuteman III missile, with its enlarged third-stage, and the development of thermonuclear weapons small enough for several to fit inside a single missile cone. MIRV's accuracy and ability to hit a small target, such as a missile silo, would serve to reduce collateral damage.[21]

Airmen work on a Minuteman III's Multiple Independently Targetable Vehicle (MIRV) System, undated. (USAF)

The Soviet Union also had missiles with multiple warheads under development. In 1968 and 1969 it tested SS–9 missiles containing three separate warheads, or multiple reentry vehicles, that could hit targets roughly 10 miles apart. The Soviets were trying to develop the more accurate MIRVs, but it remained unclear from their tests, Haig reported to Kissinger, whether their warheads could be independently targeted. For Laird, the Soviet MRV test program confirmed the need for Safeguard and continued testing of the U.S. MIRV. His concern about the Soviet's capability to develop independently targetable warheads lent weight to Laird's advocacy of the Safeguard program.[22]

The deployment of MIRVs would dramatically increase the number of U.S. strategic missile warheads to a range of 7,000 to 9,500 by the mid-1970s. Only a prohibited deployment or deferred testing could keep the MIRV out of the arsenal. Under Secretary of State Elliot Richardson argued that pressing ahead with MIRV testing might signal to the Soviets that the United States would move toward deployment and perhaps even refuse to negotiate the MIRV issue. He proposed a temporary halt to testing or stretching out the program, an idea also embraced by the ACDA.[23]

Reflecting the views of OSD and the JCS, Packard took an uncompromising position against Richardson's proposal. He contended that the ongoing U.S. testing program helped spur Soviet interest in SALT; continued testing would indicate that only an arms agreement would cause the United States to change MIRV deployments. Possession of a clearly established MIRV capability would bolster the U.S. negotiating position. Voluntary cutbacks in U.S. strategic programs might lead the Soviets to think that they could prevent U.S. strategic deployments without having to restrain their own program.[24]

Other agencies and offices joined the debate. The JCS and the director of defense research and engineering also took a dim view of a testing ban, believing that it would not stop the Soviets from developing or eventually deploying MIRVs. State, CIA, ACDA, and the Pentagon's Systems Analysis office favored a ban, contending that the Russians could not deploy MIRVs without carrying out significant additional testing and that they would not risk detection by cheating on a testing moratorium. Systems Analysis agreed with State and ACDA that, if the United States wished to include a MIRV/MRV test ban as part of a strategic arms agreement, it would have to impose a moratorium on testing during talks. After MIRVs were actually deployed, it would be difficult to verify the actual limits on their numbers without resorting to on-site inspections.[25] Many legislators also concluded that continued MIRV development and testing would escalate strategic arms competition, making it impossible to limit strategic weapons, but that a presidential ban on MIRV testing would induce "some Congressmen now on the fence" to side with the administration on the ABM.[26]

Siding with Laird, Kissinger advised Nixon to continue MIRV testing because it was in the U.S. interest to retain MIRVs to preserve strategic capabilities, especially if the United States and the Soviet Union retained a moderate level of ABMs. He thought a ban would also provide the Soviets with an excuse to delay arms talks. After news of the internal disagreement appeared in the press, Nixon, agreeing with Packard and Kissinger, established a single position for the administration. In June he decided to go ahead with MIRV testing despite opposition within his administration and the Senate.[27]

Battle for the ABM

After the House easily approved deployment of the ABM, a badly divided Senate took up the measure. Spearheading the administration's effort to win Senate backing, Laird made numerous appearances before Senate committees. His tenacious defense of the administration's position showcased his political skill. On 21 March 1969 the secretary appeared before a subcommittee of the Committee on Foreign Relations, where he clashed with Senators Fulbright and Gore, prominent opponents of missile defense. Laird testified that the Soviet nuclear missile buildup was intended to neutralize U.S. defenses in a first strike. The threat posed by the SS–9 missile as a first-strike weapon, the secretary concluded, could be met only by deploying an ABM system. He staunchly defended the Safeguard program in the face of strong, occasionally acerbic questioning. His involved, sometimes discursive answers eventually exasperated Fulbright, who complained that their length left insufficient time for additional questions. "You are such a good witness," Fulbright protested, "that we are spending much longer than usual in these hearings."[28]

Framing his criticism of the ABM in a broad context, Fulbright berated the administration for employing what he characterized as scare tactics that had exaggerated the Soviet missile threat and misled Congress and the people about the need for the ABM. Such tactics suggested desperation in trying to win public and congressional support for an unpopular system. Fulbright likened this approach to the way he thought the Johnson administration and McNamara had gulled Congress and the public about U.S. plans for Vietnam.[29]

Senator Gore posed a hypothetical question to Laird about how a sergeant or lieutenant at a missile site might report an incoming missile strike to the president and then ask him which button to push. Fulbright quickly interjected, "The panic button." His comment amused the audience but provided Laird an opening for a sharp rejoinder. Such a situation, he stated solemnly, was "not any laughing matter. It is a deadly serious question. . . . If I were sitting in the position of the President of the United States, I would like to be able to have an ABM to launch and not have to push the button for the [retaliatory] strike. I would like to have that capability of being able to intercept some incoming nuclear warheads." Gore countered that the threat of massive U.S. retaliation, not the ABM, was the real deterrent. In his estimation, two ABM missile sites would do little to protect the U.S. missile force.[30]

In testimony on 10 June 1969 before the Senate Appropriations Committee, Laird directly countered charges that the ABM would lead to an arms race. He insisted that diplomacy and public statements made clear that U.S. objectives were defensive.[31] The absence to date of any nuclear exchanges with the Soviet Union was due to what

Laird termed the strong U.S. defensive strategic weapons capability. In his view, Safeguard would stand on that foundation and represented "a building block for peace."[32]

In June 1969 the president declared in public his unwillingness to compromise on the ABM. He expected to win, believing he could count on the support of 50 or 51 senators. Senator Margaret Chase Smith, ranking minority member of the Armed Services Committee and an ABM opponent, was less certain. She informed Nixon that the vote in the deeply split committee could go either way.[33]

Senator Margaret Chase Smith (D–ME), a pivotal figure in the passage of funding for the ABM. (U.S. Senate Historical Office)

Senators trying to derail ABM deployment had a lower estimate of Soviet offensive missile capabilities, specifically the SS–9, than Nixon and Laird had. Opponents sought to demonstrate that the ABM was not needed to preserve the U.S. nuclear deterrent from the Soviet missile threat. The Soviets, they asserted, could only destroy part of the U.S. deterrent force. In support of their argument they emphasized the reported differences between CIA and DoD assessments of the capability and role of the Soviet SS–9 missile. A number of Senators against the ABM claimed that Laird had changed his views on the SS–9 to strengthen his argument for missile defense. Confirmation of a split within the administration on the Soviet missile threat would undermine the administration's case for the ABM. Fulbright and Gore wanted to bring any disagreements into the open.[34]

Laird accepted the Senate Foreign Relations Committee's request to testify about his disagreements with the CIA but shrewdly made it conditional on CIA Director Helms also appearing at the same session. The committee acceded to Laird's stipulation, but Helms' appearance meant the hearings would have to be classified. This was a deft move because there would be no public forum and no official, public airing of any rift between DoD and CIA. On 23 June 1969 Helms and Laird testified behind closed doors for nearly five hours on their respective views of the SS–9. A sanitized version of the hearing printed in July included none of Helms' answers, which remained classified. Even that bowdlerized version included many tense exchanges between Laird and Fulbright, along with other senators, frequently sparring over semantics. Laird's responses would often lead to a detailed description of the process of gathering and sharing intelligence, making it hard for Fulbright and other senators to sustain a line of questioning. At the end of the hearing Fulbright commented in exasperation to the secretary, "You have not once said yes or no."[35]

Laird proved an adept, nimble witness before congressional committees. At the same time, he respected his critics and in turn they continued to regard him highly. Disagreements were sharp but generally free of acrimony. At the session's end Gore and Laird presented differing conclusions to the public. In interviews with reporters, Gore reiterated his charge that Laird had changed his position on the SS–9 missile. Laird held two press conferences in quick succession reasserting that he had not deviated from his earlier testimony: the SS–9 had a first-strike capability. Reporters trying to get Laird to clarify his definition of what constituted a first-strike weapon had no more success than had Fulbright and Gore.[36]

Laird's appearance before the Foreign Relations Committee was in effect a prelude to formal Senate consideration of the FY 1970 military authorization bill, which included funding for the ABM. Before the Senate considered the measure, however, Senator John Stennis requested Laird's assessment of the Russian ICBM threat in writing and wanted to know whether Helms disagreed or concurred with it. Responding at length and transmitting a copy to Helms on 8 July, Laird wrote that the CIA director had "no disagreement" with his statements "concerning the potential Soviet and Chinese Communist strategic capabilities, as seen from the intelligence point of view." Again, he stated categorically that his position on the first-strike capability of the Soviet Union had not changed, and he highlighted several recent developments in the Soviet strategic forces. By continuing to deploy the SS–9, he noted, the Russians could have around 400 operational SS–9 launchers by the mid-1970s. They had also conducted three additional tests of the SS–9 with MRVs since March. Exhibiting confidence and certainty, Laird reported that the intelligence community "agreed that the USSR has the capability to start deploying hard target multiple independently targeted re-entry vehicles in 1972." With the introduction of two additional Y-class submarines and other planned deployments, the Soviets could match the SLBMs in the U.S. Polaris fleet by the mid-1970s. He termed this enhanced Soviet capability "a very grave threat to our MINUTE-MAN forces and our bomber forces in the mid-1970s." In Laird's judgment, the USSR could seriously compromise the U.S. deterrent force within a few years if the government did nothing to offset it. By the mid-1970s the Soviets could have the capability to render U.S. strategic forces incapable of retaliating with assured destruction. Until a strategic arms limitation agreement was reached, the most prudent U.S. course was to begin the first phase of the ABM. The stage was now set for the dramatic finale.[37]

On 6 August, in a session filled with unexpected turns, the Senate approved the Safeguard system by a 51–50 vote. Vice President Spiro Agnew cast the 51st vote for the ABM. At the center of the four-hour battle in the upper chamber was Maine's Senator Smith. She opposed the ABM and authorizing R&D funds to develop a missile system. Her initial amendment to the defense authorization bill prohibited all R&D spending as well as deployment of Safeguard; it was defeated convincingly, 89 to 11. Also on the docket that day, the Cooper-Hart amendment allowed continued R&D spending on Safeguard but banned its deployment. After conferring with Senators John Sherman Cooper, Philip A. Hart (D–MI), and others during the floor debate, Senator Smith agreed to support a modified version of the Cooper-Hart amendment that banned deployment and prohibited all R&D spending on Safeguard but permitted it for other missile defense systems. This revised amendment, hastily drafted during the debate, failed on a 50–50 vote. By Senate rules, the amendment needed a majority to succeed. Opponents of Safeguard tried once more that day to halt deployment. They brought the original Cooper-Hart amendment allowing continued R&D spending up again for a vote; it lost 51–49. Senator Smith voted against the amendment. She steadfastly opposed ABM and believed the Cooper-Hart amendment merely postponed a decision on a system that would prove inadequate against a Russian attack. Contemporary accounts display perplexity over Smith's seemingly contradictory votes, but there was a thread of consistency in her position. Throughout she opposed deployment and R&D spending on a missile defense system she believed was unworkable.[38]

In the end, lobbying probably helped win the narrowest possible victory for deploying the ABM system. Laird's deft handling of Senator Smith made a difference. Fearing that Safeguard would lose by one vote, he met privately with her trying to gain her support. He told her that if she did not change her vote ABM would be defeated, which would thus doom any chance of the arms control agreement she wanted. Absent a U.S. ABM system, Laird emphasized, the Soviet Union had no incentive to reach an arms agreement. She let it be known that her executive assistant and close personal associate, William C. Lewis, a brigadier general in the Air Force Reserve, had not received what she considered appropriate recognition for his service. Moreover, because of a longstanding, personal relationship with Lewis, she did not want him to be assigned away from the Pentagon. Taking her cue, Laird said he would arrange for additional appreciation of Lewis' service and continuation of his reserve assignment in the Air Force legislative affairs office. Laird's biographer, Dale Van Atta, summed up the outcome: "In a series of amendments crafted by her aide General Lewis, Smith was able to give Laird the vote he needed to secure funding, while at the same time maintaining her public opposition to the ABM."[39]

When the Senate authorized two ABM sites in the FY 1970 budget, Nixon claimed full credit for himself, giving his top assistants H. R. Haldeman, John D. Ehrlichman, and Kissinger detailed instructions on how to present to the public "the true story as to Presidential influence and the 'Nixon Style'" in winning

Senate approval. "Never in history," Nixon boasted, "has probably a President, individually and collectively, talked to more Senators on an issue than in this case." His conclusion was hard to sustain. Senator Maurice R. "Mike" Gravel (D–AK) described his one-on-one session with the president as a soft-sell approach in which Nixon basically asked him to weigh all the evidence before deciding. Other senators gave similar accounts of low-key sessions with the president. Nixon evidently assumed the weight of his arguments and the manner of his presentation would be sufficiently persuasive. He gave no credit to Laird and failed even to mention the secretary's extensive testimony. Nor did he give any credit to the arguments advanced by the pro-ABM committee with Democratic Party leanings assembled by former Deputy Secretary of Defense Paul Nitze that helped sway some votes.[40]

Laird offered a very different version of why the Senate passed the ABM. He considered Nixon an ineffective lobbyist who would talk down to senators while trying to demonstrate his superior intelligence. Moreover, the president was not forceful; he admitted that he never asked for a commitment from a senator. In contrast, Laird used the vice president's office just off the Senate floor to meet individually with senators. He recalled that he did all his own lobbying. As a former legislator and vote counter, he was willing to make deals to win support in view of the anticipated closeness of the vote.[41]

Strategic Arms Limitations

For Nixon and Laird the approval to deploy a limited ABM represented a green light to initiate arms limitation talks in which the ABM would loom as a central issue. For Laird in particular a deployable ABM system was a prerequisite for arms limitation talks. Two years earlier, in July 1968, when the Johnson administration agreed to begin preliminary discussions with the Soviet Union, Nitze had spearheaded the effort to devise an initial negotiating position to freeze offensive systems (ICBMs and SLBMs) and cap the number of potential ABM sites.[42] The Soviet invasion of Czechoslovakia in August interrupted that initiative, but the two sides later agreed that they would pursue talks to maintain a stable U.S.-Soviet strategic deterrent by limiting offensive and defensive missiles.[43]

The different strategic defensive postures and perspectives of the two super-powers would affect the negotiations. By treaties the United States was obligated to defend its distant allies in Europe and Asia. In contrast, Soviet allies were close neighbors. The USSR had built up a heavy ICBM arsenal with large payloads that could threaten U.S. land-based missiles, even those in hardened sites. Although the United States had stopped adding ICBMs to its force, it surpassed the Soviet Union in developing and testing MIRVs, which provided a U.S. advantage in the number of warheads. The United States also possessed more strategic bombers and continued to enhance its SLBM capabilities. Thus the differences between the two nations made it difficult to equate specific weapons or categories of weapons and find agreement on the terms of strategic equivalence. By the same token, neither the Soviets nor the Americans would defer acting on their military development plans while waiting for talks to begin.[44]

Before the start of the talks the Nixon administration formulated its strategic policy. In January 1969 Nixon had ordered a worldwide review of U.S. strategy and force levels (NSSM 3) for strategic and general purpose forces. That review would be completed in the fall, but its conclusions would have significance for the U.S. position at arms talks. With the U.S. lead in SLBM launchers and long-range bombers as well as an advantage in developing MIRVs, Laird advised Kissinger to reach an agreement quickly to help preserve the existing U.S. edge and slow down the Soviet Union's missile building program.[45]

In March, just before he decided to push for a limited ABM system, Nixon asked a widely representative interagency steering committee to prepare options for a U.S. negotiating position (NSSM 28), the first step toward establishing a strategic arms negotiations policy and a logical follow-on to the NSSM 3 study on U.S. strategic posture. He appointed ACDA Director Gerard Smith to chair the committee. Representing Laird were Deputy Secretary David Packard and Ivan Selin, acting head of Systems Analysis. Air Force Lt. Gen. Royal B. Allison spoke for the chairman of the JCS.[46]

Smith's committee issued its report at the end of May 1969, offering four illustrative packages of arms restrictions for developing a negotiating proposal. All options considered the number of ABM sites, retention or prohibition of MIRVs, and the means of verifying compliance.[47] The first two options froze ICBMs at current levels and banned mobile land missiles. The difference was that the second option restricted submarine launchers. Options 3 and 4 were identical to each other save that the fourth banned MIRV deployment.[48] The JCS supported the first three options if they imposed no limitations on new technology or force modernization and included provisions for verification and replacement. Not wishing to forego MIRVs, the Joint Chiefs flatly rejected the fourth option.[49]

On 11 June 1969, about the time that NSSM 28 was completed, Secretary of State Rogers formally notified Soviet Ambassador Dobrynin that the United States was willing to enter negotiations with the USSR on strategic arms limitation. He hoped that talks could start at the end of July, even though at that time the struggle over the ABM had remained undecided. The administration believed its willingness to begin arms discussions at an early date would help improve chances to obtain approval for ABM funding. Nixon appointed Gerard Smith to head the U.S. delegation and Philip J. Farley, deputy assistant secretary of state for politico-military affairs, as his alternate. Former Secretary of the Air Force Harold Brown was named senior technical member. Other members of the delegation included former ambassador to the Soviet Union Lewellyn E. Thompson, Paul Nitze (Laird's representative), and General Allison (General Wheeler's choice). Under President Johnson, Nitze had held a variety of important positions in the Pentagon—deputy secretary of defense, secretary of the navy, ASD(ISA)—and previously in the State Department, as director of the Policy Planning Staff. Laird had wanted Nitze to head ISA, but Senator Barry Goldwater had vowed to block his nomination. Because Laird felt Nitze possessed unmatched experience in arms control issues and superb negotiating skill, he selected him as his personal representative. Senate confirmation was not required.[50]

Unwilling to risk alienating allies, the administration consulted with them before embarking on arms talks with the Soviets. Any limitation on bombers and air defenses would have a great impact on NATO, whose members feared that an arms agreement could be tantamount to solidifying U.S.-USSR strategic hegemony, subordinating European interests and relegating them to the status of interested bystanders.[51] Nixon specifically sought to dispel the notion (advanced by some German officials) that the United States would decide on a negotiating position without considering the views of its allies. The president gave them an opportunity to participate in the ongoing process of analyzing SALT options. He also made clear to allies that the status of conventional and theater nuclear forces in Europe was not negotiable with the Soviets. Nixon's stand and initial consultations reassured allies that the United States would seek to protect their interests.[52]

Nixon adopted the concept of strategic sufficiency to help establish clear guidelines for SALT and for consultations with U.S. allies. Strategic sufficiency envisioned strategic forces adequate to deter an attack and to protect the United States and its allies from coercion or intimidation. The concept also emphasized the need for U.S. capability to retaliate against a nuclear attack on the United States.[53]

Laird advocated a watchful approach, advising the president to be "cautious, flexible, and probing." In July 1969 the secretary expressed his concern about the lack of agreement within the administration on what assumptions should guide U.S. participation and the uncertainty about Soviet political objectives in undertaking arms talks. Having achieved parity in numbers, the USSR, he feared, might try to consolidate its position by seizing "any opportunity for strategic superiority or advantage" during the arms talks.[54]

Verification was a central concern, dividing the administration on the question of how much reliance to place on technical verification procedures. No agreement emerged on whether or under what conditions the United States should seek on-site inspections. At the 25 June 1969 NSC meeting, Laird and Wheeler expressed unease over the ability of the intelligence community to ascertain Soviet compliance without on-site inspections. ACDA, State, and CIA disagreed, professing confidence in U.S. technical verification methods. On 21 July Nixon set up an interagency Verification Panel under Kissinger's chairmanship to assess the U.S. capability to corroborate Soviet arms control proposals and compliance with the terms of an arms agreement. The panel included Packard, Wheeler, Under Secretary of State Richardson, Gerard Smith, Richard Helms, and Attorney General John Mitchell. The group met regularly during the course of the negotiations to review analytical studies and develop negotiating options.[55]

In late October 1969 the American and Soviet governments announced that preliminary discussions on arms control would begin on 17 November in Helsinki, Finland.[56] The Soviets had delayed committing themselves to arms talks until the tensions arising from the border clashes with China in March 1969 had eased and the U.S. Senate had approved the ABM in August. Politburo chief Leonid Brezhnev instructed the head of the Soviet delegation, Vladimir Semyonov, to draw out the talks. Nixon viewed the opening sessions as an opportunity to explore Soviet intentions, not the time to put on the table any specific proposal. He wanted to be certain that the military forces at his disposal would deter a rational opponent from

President Nixon meets in the Oval Office with members of the strategic arms limitation talks delegation: Left to right, Maj. Gen. Royal Allison, Paul Nitze, Gerard Smith, Nixon, Philip Farley, and Harold Brown, 12 November 1969. (Nixon Presidential Library)

attacking the United States or threatening its allies. Nixon would accept weapon restraints only after being assured that the United States could detect Soviet violations of the limitations "in sufficient time to protect our security interests."[57]

OSD officials raised numerous concerns about strategic arms issues. In November U.S. intelligence reported a continued high rate of Soviet missile construction and production of nuclear weapons. According to newspaper accounts, the Soviets had about 300 more ICBMs than the United States, or 150 more missiles than U.S. officials had reported in the spring. With the clear U.S. advantage in MIRV technology, DoD continued to oppose a moratorium or ban on MIRV testing.[58] Wheeler and Nitze, who stressed MIRV's importance to strategic policy, pointed out that missiles armed with MIRV were needed in order to hit more than 500 additional Soviet targets. With MIRVs added to the land-based Minuteman force and the submarine-based Poseidon missiles then under development, the United States could freeze the number of launchers at current levels. A MIRV moratorium was equivalent to a ban, in Wheeler's judgment: "It would kill the Poseidon program."[59]

To probe Soviet views, Nixon's final guidance for the exploratory talks allowed the inclusion of MIRV. The Soviets, however, did not bring up MIRV during the Helsinki round of talks, leading Smith to conclude that they did not appear to want a MIRV ban.[60]

Battle for ABM Phase II

In August 1969 the Senate had authorized spending for Safeguard, but as of early December it had not yet appropriated FY 1970 funds for the first phase of a missile defense system. Until it did, Laird planned to use FY 1968 and FY 1969 funds for site acquisition, engineering, and construction of the Phase I sites in North Dakota and Montana. DoD would use some of this money also to make site selection and carry out initial engineering for potential Phase II sites. The president had decided that Phase II would begin when needed, in response to the evolving nature of the threat or to progress in arms talks. To Laird, convinced that ABM gave the U.S. negotiating leverage and a greater chance of gaining a treaty, it was essential to move toward deployment of Safegurd. He succinctly expressed this point in an interview after he left office, "If I had lost the ABM, we never would have had the [SALT] treaty."[61]

By the end of 1969 the darkening outlook for the FY 1971 budget stirred debate over how and when to proceed with Phase II construction. The possibility that budget issues might cause DoD to postpone work on the second phase until FY 1972 alarmed Nixon. Concerned that a delay could complicate his SALT negotiating position, he requested in early November an immediate review of the ABM program and associated costs.[62]

Drawing on analyses prepared by Systems Analysis, DDR&E, and the comptroller, Packard concluded that the Soviet threat had grown more serious since Nixon's March decision to move forward on the ABM. The Soviets had continued to deploy the SS–9 missile and to develop a version with three warheads. The possibility of SS-9 missiles with MIRV warheads as well as continued growth in the number of Soviet launch vehicles raised questions about the survivability of the Minuteman. Packard desired to proceed with Phase I as proposed, but for financial reasons to scale back Phase II to one or two additional sites in FY 1971. Funding the entire Phase II program as originally conceived appeared no longer affordable because of competing DoD requirements and reductions in the FY 1971 budget.[63]

For FY 1971, Packard wanted to authorize two new Phase II Safeguard sites at a cost of less than $1 billion for equipment purchases, within an overall DoD expenditure ceiling of $72.5 billion.[64]

Gerard Smith, head of the U.S. arms negotiating team, opposed DoD's proposals. In December 1969 he reminded the president that, since ABM was "the central issue in SALT," it would be advisable from a negotiating standpoint to confine Phase II to research and development in FY 1971. He acknowledged that the Safeguard program did exert pressure on the Soviets to reach an agreement but alluded to the narrow approval of Phase I. If Congress failed to approve Phase II expansion, the United States would gain no additional bargaining power and risk losing the pressure generated by Phase I.[65]

Nixon did not endorse Smith's position. He wanted to plan for two additional sites promptly and for the deployment of the remainder of the 12 later. At the end of December, Kissinger told Packard that the president desired "to get into phase 2 if only for bargaining effect." Nixon believed on the basis of reports from the Helsinki sessions that the Russians preferred a limited ABM system for defense against third-country (i.e., China) attacks. "This is what they will insist on," he wrote Kissinger. Nixon wanted something to negotiate away.[66]

Packard provided Kissinger a detailed proposal for the full ABM system, seeking FY 1971 authorization to construct two sites (Whiteman Air Force Base in Missouri and another somewhere in the Northwest). DoD also desired authorization to proceed with engineering and site selection work on three additional sites (Northeast, Michigan/Ohio, and the Washington, D.C. area) and planning for the full 12-site system. Packard believed these actions could be accomplished within DoD budget constraints of FY 1971 and later years. Total ABM expenditures between FY 1971 and FY 1974 would come to $11.7 billion. According to Packard's estimate, the 12-site ABM system if funded could be deployed by October 1977 and would come "as close to coping with the estimated Soviet and Chinese threats as funding constraints would permit." The JCS supported Packard's position.[67]

In early January 1970 Packard acknowledged that a 12-site system could reignite congressional and public controversy over the ABM and have an adverse effect on SALT. Nonetheless, he argued strongly that the fundamental requirement for DoD was to expand and deploy, just as the Soviets were doing. Failure to proceed with defensive missile systems would give the Soviets reason to delay

Laird announces the plans for the second phase of the Safeguard missile system (ABM) on 24 February 1970. With Laird are, left to right, JCS Chairman General Wheeler, Director of Defense Reasearch and Engineering John Foster, and Army Secretary Stanley Resor. (NARA)

reaching an agreement because the strategic balance was already shifting to their advantage. Only if deployed did ABMs "become real bargaining counters to trade for limitations on Soviet systems."[68] Packard's position followed that of the president and Laird.

In late February1970 Laird announced Nixon's decision to expand the ABM. The president made clear that he hoped to avoid a repeat of the close battle in the Senate over the ABM. For FY 1971 the administration wanted authorization to deploy only one additional ABM site, at Whiteman AFB in an existing Minuteman field. ABM opponents would find it difficult to prevent DoD from locating additional missiles at a site already containing ICBMs. Laird, who favored the Whiteman plan, pointed out that it enjoyed substantial congressional support and seemed the option least likely to provoke confrontation with the legislative branch. The State Department, JCS, and ACDA also preferred this option.[69] Like Laird, Nixon was convinced that no other option would pass Congress.

For Whiteman, DoD wanted FY 1971 outlays of $100 million above the amount Congress had previously approved for Phase I. The administration also sought authorization to begin site surveys, engineering, and land acquisition on five additional sites: the Northeast, the Northwest, Washington, D.C., Wyoming, and the Midwest. Laird noted that he had pledged to his former congressional colleagues that DoD would undertake the site survey only after Congress approved.

He stressed that the president's decision preserved his option to move closer to the full 12-site Safeguard system, if it proved necessary, but the decision was not necessarily a commitment to the full system. The plan was aptly characterized as "the minimum we can and must do" to attain the president's security objectives. DDR&E John Foster added that the Whiteman-only deployment represented the "minimum sustaining level for ABM." It would permit the retention of resources and personnel.[70]

To prepare for the continuation of arms talks in Vienna in late April, the NSC reviewed SALT negotiating options. Kissinger presented Nixon with four options, the product of interagency input and intensive systematic review. Option A established limits on the total number of strategic systems and would be relatively simple to verify. There would be no limitation on ABM, and medium and intermediate range missiles would be held at currently operational numbers. DoD favored this approach. Option B limited the total number of missiles and restricted the deployment of a nationwide ABM area defense, either banning all ABMs or limiting them to the defense of national capitals. MIRVs would be permitted. Option C limited both ABM and MIRV deployments, which would reduce the SS–9 threat against the Minuteman and require flight tests and an upgrade for surface-to-air missiles. DoD believed this alternative required on-site inspection. Option D required reducing the number of offensive missiles on both sides, specifically the number of SS–9 and SS–11s, in order to eliminate the disparity between the number of U.S. and Soviet missiles. Kissinger wryly noted, "The negotiability of this option is uncertain." Nixon made no decisions at the meeting but set forth his criteria for a concrete proposal that would allow for flexibility as well. He wanted an agreement, but not at the cost of putting the United States "in second position vis-à-vis the USSR."[71]

Two days after the NSC meeting, Nixon issued NSDM 51, instructing the delegation to present Option C first and then Option D, both predicated on the existence of an ABM system. In addition to an aggregate ceiling of 1,710 ICBM and SLBM missile launchers, Option C offered two choices for limiting ABMs—zero ABMs or protection of the national capital only. Option D would lower the aggregate ceiling on launchers by 100 each year for seven years, with a final January 1978 ceiling of 1,000 launchers. Deployment of ABM launchers would be prohibited. The United States would cancel Safeguard deployment but not destroy any existing radar.[72] The Soviet delegation rejected both options. They found Option C unattractive because it locked their side into a position of technological inferiority and subjected them to on-site inspections. Option D reduced the greatest Soviet advantage, their lead in the number of ICBMs.[73]

Forced to decide quickly on a new negotiating approach, at the end of July Nixon, in NSDM 74, concentrated on numerical limits on the most important strategic weapon systems. Known as Option E, it spelled out the U.S. SALT position outlined in earlier presidential decisions (NSDM 69 and NSDM 73). Option E proposed limiting the number of ICBM launchers, sea-based ballistic launchers, and heavy bombers to 1,900. Unlike previous options, this one, prepared in the NSC, did not undergo intensive interagency review. It offered two ABM alternatives of equal priority—limiting systems to defense of national capitals or totally prohibiting deployment of launchers, interceptors, and radars. This so-called zero provision required the dismantling of existing ABM launchers and associated radars.[74] Yet the contradiction was that the ABM system remained essential to the administration's bargaining strategy.

While the president revised his SALT negotiating provisions, Congress reviewed the FY 1971 defense budget, eyeing a funding cut for the ABM. The loss of Safeguard would represent a forfeiture of the primary U.S. arms limitation bargaining chip. The FY 1971 defense authorization bill, including $1.3 billion for Safeguard, passed the House in April 1970, but a tough battle for ABM funding loomed in the Senate, where the Armed Services Committee voted to restrict ABM deployment to protection of the strategic deterrent (defense of Minuteman) and opposed using funds for advance preparation of sites in the Northwest, Michigan/Ohio, Northeast, and Washington, D.C. Kissinger feared the committee's decision could kill the ABM as an area defense system and that the full Senate might even eliminate the two sites already authorized. Laird informed Chairman Stennis of his opposition to the committee's decision, noting that if DoD was restricted to the two Safeguard sites (Phase I) with no possible expansion, he would have no recourse but to request $500 million in additional funds to counter the growing Soviet strategic threat.[75]

The administration had put itself in a difficult position. As Kissinger observed, it had asked the Senate for authorization to proceed with the construction of one additional ABM site and the preparatory work on five others at the very time U.S. negotiators were proposing a total ABM ban or a system limited to the defense of national capitals, for which the administration had requested no funds and which would prove difficult to execute. John Foster fretted over the large, costly job of providing ABM protection for Washington, D.C., and argued that DoD had "no carefully thought out technical program" to carry it out. Moreover, the current U.S. negotiating stance did not allow for defense of Minuteman, the initial rationale for the ABM. "We are in a terrible trap," Foster concluded. "A complete shambles," Packard added. Given the situation, Laird feared that the administration might be forced to accept the vulnerability of the Minuteman. Because of the centrality of the missile defense system to the U.S. negotiating position, pleas to Congress by Kissinger, Laird, and Smith to retain ABM funding proved persuasive. On 12 August 1970, in a key vote, the Senate approved the administration's Phase II ABM plan for FY 1971, but it excluded the Washington site. To obtain an ABM site for the national capital, Laird would have to work more with the Senate.[76]

Toward an Arms Agreement

At the administration's review of the FY 1972 Safeguard program in mid-January 1971, Packard presented the case for funding the site in Washington, D.C. To DoD, it not only represented the next logical step toward obtaining the area defense that Nixon wanted but was also an integral part of the U.S. SALT negotiating proposal. If Congress refused to authorize the Washington site, then the administration would have to modify its defense program and its approach to SALT. Packard noted a discrepancy between the U.S. commitment to area defense under Nixon's strategic sufficiency criteria and the Option E negotiating proposal, which abandoned area defense and precluded modifications (save hardening silos) for improving the survivability of the Minuteman. Packard's request led to further assessment of the ABM program, especially its relation to the arms reduction talks.[77]

Wayne Smith of the NSC staff noted that DoD had acknowledged the underlying vulnerability of Minuteman. The four-site Safeguard deployment constituted a necessary transition to area defense, but at the same time it failed to provide sufficient protection for the Minuteman against foreseeable threats. A dedicated hard-site Minuteman defense offered greater security against more severe threats than a four-site Safeguard deployment. Moreover, the SALT Option E proposal—a capital area site or zero ABMs—left the Minuteman force at risk from a heavy or all-out assault.[78]

For Laird, who worried about the survivability of Minuteman, Option E's negotiating proposal (NSDM 74) only increased his unease. He warned Kissinger that it would "preclude all effective measures by which the United States could provide fixed land-based ICBM survivability in the long term." The continuing Soviet development of a payload for the SS–11 with three reentry vehicles, and the resumption of testing the SS–9 with a three reentry vehicle warhead, greatly upset the secretary. Foreseeing the eventual deployment of a Soviet MIRV capability against Minuteman, Laird recommended modifying the U.S. negotiating proposal, judging that the United States could not "tolerate a vulnerable Minuteman force." For FY 1972 Laird wanted to continue with the already authorized four-site Safeguard program and carry out advanced preparations for the Washington, D.C. site. The four-site program represented a commitment to build an area defense in the future and to keep pace with the developing Soviet threat. He deemed unacceptable the alternative of slowing down the program, limiting deployment to only two Minuteman sites, and undertaking design studies of the Washington, D.C. site. To Laird, it made no sense to scale back unilaterally an already authorized program before the next round of SALT.[79]

At the NSC meeting of 27 January 1971 Kissinger described how the shifting rationale of the Safeguard program created confusion. The administration initially characterized Safeguard as providing area defense, then as a program for Minuteman defense, and later at the SALT meetings as protecting the national capital. The last rationale, DoD feared, would impair the survivability of the Minuteman.[80]

Nixon decided to continue construction at the North Dakota and Montana locations and begin construction at Whiteman AFB, Missouri, in 1971. The following year he would decide either to begin advance preparation for the Washington, D.C. site or initiate construction at Warren AFB, Wyoming. The ABM faced formidable opposition. In early April the White House counted 51 senators prepared to vote against the FY 1972 ABM program.[81]

Brig. Gen. Robert Pursley, Laird's military assistant, sought to reassure the White House, outlining Laird's plan for a concerted effort to get the president's Safeguard proposal through Congress. Laird had met with Packard, Foster, and Army Secretary Stanley Resor; he appointed Jerry W. Friedheim, deputy assistant secretary for public affairs, as the principal DoD point of contact with Congress. The secretary wanted an orderly plan for congressional liaison to avoid precipitous, uncoordinated actions that would only provoke contentious, unproductive debate. DoD's effort would perforce be largely out of the public eye, because "undue public discussion and debate will at this stage be wasteful, non-productive" and likely to arouse more opposition than support. This seemed especially true since the details of the classified SALT proposals could not be discussed publicly. Laird and Packard would continue to meet in one-on-one sessions with senators and congressmen.[82]

On 20 May 1971 the United States and the Soviet Union announced jointly that they had reached an understanding on the broad outline of a strategic arms agreement. This understanding was the product of backchannel discussions between Kissinger and Ambassador Dobrynin between January and May 1971. The two nations agreed to seek an accord on limiting the deployment of ABMs. The Soviet Union would agree to halt work on ICBMs while negotiating limitations on strategic offensive weapons. Although supportive, Laird did not believe the announcement would sway many senatorial ABM opponents. He pressed Resor to keep the Safeguard construction program moving during the talks. For Laird, the ABM remained an essential bargaining chip, and he would devote considerable effort to keeping the program viable until an arms settlement was reached.[83]

Laird to the Fore

Encouraged by the May breakthrough, Nixon issued new instructions (NSDM 117) in July to the U.S. delegation looking toward an agreement to limit strategic defensive weapons and a parallel one to control strategic offensive weapons. Negotiations on offensive and defensive systems were to be conducted at the same time, and agreements on offensive and defensive systems concluded simultaneously. Laird had strong reservations about the provisions in NSDM 117 on offensive missiles, fearing they could allow the Soviet Union to build up its strategic missile force and solidify its advantage in the number of missiles and size of payloads. Moreover, if the Soviets eventually did put MIRVs on their missiles, Laird warned, then a limitation on the number of missiles would undermine the U.S. position on strategic weapons and "mean the end of U.S. sufficiency and parity." Laird and the JCS also objected to the sweeping language in NSDM 117 that would foreclose U.S. options to deploy or possibly even carry out research and development on future, not yet envisioned, ABM systems that might prove attractive or useful later on.[84] Nixon heeded their counsel and wanted the right to pursue an ABM system based on future technology. Pending further study by the Verification Panel, the president directed that an arms agreement "not prohibit deployment of possible future ABM systems other than systems employing ABM interceptor missiles, launchers, and radars."[85]

State Department and ACDA members of the SALT delegation, however, sought authorization to table a proposal banning the deployment of the ABM. The JCS representative, General Allison, and the Joint Chiefs strongly opposed it. Nitze and Assistant Secretary for International Security Affairs Warren Nutter feared that such a proposal could lead to an asymmetrical outcome: The United States would have no missile defense, but the Soviets would retain their existing SAM networks and suffer no constraints on their R&D program. Nitze and Nutter feared that prohibiting the ABM would in turn increase the pressure to ban MIRVs. The JCS flatly rejected an ABM ban as "detrimental to the security interests of the United States" and recommended that the delegation not be allowed to table such a proposal.[86]

Laird passed the JCS objections to the president, but only after adopting Assistant Secretary for Systems Analysis Gardiner Tucker's suggestions for a more flexible, nuanced approach. Tucker had cautioned Laird that the Soviets might be earnestly seeking an ABM ban or they might simply be raising the issue to obtain a favorable public reaction. He offered two reasons why Laird should make a more positive response than the JCS. First, an ABM ban might prove to be in the U.S. interest. Second, exploring the possibility of a ban would place the administration in a stronger position with Congress than reflexively rejecting the Soviet move. Moreover, he noted that Nitze would support a ban contingent on limits on offensive weapons.[87]

Heeding Tucker's position, Laird advised Nixon that the United States could benefit from an ABM ban if three conditions were met. First, the ABM ban could not be used to reopen the possibility of banning MIRVs. Second, a key issue for Laird, the ABM prohibition had to be contingent on reaching an equitable limitation on offensive missiles, firmly linking defensive and offensive strategic weapons. Third, the provisions of the ABM ban had to be "as precise, complete, and as rigorous as we know how to make them" so that both sides would be "assured that the other's capability to destroy incoming missiles is entirely dismantled." The political appeal of a conditional ABM ban, the secretary told Nixon, would be to ease congressional pressure for an unconditional ABM ban.[88]

Meeting in the cabinet room with Nixon, Kissinger, and the JCS on 10 August 1971, Laird reiterated his and the Joint Chiefs' opposition to a defensive missile ban separated from an agreement limiting offensive weapons. He warned: "We have tabled a proposition in SALT, which gives the Soviet[s] certainly an advantage as far as the long term is concerned on the offensive weapons systems. If we were to give up the capability, which we have, to go into a defensive system on down the road, by going to zero at this time, without opening up the offensive proposition that we have put on the table in the SALT talks, I believe it would . . . endanger our security planning." Kissinger thought Laird's position could lead to a second stage of negotiations in which the zero ABM option and reductions of strategic offensive weapons would be discussed. Laird demurred—there might never be a second agreement. If the United States managed to get only one agreement with the Soviet Union, it would give the Soviets the opportunity to attain superiority in 1974 and 1975. "And I don't want to be around to see the Soviet Union ever be in a position of superiority," he proclaimed. Laird thought that it would be difficult, given the U.S. political system, to set aside an interim agreement later even if it put the United States in an inferior military position vis-à-vis the Soviet Union. Nixon characterized an ABM ban, coupled with a freeze on offensive weapons at current levels, as locking the United States into an inferior position. The president lamented that the related effort to halt MIRV testing and development was even "worse than stopping ABM." MIRV was needed to offset the Soviet edge in ICBMs. Packard agreed, stating that the program was the "one advantage we have against that numbers imbalance." MIRV also offered more flexibility in hedging against a missile buildup in China. "We should not give it [MIRV] up under any conditions," Packard believed.[89]

Nixon's new instructions on the SALT negotiations (NSDM 127) embodied Laird's concerns. There would be no proposal to ban ABM at the present time; rather, that issue would be taken up later after reaching agreement on limits on defensive and offensive weapons. The U.S. delegation was not to table a proposal for an ABM ban, nor to pursue the issue later on in the current phase of the negotiations. The president decreed that "a ban on all ABM deployments remains an ultimate U.S. objective and will be a subject for negotiations after we have reached an agreement on defensive limitations and an interim agreement on offensive limitations."[90]

Throughout the late summer and fall of 1971, Laird, with support from Tucker and Moorer, continued his effort to shift the focus of the SALT negotiations from ABM to limitations on offensive weapons. On 4 September he sent Kissinger a memorandum, drafted by Tucker, advising a tough approach. The time had come to tell the Soviets that if they were unprepared to discuss limits on offensive missiles, then

Assistant Secretary of Defense for Systems Analysis Gardiner Tucker receives the DoD Distinguished Public Service Medal from Laird on 3 January 1973. Tucker influenced Laird's views on SALT. (NARA OPA)

the United States would terminate the talks and resume them only when the Soviets were ready to discuss the issue. A U.S. interim agreement proposal on offensive weapons, Laird and Tucker had concluded, would "freeze" the Soviet advantage in offensive missiles at around 550.[91]

In mid-September Laird raised the same points with Nixon. The immediate goal at the negotiations "must be to reverse the growing Soviet advantage in offensive arms while limiting or reducing ABM defenses of Soviet cities, in order to maintain clear U.S. sufficiency. The major lever we have on the Soviets is our ABM program." Laird gratuitously attached to his memorandum a list of the previous warnings he had sent to Kissinger, implying that they went unheeded.[92] Laird's memorandum elicited a bland response from Nixon, assuring the secretary that Smith would tell the Soviets of U.S. concerns about their offensive weapons and the need to discuss limits on them. Prior to the president's response, however, Kissinger had reminded Nixon that before Laird sent his missives, the SALT delegation had already been instructed to end the Helsinki sessions with very strong statements on the need to bring up limits on offensive weapons early at the Vienna meetings, the next round of SALT.[93]

Kissinger's assurances did little to assuage Laird and Moorer. At the end of September, Moorer told the secretary of his anxiety about the undiminished momentum of the Soviet ICBM, SLBM, and ABM programs and the "unyielding" stance of Soviet negotiators. Their unwillingness to make concessions, combined with the ongoing buildup, threatened to upset the strategic balance. By November the JCS believed the situation had gotten worse. The growth in Soviet offensive missiles had moved "past the parity that once would have made a freeze [on offensive weapons] militarily sound."[94]

Embracing the views of Tucker and Moorer, Laird continued to press the White House. At the end of October he wrote to Kissinger of his deep concern that the "Soviets are succeeding with their tactic of splitting an ABM agreement from any real consideration of strategic offensive limitations. We have, in effect, offered to give up our right to a strategically significant defense of our ICBMs without asking for or obtaining offensive limits that would justify this sacrifice." He thought it imperative at the next round of talks—SALT VI at Vienna from 15 November 1971 to 4 February 1972—that the United States reestablish the negotiating linkage between offensive and defensive weapons. OSD rejected an ABM agreement without an offensive freeze. At the same time, Laird proposed a new way of reacting to the Soviet strategic offensive buildup: "I believe the best action we might take now is to include in the FY 1973 budget substantial funds for early deployment of new SSBNs [nuclear ballistic missile submarines]," referring to what would later be called the Trident submarine.[95]

As Kissinger noted, the decision on whether to speed up production of an improved Poseidon SLBM or wait for the deployment of the entirely new Trident submarine in 1978 at the earliest would help determine the administration's position on SALT. If the United States decided to build more Poseidons quickly, it would seek to exclude SLBMs from any SALT limitation and try to match the number of Soviet submarines. If the decision was to adopt the Trident, then the administration would demand that SLBMs be included in SALT to freeze the number of Soviet submarines while the United States developed the new system over a five-year period. DoD wanted the Trident, because it increased the pressure to reach a quick agreement on an SLBM freeze.[96]

For the SALT VI sessions the president decided that the delegation should concentrate on discussing offensive limitations and insist that the Soviet delegation do the same. The emphasis would be to establish an overall ICBM freeze with a sub-limit on MLBMs (modern large ballistic missiles), and also include SLBMs in an interim agreement. The ABM proposal—defense of the national capital or three additional sites—would remain unchanged.[97]

In January 1972, just prior to a meeting with Kissinger, Laird pointed out to Nixon what he perceived as the shortcomings of the administration's negotiating proposal. He feared that limiting Safeguard deployments to two sites, Grand Forks and Malmstrom, would mean an inadequate defense of Minuteman, bombers, and command centers against a Soviet attack. Further, he thought that the notion of only two ABM sites would be politically difficult to defend before Congress and the public. Motivating Laird was his conviction that the continued growth of Soviet strategic forces would cause the offensive weapons balance to keep shifting in favor of the Soviet Union. He presented Nixon with a new negotiating proposal to permit one ABM site for each side and after three years the deployment of defensive missiles at two additional U.S. ABM sites, one of them for Washington, D.C., and one Soviet site. The agreement would remain in effect for five years unless superseded by a follow-on agreement. Smith and Nitze were willing to accept a three- or four-year term; five years was a bit long for an interim agreement. Laird pressed ahead, writing Nixon, "I am now convinced that defense of Washington is politically feasible if it is part of an Arms Control agreement and is accompanied by a reduction in the currently authorized SAFEGUARD program." The secretary believed his proposal would provide defenses for U.S. ICBMs, allow the modernization of offensive weapons and the transfer of more weapons from land to sea, and stop the growth in the number of Soviet strategic missiles.[98]

The key point of Laird's proposal of course linked an agreement on the ABM with an agreement limiting offensive missiles (both ICBM silos and SLBM launchers). The proposal also allowed the replacement of old SLBM launchers and ICBM silos with new SLBM launchers. The Soviets could continue to build SLBMs at a slower rate if they took out of service older ICBMs and SLBMs on a one-for-one basis. The agreement would last five years unless replaced by a follow-on agreement. Either side could withdraw from the ABM agreement should the pact on offensive missiles lapse. Laird urged that the SALT delegation be instructed to inform the Soviets that the United States wanted an agreement that permitted equal defense of ICBM fields and national capitals for each side. Philip Odeen of the NSC staff pointed out to Kissinger that if Laird was correct about the reaction of Congress, his proposal would allow Nixon the option of seeking defense of both ICBMs and the national capital. Kissinger later praised Laird's proposal as "ingenious," but it required a lengthy interagency review because of the technical questions it raised, its impact on negotiations, and the opposition of ACDA, the State Department, and the CIA. On 9 March, with Nixon's authorization, Kissinger presented the Laird proposal on SLBMs to Dobrynin through the special channel. Early in April Dobrynin gave a noncommittal answer, stating only that Soviet leaders were studying the question.[99]

Meanwhile, Laird pressed ahead with planning for the eventual deployment of the full 12-site ABM program. In his annual review of Safeguard, he urged Nixon to proceed in FY 1973 with the planned ABM defense of four Minuteman sites and continue ongoing construction at Grand Forks and Malmstrom and begin construction and procurement at the Whiteman and Warren sites. He made this recommendation even though Congress had withdrawn authorization in FY 1972 for the Whiteman site. He also proposed to initiate the early stages of preparation of the Washington, D.C. site. Noting the uncertainty about reaching a SALT agreement, Laird praised the phased ABM program as supporting "both the flexibility and the strength of the President's SALT negotiating position."[100] Once again, Laird stated his belief in the inseparable link between ABM deployment and offensive weapons talks. The JCS supported Laird, terming the four-site ABM program "the minimal acceptable military position." They also reaffirmed the need for missile defense of the national capital.[101]

The NSC met on 17 March 1972 to prepare the U.S. delegation for what would be the final round of talks in Helsinki at the end of the month. Laird again emphasized the threat of Soviet offensive missiles, stating his belief that the Soviet Union had embarked for political reasons on a program to become the superior strategic force. Nixon agreed, conjecturing that the Soviets may have been using the arms talks to help achieve this goal. In Nixon's judgment, the problem was to avoid an arms agreement that limited the United States but permitted the Soviets to attain superiority. He sought a settlement that allowed the United States flexibility. Laird argued the necessity of proceeding toward the 12-site Safeguard program because of the imperative to protect Minuteman missiles. He believed two or four ABM sites provided no strategic benefit and reiterated his judgment that Congress would support a 12-site system that included defense of Washington as part of an arms agreement. Missile defense sites for the two national capitals should remain on the table. Going into the final round, Laird's goal was to show movement toward a system with 12 ABM sites.[102]

Nitze and others kept Laird informed of developments at the negotiations, allowing the secretary to take an active role in advising the president. Looking at shifts in the Soviet position, Laird modified his view of what proposals had a strong likelihood of being included in an ABM agreement. He noted that the Soviets now seemed willing to limit future deployments of large phased array radar and also to include SLBM launchers in an interim agreement if the United States demonstrated some willingness to accommodate them in other areas. The secretary now thought that changing the U.S. position on the number of ABM sites could make an agreement with the Soviets more likely. Accordingly, on 11 April he recommended that Nixon authorize the delegation to propose an ABM agreement providing for defense of the national capital and one ICBM site for each side and eliminating the option of a second defended ICBM site for both sides. Laird wanted the U.S. delegation to press for inclusion of SLBM limits in an interim agreement on offensive missiles and to stress that the scope of the interim agreement would heavily influence the American decision on ABM.[103]

The president's negotiating instructions of 1 May (NSDM 164) incorporated Laird's position, authorizing the delegation to present a proposal limiting ABM deployments for each side to defense of the national capital and one ICBM site, contingent on Soviet agreement to include the question of SLBM launchers in the interim agreement on offensive limitations. The United States would seek to limit the Soviets to no more than 950 SLBM launchers and retain the option of replacing 54 older ICBM launchers with three ballistic missile submarines carrying 54 SLBM launchers.[104]

In late April, with still no accord at this point on some details of the agreement, Kissinger went to Moscow to discuss with Soviet officials the proposals for the 22–29 May summit meeting on SALT. In his sessions with Kissinger, Leonid Brezhnev, the Soviet leader, presented a new proposal on SALT that allowed each side to protect its capital and one ICBM site. Brezhnev advanced this idea even though he noted it meant the Soviets, given their pattern of deployments, would protect only half the number of missiles that the United States would protect. The Soviet leader also

White House cabinet room discussion on 1 May 1972. Left to right: Alexander Haig, Henry Kissinger, Admiral Thomas Moorer, Lt. Gen. Royal Allison, Richard Helms, Gerard Smith, William Rogers, President Nixon, and Secretary Laird. On this date Nixon issued NSDM 164 laying out his negotiating position on the limitation of defensive and offensive missiles. (Nixon Presidential Library)

agreed to a ceiling of 950 SLBMs and a term of five years for an offensive missile agreement. Kissinger, who had been involved in extensive private discussions on SALT with Ambassador Dobrynin in Washington, regarded these changes as a significant concession. This was the position that Laird had urged Nixon to support in January. Kissinger had introduced it to Dobrynin in March. At that time Kissinger believed the Soviet Union had expressed little interest in the idea. By late April the Soviet leadership had changed its position.[105]

On 26 May, near the end of the Moscow summit, Nixon and Brezhnev signed a breakthrough treaty on the limitation of ABM systems and an interim agreement limiting strategic offensive arms. The agreement focused on the number of missiles and missile launchers but omitted direct mention of MIRV. Both parties agreed to limit ABM systems to defense of the national capital and one ICBM site and not deploy ABMs elsewhere for the defense of national territory. The SALT agreement would last for five years and was subject to joint reviews by the signatories after five years. The five-year interim agreement on offensive arms bound the two nations not to begin construction of additional fixed land-based ICBM launchers after 1 July 1972 and to limit SLBMs. The attached binding protocol limited the United States to 710 SLBM launchers and 44 modern ballistic submarines. The Soviet Union could have no more than 950 SLBM launchers and no more than 62 modern ballistic submarines.[106]

The JCS, reluctant to support the provision that allowed the Soviets to have 950 missiles and 62 modern submarines, feared that clause would provide the USSR with the advantage of greater flexibility. JCS support would be critical for Senate ratification; removing or changing the provision in the protocol could render the entire agreement unacceptable to the Soviet Union. On 25 May, a day of frantic JCS meetings and discussions, Haig relayed to Admiral Moorer several times Nixon's insistence on reaching an arms agreement. The Chiefs finally agreed to support the agreement, but they would not "concur," because that term would require providing a justification to Congress. They told Haig they would "acquiesce," but Haig countered that the term fell short of an endorsement. Unwilling to risk scuttling the agreement, the final details of which were then being hammered out in Moscow, the JCS agreed on a statement of conditional support. If the president could not get a better agreement, their statement read, then "the Joint Chiefs of Staff are in accord—provided that we take action necessary to insure the acceleration of our ongoing offensive programs as well as improvements in existing systems."[107]

In June the JCS sent Laird a list of measures to be taken to ensure that the proposed agreement did not jeopardize the long-term security of the United States. They wanted intensive intelligence monitoring to ensure Soviet compliance with the two strategic arms agreements, and to offset any growth in the Soviet threat they wanted strongly improved R&D programs that would help maintain U.S. superiority in weapon systems technology.[108]

On the day the ABM treaty was signed, Laird directed Army Secretary Froehlke to suspend construction at Malmstrom, future work at the remaining Safeguard sites, and all R&D programs prohibited by the treaty. The Malmstrom site was to be dismantled after the treaty was ratified. At the same time Laird wanted the planning for the national capital site to proceed as quickly as possible and the deployment of the Grand Forks site to continue. Odeen estimated that the reductions in the Safeguard program would reduce DoD outlays by about $700 million in FY 1973. The new work Laird proposed would cost approximately $168 million; the net savings would be $540 million. As he had so often done on budget issues, to the consternation of the White House, Laird acted unilaterally, briefing congressional committees without seeking presidential approval or submitting his revisions to OMB.[109]

ALTHOUGH NOT INVOLVED IN NEGOTIATING with the Soviet delegation, Laird and OSD were able to shape the U.S. negotiating position, particularly in the critical months just before the Moscow summit. The secretary refused to budge from his insistence that an agreement on defensive missiles had to be an integral part of an agreement on limiting offensive weapons. The Soviet Union had no incentive to discuss offensive weapons because the United States had already stopped building them, making defensive missiles the critical issue.[110] Well before the arms talks began, Laird fully understood that the Safeguard ABM program was essential to the negotiations. Without the credible threat to deploy it, the United States would have entered the talks in a weaker position and might have had to accept an agreement that allowed the Soviet Union even greater superiority in ICBM and SLBM launchers. Laird played a vital role in getting the Senate to approve the first phase of the ABM and insisted on continuing to deploy the full 12-site system. Kissinger expressly complimented the defense secretary on his proposal for obtaining an agreement on SLBMs that allowed the United States to build the new Trident and prevented the Soviet Union from increasing its lead in SLBM launchers.

Laird's military assistant, General Pursley, who had served as an assistant also for Secretaries McNamara and Clifford, also gave high praise to Laird: "There weren't many other defense secretaries who were as knowledgeable or even as interested in arms control as Mel was. It was unusual to have a politically based secretary who was that incisive about what the arms control issues were, and his influence on the talks was seminal." Harold Brown, a member of the SALT delegation and later President Carter's Secretary of Defense, observed firsthand the interplay among Kissinger, Smith, and Laird. He concluded that the real debate on the U.S. negotiating position was between Laird, who spoke for the military, and Kissinger, who represented the president. "Because there was agreement between them in the end," Brown opined, "SALT I was signed."[111] In the Oval Office, on the day in March that Kissinger had presented Laird's proposal to Dobrynin, Nixon and Kissinger paid tribute to Laird. Complaining of Secretary Rogers' ineffectiveness on SALT, Nixon said that "you've got to hand it to old Laird. He knows the issues on SALT." Kissinger agreed, observing that Laird may have played the issue politically, "but he knows it."[112] Mastering the arcane issues and knowing how to advance SALT politically enabled Laird to make a unique contribution toward the first major arms control agreement between the superpowers since the dawn of the nuclear age.

SALT I affirmed the obligation of the United States and the Soviet Union to reduce the threat of nuclear war. The treaty's signing came only after years of difficult and complex negotiations that occurred in a prevailing atmosphere of suspicion and distrust. Arguably, the most difficult part of the process was reaching internal consensus. It is likely that Soviet decision makers dealt with the same contentious issues as the Americans in seeking agreement on a final treaty position. Achieving that internal consensus required time, energy, and creative thinking.

CHAPTER 16

Realistic Deterrence?
The FY 1973 Budget

ALWAYS IN THE BACKGROUND and often in the foreground, the budget inevitably loomed large in the making of national security policy. Laird skillfully manipulated this relationship to help achieve his goals for the Department of Defense. After two years of shrinking Defense budgets, he had won an increase in spending for FY 1972. At the start of the budget formulation process for FY 1973, he strove for still higher spending even as DoD scaled back troop levels and expenditures on Vietnam. Of continuing concern to the secretary, the cost of the All-Volunteer Force and new weapon systems shaped much of his thinking and action on the budget. As in past years, Laird and the services battled to defend their budget request against the cost-cutters in the Office of Management and Budget, the National Security Council staff, and Congress.

The FY 1973 budget took form during a period of growing unemployment, sluggish economic growth, and a ballooning budget deficit. When the previous fiscal year's budget was submitted to Congress in January 1971, the federal deficit was estimated at $11.6 billion, but by December 1971 that estimate had grown to more than $38 billion owing to shrinking revenues, spending on new programs, and revenue sharing with cities and states. The FY 1973 budget, like the previous one, was based on the hypothetical assumption of full employment, "in which spending does not exceed the revenues the economy could generate under the existing tax system at a time of full employment." This imaginative accounting exercise—the economy was not at full employment and full employment was not equated with a specific jobless rate—allowed the administration to increase spending and still claim the budget was "balanced." Proponents of the idea thought (a bit wishfully) it would act as "a self-fulfilling prophecy: By operating as if we were at full employment, we will help to bring about that full employment."[1] OMB took the concept seriously, pressing DoD to keep FY 1973 spending within the full employment level.

In the internal administration battles over the size of the president's budget request, Laird was less concerned with the notion of a full employment budget than with a DoD budget that adequately provided national security. He consistently fought OMB on this point, often taking his case directly to the president. He formulated a strategic guidance called realistic deterrence to provide a foundation for Defense spending in coming years, but that met resistance. He battled with the NSC and OMB over fiscal guidance. Laird's defense of the FY 1973 budget had a political dimension as well, advancing Nixon's reelection efforts with his public criticism of Democratic presidential nominee George McGovern's plan of dramatic cuts. As in previous years, the secretary also had to struggle with congressionally imposed cuts that in his view threatened to undermine national security.

Strategic Guidance

In view of his planned departure from the position of secretary in January 1973, the FY 1973 budget represented the last one Laird would shape from start to finish. He therefore sought to base it on a broad strategic concept when he began budget planning in the fall of 1970. The opening skirmish on the FY 1973 DoD budget occurred when the secretary sent to the president a lengthy memorandum, "Strategy for Peace: A National Security Strategy of Realistic Deterrence," in November 1970 for his eyes only. It presented Laird's view of how to implement the president's foreign policy and strategy for peace as an outgrowth of the Nixon Doctrine and a master plan for the post-Vietnam DoD. The overarching program, a strategy of peace, would carry out the president's defense policies and shape the post-Vietnam military over the coming five years. The memorandum sparked debate within the administration not just over the specifics of the DoD program but also over Laird's methodology for determining defense strategy.[2]

Realistic deterrence emphasized military strength and strong alliances as prerequisites for meaningful negotiations with American allies. U.S. military strength would be determined by what the nation could afford to spend on weapons and force structure and by a net assessment of the threat that weighed allied military capabilities against those of an adversary. Although Laird's memorandum did not describe or advocate a specific force structure, he wanted to cut personnel costs by reducing U.S. troop strength in Europe to a range of 100,000 to 150,000, withdrawing additional soldiers from South Korea, and making greater use of the reserves. Looking to the future, Laird hoped to leave only U.S. advisers in Vietnam by the middle of 1972. Not only did he advocate a smaller force, he also proposed narrower security responsibilities for U.S. forces and greater reliance on regional defense arrangements in Asia to respond to what he considered the unlikely event of a Chinese attack on South Korea or another Asian ally. The United States would provide no land forces to an ally under attack by a nation other than Communist China. Over the long term, Laird envisioned a smaller U.S. military composed entirely of volunteers, the eventual withdrawal of all U.S. ground troops from Asia, and reliance on nuclear weapons to deter Beijing. He wanted to structure general purpose forces primarily for their deterrent value, as distinguished from their war-fighting capability, a distinction derided by Kissinger who found it inconceivable that the deterrent value of a force could exceed its capability to wage war. The service secretaries, the JCS chairman, and the Army chief of staff all expressed reservations about Laird's strategic approach.

William Baroody, special assistant to the secretary and deputy secretary of defense, receives the DoD Distinguished Public Service Medal, 5 January 1973. Baroody drafted DoD's Strategy of Realistic Deterrence. (NARA OPA)

Laird placed the budget at the center of planning for national security strategy "to make the transition from war to lasting peace and freedom with a restructured U.S. military force that would require 7% or less of GNP, made up of 2.5 million volunteers or less." This size force in combination with adequate strength, partnership with allies, and progress in negotiations would be designed to deter war. Laird distinguished between this smaller future military and the draft-heavy armed forces of 3.5 million requiring more than 9 percent of GNP that Nixon inherited.[3]

Citing his experience in Congress and the Pentagon, Laird also advocated a broad role for himself in the elaboration of a comprehensive national security strategy. In his formulation, "defense planning, programming, procurement, force design (including R&D and equipment) and force deployment, employment and operations are inseparable" and properly belonged to OSD, implying a lesser role for Kissinger's Defense Program Review Committee.[4]

Although Laird wrote his exposition of national strategy for the president's eyes only, both National Security Adviser Henry Kissinger and his assistant, Wayne Smith, examined the document before Nixon did. Kissinger was critical, disparaging Laird's distinction between a National Security Strategy and a military strategy. Smith cataloged a series of omissions: no discussion of threats to U.S. interests, no assessment of whether allies would bear a larger defense burden, and no analysis of the role of U.S. forces and the risk of failure if the U.S. deterrent proved inadequate. An inescapable consequence of Laird's strategy would be greater reliance on nuclear weapons as a deterrent, which Smith alleged rested on the invalid assumption that the United States still retained the nuclear superiority it enjoyed in the 1950s. The central weakness, according to Smith, was Laird's underlying premise, reliance on a deterrent force without linking that force to its capacity to wage war. The essential point of defense planning, he concluded, was "to make sure our forces have a warfighting capability to meet possible threats to our interests." "*I believe*," he wrote Kissinger, "*he* [Laird] *makes a serious mistake in claiming that his approach can substitute for a thorough analysis of strategy and associated force structure alternatives and the presentation of such alternatives to the President for decision.*"[5]

Nixon rejected Laird's approach. Relying mainly on nuclear weapons to deter a threat, such as an attack by Warsaw Pact forces, a position long held by the European allies, was "not credible." He firmly opposed troop cuts in Europe, South Korea, and Vietnam. Like Kissinger and Smith, Nixon believed an attempt to structure

U.S. forces for their deterrent value would be a mistake; he directed Laird to revise his strategy memorandum for review by the DPRC and the NSC.[6]

Undeterred by the rebuff, Laird sent his strategy memorandum back to the president in mid-December with minor changes, informing him of his intention to move full speed ahead. Laird planned to disseminate it within DoD in the form of a tentative strategic guidance for planning future programs and budgets. After the NSC, the services, and departmental agencies reviewed the document, he would issue a revised version about 1 March 1971: "The final document would then serve as firm strategic guidance for the Department of Defense in planning its FY 73–77 Program."[7]

Laird's response flabbergasted Smith, who warned Kissinger that the revised "strategy proposal remains an alarming and conceptually inconsistent document." Laird's realistic defense strategy looked at the budget in the wrong way, Smith thought, because "'realistic' means what we think we can get. . . . The first question, I would think, is what do we think we need?"[8] Kissinger agreed but characterized the situation as "touchy": "The problem is how to handle Laird."[9] He had already circulated for review within DoD a posture statement based on his strategy proposal. Fearful that Laird might actually implement his proposal without explicit presidential approval, Kissinger reminded him that Nixon wanted the DPRC and then the NSC to review his "Strategy of Realistic Deterrence." Under pressure from Kissinger, Laird reluctantly submitted the posture statement for the DPRC to review at its 22 February 1971 meeting.[10]

The White House was not alone in finding Laird's guidance deficient. Early in February the service secretaries and the Joint Chiefs of Staff expressed to the defense secretary reservations about the notion of letting resources determine defense strategy. The JCS held that "US security interests and threats to those interests should be the prime factors in defining US military strategy. Thereafter, the military requirements of the strategy should be derived. Only after these two basic steps have been accomplished should resource constraints be imposed." They also insisted that deterrence had to be based on strength, a full array of military capabilities, and the determination to deploy them: "The possession of credible warfighting capabilities at all levels of conflict . . . is central to a credible strategy of realistic deterrence."[11] Air Force Secretary Robert Seamans and Navy Secretary John Chafee echoed the Joint Chiefs, holding that the guidance needed to provide a better description of the objectives of national strategy and required military capabilities.[12] Army Secretary Stanley Resor stressed the need for ground forces flexible and strong enough to respond to any mission. Army Chief of Staff General William Westmoreland feared that the Nixon Doctrine would lack substance without capable ground forces and the will to use them.[13]

At the 22 February 1971 DPRC session Kissinger reshaped Laird's document, eliminating the elements that had troubled him and the military services. The committee, including Packard, agreed that all forces would be based on their war-fighting capability. In turn, realistic deterrence had to be predicated on that capability and the willingness to use military power. The group reaffirmed the principle that general purpose forces should be capable of carrying out the 1½-war strategy: fighting a major Communist offensive in Europe or Asia and assisting allies in Asia or handling contingencies elsewhere. Conventional forces in Europe would continue to provide an initial defense against the Warsaw Pact. The committee wanted a working group to ensure that Laird's strategic guidance complied with presidential guidance, bringing inconsistencies or conflicts to the president's attention for review and resolution.[14] Laird's grand strategic design had encountered immovable resistance.

Fiscal Guidance

In the next step of creating the FY 1973 budget, in mid-January Packard had issued tentative fiscal guidance, based on budget data and analysis compiled by the comptroller and the Systems Analysis office. The guidance reflected Laird's intention to reduce personnel costs and wind down the U.S. military presence in Vietnam. It assumed a sharp drop in U.S. forces assigned in Southeast Asia by the end of FY 1973. By that time no Army maneuver battalions, artillery battalions, or helicopter companies would be stationed there. At the end of FY 1973 naval tactical air sorties were assumed to average 1,800 per month; Air Force tactical sorties (fighter/attack sorties) would decline to zero at the end of the fiscal year. Navy and Air Force personnel in SEA would be cut by more than half in FY 1973. In-theater Army personnel would decline from 115,000 to 29,000 in FY 1972, and total U.S. forces would fall to 43,400 by the end of June 1973.[15]

Packard's fiscal guidance established a "base case" for planning. Although higher than the amount that Nixon requested for FY 1972, it still cut targets for all services because earlier figures were "unrealistically high." Accordingly, the Army would receive $20.5 billion, or $1.1 billion less than in FY 1972; the Navy and Marine Corps,

$21.5 billion, or $200 million less than in FY 1972; and the Air Force, $21.7 billion, or $1.6 billion less than in FY 1972. All savings would come from reductions in general purpose forces. In view of the ongoing strategic arms limitation talks, Packard fenced off strategic programs, intelligence, and military support from cuts. Packard wanted the JCS Joint Force Memorandum (JFM) and the separate military service program objective memoranda, or POMs, to conform to the outlay targets.[16]

The JCS took exception to Packard's decision to exempt strategic programs, intelligence, and military assistance from budget cuts. They wanted reductions in those areas and more flexibility in preparing the JFM and POMs. Less spending for general purpose forces would weaken their credibility as a deterrent, the Chiefs concluded, and increase the willingness of the Soviets to employ their general purpose forces. Moreover, they considered Packard's force planning assumptions to be too low because they disregarded the recommendations of commanders in the field.[17]

The service secretaries likewise objected to the guidance, unanimously holding that cuts in general purpose forces would require scaling back U.S. security objectives. They believed that general purpose forces after the Vietnam War needed to be strong enough to ensure a robust NATO military that would deter the Soviets. The Army, which faced the largest reductions, maintained that it would be difficult to comply with Packard's guidance and meet national security obligations. Asked to devise "illustrative" force structure packages that allowed no cutbacks in strategic programs, intelligence, and military assistance, Army Secretary Resor presented stark alternatives. A force structure that modernized units and equipment to compensate for the Warsaw Pact's manpower advantage would require the Army to cut three divisions, leaving it with a $10^1/_3$-division force for FYs 1973–1977. An alternative force structure that kept the Army at $13^1/_3$ divisions would completely eliminate major modernization programs. Either force structure entailed risks to executing current national security plans. The U.S. commander in Europe and the JCS had agreed on the necessity of having "15 Army divisions in Europe 60 days after mobilization (M+60) and 17 Army divisions 90 days after mobilization (M+90) as the estimated minimum land force requirements for the defense of NATO." Resor wanted a "real world" force that retained essential elements of modernization and a fighting force of $13^1/_3$ divisions.[18]

Air Force Secretary Seamans also concluded that the protective fence around strategic programs, intelligence, and military assistance would erode the deterrent value of general purpose forces. He warned that the Air Force budget was so stretched that even with force cuts of "inordinate magnitudes, we cannot continue the research, development, and procurement which are in our current program." Barring a decrease in the security threat, it would be impossible "to maintain the required force for the present and provide realistic deterrence in the future if further funding reductions are imposed."[19]

Sounding equally dire, Navy Secretary Chafee contended that Packard's tentative fiscal guidance would impose personnel reductions, "result in a naval force structure even less capable of supporting the approved national strategy," and decrease the nation's ability to deter nonnuclear conflicts. The cutbacks set forth in the tentative fiscal guidance would create shortfalls in forces earmarked for NATO and "would likely bring into serious question the credibility of the U.S. commitment." Moreover, NATO would strongly oppose unilateral reductions by the United States.[20]

White House Review

Packard's guidance also raised eyebrows in the White House, where, as in previous years, the NSC strongly desired to involve itself more deeply in working out the defense program. Wayne Smith of the NSC staff feared DoD's planning cycle would rule out the president's consideration of alternative strategic or fiscal guidance. "If specific provision is not made for our involvement," he warned, "we will lose a large measure of control once 'final' fiscal guidance is issued to the Services on March 15." The DoD fiscal guidance outlay target of $79.6 billion worried Smith because it was about $6.5 billion higher than the FY 1973 budget expenditure levels specified in earlier guidance (NSDM 27 and NSDM 84). Despite of the overall spending increase, money for general purpose forces would drop. Compelled to absorb almost all expenditure reductions while faced with growing personnel costs caused by scheduled military and civilian wage and salary increases and the transition to the All-Volunteer Force, the Army would have to shrink. Smith calculated that $4 billion of the increase in outlays was "equivalent to the expected $4 billion per year decrease in Vietnam costs expected in FY 73." He argued that smaller budget outlays of $75 billion–$76 billion would still provide a credible defense.[21]

As it confronted deteriorating economic conditions, renewed inflation, and substantial federal budget deficits in 1973 and 1974, OMB sought to lower Packard's spending level below $79.5 billion. The falling cost of the Vietnam War, the elimination or postponement of some weapon systems under development, and the possible reduction of the ABM program should the strategic arms talks prove successful would allow cuts in DoD spending. Although OMB Director Shultz favored a strong national defense, he had to consider the entire federal budget and the president's desire for a full-employment balanced budget. To reach that goal, he concluded, he would have to reduce DoD spending by $2 billion–$3 billion, putting expenditures in the range of $75 billion to $76 billion, without significantly altering force structure programs. His overriding concern was that even with $3 billion cut in DoD's baseline fiscal guidance, the overall federal budget would be $9.8 billion higher than estimated full-employment revenues.[22]

Shultz's advisers pointed out that DoD budget planning assumptions (no adjustments to FY 1972 programs, no cuts in strategic programs, no base closings, and readiness at adequate levels) had forced the department into choosing between "two equally untenable" program alternatives: reducing force structure or curtailing modernization. In their view, Laird had increased his FY 1973 spending target to $79.6 billion to boost force structure and modernization programs.[23]

Resisting Shultz's call for cuts, Laird gained Kissinger's support in March 1971. He agreed to focus budget discussions in the DPRC on defense requirements to keep OMB "from whacking at" the FY 1973 fiscal guidance.[24] The tactic worked in the short run. At the meeting on 26 April, Shultz conditionally accepted Laird's figure of $79.6 billion for planning purposes, but said he would reexamine it in the summer when Congress took action on the FY 1973 budget. Even the $79.6 billion required stark trade-offs. If DoD kept the modernization program at its present level, it would have to cut manpower by 100,000; if it held manpower at its current level, modernization expenditures would fall by 12 percent.[25]

The April DPRC session also focused on Laird's interim strategic guidance of withdrawing U.S. troops from Asia, expecting U.S. allies to take up the slack, and relying on tactical nuclear weapons in an Asian conflict.[26] Such a basic change in policy, the group agreed, required the president's approval and had to be reconciled with existing policy. The DPRC asked DoD to come up with two alternative programs, one of them at the currently planned spending level of $79.6 billion and another at a lower level, for consideration in the summer.[27]

In June Laird issued revised planning guidance for the JCS and the military services. Although this guidance, prepared by the comptroller and the Systems

Analysis office, took into account the views of the JCS and the services, it anticipated a spending reduction. In line with the Nixon Doctrine's emphasis on providing military aid rather than U.S. troops to allies and the strategy of realistic deterrence, the guidance envisioned a scaled back defense program that put greater stress on diplomacy, political action, and military assistance. Accordingly, the defense program could no longer afford "to meet every threat head on." In the future, U.S. armed forces would compensate for their smaller size by enhanced readiness and modernization and a greater and more active role for the National Guard and reserve components. In what augured major change, Laird announced that "the Guard and Reserve will be the initial and primary source of augmentation of the active forces in any future emergency requiring a rapid and substantial expansion of the active forces." Reductions in the active force could "be offset by increasing the capability or modifying the structure of the Guard and Reserve forces." This guidance would constitute the DoD position in forthcoming DPRC and NSC meetings.[28]

Ever the politician, Laird advanced a number of budget proposals to different audiences, presumably as a negotiating tactic that would allow him to carry out a range of contingencies. His internal FY 1973 fiscal guidance to DoD called for expenditures of $79.6 billion, but Packard had signaled to OMB Laird's willingness to agree to a spending level of $77 billion to take effect later in the budget formulation process after the budget had been "scrubbed down." To prepare for possible cuts, Laird requested that Systems Analysis prepare a $2 billion spending decrement from the fiscal guidance, which he claimed Kissinger requested. At the same time he also pressed his case with Nixon for more money, with outlays in the range of $82 billion to $83 billion in FY 1973. He told the president that $79.6 billion in expenditures would be inadequate to support his foreign policy objectives, make it difficult in the event of war to meet the targets of NATO deployment plans, and fail to provide sufficient tactical air support to non-NATO allies. Laird argued the additional money was needed to avoid force reductions and to pay for readiness and modernization. Without extra funds, he claimed he would have to postpone military and civilian pay increases, slow the transition to an all-volunteer force, reduce air and logistic support for SEA, and close military installations. As Smith wryly observed, Laird had "come down hard on every side of the DoD budget issue," telling each party what it wanted to hear about the defense program. Smith advised Kissinger that the president should avoid getting involved with Laird's maneuvers, since no decisions were necessary at the time. Laird intended to make a persuasive case for $82 billion–$83 billion in expenditures at the 5 August DPRC meeting—before Nixon made any decisions.[29]

At the meeting, Assistant Secretary of Defense for Systems Analysis Gardiner Tucker pulled out all the stops in presenting the consequences for general purpose forces of cutting outlays below $82 billion. Manpower reductions in the Army and the Marine Corps, he contended, would force the United States to adopt a one-war strategy. The Army would lose 2⅓ active divisions; the Marine Corps, 25 percent of its combat infantry companies; and the Navy, 47 ships and 2 carriers.[30] At the $80 billion expenditure level there would not be enough soldiers and transport to reinforce NATO during an attack and also handle a conflict in Asia. To provide eight divisions to NATO, the Army would have to withhold U.S. reinforcements from Korea. At the $82 billion spending level the Army could deploy reinforcements to Korea. Several attendees expressed the fear that the U.S. military was in danger of losing credibility. Packard summed up the consequences of lower defense spending: "It could mean that we would have no ability to deploy ground forces in Asia, that we couldn't deploy in the Mediterranean, or that we couldn't go to NATO if necessary." Moorer was equally forthright: "With these reductions the President cannot have the flexibility required for a viable foreign policy in light of the Soviet build-up. We cannot gloss over the fact that this [budget] carries very high risks and reduces the President's options."[31]

Unmoved by the apocalyptic statements, Shultz insisted the spending levels under discussion were "way beyond anything that would be acceptable," in view of the president's desire for a full-employment balanced budget.[32] The inability of OMB and DoD to reach a compromise created difficulties for Nixon. Prior to the 13 August NSC meeting Kissinger sketched out the administration's dilemma. The president's balanced full-employment budget, including funds for his domestic initiatives, left only $77 billion for DoD spending. Laird, the JCS, and the services had put on record the effect grave cuts in force structure would have and the serious security risks that even the higher fiscal guidance of $79.6 billion would create.[33]

At the August NSC 1971 meeting, Laird set forth DoD's justification for nearly $82 billion in expenditures, highlighting as Tucker had the harmful effects of lower spending on general purpose forces. Unilateral cuts in strategic forces were out of the question because the United States was at strategic parity with the Soviets. He also had to get the modernization program back on track and was unwilling to shrink it. His fiscal guidance had reduced general purpose forces to help pay for higher salaries, benefits, and equipment. The secretary posed a difficult choice to Nixon: "We must either fund at the levels needed or change our strategy." Moorer amplified Laird's point, warning that the $79.6 billion spending program was "based on an either/or capability—either operating with a NATO commitment or an Asian commitment, not both." It would also eliminate the swing forces needed to carry out the NSSM 3 strategy of 1½ wars. This indeed would be a one-war strategy. Nixon responded cautiously: "There is a level beyond which defense can't be reduced—it is most important for diplomatic and psychological purposes." As was his custom, Nixon made no decision at the meeting.[34]

The president's new economic policy complicated the landscape. To cope with inflation, unemployment, a balance of payments deficit, a weakening of the dollar, and loss of U.S. gold reserves, on 15 August Nixon announced a package of far-reaching changes that temporarily suspended the convertibility of the dollar into gold (allowing the value of the dollar to float), cut federal spending by $4.7 billion, reduced foreign economic aid by 10 percent, froze wages and prices throughout the United States for 90 days, and imposed an additional tax of 10 percent on imports. The specter of a large federal deficit alarmed Laird as well. As a former legislator, he thought a deficit that could reach $40 billion would constitute a serious political liability in an election year. Although Nixon's new economic policy would create additional pressure to cut spending, Laird would continue to resist.[35]

During the fall of 1971 the White House moved closer to a decision on spending, but with less input from DoD. Although Packard met with Kissinger and OMB officials in October, he and Moorer were excluded from the White House inner circle of Kissinger, Shultz, Haig, and Smith that deliberated over the FY 1973 spending baseline. In these discussions Kissinger, who continued to push for lower spending, wanted to present Packard with a fait accompli, believing the deputy secretary could not agree to cuts "without losing enormous face with his people." Shultz pressed to reduce expenditures to $77 billion, but Kissinger was unwilling to go that low. Wayne Smith argued for $77.6 billion. In his calculations, planned reductions in DoD civilian employees, congressional and OMB budget reviews of current defense spending, and inventory drawdowns to support a smaller-scale war would automatically lower spending to $78 billion. Cuts in funding for the All-Volunteer

Force and for duplicative intelligence programs would lower total expenditures to $77.6 billion. This amount would support force levels according to Smith and equate to a DoD budget authority of about $80 billion. Budget authority comprised new obligational authority, or NOA—the authority to incur obligations—and loan authority—the authority to borrow money. Budget authority included the full costs of major procurement and construction programs whose costs would be paid over a period of years. Moreover, budget authority of $80 billion would allow room for the president to add items of his choosing, such as building four additional Poseidon submarines with the new Undersea Long-range Missile System, Smith pointed out. According to Haig, Kissinger hoped to get out a presidential directive early in December setting major force levels and a budget total "to override Laird's internal decisions" that countered Nixon's position.[36]

In October, Shultz and Kissinger came to an agreement that $77.5 billion in spending would be "sufficient to support the President's foreign policy objectives and would also be consistent with a balanced full employment budget."[37] Laird meanwhile insisted on higher spending to retain flexibility in executing the DoD program and in allocating funds to the military services.[38]

Kissinger passed the president's budget decision to Laird at the beginning of December, but only after the two had worked out a deal. They agreed on 2 December that Kissinger would send a letter to Laird informing him of Nixon's decision. Laird could more easily appeal a letter from Kissinger than a directive signed by the president. In his letter Kissinger asserted that an estimated TOA of $81 billion–$82 billion and estimated expenditures of $78 billion–$79 billion adequately supported the president's defense posture and also represented a budget increase compared with the previous year. To reach these expenditure figures, Kissinger and Shultz cut $2.4 billion (the effects of congressional action on FY 1972 spending, a budget scrub, and OMB-identified savings) from the military departments' budget submissions of $81.9 billion in expenditures. They also eliminated $1.1 billion in funds for air defense, ABM, intelligence programs, SEA sorties, and the All-Volunteer Force, but added $400 million for SLBM initiatives and for Marine Corps tactical readiness to arrive at estimated outlays of $78 billion–$79 billion. Three SLBM options were under consideration: accelerating development of the ULMS submarine and missile system, building additional 640-class submarines (carrying Poseidon missiles but incorporating new reactors and sonars), and converting attack submarines to missile launching submarines. Kissinger acknowledged that the lower spending level would compel DoD to make additional cuts but reminded Laird that the president wanted no significant reductions in current forces or their readiness.[39]

Laird persisted in his attempts to keep DoD spending above $79 billion. On 8 December he appealed to Nixon to approve outlays of $79.5 billion–$80 billion (budget authority of $83 billion–$84 billion), calling it the minimum needed to support the administration's national security and foreign policy goals. This was $1 billion more than the $78 billion–$79 billion the president approved. By cutting the budget requests of the JCS and the services, he felt he could reach an expenditure amount of $79.7 billion without compromising readiness.[40] Philip Odeen, who had replaced Laurence Lynn on Kissinger's staff, noted Laird's request would reverse a number of cuts the president had already made as well as exceed the $78.5 billion that OMB now insisted was the "absolute maximum that can be provided without upsetting the President's full employment budget balance." In April Shultz had conditionally accepted a planning figure of $79.6 billion. Odeen believed it possible to reach the lower OMB figure without compromising military capability.[41]

The continuing disagreement over defense spending exasperated Nixon, affecting as it did the availability of funds for domestic programs. On 11 December he directed Kissinger to meet that afternoon with Shultz and his chief domestic adviser John Ehrlichman to set the DoD budget: "We have to decide what the number is. . . . It has to be decided and Laird has to be told." The secretary would have no say in the decision.[42]

Kissinger, however, attempted to broker a compromise with Laird and Shultz. He informed Shultz that the president wanted to raise the Defense budget by a billion because Packard had convinced him for political reasons that additional money was needed to produce F–111s in Texas and California. He intimated to the budget director that a $500 million increase to $79 billion would suffice, but Shultz resisted, insisting that the budget was "already too big. . . . There is damned little left in the domestic budget. There is no room for new Presidential initiatives and we are having to cut back on the old ones. Defense has it all. That is what is bothering Ehrlichman."[43] Kissinger then tried to get Laird to settle for a $500 million increase, telling him that his request for more money had upset Nixon. Kissinger reassured Nixon's chief of staff H. R. Haldeman that he could get an agreement on the budget within a few days, but Shultz would have to accede to an additional $500 million.[44]

Like Shultz, Laird was in no mood to compromise. In the absence of a presidential decision on the budget, he requested again on 14 December a total of $79.5 billion–$80 billion in outlays, an extra billion for the purpose of keeping pace with the Soviets. Outlays of $78.5 billion would not provide for an accelerated ULMS program, which Laird regarded as essential for strategic arms talks, and would reduce the chance of attaining the AVF by the end of FY 1973. It would be difficult, he stressed, to demonstrate to the Soviet Union, whose military power was increasing, a serious U.S. commitment to national security when defense spending in FY 1973 would be lower in constant dollars than it was in FY 1964. Odeen doubted an additional outlay of $1 billion would "prove decisive either militarily or in political impact" and criticized Laird's criteria. "We should," he wrote Kissinger, "design our forces and budgets to meet specific strategic or diplomatic objectives not to provide an overall budget level that will compare favorably to last year's, the Soviets, or any other arbitrary yardstick."[45]

Nixon rejected Laird's plea. He decided on FY 1973 requests of around $82 billion in budget authority and $78.6 billion in expenditures. Laird wanted to keep expenditures above $79 billion. The president's decision would support a strategic force of more than 1,000 ICBMs, 600 SLBMs, and 450 B–52s. General purpose forces would consist of 13 Army and 3 Marine divisions, 21 Air Force wings, and a 575–600-ship Navy. Nixon believed that his FY 1973 request would be sufficient to protect national security and attain his economic objectives, but he needed to make reductions in a number of areas. He delayed the pay raise scheduled for October 1972 until January 1973, reducing outlays by $400 million. This postponement saved money for DoD, giving Laird some leeway in allocating funds for new programs. The president limited the Safeguard program to planning for four sites, a number that might be reduced in the event of a strategic arms limitation treaty. Strategic air defense and missile interceptors would face cuts; money for the AVF would be reduced by $350 million.[46]

Laird tried to put the best face on the lower numbers. "I can take any figure and make it work," he assured Kissinger, but nevertheless he persisted in pressing for more money in FY 1973, arguing that he had to offset the effect of inflation on DoD's buying power. Measured in constant 1971 dollars, Laird noted, defense spending would decline by $1.7 billion between fiscal years 1972 and 1973, even though nominal spending was nearly $4 billion higher in 1973. He pointed out that the reduction in AVF funding would eliminate new initiatives after the first year of the program.[47] An exasperated Kissinger reminded the secretary that the president had significantly increased DoD spending compared with the previous year and that he had omitted the declining cost of the Vietnam War from his calculations. With that decrease factored into the budget, defense spending in constant dollars would actually rise by $1 billion in FY 1973. According to Kissinger, Nixon had allocated additional funds for DoD because he wanted strong and ready forces to support his foreign policy.[48]

President's Budget Request

Nixon submitted his FY 1973 budget request to Congress on 24 January 1972, estimating total federal expenditures at $246.3 billion and receipts at $220.8 billion. Receipts at full employment were estimated at $245 billion, putting the budget "approximately in balance," which according to the president, would help stem inflation and help fund his domestic initiatives. The $78.3 billion defense expenditures request, $300 million below the amount Nixon had designated in December, would equal 31.8 percent of all FY 1973 federal expenditures, continuing the multi-year trend of declining defense spending relative to total federal spending. The $78.3 billion in outlays for spending on national defense included money for retirement system changes, civilian and military pay raises, military assistance, and atomic energy, less $692 million for offsetting receipts. Table 21 shows the DoD budget request by title. Military assistance ($600 million) and atomic energy ($2.4 billion) expenditures were in separate legislation.[49]

The president's budget request increased NOA and expenditures for personnel over the previous fiscal year for the Navy, Air Force, and Marines to pay for the November 1971 pay increase. Army personnel costs would decrease by $553 million in NOA and $646 million in expenditures because the service's average strength would fall by more than 100,000 soldiers. However, the Army would receive additional funds in both NOA and expenditures for procurement of Safeguard missiles, aircraft modernization, and the M–60 tank. The NOA request also included added money for ship modernization, naval weapons, and communications systems. The bulk of the requested money for personnel allowances would cover DoD's share of the 1972 and 1973 civilian and military pay raises. To cover the cost of proposed legislation, new FY 1973 budget requests proposed $390 million for the AVF and $290 million for military retirement system reform.[50]

Table 21. President's DoD Budget Request, FY 1973 ($ thousands)

Title	NOA	Expenditures
Military Personnel	22,414,100	22,300,000
Retired Pay	4,325,000	4,325,600
O&M	20,568,049	20,450,000
Procurement	19,313,230	16,082,000
RDT&E	8,497,800	7,923,000
Military Construction	2,040,600	1,203,300
Family Housing	977,200	799,500
Civil Defense	88,100	85,300
Special Foreign Currency Program	3,400	6,900
Allowances	3,530,000	3,425,000
Military Trust Funds	6,294	9,529
Subtotal	81,763,773	76,610,129
Offsetting receipts	(101,700)	(692,000)
Revolving Management Funds	-	(598,860)
Transfers	(6,100)	-
Subtotal	(107,800)	(1,290,860)
Total	81,655,973	75,318,669

Source: OMB, *The Budget of the United States Government, Fiscal Year 1973* (Washington, DC: Government Printing Office, 1972), 270–82.

The combined effect of personnel cuts and increased funding for FY 1973 would help stabilize DoD's budget and offset the steadily increasing personnel costs (salaries and retirement benefits) that had climbed from 42 percent of the budget in 1968 to 53 percent in 1972. A colonel's monthly pay, for example, went from $985 in 1964 to $2,057 in 1973. Owing to reductions in manpower, overall expenses for personnel would decline slightly to 52 percent of the FY 1973 budget. Higher salaries and benefits for military and civilian personnel plus the effects of inflation consumed most of the budget increases after 1964, leaving DoD with virtually no money to increase R&D and procurement spending at a time when the USSR continued to build up and modernize weapons and forces, and China was on the verge of becoming a nuclear power. These hardware accounts had no inflation-adjusted growth.[51]

Some legislators, concerned about the effect of rising personnel costs on the defense program, sought to rein in manpower spending. Senator Stennis notified

Senator William Proxmire (D–WI) clashed with Laird over defense spending. (U.S. Senate Historical Office)

Laird that the Senate Committee on Armed Services would conduct an intensive, in-depth review of military manpower: "I am concerned that the soaring manpower costs will jeopardize the modernization of our weapons systems. We must therefore make an effort to achieve compensating decreases in the numbers of personnel without affecting the over-all combat capabilities of the military services."[52]

Nixon's FY 1973 budget request immediately encountered sharp congressional criticism. Prominent Democratic senators, William Proxmire, Edward Kennedy, and Edmund Muskie faulted the increase in military spending over the previous fiscal year and asserted that defense expenditures should be shrinking because the Vietnam War was winding down. Muskie feared that the proposed deficit was large enough to spark renewed inflation.[53]

Other legislators lambasted the accounting methods on which the request was based. House Appropriation Committee chairman George Mahon ridiculed the concept of a full employment budget for providing "a very soothing and comforting approach to the problem of red-ink spending." "What one does," he said, "is to play like one has full employment and that the Government is collecting the revenue which would flow from full employment. Then one spends the funds, which of course one does not have, so one has to borrow them for the operation of the government. This strange stratagem tends to lull the Government and the citizen . . . into complacency." An apprehensive Mahon believed this practice would only create more inflation and undermine the dollar at home and abroad. Together with Senator Allen J. Ellender (D–LA), Mahon also criticized employing the unified budget concept, first used in FY 1969, to tap the surplus in the social security and highway construction trust funds to pay for normal federal operating expenses. They objected to this procedure because it made the federal deficit seem smaller than it really was. Spending surplus trust funds disregarded the obligation to repay eventually those monies to the trust funds for their designated purposes.[54]

Congressional Review

Laird's testimony before Congress in 1972, a presidential election year, took on a more political cast when he defended Nixon's military policies and the Pentagon's budget. As early as February he announced he intended to take an active role in rebutting the president's critics and would meet with people across the nation to win their support. To his staff Laird characterized the Senate as being hostile to DoD, and he expected it to vent its hostility by cutting $3.5 billion out of the Defense budget. He did not expect passage of a defense bill until after the election, but he continued to fight against additional budget cuts by Congress and even the president.[55]

There were critics aplenty who worried about the growing federal deficit and the escalating costs of developing and acquiring new weapon systems. Influential groups and individuals maintained that the Pentagon was not doing enough to shrink forces and costs for the post-Vietnam era, despite the demonstrable decline of defense spending in real terms and as a share of total federal expenditures since 1968. Two Democratic contenders for the presidential nomination, Senators George McGovern and Edmund Muskie, were the most prominent detractors of the level of defense spending. McGovern did more than denounce the high costs. At the end of January 1972 he unveiled a detailed, alternative budget that by FY 1975 would dramatically shrink defense spending to $54.8 billion, some $20 billion less than Nixon's FY 1973 outlay request and nearly $30 billion below what the president planned to spend in FY 1975 ($83.4 billion).[56]

Senator George McGovern (D–SD) proposed drastic cuts in the Defense budget and was the democratic presidential candidate in 1972. (U.S. Senate Historical Office)

Justifying the president's request for DoD spending of more than $75 billion when the FY 1973 budget deficit could reach $36.2 billion would not be an easy task, especially when many lawmakers and OMB regarded the DoD budget as a major source of cuts in federal spending. Laird tried to focus the discussion on the nation's future needs. He sought money to replace an unfair and failing conscription system with an all-volunteer force, to revitalize a modernization program vitiated by the Vietnam War, and to meet rising development and production costs. Laird argued that, absent a strategic arms limitation agreement, the Defense budget had to remain robust. To help make the case with Congress and OMB for the spending request, Comptroller Robert Moot prepared a statistical analysis of trends in defense spending to demonstrate that DoD's budget was "not the controlling factor in the over-all Federal budget."[57]

One of the new weapon programs favored by the administration was the Undersea Long-Range Missile System, a new larger submarine and a new longer-range missile for it. In December 1971 Packard had authorized an accelerated schedule to deploy the new submarine and missiles in 1978. The White House had added money to the budget request to pay for the fast-tracked program (in May 1972 the program was renamed Trident). Senators Ellender and Proxmire of the Senate Appropriations Committee saw no justification for an expensive accelerated program. Other senators questioned the need for urgency, contending the Trident was essentially a bargaining ploy to extract from the Soviet Union a mutual limitation on submarines. Laird denied this, asserting Trident's importance on its own merits. It would demonstrate to the Soviets that the United States had the resources and the resolve to counter the buildup of Soviet strategic forces and would also represent a hedge against Soviet efforts to counter the existing Polaris and Poseidon submarines.[58] Increased funding for the Navy brought complaints from Air Force Secretary Seamans, who worried that the Navy's growing share of defense spending would be at the expense of the other services, marking a shift toward a naval strategy and making the Navy the dominant service.[59]

The Vietnam War complicated Laird's efforts to win support and put added strain on his budget in 1972. North Vietnam's massive Easter Offensive, which began at the end of March, lasted through the summer, forcing the president to hike spending above planned levels. Additional air strikes, extra ship deployments to the SEA theater, increased ammunition and equipment for South Vietnam's armed

At a Pentagon press conference on 10 August 1972, Laird discusses Comptroller Robert Moot's analysis of defense expenditures and the economy. (NARA)

forces, and the continued requirement to improve and modernize Saigon's military intensified the financial pressure on the DoD budgets for FY 1972 and FY 1973.

Even as the enemy's offensive raged throughout South Vietnam and threatened to defeat Saigon's forces, some senators felt so fed up with the war that they sought to limit spending for it. Senate majority leader Mike Mansfield and other senators opposed to the administration's Vietnam strategy, however, realized the obstacles to passing legislation that would cut off funding for the war. An attempt to do so had already failed in the House. They decided instead on an indirect approach, cutting $3.5 billion from the FY 1973 budget. The timing of such a proposal in the midst of the Easter Offensive concerned Laird. He estimated that the U.S. air and naval buildup would cost $600 million–$750 million in FY 1973; logistic support and the replacement of weapon losses during the offensive could amount to $400 million–$500 million. The $100 million cost of the 1972 logistics buildup, not included in the FY 1972 budget, would have to be carried over to FY 1973. The Senate's possible cut of $3.5 billion and the unprogrammed requirements of $1.1 billion to $1.3 billion for the fighting in Vietnam, Laird warned Nixon, would have to be absorbed "within an already constrained defense budget." He feared the reductions would reduce the president's ability to pursue his foreign policy and the undergirding military strategy. In the secretary's judgment, Mansfield's plan had a better chance of success than the previous direct efforts to impose constraints by legislation.[60]

By June 1972 Senator McGovern had emerged as the clear frontrunner for his party's nomination, and the alternative Defense budget he had unveiled in January received closer scrutiny. He contended his $54.8 billion budget for FY 1975 expenditures would be sufficient "to meet foreseeable threats to our security" but with less waste and at lower cost. McGovern's cuts were significant. He would discontinue deployment of the Minuteman III and MIRV warheads, as well as efforts to upgrade the Minuteman. Even equipped with MIRVs, the Minuteman, McGovern contended, would remain vulnerable prior to launch. In any case, Soviet defenses could be penetrated without MIRVs. He would halt the Safeguard ABM system, end prototype development of the B–1 bomber, and convert no more than seven Polaris submarines to Poseidons, but he would continue to develop the ULMS. He would withdraw $2^2/_3$ divisions from Europe, leaving 130,000 U.S. soldiers on the continent, and remove the remaining U.S. division from South Korea. Active-duty military personnel would fall from more than two million in May 1972 to 1.7 million, leaving the Army with only 10 active divisions. He would reduce civilian employees from roughly a million to 761,000 in FY 1975. McGovern offered voters a stark choice regarding America's role in the world. His scaled-back program provided for defense of the United States but would probably diminish U.S. influence internationally and affect America's Cold War policy.[61]

In June Proxmire sought Laird's evaluation of McGovern's proposed budget, reminding the secretary that he had previously requested it from the DoD comptroller. In earlier testimony Robert Moot had told the committee that McGovern's budget under-calculated the cost of his defense program by $10 billion. Laird pledged to submit his analysis to Proxmire, but speaking more like a congressman than a defense secretary, he provocatively expressed his disdain for the McGovern budget. "I would say," he told the Senate Appropriations Subcommittee, "that the thing to do if you go the $30 billion reduction route is to direct the Department of Defense to spend at least a billion dollars in white flags so that they can run them up all over because it means surrender." His blast made headlines in Washington.[62]

Although Proxmire did not endorse McGovern's proposal, he bristled at Laird's provocative words. Laird answered by asserting that the Pentagon had to spend

$41 billion of its $76 billion budget on fixed expenditures for military and civilian personnel salaries and retirement benefits, leaving roughly $35 billion for everything else. With McGovern's $30 billion spending cut there would be very little money remaining. Although Proxmire's staff repeatedly asked for the promised analysis, Laird waited until 5 July to reply in some detail. Not coincidentally, this was five days before the Democratic convention opened in Miami Beach. On 6 July the secretary held a press conference and renewed his attack on McGovern's defense program. Laird professed reluctance to take up the issue. He intended to respond after the convention ended, because the Democratic platform committee had rejected the suggestion of a $20 billion–$30 billion Defense budget reduction, and he thought McGovern's proposal was dead. When Proxmire asked for his evaluation, Laird explained he was "delighted to help him in keeping this issue very much before the public." Laird devoted a large segment of the conference to tearing apart McGovern's proposal in what was a partisan political attack. Laird's comments were intended to remind the public that McGovern had proposed a defense cut too severe for even his own party, making Nixon's national security plan by contrast seem more prudent.[63]

Laird sought to garner support for the DoD program with nonpartisan analytical arguments as well. In July 1972, after the Democratic convention, DoD issued Comptroller Moot's 205-page book, "The Economics of Defense Spending: A Look at the Realities." Containing 30 tables and statistical appendixes on the Defense budget. Moot's work was widely circulated and even discussed by the media. Orr Kelly, defense correspondent for the *Washington Star*, thought the study would "become one of the more important documents of this political year." Another analyst concluded that Moot's study "established that most of McGovern's criticisms of the defense budget were primarily myths."[64] Based on current and historical budget data, Moot presented a factual context for any review of defense spending. In so doing, he debunked a number of the charges that McGovern and other critics leveled. With carefully marshaled statistical evidence, Moot tore apart the notions that the Defense budget continued to grow in real terms, that it was largest component of federal spending, and that the country was operating under a wartime economy. In FY 1953 during the Korean War defense spending ($52.8 billion) was almost twice that of all other federal agencies combined. By FY 1973 during the Vietnam War the reverse was true; nearly twice as much would go for expenditures on social and economic programs ($145.8 billion) as for defense (around $76 billion).

FY 1973 defense spending in real terms, Moot demonstrated, would account for about 31 percent of federal outlays.[65] Moot's careful and thorough analysis laid a firm statistical foundation for fending off steep cuts. Laird later acknowledged his debt to Moot's expertise on the Defense budget: "I knew the budget pretty well, but I was not a master. The master of that budget, as far as I am concerned, was Bob Moot. I would never go anywhere without Bob Moot. Even when I went over for a private meeting with the president on the budget I asked to bring Bob Moot."[66]

As the congressional committees in July weighed defense appropriations, Nixon wanted to be prepared for the worst. He requested that Laird prepare a list of possible reductions if Congress further slashed spending. In no mood to accept cuts, Laird was barely cooperative. He told Kissinger he could accept some reductions in personnel but none in operations where program costs had risen by more than $1 billion. He could recommend no cutbacks in strategic programs, general purpose forces, or any area that would impair readiness. To the contrary, he sought more money. Operations in Southeast Asia would exceed budgeted amounts, making it likely that he would seek a supplemental for FY 1973.[67]

Laird's unyielding stance made life difficult for the president, who believed that rising congressional spending for domestic programs and an expanding budget deficit might require additional cuts. Fearful that out-of-control spending could rekindle inflation, he asked Congress on 26 July to show restraint and enact a $250 billion ceiling for FY 1973 expenditures, deeming the spending limit "in the economic interest of all American citizens." This ceiling was higher than the president's January budget request of $246.3 billion, but it represented his attempt to have Congress impose a cap on spending. The president believed that he had to act and warned the lawmakers he would not allow excessive spending to force him to raise taxes or sabotage his anti-inflation program. He threatened to veto legislation with spending provisions that endangered the economy.[68]

Laird privately objected to Nixon's request to establish a spending ceiling, but not only because he had not been consulted. He complained that the president's advocacy of a ceiling would provoke deep congressional reductions in DoD's budget, in turn forcing him to cut expenditures hastily. He also pointed out that by the end of July, Congress had enacted all major appropriations save for defense and foreign aid and that overall spending would likely reach $256 billion. The upshot was that DoD would likely suffer disproportionate cuts if Congress complied with the spending ceiling. If Congress did not comply with the cap, Laird argued, then the president would be forced to cut defense to carry out his pledge. To make cuts quickly under the circumstances, Laird would have to curtail air operations in Southeast Asia and reduce manpower, inventory levels, and modernization.[69]

In public Laird was equally critical. Speaking to reporters on 31 July, he termed the spending limit "a mistake" and said, "I don't know who the hell" was responsible for it. At that point Laird also worried about McGovern's proposal to cut production of the F–15 and freeze defense spending. On 2 August he told a group of newsmen that it would be difficult and unfair to apply an expenditure limitation that would have the effect of imposing cuts on the only two appropriation bills still before Congress—defense and foreign aid. He wanted the limit applied retroactively to all appropriation measures.[70]

Laird's comments enraged the White House. Working on a spending proposal to submit to Congress, John Ehrlichman, Nixon's chief domestic adviser, and OMB Director Caspar Weinberger wanted a lid placed on federal expenditures (Weinberger replaced George Shultz as director on 12 June 1972). Weinberger thought Laird's comments bordered on insubordination and raised questions about the president's sincerity. He told Kissinger that Laird should be compelled to withdraw his statements publicly. Ehrlichman likewise called Kissinger, insisting that Laird retract his statement and that Nixon's press secretary, Ron Ziegler, would have "to repudiate him [Laird] in order to preserve our political position." Kissinger asked Laird to clarify his public position. "Well, all they need to do," the latter snapped, "is just read what I have said and read the whole transcript." Laird reiterated that the budget ceiling should not affect only the defense program, the same basic point that he had made in his memorandum to Nixon and in his comments to the press.[71]

A determined and outspoken Laird continued to battle Weinberger and OMB for more funds for Vietnam operations. At the end of September 1972 Weinberger was noticeably upset about his inability to keep Laird in check. The secretary had made a formal request for a budget supplemental of $4.1 billion to cover the cost of increased operations in Southeast Asia during the Easter Offensive through the end of 1972. Even though Weinberger had no intention of forwarding the supplemental request, he confided to Kissinger his fear that Laird would do what he had done before, simply bypass OMB. He expected the secretary to advise the congressional committees that a supplemental request was pending and then leak it to the press.[72]

Laird's persistence in battling a budget ceiling that would have harmful effects found an unlikely supporter within the NSC. Odeen, usually critical of Laird, was sympathetic. "Laird is skeptical," he told Kissinger, "that the large cuts required can be made on such short notice without impacting on defense (and I agree)." Laird criticized OMB for not being forthcoming about the actual consequences of a ceiling for DoD. He knew that enactment of a ceiling would doom DoD's supplemental request to cover Vietnam operations through the end of 1972, increasing risk at a time when the enemy was seriously threatening South Vietnam's existence.[73]

Gains and Losses

Nearly three months after the start of FY 1973, the House Appropriations Committee acted on the DoD budget, reducing new obligational authority on 11 September to $74.6 billion. This was $7.1 billion less in NOA than the president requested in January. From FY 1968 to FY 1972 the House had reduced DoD requests by more than $19 billion. On the positive side, the $74.6 billion appropriations measure represented an increase over the previous year's NOA.[74]

The House bill funded major weapon programs, including the F–14, the B–1 bomber, and the accelerated development of the Trident submarine, but it cut the ABM by $300 million, eliminating a missile site for the Washington, D.C. area. Before the committee marked up the bill, the Army had decided to terminate the Cheyenne helicopter development program because of growing costs (begun in 1963, the program had racked up estimated costs of $450 million). Money for R&D increased by $326 million over the previous year, but this amount was far less than the $1.2 billion in additional money the administration had requested. The committee also approved over $2 billion in funds to cover the high tempo of military operations to halt the North Vietnamese offensive in Vietnam.[75]

The Senate Appropriations Committee's bill of 29 September 1972 differed only marginally from the House version, adding a bit more than $27 million in NOA. For the military personnel appropriation, Laird urged passage of the Senate bill, $64 million higher than the House bill. Conference action went along with Laird's request, cutting the Senate personnel appropriation by only $5 million. The conference also supported an important element of the AVF, agreeing to provide a direct appropriation for hiring civilians to perform KP duty. Most significantly for DoD, both the Senate and the House increased NOA by more than $1.7 billion over the FY 1972 appropriation.[76] House and Senate conferees cut an additional $200 million in NOA, lowering the total to $74.4 billion. Congress granted transfer authority of $1.3 billion, bringing DoD's total funding to $75.7 billion. On 28 October, shortly before the election, Nixon signed Public Law 92-570.[77]

Although FY 1973 NOA was $6 billion below the president's January request, on balance Laird and other Pentagon leaders were pleased by the increase in NOA over the previous year and the defeat of two Democratic-sponsored budget amendments that would have made it more difficult for DoD to manage the war effort and plan the future defense program. The House had rejected an amendment requiring the withdrawal of all U.S. forces from Vietnam in four months. The Senate had turned aside McGovern's effort to hold DoD appropriations at the prior year's level. The budget that Congress enacted on the eve of the presidential election in effect repudiated the defense position of the Democratic candidate. In a political speech a day after he signed the bill, Nixon boasted that his budget would assure for the United States "a national defense second to none in the world." In contrast, the large cuts proposed by his opponent "would drastically slash away not just the fat but the very muscle of our defense."[78]

Table 22. NOA Request Compared with Appropriations (July-October 1972) ($ thousands)

	President's Request	Appropriations
Military Personnel	23,658,559	23,140,900
Retired Pay	4,358,684	4,358,684
O&M	21,634,944	21,110,624
Procurement	21,169,830	17,799,870
RDT&E	8,768,767	7,959,498
Military Construction	1,700,447	1,355,841
Family Housing	970,784	871,078
Civil Defense	88,835	83,535
Spec Foreign Currency Prog	3,400	3,400
Total	82,354,250	76,683,430

Source: OASD(C), "Appropriation Acts by Appropriation Title with Comparison to President's Budget Request, FY 1973," FAD 749/73, 9 October 1973, box 826D, Subject Files, OSD Historical Office.

Table 22 compares the amount Congress appropriated with the president's total request that includes the original proposed NOA of January 1972 of more than $81 billion plus two amendments and one additional request. The budget amendment submitted in March requested $1.87 billion in additional funds for military personnel, O&M, R&D, and civil defense. The June amendment sought $2.25 billion in added money for personnel, O&M, procurement, R&D, military construction, family housing, and civil defense. In September 1972 Nixon asked for an additional $9.85 billion for military construction. The amount for military personnel included money for the National Guard and reserve components.[79]

Table 23 shows the appropriation and active-duty military strength by service. Funds for the National Guard and reserve components totaled $1.62 million.

Table 23. Military Strength and Personnel Appropriations, FY 1973

Active	Strength	Appropriations ($ thousands)
Army	828, 900	7,528,000
Navy	601,672	5,306,749
Marine Corps	197,965	1,536,436
Air Force	700,516	7,150,575
Total	2,329,053	21,521,760

Source: P.L. 92-436, 86 Stat. 734 (1971); and P.L. 92-570, 86 Stat. 1184 (1972).

Passage of the appropriations bill in October, however, left unsettled the FY 1973 spending level, which Laird in that month estimated at $76.5 billion. Although Congress did not pass legislation imposing the $250 billion overall government spending ceiling that Nixon desired, he directed OMB to hold FY 1973 expenditures within that level. The effect of the president's decision on DoD outlays would depend to a large extent on the future cost and duration of the war, obviously unknowable in the fall of 1972. Part of that cost included the extra funds for special programs to accelerate and expand assistance to South Vietnam's armed forces before a cease-fire. If a cease-fire occurred by the end of January 1973 and Vietnam expenses dropped, it would be feasible to cut DoD spending. In the absence of a cease-fire the president would have to submit a supplemental budget request "of at least $2 billion," Odeen calculated, or, if that failed to pass, to cut back defense spending unrelated to the war. Continuation of the Vietnam War past June 1973 would require an increase in spending for FY 1974 as well. The battle lines for that fiscal year were already in place. Laird wanted $84 billion in outlays for FY 1974; OMB, nothing above $79 billion. Haig thought that even with Laird's assumption of low deployments and reduced sorties in Vietnam, the OMB figure would "degrade force levels and readiness." The long-term financial health of the force was still in play.[80]

THROUGHOUT THE LONG PROCESS of budget formulation and legislation Laird acted with independence and zeal in seeking to minimize DoD budget cuts. He stubbornly resisted OMB, deploying numerous strong arguments for higher DoD spending. He won approval for funds to cover the added expenses of stopping the Easter Offensive. His congressional experience, with the unwelcome consequences of a spending ceiling for the Defense budget, caused him to bring his disagreement with the president and OMB to the media, risking a public rebuke from the White House. Laird involved himself in the presidential campaign debates over defense spending to a greater extent than most past defense secretaries, not only making political points for Nixon but helping gain public and congressional support for his budget. Comptroller Moot, regarded by Laird as master of the Defense budget, believed the reason DoD did well in the congressional conference "was because Mr. Laird went up on the Hill and gently persuaded everybody."[81] At the same time, Laird's foray into framing a national security strategy of realistic deterrence to build the DoD budget failed to impress the White House and evoked opposition from the civilian and military leadership of the armed services.

Although expenditures started to rise during Laird's tenure, the purchasing power of those dollars fell, contributing strongly to the pressure on DoD to downsize. During Laird's tenure DoD closed military bases and installations and made significant personnel cuts to reshape itself into a smaller, but more expensive all-volunteer force for a more austere post-Vietnam environment. Between 1969 and 1973 the strength of the armed forces dropped from 3,460,000 to 2,253,000. Over that same period, the active-duty Army was nearly cut in half, from 1,512,000 to 801,000. The DoD civilian workforce declined from 1,390,000 in FY 1969 to 1,100,000 in FY 1973.[82] With the end of conscription in sight, the number of DoD personnel diminished, helping provide funds for the transition to the AVF. Along with Vietnamization, the end of the draft and the advent of the AVF fulfilled the foremost of Laird's goals as secretary of defense.

CHAPTER 17

Military Assistance

WELL BEFORE BECOMING SECRETARY of defense, Melvin Laird as a Wisconsin congressman had questioned the expense and efficacy of military assistance and even voted at times to cut the program. Referring to the Marshall Plan's success in helping rebuild Europe after World War II, he complained that by 1953 Western European countries were better off economically than before the war, yet they still sought U.S. aid. It was his conviction in the 1950s that America's allies, especially in Europe, should and could take on a greater share of the common security burden.[1]

Laird adopted a different approach upon becoming Nixon's secretary of defense. He understood that the president deemed the Military Assistance Program essential to enabling allies to assume a greater role in their own defense. Laird shared Nixon's view that without strong partnerships the nation risked exhausting its resources in a fruitless effort to dominate friends and neutralize enemies. In July 1969 the president set forth the Nixon Doctrine pledging military assistance for America's allies in the expectation that they would supply additional manpower for their defense, particularly in Asia, to reduce the high cost of Americans in uniform overseas. As secretary, Laird considered MAP essential to the president's approach, allowing the United States to honor its commitments to allies, yet reduce the need to commit U.S ground combat forces for the defense of the region. Always mindful of the DoD budget, Laird argued that "a MAP dollar is of far greater value than a dollar spent directly on U.S. forces." In support of the Nixon Doctrine, Laird expended much effort on policy issues and in seeking adequate funding to make the new doctrine viable.[2]

Military assistance was a multi-agency endeavor. Planning, programming, funding, and administering the program involved the Department of State, including the Agency for International Development (AID), and the Defense Department as well as the Bureau of the Budget (later OMB). State coordinated the overall program, ensuring that it meshed with U.S. foreign policy. Within the Pentagon, the assistant secretary of defense for international security affairs and the Joint Chiefs of Staff had key roles. ISA was responsible for developing and coordinating policy and procedures and for directing and administering both grant aid and foreign military sales. The JCS were responsible for recommending military and force objectives and equipment on a country and regional basis. Military assistance advisory groups, or MAAGs, stationed in nations receiving military assistance represented the Department of Defense. The heads of these groups made recommendations and developed military assistance plans in cooperation with the U.S. ambassador and monitored how well the program was carried out. MAAGs also administered foreign military sales transactions.[3]

The MAP assigned recipient nations to different categories. In so-called forward defense countries where the United States had commitments, MAP and the Foreign Military Sales (FMS) program were intended to reduce the requirement for American forces under existing security treaties. Nations in this group, deemed to lack the resources to provide fully for their own defense without an intolerably heavy economic burden, including Korea, Taiwan, Greece, and Turkey, were part of the MAP budget. Thailand, Laos, Iran, and Vietnam, also placed in the forward defense category, came under the DoD budget. Forward defense nations enjoyed the highest priority because improvements in their forces could reduce expenditures for U.S. forces.[4]

Congressional Critics

Each fiscal year the Defense Department had to request congressional authorization and appropriation for military assistance, but over the years the program had lost support on Capitol Hill. Many legislators criticized MAP for bolstering authoritarian, oppressive, and racist regimes as long as they were ostensibly anti-communist. They condemned arms sales as a government program to boost the profits of American companies, sell unneeded equipment to poor nations, and foster arms competition overseas. Others in Congress believed America's more prosperous allies, whose economies had recovered from the devastation of World War II, should do more on their own behalf. Even though MAP constituted a relatively small part of defense expenditures, funding dramatically declined over the years. MAP outlays (grant aid and sales) as a share of defense expenditures (also including atomic energy, selective service, and emergency preparedness) fell from a high of nearly 8 percent in FY 1953 to an estimate of less than 1 percent in FY 1969.[5]

The program was in serious trouble, lacking public support and facing strong congressional opposition, yet it was central to U.S. policy toward Latin America and part of the foundation of U.S. leadership among the industrialized nations. In June 1969 Laird testified on the FY 1970 MAP before the House Committee on Foreign Affairs, presenting it as part of "a controlled and restrained U.S. policy on arms transfers to our friends and allies." In response to critics, he noted that the Foreign Military Sales Act of 1968 had authorized changes in DoD policy on foreign military sales. The department now would "urge on no friend or ally the purchase of U.S. equipment when it is not needed, when there are better alternatives or when there are higher priority social and economic claims against limited funds." Laird believed that military assistance played an important deterrent role as an essential component of America's cold war arsenal. U.S. national security, he asserted, "is clearly weakened to the extent that the military capabilities of allied and friendly armed forces suffer from lack of adequate equipment and training."[6]

Laird meets in his office with Representative Otto Passman (D–LA). An outspoken critic of foreign aid and military assistance, Passman led the House opposition to the Military Assistance Program, undated. (OSD Historical Office)

In July, when Laird testified before the Senate Committee on Foreign Relations, which had legislative jurisdiction over foreign assistance programs, Senator William Fulbright challenged the very premises of the program. Alluding to the Truman Doctrine of 1947, the basis of the MAP, the Arkansas senator noted that more than twenty years had elapsed since its promulgation. He contended that the basic doctrine needed to be updated, especially in light of political fissures recently exposed in the Communist bloc of nations and the growing economic strength of such allies as Germany and South Korea. Fulbright's comments presaged the difficulties that the administration would confront in actually getting the MAP through his committee in the coming years, making it all the more important that the administration improve the foreign assistance program.[7]

Seeking to make the Foreign Assistance Program more effective, in March 1969 Nixon appointed an independent task force under California banker Rudolph A. Peterson to review the entire array of U.S. foreign assistance policies.[8] The Peterson task force submitted its report early in March 1970, recommending the separation of the program into distinct components for military assistance and economic development in order to pursue separate objectives. Nixon found this reorganization especially appealing.[9]

The Peterson report served as the blueprint for the president's plan. In his September 1970 reform proposal to Congress, Nixon wanted to separate the overall foreign assistance program into three parts: security assistance, humanitarian assistance, and development assistance. Calling it a complete overhaul to accompany a new foreign policy, Nixon proposed the establishment of not only three discrete organizations for the components of foreign assistance, but an International Security Assistance Program to provide support, when needed, to other nations under the Nixon Doctrine.[10]

After consultation with ASD(ISA) and the JCS, Laird worked to integrate DoD's international security programs more closely within the overall national security effort and minimize duplication of effort. Starting with the FY 1973 security assistance program, planning for military assistance and credit sales would occur within the DoD planning, programming, and budgeting system in order to correlate them with U.S. force planning and the Nixon Doctrine.

The secretary also established two new organizations to improve the department's ability to execute its planning and management of security assistance. The Defense Security Assistance Council, chaired by the ASD(ISA), would advise the secretary, coordinate security assistance programs within DoD, and be responsible for overall planning. The JCS would continue to provide military advice pertaining to military assistance. The second new organization, the Defense Security Assistance Agency, would function as the central organization for directing and supervising all operational aspects of security assistance programs within DoD. The first director, Lt. Gen. George M. Seignious, would also serve as deputy ASD(ISA) to help coordinate policy, planning, and operations. This new organization represented a departure from previous arrangements whereby regional deputy assistants in ISA had been responsible for security assistance policy. These new arrangements, Laird told the president, would allow the secretary and deputy secretary to become more directly involved in all aspects of security assistance. Nixon endorsed Laird's initiative.[11]

Laird had less success in gaining DoD control of military assistance and foreign military sales. The Peterson task force had recommended setting up a single security assistance program that included MAP, military credit sales, and the disposal of excess military supplies. Under this arrangement the State Department would set policy and coordinate operations; DoD would serve as administrator. Accordingly, Laird proposed that MAP and military sales be transferred to DoD. This change had a political benefit; it would spare the secretary of defense from having to testify before the Senate Foreign Relations Committee, eliminating a difficult hurdle. Antiwar senators routinely used the committee as a forum for attacking the administration's policies. Fulbright's committee had no authority to review the Defense budget. Laird's proposal would also shift the authority for MAP from the secretary of state to the secretary of defense.[12]

Laird thought he could win the jurisdictional battle in Congress, but both William Timmons, Nixon's assistant for congressional relations, and Henry Kissinger believed that the move would touch off a furious fight and possibly jeopardize the entire foreign assistance plan. Putting MAP and military sales in DoD would also make it more difficult to coordinate all aspects of security assistance in a single program.[13] Secretary of State William Rogers told Nixon that he emphatically opposed Laird's proposal, believing it would create difficulties in coordinating and managing the overall security assistance program.[14] In March 1971 Nixon rejected Laird's proposal to give DoD primacy in security assistance, convinced it would provoke a fight in Congress that was simply not worth waging. Nixon reaffirmed the existing allocation of Defense and State responsibilities.[15]

Battle over the FY 1971 MAP

The president's enunciation of what became the Nixon Doctrine came at a point when pressure to reduce the federal deficit threatened to shrink the military assistance program and imperil the new doctrine. Assistant Secretary of Defense (ISA) Warren Nutter informed Laird that the Defense and State Departments had agreed on a FY 1971 appropriation request of $450 million for military assistance and $272.5 million in military sales credits. However, BoB would go no higher than $350 million for MAP and $275 million for military sales. The differences involved four country programs—Taiwan, Greece, Turkey, and Spain—for which State and Defense wanted more than BoB would allow. In December Laird urged the president to approve the full appropriation request of $450 million. Alluding to the Nixon Doctrine, the secretary asserted that BoB's cuts would "raise serious doubts among our more exposed allies as to the aims and intentions of this Administration's foreign policy." The requested funds, Laird assured Nixon, were necessary "to meet high priority needs which cannot be satisfied by presently available or prospective long supply and excess stocks."[16] Budget Director Robert Mayo believed that Congress would probably provide no more than the $350 million for MAP it had authorized for FY 1970. He foresaw poor prospects for passage of a larger sum, citing Senator George Aiken's criticism of foreign aid as "a diplomatic pork barrel and a subsidy to American industry." Mayo acknowledged that $350 million for MAP would necessitate belt-tightening, but unlike Laird he expected credit sales and increases in excess stocks available for MAP to offset the reductions in part.[17]

Mayo pared the FY 1971 military assistance appropriation request to $350 million, an amount Laird considered too low to allow the president the options and flexibility to implement the doctrine and incorporate it in the FY 1972 MAP. Laird asserted that a marked increase in MAP was necessary "if we are to proceed with major U.S. defense savings by selected reductions in our overseas forces. If our strategy is to remain credible, U.S. force reductions must be counterbalanced by effective military assistance programs" to allow allied forces to assume an increased role. He noted the State Department's concurrence with his views. Laird's pleas went unheeded. The White House requested $350 million from Congress for MAP, and Congress appropriated this amount in December 1970.[18]

Months earlier additional, unanticipated requests in the summer of 1970 for military assistance bearing high price tags nearly derailed the FY 1971 MAP. A major new requirement for military assistance stemmed from the U.S. incursion in May to dislodge North Vietnam's military forces from their sanctuaries inside Cambodia. Following that, Nixon had pledged military equipment to Lon Nol's fledgling Cambodian government to help it maintain its independence, build up its armed forces, and fight the thousands of North Vietnamese Army soldiers still inside its borders. Assistance to Cambodia alone would cost at least an estimated $50 million, an amount not included in the president's January budget request for $350 million. In the absence of congressionally approved military assistance for Cambodia, funds would have to be diverted from other areas of the FY 1971 MAP. In addition, the administration had encouraged South Korea to undertake a force modernization program that would cost an additional $150 million not in the FY 1971 MAP request. Moreover, Congress threatened to curtail the dollar amount of excess U.S. military equipment transfers that supplemented the MAP. Restricting those transfers would likely hurt Taiwan, Korea, Turkey, and Greece. One of Kissinger's assistants suggested in July a supplemental MAP authorization of $200 million, but the proposal would face an uncertain fate in Congress, where critics denounced military assistance as contributing to regional arms races, propping up dictators, and imposing an economic burden on poorer nations. Senate majority leader Mike Mansfield for one had responded to the Cambodian incursion by threatening to vote against all foreign aid in the future.[19]

Laird meets with South Korean Ambassador Dong Jo Kim on 22 April 1971 to sign documents authorizing the production of the M16 rifle by the Republic of Korea. This agreement typified how the Nixon Doctrine persuaded allies to bolster their defense efforts. (OSD Historical Office)

At first the administration deferred submitting a supplemental MAP request. By September, however, analysts in the Pentagon calculated that the need for a supplemental had grown more urgent, prompting Laird to press the White House for action. Describing the grant military assistance, foreign military sales, and supporting assistance programs for FY 1971 as being in a *"real crisis,"* Laird pushed for a FY 1971 supplemental of at least an additional $260 million. Of that amount, South Korea would receive $150 million; Cambodia, $60 million; Turkey, $25 million; Taiwan, $15 million; and Greece, $10 million. On top of that, South Vietnam needed $100 million in assistance to allow the continued withdrawal of American forces, and Cambodia required $130 million to stabilize the armed forces and keep that nation from falling. As for foreign credit military sales, the secretary highlighted the serious situation with regard to Israel. With credit unavailable, the United States would have to request payment in cash from Israel for its equipment orders. The payment for FY 1971 sales totaled nearly $300 million, a sum that Israel would find difficult to pay. Thus the secretary wanted an amendment to the DoD procurement request of almost $400 million to fund credit military sales to Israel. Laird bluntly told Kissinger that "the resources currently available and being requested from Congress are inadequate to support ongoing implementation of the Nixon Doctrine and to assist in maintaining adequate balances of power throughout the world." He was convinced that an immediate MAP supplemental was imperative.[20]

Acting OMB Director Caspar Weinberger urged a delay in sending a supplemental to Congress until after the November election. Conceding that a postponement might create a gap in meeting Cambodian requirements and even necessitate diverting funds from other country programs, Weinberger pointed out that getting authorization for a supplemental would require hearings before the Senate Foreign Relations Committee that could set off an acrimonious policy debate and delay passage. Laird's total request of nearly $1 billion would also come when the administration was urging Congress to exercise restraint on budget requests. Moreover, Congress, close to its recess, would have insufficient time to handle authorizations. Estimates of Cambodia's military requirements remained uncertain, making it hard to come up with a convincing justification. The State Department, Kissinger, and Timmons all sided with OMB. Kissinger believed that essential programs could be carried out without an immediate supplemental, so Nixon deferred Laird's request.[21]

Shortly after the 1970 election Nixon requested a supplemental appropriation of $1.04 billion from Congress. It included $195 million for economic assistance, $340 million in military assistance, and a $500 million credit for Israel. In discussing the request with Senators Mike Mansfield, Hugh Scott, and Richard Russell at the White House, Nixon and Laird stressed that the supplemental was needed to implement the Nixon Doctrine in Asia and allow continuation of U.S. withdrawals from Korea and Vietnam. Russell indicated his willingness to support a request that enabled other nations to assume their own defense. Mansfield was also supportive as long as the withdrawals from Vietnam continued.[22]

At the end of November 1970 Laird testified on the need for a supplemental before the House Armed Forces Subcommittee of the Committee on Appropriations, finding a generally favorable reception. His appearance before the Senate Foreign Relations Committee in mid-December, in contrast, did not go smoothly. Before Laird could present his prepared statement, a skeptical Fulbright questioned the urgency of a supplemental. "You are not out of money," he chided Laird, contending DoD had access to enough funds to carry it through for another two months. Laird disagreed.[23]

The questioning concentrated on the provision of military assistance to Cambodia, which many senators opposed, reflecting their objections to the expansion of the war. Senator Albert Gore pressed Laird to explain how increasing military aid to Cambodia would contribute to a negotiated Vietnam settlement. Instead of responding directly, Laird began to discuss in detail military assistance under the Vietnamization program. The exasperated senator eventually gave up and withdrew his question, accusing Laird of not answering it.[24]

Despite sharp questioning from antiwar senators, in the end Congress approved a rather large FY 1971 MAP supplemental, appropriating $85 million for supplementary military assistance and $70 million for special economic assistance for Cambodia, and an added $100 million for military and economic assistance programs to replace funds that the president had already transferred to Cambodia. South Korea received a further $150 million; Jordan, an additional $30 million; Indonesia, $13 million more; Lebanon, an additional $5 million; and South Vietnam, an extra $65 million in supporting assistance. Another $17 million went for general military assistance to cover an expected shortfall in recovering unspent funds from previous years. Before the bill passed, however, legislators, who feared that aid to Cambodia would blossom into an open-ended defense commitment like the one in South Vietnam, inserted restrictive language. The funds in the supplemental authorization for Cambodia, the conference report noted, "shall not be construed as a commitment by the United States to Cambodia for its defense."[25]

Congress Rebels

In mid-December 1970, C. Fred Bergsten and Wayne Smith of the National Security Council staff met with James Schlesinger, OMB's assistant director, to review the foreign military assistance section of the president's FY 1972 foreign aid bill. They agreed that the administration should request $688 million in new obligational authority for MAP, significantly below the $786 million that Defense and State sought. They also wanted to lower military credit sales to $602 million. Secretary Rogers and Deputy Defense Secretary David Packard separately complained about the NSC and OMB cuts to President Nixon. Willing to accept some reductions, Rogers considered a minimum of $744.8 million in grant aid to be essential. In contrast to Rogers' willingness to prune the program, Packard sought an increase of $80 million over the OMB level for additional funds for Taiwan, Greece, Turkey, and Jordan. Packard's plea elicited little sympathy, because OMB's $688 million for FY 1972 represented a significant increase over the $436 million (without the MAP supplemental) for FY 1971. The disagreement over the numbers highlighted a basic problem with MAP spending. Wayne Smith saw no logical basis for the military assistance figures submitted, save for the MAP money for Vietnam and Cambodia. "We are all groping in the dark," he confessed to Kissinger, "relying on precedent and intuition, and guessing at levels and composition." He admitted he could offer no solid analysis to explain whether the MAP and FMS amounts for various nations should be increased or decreased. The Nixon Doctrine called for more military assistance, but how much money was needed to carry it out remained in question. Smith decried the lack of tools to provide an analytical answer.[26]

Laird appeared before the Senate Foreign Relations Committee on 14 June 1971 to testify for the FY 1972 foreign assistance program. By that point the administration requested $705 million for military assistance and $510 million for foreign military credit sales, a total of $1.22 billion in NOA. Nixon proposed reorganizing the security assistance program in an effort "to strengthen local defense capabilities." He aimed to provide a blend of "military and supporting economic assistance" that would "permit friendly foreign countries to assume additional defense burdens themselves without imposing undue political or economic costs."[27]

The Senate never acted on Nixon's reform proposal. Furthermore, it rejected outright his FY 1972 foreign aid authorization request by a 41 to 27 vote at the end of October. Senators critical of military assistance—notably Fulbright, Frank Church, and Stuart Symington—argued that the program failed to enhance U.S. security. In their view, MAP merely bought the support of corrupt or authoritarian allies or helped sustain anticommunist wars in Southeast Asia. Cambodia remained a flash-point for critics. Fulbright insisted that the United States had no vital interest there. Other senators feared that the Military Assistance Program for Cambodia could lead to a full-blown U.S. commitment to a shaky nation. These senators asserted Cambodia's military forces were compromised by incompetent leaders, venality, and the government's thin base of political support. Representative Wayne L. Hays (D–OH) called the effort to strengthen the Cambodian government a "catastrophic failure." Political disarray in Cambodia and Laos and persisting questions about the effectiveness of South Vietnam's forces had eroded belief in the long-term benefits of military assistance. In addition, liberals opposed military aid to authoritarian regimes in Greece and Turkey, deeming MAP an outdated Cold War program. The bill's defeat came at the hands of an unusual alliance between liberal, antiwar senators disappointed with the Cold War aspects of military assistance, and the administration's aid to Cambodia, and conservative senators philosophically opposed to foreign aid "giveaways."[28]

The defeat proved temporary. After cutting spending below the administration's request, the Senate enacted two separate bills. On 11 November it passed a military assistance bill authorizing $1.5 billion in military aid. Fulbright sought to reduce military aid to $1 billion, but the Senate did not go along. It approved the Stennis amendment to increase military aid from $1.2 billion to $1.5 billion. Senator Stennis wanted the extra money to compensate for the severe cuts imposed by the Foreign Relations Committee, because he thought those cuts could jeopardize the withdrawal of U.S. forces from South Vietnam and reduce aid to Israel, Turkey, and Korea. Ironically, the Foreign Relations Committee's decision to separate the foreign aid bill into two pieces of legislation helped dissolve the alliance that had defeated the initial aid measure and allowed passage of the smaller foreign assistance package.[29]

Hoping to avoid another bruising battle over MAP in the Senate, Laird resurrected his proposal to put all foreign security assistance under DoD. In November 1971 he recommended to George Shultz that the FY 1973 request "be restructured as Defense Authorization and Appropriation Bills" so that the administration could present the various aspects of military assistance in the context of the overall national security program and bypass the Senate Foreign Relations Committee.[30] Under the secretary's plan, DoD's budget would include the appropriation for MAP, FMS (credit), and defense supporting assistance funds related to security programs. All military assistance (hardware and training) would also be in DoD's budget, including programs for combat zones in Southeast Asia (both MAP and service-funded military assistance); forward defense nations (Korea, Taiwan, Greece, Turkey, and Israel); internal security programs in Asia, Africa, and Latin America; and base rights (Ethiopia, Morocco, Spain, and Portugal). A single appropriation would contain all material assistance (MAP, Military Assistance Service Funded, and FMS), equipment transfers, and military training assistance. Under his proposal, the State/AID appropriation would be restricted to public safety, economic support, and a contingency fund. The State Department would retain responsibility for coordinating security assistance with foreign policy.[31]

OMB analysts urged caution. First, they noted that Laird's recommendation would add $2 billion to the FY 1973 DoD budget, most likely raising the ire of senators intent on cutting defense spending. Second, OMB feared that shifting security assistance to the Defense budget could jeopardize the entire foreign aid program. Even if the jurisdictional difficulties could be overcome, OMB saw little hope of avoiding another battle over military aid in the Senate, where many members held irreconcilable differences over the program. Underlying the dispute, OMB discerned "an executive-legislative confrontation over war—and foreign policy—powers which probably cannot be avoided by budgetary maneuvers." Secretary Rogers, OMB Director George Shultz, and AID Administrator John A. Hannah urged disapproval, believing the attempt would fail.[32]

Kissinger suggested a different approach. He termed Laird's proposal an attractive alternative if the political difficulties could be overcome. Clark MacGregor, counsel to the president for congressional relations, favored the shift in principle, as did the majority of the White House Congressional Relations staff. Because of the persistence of other divisive issues on the Hill, a change in jurisdiction would require extensive preparation and would face a possibly hostile reception. Nixon agreed with Kissinger's recommendation that MacGregor consult with Senator Stennis and other leaders before he made a decision on Laird's proposal. But Stennis was unwilling to take on the additional task, advising the White House that the shift of jurisdiction would require a separate amendment.[33]

Without the support of Stennis, whose Senate Armed Services Committee would handle MAP authorization, Laird's proposal was not accepted, nor was the amount he requested for FY 1973. OMB cut the overall DoD request (NOA) for the Military Assistance Program (grants and credit sales) to $1.43 billion, at the same time slashing DoD's requested budget authority (grants and sales) from $1.34 billion to $1.24 billion. The amounts, Shultz cautioned the president, were still considerably higher than what Congress was likely to approve. The OMB director noted the rise in funds for the grant program over FY 1972. Most grant money would go to Cambodia ($225 million), Korea ($220 million), Turkey ($100 million), Thailand ($60 million), Jordan ($45 million), and Indonesia ($25 million). Credit sales would provide $300 million for Israel, $75 million for Latin America, $60 million for Greece, and $55 million for Taiwan. Kissinger termed the OMB program levels as "tight but adequate to support our foreign policy objectives" and recommended that Nixon approve them.[34]

As on other budget issues, Laird protested reductions in the DoD FY 1973 request, reminding the president that he had cut the DoD MAP request from $847.8 million (NOA) to $710 million. He also pointed out that these cuts would come on top of congressional cutbacks in the FY 1972 MAP, a total reduction of $402.8 million in NOA. The magnitude of these cuts, Laird warned, "undermines the concept of the Nixon Doctrine," leading to shortfalls in the Korean modernization program and the Cambodian program, and a weakened Vietnamization program. Laird urged the president to approve a MAP request of $907.8 million in NOA for FY 1973, including $60 million to cover the transfer of Thailand to the MAP budget. Laird's plea found a receptive ear. Nixon did increase the amount he requested from Congress. In March 1972 Nixon asked Congress for $780 million for grant military assistance and $527 million for military credit sales. Congress cut the administration's request significantly, appropriating in March 1973 $553.1 million for MAP and $400 million for foreign military sales.[35]

Table 24 summarizes executive branch requests for MAP and FMS funds and congressional action for fiscal years 1969–1973. Reflecting the importance of MAP and FMS to the Nixon Doctrine, the administration requested more funds each successive fiscal year. However, the amount that Congress appropriated reached its peak in FY 1971.

Table 24. Executive Branch MAP and FMS Requests, FYs 1969–1973 ($ thousands)

	President's Request	Appropriations
MAP		
FY 1969	420,000	375,000
FY 1970	425,000	350,000
FY 1971	690,000*	690,000
FY 1972	705,000	500,000
FY 1973	780,000	553,100
FMS		
FY 1969	120,000	296,000
FY1970	275,000	70,000**
FY 1971	772,500	700,000
FY 1972	510,000	400,000
FY 1973	527,000	400,000

Source: OASD(ISA), *Military Assistance and Foreign Military Sales Facts* (Washington, DC: Government Printing Office, May 1973), 5, 17.

*Includes FY 1971 supplemental request.

**Per continuing appropriation under Joint Resolution 33. Under P.L. 672, Congress authorized $250 million for FY 1970.

Laird, skeptical of the value of military assistance and critical of its cost as a congressman, had as secretary of defense become a staunch proponent of the program because it provided essential support for U.S allies. Laird's hope was that military assistance would help bolster America's allies and save money that DoD could use for rebuilding and reshaping the armed forces for the post-Vietnam period. Every year during his tenure, he pushed the administration to increase its budget request for military assistance and sales funds. With the exception of the FY 1971 supplemental, OMB and the White House reduced the amount that Laird wanted. Laird sought more money for MAP not just out of a desire to carry out the Nixon Doctrine. He also understood how the doctrine's emphasis on military assistance provided additional justification for continued Vietnam withdrawals and aided DoD efforts to reduce its military presence elsewhere in Asia.

The Case of Israel

U.S. military assistance faced especially stern challenges in the volatile and contentious Middle East where conflicting national security interests of the United States and Soviet Union might lead to a superpower conflict. Deep-rooted enmity between Israel and its Arab neighbors—Egypt, Jordan, and Syria—had erupted into a short war in 1967 that ended with a decisive Israeli victory. The conflict indirectly involved the two superpowers and afterward pulled the United States deeper into the region's affairs. Following the conflict, the United States sought to preserve the military balance in the region and avoid war, especially with American armed forces so heavily committed in Vietnam and Europe. U.S. arms supply policy in the Middle East represented a critical and complex element in seeking to maintain that balance, lessen violence in the region, and ensure Israel's continued existence as a nation. France, which had supplied weapons and equipment to Israel, took a pro-Arab stance after the 1967 war. The United States became Israel's main arms supplier and ally. Yet aid to Israel became the most costly, difficult, and politically charged U.S. aid program. Believing that DoD could not afford to accede to all of Israel's requests for arms, Laird sought to balance the provision of advanced weapons to help Israel in the short term with diplomatic efforts to reach a lasting Mideast political settlement.[36]

The Six-Day War of 1967 failed to settle major regional issues. Israel's complete military victory brought not political stability to the region but the prospect of superpower confrontation. Israel's defeated foes—Egypt, Syria, Jordan—rearmed with assistance from the Soviet Union and still aimed to crush Israel and gain a homeland for the Palestinians. The vanquished nations refused to recognize, negotiate, or make peace with Israel. Al Fatah, the Arab political and military organization dedicated to the liberation of Palestine, rejected any notion of compromise that would end the struggle against the Jewish state. It also had links to the commando group that attacked an Israeli airliner in January 1969 at the Athens airport. Equally adamant, Israelis would not withdraw to prewar boundaries, deeming the conquered land a necessary security buffer. After the 1967 war, the Egyptians moved closer to the Soviet Union, which during the 1960s had emerged as a major power in the Middle East. The Soviets began to build up naval forces in the eastern Mediterranean, claiming a national security need. The growing Soviet naval presence in the Mediterranean and the rapprochement with Egypt complicated the ongoing Arab-Israeli struggle, increasing regional volatility.[37]

In seeking to prevent another Arab-Israeli war and help preserve the military balance in the region, the United States carefully weighed competing interests. The nation wanted to ensure that Israel received sufficient military assistance to deter or defeat another attack but not so much that it alienated moderate Arab governments and possibly imperiled access to Mideast oil supplies. By keeping strategic missiles and nuclear weapons out of the region, the United States sought to avert a situation that might require American military intervention or lead to hostilities with the Soviet Union.[38] Israel's request in 1969 for additional advanced, attack F–4 jet fighters threatened to upset the regional military balance, posing a dilemma for Nixon in developing his Middle East policy.[39]

In July 1969 a high-ranking delegation headed by Israeli Ambassador Yitzhak Rabin met with JCS Chairman General Earle Wheeler to discuss the request to purchase an additional 100 A–4s and 25 F–4s. The Israelis wanted the planes to replace aging French jets, allowing modernization of the Israeli Air Force to keep pace with anticipated improvements in Arab air forces. Israel wanted to maintain the air superiority that had allowed it to prevail against much larger Arab forces during the 1967 war. Without air superiority Israel would be vulnerable. Wheeler advised Laird that the Israeli request had considerable merit from a military perspective, but warned that granting it could produce an arms race, spurring the Soviet Union in turn to provide more arms to Arab governments. In September 1969 Israeli Prime Minister Golda Meir pressed the issue of additional aircraft during her meeting with Nixon.[40]

When Rabin raised the matter again in October, Deputy Secretary Packard was noncommittal, reminding the ambassador that the United States had to balance support for Israel with the need to maintain good relations with other friends and allies in the region. Nutter informed Laird that U.S. intelligence agencies saw no urgency in acceding to the Israeli request. Despite the increased efforts of Soviet advisers, recent intelligence assessments held that Arab capabilities in command and control, logistics, and maintenance of aircraft had not significantly improved since 1967. Although Arab air forces outnumbered the Israeli Air Force by three to one overall, U.S. analysts believed Israel still possessed "absolute air superiority." Many Arab aircraft were not assigned to operational units; others were poorly maintained and not flyable. Arab pilots, not as well trained, lacked the experience and self-confidence of the Israelis. Moreover, the Israelis had more qualified pilots per aircraft and thus could mount more sorties. Nutter urged a broad look at U.S. arms policy in the region. To set an example for other powers, he advocated temporarily suspending the transfer of U.S. surplus military equipment. Laird endorsed these conclusions.[41]

Rising tensions in the Middle East in January and early February 1970 led to sporadic fighting between Arab and Israeli forces and indications that the USSR was increasing its military support of Egypt. Describing his talks with Soviet Foreign Minister Andrei A. Gromyko, U.S. Ambassador to Moscow Jacob B. Beam reported that the USSR showed no inclination to limit arms shipments to the region. Moreover, Moscow blamed Israel for the outbreaks of violence. Despite the fighting and the growing involvement of the Soviet Union, at the end of February 1970 Packard sent Kissinger a study concluding that Israel had no immediate requirement for additional A–4s and F–4s.[42]

Sensing no imminent danger to the military balance in the Middle East, the president concluded in March 1970 that he could wait another 90 days before making a decision about providing additional aircraft to Israel. Aware that the Soviets felt pressure from their regional allies to step up military equipment deliveries, Nixon hoped his restraint would slow down the arms race and help preserve the military balance in the Middle East. He privately assured the Israeli government that the United States "would be in a position to move quickly to maintain Israel's margin of safety" if its air superiority was threatened.[43] Nonetheless Laird remained wary. He detected a dangerous ambiguity in the statement, advising Kissinger that the Israelis could interpret it as "an open-ended obligation on our part," even allowing for direct intervention by U.S. forces to preserve that margin. He believed the administration should make clear the limits of U.S. assistance: provide equipment only.[44]

The president wanted the Pentagon to develop a contingency plan for quickly providing additional as well as replacement aircraft to Israel should an unexpected crisis occur. Seeing risks in this kind of planning, Laird's military assistant, General Pursley, urged the secretary to take a go-slow approach. There would be ample warning of a crisis, he observed, and in any event DoD needed time to analyze the issue before drafting a plan. Pursley believed it would be difficult to provide aircraft on short notice. DoD would also have to arrange for the necessary training, support, and logistics. To Pursley, the ready availability of extra aircraft might even encourage Israel to undertake high-risk air attacks, escalating the fighting. Endorsing Pursley's approach, Laird asked Kissinger for additional time so DoD could work out details and make recommendations.[45]

In March 1970 an unexpected threat to stability and American power in the region emerged that required a greater degree of engagement than Laird had advocated. The Soviet Union had shipped its most advanced air-defense missile, the SA–3, to Egypt. The Israelis were using F–4s to carry out deep penetration raids in the Nile delta and near Cairo. President Gamal Abdel Nassar appealed for the SAMs, which the Soviets agreed to supply. Furnishing the missiles was serious enough, but bringing in 1,500 Soviet military personnel to operate and maintain them represented an unprecedented expansion of Soviet presence. The USSR had a manifest interest in protecting its personnel, who might come under fire. Acutely sensitive to the Soviet move, Kissinger feared it might be only an opening gambit. Moreover, it occurred around the time that the administration had responded negatively to Israel's request for aircraft, prompting him to warn Nixon of serious implications from the Soviet assessment of U.S. resolve in the region. Indeed the Soviets, perceiving a weak U.S. response, brought in additional missiles in April and increased the number of combat personnel to 10,000. Their pilots soon began flying defensive missions over Egypt, potentially freeing up Egyptian planes for attacks along the Suez Canal. Kissinger feared combat between Soviet and Israeli pilots would become "a virtual certainty."[46]

Confronted with such disturbing news, in mid-April Nixon ordered a review of the Arab-Israeli military balance. Reversing his earlier decision, he decided to provide more planes to Israel. The Senior Review Group met twice in May to hammer out Middle East arms policy. DoD and State took opposing positions on the question of military commitments to Israel and the provision of additional F–4s and A–4s. On 21 May, Assistant Secretary of State for Near Eastern and South Asian Affairs Joseph J. Sisco, recognizing the need to set a course that kept tensions from escalating yet showed no weakness to the Soviets, recommended supplying Israel with eight additional F–4s over a two-month period. In contrast, Packard asserted the primacy of a political settlement; additional aircraft sent to Israel would make that impossible. Citing the need for a new political initiative, Nutter suggested a de facto cease-fire and the withdrawal of Israeli forces a symbolic distance from the Suez Canal.[47] At the 28 May SRG meeting his proposal went nowhere, but the group did agree that the movement of Soviet forces to the canal represented a serious concern. Soviet naval forces in the eastern Mediterranean and its missiles in Egypt in effect encircled Israel, making it imperative not to cut back deployments of the U.S. Sixth Fleet.[48]

The potential growth of Soviet influence in Jordan presented another reason for concern. To Washington, it was vital that the Hashemite kingdom, although an adversary of Israel, remain pro-Western. The administration viewed military assistance as the means to help preempt Soviet influence. In early May, when the U.S. arms package for Jordan came up for review, Secretary Rogers advised Nixon to approve it. Jordan's King Hussein needed a reasonable U.S. offer to counteract pressure from advisers who urged him to accept Soviet weapons and munitions. American policy sought to give Hussein enough military assistance to keep him reliant on the United States, permitting him to deflect those pushing him to accept Soviet support. Arms for the Jordanian army, the foundation of King Hussein's support, would help preserve his position, while a military assistance package, developed by a team of U.S. military advisers that had already gone to Jordan, would help maintain the country's pro-West stance. It was critical, Kissinger believed, for the United States to prevent the Soviet Union from establishing a foothold in Jordan, a possible first step in reorienting that country from Washington toward Moscow. Soviet influence might even eventually expand to the level it had reached in Egypt. For its part, Israel was also apprehensive about a Soviet presence in Jordan. Nixon approved the offer to Jordan, linking his decision with his resolve to provide additional arms for Israel. He wanted the Pentagon to recommend the level of additional military assistance to give Israel.[49] In Nixon's thinking, security for Israel was a prerequisite for a regional political settlement.

While the president sought aid for Jordan to keep a moderate Arab nation aligned with Washington, Laird continued to take a cautious approach to providing additional arms to the region, especially more advanced aircraft for Israel. His priority was to establish a political basis for stability in the Middle East. In June he reminded Kissinger that Israel already possessed "substantial air attack superiority over the combined air forces" of Egypt, Syria, Iraq, and Jordan because of its more skilled pilots, the lack of bombing capability on Soviet aircraft, and the inability of Arab air forces to sustain sufficient sortie rates. Laird conceded that with massive involvement and at high cost, the Soviets could achieve air superiority over Israel, but "it would take weeks or months rather than days for them to do so," providing time for the United States to respond. Laird elaborated his thinking. To preserve a balanced Middle East policy, he told Nixon that the United States should not at this time sell additional aircraft, because it would undermine the chances for long-term solutions. He observed that the F–4s had become the symbol of Israeli power in Arab eyes; use of the aircraft as attack bombers linked them to the United States. Future Israeli requirements could be met, he argued, with air defense fighters, F–5s, F–8s, or F–104s. Expanding the commitment to Israel was unacceptable to Laird, because it implied that U.S. forces would be used to support that nation directly under any circumstances.[50]

Right up to the NSC meeting on 10 June to review the Middle East situation, the State and Defense Departments clung to opposing positions. State viewed a Soviet move into the Suez Canal zone, should it occur, as a provocation requiring a clear, strong counter-signal—a statement that the United States would consider direct military intervention. DoD opposed such a commitment, favoring instead an Israeli pullback from the Suez Canal as a first step in the process toward a political settlement; it also averred that the United States should not commit itself to defending Israel's holdings in occupied territories. Defense further contended that the United States, already over-extended militarily, had no interest in the Middle East substantial enough to warrant the risk of nuclear war with the Soviet Union. With the two departments going into the 10 June session holding to established positions, the question of additional F–4s for Israel became a central issue at the June meeting.[51]

Participants assessed the Soviet military presence in the Middle East and the potential for the attrition of Israeli Air Force assets in an extended conflict with Soviet forces. That presence, plus the dispersal of Arab aircraft and the hardening of protective hangars, could negate Israel's strategy of preemptive strikes. More-over, stationing Soviet pilots in Egypt might embolden Arab nations to act rashly, possibly leading to a U.S.-Soviet clash. According to CIA Director Richard Helms' assessment, the region's military balance was seriously threatened. Under the current circumstances, Secretary Rogers saw no alternative to providing more jet fighters. Packard, who urged restraint, saw no military solution at hand and questioned whether the United States would even be in a position to intervene militarily should fighting erupt. Kissinger framed the central problem in formulating U.S. strategy: Ensuring Israel's survival required that it have some margin of military superiority, but too much of a tilt in favor of Israel would alienate Arab moderates and strengthen radicals. Following the session, Nixon decided to increase the monthly number of Phantom jets sent to Israel from four to five in September and October, on condition that deliveries not jeopardize any ongoing negotiations. Further, he directed DoD to comply with Israeli requests for logistic support for Hawk surface-to-air missiles, bombs, tanks, and radars, as well as accelerate the delivery of spare parts for F–4s and A–4s.[52] The president saw his response as a matter of urgency in a dangerously evolving situation. The arms buildup represented a form of deterrence in his judgment. It would be less likely for the Arabs to attack a strong Israel. Alluding to the serious risks in the region, Rogers asked Nixon: "How do we begin to educate the American people that the Middle East is a principal test between the US and USSR over the next few years?"[53]

In a televised interview with reporters from the major networks (ABC, CBS, and NBC) in July 1970, Nixon took the opportunity to highlight for the public the dangers in the Middle East. Comparing the region to the Balkans before World War I, he said that the two superpowers "could be drawn into a confrontation that neither of them wants." U.S. policy sought to maintain peace and the integrity of all nations in the region. War would come if the balance of power shifted so that Israel became weaker than its neighbors who desired "to drive Israel into the sea." It was in the U.S. national interest to sustain that balance. Maintaining Israel's strength was necessary not because it would enable Israel to fight a war but because it "will deter its neighbors from attacking it."[54]

The Crisis Deepens

The loss of two Israeli Phantom jets at the end of June 1970 led to the discovery that the Soviets had moved two SA–2 batteries and an SA–3 battery toward the Suez Canal and were employing new defensive tactics. The sites provided interlocking and overlapping protection of the canal. To counter the enhanced Soviet/Egyptian air defense capability, Prime Minister Golda Meir wanted quick delivery of additional aircraft and electronic equipment, for which the United States would have to extend credit because Israel lacked the cash to purchase them. After meeting with Ambassador Rabin on 8 July, Kissinger better appreciated the gravity of the changed military situation, noting the possibility that the Israelis might conduct air strikes against the SA–3 sites and thus draw Soviet aircraft into the fray. Nixon wanted DoD to act as quickly as possible.[55]

Defense continued to urge caution. Nutter, who prepared the department's response, advocated a moderate nuanced approach. The United States had to demonstrate on the one hand that it would not acquiesce in Soviet moves, but on the other it should avoid "high profile or escalatory" steps that would get the Soviets further involved. Israel's request for electronic countermeasures equipment, he noted, would give the Israelis the capability not just to defend against the SAM sites but also to conduct raids against Soviet-manned targets in Egypt. While the DoD staff studied the request, Nutter recommended that the U.S. Air Force sell Israel 30 ALQ–87 aircraft-mounted radar jammers for use only in the canal area.[56]

The Senior Review Group took up the Mideast situation and the new Israeli request on 9 July. Kissinger expressed concern that out of desperation Israel might initiate military action. His comment prompted Packard to suggest that the United States "hold back on the supply of some arms to Israel" to demonstrate to the Arabs that the United States was serious about a cease-fire. He thought it inconsistent in the short term to build up Israel's military while talking about a cease-fire. JCS Chairman Admiral Thomas Moorer added an element of ambiguity, observing that the specific equipment for Israel would depend on whether the United States expected Israel to suffer attrition during the pursuit of a cease-fire or wanted to stop the attrition so the Israelis could "hold their own." There was confusion also over the equipment that the president had already approved, because no list of specific items had been attached to the presidential decision.[57]

To ascertain Israel's weapons requirements Laird met with Rabin on 21 July. Since the end of June, Rabin reported, the Soviets had pushed the SA–2 and SA–3 missiles to within 20 to 35 miles of the Suez Canal. The ambassador said that Israel could not permit the Soviets and Egyptians to achieve air superiority over Suez and was ready to attack the missile sites employing U.S.-supplied equipment. Rabin complained to Laird that a cease-fire would allow the Soviets three months to build up their forces. Because of Soviet construction, 20 to 60 sites needed to be attacked. Israel wanted RF–4Cs (F–4s modified for photographic reconnaissance missions), drones, cluster bomb units (munitions with multiple warheads to attack armor and artillery), Shrike missiles to hit the SAM sites, and A–4s. Israel sought credit terms, because the country had numerous other bills coming due and a serious balance of payments problem. Laird introduced a note of caution, pointing to the serious pressure on the DoD budget. As usual, Laird would have to make defense program decisions to a large degree on the basis of fiscal constraints.[58]

Given the region's instability, the urgent need to review and reconcile numerous military assistance requests, and the escalation of military activity, Laird formally established in July 1970 a DoD Middle East task group to handle planning. The group would assess the department's military assistance policies and keep a current, accurate accounting of equipment deliveries. Laird reminded members of the larger objective: to maintain a regional balance of power. The department simply could not afford a Mideast arms race. A cautious Laird feared that providing sophisticated weapons to Israel could prove counterproductive, giving the Soviets a pretext for introducing new weapons to their allies throughout the world.[59]

At the time that Laird established the Middle East task group he also tried to put himself in a central policymaking position, telling Kissinger and Rogers that Nixon had asked him "to assume responsibility for the initial review of all Israeli arms requests." The rationale was to avoid confusion when a number of Israeli officials made separate, seemingly independent requests to their U.S. counterparts. DoD would maintain a list, compiled in consultation with the State Department, of items already approved in principle. Within the Pentagon, this program was dubbed Project Binge. Laird would personally review all recommendations and determine what items would be approved for sale in principle. Harold Saunders, the Middle East expert on the NSC staff, agreed on the necessity of improved coordination of arms request, but he objected to Laird's procedure because it lacked a provision for presidential review. Kissinger brusquely dismissed the defense secretary's approach. "Out of the question," he responded, "NSC must participate."[60]

Laird's assertion of authority was ignored. On 30 July, Assistant Secretary of State Sisco visited the Pentagon for briefings on providing advanced weapons to Israel. At these sessions, he presented what he termed instructions from the president. According to those in attendance, Sisco announced that Nixon had decided to provide all-out support so Israel could "completely suppress and destroy all SA–2 and SA–3 sites" on the west bank of the Suez Canal. There were to be no restraints on what was needed to suppress those sites.[61]

This decision to provide Israel with additional weapons was only one aspect of the president's policy. At the end of July Nixon announced that the Israeli cabinet had accepted a U.S. cease-fire proposal to start talks under the auspices of the U.N. peace envoy, Ambassador Gunnar V. Jarring. The Soviet Union and Egypt had already accepted this initiative. During the cease-fire, neither side was to enhance its military position, meaning no new missiles or installations or movement of forces. Israel accepted the proposal even though the Soviets had relocated some missile sites closer to the canal and increased the number of personnel stationed there. The Soviets had transformed their presence into a force capable of helping support an invasion. Israel agreed to the cease-fire, fully appreciating the political and military risks it faced. Nixon's persuasive 23 July letter to Meir helped overcome deep Israeli reservations. Skeptical about the cease-fire because the Soviets and Egyptians had shown no willingness to compromise, the Israelis believed that the Soviets had accepted the proposal only because Nixon had had taken a firm pro-Israel stance during his televised interview.[62]

Meeting with Kissinger on 5 August, Rabin expressed dissatisfaction with the cease-fire in light of recent developments along the canal. The U.S. peace initiative, he complained, had helped enable the Soviets to move surface-to-air missiles closer to the canal. At the end of June, Israel's air force had attacked these sites. Israel could not accept the eastern movement of Soviet SAMs to any closer than 40 to 60 kilometers from the canal. After Israel accepted the cease-fire proposal on 31 July, the Soviets set up a missile ambush less than 30 kilometers from the Suez. Rabin averred Israel would not accept a temporary cease-fire unless the missiles were removed. His country was prepared to carry out additional strikes if necessary to take out the forward Soviet sites. To enable such a mission, Israel persistently sought U.S. electronic jamming equipment, radars, CBUs (cluster bomb units), and Shrike missiles.[63]

Recognizing that an unfavorable shift in the military balance might tempt Israel to launch a preemptive strike, Nixon wanted to know what specific strategies the United States could support that would bolster Israel, and what their political ramifications might be if Israeli decided to move against the Soviet and Egyptian missile complexes west of the canal. Kissinger wanted DoD and State to analyze the range of strategic options and the specific equipment needed to execute the various options.[64]

At the Special Review Group meeting on 12 August, DoD agreed to provide equipment on the condition that the weapons delivered be used only if cease-fire talks broke down. In addition, the administration wanted to know how and toward what end Israel would use the equipment. Unlike previous sessions, both State and Defense agreed to provide additional military equipment to Israel if the talks proved fruitless.[65]

Less than a week after the cease-fire went into effect on 7 August, Israel charged that the Soviets and Egyptians had violated it. Accompanied by the Israeli prime minister's political adviser, Rabin met with Kissinger on 15 August. Rabin relayed Prime Minister Meir's growing apprehension over the violations and her regrets about agreeing to the cease-fire. At Kissinger's urging, Rabin met with Nixon, who approved delivery of Shrike missiles for strikes against the SA–3 complex.[66]

During August the administration found evidence of continued violations of the standstill provisions of the cease-fire. State Department Director of Intelligence and Research (INR) Ray S. Cline reported at the end of the month the presence of seven or eight SA–2 sites that had been built within 30 kilometers of the canal after the start of the cease-fire. Cline had headed the CIA Directorate of Intelligence during the Cuban missile crisis in 1962 before taking over as director of INR. U.S. protests failed to persuade the Soviets and Egyptians to stop what the United States regarded as violations of the military standstill provisions of the cease-fire. Dismayed by the infringements, Israel withdrew from the Jarring talks on 6 September.[67]

Impasse

A long-simmering internal struggle between King Hussein and Palestinian military groups living within Jordan erupted into a major crisis in September, further complicating U.S. policymaking, with special reference to military assistance. On 6 September 1970 hijackers from the Popular Front for the Liberation of Palestine commandeered three U.S. aircraft bound for New York City and flew two of them to Dawson Field, a remote airstrip in the Jordanian desert once used by the British air force. After releasing the passengers, the Popular Front commandos blew up both aircraft on 12 September. Fearing the threat of an independent Palestine Liberation Organization (PLO) in his realm, Hussein declared martial law and ordered Jordanian armor units to attack PLO military camps and the headquarters in Amman. Syrian units, in support of the Palestinians, invaded Jordan. The King's army, helped in part by the threat from Israeli forces massed along the Syrian border, beat back the invading force and expelled the Palestinian Liberation Front from Jordan. During the brief hostilities the United States sent additional war ships to the eastern Mediterranean and put the 82nd Airborne Division on alert. Laird had serious reservations about possible U.S. military intervention in the region so soon after the U.S. incursion into Cambodia. Thus he took steps to avoid the involvement of U.S. ships or aircraft during the crisis.[68]

In the midst of the Jordanian crisis, which could destabilize the region and threaten Israel's security, Nixon pledged another $500 million in aid and 18 Phantom jets to Israel. He directed Kissinger to prepare "an immediate additional arms package" for Israel; then told him to have Laird "double the package." With top priority going to antimissiles, he instructed Rogers and Laird to meet with Israeli representatives to develop a list of items to offset the advantages that violations of the standstill cease-fire had given the Egyptians. The president also wanted recommendations for Israel's long-term needs in FY 1971 and FY 1972.[69]

On 3 October Packard provided an equipment list for Israel, but urged restraint for political reasons. He believed the items under consideration "will improve Israel's position in a significant way," possibly further upsetting the Middle East military balance. The requested air-to-air refueling tankers, he noted, would give Israel a new capability, allowing it to pursue a wide-ranging antimissile strategy to outflank canal defenses. Israel had already stated its intention to use the requested equipment to attack all missile sites across the canal. Packard cautioned that the DoD package would not provide Israel "the ability to destroy the missile belt without risking significant attrition." Before approving the package he suggested that the president apply the same conditions he had attached to the initial antimissile request in August. Packard also wanted Israel to agree to resume peace talks even without a total pullback of Egyptian and Soviet missiles along the Suez. However, Nixon affixed no political conditions to his approval, but he applied the same stipulations on the use of equipment that were attached to the 14 August equipment offer. For its part, Israel showed no willingness to make political concessions. The country insisted on additional promises of U.S. financial and military assistance before agreeing to resume peace talks, a position Kissinger and Sisco supported. In November, Israel stated it wanted to buy 54 additional F–4s and 120 additional A–4s. As Nutter pointed out to Laird, this sale, given the absence of political conditions, would deprive the United States of any leverage over Israel after negotiations actually began.[70]

Laird agreed and opposed at least temporarily this sale of aircraft. The secretary urged Nixon to avoid making a specific commitment on military assistance when he met with Israeli Defense Minister Moshe Dayan in December. The equipment in the Israeli request would have to come out of DoD stocks and the budgets of the military services, forcing the department to defer what the secretary considered higher priority U.S. needs. Laird saw no immediate requirement for the additional aircraft, which in his estimation would simply add to Israel's substantial offensive advantage. He feared that Israel would get the impression it could refuse to enter talks and still obtain U.S. equipment: "We cannot afford to put Israel in a position where it can drag its feet on talks while the U.S. assures defense of its occupied territories." The secretary lamented that Israel, so absorbed by its focus on near-term security needs, failed to consider taking "a reasonable risk for peace" in the long run.[71] When Nixon and Laird met on 10 December 1970 with Dayan and Rabin, the Israelis insisted that the equipment was essential and reiterated their refusal to enter negotiations when confronted with serious violations of the cease-fire. Dayan's response clearly indicated the difficulty that the United States faced in exercising leverage over the prime beneficiary of military assistance in the Middle East.[72]

By mid-1971 the situation had come no closer to a resolution. Assessing the state of affairs for the president, Kissinger noted that the Jarring mission had made

Israeli Defense Minister Moshe Dayan arrives at the Pentagon on 11 December 1970 to discuss additional military assistance to his country. (OSD Historical Office)

no headway in moving the Arabs and Israelis toward a settlement. The effort for a modest mutual pullback of forces on the Suez Canal had reached an impasse. Soviet influence in Egypt, along with military shipments, continued to grow.[73]

Seeing current U.S. policy at a dead end, Laird concluded it was necessary to alter U.S. Middle East arms policy. He told Nixon that it was "unrealistic to talk of giving Israel enough equipment to maintain a 'balance' against present or prospective Soviet forces that may be focused on the Middle East." In Laird's mind it was more than a regional problem. It also involved NATO, the U.S. Sixth Fleet, and overall U.S. security interests. In providing weapons to Egypt, the Soviet Union also had gained greater influence over the Egyptian military. In its pursuit of regional military balance, the United States would have to continue to supply weapons to Israel but without exercising "any degree of control over Israeli capabilities." Laird concluded that additional weapons for Israel had only led to a more extensive Soviet presence in Egypt. How the United States responded to Israeli requests for additional aircraft would be the measure by which the Arab world would weigh the sincerity of U.S. efforts to reach an equitable peace settlement. Laird advocated replacing the notion of regional military balance with a less ambitious standard of assuring that Israel could defend its borders against Arab attack. He warned: "The US cannot exert sufficient leverage in the Middle East as long as it is locked rigidly into a false concept of military balance that robs the US of the initiative and does not take into account the very real differences between US and Israeli interests."[74]

Laird's initiative had little effect. At the end of December 1971, after Nixon met with Golda Meir and agreed to her request for Phantoms and Skyhawks, the president instructed Rogers to begin discussions with the Israeli ambassador aimed at concluding an agreement to deliver Phantoms and Skyhawks on a regular monthly schedule starting in February 1972. The delivery goal was three Phantom aircraft per month through calendar years 1972 and 1973; 40 A–4E Skyhawks and 10 TA–4F trainers total during 1972; and 32 A-4N Skyhawks above the 18 already provided from the production line. This decision represented a clear rebuff to Laird's attempt to change regional policy. Not only was the December memorandum not addressed to him, it took assets away from DoD, a move that affected weapons stocks, without directly informing him. The decision would have adverse consequences for U.S. force readiness and national security objectives in the region, Nutter emphasized.[75]

Laird and the Department of Defense stood in the minority on Israeli assistance. There was agreement within the administration on the need to provide military hardware to Israel but disagreement on the details. Laird judged that it was too expensive and futile to try to attain a regional military balance after the Soviets became directly involved. It would be better to pursue a long-term regional solution through negotiations and to place conditions on assistance so that the United States could exercise some leverage on Israel during negotiations. In contrast, Nixon, Kissinger, and Sisco greatly feared possible Israeli defeat and further growth of Soviet power in the Middle East, making them reluctant to impose political conditions on granting military aid to Israel. They believed that military assistance was necessary to bring Israel to the negotiating table. The disagreement in approach between Laird and the White House essentially continued as long as he was secretary of defense. Israel continued to ask for additional U.S. military equipment; Nixon granted it despite Laird's misgivings that it contributed to regional instability and depleted stocks in other theaters. Military assistance did little to enhance U.S. leverage over Israel. Its continuing requests for advanced military equipment, in Laird's view, had a potentially long-term negative effect on the readiness of U.S. forces by shifting equipment to Israel from other theaters.

LAIRD TOOK SEEMINGLY CONTRADICTORY positions on military assistance, fully embracing it under the Nixon Doctrine in Asia. The Nixon Doctrine promised net savings and a less prominent U.S. profile in Asia for the future, creating an opportunity to shift resources to Europe as the Vietnam War wound down. At the same time, he wanted to limit military assistance for Israel, over which, according to Laird and others, the United States had diminishing influence. The thread that tied these conflicting positions was Laird's intense focus on keeping defense spending in check, strengthening NATO, and avoiding an overextension of a defense establishment constrained by severe budget pressures. Laird and DoD wanted to limit the number of advanced weapons provided to Israel, believing the transfer would require the United States to take equipment out of other theaters, a move that would defer the higher priorities in Vietnam and NATO. Moreover, supplying too many arms to the Jewish state would, in Laird's judgment, only heighten military competition in the region, undermining prospects for a political settlement, and possibly even edge the United States closer to a conflict with the

Soviets. In Laird's mind, the United States was reaching the point where it could scarcely meet existing and newly imposed commitments. The nation had no Middle East security interests important enough to warrant the risk of hostilities with the Soviet Union. Greater numbers of advanced U.S. weapons in Israel only increased that risk. Laird remained consistent in his opposition to a policy that he saw as over arming Israel.

CHAPTER 18

Looking Toward the Future: The FY 1974 Budget[1]

PREPARATION OF THE FY 1974 BUDGET, the last that Laird helped put together, began in earnest in the fall of 1971 and continued until December 1972, shortly before Laird's tenure as secretary ended. As he had for the FY 1973 budget, Laird based the FY 1974 budget on the doctrine of realistic deterrence, his vision for the future that shifted defense resources from Asia and required personnel cuts to free up money for the All-Volunteer Force. Laird left office in January 1973 at about the time that President Nixon submitted his FY 1974 budget proposal to Congress, convinced that he had done his best to uphold the interests of the Department of Defense and the nation.

The financial issues facing DoD as it prepared the FY 1974 budget differed little from previous years. Even before Laird issued initial guidance on the FYs 1974–1978 defense program, the economic situation and the prospect of growing federal deficits portended the possibility of further cuts in DoD spending. In January 1971 both the Office of the Secretary of Defense and the Office of Management and Budget projected that planned defense expenditures, about a third of the total federal budget, would lead to large budget deficits in the mid-1970s, given current projections of federal revenue and nondefense spending. An increase in revenues through higher taxation or a decrease in overall spending seemed unavoidable. Intense competition for federal funds between domestic and defense programs further complicated DoD budget planning. As before, the White House pressed the Defense Department to cut its budget. It would be left to Laird's successor, Elliot Richardson, to defend the FY 1974 budget before Congress.[1]

Of special concern to White House and Pentagon officials was the rising cost of fielding military forces. Increased retirement benefits and pay, in large measure to fund the All-Volunteer Force, added to the continuing pressure to curtail spending. The president feared the effects of more expensive manpower and equipment on military strategy and national security policy. The skyrocketing costs of developing sophisticated new weapons raised knotty questions about affordability, increasing the risk that a force capable of carrying out the president's military strategy and supporting his foreign policy could become too expensive for the nation.[2]

Debate over Guidance

Laird issued the FY 1974 "Defense Policy Guidance" and "Interim Force Planning Guidance" on 23 October 1971 to the service secretaries, the chairman of the Joint Chiefs of Staff, and the directors of DoD agencies. Based on input and analysis from Systems Analysis, International Security Affairs, the JCS, and the military services, the guidance on policy and force planning constituted the foundation for volume two of the Joint Strategic Objectives Plan, the recommendations for force structure and budgets to attain five-year strategic goals. Laird wanted to link specific force levels with a variety of missions and strategies and asked the JCS to assess the inherent risks of these strategies and to propose modifications of force levels that could reduce the risks. Laird planned to use the force levels derived from the policy and force planning guidance in combination with JCS modifications to help determine his final budget guidance.[3]

Laird's strategic guidance represented a more refined version of the previous fiscal year's exposition of the concept of realistic deterrence, which envisioned allies providing more financial and military resources for their defense than in past years. With the real possibility of a smaller active-duty U.S. force structure in the future, the readiness and effectiveness of the forces in being assumed greater importance. Readiness required constant attention to maintaining and upgrading equipment and to achieving greater efficiency in logistics, command, training, intelligence, communications, and R&D. The total force concept was now embedded in national security planning. In a crisis requiring rapid and substantial mobilization, reserve and guard forces would constitute the primary, initial source for augmenting active-duty forces.[4]

Laird's force planning guidance covered in detail the roles of strategic and general purpose forces, free world forces and military assistance, Guard and Reserve forces, and mobilization planning. It handled separately the matter of the diminishing U.S. military presence in Vietnam, which was contingent on the date of a negotiated settlement. The force planning guidance reinforced the centrality of the NSDM 16 criteria for strategic sufficiency, stressing the need to sustain a reliable survivable force of land- and sea-based missiles and manned bombers. Planners were to assume completion of the full 12-site Safeguard ABM system. General purpose forces were expected to be combat ready and sufficient in numbers and capability to provide both forward deployed forces and a strategic reserve of U.S.-based forces. The armed forces had to be able to deal with three major military contingencies, first a European war between the forces of NATO and the Warsaw Pact, in which the capability to protect sea lanes to supply NATO would be essential. The second contingency posited a war against China in Northeast Asia; and the third, a conflict with China in Southeast Asia. The secretary expected war plans to include full mobilization in the event of a full-scale war with the Soviet Union or China—a reserve call-up, mobilizing civil airlift and sealift, activation of mothballed ships, and accelerated production of ships, aircraft, equipment, ammunition, and consumable items.[5]

Laird's force planning guidance envisioned a significant change over time for the role and mission of U.S. ground forces throughout Asia to allow a reemphasis on security in Europe, which, the administration deemed, was the most likely theater to erupt in a shooting war and which had suffered relative neglect during the Vietnam era. As the capabilities of Asian allies improved, Laird argued that the United States should reconfigure its ground force structure to better suit NATO requirements. America's allies throughout Asia, Laird contended in his guidance as he had on other occasions, were getting stronger and accordingly could take on more of their defense, allowing the United States to ease back on its responsibilities in the Pacific. To carry out the change, military assistance programs would expand. By FY 1977 Laird suggested optimistically, no U.S. ground forces would need to back up America's Asian allies, an assertion the White House had found unrealistic the previous fiscal year.[6]

In responding to Laird's policy and planning guidance in November 1971, the Joint Chiefs of Staff were not circumspect in stating their position. Unease pervaded their assessment. For Laird's notion of realistic deterrence to work, the JCS argued, it had to rest on a real capability to wage war, defined as the ability to inflict unacceptable damage on the war-making and industrial resources of an enemy.

"Failure of the United States to maintain a warfighting capability," the JCS concluded, "could make US deterrence illusory." That capability required the forward deployment of tactical nuclear weapons. The Chiefs found the Soviet arms buildup and simultaneous interest in strategic arms talks a problematic development. On strategic weapons, the Chiefs believed it prudent for the United States to hedge against the development of those that could lead to Soviet superiority and strategic instability. They questioned the feasibility of actually having in place by FY 1977 a security assistance program so robust that the United States would not have to provide ground forces to assist Asian allies. The JCS deemed that possibility simply too uncertain, based on questionable assumptions about adequate congressional support for security assistance and suitable progress in building up the military forces of allies. Accordingly, the United States needed to retain the option of supporting Asian allies with military forces.[7]

In mid-November 1971 Wayne Smith of Kissinger's staff obtained a bootleg copy of Laird's FYs 1974–1978 policy and planning guidance, the underlying strategy for FY 1974 DoD budget planning.[8] Like the JCS, Smith took issue with the secretary's formulation of deterrence, alleging that it "emphasizes planning to deter rather than planning to defend" and that the guidance "seems to confuse the *means* by which we hope to implement the president's strategy . . . *with the actual objectives of our national strategy.*" Smith found this especially true for Asia, a region for which the administration had not yet fully developed its long-term strategy. Laird's guidance held that Asian allies could handle threats from China "without U.S. ground forces by FY 1977." On this point, Smith emphasized, Laird's guidance conflicted with the president's views. Recognizing that Asian allies would not be self-sufficient militarily by that date, Laird had argued nonetheless that they would possess enough strength by then to deter conflict. Their future capability to exact high casualties on the Chinese would minimize the use of force by China, Laird argued. Openly skeptical, Smith noted the secretary's silence on the question of how the United States would support its allies should deterrence fail or the prospect of high casualties prove no impediment to Chinese military action.[9]

Smith had other concerns. He questioned Laird's call for greater reliance on reserve forces, doubting that DoD could fill their ranks without the incentive to volunteer that conscription provided. Moreover, Smith argued, for political reasons no president would actually take the unpopular step of mobilizing reserves, perhaps alluding to Lyndon Johnson's decision to fight in Vietnam without calling up the reserves. Laird also expected allied military capabilities to improve and regional cooperation among allies to increase. Smith thought it unlikely that Asian allies would willingly play a more prominent military role. Laird's reliance on smaller forces employing modernized weapons also raised questions of afford-ability because escalating costs of developing new weapon systems proved so hard to control. "Investment in unnecessarily expensive new weapons systems," Smith opined to Kissinger, "has already caused a dangerous erosion in military force levels and overall military effectiveness over the past ten years."[10]

In January 1972 Laird officially forwarded his Defense Policy and Planning Guidance to Kissinger, stating that it constituted definitive guidance to DoD for evaluating forces and programs. Laird asked that his guidance be reviewed to ensure that it reflected the president's views, but Philip Odeen of Kissinger's staff held that the defense guidance needed further review and revision. Kissinger agreed. Accordingly, Kissinger endorsed the secretary's policy and force planning guidance in general terms but expressed reservations on a number of issues—especially long-term planning for Asia and Laird's timetable for ending direct support of Asian allies in FY 1977. He reminded Laird that the president's policy required a U.S. capability to aid Asian allies in meeting a threat from China in either Southeast or Northeast Asia. Under the Nixon Doctrine, Kissinger noted, the president expected America's allies to assume a greater share of the mutual defense burden, but he did not envisage that they could develop a military capability sufficient to defend against a massive strike from China. Nixon also feared that further strengthening the military prowess of allied forces could upset the existing regional military bal-ance and severely burden economic development in Japan and Korea. Moreover, the 1971 version of NSSM 69 on U.S. strategy and forces for Asia had concluded that U.S. ground forces would be necessary "to support our allies against a PRC [People's Republic of China] attack even under the most favorable assumptions." Nixon wanted U.S. forces to retain the capability of reinforcing allies against a conventional Chinese attack. The president also expressed reservations about the increased reliance on reserve forces, desiring no further reductions in active forces until the reserves had demonstrated their ability to support the overall force effectively. In spite of these disagreements, Kissinger made no recommendation for Laird to change his guidance, aware he would bristle at White House revisions.

He expected the Defense Program Review Committee and the National Security Council to address the issues he raised. In April 1972 the DPRC would again discuss NSSM 69, resuming a long debate over U.S. strategy and support to Asian allies.[11]

Projected funding levels for total obligational authority and outlays formed the basis for the FYs 1974–1978 fiscal guidance that would be issued in February 1972 as part of the Defense Planning and Programming Guidance. Projected FY 1974 TOA was set at $88.9 billion ($8.7 billion higher than FY 1972) and would reach $95.1 billion in FY 1977. Projected outlays of $83.9 billion for FY 1974 ($6.4 billion above FY 1972) would climb to $97 billion by FY 1977. The guidance assumed that decreases in spending for the Vietnam War would help offset the rising personnel costs for the AVF and retired pay. The FY 1974 projections would allow increased funding for maintaining and improving major forces. Everyone involved in formulating the DoD budget understood that these numbers represented the starting point; reviews in DoD, OMB, and the NSC would reduce the initial figures well before the president submitted his budget proposal to Congress in early 1973.[12]

According to the DoD budget cycle, the department would issue its fiscal guidance for FY 1974 after the DPRC meeting in early February 1972. George Shultz, the director of OMB, was sensitive about the timing because after DoD issued its guidance it might characterize any discussions about expenditures as attempts to cut its budget. He wanted to impress upon Laird that his forthcoming guidance had to be "fiscally realistic." Rather than discuss fiscal guidance in the DPRC, of which Laird was not a member, Shultz, fearing that Laird would simply ignore DPRC recommendations as he had done on other occasions, wanted to meet with Kissinger and Laird privately to discuss the guidance.[13]

The February DPRC meeting concentrated on spending levels for the FY 1974 budget and devoted no time to assessing the impact that defense expenditures and the overall budget would have on the national economy, a matter that Laird had long maintained ought to be the committee's chief concern. As in past years, OMB and DoD clashed. OMB's starting point held defense outlays to the FY 1973 level of $82 billion. The proposed spending plan would maintain current force and readiness levels, making adjustments for higher pay, additional shipbuilding, and decreased spending in Southeast Asia. DoD's expenditure estimate of $83.9 billion included, as Comptroller Robert Moot reported, the liquidation of budget authority from previous fiscal years plus pay raises and the next increment of funding for undersea long-range missiles and the F–15 fighter. Projected spending for FY 1974 and FY 1975 would total $22 billion higher than NSDM 27 targets. Approved by Nixon in 1969, NSDM 27 established the 1½-war strategy and set planned expenditure targets for the five-year FYs 1971–1976 program (see chapter 10). The higher spending level assumed greater than anticipated rates of inflation in 1972, possible continuation of the war in Vietnam, higher funding for the AVF, and pay raises for military and civilian personnel.[14]

OMB's estimate of FY 1974 federal expenditures projected a deficit of $26 billion. Using DoD figures that estimate would climb to $28 billion. These deficit projections would force Nixon to make the difficult choice between reducing spending on planned programs, raising taxes, or accepting the deficit and giving up the idea of a balanced budget. Spending cuts would have to come from the category of controllable discretionary expenses. Nondefense controllable expenditures that could be changed by administrative action without modifying existing law or canceling existing contracts amounted to 9 percent of federal expenses. Nearly two-thirds (66 percent) of defense expenditures for FY 1974 were considered controllable, making DoD the prime target for cuts.[15]

The Pentagon and OMB agreed at the February 1972 DPRC meeting to accept for the time being military expenditures of $84 billion for planning purposes. OMB went along, expecting that budget reviews and congressional action would lower the figure eventually to $80 billion–$82 billion. The White House believed that Laird's fiscal guidance would lead to annual deficits from FY 1974 to FY 1978, leaving the president with only the option of raising taxes.[16] Laird feared that failure of the current budget formulation process to provide the chief executive with a full array of options in all areas of the federal budget—military and nonmilitary—would force the president to make arbitrary decisions in November. He did not want the DPRC to provide fiscal guidance to DoD. He wanted the president to make those decisions. Throughout his tenure as secretary he held that the DPRC needed to address the relationship of the entire federal budget and the nation's economic situation. He did not want the committee to intrude into the design or the line-by-line details of the Defense budget. JCS Chairman Admiral Thomas Moorer supported Laird, noting that the DPRC involved itself in weapons acquisition issues in too much detail.[17]

Of concern to Shultz was the growing percentage that DoD's budget devoted to training, base operations, and other support functions. In 1964 around a quarter of the budget went for support; by 1973 it had grown to a third. Over the same period military manpower levels had dropped 15 percent, but the number of civilians remained steady. A return to the support and civilian manpower ratios of 1964, OMB believed, would yield an estimated saving of $2 billion to $3 billion that could be spent on combat forces. OMB believed the incidence of relatively high support costs at a time when DoD was redeploying forces from Vietnam and reducing force structure clearly indicated that DoD had more bases and support facilities than it required.[18]

Looking ahead as was routinely done, DoD's five-year program would increase outlays by roughly $4 billion annually between FYs 1974 and 1978. The projected FY 1977 spending level of $97 billion, around $20 billion higher than the figures in NSDM 27, was largely attributable to inflation and rising payroll costs, not to an expansion of forces scheduled to remain at FY 1973 levels. DoD assumed an annual inflation rate of 3 percent, which accounted for most of the increase in projected spending over the five-year period. Taking inflation into account, Philip Odeen concluded that DoD's base five-year program (expenditures) was actually $4 billion to $5 billion lower in constant dollars than its current program but had not eliminated forces. For FY 1973 DoD planned an active-duty force of 13 Army and 3 Marine divisions at a 90 percent manning level; 22 Air Force tactical air wings, 3 Marine Corps air wings, and 67 Navy tactical air squadrons. The Navy's FY 1973 program maintained attack carriers at 14 with a fleet of 594 ships. However, the FY 1974 program would reduce the number of attack carriers to 12 and the overall ship level to 550. The modernization program for the Multiple Independently Targetable Reentry Vehicle would proceed and the full 12-site ABM program would be funded. The plan included a significant modernization program and procurement funding for the accelerated ULMS program and the procurement of the B–1 bomber. The naval ship building program called for a nuclear-powered attack carrier and a new generation of *Spruance*-class destroyers. Funds were also in the plan to develop the Air Force's Airborne Warning and Air Command System, or AWACS. The potential costs for modernization alarmed Odeen because the equipment being developed cost two- to five-times more than the equipment it would replace. Rising costs would limit the purchase of weapons more so than in the past. The likelihood of cost overruns would further intensify a problem that Odeen saw as requiring a stark choice: "Over the long term, we will simply not be able to keep up force levels unless we rely in part on quite old weapons."[19]

On 9 March 1972 Laird issued the planning and programming guidance for FYs 1974–1978 to OSD, the services, the JCS, and DoD agencies. A copy also went to Kissinger. The document included policy and fiscal guidance, materiel support planning guidance, and guidance for preparation of the POM (program objective memorandum), the basic programming and budget document for each of the armed services. It would apply to all policy and program actions for DoD. On the question of deploying U.S. forces and reserves to Asia to stem a Chinese attack, Laird hedged by stating this would be determined on a case-by-case basis, noting that his guidance would allow utilization of U.S. forces against the Chinese. With assistance from U.S. air and naval forces, he still expected that America's Asian allies would have the capability to minimize the likelihood of a conventional offensive by the Chinese. Kissinger did not sign off on the revised guidance, nor did he send it to the president. To Laird's disappointment, Kissinger stated that the DPRC and NSC would further review and clarify the guidance where appropriate. As in previous years, Kissinger's position reflected the long-term struggle between the national security adviser and the secretary over the role of the DPRC in reviewing the DoD program.[20]

Summer Stalemate

The administration debated the FY 1974 DoD budget against the worsening economic backdrop of the second half of 1972. The projected federal deficit for FY 1974, based on then current spending plans, had doubled between February and July 1972. The added danger for DoD was not just less money, but having its force size determined by near-term economic considerations rather than by the military capabilities needed to defend the country and carry out the president's foreign and national security policy. That prospect naturally also caused great concern to the NSC. In pursuit of Nixon's goal of a full employment balanced budget OMB firmly insisted on defense cuts. Laird, having won increases in DoD's budget (TOA and outlays) in the two previous fiscal years, resisted. He sought sufficient funds to modernize the weapons and equipment of the armed forces for the post-Vietnam era and to pay for the AVF.[21]

Looking ahead to conditions in Nixon's expected second term, Odeen warned in July 1972 of a looming budget crisis that would likely surface in FY 1974 and worsen during the remainder of Nixon's second term. The deficit under the full employment budget could reach $30 billion by FY 1977 even if the administration undertook no new programs. He attributed the pending plight in large measure to past tax reductions and the growth of nondefense spending "faster than revenues or the overall budget." Measured in constant FY 1973 dollars, expenditures for social security and health care had expanded 141 percent in the period from 1965 to 1973; spending on income maintenance programs during that time had jumped 82 percent; and growth in other categories of nondefense spending had reached around 102 percent. The executive branch had little control over most of this non-defense spending. In contrast, expenditures for defense over that period had fallen by 1 percent. Facing a tough economic situation, the president hardly relished the prospect of raising taxes in an election year.[22]

Maj. Gen. Robert Pursley, Laird's military assistant, gathered input from OSD offices to help the secretary prepare for budget battles with the White House and OMB. To counter arguments for cutting the DoD budget, Pursley made the obvious point that cutting defense outlays too severely would compromise the president's ability to attain his foreign policy goals. As the key talking point, he believed, Laird ought to emphasize the impact of cuts on Nixon's foreign policy options and highlight that immediate savings could be elusive. Cutting support functions without reducing troop strength, he noted, would produce little immediate financial benefit in early FY 1974. Nor would lowering the quality of new weapons under development and less so-called gold plating, or over design of weapons and equipment, yield large or early savings in the procurement account. Requiring current manpower on active duty to carry out additional duties in the name of economy could harm the well-being of military personnel and compromise attainment of the AVF, according to Pursley.[23]

Laird employed these arguments in pressing his case. To fulfill the president's goals, Laird argued that DoD required at least $84 billion. A lower spending level, he informed Nixon, "will increasingly constrain your flexibility and diminish options in the future." But Laird also emphasized the budgetary losses that DoD had already incurred. From its 1968 war peak, DoD had already cut military and civilian personnel by 30 percent and reduced purchases by 40 percent, bringing spending in real terms "to the lowest levels since 1951." Further cuts would likely discourage U.S. allies from allocating a larger share of their budgets for defense, a key element of the Nixon Doctrine. Moreover, defense spending had to be assessed, Laird insisted as he had before, within the context of the entire federal budget, a necessary approach from the secretary's perspective. Recent increases in nondefense spending combined with the growth of federal grants to state and local governments meant that by 1978 the annual federal deficit would nearly equal the Defense budget. To make his point more dramatically, Laird, unlike Odeen, did not use the numbers associated with the concept of the budget being in balance on the assumption of full employment. Accordingly, his calculation of the annual projected deficit was significantly higher than Odeen's. He urged the administration to examine the growing deficit in a broader way. From Laird's perspective, "federal fiscal problems are bigger than the defense budget, are not caused by the defense budget, and cannot be solved by the defense budget. . . . Only long term curtailment of the rate of growth of non-defense expenditures, including those for currently legislated programs, can restore economic health." In a July meeting with Caspar Weinberger, the new head of OMB, Laird reiterated the arguments that he used with Nixon, specifically that DoD had difficulty in implementing presidential policy within its fiscal guidance and that it was not the place to seek budget savings. Nixon's response to Laird implied that cuts would be forthcoming. The president noted that upcoming reviews would help develop alternative DoD programs and assess their strategic implications.[24]

OMB Director Caspar Weinberger sparred with Laird over FY 1974 defense spending.
In 1981 Weinberger became President Ronald Reagan's secretary of defense.
(Nixon Presidential Library)

To prepare the DoD budget, in July 1972 Systems Analysis under Assistant Secretary of Defense Gardiner Tucker examined the military service and defense agency budget submissions (POMs), assessing what military capabilities a specific funding level would support, and assembled material for the DPRC meeting later in July. For the FY 1974 budget, Deputy Secretary of Defense Kenneth Rush would head the budget review, slated to be completed by the end of August.[25] Rush, previously U.S. ambassador to Germany and Nixon's former Duke University law school professor, had replaced David Packard at the end of February 1972. The president wanted Rush to serve in DoD because of his knowledge of strategic arms limitations and mutual balanced force reductions in Europe. He also expected him to be more compliant than Packard or Laird. In discussing Rush's appointment, Nixon told Laird that Rush wanted to be a team player, hinting that he found Packard and Laird too independent. The president conceded that Rush lacked familiarity with defense issues such as procurement and the budget and would have to rely on Comptroller Robert Moot and the service secretaries. Laird supported Rush's appointment, but he had not been the secretary's first choice. In November 1971 he had recommended Air Force Secretary Robert Seamans for the position, telling Nixon he was tough and a good administrator.[26]

The DPRC discussed the DoD program at the end of July 1972. Laird, holding out for expenditures of $84 billion, did not permit OSD to present an alternate program at the meeting or to offer trade-offs between forces and missions. At the time of the session he and Rush were still reviewing the budget proposals of the armed services. The session proved inconclusive. Using arguments at the meeting that Laird and Moot had advanced for increased spending for previous budgets, Rush reminded the attendees that DoD's expenditures had declined as a share of GNP and that it had significantly reduced personnel, industrial purchases, and expenditures in recent years. Rush and Moot noted that increased personnel costs, pay raises, and retirement benefits had accounted for the increase in spending in recent years. The JCS considered $84 billion in expenditures a "marginal" amount relative to real security needs, arguing the need for $102 billion. Not even OSD would argue for the latter figure.[27]

Weinberger countered the DoD position, stressing the president's desire to lower inflation by cutting $20 billion from the federal budget, an action that would force cuts in defense spending. He told Rush that DoD would have to help attain Nixon's goal of full employment budget balance. "The personnel costs are so high

Laird presents the DoD Distinguished Public Service Medal to Deputy Defense Secretary Kenneth Rush, January 1973. (NARA OPA)

now," he stated, "that you must seek new reductions in manpower. . . . We must have more efficient use of our expensive manpower; this is where we can save money." Yet during the DPRC session OMB remained reluctant to provide official or even informal information on the overall budget situation in order to increase its leverage in setting the budget totals. In OMB's view, the federal fiscal situation, not a consideration of DoD's recent reductions, should determine the DoD budget.[28]

Rather than attempt to bridge the differences between DoD and the budget office, Kissinger at this point preferred to settle on a strategic framework for DoD and then develop a process for completing the budget. His goal was to avoid having Laird submit in September a detailed program insufficiently responsive to overall strategic objectives. He expected DPRC to "determine the overall strategic objectives" and then let DoD determine the forces required to carry out those objectives. At the July meeting the DPRC agreed with Kissinger's approach. Defense was to

prepare by early September a paper for the DPRC that assessed the strategic implications of various programs for FYs 1974–1978. The DPRC would then define the
broad strategic objectives before DoD worked out the details of the budget.[29]

After the meeting Kissinger reassured Laird that unlike Weinberger he did
not favor cutting the Defense budget. He reiterated that DoD should develop its
spending plans in relation to national objectives and avoid nitpicking debates over
every item in the budget. Instead of having the DPRC debate the Defense budget,
Kissinger preferred that he, Laird, and Weinberger discuss the issues privately.[30]

Weinberger, however, continued to press relentlessly for cuts. In a telephone
conversation on 5 August he sought Kissinger's approval to require Laird to submit
a budget in the range of $80 billion to $81 billion in spending. The OMB director
thought that if DoD was given guidance to prepare a budget at the $84 billion level
only, then the department would have no incentive to go below that figure. By
forcing DoD to plan for a lower target, Weinberger hoped to prevent Laird from
ignoring calls to reduce the budget. Kissinger acknowledged that Laird was hard to
pin down in budget negotiations. "If you get sucked into an individual review," he
warned Weinberger, "he'll [Laird] kill you every time." Weinberger agreed: "If we
aren't lined up ahead of time, Mel can do all kinds of machinations." Yet Kissinger
supported the secretary's underlying point that further defense cuts would actually
start to jeopardize national security. Weinberger countered that additional cuts
would not affect military capability, but Kissinger doubted that was the case.[31]
When the three met in early August, Kissinger opposed Weinberger's arbitrary
spending ceiling, insisting that the "only sound approach would be a careful strategic analysis of the implications of additional cuts." Laird said he would submit
alternate budgets that spelled out precisely the strategic implications of different
spending levels.[32]

Odeen thought it possible to bridge the differences between Laird and Weinberger. He told Kissinger in August that a variety of spending adjustments could
produce savings of $1.8 billion without making significant programmatic changes
or creating bureaucratic problems for Laird. Small additional expenditure reductions in air and missile defense, reserves, and intelligence could yield an additional
$87 million in savings that would lower estimated FY 1974 outlays to around $82
billion, a figure no longer acceptable to OMB.[33] Weinberger wanted to lower FY
1974 DoD outlays to $78 billion–$79 billion. This spending, Odeen believed, crossed

a significant threshold. He concluded that it would require changes to planned programs and have "significant strategic implications."[34]

To gain support for $84 billion in spending and to drive home the point that defense spending had not grown, Laird and others in OSD continued to emphasize the long, steady decline in military spending, as measured in constant dollars. Measured in FY 1973 dollars, DoD outlays were 7 percent lower than in FY 1964, before the start of the Vietnam War. Laird made such comparisons central to his effort to sell his $84 billion program in an adverse political climate. But comparisons between current and past spending failed to sway the White House seeking to reduce the deficit and craft a specific budget to carry out the president's strategy.[35]

The ingrained formulaic aspects of the DoD budget-building process imposed a degree of rigidity that made it more difficult to correlate the budget with the president's strategy. The increased cost of manpower affected the Army the most, but the relative allocation of funds among the services from year to year remained relatively inflexible. With the exception of the years of the Vietnam buildup, the percentage of the Defense budget allocated to land forces (Army and Marines) had remained relatively constant at 9–10 percent over the past 12 to 16 years, forcing cuts in ground forces as the costs of manpower and new equipment rose. The growing allocation of funds to cover military pay and retirement benefits over the years had forced the services to make trade-offs by reducing manpower and easing back readiness in exchange for qualitative improvements. As Odeen noted, the increased share of the budget devoted to personnel costs had caused a decline in the percentage of funds available for investment. Between FY 1964 and FY 1973 funds allocated for military pay and related spending had jumped from 43 percent to 56 percent of TOA. Money allocated for procurement; civilian pay; research, development, and test and evaluation; and construction had fallen from 45 percent to 30 percent of TOA. Over the years the Army had given up divisions and maneuver battalions to help pay for helicopters and modernization. The Air Force and Navy had made similar sacrifices of manpower.[36]

Despite Laird's professed willingness to submit an alternate spending plan to the DPRC, he was in no hurry and continued his long-standing resistance to the committee's role. He told his staff at the end of October 1972 to regard the FY 1974 budget preparation as an internal affair. At that point he did not want people from OMB, NSC, State, and other staffs reviewing DoD's working papers. As reasons he cited the uncertainty about the pending outcome of the fight over the FY 1973 budget and the president's FY 1973 expenditure limitation, both of which had a powerful bearing on the FY 1974 budget deliberations. In October the comptroller's office was still reviewing budget estimates submitted by the services. In view of the administration's fiscal problems, Moot expected great pressure from OMB and the president to cut forces and weed out waste, mismanagement, and duplicative programs.[37]

As he approached his January 1973 date for leaving DoD, Laird envisioned a diminishing role for himself in the final preparation of the FY 1974 budget. At the beginning of November he made clear to Nixon, OMB, and his OSD staff that he would not extend his time in office. A new secretary would make any decisions on the budgets submitted by the services and would defend the president's FY 1974 budget submission before Congress during April and May 1973. As he had stated numerous times, Laird would leave at the end of Nixon's first term.[38]

The debate over outlays came to a head in November 1972. Although Laird had been reluctant to lower defense spending, it was clear by this time that OMB held a stronger position than DoD. The size of the budget deficit, combined with the president's determination and campaign pledge to avoid a tax increase, made it unlikely that Laird, who would leave in a few months, could keep DoD outlays at $84 billion. By the end of November Laird had accepted an expenditure level of $82.7 billion, but even that amount remained too high for OMB, which wanted additional cuts of $4.1 billion to push outlays down to $78.6 billion. Under great pressure, DoD accepted OMB's reductions. As in years past, Moot took the lead in negotiating with White House officials the review of outlays on a line-by-line basis. In discussing the FY 1974 budget with NSC staff at the end of November, Moot stated that he believed the department could protect current force levels in FY 1974 at an estimated spending level of $79 billion by making what he termed minor cuts in intelligence programs and R&D. His conclusion also assumed that Vietnam operations would end in early January and that base closures would produce savings of $800 million, certainly optimistic projections. There was no guarantee in November that the war would end in January 1973 or that base closures would produce immediate, significant savings.[39]

At the 4 December 1972 staff meeting Laird reported his agreement to cut $3 billion from the initial FY 1974 budget estimate of $84 billion, bringing spending down to $81 billion. He seemed unwilling to announce a lower figure at this point but implied that it was a possibility because of the unknown savings that would result from base closures and associated civilian and military reductions, the

FY 1974 costs of the Vietnam War, and the ongoing costs of Enhance Plus, the program to accelerate the shipment of arms and equipment to South Vietnam's armed forces. OSD had not even completed its review of the base closure program. By mid-December DoD submitted the FY 1974 budget proposal to the White House. After this time only the president could make changes before it went to Congress. For planning purposes, that budget cautiously assumed no Vietnam cease-fire in FY 1974 and no changes in force structure. The budget did not include savings from base closures, an issue Nixon had decided to defer. In final discussions with OMB and NSC representatives at the end of December, Moot agreed to set TOA at $85 billion, an increase of $5 billion over FY 1973. He reported, however, that a final figure for outlays had not yet been reached.[40]

President's Budget

On 29 January 1973 Nixon presented his budget to Congress. He boasted that his budget would not require a tax hike or drive prices higher because he had kept a firm hand on excessive spending, "the greatest threat to our new prosperity." Nixon urged Congress to set a "rigid ceiling on spending, limiting total outlays in FY 1974 to $268.7 billion," the figure in his recommended budget. The share of the gross national product for national defense had fallen by 25 percent from 1955 to 1972. Nixon touted the Nixon Doctrine, Vietnamization, reductions in manpower, and the shift to the AVF as important steps in holding down defense expenditures. DoD outlays in FY 1974 "will be substantially the same as in 1968," the president asserted.[41]

Although Nixon had scaled back Laird's spending request of $84 billion, the DoD budget continued its growth of recent years. Defense outlays in the president's budget submission (including money for military assistance) had increased from $74.8 billion in FY 1973 to $79 billion in FY 1974. TOA (including funds for military assistance) had gone up from $79.7 billion in FY 1973 to $85.1 billion in FY 1974.[42] Higher pay and rising prices accounted for most of the increase from the previous fiscal year so that growth in spending allowed no expansion of forces. Estimated outlays for manpower increased by $2.1 billion in FY 1974; operating costs went up by $300 million; RDT&E, procurement, and construction spending grew by $1.8 billion. The president's budget proposal would fund the All-Volunteer Force.[43] Tables 25 and 26 on page 510 show Nixon's budget submission by TOA and by outlays. The TOA figure of $85.1 billion and the outlay figure of $79 billion both represented large increases over FY 1973 (Public Law 92-570). (See chapter 15 for details.)

Table 25. Total Obligational Authority, FY 1974 ($ millions)

By Function	TOA
Military Personnel	22,649
Retired Military	4,706
O&M	22,405
Procurement	18,806
RDT&E	8,555
Military Construction & Other	3,036
Pay Raises	2,885
AVF	150
Retirement Reform	390
Military Assistance	1,684
Offsetting Receipts	(101)
Total	85,165

Source: OMB, *The Budget of the United States Government, Fiscal Year 1974* (Washington, DC: Government Printing Office, 1973), 345.

Table 26. Outlays, FY 1974 ($ millions)

By Function	Outlays
Military Personnel	22,500
Retired Military	4,706
O&M	21,662
Procurement	16,490
RDT&E	8,069
Military Construction & Other	1,684
Pay raises	2,680
AVF	140
Retirement Reform	370
Military Assistance	800
Offsetting Receipts	(101)
Total	79,000

Source: OMB, *Budget of the United States Government, Fiscal Year 1974*, 345.

To help control the rising manpower costs attributable to the AVF and pay raises, the president's budget submission reduced military personnel and trimmed the size of the raises compared with previous years. Headquarters personnel, training, and support functions were sliced to help lower overhead. The budget included funds for modernizing weapons and developing the force structure for the post-Vietnam era. For ground forces specifically, the budget allowed for the purchase of additional M–60 tanks and wire-guided antitank missiles. The Navy would have money for ship modernization, procurement of five nuclear submarines, construction of a nuclear aircraft carrier, development of a strategic submarine-launched cruise missile, and deployment of the F–14 fighter. The Air Force would have funds to purchase additional F–15 fighters and develop the B–1 bomber and the A–X close air support system. The Marine Corps could modernize its air wings with the purchase of the newest versions of the F–4 and the A–4 attack aircraft and the development of the AV–8 Harrier, a vertical takeoff and landing aircraft. The budget request included funds for upgrading air-launched munitions through procurement of guided bombs and missiles.[44]

Nixon's budget submission would provide a nuclear deterrent deemed sufficient by the administration's criteria. The FY 1974 budget allowed completion of the Safeguard ABM site in North Dakota, but resulted in halting construction of the Montana site in accordance with the terms of the SALT agreement of May 1972. Funds for the deployment of the ABM defense of Washington, D.C., were omitted. Over $7 billion in TOA went for strategic forces, providing funding for continued development of the Trident submarine-launched ballistic missile and the B–1 bomber, conversion of ballistic missiles to Minuteman IIIs and Poseidons, development of an SLBM cruise missile, R&D, on-site defense, improvement of early warning detection of incoming ballistic missiles, and upgrading the strategic command and control system through the development of AWACS and satellite communications.[45]

Nixon's FY 1974 budget largely preserved existing force structure but cut military personnel strength for all services from FY 1973 levels. The number of ground force divisions remained unchanged, as did the number of air squadrons and air wings. However, with the removal of older ships from service, there would be fewer ships in the Navy's fleet in all categories of vessels save nuclear attack submarines, which would grow by four, owing in part to an increase in funding for

Undated aerial view of the Stanley Mickelson Safeguard Complex near Grand Forks, North Dakota. (Library of Congress)

development of the Trident. The number of aircraft carriers included both attack and antisubmarine carriers.

In his interactions with OMB and the White House over the FY 1974 budget, Laird looked to the future, striving to maintain outlays at levels he believed were necessary to sustain the president's security program and the strategy of realistic deterrence. Laird failed to get White House support for his strategy and was forced to cut outlays. Given the unsettled domestic economic conditions, the looming budget deficit, and the desire to preserve a relatively balanced budget, money battles naturally emphasized outlays, which had an immediate impact on the budget and the economy, rather than TOA, which had a greater economic effect in future years. Without an adequate level of expenditures in FY 1974, Laird understood it would become that much harder in the future to rebuild the force or modernize it, but he had to back down from his initial spending goals. The starting point for future DoD budgets would begin at a lower level.

Table 27. Active Military Personnel and Forces, FYs 1973–1974

	FY 1973 (est.)	FY 1974 (est.)
End Strength		
Army	825,000	804,000
Navy	574,000	566,000
Marine Corps	197,000	196,000
Air Force	692,000	666,000
Total	2,288,000	2,232,000
Land Forces		
Army Divisions	13	13
Marine Corps Divisions	3	3
Air Forces		
Strategic Squadrons	13	13
Tactical Air Force Wings	21	21
Tactical Navy Wings	14	14
Tactical Marine Corps Wings	3	3
Naval Forces		
Aircraft Carriers	16	15
Nuclear Attack Submarines	60	64
Other Warships	244	191
Amphibious Assault Ships	65	65
Airlift and Sealift		
C–5A Squadrons	4	4
Troop and Cargo Ships, Tankers	63	57

Source: OMB, *Budget of the United States Government, Fiscal Year 1974*, 79.

AT THE START OF THE BUDGET PROCESS, the secretary had been active in laying out the strategic framework for the future defense program. During the FY 1974 budget process Laird continued to battle Kissinger and his staff over the role of the DPRC, a conflict dating from the early days of the administration. From the beginning of his tenure, Laird strongly resisted efforts to give the DPRC broader authority over the shaping of the DoD budget. In November he accepted an $81 billion spending level after an internal scrub, but he never presented to the DPRC the alternative budget that Kissinger wanted, ensuring that Kissinger could not consider alternative budgets. Odeen ruefully concluded that Laird's failure to even consider a second program was an act of noncompliance that spoke clearly of the secretary's ability to sidestep Kissinger.[46]

In the fall of 1972, with just months to serve after Nixon's reelection, Laird largely disengaged from the battle over the FY 1974 budget. He knew that the preparation of Nixon's FY 1974 budget submission, a tense argument about the numbers the president would send to Congress, was only the first act. Supported by the OSD staff, the next secretary would have to defend the defense program before Congress. Given the short period that he would remain in office, in September 1972 Laird focused instead on getting the FY 1973 budget through Congress, the critical, concluding act of the marathon budget process. With his congressional experience and unique political skills he knew he could make a difference in getting the 1973 budget passed. To the end of his tenure, Laird worked hard and successfully to preserve the budget-making prerogatives of his office and leave the future defense program on a sound footing.

CHAPTER 19

Fixing the Fraying Force

AS SECRETARY OF DEFENSE in a time of war and social and cultural upheaval, Melvin Laird faced unusual, multiple challenges. Since the mid-1960s U.S. naval, air, and ground forces in Vietnam had been engaged in fighting an inconclusive conflict that exacted an increasingly hard toll from warfighters, equipment, and supply stocks. Yet Laird contended with more than managing logistics and operations in Vietnam and staving off continual pressure to cut the Defense budget. He especially had to consider the long term to ensure that the U.S. military would remain a cohesive force, well equipped and trained after the war, ready and disciplined.

The Vietnam era witnessed the emergence of largely unexpected problems— notably racial discord, indiscipline, and drug abuse—that threatened to jeopardize the military's ability to perform its mission and fulfill the nation's treaty and alliance commitments. (The problems caused by the existing conscription system and the transition to an all-volunteer force are discussed in chapter 13.) The contrast between the highly trained, professional military units that had confidently entered Vietnam in 1965 and those fighting there in 1970–1971 was a striking development that Army historians particularly found alarming. One official historian, Ronald Spector, observed that five years after the initial deployment "the complex fabric of custom, law, discipline, esprit, and coercion which had held the Army together had disintegrated." Army historian Graham Cosmas discerned "a general deterioration in the professional standards, leadership, discipline, and morale of American forces in Vietnam."[1]

The damaging stresses within U.S. military forces manifested themselves most dramatically in Vietnam. The murder of scores of South Vietnamese civilians by a company of the U.S. American Division during an operation at My Lai hamlet in March 1968, attributable in part to marginally competent leaders, was morally reprehensible in itself. The subsequent cover-up of the crime by division officers was infinitely worse, demonstrating a collapse of military discipline, ethics, and professionalism that reached as high as the division's commander, Maj. Gen. Samuel W. Koster. He was reduced in rank and forced to retire for failing to investigate and report the incident to higher headquarters. The September 1968 riot at the Long Binh Jail, the largest U.S. military stockade in South Vietnam, exposed the racial tensions within the Army. The rioters, most of whom were black, held a number of white guards as hostages. At the start of 1969 U.S. Army and Senate investigations uncovered racketeering and black market activities in the officer and enlisted clubs and post-exchange system of the U.S. Military Assistance Command, Vietnam. Among the indicted was the command sergeant major of the Army, the service's highest ranking noncommissioned officer.[2] The spreading use of illegal drugs in the armed forces, reflecting in part profound social and cultural changes in the United States, became a serious problem not only in Vietnam but elsewhere as well.[3]

Disillusionment with the war contributed in part to the breakdown of discipline in Vietnam. Desertions increased, and in some units soldiers attacked or even killed their commanding officers with fragmentation grenades, the so-called practice of "fragging," a clear manifestation of morale and discipline problems as well as anger against superiors that sometimes involved racial issues or drug abuse. Especially to those draftees who felt alienated from career NCOs and officers, fighting and risking death seemed pointless for a cause many soldiers no longer believed in and for a war from which the United States sought to extricate itself. Many draftees, recent high school graduates from poor or working class backgrounds, served in combat units in Vietnam where they could face hostile fire for their entire 12-month tour. Differing in age and outlook, many draftees and noncareer personnel identified themselves as a separate group, antithetical in values and outlook to the "lifers," a derisive term applied to the officers and enlisted men making the military a career. Many observers commented on the discrepancy that ordinary soldiers perceived between the lofty, optimistic official pronouncements on the war by policymakers and top-level military commanders and the harsh and inescapable reality of the war they actually fought in the villages and rice paddies.[4]

With the end of both the war and the draft in view, Laird focused on preparing U.S. forces for the post-Vietnam era. During Laird's tenure, the department handled difficult and unexpected challenges to military effectiveness that necessitated setting in motion social, cultural, and institutional changes to tackle a growing number of social problems.

Who Fights in Vietnam

In Congress during the mid-1960s, Laird had objected to the way President Lyndon Johnson and Secretary of Defense Robert McNamara conducted the war, arguing for the increased use of air and sea power and a reduced role for U.S. ground forces. Over time, Laird openly opposed the administration's Vietnam policy, condemning it for needlessly wasting lives and treasure in an endeavor that offered no hope of victory.[5] When U.S. troops began deployments to Vietnam in 1965, Johnson had made a decision with long-lasting ramifications for the armed forces, particularly the Army. In July of that year, to avoid stirring up domestic antiwar sentiment, the president chose not to call up the National Guard and reserve components to serve in Vietnam, instead putting the entire burden to train, deploy, and fight the ground war on regular Army and Marine forces. Carried out in phases, the troop buildup of 1965 and 1966 committed virtually all combat-ready Army and Marine Corps units in the United States to the war. Without recourse to mobilize the reserves, the Army had only active-duty units to fight the war in Vietnam and fulfill U.S. treaty and alliance commitments abroad.[6] As secretary of defense, Laird would have to deal with the consequences of Johnson's decision to keep the reserves on the sidelines.

Laird was also burdened by McNamara's cost-efficient management of the war. His predecessor's approach presented serious problems in regards to active-duty armed forces and the strategic reserve, the forces needed to meet treaty commitments in Europe and Asia. To support Vietnam operations, McNamara had pulled manpower from Army units stationed outside the war theater. The seven Army divisions based overseas and not assigned to Vietnam were deliberately kept at 60–70 percent of assigned strength to make manpower and materiel available for Vietnam. As a consequence, personnel turnover rates in these divisions averaged 150–200 percent annually, weakening readiness and unit cohesion. Increased draft calls filled the ranks mostly with recently trained draftees. Personnel turbulence and shortages of trained and specialized personnel lowered combat readiness. Without corrective action, the JCS feared that the Vietnam deployments of 1965 and 1966 would undermine U.S. ability to maintain its force commitment to NATO, counter possible Chinese Communist intervention in Southeast Asia or Korea, and handle a minor emergency. Not a single Army division remaining in the United States, the JCS reported in March 1966, was ready for deployment. Moreover, the Air Force had no deployable tactical fighter or reconnaissance squadrons in Strike Command. The Navy would need additional carriers, air squadrons, warships, and support units to fulfill its war and alliance requirements. During the buildup American military units throughout the world had sent their reserve stocks of equipment and ammunition to units engaged in Vietnam. Laird would have to deal with the consequences of McNamara's policies: hollowed out U.S. forces in Europe that made them less capable in the event of a Warsaw Pact invasion and the deteriorating condition of ground forces in Vietnam.[7]

The problems evident in 1966 grew more severe, and by the spring of 1968, after the Tet offensive in Vietnam and the *Pueblo* incident in North Korean waters, the combat readiness of active divisions in the United States fell even lower. In May, the JCS warned Defense Secretary Clark Clifford of the serious risks owing to decreased readiness and limitations on strategic capability. At this point, nearly all U.S. Army units in Europe were rated as marginal or not combat-ready because of serious equipment shortages and lack of spare parts. The Navy's Atlantic Fleet and the U.S. Air Force in Europe faced similar readiness problems.[8]

From the beginning of his tenure, Laird dealt with the dire consequences of McNamara's war policies. Deteriorating readiness and weakened strategic capability gave clear warning of the physical unraveling of the whole military force from the long, hard war in Vietnam. Added to those complications, Laird's Pentagon also tackled something new: the manifestation of deep cultural and psychological changes that affected morale and readiness. Secretary Laird had to address these challenges to combat effectiveness in order to preserve the armed forces in the present and prepare them for the future.

Drug Abuse

During the early 1960s the public image of the American armed forces remained positive. Rarely were concerns voiced about the character or motivation of those in uniform. By the mid-to-late 1960s, with the Vietnam War becoming less popular and cultural norms becoming more permissive, that image changed drastically. U.S. military commands gradually became aware of drug abuse in the ranks, even if commanders tended to shrug off initial news reports. With the passage of time, however, drug use in the military became impossible to ignore. The use of illegal drugs in civil society and in the armed forces grew in tandem as social changes reached into military ranks.[9]

Although the absence of reliable statistical information made the drug problem hard to measure accurately, it had clearly grown in scope and severity during the Johnson administration. The number of investigations of drug abuse within the armed forces (certainly not a complete measure of total illegal drug use) was a commonly used metric and could be consistently counted over time. The situation in Vietnam drew the most attention and could provide fairly accurate statistics. Investigations of marijuana users in Vietnam increased from 43 in 1965 to over 3,200 in 1968. The Uniform Code of Military Justice (UCMJ) regarded drug offenses as "conduct prejudicial to good order and military discipline" and subject to punishment.[10]

In November 1967 the Department of Defense set up a task force to study the burgeoning problem of illegal drug use in the armed forces. Dividing drugs into three groups: marijuana, narcotics (opiates and cocaine), and dangerous drugs (hallucinogens, depressants, and stimulants), the task force uncovered disquieting trends. Enlisted men, aged 19–24, composed the largest group of marijuana users. Statistics showed an increase in the number of inductees disqualified from military service because of drug abuse, the number of general courts-martial for drug offenses, and the number of administrative discharges for drug abuse. Marijuana use was highest in the United States and Southeast Asia, but dangerous drugs—heroin, cocaine, and hallucinogens—were more prevalent in the United States than overseas. The report ruefully acknowledged that the real incidence of abuse was most likely greater than the statistics indicated.[11]

In response, the secretary of defense approved in February 1968 a department-wide directive for the prevention and elimination of drug abuse, establishing under the assistant secretary for manpower and reserve affairs a program of education and enforcement as well as a DoD drug abuse control committee. The need for the directive was compelling. Military investigative agencies reported "a sharply increasing drug abuse problem in the Armed Services." Over the same period investigations of hard drug usage among the armed forces stationed in the United States had climbed from 1,078 to 1,849.[12]

As a congressman, Laird was certainly aware of official and media reports of illegal drug use in the military. By the time that he became secretary in January 1969, the issue had become a major problem. Routine reports and public testimony by DoD officials made it clear that the drug problem was not confined to Army personnel or to members of the armed forces stationed in Vietnam. In 1969 and 1970 the Navy discharged over 3,800 sailors for illegally using or pushing drugs. Navy Chief of Personnel Vice Adm. Charles K. Duncan ruefully testified before a House committee in April 1970 that drug abuse in the Navy was no higher in Vietnam than it was in Norfolk or San Diego.[13]

Still, MACV Commander General Creighton Abrams seemed not fully aware of the extent and seriousness of the problem. In October 1970 he apologized to Admiral John McCain, the CINCPAC commander, for "suddenly and without prior indication" informing him of a significant number of deaths from drug abuse in his command. The U.S. Army in Vietnam surgeon general had released the information to an investigator for a Senate committee but had not yet shared it with the MACV commander. Alarmed by reports of "very heavy use of drugs by servicemen in Vietnam," President Nixon demanded that Laird tell him what DoD was doing to handle the problem.[14]

Laird's response to the president framed the issue in a larger context that highlighted the correlation between drug abuse in the services and the recruitment of personnel from metropolitan areas where illegal drug usage was growing. The first line of defense was to prevent drug users, suppliers, and addicts from entering the services. To deal with drug abusers already in the ranks, Laird advocated not just disciplinary measures but also a strengthened drug education and prevention program and rehabilitation. To help reach those objectives, Laird informed the president that he had established a task force under Assistant Secretary of Defense (MRA) Roger Kelley to review DoD policy (the 1968 directive).[15]

Seeking a new approach to the drug problem, Kelley reviewed the entire range of discipline, treatment, and rehabilitation issues. He believed that recent research and changing social attitudes made it abundantly clear that the current policy, which concentrated on punitive measures, had proved out of date and inadequate to deal with a growing drug abuse problem among the armed forces, civilian employees, and dependents. Where education and screening failed, drug abusers in the armed forces needed to be dealt with quickly, firmly, and fairly. Significantly,

Kelley's report suggested a new approach that called for reasonable efforts to rehabilitate those who could have a reasonable future in the military. The 1968 DoD policy had not provided for an amnesty program whereby service members with a drug problem could turn themselves in for treatment and rehabilitation. In addition, Kelley concluded that those discharged from the military should also have access to further treatment and rehabilitation. He proposed that revisions to the 1968 DoD directive incorporate these findings. On 18 August Laird approved Kelley's recommendations and authorized him to prepare a new directive.[16]

In giving Kelley a green light, Laird responded not just to the drug problem itself but to increasing public awareness of the problem. Numerous press stories about drug abuse in the military had appeared, and Congress expressed concern about the problem and interest in rehabilitation. The chairman of the Senate Subcommittee to Investigate Juvenile Delinquency, Senator Thomas J. Dodd (D–CT), who aced a tough reelection fight, planned to hold hearings on the problem. Dodd wanted to examine DoD measures to rehabilitate victims of drug abuse, whom he characterized as needing treatment, not punishment. Senator Richard S. Schweiker (R–PA) also suggested that Laird implement a DoD-wide rehabilitation program.[17]

The notion of rehabilitation also gained momentum within the military. On its own initiative, the Army was already testing this approach, having set up amnesty programs in 1970 at several installations, including Fort Bragg, North Carolina, at the behest of base commanders. Believing that the drug problem reduced military effectiveness, the 4th and 25th Infantry Divisions in Vietnam had adopted non-punitive amnesty programs to help drug users overcome addiction. The new DoD drug directive then being drafted would help preempt Dodd's investigation and defuse possible Senate criticism.[18]

Promulgated on 23 October 1970, the revised directive on the "Illegal or Improper Use of Drugs" covered all DoD components. The new policy aimed "to prevent and eliminate drug abuse within the armed forces and to attempt to restore members so involved to useful service." Abuse was defined as "the illegal, wrongful or improper use of any narcotic substance, marijuana, or dangerous drug, or the illegal or wrongful possession, transfer, or sale of the same." Proscribed drugs included marijuana, opiates, cocaine, LSD, and other hallucinogens. The directive sought to distinguish between the experimenter, the user, and the addict, and applied different administrative and disciplinary measures accordingly. It further encouraged military services "to develop programs and facilities to restore and rehabilitate members who are drug users or drug addicts when such members desire and are willing to undergo such restoration." The services also received authority to establish amnesty programs on a trial basis, including medical assistance and suspension of action under the UCMJ against users sincerely seeking rehabilitation or voluntarily admitting to drug abuse.[19]

By the time DoD issued the 1970 directive there could be no denying the gravity and scope of the drug problem in the armed forces. The MACV surgeon general informed Alexander Haig during his visit to Vietnam in December 1970 that half of the U.S. troops arriving in Vietnam by 1970 had some association with drugs before reaching the war theater. The use of heroin was on the increase for several reasons: low prices, easy availability, and the purity and potency of the drug sold in South Vietnam. An NBC television news report of 24 January 1971 showing U.S. soldiers "purchasing heroin openly from a South Vietnamese" and reports of deaths among heroin users in MACV prompted Laird to request that JCS Chairman Admiral Thomas Moorer take a closer look at the allegations. Vietnam was only part of the problem. Military usage of hard narcotics, marijuana, and dangerous drugs had increased worldwide. Lt. Gen. Robert C. Taber, principal deputy for MRA, reported to Laird that hashish and marijuana were the preferred drugs for the U.S. military stationed in Germany, with U.S. service personnel consuming an estimated 80 percent of the hashish on the market.[20]

Increasing drug abuse in the military spilled over into domestic politics. Then-Georgia Governor Jimmy Carter, for one, worried about the effect of the drug problem in view of his state's large military population and the financial and social costs of dealing with addicted servicemen returning home from Vietnam. He wanted more information on the military drug problem. As the nation's top law enforcement official, Attorney General John Mitchell also had deep concerns about the considerable numbers of addicted Vietnam veterans. A member of Nixon's inner circle, Egil Krogh Jr., deputy presidential assistant for domestic affairs, deemed the problem so serious that it required a solution at the highest levels of government. In April 1971 he proposed to John Ehrlichman, his boss, the formation of an inter-agency White House working group composed of cabinet members.[21]

The president directed that an interagency group develop a drug prevention program by early June. Nixon sought to emphasize that the problem was national in scope and not limited to the armed forces in Vietnam. Kelley alerted Laird on DoD's role in this new program. Before publicly announcing his program, Nixon directed Laird to take immediate action to deal with heroin addiction in Vietnam, requiring identification and detoxification treatment of addicts prior to their return to the United States, and referral to the Veterans Administration of military personnel scheduled to be discharged who had refused treatment.[22]

Meanwhile, the department continued to refine its programs. Vietnam returnees were to undergo urine testing for detection. As Kelley noted, the burden for treating users fell disproportionately on DoD, because it had more facilities than the Veterans Administration. He believed the typical heroin user in Vietnam required different treatment from that of a mainlining drug addict in the United States, asserting somewhat optimistically that users in Vietnam took drugs out of boredom and because they were readily available and cheap.[23]

In June 1971 Nixon unveiled his comprehensive policy, calling drug abuse "America's public enemy number one." Rehabilitation of drug addicts had become top priority. He sought $155 million in new funding for enforcement and treatment programs, and ordered immediate testing procedures and rehabilitation efforts to begin in Vietnam. He directed DoD to provide rehabilitation programs to all service personnel returning home for discharge desiring help. "All of our servicemen must be accorded the right to rehabilitation," the president declared in a dramatic shift from earlier policies.[24]

Given the gravity of the drug problem, Nixon decided the White House would handle the government's efforts. To that end, he appointed as special consultant to the president for narcotics and dangerous drugs Dr. Jerome H. Jaffe, who would report directly to him and have the responsibility of coordinating the work of all government agencies dealing with drug rehabilitation. Nixon established the office by executive order, considering it an emergency response to a national problem. He selected Jaffe, fully aware that he was "controversial," "blunt," and "abrasive." "He is going to knock heads together. . . . He will have the total backing of the White House and our total interest," the president said.[25]

On the day that Nixon announced his drug policy to Congress, Laird requested that the military services and the JCS develop plans to address specifically "heroin use among members of the armed forces in Vietnam," stressing that more needed to be done immediately. The plans required the identification within seven days of servicemen who were using or were dependent on narcotics. The men would be enrolled in a 5-to-7-day detoxification treatment program before returning to the United States. Personnel nearing the end of their terms who desired treatment would have the opportunity for a minimum 30-day treatment in military facilities in the United States when Veterans Administration or civilian programs were unavailable. Those with service time remaining were to be treated in military programs in the United States "and afforded the opportunity for rehabilitation." The aim was to focus first on drug-dependent servicemen departing from Vietnam and then expand drug-treatment programs to all of Southeast Asia and later worldwide. With no additional funding expected, DoD would have to provide personnel, resources, funds, and logistical support from available sources. The DoD program represented the first attempt at large-scale government drug testing.[26]

Although in May 1972 Nixon credited Laird for creating an effective program to detect and deter drug abuse, no one expected the drug problem to go away. Over the years, the DoD testing regimen would be refined but continue without interruption, an acknowledgment of the reality of continuing widespread drug abuse. All knew it would require long-term vigilance and regular testing to identify and rehabilitate users. The DoD and Nixon drug policy reforms represented only the initial attempts to deal with what would prove to be a serious, persistent societal problem that defied easy answers.

Racial Discord

Despite outbreaks of violent and destructive racial disturbances in major U.S. cities—Philadelphia, Los Angeles, Newark, and Detroit—from 1964 to 1968, and especially after the assassination of Martin Luther King, U.S. armed forces seemed for a time largely unaffected by the racial strife.[27] *Time Magazine* reported in May 1967 that it saw few manifestations of racial trouble among troops in Vietnam. In the spring of 1968 General Abrams, then the deputy U.S. commander in Vietnam, described racial problems within MACV as negligible. That was not the view of L. Howard Bennett, a DoD civil rights official visiting Vietnam in the fall of 1968, who warned that black-white tensions were near the breaking point, a finding some top-level officials dismissed as alarmist. Bennett found little evidence of unrest in combat areas, where common dangers united black and white soldiers. However, troubled relations resided in rear areas, where blacks complained that the military

President Nixon meets with Special Assistant for Civil Rights Robert Brown whose concern about troubled race relations in the military was a catalyst for policy changers, undated. (Nixon Presidential Library)

justice system was biased against them and that the chain of command was deaf to their grievances about promotions, military justice, and unequal treatment. As one black enlisted soldier serving at a base camp at Cu Chi northwest of Saigon noted, after the Tet offensive of 1968 "you could feel the racial tension begin to tighten." In his view, the assassination of Martin Luther King in April that year had a significant impact on the attitudes of black soldiers. He was not surprised when "there was a full-scale race riot at Cu Chi."[28]

Another indication of problems in race relations came in early March 1969. Robert J. Brown, Nixon's special assistant for civil rights, sent the president a memorandum on the status of minorities, primarily blacks, in the armed forces, warning that minority newspapers had voiced concern about the uneasy relationship between the military and minority groups. He feared that the Vietnam War would "divert funds, and perhaps attention, from the problems experienced by members of minority groups and the disadvantaged." The complaints centered on two allegations: that blacks and other minorities in the military were frequently not treated equally, and that minority groups incurred a disproportionate share of combat duty, fatalities, and injuries. Links between black militants and the antiwar movement at home, he predicted, would likely mean that racial unrest "will continue to grow" in the military, so he advised DoD to form a special panel to deal with the issue.[29]

Nixon's chief domestic adviser, John Ehrlichman, opposed the idea, suggesting instead that Laird issue public statements supporting the principle of equal treatment of all minority groups in the military and also include prominent blacks on the panel studying the draft. At the time Nixon expressed no interest in convening a special body, believing it would duplicate the ongoing study of conscription and possibly interfere with the work of the DoD inspector general in examining racial complaints.[30] Unwilling to drop the matter, the persistent Brown sent Ehrlichman a second memorandum in August asking him to reconsider setting up a panel because racial difficulties were now "a serious reality" on military bases. His warning about coming racial strife proved prescient.[31]

In May 1969 Laird issued to all military personnel a public statement on equal opportunity and treatment in the armed forces. It reflected proudly and almost complacently on the integration of the armed forces following President Truman's executive order ending segregation, but it sounded no alarms about difficulties ahead: "No sector in American life has achieved the measure of equal opportunity and treatment that has been realized in the Armed Forces." Laird stated his commitment to removing "every vestige of discrimination," according equal opportunity and treatment to all, regardless of color, religion, national origin, or other irrelevant factor. Equal opportunity applied to training, education, assignment, promotion, and the chance to reach the highest leadership positions. It soon became clear that DoD had to do more in the area of race relations than issue proclamations.[32]

In July 1969 an outbreak of violence at Camp Lejeune, North Carolina, between white and black Marines led to the death of a white corporal. Racial assaults occurred about four times a week on the base. At Fort Bragg, North Carolina, in August, 25 soldiers were hospitalized after a clash involving 200 black and white troops. Flare-ups were reported on other Army, Navy, and Marine Corps installations at home. In Vietnam, racial incidents requiring the intervention of Military Police to restore order and discipline took place at Saigon, Danang, and elsewhere. No longer could DoD ignore the existence and severity of racial strife. After a second visit to Vietnam, Bennett concluded that unless the armed forces found ways to improve communications and relations between whites and blacks the likelihood of additional clashes would grow. White officers, he believed,

Laird, flanked by service chiefs and the chairman of JCS, announces DoD's Human Goals campaign. Left to right: General Robert Cushman, USMC commandant; Admiral Thomas Moorer, CNO; General Earle Wheeler, JCS chairman; General William Westmoreland, Army chief of staff; and General John Ryan, Air Force chief of staff, undated. (OSD Historical Office)

were insensitive and lacked understanding and knowledge of the current mood of black servicemen.[33]

Advising Laird that something stronger than another exhortation was needed, Kelley suggested that DoD issue a charter, a guarantee of rights, that would have far greater import than another memorandum. Laird agreed and in August issued a sweeping DoD charter on Human Goals pledging to make the department "a model of equal opportunity for all regardless of race or creed or national origin." His underlying goal was pragmatic—the nation needed a cohesive, well-trained force. The charter stated, "To provide such a force we must increase the attractiveness of a career in Defense," allowing everyone in uniform and every civilian to take great pride in themselves and their work. The charter would be republished annually. Signed by the Pentagon's top military and civilian leaders and displayed prominently in defense installations around the world, it was also reproduced on the back cover of Laird's annual reports to Congress. The charter was not intended to be panacea or a public relations gimmick, but a set of objectives against which DoD efforts could be evaluated.[34]

Secretary Laird demonstrated unwavering commitment to the charter's principles. In January 1970 he had Bennett brief the Armed Forces Policy Council on racial issues. Bennett acknowledged the progress that had occurred: More black officers received promotions to higher ranks in all services; more enlisted blacks had reached mid-level management positions; and more blacks were enrolled in the three service academies. The perceptions of blacks, Bennett observed, had changed. They now manifested a new-found racial pride derived from the civil rights movement and growing confidence that they had the means to improve their situation. Yet he found a worrisome difference in outlooks on the part of blacks and whites, high officials, and rank and file. Although Laird and Bennett could legitimately refer to DoD's progress over the years in racial relations, many people entering the service were simply unaware of or indifferent to past gains, yet conscious of continuing discrimination in the present. Bennett found growing black-white tensions during his visits to Vietnam and Thailand, residual racial discrimination, and racism on the part of both blacks and whites. As he noted, "The Armed Forces mirror and reflect the patterns of Black-white relationships that exist in the nation's civilian community." The two most common complaints again pointed to discrimination in promotions and assignments and a sense that the administration of military justice was unfair to blacks.[35] Bennett averred that the armed forces were integrated only on the surface; on a functional or operational level, "we have not yet achieved . . . fraternal and spiritual integration." To him this was the ultimate goal and Laird agreed, reiterating DoD's goal "to make military service a model of equal opportunity."[36]

Equal opportunity and antidiscrimination involved more than the armed forces. Equal Employment Opportunity (EEO) regulations and the Human Goals Charter applied to contracts for acquiring weapons and materiel. Throughout 1968 the three largest suppliers of textiles to DoD (J. P. Stevens Mills, Dan River Mills, and Burlington Industries) had failed to submit acceptable affirmative action plans on minority hiring as required by law. In February 1969 the three companies were formally cited for not complying with EEO regulations. If these firms remained noncompliant, DoD would refuse to do business with them, a move that would create a major supply disruption of fabric for service uniforms. No satisfactory alternative manufacturers could meet DoD's requirements for textiles. Without uninterrupted production by these three companies, supply failures would be inevitable. Considering the problem serious, the head of the Defense Supply Agency, Lt. Gen. Earl C. Hedlund, urged Laird to take immediate steps to pressure the companies to comply with the regulations.[37]

Laird called on his deputy, David Packard, the former CEO of Hewlett-Packard, to handle the EEO issue, over which the government and the companies had been deadlocked since August 1968. Based on his experience in running his own company and setting up EEO programs, Packard saw the need for new affirmative action programs to reach EEO goals. At the end of March 1969, he and Burlington Industries chairman Charles F. Myers Jr. announced a new agreement for a revised affirmative action plan "to ensure that job recruitment, hiring, placement and promotion occur without discrimination because of race or sex." Significantly, the agreement also included new reporting procedures to monitor compliance and was followed by agreements with other textile firms. Two years after reaching the agreement, DoD reported substantial increases in minority employment in plants operated by Burlington Industries, Dan River Mills, J. P. Stevens Mills, Fieldcrest Mills, and Spring Mills. From 1968 to 1971 the total minority workforce at these firms, mostly blacks, increased by more than 10,000, a jump of 48.3 percent.[38]

At the time of the Burlington settlement, Packard sent a memorandum to Kelley requesting a fresh examination of DoD's record on minority hiring. Noting that he was involved in this issue with government contractors, Packard thought it important to ensure that the department also had an effective affirmative action plan. Fully supporting Packard, Laird made it policy to extend the principles of affirmative action to ensure equal opportunity for all civilian DoD employees in recruitment, career development, promotions, training, selection for supervision, awards, and other forms of recognition.[39]

The Pentagon's efforts at affirmative action constituted a noteworthy part of an administration-wide program. Nixon appointed George Shultz, an advocate of using federal guidelines to advance the hiring of minorities and women, as his secretary of labor. He helped revive and then expand the Philadelphia Plan, which required federal contractors in the construction industry to hire minority workers, to nine additional cities. President Nixon's executive order of 8 August 1969 broadened the government's reach, making it U.S. policy to provide equal opportunity for federal civilian employment and requiring each agency and department to establish affirmative action programs. The policy covered all government contractors. The Labor Department's Office of Contract Compliance issued an order on affirmative action programs dated 30 January 1970 that applied to all government contractors or subcontractors with 50 or more employees and a contract of $50,000 or higher. These programs specified the procedures that bound contractors to provide equal employment opportunity. Contractors were also required to develop written affirmative action compliance programs that included analysis of deficiencies in using minorities and corrected goals and timetables. Laird fully embraced the president's initiative, admonishing the military departments and defense agencies involved with contracts to embrace the "moral intent of equal opportunity" as well as administrative and procedural steps "to insure full compliance" with the legal provisions.[40]

Laird did more than issue policy guidance. He thrust himself into the middle of an affirmative action contract dispute with McDonnell-Douglas, the contractor for the F–15 and its electronics. Late in January 1970, just after the firm was awarded the contract, Rev. Theodore M. Hesburgh, president of the University of Notre Dame and chairman of the U.S. Civil Rights Commission, informed Laird that DoD's contract compliance office had failed to conduct the required compliance review of the McDonnell Douglas Corporation's equal employment opportunity practices before signing the F–15 contract, which contained an equal employment opportunity clause. In February Laird personally directed Air Force Secretary Seamans to travel immediately from Puerto Rico, where he was attending a commanders' conference at an Air Force installation, to St. Louis, where McDonnell Douglas manufactured the aircraft. He was to make sure that the appropriate affirmative action compliance clause was added to the contract by the end of the day. Otherwise, Laird would ask the Air Force to rebid the jet fighter contract.[41]

Laird's intervention had the desired impact. When Seamans arrived, he found that the company had not submitted a compliance program for approval, a matter that seemed to surprise DoD and McDonnell Douglas upper management. The company agreed to amend the contract. DoD and the Labor Department reached agreement on an affirmative action program with McDonnell Douglas. With assistance from Labor, the company prepared a new EEO program that applied to all of the firm's work, not merely the F–15. McDonnell Douglas pledged to take "vigorous new action to insure equal opportunity in recruiting, hiring, training, transfer, and upgrading of all personnel." It "established targets for hiring or upgrading minority-group persons under certain job categories, including technical, professional, supervisory, and management positions."[42]

At roughly the same time as the McDonnell Douglas incident, Laird concluded that improved education and communications remained critical to improving race relations. He directed the services to establish the Inter-Service Task Force on Education in Race Relations, which required each service to report on its efforts to ameliorate race relations. Acting Air Force Secretary John L. McLucas reported that his service had already established a number of boards and councils and had appointed equal opportunity officers at major commands and many bases to provide dialogue on race relations. He referred to the Air Force Equal Opportunity Policy Review Committee set up at the Air Staff level to monitor all aspects of race relations. Navy Secretary John Chafee cited a SecNav instruction that "encourages commanders to establish bi-racial command-community relations committees" to work for equal treatment and racial harmony. Army Secretary Stanley Resor, who provided a more complete and frank response, admitted that "the state of race relations in the Army gives cause for concern" and laid out a detailed program for providing better opportunities and better communication as ways to ameliorate the situation.[43]

Given the responses to Laird's initiative, Assistant Secretary for Administration Robert Froehlke remained skeptical of achieving full compliance or meaningful improvements in training and promotion opportunities without continued support and active participation from the top echelons of OSD. Kelley indicated to Laird that OSD itself needed to set a better example. Minorities were seriously underrepresented at the higher levels of DoD, comprising 11.3 percent of total DoD civilian employment but just 4.5 percent of grades GS-12 to GS-15 and 0.6 percent of grades GS-16 to GS-18. Laird agreed and urged Kelley to do more to improve equal employment opportunity throughout DoD.[44]

Official proclamations, regulations, and programs to improve communications regarding racial issues were necessary but hardly sufficient. Follow-through to ensure compliance remained critical, and as Froehlke and Kelley had advised it was often inadequate. Roy Wilkins, chairman of the Leadership Conference on Civil Rights, met with Laird in August 1970 to discuss compliance matters. Wilkins headed a delegation that raised questions about contract compliance, DoD's employment practices, and discrimination in off-base housing, a major issue. Because no military installation could offer on-base housing for everyone assigned to the post, most service personnel had to rent living quarters on the civilian market. Off-base housing policy expressly forbade discrimination by landlords, who were required to sign a pledge that they would not discriminate against blacks or other minorities. As Wilkins stressed, required written assurances provided no guarantee of compliance. Some landlords signed the statement of nondiscrimination but then refused to rent to black service members. Wilkins thought that DoD policy should require base commanders to verify compliance by landlords, cooperate with local civil rights and fair housing groups to help ensure compliance with fair housing laws, and meet with black personnel to explain their rights and hear complaints. Wilkins also urged that a contractor's affirmative action plans be made public and a company's compliance evaluated.[45]

Laird acknowledged the need to better enforce compliance with fair housing laws, but he informed Wilkins that current policy relied on local military personnel to report instances of housing discrimination up the chain of command to DoD for enforcement. Local officials gathered evidence, but they were not authorized to take steps to compel landlords to comply and could not impose sanctions. When it had proof of discrimination, DoD could impose sanctions and forbid service personnel from signing leases or rental agreements with landlords. Laird understood the issue Wilkins raised, but existing policy limited his options.[46]

In the fall of 1970 a joint DoD military services team under Deputy Assistant Secretary of Defense for Equal Opportunity Frank W. Render II visited Air Force, Navy, and Army installations in Western Europe to assess the effectiveness of current DoD programs and policies related to equal opportunity and make recommendations to Secretary Laird, who had recently appointed Render, a black, to the post. The team focused on "the black minority as representative of minority problems." In planning for the trip, the group thought it understood the range of issues that created racial tension, but on arrival members discovered an unanticipated "level of frustration and anger among blacks." In some meetings with military personnel dialogue proved impossible because of the total alienation of some individuals. "They had given up on . . . the establishment of the Armed Forces and the system that represents the American way of life," the report concluded. Some blacks in uniform expressed a desire to return to the United States so they could fight to "free their black sisters and brothers" from the ghettos, racial bigotry, and

Assistant Secretary of Defense for Manpower and Reserve Affairs Roger Kelley on 4 June 1970 introduces Frank Render, the nominee for deputy ASD for manpower and reserve affairs for civil rights, to Laird. Kelley took the lead in developing policies to improve race relations in the armed services; Render submitted an influential report on race relations in the military. (OSD Historical Office)

oppression. Render attributed part of the responsibility for the anger and alienation on the failure of command leadership to exercise its authority in dealing with racial problems. According to his report, some racial incidents had occurred to the surprise of commanders, who naively wondered how such things could happen in their commands. Render recommended improved programs of race relations and education among other things. Kelley endorsed the report and sent it to Laird.[47]

Laird's meeting with Wilkins and other civil rights leaders and Render's report directly influenced the secretary. On 14 December 1970, about one month after Render made his recommendations, the department issued DoD Directive 1100.15 on equal opportunity. Representing a major change in race relations in DoD, the directive contained two new significant policies. First, it established leadership in operating a successful equal opportunity program as a criterion for evaluating the promotion of military and civilian officials. The directive imposed sanctions against officials failing to produce satisfactory results. Equal opportunity provisions pertaining to race, color, sex, religion, and national origin applied to military, civilians, dependents, and contractors. Second, numerical goals and timetables in hiring, placing, and promoting civilian employees were to be established to ensure equal opportunity for minorities and women. The service secretaries and directors of the principal DoD agencies were to be held accountable for results. Moreover, in a major policy change commanders worldwide received the authority to impose sanctions on property owners who discriminated against minorities, addressing Wilkins' criticism of how DoD executed its policy of nondiscrimination in housing. Instead of simply reporting the problems in off-base housing to higher headquarters, local commanders were empowered to take corrective action against landlords who discriminated overseas or in the United States. They also had the authority to place clubs and restaurants off limits to all service members. The 1970 directive gave teeth to Laird's goal of making DoD a model of equal opportunity.[48]

As an outgrowth of Laird's emphasis on improving race relations within DOD and in keeping with his Human Goals program of 1969, DoD set up a new organization in June 1971 to provide formal training in race relations for all members of the armed forces. To train instructors in race relations, the department established the Defense Race Relations Institute at Patrick Air Force Base in Florida. The Air Force provided the operating funds. Composed of military officers, enlisted personnel, and civilians from the Army, Navy, and Air Force, the institute began its first class in October 1971. In the years following, thousands of students received training in equal opportunity and race relations. At that time no other public or private institution had embarked on such a far-reaching step to promote racial understanding. In a significant change, the institute was later renamed the Defense Equal Opportunities Management Training Institute to reflect it broader mission after gender issues were incorporated into the curriculum.[49]

Laird took up the fairness question of the administration of military justice, which had long bothered civil rights groups, the Congressional Black Caucus, and minority service members. President Nixon also hoped for a better understanding of the issue. Accordingly, in January 1972 Laird asked Kelley to establish a task force of military and nongovernmental legal personnel, including minorities, to identify the scope of racial discrimination in the administration of military justice, the reasons for the disparity in punishment rates "between racially iden-tifiable groups," and "the impact of racially related patterns or practices" adversely affecting the equitable administration of military justice. He authorized the task force in April 1972 to make recommendations that would remedy deficiencies and "enhance the opportunity for equal justice for every American serviceman and servicewoman." The task force represented another step by Laird toward institu-tionalizing the principle of equal opportunity and equal treatment within DoD. In September he urged the military secretaries to make institutionalizing equal opportunity programs "a priority management function."[50]

The task force, co-chaired by Lt. Gen. Claire E. Hutchin, commanding gen-eral of the First U.S. Army, and Nathaniel Jones, general counsel of the NAACP (National Association for the Advancement of Colored People), issued its report on 30 November 1972. General Hutchin noted the need to make changes to ease the path to the All-Volunteer Force. Among the panel's recommendations were improvements in educational opportunities for all minorities, establishment of an equal opportunity official at the assistant secretary of defense level, and numerous procedural changes to the military justice system, especially in regard to nonjudicial punishment (NJP)—minor infractions handled by a commanding officer rather than the military court system. The goal was to eliminate command influence in the judicial process, a change that Jones asserted could be accomplished without compromising command authority or military discipline. The judge advocates general of the military services filed minority reports, alleging that changes to the NJP regulations risked weakening military discipline. Summarizing the report for Admiral Moorer, Col. Robert Lucy, a JSC staff officer, observed that the military judicial system had to take into account the unique problems of maintaining order and discipline wherever U.S. forces were stationed. Preserving flexibility in admin-istering NJP was a critical element to be preserved. As Laird noted, it would take time to make changes that satisfied critics and the services.[51]

Knowing that it was the right thing to do and would send a clear message that DoD was serious about equal opportunity, Laird ensured that black officers were promoted to flag rank. He would take no action on the promotion lists given to him until qualified blacks were included. In April 1971 Laird stressed to Nixon the need to promote black officers to flag rank and stated that he would send the president a list of qualified black officers. Nixon supported Laird because he wanted a good representation of American society at all ranks of the military. Before the Nixon administration, only two blacks held the rank of general. By mid-1970, the Army had three black generals; the Air Force Reserve and the Army Reserve, one each. Since most Army generals were assigned to office jobs, only a select few ever commanded a division. It was therefore significant when Laird approved the appointment of the first black Army division commander—Maj. Gen. Frederic E. Ellis who became the 8th Division commander in April 1972. Laird pushed the career of Daniel Chappie James Jr., the first black Air Force general. Laird so valued James' abilities that he endorsed his promotion to a second and then a third star. Even after Laird left DoD he continued to be an advocate for James, helping persuade President Gerald Ford to promote him to four-star general in the U.S. military. Laird had to lean on the Navy, the most tradition-bound service and the service with the fewest number of blacks eligible for flag rank. The Navy promoted Capt. Samuel L. Gravely Jr., the first black to command a warship, to the rank of rear admiral in June 1971.[52]

Laird's tenure was marked by serious efforts to overcome discrimination and promote equal opportunity. He believed that issuing directives on affirmative action and equal opportunity, establishing organizations to provide equal treatment, and educating personnel on race relations would not only promote fairness but also help remedy shortcomings in policy and compliance. The secretary believed in the justice of these measures for the present and as essential steps to prepare the armed forces for the future. Without better race relations and the reality of equal opportunity for all, Laird knew he could not attain his goal of a viable all-volunteer force. By addressing the serious racial divisions in the military, as he had done in the Human Goals Charter, Laird could hope to build the armed forces of the future.

New Opportunities for Women

Women had a long but unequal association with the armed forces, over the years gaining greater recognition and responsibility. During Laird's tenure, a period of continuing growth of the feminist movement, women in the military achieved notable gains. He recognized that women would need to play a prominent role in an all-volunteer force. Moreover, to attract women to military service the opportunities for promotion and meaningful careers had to expand.

Although women had joined the Army surreptitiously during the American Revolution and the Civil War, supporting the military as civilian cooks, laundresses, and nurses, none had served as official members of the military until the first decade of the twentieth century. The Army Nurse Corps (Female) was established in 1901 as part of the Army Medical Department of the Regular Army; and the Navy Nurse Corps, in 1907. At that time nurses held "relative rank," the equivalent of the military pay grade of a lieutenant, captain, or major, but did not receive commissions as officers and lacked most of the privileges of officers. During World War I, the Navy recruited about 13,000 women for active duty to fill clerical jobs, but after the war disbanded the group. The Army had authority to enlist women during the war but chose to hire nearly 36,000 women under contract, mostly as typists and telephone operators, fields that women dominated. After the war, the Army staff circulated proposals to establish a permanent women's Army corps, but those papers "were filed and forgotten," according to the official historian of women serving in the Army. With the approach of World War II and the potential shortage of males to fully staff the armed services, the notion of calling on women and setting up a formal women's military organization received renewed attention. In 1942 the Women's Army Auxiliary Corps (WAAC) was established. Its name was later changed to the Women's Army Corps, or WAC. During World War II, women served in the Army and in the Army Air Forces, the precursor of the Air Force, at home and abroad. The Navy obtained authority from Congress to enlist and appoint females to the women's sections of the Navy, Marine Corps, and Coast Guard Reserves. The sea services then established components for women during the war and called reservists to active duty. These women received the pay and benefits of regulars but were restricted to noncombatant duties ashore in the continental United States.[53]

After World War II, women continued to gain increased status in the military. The Women's Armed Services Integration Act of 1948 bestowed regular and reserve status on women serving in all services, including the newly formed Air Force. Under the act, women would not be restricted to membership in the reserves. While the new law made females an integral part of the defense establishment, it did not give them equal status with men; promotions were capped at the grade of lieutenant colonel for the Army and Air Force and commander for the Navy. Restricted to noncombat duties, women could exercise command authority only over members of their sex. Moreover, the size of the female component of each service was limited to 2 percent of the enlisted strength of that service. In August 1951 women gained representation at the DoD level when Secretary of Defense George C. Marshall established the Defense Advisory Committee on Women in the Services (DACOWITS), comprising fifty female civilian leaders to provide advice on issues affecting military and civilian women. DACOWITS, which reported to Assistant Secretary of Defense for Manpower and Personnel Anna M. Rosenberg, helped her develop policies and standards for women in recruiting, utilization, housing, education, and recreation.[54]

During the Vietnam War, the role and numbers of women in the military expanded. Between 1966 and 1969 the WAC was scheduled to increase by more than 3,500; the WAVES (Women Accepted for Volunteer Emergency Service), by 1,100; women Marines, by 900; and the Women in the Air Force (WAF), by over 3,200. The Army Nurse Corps assigned female nurses to serve in military hospitals in Vietnam and to help organize and train South Vietnam's Women's Armed Forces Corps. In November 1967 President Johnson signed significant legislation eliminating the ceiling on women's rank and the 2 percent limitation for each service. In 1969 the "Army 75 Personnel Concept Study" argued for the expansion of women's role in the Army, demonstrating that traditional views were changing. These steps had little immediate follow-through. Maj. Gen. Jeanne M. Holm, the first female Air Force general (promoted in June 1971), complained that Secretaries McNamara and Clifford failed to take advantage of the legislative changes and did not do enough to promote the cause of women in the military. Holm contended that women were still treated as a separate but not equal category in DoD, just as in the larger society. When Laird arrived at the Pentagon, she noted improvements.[55]

Laird also complained about the absence of women in the honor guards and bands at the public ceremonies where he presided. Including women in these units represented a small but symbolically important step. Of greater significance was promoting females to flag rank, making it unmistakable to all that women would no longer be held back at the level of field grade officer. Getting the services to advance women to flag rank proved a challenge for Laird, since each service compiled its own list of candidates for promotion, ran its own promotion boards, and selected persons for promotion according to its own procedures and regulations. The secretary, the president, and then Congress each reviewed and approved the lists of each service.

Laird poses in January 1973 with some of the women who achieved flag rank while he was secretary. Left to right: retired Army Brig. Gen. Anna Hays, former chief of the Army Nurse Corps; Army Col. Bettie Morden, author of the official history of the Women's Army Corps; Air Force Brig. Gen. Jeanne Holm, director of the WAF; Army Brig. Gen. Mildred Bailey, director of the WAC; retired Army Brig. Gen. Elizabeth Hoisington, former director of the WAC; Brig. Gen. E. Ann Hoefly, chief of the Air Force Nurse Corps, and Rear Adm. Alene Duerk, chief of the Navy Nurse Corps. (OSD Historical Office)

Usually the civilian leadership endorsed the lists presented to them, but Laird took a more active role, refusing at times to accept a promotion list until a woman's name was added. The first service to raise women to the rank of general, the Army selected Col. Anna M. Hays, chief of the Army Nurse Corps, and Col. Elizabeth P. Hoisington, the WAC director, for promotion to brigadier general in April 1970. After confirmation by the Senate, the two women were promoted on 11 June.[56]

In 1972 the Navy promoted its first woman to flag rank. Admiral Elmo Zumwalt, the chief of naval operations, a pioneer in helping reshape the traditional culture of his service, defended the Navy, claiming in his memoir that bureaucratic disagreements with Laird had delayed Navy reforms and that in any event Nixon was lukewarm about the women's movement. For his part, Laird repeatedly pressured Navy Secretary John W. Warner to include women on promotion lists and returned any list without a woman nominee to the Navy secretary as incomplete. In public speeches, Laird proclaimed that he intended to appoint a female admiral before he left office. To the president, Laird stated his objections to the Navy's discrimination against women. In effect, he forced the Navy's hand and obtained the desired result. The Navy nominated Capt. Alene B. Duerk, chief of the Navy Nurse Corps, to the rank of rear admiral. She was promoted to that rank on 1 June 1972.[57]

After the initial round of promotions, the pace of change quickened. By the time Laird left office, the Navy was sending women to sea on warships, and the Air Force had placed a woman in command of a unit composed of men and women. Seven women had become admirals or generals. In August 1972 Army Secretary Froehlke announced that the WAC would expand in FY 1973 and then double in size by the end of FY 1978. Training facilities at the WAC Center at Fort McClellan, Alabama, would also be expanded. Enlisted women would henceforth receive Advanced Individual Training alongside men at Army training centers and service schools. WAC officers would attend advanced courses within other Army branches. In addition, more military occupational specialties (MOS) were opened to women. However, females could not be assigned to the 48 combat-related MOS categories.[58]

As the movement for equal treatment of women grew in strength and prominence in the late 1960s, so too did the role and stature of women in the civil service. In April 1971 President Nixon directed the heads of all departments and agencies to develop and put into action plans to increase the number of women serving in his administration at the top levels (GS-16 up through presidential appointees) by the end of the calendar year. Plans also specified the inclusion of greater numbers of women at mid-level positions (GS-13 to GS-15) and greater representation of women on advisory boards and commissions. The president wanted the plans submitted by mid-May. Stressing a firm commitment to women's rights, Nixon declared, "We must now clearly demonstrate our recognition of the equality of women by making greater use of their skills in high level positions."[59]

Laird developed a DoD plan setting objectives to attract more civilian women to appointive positions (GS-16 and above), more in mid-level positions, and more as appointees on advisory boards and committees. In June 1971 he informed the president of his intention to establish "aggressive, affirmative action programs," specifically including women in federal service. He prescribed for DoD components minimum requirements to make greater use of women in high-level positions and appointed his special assistant, Carl S. Wallace, to coordinate the project. Laird's efforts to enhance the position of women in the military established a firm foundation for more sweeping changes in the future.[60]

EVEN BEFORE THE WAR ENDED with South Vietnam's defeat in 1975, America's involvement had left a troubling legacy for the U.S. military, whose health by 1970 was certainly of growing concern. Drug abuse, low morale, disciplinary problems, and volatile race relations revealed an institution under strain, no doubt aggravated by the war. The clearly visible problems were a cause of foreboding, although as the U.S. role in the war waned there had been no diminution of combat capability in Vietnam to that point. DoD had to deal with drug abuse and racial tensions, but it was also imperative that traditional military culture adapt to new attitudes and conditions about race and gender issues. The problem went far beyond bad behavior by individuals.

The U.S. culture from which armed forces personnel were drawn underwent rapid change during the war. The military in turn underwent a transformation under Laird from a conscripted to an all-volunteer force. Laird understood that traditional military culture, with its unequal treatment of minorities and women, had to change fundamentally, and he worked to create equal opportunity for men and women, blacks and whites. He knew that the armed forces had to extricate from Vietnam not only because the war was unpopular, but because it was so costly in lives, money, and equipment and contributed to unraveling the moral fiber of the institution. Laird intended to restore and burnish the military's reputation tarnished by Vietnam. With growing antimilitary sentiment in public and in Congress and shrinking Defense budgets, Laird stood up to the challenge of preparing the armed forces to meet future national security needs.

CHAPTER 20

Laird's Legacy

ON 8 NOVEMBER 1972, shortly after Nixon's election to a second term, Melvin Laird, as planned since the day he had accepted the post of secretary of defense, requested that the president accept his resignation "effective January 20, 1973." Even before joining the administration, Laird believed, especially after observing Robert McNamara during his long service as secretary, no person should serve in the position for more than one presidential term. Looking back, Laird characterized his tenure as a time of conscious transition "from war to peace . . . from reliance on an inequitable selective service system to zero draft and an all-volunteer force, from federal budgets dominated by defense expenditures to budgets dominated by spending on human resources without sacrificing essential national security." Laird expressed his gratification for Nixon's "unfailing support . . . in the difficult tasks I have had to face," a tactful characterization of their relationship. Laird indeed had Nixon's support on the antiballistic missile, the AVF, and the efforts to stabilize a deteriorating military force and improve opportunities for minorities and women, but he encountered presidential opposition in other areas. He often sharply disagreed with the president and Henry Kissinger on the pace of troop withdrawals from Vietnam, defense spending, the Cambodian bombing, and the appropriate response to the EC–121 crisis.[1]

In accepting Laird's resignation, Nixon paid tribute to a long relationship, calling him "the indispensable man—the right man for the right place, at the right time." The president stated that Laird was uniquely qualified for the job by virtue of his years of service on the House Defense Appropriations Subcommittee and his "enormous skill in handling difficult political problems."[2] No doubt he was referring to Laird's role in the fight to win approval of the ABM, his efforts to fend off drastic congressional cuts in defense spending, his handling of morale and social problems in the armed forces, the campaign ending conscription, his efforts to foster the future growth of the armed forces, and most of all the change in Vietnam policy that led to the withdrawal of U.S. forces from Vietnam. In good measure owing to Laird's efforts, Vietnam did not pose a major political liability for Nixon in the 1972 presidential election. U.S. forces in Vietnam had shrunk to a small number, and the public found less reason to protest against an unfair selective service system.[3]

Perhaps influenced by his experience as Dwight Eisenhower's vice president in the 1950s, Nixon may have expected Laird to be a deferential defense secretary. After all, two of Eisenhower's three selections, Charles E. Wilson and Neil H. McElroy, had accepted the role of managers from the start, essentially loyalists carrying out the president's major defense policy decisions. By contrast, Laird fully remained his own man, staking out independent positions that sometimes challenged the president—especially on the Defense budget and the pace and timing of Vietnam withdrawals— and defending and implementing them skillfully.

Laird had forged his basic views on major national security issues during his years in Congress. He had grown uneasy over the state of America's national security under Lyndon Johnson. The long, costly Vietnam War had weakened the U.S. economy, its armed forces, and the military commitment to NATO. In Laird's judgment, the conflict was peripheral to core U.S. security interests and provided an opportunity for the Soviets to enhance their conventional and strategic power in the second half of the 1960s.

A key advantage in Laird's leadership of the Pentagon was his unflagging connection with Congress. His military assistant Robert Pursley observed that he maintained close ties with people on both sides of the aisle: "He had a large number of very close Democratic friends and he used those relationships a lot."[4] Laird later recalled how he maintained his congressional ties, briefing Congress regularly, trying to keep the White House informed of sensitive congressional issues, and spending time with his former colleagues. He claims he was the only secretary of defense to sit with Representative George Mahon at executive sessions of the House Appropriations Committee as it reviewed the DoD appropriation bill. These relationships helped in gaining approval for the incentives that were part of the AVF. "I had 100 percent support from the Congress, from my old colleagues in both the House and the Senate," he asserted.[5]

Robert Moot, who began his tenure as DoD comptroller in August 1968 under Clark Clifford and served until January 1973, noted dramatic improvement in relations with Congress over the course of Laird's tenure. According to Moot, the secretary helped to restore public confidence and mend relations with Congress, especially the Armed Services and Appropriations committees. Laird also made special efforts to inform other agencies and departments about the Defense budget. As he continued to cultivate personal relationships with committee chairmen, they tended to accept Laird's priorities when considering program cuts. Owing to the secretary's congressional experience, Moot observed, he "fully understood the individual interests of Committee members. This knowledge was employed as leverage in conference action, and in building good will in other areas." Laird handled his relationship with Congress respectfully, emphasizing its status as a co-equal branch of government. Using key members of OSD in a team effort to improve the connection with Congress, Laird emphasized the need to transform the relationship with the legislature, as noted by Assistant Secretary of Defense for Systems Analysis Gardiner Tucker, "from a kind of adversary confrontation to a partnership in which they share in facing and solving some of our problems, not just in criticizing our actions and proposals."[6] The good relations with Congress certainly helped preserve DoD's budget from even steeper cuts.

Under his eponymous doctrine, Nixon envisioned no future U.S. ground force involvement in Asian wars such as Vietnam and scaled down commitments for a time of scarce resources. The doctrine represented a necessary pragmatic pulling back (for financial and political reasons) from the broad notion of the United States as the world's policeman and the lofty ambition expressed in President Kennedy's inaugural address "to bear any burden, fight any foe, anywhere, anytime." Laird interpreted the Nixon Doctrine as a way to help him control spending as he worked to hold down the cost of new weapons through acquisition reform and began to implement the total force concept, making greater use of the National Guard and the reserve components, to economize and increase force effectiveness. He leaned on NATO allies to contribute more resources to the alliance and sought to reduce the number of U.S. troops stationed in Europe and South Korea.

Laird articulated a strategy of realistic deterrence to describe his position on national security. Former Secretary of Defense James Schlesinger later characterized Laird's conception as less a substantive strategy than a way of handling budget reductions. But coping with diminished resources and preserving U.S. deterrence capability required a strategic vision. Laird adopted the less ambitious but more executable defense strategy of preparing for 1½ wars in keeping with the foreign policy climate of détente. The overall Nixon-Laird approach sought to reduce the threat in order to permit a reduction of the military.[7]

At the beginning of his administration, Nixon intended to change the character of U.S. relations with the Soviet Union from one of confrontation to one of negotiation and to seek talks on strategic arms. Laird fully supported the president's and Kissinger's efforts to reorient relations with the Soviet Union. However, Kissinger effectively excluded Laird from substantive involvement in the opening of China. Still, the larger vision the three men shared made it logical to seek an arms agreement with the Soviets, whose strategic arsenal was growing, and to widen the Sino-Soviet rift by seeking to develop relations with China. The opening to China represented an attempt to diminish the threat from that country and at the same time give the Soviet Union a powerful inducement to negotiate an agreement with the United States on strategic arms. In an era of shrinking Defense budgets, the Strategic Arms Limitation Agreement of 1972, whose passage Laird helped secure, would reduce potential threats to the United States.

American involvement in Vietnam had provided the USSR an opportunity to expand its strategic missile arsenal. From intelligence reports Laird knew that the continuing Soviet buildup could at some point jeopardize the U.S. nuclear edge. The Soviet threat induced him to advocate arms limitation talks as being in America's interest. Delay in reaching an agreement would work to the Soviet Union's advantage. Thus Laird became a leading advocate not just of deploying the Safeguard antiballistic missile system for defensive purposes but of using planned ABM deployments as a bargaining chip in arms negotiations. He was instrumental in getting the Senate to approve the deployment of the ABM in the summer of 1969. In subsequent years he battled to keep the program alive and funded so it could remain central to the arms limitation negotiations with the Soviets. Director of Defense Research and Engineering John Foster contended in 1972 that the United States would "be in an unacceptable position" had Laird been unable to convince Congress to continue funding the MIRV (Multiple Independently Targetable Reentry Vehicle) and the Safeguard ABM. In his first two years Laird accepted his role as a lightning rod for criticism of these programs and successfully defended them in public and in Congress. His efforts, Foster believed, led to the deployment of the ABM and advanced an understanding of the future possibilities of missile defense.[8]

Laird helped shape the U.S. negotiating position by insisting that defensive missiles be an integral part of an agreement limiting offensive weapons. To Laird, the obvious reason was that the Soviet Union had no incentive to discuss offensive weapons because the United States had already stopped building them. He also influenced the Senate passage of the 1972 SALT I accord, a contribution that Kissinger acknowledged. Throughout preparations for the strategic arms talks and the talks themselves, Laird relied on his deputy David Packard and his personal representative Paul Nitze to speak for the department and coordinate the DoD position.[9]

Despite the decline in overall defense spending, Laird protected the funding for a new generation of weapons essential for waging future conflicts. Foster pointed to the number of advanced systems long under development that were deployed in Vietnam. Some would prove to be revolutionary: night vision devices for soldiers, MIRVs, refined remote sensors for monitoring enemy activity (particularly traffic along the Ho Chi Minh Trail), and so-called smart weapons such as laser-guided munitions that had already proved effective during the North Vietnamese Easter Offensive. The new *Ohio*-class submarine and associated Trident missiles represented a major achievement in sea-based deterrence. The new B–1 bomber had moved into its development phase. After tense negotiations and congressional hearings, the financially endangered Lockheed Aircraft Corporation was saved from bankruptcy and with it the C–5A cargo plane that became key component of U.S. efforts to project power and assist allies overseas.[10]

Under Laird, the Defense budget and the military forces endured significant cuts. Defense outlays in current dollars fell from $77.79 billion (FY 1969) to $73.22 billion (FY 1973), a drop of 6 percent that masked the deleterious effect of inflation on spending. Measured in inflation-adjusted *constant* FY 2014 dollars, outlays declined by 27 percent between FY 1969 and FY 1973. In addition, the armed forces shrank dramatically in size from 3,460,000 personnel in FY 1969 to 2,253,000 in FY 1973. Each service also experienced severe cuts to force structure. The Army went from 18 to 13 divisions; U.S. Navy ships, from 885 to 641; and the number of Air Force wings, from 180 to 153. The Marine Corps lost one of its four divisions.[11]

Laird never claimed to be a master of the enormously complex budget process, but he was a master politician. This attribute served him well in his budget battles with the military services and the JCS, always seeking more than they could reasonably expect; with an ambitious Henry Kissinger and his NSC staff, eager to have greater authority over the DoD budget; and with OMB, the president's fiscal watchdog, dedicated to tightly controlling expenditures. Greater obstacles lurked beyond these—a president seeking to carry out his political and economic agenda for the country, and a Congress prone to pursue its own interests and preferences and having the final say. The annual budget battle produced major drama in Washington, and the Defense Department typically took center stage. Experienced in both the legislative and executive branches, Laird proved adept in marshalling facts and figures and influencing legislators to attain most of the goals he set for the Defense Department. In helping Laird manage the budget process within DoD, no one was more important than his comptroller, Robert Moot.[12]

No selection was more critical to Laird's tenure than that of his deputy, David Packard, who handled acquisition reform and the details of budget preparation in the Pentagon. The choice of Hewlett-Packard's cofounder and CEO, a successful businessman with expertise in technology and defense research and development, meant a proven leader had arrived at the Pentagon. Packard's background allowed Laird to concentrate on relations with the Joint Chiefs, the armed services, the White House, Congress, U.S. allies, and the public on a range of critical issues, particularly Vietnam, the Defense budget, and the draft. Packard's replacement as deputy, Kenneth Rush, served for a shorter period and proved less influential and effective.[13]

Likewise, the departure in 1972 of Brig. Gen. Robert Pursley, Laird's military assistant, represented a significant loss to the secretary. Beginning with McNamara, Pursley had served as a military assistant to three successive secretaries of defense, prima facie evidence of his usefulness and skill. The White House, however, did not appreciate Pursley's service. Nixon, Kissinger, and Haig, in varying degrees, believed that he exerted a strong, even negative influence over Laird, encouraging him to counter the president's wishes. That they could entertain such suspicions perhaps reflected their frustration with Laird's independence.[14]

Laird maintained his control in running the department, especially in regard to the Defense budget. Through the NSC and the Defense Program Review Committee, Kissinger tried to gain authority in shaping the details of the DoD budget. Using delaying tactics and providing incomplete responses to requests for budget plans, Laird and Packard ensured that Kissinger's DPRC acquired no real authority over the formulation of the Defense budget. Kissinger never attained his ambitious goals for the DPRC. On the positive side, the committee did provide budget analysts a forum for evaluating long-term projections and resource allocations within the executive branch.[15]

From the start, Laird made clear to the president, JCS, and OSD that he wanted all Pentagon communications with the White House and the NSC to go through his office. Since the Eisenhower administration, the NSC staff had direct contact with the JCS, giving the Chiefs the ability to bypass the secretary and even go directly to the Congress on some matters. When Laird became secretary, he expected presidential decisions and NSC memoranda to come to him for dissemination within the Pentagon on a need-to-know basis. He sent Nixon numerous memoranda about using his OSD office as the single point of liaison between the White House and the Pentagon to optimize coordination with the White House and within DoD. Laird's intent was to establish clear lines of responsibility without restricting the chairman's role as military adviser to the president. From Laird's perspective, this area represented the core of his relationship with the president and the JCS. Laird's entreaties did not stop Nixon, Kissinger, and the JCS from using private channels to bypass him, although the secretary was aware of their existence and often what was being discussed. Laird claimed that sources loyal to him in the National Security Agency and Defense Intelligence Agency kept him informed about Kissinger's contacts with the Soviets, Chinese, and North Vietnamese, and even provided advance knowledge about Kissinger's secret trip to Beijing. To exercise their freedom of action and to keep Laird in the dark, especially after Laird helped thwart Nixon's desire to retaliate against North Korea during the EC–121 crisis, Nixon and Kissinger used backchannels to communicate with the JCS chairman, Ambassador Ellsworth Bunker in Saigon, and General Creighton Abrams, the commander in Vietnam, about the initial decisions and preliminary planning to embark on offensives in Cambodia and Laos.[16]

The use of private channels came to a head in December 1971 during the India-Pakistan War. *Washington Post* journalist Jack Anderson published information from several sensitive crisis management meetings about the White House's handling of the matter, enraging Nixon and Kissinger. Investigators traced the leak to an enlisted man assigned to the JCS liaison office, Yeoman Charles Radford, who without authorization made copies of sensitive documents and provided them to Admiral Moorer, the JCS chairman. Laird never saw any of this material that came through a channel designed to bypass him. He had surmised from what the JSC said from time to time "that somebody was giving them information, even ahead of the time that I got it in the decision memorandums from the President." Laird deemed the arrangement a breach of trust. He launched an investigation by his general counsel Fred Buzhardt and closed down the JCS liaison office. Nixon, however, refused to take punitive action against the chairman. By keeping silent about Moorer's involvement, Nixon ensured that the chairman would continue to support White House efforts to keep Laird in check. This unfortunate episode strained relations between Laird and Moorer and exposed the level of distrust between the White House, civilian leaders in the Pentagon, and the JCS.[17]

Laird presents the Defense Distinguished Service Medal to General Counsel Fred Buzhardt, January 1973. Laird had Buzhardt prepare a detailed report on the Yeoman Radford episode. (NARA OPA)

Of all the divisive issues that confronted Laird, the Vietnam War was the primary one for DoD and the nation. Under McNamara, the Pentagon had shifted resources (troops, equipment, and ammunition) to MACV from other commands, weakening their readiness. The protracted, controversial war diminished DoD's public reputation and eventually contributed to reductions of its budget and delays in some modernization programs.

The secretary made a signal policy contribution toward ending U.S. military involvement by developing the U.S. program to improve and modernize South Vietnam's forces so they could assume a growing share of the combat role and allow U.S. forces to withdraw. A much discussed topic during the election campaign, troop withdrawal became a priority for Laird soon after he arrived in the Pentagon. He assumed that the new administration had a short breathing spell to work out its position on Vietnam before war critics resumed their attacks. Public frustration and disaffection with the stalemated conflict and ever-mounting U.S. casualties made it imperative to get American forces out of Vietnam. Laird supported a negotiated settlement but doubted whether one could materialize before public and congressional opinion turned hostile. With a U.S. victory in the near term unachievable, Laird advocated Vietnamization as militarily feasible and politically pragmatic. Vietnamization also represented a step in implementing the Nixon Doctrine. During Laird's tenure, South Vietnam's armed forces doubled in size while the U.S. military forces in Vietnam dropped from 540,000 troops in 1969 to 23,335 at the time the Paris Peace agreement was signed in January 1973.[18]

Vietnamization required a major U.S. logistical effort in the midst of ongoing combat and troop withdrawals. Assistant Secretary of Defense for Installations and Logistics Barry Shillito estimated that the United States delivered over $5.3 billion of new equipment to Saigon's armed forces. U.S. advisers trained South Vietnamese forces and assumed responsibility for combat and logistic support for the equipment and supplies the United States provided— including the additional unprogrammed equipment sent by DoD to hold off the advance of North Vietnamese forces during the 1972 Easter Offensive. The influx of equipment stretched the capability of the South Vietnamese military logistic system to the limit. Shillito conceded that the United States would need to provide financial support to the Vietnamese for an indefinite period in order to sustain their logistical system. Moreover, South Vietnam would continue to require petroleum, ammunition, repair parts, and technical assistance. Designed to provide essential support, not ensure self-sufficiency, Viet-namization came with significant risks. North Vietnam was not likely to abandon its effort to conquer South Vietnam, and the past performance of South Vietnam's leadership had raised many doubts of its efficacy.[19]

Leonard Sullivan, deputy DDR&E for Southeast Asian matters, had reached a similar conclusion after a visit in 1971 to South Vietnam (see chapter 8). Jeffrey Clarke, author of the official Army history of Vietnamization, found that South Vietnam's military in 1973 was undeniably larger and better equipped than it was in 1969, but it was still hampered by a lack of mobility and weak leadership, prob-lems that had resisted the ministrations of U.S. leaders and advisers since 1965. The quantities of modern arms and equipment, the extensive training that the Pentagon provided, and the growing size of Vietnam's armed forces "gave the impression that great progress had been made in revitalizing and improving South Vietnam's military forces, when many of the measures were only props intended to shore up a flawed piece of architecture." South Vietnam's force structure was designed to fight a defensive war with military deficiencies compensated by U.S. air and naval power. The possibility that U.S. support might be reduced or eliminated was not consid-ered by MACV or South Vietnam's Joint General Staff. Graham Cosmas, author of a detailed official Army history of MACV, concluded it would take a generation or more to transform South Vietnam into an effective government, far more time than the United States was willing to provide.[20]

Even if Vietnamization had rebuilt South Vietnam's military into an effective force, it would not have assured the South's final victory. At the time of the 1973 cease-fire, there were serious doubts about South Vietnam's political will and the durability of security in the countryside. Would the central government prove capa-ble of sustaining itself and establishing popular support in the villages? Or would the weakened but not defeated Viet Cong insurgency continue to threaten Saigon's legitimacy in rural areas? North Vietnam's army remained formidable, and some of its units were stationed within South Vietnam. When South Vietnam's military proved unable to cope with the North Vietnamese invasion in 1975, Congress decided to write no more checks, a step that Laird opposed.[21]

Laird and the White House disagreed over the pace of Vietnamization. For political and budgetary reasons the secretary wanted a steady, well-managed transfer of responsibility for the war to the South Vietnamese. Nixon and Kissinger, supported by the Joint Chiefs, sought to proceed more slowly and to retain sufficient American military power in-theater to maintain military pressure on the enemy. Laird considered the White House approach as politically risky, most likely leading to more U.S. casualties and a prolonged U.S. military engagement at a time of growing war weariness. A slower redeployment schedule would also delay the inevitable and necessary process of reshaping and restoring the armed forces for the postwar era. Yet the White House had valid reasons to proceed slowly. Kissinger feared that regular withdrawals would be taken for granted, thus weakening any incentive for the North Vietnamese to make concessions and negotiate.[22] Emphasizing the impact of declining budgets on the ability of the United States to maintain troop levels in Vietnam, Laird outmaneuvered Kissinger and even the president in battles over the pace of withdrawal.[23]

During the 1972 Easter Offensive, Laird stood virtually alone in the administration in arguing that the cumulative effect of the improvement and modernization programs had given South Vietnam's armed forces the weapons and equipment to defend their country. He saw the offensive as a test of South Vietnam's will, its leadership, and the effectiveness of its forces. In his view, South Vietnam would not prevail unless its leadership mastered the challenges it faced; in the long run South Vietnam's fate was in South Vietnamese hands. Moreover, providing the country with still more resources would compromise U.S. defenses in Europe and reduce U.S. leverage with the Soviet Union and China.[24] Laird walked a fine line, arguing that improvements in South Vietnam's armed forces over the long term had justified continuation of U.S. withdrawals. If he had said that South Vietnam could not defeat the Easter Offensive without American airpower, he would be undermining his own claim that South Vietnam's forces had measurably improved. However, he left unanswered the question of whether he really believed the South Vietnamese were strong enough on their own to withstand the North Vietnamese onslaught. In contrast, a skeptical Nixon had less confidence in South Vietnam's army than Laird and would not risk South Vietnam's defeat by allowing the ARVN to fight without additional U.S. air support.[25]

While the American withdrawal from Vietnam proceeded apace, Laird made significant changes in the military's approach to personnel. Laird's conception of the total force, relying on the National Guard and reserve components to perform essential missions, was part of the foundation of the All-Volunteer Force and the post-Vietnam military. But those forces in general were not yet ready for that role, for both the Army Reserve and Guard had fallen into a state of neglect that threatened their credibility as a back-up force. Assistant Secretary of Defense for Manpower and Reserve Affairs Roger Kelley noted that many units had little or no usable equipment and force structure, and missions were poorly defined. Active forces had relied on the draft as the primary means of augmenting their ranks for so many years that few officials in DoD believed that the guard and the reserves would ever be called to active duty. President Johnson's decision not to mobilize them for service in Vietnam led many new enlistees to view National Guard/reserve service as a safe haven from military combat duty. Starting in 1969, congressional mandates forced the services to take steps to improve the status of reserve forces, but questions remained about their ability to deal with emergencies.[26]

Laird's total force approach of 1970 called for improvements in manning, training, and equipping the guard and reserves so that they could serve as the initial and primary source of augmentation for the active force in future emergencies. The funds in the Defense budget allocated to the guard and reserves rose from $2.1 billion in FY 1969 to $4.1 billion in FY 1973. Their combat usable equipment had an estimated value of $300 million in FY 1970. By FY 1973 that value exceeded $1 billion. Army Secretary Robert Froehlke concluded at the end of Laird's tenure that the reserves were indeed improving but "are not sufficiently ready." Laird's effort had the overall effect of establishing securely the concept of total force planning, although full implementation remained an elusive target in part because the regular forces were reluctant to increase resources to the reserves to increase their effectiveness. Improving the the guard and reserves and achieving a combat ready total force would concern future secretaries of defense in the decades to come.[27]

Laird oversaw a fundamental, far-reaching change in personnel policy. Along with the measures taken to rebuild the guard and reserve forces, the elimination of the draft and compulsory military service, the military pay raise, quality-of-life improvements in the military, and a reinvigorated recruiting system transformed the nature of military service, whose restructuring would only be realized fully after the Vietnam War. Under Laird's leadership, the Pentagon acted to combat racial discrimination, improve race relations, handle a growing drug abuse problem, and improve opportunities for women serving in uniform. Spurred by an ongoing social and cultural transformation, the changes set in motion under Laird pointed to a

Kissinger and Laird share a laugh during their last breakfast in Laird's Pentagon office, 25 January 1973. (OSD Historical Office)

future that allowed no return to the conscripted armed forces of the past, which had restricted the role of women and minorities.[28]

The constants in Laird's positions as secretary were to carry out policies that the nation could afford financially, to keep the nation's defenses strong, and to weigh the political costs of defense policies to the nation and his party. Laird believed Nixon won reelection in large measure on how he handled the Vietnam War. A president who had won a narrow electoral victory in 1968 and had confronted widespread antiwar protests early in his first term easily went on to reelection in 1972. Nixon's political victory owed much to Laird's handling of the withdrawals and the end of conscription.

Vietnam did not tarnish or undermine Laird's reputation as it had McNamara's. Unlike McNamara, the architect of the Vietnam buildup who came to doubt his own policies and actions, Laird, the architect of Vietnam withdrawals, remained convinced that his policies were the right ones. Believing it necessary to extricate America's armed forces from the Vietnam morass, he engineered a change in the mission of U.S. forces in Vietnam from waging war to withdrawal and improving South Vietnam's military. Unlike McNamara, he left office on his own terms as he had stated when he assumed office.[29]

Having achieved his primary goals—withdrawing all U.S. combatant forces from Vietnam and helping end an unfair conscription system—Laird helped

Laird with his successor, Elliott Richardson, 23 January 1973. (Nixon Presidential Library)

prepare the armed forces and DoD for the post-Vietnam era. He strengthened ties with U.S. military allies in Western Europe and Asia and improved relations with Congress and the JCS. In the end he proved a worthy rival to Kissinger, making adroit use of his political base and political skills to retain autonomy in a some-times dysfunctional administration that sought to stifle the independent secretary. Fortunately for Nixon and Kissinger, they failed to neutralize Laird. The president depended on Laird to help curb personnel cuts, to stem declines in defense spend-ing, and to help push SALT I, the ABM, and the AVF through Congress.[30]

Nixon even turned to Laird in a sensitive moment in his presidency. When the president's culpable aides, Haldeman and Ehrlichman, were forced to resign during the Watergate scandal, Nixon called back the former defense secretary to run his domestic programs. Laird resigned from his position as counselor to the president for domestic affairs several months after he learned of Nixon's involvement in the Watergate cover up, but not before he played a role in securing Gerald Ford's selection as vice president. Laird's connections in Congress helped him advance important domestic legislation, such as the federal budget, during his time as Nix-on's domestic counselor.[31]

Laird was proud of his achievements as secretary of defense. He viewed his obligation to serve the best interests of the nation as surpassing any other consideration—personal, political, economic, or bureaucratic. He entered office with the determination to disengage the United States from the war in Vietnam. And in doing so, he tried to ready the armed forces for the future.

In retrospect, Laird's measures to improve race relations, handle the drug issue, and increase opportunities for women represented initial solutions to problems that over time would reveal their complexity and require more extensive changes. Nevertheless, these efforts helped to establish a firm foundation for Nixon's second term. On Vietnam, the single most critical issue for Laird and Nixon, there was no firm foundation. The ignominious, rapid collapse of South Vietnam in 1975 brutally exposed the weaknesses of its armed forces and raised anew questions about the validity and accomplishments of the Vietnamization program. In most areas of his tenure as secretary, Laird's political focus served him well, but less so in regard to Vietnam. He helped end U.S. involvement there, but not the rancorous disagreements throughout the nation about the U.S. government's involvement in the divisive, costly war.

ABM	Antiballistic Missile
ACDA	Arms Control and Disarmament Agency
AFB	Air Force Base
AFPC	Armed Forces Policy Council
AMSA	Advanced Manned Strategic Aircraft
ARVN	Army of the Republic of Vietnam
ASD	Assistant Secretary of Defense
ASD(C)	Assistant Secretary of Defense (Comptroller)
ASD(I)	Assistant Secretary of Defense (Intelligence)
ASD(ISA)	Assistant Secretary of Defense (International Security Affairs)
ASD(I&L)	Assistant Secretary of Defense (Installations and Logistics)
ASD(MRA)	Assistant Secretary of Defense (Manpower and Reserve Affairs)
ASD(SA)	Assistant Secretary of Defense (Systems Analysis)
ASW	Antisubmarine Warfare
AVF	All-Volunteer Force
AWACS	Airborne Warning and Control System
AWOL	Absent Without Leave
BoB	Bureau of the Budget
CBU	Cluster Bomb Unit
CBW	Chemical Biological Warfare
CDC	Center for Disease Control
CIA	Central Intelligence Agency
CINCEUR	Commander in Chief, European Command
CINCPAC	Commander in Chief, Pacific Command
CJCS	Chairman, Joint Chiefs of Staff
CM	Chairman, Joint Chiefs of Staff memorandum
CMH	U.S. Army Center of Military History
CNO	Chief of Naval Operations

CONAD	Continental Air Defense
CONUS	Continental United States
CORDS	Civil Operations and Revolutionary Development Support
COSVN	Central Office for South Vietnam
Cong. Rec.	*Congressional Record*
CRAF	Civil Reserve Air Fleet
CRS	Congressional Research Service
CSA	Chief of Staff, Army
CW	Chemical Weapons
DACOWITS	Defense Advisory Committee on Women in the Services
DASD	Deputy Assistant Secretary of Defense
DCAA	Defense Contract Audit Agency
DCI	Director of Central Intelligence
DDI	Director of Defense Intelligence
DDR&E	Director of Defense Research and Evaluation
DepSecDef	Deputy Secretary of Defense
DIA	Defense Intelligence Agency
DMZ	Demilitarized Zone
DoD	Department of Defense
DPM	Draft Presidential Memorandum
DPQ	Defense Planning Questionnaire
DDR&E	Director of Defense Research and Engineering
DPRC	Defense Program Review Committee
DSA	Defense Supply Agency
DSARC	Defense Systems Acquisition Review Council
EEO	Equal Employment Opportunity
E.O.	Executive Order
EUCOM	European Command
FAD	Financial Accounting Document
FBI	Federal Bureau of Investigation
FDL	Fast Deployment Logistics
FMS	Foreign Military Sales
FRUS	*Foreign Relations of the United States*
FY	Fiscal Year

FYDP	Five-Year Defense Plan
GAO	Government Accounting Office
GNP	Gross National Product
GRC	Government of the Republic of China (Taiwan)
GVN	Government of (South) Vietnam
H	U.S. House of Representatives
HCA	House Committee on Appropriations
HCAS	House Committee on Armed Services
HCFA	House Committee on Foreign Affairs
HEW	Health, Education, and Welfare
HP	Hewlett-Packard Company
HSCA	House Subcommittee on Appropriations
I&L	Installations and Logistics
I&M	Improvement and Modernization
ICBM	Intercontinental Ballistic Missile
INR	Bureau of Intelligence and Research, Department of State
ISA	International Security Affairs
JCS	Joint Chiefs of Staff
JCSM	Joint Chiefs of Staff memorandum
JFM	Joint Force Memorandum
JSOP	Joint Strategic Objectives Plan
LANTCOM	Atlantic Command
LBJ	Lyndon B. Johnson
LC	Library of Congress
LOC	Line of Communication
Ltr	Letter
MAAG	Military Assistance Advisory Group
MACV	Military Assistance Command, Vietnam
MAP	Military Assistance Program
MASF	Military Assistance Service Funded
MBFR	Mutual and Balanced Force Reduction
MBT	Main Battle Tank
MIRV	Multiple Independently Targetable Reentry Vehicles
MIT	Massachusetts Institute of Technology

MLBM	Modern Large Ballistic Missile
MOL	Manned Orbiting Laboratory
MOS	Military Occupational Specialties
MRA	Manpower and Reserve Affairs
Msg	Message
Mtg	Meeting
NAACP	National Association for the Advancement of Colored People
NASA	National Aeronautics and Space Administration
NATO	North Atlantic Treaty Organization
NIE	National Intelligence Estimate
NJP	Nonjudicial Punishment
NLF	National Liberation Front (Viet Cong)
NMCC	National Military Command Center
NOA	New Obligational Authority
NPG	Nuclear Planning Group
NSA	National Security Agency
NSC	National Security Council
NSDM	National Security Decision Memorandum
NSSM	National Security Study Memorandum
NVA	North Vietnamese Army
OASD	Office of the Assistant Secretary of Defense
O&M	Operations and Maintenance
OMB	Office of Management and Budget
OSD	Office of the Secretary of Defense
OSD/HO	Office of the Secretary of Defense/Historical Office
OST	Office of Science and Technology
P.L.	Public Law
PACOM	Pacific Command
PAR	Perimeter Acquisition Radar
PFIAB	President's Foreign Intelligence Advisory Board
PLO	Palestine Liberation Organization
PMDL	Provisional Military Demarcation Line
POL	Petroleum, Oil, and Lubricants
POM	Program Objective Memorandum

PPBS	Planning, Programming, and Budgeting System
PRC	People's Republic of China
R&D	Research and Development
RDT&E	Research, Development, Test and Evaluation
REDCOSTE	Reduction of Costs in Europe
RF/PF	Regional Force/Popular Force
RG	Record Group
ROK	Republic of Korea
RVNAF	Republic of Vietnam Armed Forces
S	U.S. Senate
S&L	Supply and Logistics
SA	Systems Analysis
SAC	Strategic Air Command
SACEUR	Supreme Allied Commander, Europe
SACLANT	Supreme Allied Commander, Atlantic
SALT	Strategic Arms Limitation Talks
SAM	Surface-to-Air Missile
SCA	Senate Committee on Appropriations
SCAS	Senate Committee on Armed Services
SCFR	Senate Committee on Foreign Relations
SecArmy	Secretary of the Army
SecAF	Secretary of the Air Force
SecDef	Secretary of Defense
SecNav	Secretary of the Navy
SIG	Senior Interdepartmental Group
SIOP	Single Integrated Operational Plan
SLBM	Submarine-Launched Ballistic Missile
SMOF	Staff Member and Office Files
SNIE	Special National Intelligence Estimate
SOUTHCOM	Southern Command
SRAM	Short-Range Attack Missile
SRG	Senior Review Group
SRG	Special Review Group
SSBN	Ballistic Missile Submarine (Nuclear Powered)

SSC	Senate Subcommittee
SSCA	Senate Subcommittee on Appropriations
STRICOM	Strike Command
Telcon	Telephone Conversation
TF	Task Force
TFX	Tactical Fighter Experimental
TOA	Total Obligational Authority
TOW	Tube-launched Optically-tracked Wire-guided Missile System
TPP	Total Package Procurement
UCMJ	Uniform Code of Military Justice
ULMS	Undersea Long-range Missile System
UPI	United Press International
USIA	United States Information Agency
USUHS	Uniformed Services University of the Health Sciences
VC	Viet Cong
VN	Vietnam
VNCF	Vietnam Country Files
VNSF	Vietnam Subject Files
VOLAR	Volunteer Army
VSSG	Vietnam Special Studies Group
WAAC	Women's Army Auxiliary Corps
WAC	Women's Army Corps
WAF	Women in the Air Force
WAVES	Women Accepted for Volunteer Emergency Service
WH	White House
WHCF	White House Central Files
WHSF	White House Special Files
WNRC	Washington National Records Center
WSAG	Washington Special Actions Group

1. Change Comes to the Pentagon

1. *Department of Defense (DoD) Annual Report for Fiscal Year 1968* (Washington, DC: Government Printing Office, 1968), 532, 543.

2. Office of the Secretary of Defense, Historical Office (OSD/HO), *Department of Defense Key Officials, 1947–2000* (Washington, DC: 2000), tables 1, 2, 5, 6. The figure for Southeast Asia (SEA) costs comes from Office of Management and Budget (OMB), *The Budget of the United States Government, Fiscal Year 1970* (Washington, DC: Government Printing Office, 1969), 27, 73.

3. For more on the growth of the defense establishment, see Alex Roland, *The Military-Industrial Complex* (Washington, DC: American Historical Association, 2001).

4. Lawrence S. Kaplan, Ronald D. Landa, and Edward J. Drea, *The McNamara Ascendancy, 1961–1965* (Washington, DC: OSD Historical Office, 2006), 536–39; Edward J. Drea, *McNamara, Clifford, and the Burdens of Vietnam, 1965–1969* (Washington, DC: OSD Historical Office, 2011); Dale Van Atta, *With Honor: Melvin Laird in War, Peace, and Politics* (Madison: University of Wisconsin Press, 2008); Julius Duscha, "The Political Pro Who Runs Defense," *New York Times Magazine*, 13 Jun 1971.

5. ASD(A) DoD Brief of the Organization and Functions, Apr 1968, folder Transition, box A98, William J. Baroody Papers, Gerald R. Ford Presidential Library and Museum, Ann Arbor, MI [hereafter Ford Library].

6. Van Atta, *With Honor*, 3–4, 31–33; Personal Data Sheet, folder Transition, box A96, Baroody Papers, Ford Library. Laird sent Bryce Harlow, Nixon's assistant, recommendations for every cabinet position. See ltr, Laird to Harlow, n.d., ibid. The society was founded in 1949 by 15 Republican congressmen opposed to monthly bonuses for war veterans because of the cost.

7. Richard M. Nixon, *RN: The Memoirs of Richard Nixon* (New York: Grosset & Dunlap, 1978), 339; Melvin Laird, interview by Maurice Matloff and Alfred Goldberg, 2 Sep 1986, 1–2 (quote); Laird, interview by Alfred Goldberg and Richard Hunt, 11 Oct 2001, 5–6, OSD/HO; ltr, Nixon to Laird, 17 Nov 1972 (quotes), folder Laird, box 10, Name/Subject File, President's Personal Files, Richard Nixon Presidential Library and Museum, Yorba Linda, CA [hereafter Nixon Library].

8. Nixon, *Memoirs*, 289 (quote). See also, Van Atta, *With Honor*.

9. News conference, 13 Dec 1968, OSD Historical Office, comp., *Public Statements of Melvin R. Laird, Secretary of Defense, 1969*, 1:3; James D. Hessman, "DoD After Two Years

of Laird," *Armed Forces Journal* 108 (21 Dec 1970); *Time*, 9 May 1994, Time Magazine Archive, <http://content.time.com/time/archive/>.

10. Melvin Laird, interview by Maurice Matloff and David Trask, 18 Aug 1986, 3–4, 14, 20, OSD/HO.

11. Ibid., 9.

12. Memo, Haig for Kissinger, 1 Feb 1969, folder DoD vol. 1, box 220, Agency Files, NSC, Nixon Library; Minutes, SecDef Staff Meeting, 31 Jan 1969, folder Staff Mtgs 27 Jan 1969–Mar 1969, box 13, Acc 330-77-0062, Records of the Office of the Secretary of Defense, Record Group 330, Washington National Records Center (WNRC), Suitland, MD.

13. Laird interviews, 18 Aug 1986, 15–16 (quotes); 2 Sep 1986, 5–7; Van Atta, *With Honor*, 316.

14. Laird interview, 18 Aug 1986, 7, 27; Duscha, *New York Times Magazine*, 13 Jun 1971.

15. Press conference, 30 Dec 1968, OSD Historical Office, comp., *Public Statements of David Packard, Deputy Secretary of Defense, 1969*, 1:1–18.

16. Ibid., 1:2 (quote); Laird interview, 2 Sep 1986, 15.

17. Laird interview, 11 Oct 2001, 9; ltr, Nixon to Laird, 17 Nov 1972 (quote), cited in note 4.

18. News conference, 30 Dec 1968, *Packard Public Statements 1969*, 1:1, 4–5; Senate Committee on Armed Services (SCAS), *Nominations of Laird, Packard, and Darden: Hearings*, 91st Cong., 1st sess., 15 Jan 1969, 37.

19. Press conference, 30 Dec 1968, *Packard Public Statements 1969*, 1:4–9, 14.

20. Richard Lyons, "Packard Is Confirmed," *Washington Post*, 24 Jan 1969, 4.

21. Orr Kelly, "Laird Likely to Retain Foster, Moot," *Washington Star*, 13 Jan 1969, 5.

22. Van Atta, *With Honor*, 10, 141–42; Laird interview, 11 Oct 2001, 4. Clifford urged Laird to retain Moot, Resor, and Foster; see memo, Clifford for Johnson, 23 Dec 1968, folder Transition Materials, box A98, Baroody Papers, Ford Library. Information on the tenure of high-ranking officials comes from *DoD Key Officials, 1947–2004*.

23. Laird interview, 2 Sep 1986, 39; Robert Pursley, interview by Alfred Goldberg and Roger Trask, 15 Aug 1997, 14, OSD/HO; Drea, *McNamara, Clifford, and the Burdens of Vietnam*, 9.

24. *DoD Key Officials*, 58–61.

25. George C. Wilson, "3 Service Secretaries Named," *Washington Post*, 7 Jan 1969, carried three stories on Laird's selections.

26. Alice C. Cole et al., *The Department of Defense: Documents on Establishment and Organization, 1944–1978* (Washington, DC: OSD Historical Office, 1978), 248–49; ltrs, Rivers to Laird, 7 Feb 1969; Laird to Rivers, 14 Feb 1969: both in folder 54, box 5, Records from SecDef Vault, Acc 330-74-142, WNRC.

27. Kaplan et al., *McNamara Ascendency*, 8, 13, 74–75. For a defense and explanation of the role of systems analysis under McNamara, see Alain C. Enthoven and K. Wayne

Smith, *How Much Is Enough? Shaping the Defense Program, 1961–1969* (New York: Harper & Row, 1971).

28. House Committee on Armed Services (HCAS), *Hearings on Military Posture*, 91st Cong., 1st sess., 27 Mar 1969, H. Rept. 91-14, pt. 1:1710.

29. Ltr, Rivers to Packard, 7 May 1969, attached to ltr, Rivers to Packard, 28 May 1969, folder 54, box 5, Records from SecDef Vault, Acc 330-74-142.

30. Ltr, Packard to Rivers, 26 May 1969, attached to ltr, Rivers to Packard, 28 May 1969, ibid.

31. Ltr, Rivers to Packard, 21 Nov 1969, attached to ltr, Packard to Rivers, 2 Dec 1969, folder 54, box 5, Records from SecDef Vault, Acc 330-74-142.

32. Ltr, Packard to Rivers, 2 Dec 1969, cited in note 31. Packard provided Rivers with a copy of DoD Instruction 7045.7, dated 29 October 1969, which spelled out the new procedures for the PPBS.

33. Memo for the Record, 10 Jul 1969, signed by Packard, Wheeler, Resor, Chafee, and Seamans, in Adm. Thomas H. Moorer Diary, 10 Jul 1969, box 2, Acc 218-05-006, Records of the Joint Chiefs of Staff, Record Group 218, National Archives and Records Administration (NARA) II, College Park, MD.

34. C. Vance Gordon et al., "Revolution, Counter-Revolution, and Evolution: A Brief History of the PPBS," 12, copy in Author Files, OSD/HO.

35. Laird interview, 2 Sep 1986, 11; memo, Haig for Kissinger, 21 Oct 1969, folder DoD, box 1000, Haig Special File, NSC, Nixon Library. Kissinger wrote his comments on this memo.

36. Drea, *McNamara, Clifford, and the Burdens of Vietnam*, 5–6; memo, Laird for Service Secretaries, 25 Jan 1969, box 44, SecDef Records, Acc 330-75-089, WNRC; David Packard, interview by Alfred Goldberg and Maurice Matloff, 9 Nov 1987, 7; Laird interview, 2 Sep 1986, 11.

37. Laird interview, 11 Oct 2001, 18.

38. Laird interview, 2 Sep 1986, 12–13.

39. Richard A. Ware, "The Pentagon's Office of International Security Affairs, 1969–1973" (American Enterprise Institute for Public Policy Research, 1986), 7. Ware was Nutter's deputy. Vernon E. Davis, *The Long Road Home: U.S. Prisoner of War Policy and Planning in Southeast Asia* (Washington, DC: OSD Historical Office, 2000), 178, 198; Van Atta, *With Honor*, 142. Laird's papers at the Ford Library contain an extensive collection of Memoranda for the Record of the numerous meetings on Vietnamization.

40. Memo, Laird for DDR&E et al., 27 Mar 1969, attached to ltr, Laird to Rep. F. Bradford Morse (R–MA), 17 May 1969, folder Procurement 2–5, box 21, Melvin R. Laird Papers, Ford Library. See chapter 3 for Nixon's budget cuts.

41. Packard, "Improving the Development and Procurement of New Weapons," attached to ltr, Packard to Laird, 14 Jan 1972, 1–2, 23–24, folder Procurement Summary,

box 42, Laird Papers, Ford Library. Packard sent this report to Laird after he left his post as deputy.

42. Memo, Packard for Service Secretaries, 31 Jul 1969, folder Procurement 6–11, box 21, Laird Papers, Ford Library.

43. Memo, Packard for Service Secretaries, 15 Apr 1969, folder Procurement 2–5; memo, Packard for Service Secretaries et al., 30 May 1969 (quote), folder Procurement 6–11: both in ibid.; Packard, "Improving the Development," 24 (quote), cited in note 41.

44. Orr Kelly, "Laird Planning Major Review at Pentagon," *Washington Star*, 14 Dec 1968, 3 (quote); News conference, 30 Jun 1969, *Laird Public Statements 1969*, 5:1871–86.

45. DoD News Release, 605–69, 19 Jul 1969, OSD/HO; *Cong. Rec.*, 12 Aug 1969, S 9852.

46. *Cong. Rec.*, 28 Oct 1969, S 13365–67.

47. Memo, Haig for Kissinger, 10 Jun 1970 (quote), folder Blue Ribbon Defense Panel, box 239, Agency Files; telcon, Kissinger and Moorer, 16 Jun 1970 (quote from Moorer), folder 9, box 5, HAK [Henry A. Kissinger] Telcons; ltr, Laird to Kissinger, 26 May 1970, attached to memo, Haig for Kissinger, 10 Jun 1970; memo, Kissinger for Nixon, re meeting w/Fitzhugh, 17 Jun 1970 (quote), folder Haig Chron Jun 11–22, 1970 [1 of 2], box 968, Alexander M. Haig Chronological Files [hereafter Haig Chron Files]; ltr, Fitzhugh to Nixon, 22 Jun 1970; memo, Kissinger for Nixon, 11 Jul 1970 (Nixon quote): both attached to memo, Haig for Kissinger, 10 Jul 1970, folder Blue Ribbon Panel, box 239, Agency Files; memo, Kissinger for Nixon, 14 Jul 1970, ibid.; telcon, Kissinger and Laird, 21 Jul 1970 (Laird quote), folder 2, box 6, HAK Telcons: all in NSC, Nixon Library.

48. News conference, 27 Jul 1970, *Laird Public Statements 1970*, 4:1794–1802.

49. "Report to the President and the Secretary of Defense on the Department of Defense," by the Blue Ribbon Defense Panel, 1 Jul 1970, 1, box 555, Subject Files, OSD/HO.

50. Ibid., 1–4, 7, 24, 200, 207 (quote); Mark M. Lowenthal, "Defense Department Reorganization: The Fitzhugh Report, 1969–1970," Congressional Research Service (CRS), 19 Aug 1976, 12–13, folder Blue Ribbon Panel Status 1969–1970, box 549, Subject Files, OSD/HO. Retired Admiral Arleigh Burke told Nixon that implementing the reorganization proposal of the report would reduce military effectiveness and jeopardize U.S. security. Ltr, Burke to Nixon, 28 Jul 1970, attached to memo, Campbell for Haig, 29 Jul 1970, folder Blue Ribbon Defense Panel, box 239, Agency Files, NSC, Nixon Library.

51. Blue Ribbon Defense Panel Report, cited in note 49.

52. Moorer Diary, 15 Jul 1970 (quote), folder Jul 1970, box 1, Acc 218-05-006; memo, Kissinger for Nixon, 10 Sep 1970, folder Blue Ribbon Defense Panel, box 239, Agency Files, NSC, Nixon Library.

53. Memo, Harlow for Haig, 6 Aug 1970 (quote), attached to memo, Howe for Haig, 8 Aug 1970, folder DoD vol. 8, box 225; memo, Lynn for Kissinger, 5 Oct 1970, folder Blue Ribbon Defense Panel, box 239; memo, Kissinger for Nixon, 29 Oct 1970 (quotes); and ltr, Nixon to Laird, 5 Nov 1970, both attached to memo, Smith for Kissinger, 21 Oct 1970, folder DoD vol. 9, box 225: all in NSC, Nixon Library.

54. Memo, Laird for Nixon, 14 Nov 1970 (quotes), folder Blue Ribbon Defense Panel, box 239; telcons, Kissinger and Laird, 8 Jul 1970, folder 1; 21 Jul 1970, folder 2: both in box 6, HAK Telcons, NSC, Nixon Library.

55. DoD News Releases 698-70, 26 Aug 1970, and 713-70, 1 Sep 1970, folder Blue Ribbon Panel Clips, box 549, Subject Files, OSD/HO. The committee included David O. Cooke, DASD for Administration; Vice Adm. John P. Weinel, director of plans and policy for the Joint Staff; Army Lt. Gen. William E. DePuy, USA, assistant vice chief of staff; Rear Adm. Frank W. Vannoy, assistant deputy CNO for Plans and Policy; Maj. Gen. George J. Eade, USAF, director of plans; and Brig. Gen. Herbert L. Beckington, USMC, assistant director of personnel. Memo, Smith for Kissinger, 27 Nov 1970, folder Blue Ribbon Defense Panel, box 239, Agency Files, NSC, Nixon Library.

56. Memo, Laird for Nixon, 2 Feb 1971, attached to memo, Nixon for Laird, 22 Feb 1971, folder DoD vol. 10, box 226, Agency Files, NSC, Nixon Library; Laird interview, 2 Sep 1986, 16 (quote).

57. News briefing, Fitzhugh and Buzhardt, 27 Jul 1970, 10–11, folder Blue Ribbon Defense Panel, box 549, Subject Files, OSD/HO; News conference, Laird and Packard, 27 Jul 1970, *Laird Public Statements 1970*, 4:1794–1802 (quote).

58. Laird Statement on FY 1972–76 Defense Program and the FY 1972 Defense Budget Before SCAS," 15 Mar 1971, 124–25 (quote), OSD/HO; memo, Smith for Kissinger, 3 Apr 1971 (quote), folder DoD vol. 11, box 226, Agency Files, NSC, Nixon Library.

59. "Blue Ribbon Defense Panel Report on National Command and Control and Defense Intelligence," Executive Summary, n.d., folder Blue Ribbon Defense Panel, box 239, Agency Files, NSC, Nixon Library.

60. Memo, Lynn for Kissinger, 7 Aug 1970, ibid.

61. "Blue Ribbon Panel Report," Executive Summary, cited in note 59.

62. Memo, Lynn for Kissinger, 7 Aug 1970, cited in note 60.

63. Memo, Smith for Kissinger, 23 Sep 1970; JCSM-514-70 for Laird, 7 Nov 1970: both in *Foreign Relations of the United States [FRUS], 1969-1976* (Washington, DC: Government Printing Office), 2:452–55, 464–66.

64. Roger R. Trask and Alfred Goldberg, *The Department of Defense, 1947–1997: Organization and Leaders* (Washington, DC: OSD Historical Office, 1997), 35.

65. Memo, Nixon for Laird, 28 May 1971, folder DoD vol. 7, box 227, Agency Files, NSC, Nixon Library.

2. Organizing National Security in a New Administration

1. A number of studies have examined the evolution of the role of the NSC and the national security adviser. Among the notable ones are John Prados, *Keeper of the Keys: A History of the National Security Council from Truman to Bush* (New York: Morrow, 1991); I. M. Destler, *Presidents, Bureaucrats, and Foreign Policy: The Politics of Organizational*

Reform (Princeton, NJ: Princeton University Press, 1974); Ivo Daalder and I. M. Destler, *In the Shadow of the Oval Office: Profiles of the National Security Advisers and the Presidents They Served—From JFK to George W. Bush* (New York: Simon & Schuster, 2009); Peter Rodman, *Presidential Command: Power, Leadership, and the Making of Foreign Policy from Richard Nixon to George W. Bush* (New York: Knopf, 2009); and David J. Rothkopf, *Running the World: The Inside Story of the National Security Council and the Architects of American Power* (New York: Public Affairs, 2004). For differing views of the Nixon Kissinger approach to foreign affairs, see William P. Bundy, *A Tangled Web: The Making of Foreign Policy in the Nixon Presidency* (New York: Hill & Wang, 1998); Robert Dallek, *Nixon and Kissinger: Partners in Power* (New York: Harper, 2007); Seymour M. Hersh, *The Price of Power: Kissinger in the White House* (New York: Summit Books, 1983); and Van Atta, *With Honor*.

2. Nixon, *Memoirs*, 339.

3. Marvin L. Kalb and Bernard Kalb, *Kissinger* (Boston: Little, Brown, 1974), 89–90; Van Atta, *With Honor*, 136.

4. Ibid., 340–41 (quotes). For Kissinger's pre-inauguration contacts with Nixon's entourage, see Hersh, *Price of Power*, chap. 1; and Bundy, *Tangled Web*, 52.

5. Henry A. Kissinger, *White House Years* (Boston: Little, Brown, 1979), 38–39; Prados, *Keeper of the Keys*, 261.

6. Andrew Goodpaster, interview by Alfred Goldberg and Maurice Matloff, 7 Feb 1984, 31, OSD/HO; memo, Goodpaster for Kissinger, 15 Dec 1968, 4–5, folder Gen. Goodpaster, box 1 Henry A. Kissinger (HAK) Administrative and Staff Files, NSC, Nixon Library.

7. Prados, *Keeper of the Keys*, 262. Halperin, a Harvard colleague of Kissinger, served as deputy assistant secretary of defense for policy planning and arms control during the Johnson administration; see *FRUS 1964–1968*, 2:xxxii.

8. Memo, Kissinger for Nixon, 27 Dec 1968, *FRUS 1969–1976*, 2:1–10.

9. Kissinger wrote in *White House Years*, page 44, that Nixon approved the reorganization on 27 December before discussing it with Laird and Rogers on 28 December 1968. A handwritten annotation on the Kissinger memo of 27 December, cited in note 8, dated the document 27 December 1968 and noted that Nixon approved it on 30 December.

10. Destler, *Presidents, Bureaucrats, and Foreign Policy*, 104–05; Kissinger, *White House Years*, 42–43; Bundy, *Tangled Web*, 54–55.

11. Van Atta, *With Honor*, 155–56.

12. Paper Prepared by the Under Secretary of State-Designate (Richardson), n.d., *FRUS 1969–1976*, 2:15–18; U. Alexis Johnson recounted his misgivings in his memoir, *The Right Hand of Power* (Englewood Cliffs, NJ: Prentice Hall, 1984), 513–14.

13. Memo, Kissinger for Nixon, 7 Jan 1969, *FRUS 1969–1976*, 2:11–14; memo, Nixon for Kissinger, 13 Jan 1969, ibid., 2:25–26; draft memo, Kissinger and Goodpaster for president-elect, n.d., folder Goodpaster, box 1, HAK Administrative and Staff Files, NSC, Nixon Library.

14. Van Atta, *With Honor*, 155–59.

15. Memo, Kissinger for Nixon, 27 Dec 1968, cited in note 8; NSDM 2, 20 Jan 1969, *FRUS 1969–1976*, 2:30–33.

16. NSSM 3, subj: U.S. Military Posture and the Balance of Power, 20 Jan 1969, attached to memo, Kissinger for Laird, 21 Jan 1969 (quote), folder DoD vol. 1, box 220, Agency Files, NSC, Nixon Library.

17. Kissinger, *White House Years*, 44–45; memo, Laird for Kissinger, 9 Jan 1969, *FRUS 1969–1976*, 2:22–24 (quotes).

18. NSDM 2, 20 Jan 1969, *FRUS 1969–1976*, 2:30–33.

19. Minutes of First Meeting of NSC, 21 Jan 1969, ibid., 2:38–41. See also memo, Kissinger for Vice President et al., 23 Jan 1969, folder NSC Procedures and Meeting Schedule 1/12/69, box H-019, NSC Institutional Files [hereafter H-Files], Nixon Library.

20. Also in the office of the assistant to the president for national security affairs were Lawrence S. Eagleburger, Richard M. Moose, Robert Houdek, and Arthur McCafferty; see memo, Haig for Kissinger, 11 Feb 1969, folder National Security Adviser, box 40, Kissinger/Scowcroft Files, 1969–1977, NSC Organization, Ford Library.

21. Alexander Haig, interview by Alfred Goldberg and Ronald Landa, 14 Feb 1996, 3–4, OSD/HO; memo, Haig for Kissinger, 8 Jan 1969, *FRUS 1969–1976*, 2:19–21; memo, Kissinger for Laird, 29 Jan 1969 (quote), folder DoD vol. 1, box 220, Agency Files, NSC, Nixon Library.

22. Memo, Haig for Kissinger, 7 Feb 1969, folder Haig Chron Feb 1–15, 1969, box 955, Haig Chron Files, NSC, Nixon Library. Haig labeled the memo "Eyes Only-Private."

23. Memo, Haig for Kissinger, 11 Feb 1969, cited in note 20. Haig had to wait until June 1970 before formal promotion to deputy, even though he seemed to exercise that authority well before that date.

24. Memo, Laird for Kissinger, 7 May 1969, *FRUS 1969–1976*, 2:93–94; talking points on NSC organization, 9 May 1969, folder NSC Org-4, box 40, Kissinger/Scowcroft Files, Ford Library. Haig, the likely author of the talking points, proposed that he be relieved of responsibility for substantive projects and be granted "complete authority for staff supervision" so he could concentrate on running the NSC staff, handling personnel problems, and transmitting Kissinger's guidance.

25. Memo, Laird for Kissinger, 4 Aug 1970, *FRUS 1969–1976*, 2:254–57.

26. Memo, Rogers for Kissinger, 26 Feb 1971, ibid., 2:300.

27. Comment by Kissinger submitted to the Subcommittee on National Security and International Operations of the Senate Committee on Government Operations, 3 Mar 1970, folder Haig Chron Aug 17–21, 1970 [2 of 2], box 970, Haig Chron Files, NSC, Nixon Library.

28. Personal memo, Sonnenfeldt for Kissinger, 30 Apr 1969 (quotes), attached to memo, Haig for Kissinger, 3 May 1969, folder NSC Org-4, box 40, Kissinger/Scowcroft Files, Ford Library; memo, Halperin, 5 Aug 1969 (quotes), folder Halperin, box 817, Name Files, NSC, Nixon Library. Halperin told Kissinger he would remain "for a two-month trial period provided we can reach a clear understanding of my functions and

provided that you communicate this understanding at a staff meeting. . . ." Ltr, Halperin to Kissinger, 22 Aug 1969, folder NSC Org-5; memo, Watts for Kissinger, 1 Dec 1969, folder NSC Org-6: both in box 40, Kissinger/Scowcroft Files, Ford Library. On 3 April 1970, Watts and Richard Kennedy sent Kissinger recommendations to improve the NSC. *FRUS 1969–1976*, 2:225–29.

29. NSDM 8, 21 Mar 1969, ibid., 2:76–77.

30. Memo for Haig, 17 Apr 1969, folder North Korean Reconnaissance Shootdown Haig vol. 2, box 434, Korea: EC–121 Shootdown File [hereafter EC–121], NSC, Nixon Library; Richard A. Mobley, *Flash Point North Korea: The Pueblo and EC–121 Crises* (Annapolis, MD: Naval Institute Press, 2003), 99–103.

31. The chronology of the EC–121 incident is largely based on the State Department Historical Office's report "North Korean Downing of a U.S. Reconnaissance Plane: The EC–121 Incident, April 1969," prepared by Allen H. Kitchens in October 1969. State sent this report to Kissinger in November, memo, Eliot for Kissinger, 13 Nov 1969, folder Chronology of EC-121M Shootdown [1], box 439, EC–121, NSC, Nixon Library. Another chronology is the "Sequence of Notification–Korean Incident," folder Chronology of EC–121 Shootdown, box 436, ibid. Information on equipment comes from General Wheeler's testimony before a subcommittee of the House Committee on Armed Services; see HCAS, Special Subcommittee, *Inquiry into the U.S.S. Pueblo and EC–121 Plane Incidents: Report*, 91st Cong., 1st sess., 28 Jul 1969, H. Rept 91-12, 1675; Mobley, *Flash Point,* 107.

32. Nixon, *Memoirs*, 382–85; Hersh, *Price of Power*, 69; Kissinger, *White House Years*, 313–21; Alexander Haig, interview by Alfred Goldberg and Ronald Landa, 2 May 1996, 19 (quote), OSD/HO.

33. Memo, Kissinger for Laird, 15 Apr 1969, folder North Korean Reconnaissance Shootdown Haig vol. 1, box 434, EC–121, NSC, Nixon Library. The memo was sent to Laird at 11:29 p.m. Memo, Kissinger for the Vice President et al., 15 Apr 1969, folder EC–121 1–4, box 6, Laird Papers, Ford Library; telcon, Nixon and Kissinger, 15 Apr 1969, 10 p.m.; memo, Laird for Kissinger, 15 Apr 1969: both in folder Haig vol. 1, box 434, EC–121, NSC, Nixon Library.

34. Memo, Kissinger for Nixon, 15 Apr 1969, folder North Korean Reconnaissance Shootdown Haig vol. 1, box 434, EC–121, NSC, Nixon Library; Memo for the Record, subj: NSC Meeting on North Korean Downing of U.S. EC–121 Reconnaissance Aircraft, 16 Apr 1969, folder NSC Minutes Originals 1969 [3 of 5], box H-109, H Files, NSC, Nixon Library.

35. Nixon, *Memoirs*, 383–84; Kissinger, *White House Years*, 317.

36. Msg, CINCPAC to CINCPACFLT, 181825Z Apr 1969, folder General Materials, box 438, EC–121, NSC, Nixon Library.

37. H. R. Haldeman, *The Haldeman Diaries: Inside the Nixon White House* (New York: G.P. Putnam's Sons, 1994), 50; telcon, Kissinger and Laird, 2:10 p.m., 16 Apr 1969 (quotes), folder Chronology, box 436, EC–121, NSC, Nixon Library.

38. Memo, Kissinger for Nixon, 16 Apr 1969, folder Presidential Approvals vol. 1, box 435, EC–121, NSC, Nixon Library. When Kissinger later criticized Nixon's crisis management

as slow, he neglected to mention that he had proposed the timetable for Nixon; see Kissinger, *White House Years*, 316.

39. Telcon, Nixon and Kissinger, 8:00 p.m., 17 Apr 1969, folder Haig vol. 2, box 434, EC-121, NSC, Nixon Library.

40. Fact Sheet, subj: Logistic Support of Hostilities in Korea, 17 Apr 1969, ibid.

41. Memo for the Record, NMCC, 18 Apr 1969, folder EC-121 Shootdown Apr 18–19, box 439, ibid.; JCSM-247-69 for SecDef, 24 Apr 1969, folder North Korean Reconnaissance Shootdown Haig vol. 3, box 435, ibid.; Kissinger, *White House Years*, 318.

42. Telcon, Nixon and Kissinger, 9:15 a.m., 18 Apr 1969, folder North Korean Reconnaissance Shootdown Haig vol. 3, box 435, EC-121, NSC, Nixon Library.

43. *Public Papers of the Presidents of the United States: Richard Nixon, 1969* (Washington, DC: Government Printing Office, 1971), 1969, 299; memo, Haig for Kissinger, 17 Apr 1969, folder North Korean Reconnaissance Shootdown Haig vol. 2, box 434; memo, Haig for Kissinger, 18 Apr 1969, folder Haig vol. 3, box 435: both in EC-121, NSC, Nixon Library.

44. Memo, Nixon for Rogers et al., 14 Apr 1969, folder HAK/President Memos 1969–1970, box 341, Subject Files, NSC, Nixon Library; memo, Laird for Nixon, 18 Apr 1969 (quote), folder General Materials, box 438, EC-121, NSC, Nixon Library.

45. Memo, Laird for Nixon, 18 Apr 1969, cited in note 44.

46. Nixon, *Memoirs*, 383; Kissinger, *White House Years*, 319–20; memo, Sneider for Kissinger, 18 Apr 1969, folder General Materials, box 438, EC-121, NSC, Nixon Library; *Haldeman Diaries*, 51.

47. Telcon, Kissinger and Rogers, 19 Apr 1969, 9:25 a.m., folder Chronology, box 436; Memo for the Record, Haig, 21 Apr 1969, folder EC-121 Shootdown – Apr 20–, box 439: both in NSC, Nixon Library.

48. Memo, Laird for President, 22 Apr 1969, folder North Korean Reconnaissance Shootdown Haig vol. 3, box 435, EC-121, ibid. Laird and Kissinger discussed these studies in detail; see memo, Kissinger for Nixon, 24 Apr 1969, ibid.

49. JSCM-248-69 for SecDef, 24 Apr 1969, attached to memo, Laird for Kissinger, 24 Apr 1969, ibid. Wheeler recommended less extensive coverage using aircraft from bases in South Korea to provide reasonable protection from North Korean attacks.

50. Telcon, Kissinger and Rogers, 24 Apr 1969, 5:20 p.m.; memo, Kissinger for Laird, 25 Apr 1969: both in ibid. The memo was transmitted to Laird by "LDX" at 5:15 p.m. according to a notation on the document.

51. Memo, Laird for Kissinger, 25 Apr 1969, ibid. Attached were Laird's memos to Chairman, Joint Chiefs of Staff (CJCS) and DDR&E.

52. Telcon, Kissinger and Packard, 25 Apr 1969, 6:40 p.m., folder Chronology, box 436, ibid.; telcons, Kissinger and Laird, 28 Apr 1969, 11:35 a.m., 7:15 p.m.: both in folder North Korean Reconnaissance Shootdown Haig vol. 3, box 435, ibid.

53. Memo, Kissinger for Nixon, 30 Apr 1969 (quotes); memo, Kissinger for Rogers, Laird, et al., subj: Resumption of Regularly Scheduled Reconnaissance Operations in the

Pacific Area, 29 Apr 1969; memo, Kissinger for Rogers, Laird et al., 30 Apr 1969; memo, Kissinger for Packard, 28 Apr 1969: all in folder Presidential Approvals Haig vol. 1, ibid.

54. *FRUS 1964–68*, 30: 77n2; memo, Haig for Kissinger, 28 Apr 1969 (quote), folder North Korean Reconnaissance Shootdown Haig vol. 3, box 435, EC–121, NSC, Nixon Library.

55. Ltr, Johnson to Kissinger, 21 Apr 1969; memo, Nutter for Kissinger, 26 Apr 1969: both in folder North Korean Reconnaissance Shootdown Haig vol. 3, box 435, EC–121, NSC, Nixon Library; Kissinger, *White House Years*, 319.

56. Nixon, *Memoirs*, 384–85.

57. Memo, Karamessines for Kissinger, 21 Apr 1969 (quote); memo, U. Alexis Johnson, 28 Apr 1969 (quote), attached to memo, Johnson for Kissinger, n.d.: both in folder North Korean Reconnaissance Shootdown Haig vol. 3, box 435, EC–121, NSC, Nixon Library.

58. Memo, Kissinger for Nixon, 17 Sep 1969, folder DPRC & Def Budget 1969, box 234, Agency Files, NSC, Nixon Library.

59. Pursley, interview by Goldberg and Trask, 15 Aug 1997, 36–37, OSD/HO; memo, Laird for McCracken, 23 Dec 1969 (quotes), folder 77, box 7, Records from SecDef Vault, Acc 330-74-142, WNRC.

60. Melvin Small, *The Presidency of Richard Nixon* (Lawrence: University Press of Kansas, 1999), 52–53; Kissinger, *White House Years*, 394–96. Nixon's memoir does not discuss the DPRC.

61. Memo, Laird for Kissinger, 5 Sep 1969, folder NATO vol. 6, box 257, Agency Files, NSC, Nixon Library.

62. Memo, Lynn for Kissinger, 10 Sep 1969 (quote), attached to memo, Kissinger for Nixon, 17 Sep 1969, cited in note 58.

63. Memo, Kissinger for Nixon, 17 Sep 1969 (quote), folder DPRC & Def Budget 1969, box 234, Agency Files, NSC, Nixon Library; HAK Talking Points, meeting w/Shultz, Ehrlichman, n.d. (quotes), folder DPRC & Def Budget 1970 vol. I, box 235, Agency Files, NSC, Nixon Library. The Talking Points paper, which recounts the reasons for establishing DPRC, was drafted by Larry Lynn probably in June 1970.

64. NSDM 26, 11 Oct 1969, *FRUS 1969–1976*, 2:166–67. Laird's views were contained in memo, Pursley for Kissinger, attached to memo, Pursley for Haig, 24 Sep 1969, folder Haig Chron Sep 1969 [1 of 2], box 958, Haig Chron Files, NSC, Nixon Library.

65. NSDM 27, 11 Oct 1969, folder NSDM 1-50, box 363, Subject Files, NSC, Nixon Library.

66. Memo, Laird for Service Secretaries, CJCS et al., 28 Oct 1969, *FRUS 1969–1976*, 2:176–77.

67. Memo, Lynn for Kissinger, ibid., 168–172; memo, Lynn for Kissinger, 24 Oct 1969, folder 1971 Budget Procedures, box 309, Subject Files, NSC, Nixon Library.

68. Memo, Haig for Kissinger, 4 Nov 1969, folder DPRC & Def Budget 1969, box 234, Agency Files, NSC; memo, Haig for Kissinger, 11 Nov 1969, folder Haig Chron Nov 1969 [2 of 3], box 959, Haig Chron Files, NSC; memos, Lynn for Kissinger, 8 Dec 1969; Laird for

Kissinger, 25 Nov 1969: both attached to memo, Haig for Kissinger, 8 Dec 1969, folder Haig Chron Dec 1–8, 1969, box 960, Haig Chron Files, NSC, Nixon Library.

69. Memo, Laird for Kissinger, 1 Dec 1969 (quote), attached to "Talking Points," 11 Dec 1969, folder DoD vol. 3, box 221, Agency Files, NSC, Nixon Library; memos, Lynn for Kissinger, 8 Dec 1969 (quote); Laird for Kissinger, 25 Nov 1969: both attached to memo, Haig for Kissinger, 8 Dec 1969, cited in note 68; memo, Haig for Kissinger, 1 Dec 1969 (quotes), *FRUS 1969–1976*, 2:194–95.

70. Ed. note, *FRUS 1969–1976*, 2:201–02; memo, Lynn for Kissinger, 8 Dec 1969, cited in note 67; "Talking Points," 11 Dec 1969, cited in note 69.

71. Memo, Packard for Kissinger, 3 Dec 1969 (quotes), attached to memo, Haig for Kissinger, 8 Dec 1969, cited in note 68.

72. Memo, Kissinger for Nixon, 24 Dec 1969, folder BoB vol. 1, box 206, Agency Files, NSC, Nixon Library.

73. Memo, Kissinger for Under SecState et al., 26 Feb 1970, attached to memo, Lynn for Kissinger, 26 Mar 1970, folder DPRC & Def Budget 1970 vol. 1, box 235, ibid.; memo, Laird for Kissinger, DPRC Working Group Procedures, 14 Mar 1970 (quote), folder 70, box 6, Records from SecDef Vault, Acc 330-74-142. Laird sent Kissinger a second memo on 14 March. See memo, Laird for Kissinger, attached to memo, Lynn for Kissinger, subj: DPRC, 26 Mar 1970 (quotes), folder DPRC & Def Budget 1970 vol. 1, box 235, Agency Files, NSC, Nixon Library. General Wheeler objected to having the DPRC working group prepare all the issue papers. Wheeler recommended that the department "retain responsibility" for preparing papers involving "matters under its primary cognizance" and that the review group only prepare studies on topics outside the purview of DoD. See memo, Wheeler for Laird, 22 Jan 1970, folder 77, box 7, Records from SecDef Vault, Acc 330-74-142.

74. Memo, Haig for Kissinger, 14 Mar 1970, folder Haig Chron Mar 12–20, 1970 [2 of 2], box 963, Haig Chron Files, NSC, Nixon Library. Haig addressed this memo to "Henry."

75. Memo, Kissinger for Nixon, n.d., attached to memo, Lynn for Kissinger, 26 Mar 1970 (quote) cited in note 72; memo, Nixon for Chairman DPRC, 2 Apr 1970 (quote), folder DPRC & Def Budget 1970 vol. 1, box 235, Agency Files, NSC, Nixon Library. Kissinger drafted the memorandum.

76. Effective 1 July 1970, the Office of Management and Budget (OMB) assumed the duties of BoB, which ceased to exist. George P. Shultz became director of OMB. HAK Talking Points, meeting w/Shultz, Ehrlichman, n.d., folder DPRC& Def Budget 1970 vol. 1, box 235 Agency Files, NSC, Nixon Library; memo, Odeen for Kissinger, 3 Feb 1972, in note, *FRUS 1969–1976*, 2:342 (quotes).

77. Walter S. Poole, *The Joint Chiefs of Staff and National Policy, 1969–1972* (Washington, DC: Office of Joint History, Office of the JCS, 2013), 15; memo, Spiers for Irwin, 3 Mar 1971, *FRUS 1969–1976*, 2:301–303.

78. Memo, Spiers for Irwin, 28 Feb 1972, *FRUS 1969–1976*, 2:343–44.

79. HAK Talking Points, cited in note 75. Lynn, who advised Kissinger on the DPRC, wrote this memo. *FRUS 1969–1976*, 2:239–43.

80. Michel Warner, "Reading the Riot Act: The Schlesinger Report, 1971," *Intelligence and National Security* 24, no. 3 (Jun 2009): 387–93.

81. "Report on Defense Intelligence," 29 Jul 1969, attached to memo, Laird for Service Secretaries et al., 1 Aug 1969, *FRUS 1969–1976*, 2:392–403.

82. Ed. note, *FRUS 1969–1976*, 2:446–47, discusses the president's meeting w/PFIAB on 18 July 1970.

83. Study by OMB and NSC Staffs, "A Review of the Intelligence Community," 10 Mar 1971, *FRUS 1969–1976*, 2:494–513; memo, Schlesinger for DirOMB, 11 May 71, ibid., 513–16. For background on the 1947 act, see Steven L. Rearden, *The Formative Years, 1947–1950* (Washington, DC: OSD Historical Office, 1984), 22–27.

84. Memo, Nixon for Kissinger, 30 Nov 1970, *FRUS 1969–1976*, 2:467 (quotes); ed. note (quote), ibid., 482–83; Andrew W. Marshall, interview by Alfred Goldberg and Maurice Matloff, 1 Jun 1992, 13–14, OSD/HO.

85. Warner, "Reading the Riot Act," 387–417; Benjamin Welles, "Nixon Reported Weighing Revamping of Intelligence Services," *New York Times*, 11 May 1971, 2.

86. Memo, Schlesinger for Shultz, 11 May 1971, *FRUS 1969–1976*, 2:513–16; telcon, Kissinger and Laird, 20 Jan 1971, cited in note 83; memo, Laird for Froehlke, 5 Aug 1971, folder Pursley Chron May–Oct 1971, box 3, Pursley Files, Acc 330-75-104, WNRC.

87. Schlesinger, "A Review," 10 Mar 1971, cited in note 83.

88. Telcon, Kissinger and Laird, 9 Nov 1971, folder 1, box 12, HAK Telcons, NSC, Nixon Library (quotes); telcons, Kissinger and Symington, Kissinger and Fulbright, both on 11 Nov 1971, ibid.; Moorer Diary, 26 Nov 1971 (quote), box 2, Acc 218-05-006, NARA II. According to Moorer, Laird had seen a copy of the reorganization in advance but was angry because none of his recommended changes was accepted.

89. Ltr, Nixon to Helms, 1 Nov 1971, *FRUS 1969–1976*, 2:537; memo, Cline for Richardson, 1 Dec 1971, ibid., 552–558; White House Press Release, 5 Nov 1971, folder Intell 1971, box 740, Subject Files, OSD/HO.

90. Memo, Nixon for SecState et al., 5 Nov 1971, *FRUS 1969–1976*, 2:539–44; see also memo, Laird for Service Secretaries, 29 Dec 1971, ibid., 587–88; and memo, Laird for Service Secretaries et al., 10 Nov 1971, folder Intell 1971, box 740, Subject Files, OSD/HO.

91. Draft memo, Moot for Laird, n.d., *FRUS 1969–1976*, 2:567–71; JCSM-546-71 for Laird, 10 Dec 1971, ibid., 571–73; memo, Packard for Service Secretaries et al., 3 Nov 1971, *FRUS 1969–1976*, 2:538–39; DoD News Release 943-71, 6 Nov 1971, *Laird Public Statements 1971*, 6:2114–15.

92. DoD Directive 5115.1, 18 Jan 1972, *FRUS 1969–1976*, 2:591–94.

93. Memo, Seamans for Laird, 7 Jan 1972, ibid., 594, note 3.

94. Marshall interview, 1 Jun 1992, 14–15; memo, Hall for Laird, 23 Feb 1972, *FRUS 1969–1976*, 2:600–02.

95. Memo, Nixon for Haldeman, 18 May 1972, *FRUS 1969–1976*, 2:620–21.

96. Memo, Kissinger for Nixon, 15 Feb 1969, folder USSR Memcons, box 340, Subject Files, NSC, Nixon Library; Nixon, *Memoirs* 369–370 (quote); Kissinger, *White House Years*, 138–41; *Haldeman Diaries*, 30.

97. This author has not found documentation on the origins of these channels but has copies of numerous private exchanges between Kissinger and Bunker and Abrams.

98. Memo, Pursley for Laird, 20 Jan 1969, *FRUS 1969–1976*, 2:26–29.

99. Memo, Laird for Service Secretaries et al., 25 Jan 1969, folder NSC Materials, box 3, Pursley Files, Acc 330-75-104; memo, Laird for CJCS and ASD (ISA), 22 Jan 1969, attached to memo, Pursley for DirDIA, 9 Jan 1970, folder Miscellaneous Correspondence, box D17, Laird Papers-03, Ford Library.

100. Ltr, Laird to DuBridge, 12 Jun 1969, attached to memo, Laird for Wheeler, 11 Jun 1969 (quote), Moorer Diary, box 1, Acc 218-05-006.

101. Memos, Laird for Kissinger, 22 Jan 1969; Kissinger for Laird, 25 Jan 1969: both in folder NSC-Org-1, box 40, Kissinger/Scowcroft Files, Ford Library.

102. Memo, Laird for Service Secretaries, 12 Sep 1969, attached to memo, Pursley for DirDIA, 9 Jan 1970, cited in note 99.

103. Memo, Laird for Nixon, 15 Mar 1971; memo, Nixon for Laird, 8 Apr 1971: both in folder Staff Mtgs Apr–Jun 1971, box 14, Acc 330-77-0062, WNRC.

104. Memo, Haig for Kissinger, 20 Jan 1969, folder Chron Haig Jan 1969, box 955, Haig Chron Files, NSC, Nixon Library; telcons, Nixon and Kissinger, 13 Dec 1969 (quotes), 2:07 p.m., folder 9–16 Dec 1969, box 3; Kissinger and Laird, 5 Feb 1969, 2:10 p.m., box 1: all in HAK Telcons, ibid.

105. Memo, Nixon for Kissinger, 12 Nov 1971, folder Memos from the President 1971, box 140, Haldeman Files, White House Special Files (WHSF), Nixon Library.

106. Andrew Goodpaster, interview by Goldberg, Matloff, and Robert Watson, 19 Jan 1984, 36, OSD/HO.

3. How Much for Defense? The FY 1970 Budget

1. For further information on the international and domestic economic issues of the period, see Francis Gavin, *Gold, Dollars and Power: The Politics of International Monetary Policy Relations, 1958–1971* (Chapel Hill: University of North Carolina Press, 2007); Thomas Zeiler and Alfred Ickes, *American Trade and Power* (New York: Columbia University Press: 1992); and *Globalization and the American Century* (Cambridge: Cambridge University Press, 2003); and Allen Matusow, *Nixon's Economy: Booms, Busts, Dollars, and Votes* (Lawrence: University of Kansas Press, 1998).

2. "Economic Report of the President—Message from the President" (H. Doc. 91-28), in *Cong. Rec.*, 16 Jan 1969, S 389–94.

3. Ibid.

4. Tab D, memo, DirBoB for President, 16 Dec 1968, attached to T/C, folder 97, FY 70 budget, box 8, Records from SecDef Vault, Acc 330-74-142, WNRC. Secretary Clifford responded to this document on 18 December in a memo for the president. Laird saw this document on 29 January 1969, according to a stamp on the document.

5. Memo, Clifford for President, 2 Oct 1968, folder Vietnam Calendar B 1–46, box 30, Laird Papers, Ford Library.

6. The Fiscal Year 1970–74 Defense Program and 1970 Defense Budget, 15 Jan 1969, OSD Historical Office, comp., *Public Statements of Clark Clifford, Secretary of Defense, 1968*, 4:1 (emphasis in original).

7. Tab E, CM-3811-68 for SecDef, 19 Dec 1968, attached to T/C, cited in note 2.

8. Tab D, memo, SecDef for President, 18 Dec 1968, ibid.

9. Tab B, ASD(C) Fact Sheet—Defense Budget, 5 Jan 1969, ibid.; Richard M. Leighton, *Strategy, Money, and the New Look, 1953–1956* (Washington, DC: OSD Historical Office, 2001), 50; Executive Office of the President, OMB, *The U.S. Budget in Brief, Fiscal Year 1973* (Washington, DC: Government Printing Office, 1972), 4, 74.

10. *FRUS 1969–1976*, 3:iv–v.

11. Edwin L. Dale Jr., "Inflation and Vietnam," *New York Times*, 25 Jun 1969, gave the inflation rates for 1958–1965 and three months in 1969. Senate Committee on Foreign Relations (SCFR), *Hearings: Impact of the War in Southeast Asia on the U.S. Economy*, 91st Cong., 2nd sess., 15 and 16 Apr 1970, pt.1:55, lists the consumer price index from 1960 to 1970.

12. Warren Unna, "Doubts Rise on Hill Over Arms Needs," *Washington Post*, 23 Mar 1969.

13. Table 1, Statement of ASD(C) Robert Moot to Subcommittee on Economy in Government of the Joint Economic Committee, 6 Jun 1969, folder DoD Budget General Jan-Jun 1969, box 787, Subject Files, OSD/HO.

14. Lawrence J. Korb, *The Fall and Rise of the Pentagon: American Defense Policies in the 1970s* (Westport, CT: Greenwood Press, 1979), 17.

15. *U.S. News & World Report*, 25 Nov 1968; William Beecher, "Military Asking for $20-Billion More," *New York Times*, 19 Dec 1968, 30.

16. Korb, *The Fall and Rise of the Pentagon*, 28–32.

17. Nixon, "The All-Volunteer Armed Force," 17 Oct 1968, folder AVF 1–3, box 1, Laird Papers, Ford Library. The speech was given on the CBS radio network.

18. Matusow, *Nixon's Economy*, 37–39.

19. OMB, *The Budget of the United States Government, Fiscal Year 1977* (Washington, DC: Government Printing Office, 1996), Historical Tables, 45–46.

20. Special msg to Congress on fiscal policy, 26 Mar 1969, *Nixon Public Papers 1969*, 254; Matusow, *Nixon's Economy*, 39, 53; Nixon, Memorandum on the Need for a Review of the Budget, 27 Jan 1969, *Nixon Public Papers 1969*, 23–24.

21. *DoD Annual Report FY 1968*, 67–68 (quote); memo, Fitt for Laird, 21 Jan 1969 (quotes), folder 97 FY 70 Budget, box 8, Records from SecDef Vault, Acc 330-74-142; Memo

for the Record, ASD(MRA), 29 Jan 1969, folder Mil Pay Bill, box A 79, Baroody Papers, Ford Library. Details of the Hubbell Plan come from Fitt's memo.

22. Memo, Fitt for Laird, 21 Jan 1969, cited in note 20; ltr, Packard to Mayo, 7 Mar 1969, folder FY 70 Budget, box 81, ASD(C) Files, OSD/HO.

23. Memo, Fitt for Laird, 21 Jan 1969, cited in note 20; Minutes, SecDef Staff Meeting, 10 Feb 1969, 6, folder Staff Mtgs 27 Jan 1969–Mar 1969, box 13, Acc 330-77-0062, WNRC. The civilian and military leadership routinely attended Laird's staff meetings. Staff Secretary R. Eugene Livesay usually drafted the notes for the weekly sessions. Memo, Mayo for Kissinger, 24 Mar 1969, folder DoD Budget, box 238, Agency Files, NSC, Nixon Library.

24. Minutes, SecDef Staff Meetings, 17 Mar 1969, 7–9 (quotes); 17 Feb 1969, 4: both in folder Staff Mtgs 27 Jan 1969–Mar 1969, box 13, Acc 330-77-0062. Admiral Hubbell briefed the group on his pay reform package on 17 February.

25. For information on McNamara's budget process and how he funded the war, see Drea, *McNamara, Clifford and the Burdens of Vietnam*, chaps. 4, 6, and 9.

26. Minutes, SecDef Staff Meeting, 27 Jan 1969, 4, folder Staff Mtgs 27 Jan–Mar 1969, box 13, Acc 330-77-0062.

27. Minutes, SecDef Staff Meeting, 17 Feb 1969, 1–3 (quote 2), cited in note 24; "General Policy Guidance for the Review of the FY 1969 Supplemental and FY 1970 Budget," 14 Feb 1969, attached to minutes, ibid.

28. Memo, ASD(SA) for SecDef, 5 Feb 1969, folder SA Fact Sheets, box 80, ASD(C) Files, OSD/HO.

29. See for example, Thomas C. Thayer, *War Without Fronts: The American Experience in Vietnam* (Boulder, CO: Westview Press, 1985), 90–91. Thayer analyzed data on the war for the Systems Analysis office during the Johnson and Nixon administrations.

30. Memo, Laird for Kissinger, 1 Mar 1969, folder 21, box H-021, H Files, NSC, Nixon Library

31. "General Policy Guidance," 14 Feb 1969, cited in note 27.

32. Ltr, Packard to Mayo, 7 Mar 1969, folder FY 1970 Budget, box 81, ASD(C), OSD/HO. Laird was in Vietnam 5–12 March. The copy of this document in the ASD(C) Files does not contain the schedules enclosed with the original. See House Committee on Appropriations (HCA), Subcommittee on Department of Defense, *Department of Defense Appropriations for 1970: Hearings*, 91st Cong., 1st sess., 19 Mar 1969, table 2, pt.1:367; Executive Office of the President, OMB, *The U.S. Budget in Brief, Fiscal Year 1970* (Washington, DC: Government Printing Office, 1969), 4.

33. Matusow, *Nixon's Economy*, 10–11; Minutes, SecDef Staff Meetings, 3 Mar 1969, 4–5, 10 Mar 1969, 4, folder Staff Mtgs 27 Jan–Mar 1969, box 13, Acc 330-77-0062.

34. President's News Conference of 14 Mar 1969, *Nixon Public Papers 1969*, 211–12 (quote); Special Message to Congress on Fiscal Policy, 26 Mar 1969, ibid., 253–54 (quote).

35. SecDef Press Conference, 9 Mar 1969, *Laird Public Statements 1969*, 1:244–46 (quote); memo, Laird for Nixon, 13 Mar 1969, folder 3, box 3, Records from SecDef Vault, Acc 330-74-142.

36. SCAS, *Authorization for Military Procurement, Research and Development, Fiscal Year 1970, and Reserve Strength: Hearings*, 91st Cong., 1st sess., 19 Mar 1969, pt. 1:95–96; Fact Sheet "FY 1970 Budget Development," folder FY 1970 Budget, box 81, ASD(C) Files, OSD/HO.

37. Memo, Schlesinger for Packard, 18 Mar 1969, attached to memo, Haig for Kissinger, 24 Mar 1969, folder DoD Budget, box 238, Agency Files, NSC, Nixon Library.

38. Memo, Schlesinger for Haig, 24 Mar 1969, attached to memo, Haig for Kissinger, 24 Mar 1969 (quotes), ibid.

39. Memo, Laird for President, 20 Mar 1969; memo, Mayo for President, 21 Mar 1969: both in ibid.

40. Minutes, SecDef Staff Meeting, 24 Mar 1969, 8–9, folder Staff Mtgs 27 Jan 1969–Mar 1969, box 13, Acc 330-77-0062.

41. Memo, Mayo for Kissinger, 24 Mar 1969, folder DoD Budget, box 238, Agency Files, NSC Nixon Library. The memo was marked personal and confidential.

42. Telcon, Kissinger and Packard, 24 Mar 1969, ibid.

43. Memo, Haig for Kissinger, 24 Mar 1969, cited in note 37.

44. Memo, President for Mayo, 24 Mar 1969, attached to memo, DirBoB for Heads of Executive Departments and Agencies, 28 Mar 1969, folder 2d Revised FY 70 Budget Review, box 82, ASD(C) Files, OSD/HO.

45. Memo, Mayo for Kissinger, 25 Mar 1969, folder DoD Budget, box 238, Agency Files, NSC, Nixon Library.

46. Telcon, Packard and Kissinger, 25 Mar 1969, ibid.

47. Memo, Mayo for Laird, 26 Mar 1969, folder 2d Revised FY 70 Budget Review, box 82, ASD(C) Files, OSD/HO.

48. Ltr, Packard to Mayo, 27 Mar 1969, ibid.

49. Laird remarks to the press, 27 Mar 1969, *Laird Public Statements 1969*, 2:871.

50. Statement on the Balance of Payments, 4 Apr 1969, *Nixon Public Papers 1969*, 265–67; Statement on Proposed Changes in the 1970 Budget, 12 Apr 1969, ibid., 278–80.

51. Ltr, Mayo to Laird, 23 Apr 1969, folder 2d Revised FY 70 Budget Review, box 82, ASD(C) Files, OSD/HO.

52. Ltr, Mayo to Laird, 23 May 1969; memo, Mayo for Dept Heads, 27 Jun 1969: both in folder FY 1970 Budget, box 81, ibid.

53. Statement on the 1970 Budget, 22 Jul 1969, *Nixon Public Papers 1969*, 536–38.

54. R. Cargill Hall and Jacob Neufeld, eds., *The U.S. Air Force in Space: Proceedings, Air Force Historical Foundation Symposium, Andrews Air Force Base, Maryland, September 21–22, 1995* (Washington, DC: Government Printing Office, 1998), 70–73; telcon, Packard

and Kissinger, 14 Apr 1969 (quote), folder DoD Budget, box 238, Agency Files, NSC, Nixon Library.

55. Ltr, Packard to Rivers, 10 Jun 1969, folder 54, box 5, Records from SecDef Vault, Acc 330-74-142; Laird remarks to the press, 10 Jun 1969, *Laird Public Statements 1969*, 4:1683; Packard statement to the press, 10 Jun 1969, DoD News Release 491-69, *Packard Public Statements 1969*, 3:880.

56. Ltrs, Stennis to Laird, 14 Aug 1969; Laird to Stennis, 27 Aug 1969 (quotes): both in folder FY 1970 Budget, box 81, ASD(C) Files, OSD/HO.

57. Laird news conference, 21 Aug 1969, *Laird Public Statements 1969*, 5:2047.

58. Ibid. (quote), DoD News Release 699-99, 21 Aug 1969, *Laird Public Statements 1969*, 5:2046–49. George C. Wilson, "Laird to Cut Defense Funds by $3 Billion," *Washington Post*, 22 Aug 1969 (quote) reported on Laird's manner of speaking.

59. Memo, Haig for Kissinger, 14 Aug 1969 (quote), folder Items to discuss with the President 8/13/69 to 12/30/69, box 334, Subject Files, NSC, Nixon Library; Laird news conference, 21 Aug 1969, DoD News Release 699-99, 21 Aug 1969, 2062 (quote), cited in note 57.

60. Orr Kelly, "Behind a Senatorial Revolt Against the Military," *Washington Star*, 7 Sep 1969. Eagleton's comments appeared in the *Washington Post* on 24 August 1969.

61. The *Washington Post* carried two stories on the Moynihan report on the peace dividend on 26 August 1969: Carroll Kilpatrick, "Big Surplus After War Discounted," and UPI, "Moynihan Prediction Stirs Demand for Change in National Priorities." News conference with ASD (Comptroller) Robert Moot, 20 Oct 1969, box 81, ASD(C) Files, OSD/HO.

62. Ltr, Laird to Mayo, 19 Sep 1969, folder FY 70 Budget, box 81, ASD(C) Files, OSD/HO.

63. DoD News Release 921-69, 27 Oct 1969, in *Laird Public Statements 1969*, 6:2389; Van Atta, *With Honor*, 310; Laird interview, 15 Oct 2001, 2–3.

64. For the congressional reduction in FY 1970 appropriations, see *Cong. Rec.*, 18 Dec 1969, H 12706 and HCA, Subcommittee on the Department of Defense, *Department of Defense Appropriations for 1970: Hearings*, 91st Cong., 1st sess., 17 Nov 1969, pt. 7:358–60. The FY 1970 Authorization Act, P.L. 91-121, 83 Stat. 204, was signed into law on 19 November 1969.

65. Rowland Evans and Robert Novak, "Defense Budget-Cutting Miracle," *Washington Post*, 31 Dec 1969.

66. *Hearings*, cited in note 64, 362–63, table 1, 366.

67. Ibid., 363–65.

68. Ibid., table 3, 367.

69. Ibid., 381–84.

70. *Cong. Rec.*, 8 Dec 1969, H 11865–69.

71. George Wilson, "Congress Leading Way on Military Cutbacks," *Washington Post*, 8 Dec 1969, A1; Wilson, "$69.9 Billion Voted For Arms in House," *Washington Post*, 9 Dec 1969, A1. See *Cong. Rec.*, 8 Dec 1969, H 11865–908 for the House debate on the appropriation bill for FY 1970 (quote 11893).

72. Senate Subcommittee on Appropriations (SSCA), *Department of Defense Appropriations for Fiscal Year 1970: Hearings*, 91st Cong., 1st sess., 9 Dec 1969, pt. 6:36–42.

73 Ibid., 80; "Laird Asks Senate to Restore Funds," *Washington Post*, 10 Dec 1969.

74. *Cong. Rec.*, 15 Dec 1969, S 16744.

75. Ibid., 18 Dec 1969, H 12706. See ibid., 8 Dec 1969, H 11868–69 for the creation of Title II. Table 3 numbers appear as printed in the *Congressional Record*, but the total for the change from the revised budget by service is incorrect. The reductions by service add up to 5,637,532,000. The DoD FY 1970 Appropriations Act, P.L. 91-71, 83 Stat. 469, passed on 29 December 1969.

76. George C. Wilson, "Public's New Tune Spurs Mahon to Cut Arms Funds by $5 Billion," *Washington Post*, 22 Dec 1969, 1.

77. NSSM 3, 20 Jan 1969, folder NSSM 1–4, box 16, NSC, OSD/HO.

78. NSDM 27, 11 Oct 1969, folder NSDM 1–50, box 363, Subject Files, NSC, Nixon Library.

79. Memo, Haig for Kissinger, 22 Dec 1969, folder Haig Chron Dec 21–31, 1969 [2 of 2], box 961, Haig Chron Files, ibid. Laird's letter is cited in note 63.

80. *Cong. Rec.*, 8 Dec 1969, H 11874.

4. The Predicament of Vietnam

1. Memo, Pursley for Clifford, 19 Dec 1968, folder 15, box 2, Records from SecDef Vault, Acc 330-74-142, WNRC.

2. Willard J. Webb, *The Joint Chiefs of Staff and the War in Vietnam, 1969–1970* (Washington, DC: Office of Joint History, Office of the JCS, 2002), 1, 15.

3. Richard A. Hunt, *Pacification: The American Struggle for Vietnam's Hearts and Minds* (Boulder, CO: Westview Press, 1995), 208–09.

4. Memo, Taylor for Kissinger, 13 Jan 1969, folder Taylor Memos/Vietnam; memo, Ginsburgh for Kissinger, 17 Jan 1969, folder Reappraisal of VN Commitment: both in box 64, Vietnam Subject Files (VNSF), NSC, Nixon Library.

5. Memo, ASD(ISA) for SecDef, 25 Jan 1969, folder Vietnam 9–10, box 31, Laird Papers, Ford Library.

6. OASD(C), "War Termination Plan," 2 Jan 1969, folder 65, box 6, Records from SecDef Vault, Acc 330-74-142.

7. Memo, Selin for Laird, 4 Mar 1969, folder Vietnam 14–19; memo, Selin for Laird, 14 Mar 1969, folder Vietnam 24–29: both in box 31, Laird Papers, Ford Library.

8. Thayer, *War Without Fronts*, 103–04. During the Vietnam War, Thayer compiled and analyzed statistical data for Systems Analysis in OSD.

9. Webb, *JCS and the War in Vietnam 1969–1970*, 15–19, 259; Hunt, *Pacification*, 197.

10. Andrew L. Johns, *Vietnam's Second Front: Domestic Politics, the Republican Party, and the Cold War* (Lexington: University Press of Kentucky, 2010), 69, 73–73. Johns' book

and Van Atta's *With Honor* chart the course of Congressman Laird's views on Vietnam. Newspaper accounts of Laird's positions on the war are in folder 67, box 6, Records from SecDef Vault, Acc 330-74-142. Quotes come from "GOP May End Support of Policy in Vietnam," *Waukesha Daily Freeman*, 29 Nov 1965, and "Laird Wants Ground War Eased," *Milwaukee Journal*, 8 Jul 1967.

11. *Cong. Rec.*, 13 Jun 1967, H 7077.

12. Alfred Maund, "Window on Washington," *Madison Capital Times*, 24 Jul 1967, folder Vietnam Statements 2, box A19, Baroody Papers, Ford Library.

13. Van Atta, *With Honor*, 123–25.

14. Hersh, *Price of Power*, 48–50; Jeffrey Kimball, *Nixon's Vietnam War* (Lawrence: University Press of Kansas, 2002), 91–94.

15. NSSM 1, Situation in Vietnam, 21 Jan 1969, folder 45 NSSM 1, box 4, Records from SecDef Vault, Acc 330-74-142.

16. Hunt, *Pacification*, 209; Talking Paper for SecDef and CJCS for NSC meeting on 25 Jan 1969, folder Vietnam 9–10, box 31, Laird Papers, Ford Library; Kissinger, *White House Years*, 238.

17. Talking Points, attached to memo, Kissinger for Nixon, 24 Jan 1969, folder VN Alternatives, box H-019, H Files, NSC, Nixon Library; Minutes, NSC Meeting, 25 Jan 1969 (quote, 28), folder 1, box H-109, H Files, ibid.

18. Vietnam Policy Alternatives, attached to memo, Kissinger for Nixon, 24 Jan 1969 cited in note 17; memo, Bundy for Rogers, 24 Jan 1969, folder Vietnam (VN) Alternatives, box H-019, H Files, NSC, Nixon Library; Talking Paper for SecDef and CJCS, 25 Jan 1969, cited in note 16; Minutes, NSC Meeting, 25 Jan 1969, 30 (quote), 32–33, cited in note 17.

19. Vietnam Policy Alternatives, cited in note 18.

20. CM-3887-69 for Laird, 23 Jan 1969, folder 108, box 9, Records from SecDef Vault, Acc 330-74-142.

21. Minutes, NSC Meeting, 25 Jan 1969 32, 33, (37 quote), cited in note 18.

22. Memo, Kissinger for Nixon, 29 Jan 1969, folder VN Alternatives, box H-019, H Files, NSC, Nixon Library.

23. Memo, meeting between Kissinger, Laird, and Wheeler on 30 Jan 1969, 6 Feb 1969 (quotes), attached to ltr, Kissinger to Laird, 6 Feb 1969, folder Miscellaneous Correspondence, box D17, Laird Papers, Ford Library; Henry A. Kissinger, *Ending the Vietnam War: A History of America's Involvement in and Extraction from the Vietnam War* (New York: Simon and Schuster, 2003), 58.

24. Memo, Haig for Kissinger, 5 Feb 1969, folder Haig Chron Feb 1–15, 1969, box 955, Haig Chron Files, NSC, Nixon Library.

25. List of Specific Actions Agreed to at 30 Jan Meeting, attached to ltr, Kissinger to Laird, 6 Feb 1969, cited in note 23.

26. Memo, Nixon for Kissinger, 1 Feb 1969 (quotes), attached to memo, Kissinger for Laird, 5 Feb 1969, folder Haig Chron Feb 1–15, 1969, box 955, Haig Chron Files, NSC,

Nixon Library. Nixon would occasionally send personally written memos directly to his staff requesting specific actions.

27. Memo, Kissinger for Laird, 5 Feb 1969, attached to memo, Laird for Kissinger, 11 Feb 1969 (quote), folder Personal file, box D17, Laird Papers, Ford Library.

28. Memo, Kissinger for Nixon, 11 Feb 1969 (quote), folder Vietnam vol. 1, box 136, Vietnam Country Files (VNCF), NSC, Nixon Library. Talking Points attached.

29. Memo, Haig for Kissinger, 2 Mar 1969 (quotes), folder Haig Vietnam vol. 1 [1 of 2], box 1007, Haig Special File, NSC, Nixon Library. The JCS plan and Laird's cover memo were attached. Memo, Kissinger for Laird, 3 Mar 1969 (quote), folder Haig Chron Mar 1969 [1 of 2], box 955, Haig Chron Files, ibid., contains Kissinger's reaction to the plans.

30. Memo, Laird for Nixon, 4 Mar 1969, folder 37, box 3, Records from SecDef Vault, Acc 330-74-142; Webb, *JCS and the War in Vietnam 1969–1970*, 28.

31. Memo, Laird for Kissinger, 11 Apr 1969 (quotes); Memo for the Record, Laird, 12 Apr 1969; memo, Wheeler for Laird, 11 Apr 1969: all attached to memo, Pursley for Laird, 22 Apr 1969, folder NSC Materials, box 3, SecDef Files, Acc 330-75-104, WNRC. In his memo for Laird, Wheeler stated that he believed Kissinger had previously discussed the plan with Laird. The mining plan was attached to Wheeler's memo. Memo, Kissinger for Laird, VN Feint Operations, 12 Apr 1969 (quotes), folder Vietnam vol. 3, box 136, VNCF, NSC, Nixon Library. Hersh, *Price of Power*, 120 (explanatory note).

32. Memo, Haig for Kissinger, 10 Sep 1969 (quotes), folder Haig Chron Sep 1969 [2 of 2], box 958, Haig Chron Files, NSC, Nixon Library; Hersh, *Price of Power*, 120 (explanatory note); memo, Kissinger for Laird, 5 Feb 1969, attached to memo, Laird for Kissinger, 11 Feb 1969, cited in note 28. See also chapter 2.

33. Memo, Laird for Nixon, 5 Feb 1969, attached to memo, Haig for Kissinger, 10 Feb 1969, folder Haig Chron Feb 1–15, 1969, box 955, Haig Chron Files, NSC, Nixon Library; Kissinger, *Ending the War*, 58 (quote).

34. Nixon, *Memoirs*, 370.

35. Memo, Laird for Nixon, 4 Mar 1969, attached to memo, Kissinger for Nixon, 13 Mar 1969, folder Vietnam vol. 1, box 136, VNCF, NSC, Nixon Library. Nixon's comments appear on Kissinger's memo.

36. Van Atta, *With Honor*, 175–78. Froehlke had traveled to Thailand and was not part of the group writing the report.

37. Memo, Laird for Nixon, 13 Mar 1969, folder 3, box 3, Records from SecDef Vault, Acc 330-74-142; Jeffrey J. Clarke, *Advice and Support: The Final Years, 1965–1973* (Washington, DC: U.S. Army Center of Military History, 1988) 347.

38. Memcons, Laird w/Huong and Vy, 8 Mar 1969; Laird w/Thieu, 8 Mar 1969, attached to memo, Laird for Nixon, 13 Mar 1969, cited in note 37; msg, 28120, State to Saigon (Laird to Bunker), 21 Feb 1969, Laird's Briefing for Nixon, 20 Feb 1969, attached to Table of Contents, JCS meeting, 24 Feb 1969, folder 21, box 2, Records from SecDef Vault, Acc 330-74-142.

39. Memo, Laird for Nixon, 13 Mar 1969, cited in note 37.

40. *Nixon Public Papers, 1969*, 215.

41. Clarke, *Advice and Support*, 345; Summary of Responses to NSSM 1, n.d., folder Vietnam 3/28/69 [1 of 2], box H-021, H Files, NSC, Nixon Library.

42. Summary of Responses to NSSM 1, n.d., folder Vietnam-2, box H-021, H Files, NSC, Nixon Library.

43. Msg, MAC 3743, Abrams to Goodpaster, 23 Mar 1969, folder Abrams Cables, box 65, VNSF, NSC, Nixon Library; Clarke, *Advice and Support*, 348.

44. NSSM 29, Papers for Vietnam Negotiations, 12 Mar 1969, folder 107, box 9, Records from SecDef Vault, Acc 330-74-142; Minutes, NSC Meeting, 28 Mar 1969, folder Meeting Mar 29, 1969, box H-121, H Files, NSC, Nixon Library. The discussion of the 28 March meeting is based on these minutes, which were probably taken by Haig. Memo, Kissinger for Nixon, 28 Mar 1969, folder Vietnam-2 , box H-021, H Files, NSC, Nixon Library; Memo for the Record, McConnell, 31 Mar 1969, folder Vietnam vol. 1, box 19, Laird Papers, Ford Library.

45. Minutes, NSC Meeting, 28 Mar 1969, cited in note 44; Van Atta, *With Honor*, 182.

46. Minutes, NSC Meeting, 28 Mar 1969, cited in note 44.

47. Ibid.; NSDM 9, 1 Apr 1969, folder NSDMs 1–50, box 363, Subject Files, NSC, Nixon Library.

48. NSDM 9, 1 Apr 1969 (quote); Memo for the Record, McConnell, 31 Mar 1969, cited in note 44.

49. Webb, *JCS and the War in Vietnam 1969–1970*, 14 (quote); Nixon, *Memoirs*, 392 (quotes).

50. NSDM 9, 1 Apr 1969, cited in note 47.

51. NSSM 36, 10 Apr 1969, folder NSSM 36 1 of 2, box H-142, H Files, NSC, Nixon Library; Webb, *JCS and the War in Vietnam 1969–1970*, 65.

52. NSSM 37, 10 Apr 1969, folder Vietnam 36–42, box 31, Laird Papers, Ford Library.

53. President's news conferences, 6 Feb 1969, 4 Mar 1969, 14 Mar 1969, *Nixon Public Papers 1969*, 67–68, 189 (quote), 215; memo, Nixon for Rogers et al., 14 Apr 1969, folder NSC Materials, box 3, SecDef Files, Acc 330-75-104; Clarke, *Advice and Support*, 346–47.

54. Memo, Moorer for Sneider, 19 Mar 1969, folder Vietnam-1, box H-021, H Files, NSC, Nixon Library. Moorer attached a draft memo to bring this issue to Kissinger.

55. Memo, Taylor for Kissinger, 19 Mar 1969 (quote), attached to memo, Haig for Kissinger, 27 Mar 1969, folder Taylor Memos/Vietnam, box 64, VNSF, ibid.

56. Televised address, 14 May 1969, *Nixon Public Papers 1969*, 370, 372–73; memo, Selin for Laird, 13 May 1969, folder Vietnam 47–50, box 32, Laird Papers, Ford Library; memo, Laird for Service Secretaries, 21 May 1969, attached to memo, Lemnitzer for Haig, 22 May 1969, folder Haig's Vietnam File Apr–Oct 1969 vol. 2 [2 of 2], box 1008, Haig Special File, NSC, Nixon Library.

57. Memo, Laird for Nixon, 2 Jun 1969, w/attached memo, Richardson for Laird, 2 Jun 1969, folder Vietnam 58–62, box 32, Laird Papers, Ford Library; Webb, *JCS and the War in Vietnam 1969–1970*, 66–67.

58. Memo, Haig for Kissinger, 21 May 1969 (quote), folder Items to Discuss Feb 15–Jul 14, 1969, box 334, Subject Files, NSC, Nixon Library; William M. Hammond, *Public Affairs: The Military and the Media, 1968–1973* (Washington, DC: U.S. Army Center of Military History, 1996), 85–87; Memo for the Record by NMCC, 21 May 1969. See Samuel Zaffiri, *Hamburger Hill* (New York: Presidio Press, 1988) for an account of the battle and the public reaction.

59. Excerpts from Kennedy's Senate speech, attached to memo, Haig for Kissinger, 21 May 1969, cited in note 58. Kennedy's speech is in *Cong. Rec.*, 20 May 1969, S 13003. Hammond, *Military and the Media*, 87.

60. Memo, Haig for Kissinger, 21 May 1969 (quotes), cited in note 58; memo, Laird for Nixon, 21 May 1969, folder Hamburger Hill, box 67, VNSF, NSC, Nixon Library; Hammond, *Military and the Media*, 88.

61. *Haldeman Diaries*, 57–59.

62. Memo, Haig for Kissinger, 27 May 1969, folder Haig Chron May 1969 [1 of 2], box 956, Haig Chron Files, NSC, Nixon Library; memo, Kissinger for Nixon, subj: Secretary Rogers' Trip, 6 May 1969; memo, Kissinger for Nixon, Guidance for Sec Rogers' Visit to Saigon, 6 May 1969: both in folder State vol. 2, box 279, Agency Files, ibid.; memo, Possibility President Thieu may discuss withdrawal of US forces w/Nixon, 2 Jun 1969, folder Vietnam vol. 6, box 137, VNCF, NSC, ibid.; Hammond, *Military and the Media*, 89–90; Webb, *JCS and the War in Vietnam 1969–1970*, 68.

63. Kissinger, *Ending the Vietnam War*, 82–83; Webb, *JCS and the War in Vietnam 1969–1970*, 68; SecDef Briefing for President, 7 Jun 1969, folder Vietnam 58–62, box 32, Laird Papers, Ford Library; Memcon, Midway Island, 8 Jun 1969, folder State vol. 3, box 280, Agency Files, NSC, Nixon Library. This meeting included the two leaders plus Kissinger and Nguyen Phu Duc, Thieu's personal assistant.

64. Nixon remarks at Midway, 8 Jun 1969, *Nixon Public Papers* 1969, 443.

65. Memo, Laird for Resor, 12 Jun 1969, folder Vietnam 63–68; memo, Laird for Nutter et al., 17 Jun 1969, folder Vietnam 69–73; memo Laird for Nixon, 18 Jun 1969, folder Vietnam 69–73: all in box 32, Laird Papers, Ford Library; ltr, Laird to Kissinger, 22 Sep 1969, *FRUS 1969–1976*, 2:159–60.

66. *Nixon Public Papers 1969*, 471–72.

67. Kissinger, *White House Years*, 274–75; *Haldeman Diaries*, 65; msg, 102403, State to Bangkok, 21 Jun 1969, attached to memo, Sneider for Kissinger, 20 Jun 1969, folder Vietnam vol. 7, box 138, VNCF, NSC, Nixon Library.

68. Memo, Wheeler for Laird, 21 July 1969 (quotes), attached to memo, Kissinger for Nixon, 22 Jul 1969, folder Haig Chron Jul 1969 [1 of 2], box 957, Haig Chron Files, NSC, Nixon Library.

69. Memcon, Nixon, Thieu, Kissinger, Bunker, Nguyen Phu Duc, 30 Jul 1969, *FRUS 1969–1976*, 6:321–26.

70. *Nixon Public Papers 1969*, 370 (quote); Webb, *JCS and the War in Vietnam 1969–1970*, 55–56.

71. Memo, Kissinger for Nixon, 7 Jul 1969, folder 2, H-023, H Files, NSC, Nixon Library; *Haldeman Diaries*, 69–70 (quote).

72. Memos, Rogers for Nixon, 24 Jun 1969; Nixon for Rogers, 2 Jul 1969 (quote), attached to memo, Kissinger for Rogers et al., 3 Jul 1969, folder Haig's Vietnam File Apr–Oct 1969 vol. 2 [2 of 2], box 1008, Haig Special File, NSC, Nixon Library; *Haldeman Diaries*, 69–70 (quote); Kissinger, *White House Years*, 276.

73. Table, "Comparison of Enemy Offensives," folder 37, box 3, Records from SecDef Vault, Acc 330-74-142; memo, Kissinger for Nixon, 7 July 1969 (quotes), cited in note 71.

74. Kissinger, *White House Years*, 276; Webb, *JCS and the War in Vietnam 1969–1970*, 56 (Wheeler's comments).

75. Memo, Laird for ASD(ISA), 14 Jul 1969 (quotes), attached to memo, Kissinger for Nixon, 22 Jul 1969, folder DoD vol. 3 May–Aug 1969, box 221, Agency Files, NSC, Nixon Library. Emphasis in original.

76. Memo, Wheeler for Laird, 21 Jul 1969, attached to memo, Kissinger for Nixon, 22 Jul 1969, cited in note 68.

77. Memo, Kissinger for Nixon, 22 Jul 1969, cited in note 68, a copy of Pursley's proposed change was attached; memo, Laird for Nixon, 7 Aug 1969 (quote), folder Vietnam Memos & Misc vol. XI-A, box 139, VNCF, NSC, Nixon Library; memo for President, n.d., attached to memo, Kissinger for Nixon, 22 Jul 1969, cited in note 68; Kissinger, *White House Years*, 276; Kimball, Nixon's *Vietnam War*, 151.

78. Hunt, *Pacification*, 86–87; Frank Jones, *Blowtorch*, chap. 5.

79. Memo, Clifford for President, 2 Oct 1968, folder Vietnam Calendar, B 1-46, box 30, Laird Papers, Ford Library; Clarke, *Advice and Support*, 280–82, 293–95, 301–02; Webb, *JCS and the War in Vietnam 1969–1970*, 111–12.

80. Memo, Resor for Laird, 14 Mar 1969 (quotes), folder Vietnam 24–29; memo, Resor for Laird, 22 Apr 1969 (quote), folder Vietnam 36–42: both in box 31, Laird Papers, Ford Library.

81. Memo, Packard for Service Secretaries, 28 Apr 1969 (quotes), folder 2d Revised FY 70 Budget Review, box 82, ASD(C) Files, OSD/HO; Webb, *JCS and the War in Vietnam 1969–1970*, 112–15.

82. Clarke, *Advice and Support*, 351–53; Webb, *JCS and the War in Vietnam 1969–1970*, 116–17.

83. Memo, Laird for Service Secretaries, 12 Aug 1969, folder Vietnam 85–92, box 32, Laird Papers, Ford Library.

84. Memo, Lake for Kissinger, 7 Sep 1969, folder Tony Lake Chron File Jun 1969–May 1970 [5 of 6], box 1048, Staff Files–Lake Chron, NSC, Nixon Library. Kissinger's

handwritten annotations appear on this memo. Memo, Kissinger for Nixon, 10 Sep 1969 (quotes), folder Lake–Miscellaneous Material Sep 1969–Jan 1970, box 1047, ibid. Kissinger reproduced this memo in full in his *White House Years*, 1480–82. Nixon's copy, in which he underlined certain passages, is in folder Special NSC Meeting 9/12/69, box H-024, H Files, NSC, Nixon Library.

85. *Haldeman Diaries*, 86; Kissinger, *White House Years*, 283; Minutes NSC Meeting, 12 Sep 1969, 22–25 (quote), folder NSC Minutes Originals 1969 [4 of 5], box H-109, H Files, NSC, Nixon Library. The minutes are incomplete with numerable omissions in the discussion about withdrawals, making it difficult to analyze the debate.

86. *Nixon Public Papers 1969*, 718; DoD News Release 762-69 and news conference, 17 Sep 1969, *Laird Public Statements 1969*, 6:2133–43; memo, Kissinger for Nixon, 25 Sep 1969 (quote), folder DoD vol. 4, box 222, Agency Files, NSC, Nixon Library.

87. *Nixon Presidential Papers 1969*, 731; *Laird Public Statements 1969*, 6:2158–63; DoD News Release 489-70, 11 Jun 1970, folder Draft Reform, box 319, Subject Files, NSC, Nixon Library.

88. Memo, Kissinger for Nixon, 23 Oct 1969, folder Lake Chron Oct 1969, box 1046, Staff Files–Lake Chron, NSC, Nixon Library.

89. Memo, Laird for Kissinger, 8 May 1969, folder Haig Vietnam vol. 2 [2 of 2], box 1008, Haig Special File, ibid.

90. Nixon, *Memoirs*, 393 (quotes); Kissinger, *Ending the Vietnam War*, 92–93. Hersh, *Price of Power*, 120 (explanatory note), states that Robinson's White House liaison office kept much of the planning for Duck Hook from Laird. For more on Duck Hook, see John Prados, *Vietnam: History of an Unwinnable War, 1945–1975* (Lawrence: University Press of Kansas, 2009), 308–12.

91. Memo, Laird for Nixon, 8 Oct 1969 (quotes); JCS memo JCSM-600-69 for Laird, 1 Oct 1969: both attached to note by Haig, 11 Oct 1969, folder JCS I, box 245, Agency Files, NSC, Nixon Library.

92. Memo, Kissinger for Nixon, n.d., attached to note by Haig, 11 Oct 1969, folder JCS I, box 245, Agency Files, NSC, Nixon Library; Kissinger, *White House Years*, 284–85. A secret global nuclear alert in October may have been related to Duck Hook. See Jeffrey Kimball, *The Vietnam War Files* (Lawrence: University Press of Kansas, 2004), 110–20.

93. Nixon, Address to the Nation, 3 Nov 1969, *Nixon Public Papers 1969*, 901–09; unsigned ltr, Nixon to Rogers and Laird, 4 Nov 1969; memo, Kissinger for Rogers and Laird, 7 Nov 1969: both in folder State vol. 4, box 280, Agency Files, NSC, Nixon Library; Bundy, *Tangled Web*, 80–83; Jack Anderson, "The Washington Merry-Go-Round," *Washington Post*, 15 Oct 1969; "Hanoi Paper Lauds Protest," *New York Times*, 15 Oct 1969.

94. Memo, Kissinger for Nixon, 15 Nov 1969, folder Vietnam vol. XII, box 140, VNCF, NSC, Nixon Library; Memo for the Record by Haig, 19 Nov 1969, folder Haig's Vietnam File Nov-Dec 1969 vol. 3 [2 of 2], box 1008, Haig Special File, ibid.; *Haldeman Diaries*, 108.

95. Memo, Haig for Kissinger, Phase III Withdrawals, 24 Nov 1969, folder Haig's Vietnam File Nov–Dec 1969 vol. 3 [2 of 2], box 1008, Haig Special File, NSC, Nixon Library; memo, Wheeler for Laird, Force Planning, 29 Nov 1969, attached to memo, Haig for Kissinger, Force Planning, 20 Dec 1969, folder DoD vol. 5, box 223, Agency Files, NSC, ibid.

96. Memo, Laird for Kissinger, Force Planning, 12 Dec 1969, attached to memo, Haig for Kissinger, Force Planning, 20 Dec 1969, folder DoD vol. 5, box 223, Agency Files, NSC, Nixon Library.

97. Address to the Nation, *Nixon Public Papers 1969*, 1025–28.

98. Memo for the Record, OSD, Status of the FY 1971 Defense Budget, 8 Dec 1969, folder DPRC & Def Budget 1969, box 234, Agency Files, NSC, Nixon Library.

99. Memos, Laird for Nixon, 20 Dec 1969 (quote); Nixon for Laird, 27 Dec 1969 (quote), both attached to memo, 26 Dec 1969, folder BoB vol. 1, box 206, ibid. In his memo to Nixon, Kissinger thought Laird's plan was sound.

5. The Battle over Troop Withdrawals

1. Memo, Laird for Nixon, 17 Feb 1970, attached to memo, Haig for Kissinger, 24 Feb 1970, folder DoD vol. 6, box 244, Agency Files, NSC, Nixon Library.

2. Memo, Laird for Nixon, 17 Feb 1970, cited in note 1 (quote); Lewis Sorley, ed., *Vietnam Chronicles: The Abrams Tapes, 1968–1972* (Lubbock, TX: Texas Tech University Press, 2004), 370.

3. Memo, Laird for Nixon, 17 Feb 1970, cited in note 1 (quote).

4. Memo, Morrill, Fiscal Outlook 1972–76, 21 Mar 1970, folder AVAF–DPRC 69–70, box 37, Anderson Files, Staff Member and Office Files (SMOF), WHSF, Nixon Library.

5. Memo, Laird for Nixon, 17 Feb 1970, cited in note 1 (quote); Sorley, *Abrams Tapes*, 370.

6. Ibid.

7. Memo, Kissinger for Nixon, 15 Dec 1969, folder Items for Haig Trip, box 1012, Haig Special File, NSC, Nixon Library; memo, Haig for Kissinger, 24 Feb 1970, cited in note 1 (quotes).

8. Memo, Kissinger for Nixon, 16 Jan 1970 (quotes), folder T. Lake Chron Jan 1970, box 1046, Staff Files–Lake Chron, NSC, Nixon Library; Kissinger, *Ending the Vietnam War*, 109–10.

9. Memo, Kissinger for Nixon, 19 Mar 1970, folder 1, box H-002, H Files, NSC, Nixon Library; Hunt, *Pacification*, 210–11.

10. Memo, Laird for Nixon, 27 Feb 1970, folder 1, box H-002, H Files, NSC, Nixon Library.

11. Ibid.

12. Ibid.

13. JCS Paper, "Phase IV Troop Withdrawals," attached to memo, Haig for Kissinger, 17 Mar 1970, folder Haig's Vietnam File vol. 5 [2 of 2], box 1009, Haig Special File, NSC, Nixon Library.

14. Msg, MAC 3303, Abrams to Wheeler, 13 Mar 1970 (quotes), attached to memo, Laird for Kissinger, 7 Apr 1970, folder 13, box 2, Records from SecDef Vault, Acc 330-74-142, WNRC.

15. JCSM-15-70 for SecDef, 3 Apr 1970 (quote), folder Haig Chron Files Apr 13–15, 1970 [2 of 2], box 965, Haig Chron Files, NSC, Nixon Library; memo, Laird for Kissinger, 7 Apr 1970 (quote), cited in note 10 w/attachment JCSM-117-70 for SecDef, 16 Mar 1970.

16. Msg, WHS0016, Kissinger to Bunker, 6 Apr 1970 (quotes); msgs, WHS 0019 and 0020, Kissinger to Bunker, 8 Apr 1970; msgs, Saigon 948 and 949, Bunker to Kissinger, 8 Apr 1970: all in folder Backchannel Msgs, 1970 Southeast Asia (SEA), box 410, Backchannel, NSC, Nixon Library.

17. Memo, Laird for Nixon, 7 Apr 1970, folder 13, box 2, Records from SecDef Vault, Acc 330-74-142.

18. Memo, Kissinger for Nixon, 13 Apr 1970, folder Haig Chron Apr 13–15, 1970 [2 of 2], box 965, Haig Chron Files, NSC, Nixon Library. It is not clear whether this meeting was actually held, because problems with Apollo XIII mission came to light that day, forcing Nixon to postpone his speech on Vietnam withdrawals until 20 April (*Haldeman Diaries*, 150).

19. *Nixon Public Papers 1970*, 374; msg, WHS 0022, Kissinger to Bunker, 11 Apr 1970, folder Backchannel Msgs 1970 SEA, box 410, Backchannel, NSC, Nixon Library.

20. Telcons, Kissinger and Laird, 20 Apr 1970, 12:40 p.m., 3:55 p.m. (quotes), and 4:20 p.m.: all in folder 1, box 5, HAK Telcons, NSC, Nixon Library.

21. Msgs, WHS 0029, Kissinger to Abrams, 21 Apr 1970; Saigon 166, Bunker to Kissinger, 22 Apr 1970: both in folder Backchannel Msgs 1970 SEA, box 410, Backchannel, NSC, Nixon Library; Kissinger, *Ending the Vietnam War*, 145–46.

22. Memo, Laird for Wheeler, 24 Apr 1970, folder Vietnam 166–171, box 33, Laird Papers, Ford Library.

23. Memos, Laird for Nixon, 30 May 1970 (quotes); Nixon for Laird, 2 Jun 1970: both attached to memo, Kissinger for Nixon, 1 Jun 1970; memo, Laird for Nixon, 5 Jun 1970: all in folder DoD vol. 7, box 224, Agency Files, NSC, Nixon Library.

24. Memo, Odeen (SA) for Pursley, 23 Apr 1970, folder 2, box 2, Records from SecDef Vault, Acc 330-74-142; memo, Resor for Laird, 30 Apr 1970, folder Vietnam 166–171, box 33, Laird Papers, Ford Library; DoD News Release 548-70, 1 Jul 1970 (folder Draft Calls 1969–72, box 1090, OSD/OH) gives draft calls for Jan–Aug 1970; JCSM-266-70 for Laird, 2 Jun 1970, tab c, folder 12, box 2, Records from SecDef Vault, Acc 330-74-142.

25. Ibid.

26. JCSM-266-70 for Laird, 2 Jun 1970, cited in note 24.

27. Memo, Resor for Laird, 23 July 1970, folder Vietnam 209–210, box 33, Laird Papers, Ford Library.

28. Sorley, *Abrams Tapes*, 444–47 (Resor quotes, 444, 446; Rosson quote, 446). Emphasis in original. Memo, Resor for Laird, 12 Aug 1970 (quote), folder JCS vol. 1, box 245, Agency Files, NSC, Nixon Library.

29. Memo, Resor for Packard, 16 Jul 1970, Moorer Diary, folder Jul 1970, box 1, Acc 218-05-006, NARA II; memo, Resor for Laird, 23 July 1970, folder Vietnam 209–210, box 33, Laird Papers, Ford Library; memo, Kissinger for Nixon, 31 May 1970, attached to memo, Kissinger for Nixon, 1 Jun 1970, cited in note 23; memo, Kissinger for Richardson et al., 13 Jun 1970, folder DPRC & Def Budget 1970 vol. 1, box 235, Agency Files, NSC, Nixon Library.

30. Memo, Kissinger for Nixon, 26 Jul 1970 (quote), folder Haig Chron Jul 23–31, 1970, box 969, Haig Chron Files, NSC, Nixon Library; *Haldeman Diaries*, 180.

31. Memo, Laird for Moorer, 30 Jul 1970, folder Vietnam 215–216, box 34, Laird Papers, Ford Library.

32. Memo, Haig for Kissinger, 9 Aug 1970 (quotes), folder Items to Discuss w/President 16 Jun to 8 Sep 1970, box 335, Subject Files, NSC, Nixon Library; DoD News Release 548-70, 1 Jul 1970 (quote) cited in note 19; Fred Farrar, "Laird Plans for Draft Call Cuts," *Chicago Tribune*, 24 Jul 1970, 1; memo, Kissinger for Nixon, 17 Aug 1970 (quote), folder Haig Chron Aug 11–17, 1970, box 970, Haig Chron Files, NSC, Nixon Library.

33. Memo, Laird for Kissinger, 20 Aug 1970, attached to memo, Haig for Kissinger, 20 Aug 1970 (quote), folder Haig Chron Aug 17–21, 1970 [1 of 2], box 970, Haig Chron Files, NSC, Nixon Library.

34. Ibid.; memo, Robinson for Moorer, 21 Aug 1970 (quote), Moorer Diary, folder Aug 1970, box 1, Acc 218-05-006; memo, Kissinger for Laird, SEA Redeployments, 4 Sep 1970, folder Vietnam 232–235, box 34, Laird Papers, Ford Library.

35. Memo, Laird for Kissinger, 17 Sep 1970, folder Vietnam 245A–250, box 34, Laird Papers, Ford Library.

36. Memo, Smith for Kissinger, 24 Sep 1970 (quotes, emphasis in original), folder Haig Chron Sep 19–24, 1970 [1 of 2], box 972, Haig Chron Files, NSC, Nixon Library; *Nixon Public Papers 1970*, 836.

37. Memo, Haig for Kissinger, 20 Aug 1970, folder Haig Chron Files Aug 17–21, 1970 [1 of 2], Haig Chron Files, NSC, Nixon Library; memo, Robinson for Moorer, 21 Aug 1970, cited in note 34; memo, Laird for Kissinger, 17 Sep 1970, folder Vietnam 245A–250, box 34, Laird Papers, Ford Library.

38. Memo, Resor for Laird, 26 Oct 1970 (quotes), folder Vietnam 271–275, box 34, Laird Papers, Ford Library; memo, Smith for Kissinger, 19 Oct 1970 (quote), folder DoD vol. 9, box 225, Agency Files, NSC, Nixon Library. Smith contended that money was not a problem in the near term since the FY 1971 budget request provided more funds for personnel than could be used "under current projections." Copy msg, JCS to CINCPAC, n.d., folder 5, box H-100, H Files, NSC, Nixon Library. Abrams received an information copy of this message.

39. Minutes, DPRC Meeting on Military Manpower–24 Nov 1970, attached to memo, Davis for Kissinger, 3 Dec 1970, folder DPRC Minutes [1 of 3], box H-118, H Files, NSC, Nixon Library.

40. Memo, Packard for Kissinger, 4 Dec 1970, folder 5, box H-100, H Files, NSC, Nixon Library.

41. JCSM-576-70 for Laird, 17 Dec 1970, folder Vietnam 299–299B; JCSM-59-71 for Laird, 16 Feb 1971, folder Vietnam 321–324: both in box 35, Laird Papers, Ford Library.

6. Taking the Fight into Cambodia

1. Recent accounts that discuss U.S. military actions in Cambodia include Dallek, *Nixon and Kissinger*; Prados, *Vietnam*; and John M. Shaw, *The Cambodian Campaign: The 1970 Offensive and America's Vietnam War* (Lawrence: University Press of Kansas, 2005).

2. Webb, *JCS and the War in Vietnam 1969–1970*, 131–35; Paper, "Hanoi's Use of the Cambodian Base System in the Vietnam War," n.d., folder Background Briefing Book on Cambodia, box 587, Cambodian Operations (1970), NSC, Nixon Library; CIA Rept. 0550-69, "The Situation in Vietnam," 24 Jan 1969, folder 5, box H-019, H Files, NSC, Nixon Library.

3. Memos, Nixon for Kissinger, 8 Jan 1969 (quote); Kissinger for President-Elect Nixon, 13 Jan 1969: both in folder Gen. Goodpaster, box 1, HAK Office Files, NSC, Nixon Library.

4. Memo, Rogers for Nixon, 5 Feb 1969; OSD/Joint Staff Comments on a Memo for the President, n.d.: both attached to memo, Kissinger for Nixon, 12 Feb 1969, folder HAK 1, box 84, HAK Office Files, NSC, Nixon Library.

5. Webb, *JCS and the War in Vietnam 1969–1970*, 139–40.

6. Hammond, *Military and the Media*, 64 65.

7. Msg, JCS 01836, McConnell to Abrams, 11 Feb 1969 (quote), folder Operation Menu, box D18, Laird Papers, Ford Library; msg, 023875, State to Saigon, 14 Feb 1969 (quote), folder Personal File, box D17, ibid.; memo, Haig for Kissinger, 13 Feb 1969, folder Haig Chron Feb 1–15, 1969, box 955, Haig Chron Files, NSC, Nixon Library; msg, JCS 01915, McConnell to Abrams, 13 Feb 1969, folder Operation Menu, box D18, Laird Papers, Ford Library. Accounts based on unclassified sources include, Prados, *Vietnam*; Shaw, *Cambodian Campaign*; and Kimball, *Nixon's Vietnam War*.

8. "Chronology," handwritten notes by Pursley (quote), folder Menu 1, box D18, Laird Papers, Ford Library; memo, Kissinger for Nixon, 19 Feb 1969 (quotes), folder Planning for Strike, box 104, VNSF, NSC, Nixon Library. Kissinger's memo does not indicate which persons supported which bombing options.

9. Memo, Kissinger for Nixon, 19 Feb 1969, cited in note 41; memo, Kissinger for Laird, 22 Feb 1969, folder Operation Menu, box D18, Laird Papers, Ford Library.

10. Msg, JCS, 02248, Wheeler to Abrams, 22 Feb 1969 (quote), attached to memo, Kissinger for Laird, 22 Feb 1969, cited in note 8; memo, Wheeler for Kissinger, 20 Feb 1969 (quotes), folder Planning for Strikes, box 104, VNSF, NSC, Nixon Library.

11. Memo, Pursley for Laird, 19 Feb 1969, folder Menu 1, box D20–D21, Laird Papers, Ford Library.

12. Memo for the Record, Meeting re Breakfast Plan, 25 Feb 1969 (quote), attached to memo, Haig for Pursley, 25 Feb 1969; memo, Kissinger for Laird, 22 Feb 1969 (quote): all in folder Operation Menu, box D18, Laird Papers, Ford Library. Haig warned Pursley

not to reproduce the memo for the record and only show it to Laird, Wheeler, Colonel McAuliffe, and Colonel Sitton. Nixon, *Memoirs*, 380–81; Kissinger, *White House Years*, 242–43; *Haldeman Diaries*, 33.

13. Memo, Haig for Pursley, 26 Feb 1969, folder Operation Menu, box D18, Laird Papers, Ford Library; Nixon, *Memoirs*, 380–81; Memo for the Record by Nixon, 15 Mar 1969, attached to memo, Nixon for Rogers and Laird, 15 Mar 1969 (quote), folder Vietnam vol. 1, box 136, VNCF, NSC, Nixon Library.

14. Msg, Packard to Laird, 8 Mar 1969, folder 4, box D31, Laird Papers, Ford Library; Nixon, *Memoirs*, 381 (quote); telcons, Nixon and Kissinger, 15 Mar 1969, folder Breakfast Plan, box 89, Vietnam; Nixon and Kissinger, 15 Mar 1969, 3:45 p.m. (quote), folder 5, box 1, HAK Telcons: both in NSC, Nixon Library.

15. Telcons, Kissinger and Laird, 15 Mar, 5:40 p.m., and 16 Mar 1969, 9:30 a.m. (quote), folder 5, box 1, HAK Telcons, NSC, Nixon Library; Kissinger, *White House Years*, 245–47. In his memoir, Nixon said he made the decision to bomb during a 16 March White House meeting with Rogers, Wheeler, Laird, and Kissinger. This is technically not correct. As Kissinger wrote in *White House Years*, Nixon used the 16 March meeting as a forum for discussing an issue that he had actually decided the previous day.

16. Memo for the Record, 25 Feb 1969, cited in note 45; Checklist for meeting w/ President, 16 Mar 1969 (quotes), folder Planning for Strikes, box 104, VNSF, NSC, Nixon Library; memo, Kissinger for Laird, 16 Mar 1969, folder Personal File, box D17, Laird Papers, Ford Library.

17. Nixon, *Memoirs*, 382.

18. Laird interview, 11 Oct 2001, 35, OSD/HO.

19. Webb, *JCS and the War in Vietnam 1969–1970*, 136–37 (quotes); memo, Laird for Nixon, 24 Mar 1970 (quote), folder 13, box 2, Records from SecDef Vault, Acc 330-74-142, WNRC; DoD, "Report on Selected Air and Ground Operations in Cambodia and Laos," 10 Sep 1973, folder Cambodia, box D17, Laird Papers, Ford Library. The records give no indication of who devised the reporting arrangements.

20. Memo, Haig for Kissinger, 11 Jun 1969 (quote), folder Planning for Strike, box 104, VNSF, NSC, Nixon Library; Kissinger, *White House Years*, 253.

21. Kissinger, *White House Years*, 253 including explanatory note; DoD Report, 10 Sep 1973, 7 cited in note 19.

22. Three memos, Hoover for Tolson et al., 9 May 1969, 10:35 a.m., 11:05 a.m., and 5:05 p.m., *FRUS 1969–1976*, 2:94–99; memo, Sullivan for DeLoach, 11 May 1969, ibid., 99–100; ltr, Sullivan to Hoover, 20 May 1969, 103–04; memo, Sullivan for DeLoach, 28 May 1969, ibid., 104–05.

23. Laird interview, 11 Oct 2001, 35.

24. Ltrs, Pursley to Laird, 11 Sep 1980; Pursley to Beecher, 4 Sep 1980; Beecher to Pursley, 8 Sep 1980 (quote): all in folder News Leaks, box D18, Laird Papers, Ford Library.

25. Memos, Laird for CJCS, 30 Sep 1969; CM-4617-69 for Laird, 7 Oct 1969; Pursley for Laird, 7 Oct 1969: all in folder Op Menu, ibid.; telcon, Kissinger and Laird, 4 Nov 1969 (quote), folder 3, box 3, HAK Telcons, NSC, Nixon Library.

26. CM-4953-70 for Laird, 12 Mar 1970; CM-4958-70 for Laird, 14 Mar 1970 (quotes): both in folder Op Menu, box D18, Laird Papers, Ford Library; memo, Laird for Nixon, 24 Mar 1970 (quote), attached to memo, Kissinger for Nixon, 27 Mar 1970, folder General Memos on B–52 Strikes, box 105, VNSF, NSC, Nixon Library.

27. Memo, Kissinger for Nixon, 17 Mar 1970, folder Cambodia vol. 2, Sep 1969–9 Apr 1970, box 506, CF–Far East, NSC, Nixon Library; memo, Haig for Kissinger, 24 Feb 1970, folder Haig Chron Mar 1–11, 1970 [1 of 2], box 963, Haig Chron Files, NSC, Nixon Library; Webb, *JCS and the War in Vietnam 1969–1970*, 142–43; T. D. Allman, "Sihanouk Tries to Ease Out Hanoi's Troops," *Washington Post*, 3 Feb 1970.

28. Fact Sheet, Cambodian Incursion, 29 Nov 1972, folder Summary Papers Tab E, box 43, Laird Papers, Ford Library; memo, Eliot for Kissinger, 30 Mar 1970, folder Vietnam Mar 1970, box 144, VNCF, NSC, Nixon Library; Reuters, "Cambodians Sack Offices of VC, Hanoi," *Washington Post*, 12 Mar 1970, A1; Stanley Karnow, "Hanoi, Peking Join Sihanouk Call for War," 24 Mar 1970, A1; UPI, "Demand Made to Viet Cong and Hanoi," *Washington Star*, 13 Mar 1970, 1.

29. Memos, Laird for CJCS, 25 Mar 1970; Laird for Nixon, 26 Mar 1970 (quote): both in folder Cambodia 1–6, box 2, Laird Papers, Ford Library; Van Atta, *With Honor*, 258–59; Prados, *Vietnam*, 363; Webb, *JCS and the War in Vietnam 1969–1970*, 144–45.

30. *Cong. Rec.*, 26 Mar 1970, S 4573–74; UPI, "2 on Hill Seek to Ban GIs in Cambodia," *Washington Post*, 12 Apr 1970.

31. President's News Conference of 21 Mar 1970, *Nixon Public Papers 1970*, 292.

32. Memo, Kissinger for Nixon, 19 Mar 1970 (quote), folder Cambodia vol. 2, Sep 1969–9 Apr 1970, box 506, CF–Far East, NSC, Nixon Library; memo, Kissinger for Nixon, 22 Apr 1970, folder Howe Chron Apr 1970, box 1074, Howe Chron Files, NSC, Nixon Library; telcon, Nixon and Kissinger 20 Mar 1970, box 1, HAK closed telcons, NSC, Nixon Library; memo, Laird for CJCS, 25 Mar 1970, folder 36, box 3, Records from SecDef Vault, Acc 330-74-142; memo, Kissinger for Laird, 26 Mar 1970, folder Cambodia 1–6, box 2, Laird Papers, Ford Library; Webb, *JCS and the War in Vietnam 1969–1970*, 145–46.

33. Memo, Abrams, 30 Mar 1970, folder Howe Chron Apr 1970, box 1074, Howe Chron Files, NSC, Nixon Library. This memo summarizes Abrams' message.

34. Ltr, Laird to Rogers, 31 Mar 1970, folder Haig Chron Mar 27–31, 1970, box 964, Haig Chron Files, NSC, Nixon Library; memo, Haig for Kissinger, 1 Apr 1970 (quotes), folder DoD vol. 6, box 224, Agency Files, NSC, Nixon Library; msg, WHS 0012, Haig to Bunker, 31 Mar 1970, folder Backchannels SEA 1970, box 410, Backchannel, NSC, Nixon Library.

35. Ltr, Laird to Rogers, 31 Mar 1970; memo, Rogers for Nixon, 31 Mar 1970 (quotes): both attached to ltr, Rogers to Laird, 2 Apr 1970, folder 36, box 3, Records from SecDef Vault, Acc 330-74-142; memo, Kissinger for Nixon, 31 Mar 1970 (quote), folder Vietnam

Mar 1970, box 144, VNCF, NSC, Nixon Library; msg, 04725, Saigon to State, 30 Mar 1970, attached to memo, Haig for Holdridge, 30 Mar 1970, folder Haig Chron Mar 27–31, 1970, box 964, Haig Chron File, NSC, Nixon Library.

36. Msg, 933, Saigon to State (Bunker to Kissinger), 8 Apr 1970, folder Backchannel Msgs SEA 1970, box 410, Backchannel, NSC, Nixon Library. Laird and Rogers did receive the ambassador's assessment of the situation in Cambodia, which he transmitted through regular State Department channels.

37. Webb, *JCS and the War in Vietnam 1969–1970*, 149; memo, ISA for Laird, n.d., attached to memo, Murphy for Laird, 22 Apr 1970, folder 36, box 3, Records from SecDef Vault, Acc 330-74-142; Memo for the Record, Remarks by Kissinger on the Cambodian Decision, 12 May 1970 (quote), folder Howe Chron May 1970, box 1075, Howe Chron Files, NSC, Nixon Library; memo, Kissinger for Nixon, n.d. (quote), folder Cambodia vol. 3, 10 Apr 1970–23 Apr 1970, box 506, CF–Far East, NSC, Nixon Library.

38. Memo for the Record, 14 Apr 1970 WSAG Meeting; memo, Davis for Packard, 16 Apr 1970, w/attached WSAG Meeting Summary of Conclusions, 15 Apr 1970: both in folder 36, box 3, Records from SecDef Vault, Acc 330-74-142; Webb, *JCS and the War in Vietnam 1969–1970*, 151–52.

39. Murrey Marder, "U.S. Calls War in Cambodia An 'Invasion,'" *Washington Post*, 25 Apr 1970 (quote), A1; CM-5063-70 for Laird, 21 Apr 1970 (quote), folder 36, box 3, Records from SecDef Vault, Acc 330-74-142; Webb, *JCS and the War in Vietnam 1969–1970*, 152.

40. Msgs, MAC 5307, Abrams to McCain, 21 Apr 1970, attached to memo, Pursley for Kissinger, 21 Apr 1970; JCS 5455, Wheeler to Abrams, 21 Apr 1970 (quote): all in folder 36, box 3, Records from SecDef Vault, Acc 330-74-142; Laird interview, 15 Oct 2001, 17 (quote).

41. *Haldeman Diaries*, 152 (quotes); Kimball, *Nixon's Vietnam War,* 202; Haldeman note cited in Kimball, *Vietnam War Files*, 131 (quote); *Nixon Public Papers 1970*, 375 (remaining quotes).

42. Memo, Nixon for Kissinger, 22 Apr 1970, folder HAK/President Memos 1969–1970, box 341, Subject Files, NSC, Nixon Library.

43. NSDM 56, 22 Apr 1970, folder NSDM 51–96, box 363, ibid.; memo, CJCS for Laird, 22 Apr 1970, attached to memo, Pursley for Kissinger, 22 Apr 1970, folder 36, box 3, Records from SecDef Vault, Acc 330-74-142; telcon, Kissinger and Laird, 23 Apr 1970, 1:35 p.m., folder 1, box 5, HAK Telcons, NSC, Nixon Library; *Haldeman Diaries*, 153–54 (quote).

44. *Haldeman Diaries*, 154.

45. Memo, Kissinger for Nixon, 26 Apr 1970 (quote), folder Haig Chron Apr 16–30, 1970 [1 of 3], box 965, Haig Chron Files, NSC, Nixon Library; telcon, Kissinger and Wheeler, 24 Apr 1970, 7:25 p.m., folder 1, box 5, HAK Telcons, ibid.; Webb, *JCS and the War in Vietnam 1969–1970*, 158–59.

46. Memos, Laird for Nixon, 27 Apr 1970 (quote); Kissinger for Nixon, 27 Apr 1970: both attached to memo, Haig for Kissinger, 27 Apr 1970, folder Haig Chron Apr 16–30,

1970 [1 of 3], box 965, Haig Chron Files, NSC, Nixon Library. Haig characterized Laird's memo as "loaded with distortions and misstatements."

47. Memo, Laird for Nixon, 27 Apr 1970, cited in note 46.

48. NSDM 57, 26 Apr 1970, folder NSDM 51–96, box 363, Subject Files, NSC, Nixon Library; Laird interview, 15 Oct 2001, 18–19; *Haldeman Diaries* cited in Kimball, *Vietnam War Files*, 132 (quote); Webb, *JCS and the War in Vietnam 1969–1970*, 158.

49. *Haldeman Diaries* cited in Kimball, *Vietnam War Files*, 133; telcons, Kissinger and Laird, 27 Apr 1970, 10:25 a.m.; Kissinger and Haldeman, 27 Apr 1970, 10:35 a.m.: both in folder 2, box 5 HAK Telcons, NSC, Nixon Library; memo, Laird for Nixon, 27 Apr 1970, cited in note 46.

50. Msgs, WHS 0033, Nixon to Bunker, 27 Apr 1970 (quotes); Saigon 251, Bunker to Nixon, 27 Apr 1970 (quote), NSDM 58, 28 Apr 1970: all attached to memo, Kissinger for Rogers et al., 28 Apr 1970, folder NSDM 51–96, box 363, Subject Files, NSC, Nixon Library.

51. Memo of Meeting, Cambodia/South Vietnam, 28 Apr 1970 (quotes), folder Haig's Vietnam File vol. 5 [2 of 2], box 1009, Haig Special File, NSC, Nixon Library; msg, JCS 05812, Wheeler to McCain, 28 Apr 1970, folder 2, box 590, Cambodian Operations (1970), NSC, Nixon Library.

52. DoD News Release 362-70, 29 Apr 1970; Kimball, *Nixon's Vietnam War*, 210–11.

53. *Nixon Public Papers 1970*, 405–10.

54. Cooper-Church amendment attached to memo, Kenneth E. BeLieu (Deputy Assistant to the President for Congressional Relations) for Kissinger, 8 May 1970, folder Cambodia vol. 5, 8 May 1970–22 May 1970, box 508, CF–Far East, NSC, Nixon Library.

55. Hammond, *Military and the Media*, 307–19; Paul J. Scheips, *Role of Federal Military Forces in Domestic Disorders, 1945–1992* (Washington, DC: U.S. Army Center Military History, 2012), 404, 410–11.

56. *Nixon Public Papers 1970*, 476–80 (quote); memo, Kissinger for Nixon, 22 Aug 1970, folder Cambodia vol. 9, 21 Jul–31 Aug 1970, box 510, CF–Far East, NSC, Nixon Library.

57. Memo, Kissinger for Nixon, 22 May 1970, folder Howe Chron May 1970, box 1075, Howe Chron Files; memo, Kissinger for Nixon, 26 May 1970, folder Vietnam May 1970, box 146, VNCF; memo, Kissinger for Nixon, 22 Oct 1970, folder Cambodia vol. 10, 1 Sep 1970–31 Oct 1970; memo, Kissinger for Nixon, 15 Dec 1970, attached to note, HAK, 16 Dec 1970, folder Cambodia vol. 11, 1 Nov 1970–Jan 1971: both in box 511, CF–Far East; NSDM 89, 26 Oct 1970, folder 4, box 363, Subject Files; memo, Laird for Moorer, 8 Dec 1970, attached to memo, Pursley for Eliot, 29 Dec 1970, folder Cambodia vol. 11, 1 Nov 1970–Jan 1971, box 511, CF–Far East: all in NSC, Nixon Library.

7. The War in Laos

1. For the developments in Laos in the 1950s and 1960s, see Kaplan, Landa, Drea, *McNamara Ascendancy, 1961–1965*; Jacob Van Staaveren, *Interdiction in Southern Laos, 1960–1968* (Washington, DC: Air Force History and Museums Program, 1993); Charles

A. Stevenson, *The End of Nowhere: American Policy Toward Laos Since 1954* (Boston, MA: Beacon Press, 1972); Martin E. Goldstein, *American Policy Toward Laos* (Hackensack, NJ: Fairleigh Dickinson University Press, 1973); Jane Hamilton-Merritt, *Tragic Mountains: The Hmong, the Americans, and the Secret Wars for Laos, 1942–1992* (Bloomington: Indiana University Press, 1993); and Arthur J. Dommen, *Laos: Keystone of Indochina* (Boulder, CO: Westview Press, 1985).

2. Kissinger, *White House Years*, 448–51; Webb, *JCS and the War in Vietnam 1969–1970*, 173–74.

3. Kissinger, *White House Years*, 448–51 (quote 451).

4. Thayer, *War Without Fronts*, 82–84; Bundy, *Tangled Web*, 68–69; memo, Sullivan for Kissinger, 10 Jun 1969, attached to memo, Kissinger for Nixon, 16 Jun 1969, folder Laos vol. 1, box 545, CF–Far East, NSC, Nixon Library.

5. Ltr, Wheeler to Rostow, 18 Jan 1969, attached to memo, Lemnitzer for Kissinger, 21 Jan 1969; memo, Ginsbergh for Kissinger, 17 Jan 1969; memo, Kissinger for Nixon, 15 Apr 1969; ltr, Warnke to Bundy, 11 Nov 1968, attached to memo, Wright for Rostow, 15 Jan 1969: all in folder Laos vol. 1, box 545, CF–Far East, NSC, Nixon Library.

6. Memo, Sullivan for Kissinger, 10 Jun 1969, cited in note 4.

7. William W. Momyer, *Airpower in Three Wars* (Washington, DC: Air Force History and Museums Program, 1978), 85.

8. Msg, CJCS 09447, Wheeler to McCain, 31 Jul 1969 (quote); memo, Laird for Kissinger, 31 Jul 1969: both attached to memo, Haig for Pursley, 31 Jul 1969 (quote), folder Laos vol. 1, box 545, CF–Far East, NSC, Nixon Library; msg, Haig to Lake, 31 Jul 1969 (quote), folder Haig Chron Jul 1969 [1 of 2], box 957; memo, Haig for Pursley, 1 Aug 1969, folder Haig Chron Aug 1969, box 958: both in Haig Chron Files, ibid.

9. Msg, ToHAK 164, Haig to Lake for Kissinger, 1 Aug 1969; memo, Richardson for Haig, 5 Aug 1969 (quote): both in folder Laos vol. 2, box 545, CF–Far East, ibid.

10. Memo, Laird for Nixon, 19 Aug 1969 (quotes), attached to memo, TL [Tony Lake] for Kissinger, 29 Aug 1969, ibid.

11. Memo, TL [Tony Lake] for Kissinger, 29 Aug 1969 (quote), cited in note 10; memo, Kissinger for Nixon, 2 Sep 1969 (quotes), attached to memo, Howe for Holdridge, 6 Sep 1969 (Kissinger quote), Laos vol. 2, box 545, CF–Far East, NSC, Nixon Library; NSSM 74, Planning for Laos, 17 Sep 1969 (quote); memo, Kissinger for Laird, 15 Sep 1969, folder Laos 0A-OC, box 9, Laird Papers, Ford Library.

12. *Cong. Rec.*, 19 Sep 1969, S 10981 (quote). The Symington subcommittee was part of the Senate Foreign Relations Committee. Bundy, *Tangled Web*, 69 (quotes); Roger Warner, *Back Fire: The CIA's Secret War in Laos and Its Link to the War in Vietnam* (New York, Simon & Schuster: 1995), 276–77.

13. Memos, Kissinger for Nixon, 25 Sep 1969 (quote); Kissinger for Nixon, 1 Oct 1969: both in folder 1, box 398, Subject Files, NSC, Nixon Library.

14. *Cong. Rec.*, 29 Oct 1969, S 13434.

15. Wilson, "Conferees on Military Funds," *Washington Post*, 19 Dec 1969; President's Statement About the Situation in Laos, 6 Mar 1970, *Nixon Public Papers 1970*, 248; Bundy, *Tangled Web*, 69–71; DoD Appropriations Act, 1970, P.L. 91-171, 83 Stat. 487 (1969).

16. Memo, Laird for Kissinger, 25 Sep 1969, folder Laos vol. 2, box 545, CF–Far East, NSC, Nixon Library; Minutes, WSAG Meeting, 29 Sep 1969 (quote), folder WSAG 69 and 70 [6 of 6], box H-114, H Files, ibid.

17. Memo, Laird for Nixon, 6 Oct 1969, attached to memo, Haig for Kissinger, 7 Oct 1969 (quote), folder Laos vol. 2, box 545, CF–Far East, ibid.; memo, Holdridge for Kissinger, 7 Oct 1969, attached to memo, Kissinger for Nixon, 23 Oct 1969 (quote), folder Laos vol. 3, box 546, ibid.; memo, Kissinger for Rogers, Laird, and Helms, 6 Dec 1969, attached to memo, Kissinger for Nixon, subj: Formation of an Interagency Ad Hoc Group on Laos, 2 Dec 1969, ibid.; ltr, Marshall Green to Kissinger, 9 Jan 1970, ibid.

18. Hamilton-Merritt, *Tragic Mountains*, 230–31; Bundy, *Tangled Web*, 145–46.

19. Ltr, Symington to Rogers, 3 Feb 1970, attached to Point Paper for the CJCS, folder 106, box 9, Records from SecDef Vault, Acc 330-74-142, WNRC; "Statement on Laos" by Senator Fulbright, 2 Mar 1970 (quotes), folder NSC Meeting 2/27/70 Laos, box H-027, H Files, NSC, Nixon Library; Bundy, *Tangled Web*, 145–46.

20. Memo, STU for Nutter, 27 Feb 1970, folder 106, box 9, Records from SecDef Vault, Acc 330-74-142. There is no further identification of "STU" on the memo, but it might be Stuart P. French, who was Nutter's principal assistant.

21. Laird's military assistant, Colonel Pursley, thought the NSC principals should consider other options as well, among them a new official public statement about U.S. policy and activities. Both Pursley and Daniel Z. Henkin, assistant secretary of defense for public affairs, recommended this option to Laird. Memo, Pursley for Laird, NSC Meeting on Laos, 27 Feb 1970, folder 106, box 9, Records from SecDef Vault, Acc 330-74-142.

22. Minutes, NSC Meeting on Laos, 27 Feb 1970 (Harlow, Rogers, Laird, and Nixon quotes), folder 1, box H-110, H Files, NSC, Nixon Library; memo, Kissinger for Nixon, 27 Feb 1970 (Kissinger quotes), folder NSC Mtg 2/27/70, box H-027, ibid.

23. *Nixon Public Papers 1970*, 244–49.

24. Tab C, memo Grant for Kissinger, 16 Mar 1970, folder Laos vol. 4, box 546, CF–Far East, NSC, Nixon Library.

25. Memo, Nixon for Kissinger, 2 Mar 1970 (quote), attached to memo, Haig for Kissinger, 3 Mar 1970 (quotes), folder Haig Chron Mar 1–11, 1970 [2 of 2], box 963, Haig Chron Files, NSC, Nixon Library.

26. Summary minutes, Ad Hoc Group Meeting on Laos, 12 Mar 1970 (quote), attached to memo, Grant for Kissinger, 14 Mar 1970, folder Laos vol. 4, box 546, CF–Far East, ibid; memo Laird for Nixon, 7 Mar 1970, folder Laos 5–8, box 9, Laird Papers, Ford Library.

27. Draft memo, Kissinger for Nixon, 18 Mar 1970, folder Haig Chron Mar 12–20, 1970 [1 of 2], box 963, Haig Chron Files, NSC, Nixon Library. It is not clear whether this memo went to Nixon. Memo, Kissinger for Nixon, 19 Mar 1970 (quote), folder Laos vol. 4,

box 546, CF–Far East, ibid. A handwritten note at the top of this memo reads "Dictated by Gen Haig but not sent." Memo, Haig for Kissinger, 19 Mar 1970 (quote), folder Haig Chron Mar 12–20, 1970 [1 of 2], box 963, Haig Chron Files, ibid.

28. Memo, Davis for Laird w/attached Summaries of Conclusions of WSAG Meetings on Laos and Cambodia on 19 Mar 1970, 6 Apr 1970, folder 36, box 3, Records from the SecDef Vault, Acc 330-74-142; memo, Kissinger for Nixon, 19 Mar 1970; memo, Kissinger for Rogers and Laird, 19 Mar 1970: both in folder Haig Chron, Mar 12–20,1970 [1 of 2], box 963, Haig Chron Files, NSC, Nixon Library; ltr, Packard to Helms, 13 Jun 1970, folder Laos 11–13, box 9, Laird Papers, Ford Library.

29. Memo, Holdridge for Kissinger, 17 Dec 1970, folder Vietnam Dec 1970, box 151, VNCF, NSC, Nixon Library.

30. Memcon, 31 May 1970, folder 2, box 339, Subject Files, ibid.

31. See William C. Westmoreland's memoir, *A Soldier Reports* (New York: Doubleday, 1976).

32. Bruce Palmer, *The 25-Year War: America's Military Role in Vietnam* (New York: Simon & Schuster, 1985), 105; memo, Laird for Kissinger, 30 Nov 1970, folder 31, box 3, Records from the SecDef Vault, Acc 330-74-142. Vietnam's climate was governed by monsoons. During the May-September southern monsoon, Vietnam experienced abundant rainfall. During the October-April northern monsoon, the country had relatively little rain.

33. Msg, McCain to Moorer, 10 Nov 1970, Messages, Creighton Abrams Papers, U.S. Center of Military History (CMH), Washington, DC; Webb, *JCS and the War in Vietnam 1969–1970*, 15–16.

34. Telcon, Moorer and McCain, 4 Dec 1970; msg, Moorer to McCain, n.d. (quote): both in Moorer Diary, box 2, Acc 218-05-006, NARA II. Moorer refers to Haig's planned arrival in Saigon in a week, which would mean the message was sent around 4 December.

35. Memcon, Meeting R. C. Robinson w/Kissinger and Haig, 5 Dec 1970, ibid.

36. Telcon, Nixon and Kissinger, 9 Dec 1970, folder 1, box 8, HAK Telcons, NSC, Nixon Library.

37. Msg, MAC 15808, Abrams to McCain, 12 Dec 1970, folder Lam Son 719 6 Jan–8 Feb 1971, box 110, Acc 218-92-0029, NARA II; msg, McCain to Moorer, 15 Dec 1970, Messages Abrams Papers, CMH; Moorer Diary, entries for 14, 15 (quote), 18 Dec 1970 (quote), box 2, Acc 218-05-006. Emphasis in original. According to the finding aid for the institutional files of the NSC, the WSAG met twice in December. The only meeting on the war occurred 11 December. The description of Westmoreland's plan comes from the discussion he had with Kissinger on 23 February 71; see Kissinger, *Ending the Vietnam War*, 201.

38. Moorer Diary, 18 Dec 1970, box 2, Acc 218-05-006; telcon, Nixon and Kissinger, 19 Dec 1970 (quote), folder 2, box 29, HAK Telcons, NSC, Nixon Library.

39. Moorer Diary, 21 Dec 1970 (quote), box 2, Acc 218-05-006; telcon, Nixon and Kissinger, 19 Dec 1970 (quotes), folder 2, box 29, HAK Telcons, NSC, Nixon Library.

40. Memcon Robinson, 22 Dec 1970, noon, Moorer Diary, box 2, Acc 218-05-006.

41. Ibid.

42. Memo for the Record, Robinson, 22 Dec 1970, 1630 hours, ibid.

43. I have found no information about Laird's reaction to the early planning by Kissinger, Abrams, Haig, and Moorer; or even if he discovered it. Van Atta, Laird's biographer, based his account on secondary sources and does not mention the effort to keep Laird in the dark about the early planning (p. 346). His account suggests that Laird was unaware of the planning done behind his back. Van Atta makes no mention of the 22 December meeting with Nixon that discussed how to inform Laird of the plan at the 23 December meeting.

44. Memo for the Record, Moorer, 23 Dec 1970 (quote), ibid.

45. CM-449-70 for Laird, 4 Jan 1971, folder CM 437-70 to CM 481-70, box 1, Acc 218-92-0029.

46. Memo, Laird for Nixon, 16 Jan 1971, (quotes 4, 9), folder 41, box 4, Records from SecDef Vault, Acc 330-74-142. Emphasis in original. Paper, "Meetings Associated w/Laotian Decision," n.d., folder Howe Chron Feb 1971, box 1077, Howe Chron Files, NSC, Nixon Library; Moorer Diary, 9 Jan 1971, box 2, Acc 218-05-006.

47. Memcon, Laird and Thieu, 11 Jan 1971 (quotes), folder Haig Chron Jan 13–17, 1971 [1 of 2], box 975; memo, Kissinger for Nixon, 23 Jan 1971, folder Haig Chron Jan 18–24, 1971 [1 of 2], box 976: both in Haig Chron Files, NSC, Nixon Library. The memcon does not indicate that Laird and Thieu discussed the duration of the operation in Laos.

48. "Meetings Associated w/Laotian Decision," cited in note 47; msg, JCS 1475 to CINCPAC, 19 Jan 1971 (quote); Moorer Diary, box 2, Acc 218-05-006. Laird wrote "OK" on each page of the message. Moorer Diary, 18 Jan 1971 (quotes), ibid. Moorer's diary entry for 19 January indicated he brought the message on Tchepone to Laird at 9:03 a.m.

49. Memo for the Record, Moorer, 23 Jan 1971; msg, JCS 2225, Moorer to McCain, 28 Jan 1971: both in Moorer Diary, box 2, ibid.

50. Memo, Kissinger for Nixon, 26 Jan 1971, folder JCS vol. 1, box 245, Agency Files, NSC, Nixon Library; Moorer Diary, 28 Jan 1971, 27 (quote); telcon, Moorer and McCain, 27 Jan 1971: both in Moorer Diary, box 2, Acc 218-05-006.

51. Hammond, *Military and the Media*, 408–13; memo, Haig for Kissinger, 29 Jan 1971, folder Haig Chron Jan 25–31, 1971, box 976, Haig Chron Files, NSC, Nixon Library.

52. Memo, Haig for Kissinger, 29 Jan 1971 (quote), cited in note 46; memo, Kissinger for Rogers et al., 2 Feb 1971, folder Laos 40–45, box 9, Laird Papers, Ford Library; Moorer Diary, 2 Feb 1971, box 2, Acc 218-05-006.

53. CIA Special Operations Reports, 1 and 5 Feb 1971: both in folder Lam Son 719 6 Jan–8 Feb 1971, box 110, Acc 218-92-0029.

54. Moorer Diary, 2 and 3 (quote) Feb 1971, box 2, Acc 218-05-006; telcon, Kissinger and Laird, 2 Feb 1971, folder 8, box 8, HAK Telcons, NSC, Nixon Library; msg, JCS 3244, Moorer to McCain and Abrams, 4 Feb 1971, copy in Moorer Diary, box 2, Acc 218-05-006. Quote from message, which Moorer released and Laird approved. Kissinger (quote), Moorer

Diary, 4 Feb 1971, ibid. Official English Text of Statement Broadcast by President Thieu, 8 Feb 1971, folder 40, box 4, Records from SecDef Vault, Acc 330-74-142.

55. Hammond, *Military and the Media*, 428–29 (quote).

56. Ibid., 441, 443–44; msgs, QTR 0064, Sutherland to Abrams, 12 Feb 1971; MAC 01554, Abrams to Sutherland, 13 Feb 1971; DNG 0448, Sutherland to Clay, 14 Feb 1971: all in Messages, Abrams Papers, CMH; Moorer Diary, 12 Feb 1971; telcon, Moorer and Kissinger, 20 Feb 1971: both in Moorer Diary, box 2, Acc 218-05-006; Phillip B. Davidson, *Vietnam at War: The History, 1946–1975* (Novato, CA: Presidio Press, 1988), 645–46.

57. Moorer Diary, 22 Feb 1971 (quote); telcons, Kissinger and Moorer, 22 Feb 1971, 1700 hours (quotes); Nixon and Moorer, 22 Feb 1971, 1945 hours (quote): all in Moorer Diary, box 2, Acc 218-05-006. For information on helicopter losses, see Hammond, *Military and the Media*, 450.

58. Kissinger, *Ending the Vietnam War*, 200–02. Kissinger asked for Westmoreland's briefing when Moorer was away from Washington.

59. Telcon, Kissinger and Laird, 25 Feb 1971 (quote), folder 9, box 8, HAK Telcons, NSC, Nixon Library; Moorer Diary, 23 Feb 1971 (quotes); Memo for the Record, JCS Meeting, 24 Feb 1971 (quotes): both in Moorer Diary, box 2, Acc 218-05-006.

60. Van, Atta, *With Honor*, 347–48.

61. Memo for the President from Haig, President's Meeting w/Moorer and Kissinger, 25 Feb 1971, folder Howe Chron Feb 1971, box 1077, Howe Trip Files, NSC, Nixon Library; memcon, President et al., 26 Feb 1971, folder NSC Minutes 1971 [4 of 5], box H-110, H Files, ibid.

62. Msg, WHS 1010, Kissinger to Bunker, 1 Mar 1971, folder Haig Chron Mar 1–6, 1971 [2 of 2], box 977, Haig Chron Files, ibid.; Conversation 459-2, Nixon and Kissinger, 27 Feb 1971, Nixon Tapes, Nixon Library.

63. Memo, Kissinger for Nixon, 3 Mar 1971 (quotes), ibid.; telcon, Nixon and Moorer, 3 Mar 1971; Moorer Diary, 3 Mar 1971 (quote): both in Moorer Diary, box 2, Acc 218-05-006.

64. Telcon, Nixon and Moorer, 6 Mar 1971 (quotes), in ibid.; telcon Nixon and Kissinger, 6 Mar 1971, folder 3, box 9, HAK Telcons, NSC, Nixon Library.

65. Telcon, Nixon and Kissinger, 3 Mar 1971, folder 3, box 9, HAK Telcons, NSC, Nixon Library.

66. Telcons, Kissinger and Laird, 9 Mar 1971, 6:45 p.m.; Kissinger and Moorer, 9 Mar 1971, 6:50 p.m., 8:08 p.m. (quote); Moorer and Abrams, 9 Mar 1971, 7:55 p.m. (quote); memo, Laird for Moorer, 11 Mar 1971: all in Moorer Diary, 9 and 11 Mar 1971, box 2, Acc 218-05-006; memo, Laird for Moorer, 26 Mar 1971, folder Laos 47–50, box 9, Laird Papers, Ford Library.

67. Telcon, Moorer and Abrams, 9 Mar 1971, 7:55 p.m., cited in note 66.

68. Davidson, *Vietnam at War*, 648–49.

69. Msg, Kissinger to Bunker, 9 Mar 1971, attached to memo, Robinson for Moorer, 10 Mar 1971, Moorer Diary, box 2, Acc 218-05-006.

70. Msg, Saigon 0458, Bunker to Kissinger, 10 Mar 1971, ibid.

71. Memo of Laos/Cambodia Briefing, 11 Mar 1971 (quote), folder Haig Chron Mar 10–20, 1971 [1 of 2], box 977, Haig Chron Files, NSC, Nixon Library; "S. Viets See Aims Fulfilled," news dispatch, 14 Mar 1971 (quote), folder Lam Son 719, box 292, Subject Files, OSD/HO.

72. "Pullback Planned in Laos," 14 Mar 1971; "S. Viets Continue Pullback," AP press release, 18 Mar 1971: both in folder Lam Son 719, box 292, Subject Files, OSD/HO; telcon, Kissinger and Rogers, 17 Mar 1971 (quote), folder 4, box 9, HAK Telcons, NSC, Nixon Library.

73. Moorer Diary, 17 Mar 1971, box 2, Acc 218-05-006; telcons, Kissinger and Moorer, 17 Mar 1971, 11:07 a.m., 6:55 p.m., folder 4, box 9, HAK Telcons, NSC, Nixon Library; memo, Moorer for Laird, 16 Mar 1971 (quote), folder CM 701-71 to CM 751-71, box 2, Acc 218-92-0029.

74. Hammond, *Military and the Media*, 472; msg, JCS 6505, Moorer to McCain and Abrams, 17 Mar 1971 (quote), folder Laos–Lam Son 719, box 19, Acc 218-92-0029; Moorer Diary, 18 Mar 1971 (quote), box 2, Acc 218-05-006; telcons, Nixon and Kissinger, 17 Mar 1971; Kissinger and Moorer, 18 Mar 1971 (quote): both in folder 4, box 9, HAK Telcons, NSC, Nixon Library; msg, Kissinger to Haig, 17 Mar 1971; msg, Kissinger to Bunker, Mar 1971 (quote): both in folder Haig SEA Trip Mar 1971, box 1013, Haig Special File, ibid.

75. Telcons, Laird and Kissinger, 23 Feb 1971, 8:55 a.m., 5:05 p.m. (quote), folder 1, box 9, HAK Telcons, ibid.

76. Msg, Kennedy to Haig in Saigon, 17 Mar 1971; msg, Haig to Kissinger, 19 Mar 1971 (quotes), both attached to memo, Kissinger for Nixon, 19 Mar 1971, folder Haig Chron Mar 10–20, 1971 [1 of 2], box 977, Haig Chron Files, NSC, Nixon Library; msg, Saigon 641, Haig to Kissinger, 19 Mar 1971 (quotes), folder 6, box 977, ibid.

77. Telcons, Kissinger and Rogers, 19 Mar 1971, 9:35 a.m. (quote); Kissinger and Nixon, 19 Mar 1971, 11:10 a.m. (quotes): both in folder 5, box 9, HAK Telcons, ibid.; telcon, Kissinger and Nixon, 20 Mar 1971, 10:30 a.m. (quote), folder 4, box 29, ibid. Kissinger expressed the same point to Moorer, "I think we were within a division . . . of ending this goddamn thing." Telcon, Kissinger and Moorer, 21 Mar 1971, ibid.

78. Two telcons, Kissinger and Laird, 21 Mar 1971 (quotes); telcon, Nixon and Kissinger, 21 Mar 1971: all in ibid. There are two transcribed telephone conversations between Kissinger and Laird for this date, but they give no indication of the time. The first conversation ends abruptly because Nixon telephoned Kissinger. The second conversation begins after the president's call. These conversations appear to have been transcribed at least one day after the conversation. Davidson, *Vietnam at War*, 649. On the U.S. withdrawal, see Prados, *Vietnam*, 415, and Clarke, *Advice and Support*, 475.

79. Memo, Kissinger for Nixon, w/attached memo, Abrams for McCain, Assessment by Gen. Abrams, 22 Mar 1971, folder Haig Chron Mar 21–31, 1971 [2 of 2], box 978, Haig Chron Files, NSC, Nixon Library; two telcons, Kissinger and Nixon, 21 Mar 1971, folder

4, box 29, HAK Telcons, ibid. One telephone conversation occurred at 10:00 a.m. (quote); the date of the second is annotated with a question mark.

80. Ltr, Kissinger to Rep. Hale Boggs, 29 Mar 1971, folder Haig Chron Mar 21–31, 1971 [1 of 2], box 987, Haig Chron Files, ibid.; *Nixon Public Papers 1971*, 522–27 (quotes 523–24).

81. Memo, Haig for Kissinger, n.d., folder Haig SEA Trip Mar 14–21, 1971 [2 of 2], box 1013, Haig Chron Files, NSC, Nixon Library.

82. Moorer Diary, 10 Apr 1971, box 2, Acc 218-05-006; telcon, Kissinger and Westmoreland, 12 Apr 1971 (quotes), folder 5, box 29, HAK Telcons, NSC, Nixon Library. Sorley's unfairly critical biography, *Westmoreland: The General Who Lost Vietnam* (New York: Houghton Mifflin Harcourt, 2011), fails to even mention Westmoreland's concept for an offensive in Laos.

83. Moorer Diary, 21 Apr 1971, box 2, Acc 218-05-006.

84. Telcon, Nixon and Kissinger, 25 Mar 1971, folder 6, box 9, HAK Telcons, NSC, Nixon Library.

85. Stewart Alsop, "The Tchepone Test," Newsweek, 22 Feb 1971.

86. Minutes WSAG Meeting, Evaluation of Lam Son Operation, 23 Mar 1971, folder 3, box H-115, H Files, NSC, Nixon Library.

87. Telcon, Nixon and Kissinger, 7 Feb 1971 (quote), folder 8, box 8, HAK Telcons, ibid.

88. Hammond, *Military and the Media*, 488–90; *Haldeman Diaries*, 259 (quote).

89. Telcons, Kissinger and Laird, 6:55 p.m., Kissinger and Moorer, 8:35 p.m., Nixon and Kissinger, 8:25 p.m. (quotes), all 14 Sep 1971: all in folder 5, box 11, HAK Telcons, NSC, Nixon Library; Moorer Diary, 15 Sep 1971, box 2, Acc 218-05-006.

90. Telcon, Kissinger and Laird, 15 Sep 1971, 8:40 a.m. (quote), folder 5, box 11, HAK Telcons, NSC, Nixon Library.

91. White House Conversation 464-23, 17 Mar 1971 between Nixon and Kissinger, White House Conversations, Nixon Library.

92. Van Atta, *With Honor*, 350; Minutes, SecDef Staff Meeting, 29 Mar 1971, folder Staff Mtgs Jan-Mar 1971, box 14, Acc 330-77-0062, WNRC.

93. White House Conversation 472-13, 23 Mar 1971 between Nixon, Kissinger and Haldeman, White House Conversations, Nixon Library.

8. Preparing South Vietnam to Stand Alone

1. Memo, Haig for Kissinger, 8 Apr 191970, folder Haig's Vietnam File vol. 5 [1 of 2], box 1009, Haig Special File, NSC, Nixon Library.

2. Memo, Kissinger for Nixon, 16 Apr 191970 (quote), memo Laird for Kissinger, 27 Apr 191970, both attached to note Lord to Kissinger, 27 Apr 1970, folder Vietnam Apr 1970, box 145, VNCF, ibid.

3. Msg, Kissinger to Bunker (Back Channel), n.d., folder 2, box 975, ibid.; msgs, WHS 1004, Kissinger to Bunker, 16 Jan 1971; Saigon 544, Bunker to Kissinger, 16 Jan 1971: both in folder 6, ibid.

4. Memo, Laird for Nixon, 16 Jan 1971 (quote on p 10), folder 41, box 4, Records from SecDef Vault, Acc 330-74-142, WNRC. Emphasis in original.

5. Memo, Robinson for Kissinger, 8 Jan 1971 (quote), attached to note Haig to Kissinger, 9 Jan 1971, folder Vietnam 1 Jan–10 Feb 1971, box 152, VNCF, NSC, Nixon Library; memo, Haig for Kissinger, 15 Jan 1971, folder 6, box 975, ibid.

6. Memo, Laird for Nixon, 16 Jan 1971 (quote), cited in note 4; memo Holdridge for Kissinger, 14 Jan 1971 (quote), folder Vietnam 1 Jan–10 Feb 1971, box 152, VNCF, NSC, Nixon Library.

7. CM-526-71 for Laird, Trip Report (quotes), n.d., Moorer Diary, folder 9, box 2, Acc 218-05-006, NARA II.

8. Msg, Kissinger to Bunker, 27 Mar 1971 (Backchannel) (quotes), folder 3, box 103, HAK Office Files, NSC, Nixon Library; telcon, Kissinger and Moorer, 11 Mar 1971, folder 3, box 9, HAK Telcons, ibid.

9. Msg, Saigon 938 Bunker to Kissinger, 2 Apr 1971, folder 3, box 103, HAK Office Files, ibid.; msg, Kissinger to Bunker (Backchannel), 2 Apr 1971, folder 4, box 978, ibid.

10. Memo, Laird for Nixon, 3 Apr 1971 (quotes), attached to note to Haig, 4 Apr 1971 (quote), folder Troop Withdrawals, box 103, HAK Office Files, ibid. Emphasis in original. JCSM-145-71 for Laird, 26 Mar 1971, folder Troop Withdrawals-1, box 3, Kissinger/Scowcroft Files, Ford Library.

11. Msg, Haig to Kissinger, 16 Mar 1971, attached to memo, Kissinger for Nixon, n.d., folder Haig SEA Trip Mar 1971 [1 of 2], box 1013, Haig Special File, NSC, Nixon Library; President's Address to the Nation, 7 Apr 1971; President's News Conference, 12 Nov 1971: both in *Nixon Public Papers 1971*, 522, 524, 1101; memo, Laird for Moorer, 15 Nov 1971, folder Vietnam Nov–Dec 1971 [2 of 2], box 158, VNCF, NSC, Nixon Library. Calculations are based on the maximum strength of over 549,000.

12. President's Remarks, 13 Jan 1972, *Nixon Public Papers 1972*, 30; memo, Laird for Kissinger, 30 Jul 1971, attached to memo, Haig for Kissinger, 30 Jul 1971, folder Haig Chron Jul 27–31, 1971, box 984, Haig Chron Files, NSC, Nixon Library.

13. JCSM-42-1970 for Laird, 29 Jan 1970, folder 39, box 4, Records from SecDef Vault, Acc 330-74-142, WNRC; memo, Laird for Wheeler, 13 Mar 1970, folder Vietnam 152–153, box 33, Laird Papers, Ford Library; Clarke, *Final Years*, 355–56; Dale Andrade, *Trial By Fire: The 1972 Easter Offensive, America's Last Vietnam Battle* (New York: Hippocrene Books, 1995), 2.

14. Bernard C. Nalty, *The War Against Trucks: Aerial Interdiction in Southern Laos* (Washington, DC: Air Force History and Museums Program, 2005), 237–38; Leonard Sullivan, interview by Alfred Goldberg and Roger Trask, 4 May 1966, 4, OSD/HO.

15. Memo, Laird for Nixon, 5 Jun 1970, folder Vietnam 186–187, box 33, Laird Papers, Ford Lirary.

16. Memo, Laird for Kissinger, attached to memo, Kissinger for Nixon, 26 Mar 1971, folder 11 Feb–28 Mar 1971, box 153, VNCF, NSC, Nixon Library; memo Kissinger for Laird, 1 Apr 1971 (quote), folder Vietnam 357–359, box 35, Laird Papers, Ford Library.

17. Memos, Laird for Wheeler, 5 Jun 1970, folder Vietnam 186–187, box 33; Laird for Moorer, 17 Aug 1970 (quotes), folder Vietnam 227–231, box 34: both in Laird Papers, Ford Library.

18. Memos, Kissinger for Laird et al., NSSM-99, 17 Aug 1970 (quote), folder Vietnam 227–231; Laird for ASD (ISA), 27 Aug 1970, folder Vietnam 232–235: both in box 34, Laird Papers, Ford Library; memo, Laird for Kissinger, 19 Feb 1971, folder Vietnam 329–333, box 35, ibid.

19. Memo, Kissinger for Laird, n.d., attached to note, Haig to Kissinger, 27 Feb 1971, folder DoD vol. 11, box 226, Agency Files, NSC, Nixon Library; memo, Nutter for Laird, 23 Mar 1971, folder 41, box 4, Records from SecDef Vault, Acc 330-74-142; memo, Kissinger for Laird, 15 Jun 1970, folder 188–192a, box 33, Laird Papers, Ford Library; memo, Kissinger for Laird et al., NSDM 79, 13 Aug 1970, folder NSDM 51–96, box 363, Subject Files, NSC, Nixon Library.

20. Memo, Laird for Moorer, 17 Aug 1970, cited in note 17; memo, Kissinger for Nixon, 31 May 1971 (quote), folder Vietnam May 1971, box 154, VNCF, NSC, Nixon Library. Second quote found in Nixon's notations on the memo. Paper, "Mission of US Forces," attached to memo, Haig for Kissinger, 15 May 1971 (quote), folder May 11–18, 1971 [1 of 2], box 980, Haig Chron Files, ibid.

21. Memo, Laird for Wheeler, 5 Jun 1970 (quotes), attached to memo, Laird for Nixon, 5 Jun 1970, folder Vietnam Jun 1970, box 147, VNCF, ibid.; memo, Pursley for Nutter, 25 May 1970, attached to memo, Laird for Nixon, 5 Jun 1970, folder Vietnam 186–187, box 33, Laird Papers, Ford Library.

22. Memo, Laird for Kissinger, 5 Apr 1971, folder Vietnam 360–367, box 35, Laird Papers, Ford Library.

23. Memo, Laird for CJCS and Service Secretaries, 19 Feb 1971, folder Vietnam 325–328, ibid.

24. Clarke, *Final Years*, 455–56; JCSM-347-71 for Laird, 24 Jul 1971, folder Vietnam 487–492, box 37, Laird Papers, Ford Library.

25. Paper "VNAF Modernization," n.d. (bears the notation "SecDef has seen 18 Feb 1971"), folder 41, box 4, Records from SecDef Vault, Acc 330-74-142; CM-489-71 for Laird, 21 Jan 1971, folder Vietnam 307–311, box 35, Laird Papers, Ford Library.

26. Memo, Kissinger for Nixon, 26 Mar 1971, folder DoD vol. 11, box 226, Agency Files, NSC, Nixon Library; memo, Sullivan for DDRE, 14 Apr 1971, attached to memo for Laird, 15 Apr 1971, folder Laos 52–54, box 9, Laird Papers, Ford Library; memo, Packard

for CJCS and Service Secretaries, 10 May 1971, attached to memo, Karhohs for Pursley, 7 May 1971, folder Vietnam 410–412, box 36, ibid.; Nalty, *War against Trucks*, 238–40, 249.

27. Memo, Laird for CJCS and Service Secretaries, 2 Jul 1971, folder Vietnam Jul–Aug 1971, box 27, Acc 218-92-0029, NARA II.

28. Msg, 220105Z, McCain to Moorer, 22 Jul 1971 (quote), folder Vietnam Jul–Aug 1971, ibid.; memo, Laird for Moorer, Vietnamization of Interdiction, 8 Oct 1971 (quotes), folder 94, box 8, Records from SecDef Vault, Acc 330-74-142.

29. Memo, Laird for Moorer, 8 Oct 1971, cited in note 28.

30. Memo, Haig for President File, President's Meeting w/Laird et al., 26 Mar 1971, folder 11 Feb–28 Mar 1971, box 153, VNCF, NSC, Nixon Library; memo, Nutter for Laird, 23 Mar 1971, folder 41, box 4, Records from SecDef Vault, Acc 330-74-142.

31. Memo, Laird for Nixon, 18 May 1971 (quote), attached to memo, Smith for Kissinger, 19 May 1971, folder Vietnam May 1971, box 154, VNCF, NSC, Nixon Library.

32. Memo, Smith for Kissinger, 19 May 1971, cited in note 31; msg, Saigon 0043, Bunker to Kissinger, 22 May 1971, folder 5, box 980, NSC, Nixon Library.

33. Summary of Conclusions, Senior Review Group Meeting, 24 May 1971, folder 4, box H-112, H Files, NSC, Nixon Library; Memo for the Record by Karhohs, SRG Meeting, 24 May 1971, folder Vietnam 424–431, box 36, Laird Papers, Ford Library. Major General Karhohs was director of the Vietnam Task Force in DoD. Memo, Welander for Moorer, 8 Jun 1971 (quote), Moorer Diary, folder 14, box 3, Acc 218-05-006.

34. Memo, Kissinger for SRG, folder Vietnam 424–431, box 36, Laird Papers, Ford Library; memo Smith for Walsh et al., 28 May 1971, folder SRG Meeting 4 Jun 1971, box H-056, H Files, NSC, Nixon Library.

35. Summary of Conclusions, Senior Review Group Meeting, 9 Jun 1971, folder 3, box H-112, H Files, NSC, Nixon Library; memo, Packard for SRG, 18 Jun 1971, folder SRG Meeting 22 Jun 1971 [2 of 2], box H-055, H Files, NSC, Nixon Library; memo, President for SecDef, SecState, NSDM 118, 3 Jul 1971, folder Vietnam 472–478, box 36, Laird Papers, Ford Library; memo, Smith for Kissinger, 21 Jul 1971, attached to memo, Kissinger for Laird, 21 Jul 1971 (quotes), folder Vietnam Jul 1971, box 155, VNCF, NSC, Nixon Library; Clarke, *Final Years*, 456–57.

36. CM-995-71 for Laird, 23 Jun 1971, attached to memo, Laird for Moorer, 29 Jun 1971 (quote), folder Vietnam Jul 1971, box 155, VNCF, NSC, Nixon Library; memos, Laird for Moorer, 3 Jun 1971, folder Vietnam 434–438; Laird for Kissinger, 1 Jul 1971 (quote, emphasis in original), folder 467–471: both in box 36, Laird Papers, Ford Library.

37. Memos, Laird for Moorer, 23 Jun 1971, folder 454–460A; Laird for Moorer, 20 Jul 1971, folder Vietnam 479–483: both in box 36, Laird Papers, Ford Library.

38. JCSM-379-71 for Laird, 17 Aug 1971 (quote), folder Vietnam 510; memo, Laird for Moorer, 4 Sep 1971 (quote), folder Vietnam 530–536: both in box 37, ibid.

39. Memo, Laird for Nixon, 4 Sep 1971, folder Vietnam 530–536, ibid.

40. Memo for the Record, NSC Meeting on Vietnam, 20 Sep 1971, folder 4, box H-110, H Files, NSC, Nixon Library.

41. Memos, Foster for Laird, n.d. (quote), attached to Sullivan for Pursley, 27 Oct 1971; Sullivan for Pursley, 1 Nov 1971: all in folder 94, box 8, Records from SecDef Vault, Acc 330-74-142.

42. CM-1320-71, Memo for the Record, Visit by CJCS to SVN, 18 Nov 1971, folder CM 1272-71 to CM 1359-71, box 3, Acc 218-92-0029; memo, Laird for Nixon, 8 Nov 1971 (quotes), folder Vietnam Nov–Dec 1971 [2 of 2], box 158, VNCF, NSC, Nixon Library.

43. Memo, Laird for Nixon, 8 Nov 1971, cited in note 43.

44. Memo, Laird for Nixon, 3 Dec 1971, folder Vietnam 603–607, box 38, Laird Papers, Ford Library.

45. Memo, Haig for President File, President's Meeting w/Laird, 13 Jan 1972, folder Haig Chron Jan 1–21, 1972, box 990, Haig Chron Files, NSC, Nixon Library.

46. James H. Willbanks, *Abandoning Vietnam: How America Left and South Vietnam Lost Its War* (Lawrence: University Press of Kansas, 2004), 122–23; Hunt, *Pacification*, 252–53.

47. Willbanks, *Abandoning Vietnam*, 124–26; Andrade, *America's Last Vietnam Battle*, 3; Randolph, *Powerful and Brutal Weapons*, 24.

48. Memo, Laird for Moorer, 6 Jan 1972 (quote), attached to memo, Laird for Kissinger, 12 Jan 1972, folder DoD vol. 15, box 230, Agency Files, NSC, Nixon Library; memo, Odeen for Kissinger, 5 Jan 1972 (quote), folder Vietnam Jan–Feb 1972 [1 of 3], box 158, VNCF, NSC, Nixon Library; Randolph, *Powerful and Brutal Weapons*, 49–50. Before joining Kissinger's staff, Odeen worked in the Systems Analysis office in OSD.

49. Paper, "Conclusions Regarding Enemy versus Friendly Capabilities," attached to CM-1440-72 for Laird, 10 Jan 1972, folder Vietnam 640–644, box 38, Laird Papers, Ford Library; msg, Kissinger to Bunker, 11 Jan 1972, folder Haig Chron Jan 1–21, 1972, box 990, Haig Chron Files, NSC, Nixon Library.

50. Msg, Saigon 0017 Bunker to Kissinger, 17 Jan 1972, folder 8, box 103, HAK Office Files, NSC, Nixon Library.

51. Msg, Abrams to McCain, 200945Z Jan 1972 (quotes), attached to CM-1468-72 for Laird, 20 Jan 1972, folder Vietnam 654–656, box 38, Laird Papers, Ford Library; Moorer Diary, 20 and 22 Jan 1972, folder 21, box 4, Acc 218-05-006.

52. Moorer Diary, 22 Jan 1972, cited in note 51.

53. Memo, Odeen/Negroponte for Kissinger, 22 Jan 1972 (quote), folder NSC Meeting Vietnam 2/2/72, box H-032, H Files, NSC, Nixon Library; memo, Odeen for Kissinger, 26 Jan 1972 (quote), folder Vietnam Jan–Feb 1972 [1 of 3], box 158, VNCF, ibid.

54. Memo, Laird for Kissinger, 26 Jan 1972, folder Vietnam Jan–Feb 1972 [2 of 3], box 158, VNCF, ibid.

55. Memos, Nixon for Laird, 1 Feb 1972 (quote); Kissinger for Nixon, 29 Jan 1972 (quote): both attached to memo, Odeen/Kennedy for Kissinger, 27 Jan 1972, ibid.

56. Memos, Odeen for Kissinger, 29 Jan 1972; Kissinger for Nixon, n.d., bears the stamp: "The President has seen" (quote, emphasis in original): both in folder NSC Meeting Vietnam 2/2/72, box H-032, H Files, ibid.

57. Memo for the Record, Moorer, NSC Meetings 2 Feb 1972 (quote), 4 Feb 1972, Moorer Diary, folder 22, box 4, Acc 218-05-006; memo, Kissinger for Laird, NSDM 149, 4 Feb 1972 (quotes), attached to memo Laird for Nixon, 8 Mar 1972, folder Haig Chron Mar 7–15, 1972, box 992, Haig Chron Files, NSC, Nixon Library.

58. Moorer Diary, 3 (quotes), 4 (quote), and 5 Feb 1972 (quote), folder 22, box 4, Acc 218-05-006.

59. Memo, Laird for Moorer, 2 Feb 1972, Moorer Diary, ibid.; CM-1521-72 for Laird, 7 Feb 1972, folder CM 1521-72 to CM 1586-72, box 3, Acc 218-92-0029; memo, Laird for Nixon, 8 Mar 1972, cited in note 76; memo, Seamans for Laird, 4 Feb 1972, folder Personal File, box D17, Laird Papers, Ford Library.

60. Memo, Laird for Moorer, 3 Mar 1972, folder Vietnam 19702–19707, box 39, Laird Papers, Ford Library; CM-1610-72 for Laird, 7 Mar 1972, folder Vietnam Mar 1972, box 218, Acc 218-92-0029.

61. Msg, MACV 69866, Abrams to Moorer, 8 Mar 1972; CM-1625-72 for Laird, 9 Mar 1972: both attached to memo, Laird for Kissinger, 10 Mar 1972, folder Haig Trip Papers 4/14–4/19/72 [1 of 2], box 1014, Haig Special File, NSC, Nixon Library. Bunker endorsed Abrams' request in msg, Saigon 0050, Bunker to Kissinger, 10 Mar 1972, folder 1, box 992, ibid.; memo, Laird for Nixon, 14 Mar 1972, folder Vietnam Mar 1972 [1 of 2], box 159, VNCF, ibid.; memo, Kissinger for Nixon, 18 Mar 1972, folder Haig Trip Papers 4/14–4/19/72 [1 of 2], box 1014, Haig Special File, ibid.; memo, Nixon for Laird, 18 Mar 1972 (quote), folder Vietnam 722–729, box 39, Laird Papers, Ford Library.

62. Memo, Laird for Moorer, 22 Mar 1972, Moorer Diary, box 4, Acc 218-05-006.

63. Memo, Haig for Nixon, n.d. (quote), attached to memo, Stearman for Haig, 25 Mar 1972, folder Vietnam Mar 1972 [1 of 2], box 159, VNCF, NSC, Nixon Library. It is unclear whether Haig sent this report to Nixon.

64. Msg, Vann to Abrams, 270151Z Mar 1972 (quotes), folder 11600–11799, Messages, Abrams Papers, CMH.

65. Moorer Diary, 28 Mar 1972, folder 23, box 4, Acc 218-05-006; *New York Times*, 31 Mar and 3 Apr 1972; Clarke, *Final Years*, 481.

9. A Time of Trial: The Easter Offensive and Vietnamization

1. Andrade, *America's Last Battle*, 29; Willbanks, *Abandoning Vietnam*, 126–29.

2. Notable recent treatments of the offensive include Andrade, *America's Last Battle*; Prados, *Vietnam*; Stephen Randolph, *Powerful and Brutal Weapons: Nixon, Kissinger, and the Easter Offensive* (Cambridge, MA: Harvard University Press, 2007); Willard J. Webb and Walter S. Poole, *The Joint Chiefs of Staff and the War in Vietnam, 1971–1973* (Washington,

DC: Office of Joint History, Office of the JCS, 2013); and Willbanks, *Abandoning Vietnam*. For an assessment of how the offensive affected pacification, see Hunt, *Pacification*.

3. See chapter 2 for more on the EC-121 crisis.

4. Randolph's *Powerful and Brutal Weapons* lays out the conflicts within the administration. This chapter focuses on how these conflicts affected Laird's role during the Easter Offensive.

5. *FRUS 1969–1976*, 8:641–42.

6. Msgs, Kroesen to Abrams, 310415Z Mar 1972; Kroesen to Abrams, 311215Z Mar 1972 (quote) emphasis added: both in folder 11600–11799, Messages, Abrams Papers, CMH. The time in Washington of the first message was 2315 hours on 30 March; the second message, 0715 hours on 31 March. See *FRUS 1964–1968*, 6:408–09, for a summary of the understanding.

7. *FRUS 1969–1976*, 8:153–57

8. Telcon, Kissinger and Moorer, 31 Mar 1972 (quotes), folder 7, box 13, HAK Telcons, NSC, Nixon Library; Kissinger, *White House Years*, 1097.

9. Kissinger, *Ending the Vietnam War*, 233–34 (1st and 2nd quotes); telcon, Kissinger and Moorer, 3 Apr 1972 (3rd quote), folder 8, box 13, HAK Telcons, NSC, Nixon Library.

10. Willbanks, *Abandoning Vietnam*, 129–34; Moorer Diary, 2 Apr 1972; telcon, Moorer and Laird, 2 Apr 1972, 9:10 a.m. (quote): both in Moorer Diary, folder 24, box 4, Acc 218-05-006, NARA II.

11. In *White House Years*, 1108–23, and *Ending the Vietnam War*, 243–55, Kissinger lays out the administration's thinking. See also Randolph, *Powerful and Brutal Weapons*, 156–57.

12. Nixon, *Memoirs*, 586–89 (quote 589); Willbanks, *Abandoning Vietnam*, 133–34; Kissinger, *White House Years*, 1098–99; telcon, Moorer and Kissinger, 2 Apr 1972, in Moorer Diary, folder 24, box 4, Acc 218-05-006; telcon, Kissinger and Moorer, 3 Apr 1972, folder 8, box 13, HAK Telcons, NSC, Nixon Library.

13. Kissinger, *Ending the Vietnam War*, 234; Wayne Thompson, *To Hanoi and Back: The United States Air Force and North Vietnam, 1966–1973* (Washington, DC: Air Force History and Museums Program, 2000), 220–22; Webb and Poole, *JCS and Vietnam 1971–1973*, 353; Moorer Diary, 2 Apr 1972; telcons, Kissinger and Moorer, Moorer and Rush, 2 Apr 1972: both in Moorer Diary, folder 24, box 4, Acc 218-05-006.

14. Memo for the Record, Moorer, Meeting w/President Nixon, 3 Apr 1972 (quote); Memo for the Record, Moorer, 3 Apr 1972; memo, Nixon for Laird, 3 Apr 1972: all in Moorer Diary, folder 24, box 4, Acc 218-05-006.

15. Memo, Haig for Kissinger, 3 Apr 1972, folder Haig Trip Papers 4/14–4/19/72 [1 of 2], box 1014, Haig Special File, NSC, Nixon Library; Memo for the Record, Moorer, 4 Apr 1972, Moorer Diary, folder 24, box 4, Acc 218-98-33, NARA II; telcon, Kissinger and Laird, 3 Apr 1972, folder 8, box 13, HAK Telcons, NSC, Nixon Library.

16. Telcon, Nixon and Kissinger, 3 Apr 1972 (quote), folder 8, box 13, HAK Telcons, NSC, Nixon Library; Memo for the Record, Moorer, 4 Apr 1972, cited in note 15.

17. Telcon, Moorer and Rush, 2 Apr 1972, cited in note 13 (1st quote); msg, Kissinger to Haig (in Saigon), 1 July 1972 (2nd quote), folder Haig Chron Jun 30–Jul 18, 1972, box 994, Haig Chron Files, NSC, Nixon Library.

18. Memo, Haig for Kissinger, 19 Aug 1972, folder Haig Chron Aug 10–24, 1972 [1 of 2], box 995, Haig Chron Files, NSC, Nixon Library.

19. Telcons, Moorer and Kissinger, 2 Apr 1972; Moorer and Rush, 2 Apr 1972; Moorer Diary, 3 Apr 1972: all in Moorer Diary, folder 24, box 4, Acc 218-05-006; telcon, Nixon and Kissinger, 3 Apr 1972, folder 8, box 13, HAK Telcons, NSC, Nixon Library; Thompson, *To Hanoi and Back*, 222.

20. Memo for the Record, Moorer, 4 Apr 1972, Moorer Diary, folder 24, box 4, Acc 218-98-33.

21. Moorer Diary, 5 May 1972 (1st quote), folder 25, box 5, ibid.; memo, Haig for Kissinger, 5 May 1972 (2nd quote), folder Haig Chron File May 1–20, 1972 [2 of 2], box 993, Haig Chron Files, NSC, Nixon Library; Moorer Diary 26 Jul 1972, folder 26, box 5, ibid.; Randolph, *Powerful and Brutal Weapons*, 20; *FRUS 1969–1976*, 7:80–82.

22. Msg, JCS 6826, Moorer to McCain, 4 Apr 1972, Moorer Diary, folder 24, box 4, Acc 218-05-006; msg, Kissinger to Bunker, 4 Apr 1972, folder Haig Chron Apr 1–21, 1972, box 992, Haig Chron Files, NSC, Nixon Library; Nixon, *Memoirs*, 588.

23. Memo for the Record, Moorer, 5 Apr 1972, Moorer Diary, folder 24, box 4, Acc 218-05-006. Moorer wrote that Kissinger and Rush heard his conversation with Abrams.

24. Memo for the Record, Laird, 15 May 1972, folder SecDef Correspondence, box D17, Laird Papers, Ford Library; Thompson, *To Hanoi and Back*, 199–202; memos, Laird for Moorer, 30 Mar 1972; Moorer for Laird, 31 Mar 1972; Moorer Diary, 28 Mar 1972: all in Moorer Diary, folder 23, box 4, Acc 218-05-006.

25. Moorer Diary, 5 Apr 1972 (1st quote), folder 24, box 4, Acc 218-05-006; *Haldeman Diaries*, 436 (2nd quote), 437; telcon, Nixon and Kissinger, 5 Apr 1972, folder 8, box 13, HAK telcons, NSC, Nixon Library; Thompson, *To Hanoi and Back*, 221.

26. Moorer Diary, 4 Apr 1972, 5 Apr 1972 (quote), 7 Apr 1972: all in folder 24, box 4, Acc 218-05-006; Thompson, *To Hanoi and Back*, 221; Randolph, *Powerful and Brutal Weapons*, 18, 98–99.

27. Memo, Odeen for Haig, 6 Apr 1972, folder Vietnam Apr 1972, box 159, VNCF, NSC, Nixon Library; Willbanks, *Abandoning Vietnam*, 135.

28. Moorer Diary, 4 Apr 1972, cited in note 26.

29. Memos, Laird for Kissinger, 6 Apr 1972 (quotes); Kissinger for Laird, 6 Apr 1972, both attached to memo, Haig for Kissinger, 6 Apr 1972, folder Haig Trip Papers 4/14–4/19/72 [1 of 2], box 1014, Haig Special File, NSC, Nixon Library.

30. Moorer Diary, 7 Apr 1972 (1st quote); msg, Abrams to Moorer, 080750Z Apr 1972 (2nd quote): both in Moorer Diary, folder 24, box 4, Acc 218-05-006.

31. Telcon, Nixon and Kissinger, 8 Apr 1972, folder 9, box 13, HAK Telcons, NSC, Nixon Library; Randolph, *Powerful and Brutal Weapons*, 119–20.

32. Msg, JCS 3492, Moorer to McCain and Abrams, 8 Apr 1972 (quotes); Moorer Diary, 8 Apr 1972: both in Moorer Diary, folder 24, box 4, Acc 218-05-006.

33. Telcon, Kissinger and Laird, 8 Apr 1972, folder 9, box 13, HAK Telcons, NSC, Nixon Library.

34. Msgs, 0147, Vann to Abrams, 19 Feb 1972, folder 11103–11299; 0243; Vann to Abrams, 19 Feb [?] 1972, folder 11301–11599: both in Messages, Abrams Papers, CMH; Webb and Poole, *JCS and Vietnam 1971–1973*, 352; Willbanks, *Abandoning Vietnam*, 133–42; Hunt, *Pacification*, 255.

35. Msgs, Abrams to Moorer, 140545Z Apr 1972; McCain to Moorer, 140642Z Apr 1972; Memo for the Record, Moorer, 14 Apr 1972: all in Moorer Diary, folder 24, box 4, Acc 218-05-006. The CINPAC message outlining the plan's concept was attached. Msg, Clarey for McCain, 140735Z Apr 1972, also in Moorer Diary, folder 24, ibid.

36. Webb and Poole, *JCS and the War in Vietnam 1971–1973*, 159.

37. Memo for the Record, Moorer, North Vietnamese Offensive, 14 Apr 1972 (quotes); Memo for the Record, Moorer, Follow-on to Decisions, 15 Apr 1972: both in Moorer Diary, folder 24, box 4, Acc 218-05-006; Randolph, *Powerful and Brutal Weapons*, 123. Haig described his session with Abrams as a long and fruitful exchange of views. See msg, Haig to Kissinger, 22 Apr 1972, folder Haig Trip Papers 4/14–4/19/72 [2 of 2], box 1014, Haig Special Files, NSC, Nixon Library.

38. Telcon, Kissinger and Laird, 15 Apr 1972 (quote), folder 10, box 13, HAK Telcons, NSC, Nixon Library; Memo for the Record, Moorer, 15 Apr 1972, cited in note 32.

39. Memo for the Record, Haig, Meeting w/Kissinger and Laird, 11 Aug 71, folder 30, box 1025, Haig Special Files, NSC, Nixon Library; memo, Howe for Haig, 2 Dec 1971 (quote), folder Army vol. 2, box 201, Agency Files, NSC, Nixon Library.

40. Telcon, Kissinger and Laird, 17 Mar 1972 (quote), folder 6, box 13, HAK Telcons, NSC, Nixon Library; Lewis Sorley, *Thunderbolt: General Creighton Abrams and the Army of His Times* (New York: Simon & Schuster, 1992), 333–35.

41. Ltr, Wheeler to Laird, 28 Feb 1972, folder Personnel, box D18, Laird Papers, Ford Library; memo, Froehlke for Laird, n.d.; memcon by Laird, 21 Mar 1972 (quotes): both in folder SecDef Correspondence, box D17, ibid. Laird had Carl Wallace and Pursley witness the call to Abrams that Laird made from his office.

42. Memo, Laird for Nixon, 15 Jun 1972, folder SecDef Correspondence, box D17, Laird Papers, Ford Library. Haig was sworn in as vice chief on 4 January 1973.

43. Memos, Laird for Kissinger, 21 Apr 1972 (quotes), folder Vietnam 798–801, box 39; Kissinger for Laird, 28 Apr 1972, folder Vietnam 825–828, box 40: both in Laird Papers, Ford Library.

44. President's Address to the Nation, 26 Apr 1972, *Nixon Public Papers 1972*, 550–54 (quote 553); telcons, Kissinger and Laird, 26 Apr 1972, 28 Apr 1972: both in folder 11, box 13, HAK Telcons, NSC, Nixon Library.

45. Memos, Chafee for Laird, 26 Apr 1972, folder Vietnam 817, box 40; Seamans for Laird, 24 Apr 1972, folder Vietnam 808, box 39, Laird Papers, Ford Library.

46. Memo, Laird for Moorer, 26 Apr 1972 (1st quote), folder Vietnam, box 28, Acc 218-92-0029, NARA II; telcon, Kissinger and Laird, 28 Apr 1972 (2nd quote), folder 11, box 13, HAK Telcons, NSC, Nixon Library.

47. Memo, Laird for Nixon, 2 May 1972 (quote), attached to memo, Kissinger for Laird, 12 May 1972, folder DPRC & Def Budget Jan–Jul 1972, box 237, Agency Files, NSC, Nixon Library.

48. Ltr, Laird to Shultz, 13 May, folder Vietnam 880, box 40, Laird Papers, Ford Library.

49. Msgs, Haig to Kissinger, both dated 1 Jun 1972, folder Haig Chron Jun 1–12, 1972, box 993, Haig Chron Files, NSC, Nixon Library; Livesay notes, SecDef Staff (AFPC) Meeting, 30 May 1972 (quote), folder Staff Mtgs Apr–Jun 1972, box 15, Acc 330-77-0062, WNRC.

50. Msg, TOHAK 261, Haig to Kissinger, 30 May 1972, folder Haig Chron May 21–31, 1972 [1 of 2], box 993, Haig Chron Files, NSC, Nixon Library; HCA, Subcommittee on the Department of Defense, *Department of Defense Appropriations for 1973*, 92nd Cong., 2nd sess., 5 Jun 1972, 364.

51. Memo, Kissinger for Nixon, 3 Jun 1972, folder Haig Chron Jun 1–12, 1972, box 993, Haig Chron Files, NSC, Nixon Library; telcons, Kissinger and Laird, Kissinger and Shultz, 2 Jun 1972: both in folder 7, box 14, HAK Telcons, ibid.; memo, Laird for Kissinger, 1 Jun 1972, attached to msg, Haig to Kissinger, 1 Jun 1972, folder Haig Chron Jun 1–12, 1972, box 993, Haig Chron Files, ibid.

52. Memo, Cook for Nixon, 7 Jun 1972, folder DoD vol. 17, box 231, Agency Files, NSC, Nixon Library; HCA, *DoD Appropriations for 1973*, 5 Jun 1972, 364.

53. Ltr, Laird to Weinberger, 9 Jun 1972, attached to memo, Rear Adm. Daniel Murphy for Haig, 10 Jun 1972, folder OMB 1971–72, box 268, Agency Files, NSC, Nixon Library; Livesay notes, SecDef Staff Meeting, 12 Jun 1972, folder Staff Mtgs Apr–Jun 1972, box 15, Acc 330-77-0062.

54. Memo, Laird for Kissinger, 15 Jun 1972 (1st quote), attached to memo, Haig for Kissinger, 15 Jun 1972, folder Vietnam Jun–Jul 1972 [2 of 2], box 160, NSC, Nixon Library; memo, Kissinger for Nixon, 26 Jun 1972 (2nd quote, emphasis in original), attached to memo, Odeen for Kissinger, 24 Jun 1972, folder DPRC & Def Budget Jan–Jul 1972, box 237, Agency Files, ibid.; memo, Kissinger for Nixon, 25 Sep 1972, folder DPRC & Def Budget Aug–Dec 1972, box 237, Agency Files, ibid.

55. Willbanks, *Abandoning Vietnam*, 143; memo, Laird for Nixon, 1 May 1972 (quotes), folder Vietnam 839–844, box 40, Laird Papers, Ford Library; msg, MAC 04021, Abrams to Laird, 1 May 1972, in Moorer Diary, box 4, Acc 218-05-006; *Haldeman Diaries*, 450.

56. Msg, MAC 04039. Abrams to Laird, 2 May 1972, Messages, Abrams Papers, CMH.

57. Memo, Laird for Nixon, 2 May 1972, folder Vietnam 839–844, box 40, Laird Papers, Ford Library.

58. Telcons, Kissinger and Moorer, 2 May 1972, 9:45 p.m.; Kissinger and Laird, 2 May 1972, 10:10 p.m.: both in folder 1, box 14, HAK Telcons, NSC, Nixon Library.

59. Telcons, Kissinger and Laird, 2 May 1972, 9:45 p.m. (1st and 3rd quotes); 2 May 1972, 10:10 p.m. (2nd and 4th quotes), both cited in note 58; Thompson, *To Hanoi and Back*, 223–24.

60. Telcons, Kissinger and Nixon, 2 May 1972, 3 May 1972 (quotes), folder 1, box 14, HAK Telcons, NSC, Nixon Library; Kissinger and Moorer, 19 Apr 1972, Moorer Diary, box 4, Acc 218-05-006; Kissinger, *Ending the Vietnam War*, 270.

61. Memo, Nixon for Kissinger, 30 Apr 1972, folder HAK/President Memos 1971–, box 341, Subject Files, NSC, Nixon Library; telcon, Kissinger and Moorer, 1 May 1972, folder 1, box 14, HAK Telcons, ibid.; Moorer Diary, 1 May 1972, box 4, Acc 218-05-006.

62. Msgs, Abrams to Moorer, 040425Z May 1972; McCain to Moorer, 040805Z May 1972: both in folder Bunker Backchannels 1972, box 414, NSC, Nixon Library; Moorer Diary, 4 May 1972, Acc 218-05-006; Thompson, *To Hanoi and Back*, 227–28.

63. Msg, WHS 2063, Kissinger to Bunker, 4 May 1972 (quotes), folder Bunker Backchannels 1972, box 414, NSC, Nixon Library.

64. Kissinger, *Ending the Vietnam War*, 271.

65. Nixon, *Memoirs*, 601–02; Kissinger, Kissinger, *White House Years*, 1174–76; *Haldeman Diaries*, 4 May 1972, 453–55.

66. Telcons, Kissinger and Moorer, 4 May 1972, 5 May 1972; Moorer Diary, 4 May 1972 (quotes), 5 May 1972, box 4, Acc 218-05-006; *Haldeman Diaries*, 454–55; Van Atta, *With Honor*, 393. Kissinger made his observations about Rush in a conversation with Nixon in the Executive Office Building on 3 Apr 1972. See White House Conversation 328–25, White House Tapes, Nixon Library.

67. Moorer Diary, 6 May 1972 (1st quote); telcons, Moorer and Rush, 6 May 1972; Moorer and Kissinger, 6 May 1972: both in box 4, Moorer Diary, Acc 218-98-33; telcons, Nixon and Kissinger, 6 May 1972, 10:27 a.m.; Kissinger and Nixon, 6 May 1972, 1:45 p.m. (2nd quote), 3:30 p.m., and 5:05 p.m.; Kissinger and Laird, 6 May 1972 (3rd quote): all in folder 2, box 14, HAK Telcons, NSC, Nixon Library.

68. Briefing by DCI, 8 May 1972, folder 1, box H-33, H Files, NSC, Nixon Library; Memo for President Files, NSC Meeting, 8 May 1972 (quotes), folder NSC Minutes Originals 1971 [2 of 5], box H-110, ibid.

69. Memo for President Files, 8 May 1972, cited in note 68.

70. Ibid. (quotes); telcon, Colson and Laird, 10 May 1972, Nixon Conversation 24-63, White House Tapes, Nixon Library.

71. Nixon, Address to the Nation, 8 May 1972 (quotes), *Nixon Public Papers 1972*, 583–58; Thompson, *To Hanoi and Back*, 229.

72. Telcons, Nixon and Laird, 9 May 1972, Nixon conversation 24-40; Nixon and Moorer, 9 May 1972 (quote), Nixon conversation 24-59: both in White House Tapes, Nixon Library.

73. Sorley, *Thunderbolt*, 323–26.

74. Randolph, *Powerful and Brutal Weapons*, 216–17.

75. Mark Clodfelter, *The Limits of Air Power: The American Bombing of North Vietnam*. New York: London: Collier Macmillan, 1989), 157–59; msg, Moorer to McCain, 152340Z May 1972, folder Vietnam May 1972, box 28, JCS Records, Acc 218-03-001; memos, Nixon for Haig, 18 May 1972, 20 May 1972 (quote), both in HAK/President Memos 1971–, box 341, Subject Files, NSC, Nixon Library.

76. Thompson, *To Hanoi and Back*, 230–33; Clodfelter, *Limits of Airpower*, 161; memo, Moorer for Laird, 11 Oct 1972, folder Vietnam 1100–1105, box 42, Laird Papers, Ford Library.

77. Willbanks, *Abandoning Vietnam*, 150–52, 160.

78. Memo, Laird for Nixon, n.d. (quote), attached to memo, Kissinger for Nixon, 19 May 1972, folder Vietnam May 1972 1 of 2, box 160, VNSF, NSC, Nixon Library; NSDM 168, Military Assistance to the RVN, 19 May 1972, folder WSAG Meeting 20 Jun 1972, box H-088, H Files, ibid.

79. Memo, Laird for Nixon, 12 Jun 1972, folder Vietnam 949-1, box 41, Laird Papers, Ford Library.

80. Memo, Nixon for Kissinger and Haig, 19 May 1972, folder HAK/President Memos 1971–, box 341, Subject Files, NSC, Nixon Library.

81. Memo, Shillito for Laird, 7 Jun 1972, folder Vietnam 938–943, box 41, Laird Papers, Ford Library; msg, JCS to CINCEUR, 271716Z Oct 1972, Enhance Plus, folder Oct 1972, box 29, Acc 218-03-001; memo, Laird for Nixon, 17 Nov 1972, folder Vietnam 1168–1173, box 43, Laird Papers, Ford Library; Clarke, *Final Years*, 452–53.

82. Clarke, *Final Years*, 455, 468–69, 489–90; Willbanks, *Abandoning Vietnam*, 162.

83. Weyand's report is summarized in Clarke, *Final Years*, 493–95.

84. Memo, Nixon for Kissinger and Haig, 15 May 1972 (1st and 2nd quotes), folder HAK/President Memos 1971–, box 341, Subject Files, NSC, Nixon Library; memo, Nixon for Kissinger and Haig, 19 May 1972 (3rd and 4th quotes), cited in note 78.

10. Looking Beyond Vietnam: The FY 1971 Budget

1. Drea, *McNamara, Clifford, and the Burdens of Vietnam*, 6.

2. Korb, *Fall and Rise of the Pentagon*, 84–87; HAK Talking Points, n.d. (c. mid-Nov 1969), folder DPRC & Defense Budget vol. 1, box 235, Agency Files, NSC, Nixon Library; Robert Moot, "The Defense Budget," n.d., folder FY 71 Budget, box 84, ASD(C) Files, OSD/ HO. For a review of McNamara's Defense budgets, see Drea, *McNamara, Clifford, and the Burdens of Vietnam*, especially chapters 4 and 9.

3. Memo, Mayo for Nixon, 14 May 1969, attached to memo, Bull for Laird, 28 May 1969, folder FY 71 Budget, box 84, ASD(C) Files, OSD/HO; Korb, *Fall and Rise of the Pentagon*, 86.

4. Ltr, Laird to Mayo, 12 Jun 1969, ibid.; memo, Mayo for Laird, 30 Oct 1969, folder 1971 Budget Procedures, box 309, Subject Files, NSC, Nixon Library.

5. SecDef MPM, Land Forces, 14 May 1969, attached to memos, Packard for CJCS, Service Secretaries et al., folder 10, box 1, Records from SecDef Vault, Acc 330-74-142, WNRC.

6. Moot, "The Defense Budget," cited in note 2; SecDef MPM, Manpower and Support Programs, 23 Jul 1969, attached to memo, Packard for DDR&E et al., 24 Jul 1969, folder 10, box 1, Records from SecDef Vault, Acc 330-74-142; memo, Packard for CJCS, Service Secretaries et al., 1 Mar 1969, folder FY 71 Budget, box 84, ASD(C) Files, OSD/HO.

7. SecDef MPM, Land Forces, 14 May 1969, cited in note 5.

8. Ibid.; memo, Packard for SecNav, 27 Jun 1969, attached to memo, Packard for DDR&E et al., 24 Jul 1969, folder 10, box 1, Records from SecDef Vault, Acc 330-74-142.

9. Ibid.

10. SecDef MPM on Naval Forces, 25 Jun 1969 (quotes), attached to memo, Packard for DirDDE, 27 Jun 1969, cited in note 8.

11. MPM, Mobility Forces, 11 Jun 1969, attached to memo, Packard for SecAF, 11 Jun 1969, folder 10, box 1, Records from SecDef Vault, Acc 330-74-142.

12. Memo, Packard for CJCS, 11 Jun 1969 (2nd quote); memo, Packard for SecNav, 11 Jun 1969; SecDef MPM, Mobility Forces, 11 Jun 1969 (1st quote): all attached to memo, Packard for SecArmy, 11 Jun 1969, folder 10, box 1, Records from SecDef Vault, Acc 330-74-142.

13. Memo, Packard for SecArmy, w/attached MPM, Land Forces, 14 May 1969 (quotes), cited in note 5.

14. SecDef MPM, Tactical Air Forces, 4 Jun 1969 (quotes), attached to memo, Packard for SecNav, 4 Jun, 1969, folder 10, box 1, SecDef Records, Acc 330-74-142.

15. Memos, Packard for SecState et al., 31 Jan 1969, folder 3, box H-126; Kissinger for Nixon, n.d., folder NSSM 3, box H-023: both in H Files, NSC, Nixon Library.

16. Memo, Lynn for Kissinger, 11 Sep 1969, ibid.; NIE 11-69, 27 Feb 1969, *FRUS 1969–1976*, 12:70, 79 (quote), 82; Editor's note, *FRUS 1969–1976*, 12:86–87.

17. Memo, Kissinger for Nixon 30 Jun 1969, folder 4, box 392, NSC, Nixon Library. Nixon's handwritten comments are in the margin.

18. Memo, Kissinger for Nixon 29 Sep 1969, folder 3, box 958, Haig Chron Files, NSC, Nixon Library; SNIE 11-9-69, 17 Jul 1969, *FRUS 1969–1976*, 12:210 (quote).

19. The interagency report on strategic forces was issued on 8 May 1969, and the NSC reviewed strategic posture on 29 May.

20. Memo, Kissinger for Nixon, n.d., cited in note 15.

21. NSSM 3, General Purpose Forces Section, 5 Sep 1969, attached to NSSM 3, 20 Jan 1969, folder NSSM 1–4, box NSSM (1969) 1–49, OSD/HO.

22. Memo, Laird for Nixon, 19 Sep 1969, folder Haig Chron Sep 1969 [2 of 2], box 958, Haig Chron Files, NSC, Nixon Library; memos, Kissinger for Nixon, 24 Sep 1969, folder DoD vol. 4, box 222; Lynn for Kissinger, 24 Oct 1969; HAK Talking Points, n.d.: both in folder DPRC & Def Budget 1970 vol. 1, box 235, ibid.

23. Memo, Kissinger for Nixon, 24 Sep 1969, cited in note 22.

24. NSDM 27, 11 Oct 1969, folder NSDM 1–50, box 363, Subject Files, NSC, Nixon Library; ltr, Packard to Kissinger, 29 Oct 1969 (quote), folder DPRC Meeting 13 Nov 1969, box H-099, H Files, ibid.; HAK Talking Points, n.d., cited in note 22.

25. Kissinger, *White House Years*, 22–22.

26. DPRC Meeting, 13 Nov 1969, folder DPRC Minutes [1 of 3], box H-118, H Files, NSC, Nixon Library; memo, Packard for Wheeler, 6 Nov 1969, folder FY 71 Budget, box 84, ASD(C), OSD/HO; HAK Talking Points, n.d., cited in note 22; memo, Lynn for Kissinger, 10 Nov 1969, folder DPRC Meeting 13 Nov 1969, box H-099, H Files, NSC, Nixon Library.

27. DPRC Meeting 13 Nov 1969 (quotes), cited in note 26.

28. Memo for the Record, 8 Dec 1969, folder FY 1971 Budget, box 84, ASD(C) Files, OSD/HO; memos, Lynn for Kissinger, 21 Nov 1969, 6 Dec 1969: both in folder DPRC Meeting 9 Dec 1969, box H-099, H Files, NSC, Nixon Library.

29. Memo for the Record, 8 Dec 1969, cited in note 28; memo, Lynn for Kissinger, 10 Dec 1969, folder DPRC Meeting 9 Dec 1969, box H-099, H Files, NSC, Nixon Library.

30. Memo, Laird for Kissinger, 20 Dec 1969 (quotes), folder 77, box 7, Records from SecDef Vault, Acc 330-74-142; memo, Haig for Kissinger, 20 Dec 1969, folder DPRC & Def Budget 1969, box 234, Agency Files, NSC, Nixon Library.

31. Memo, Haig for Kissinger, 22 Dec 1969, folder Haig Chron Dec 21–31, 1969 [2 of 2], box 961, Haig Chron Files, NSC, Nixon Library; memo, Laird for Nixon, 20 Dec 1969, folder Haig's Vietnam File vol. 3 [1 of 2], box 1008, Haig Special File, ibid.

32. Memo, Nixon for Laird, 27 Dec 1969, folder Vietnam vol. 13-2, box 141, VNCF, NSC, Nixon Library.

33. Memos, Nixon for Laird, 27 Dec 1969 (quote), folder Work File Budget I, box 112, Acc 218-92-0029, NARA II; Packard for Nixon, 29 Dec 1969, folder FY 71 Budget, box 84, ASD(C) Files, OSD/HO.

34. Telcon, Packard and Kissinger, 30 Dec 1969, folder 6, box 3, HAK Telcons, NSC, Nixon Library.

35. Telcons, Kissinger and Laird, Kissinger and Mayo, 30 Dec 1969, ibid.

36. Msg, OSD 16439, Laird to Kissinger, 31 Dec 1969, folder DoD vol. 5, box 223, Agency Files, NSC, Nixon Library; telcons, Kissinger and Laird, 31 Dec 1969, 10:10 a.m. and a.m. (no time cited): both in folder 6, box 3, HAK Telcons, ibid.

37. Memo, Haig for Kissinger, 14 Jan 1970, folder 1971 Budget Procedures, box 309, Subject Files, ibid.; telcon, Kissinger and Packard, 14 Jan 1970, folder 7, box 3, HAK Telcons, ibid.; telcon, Nixon and Kissinger, 14 Jan 1970, 5:40 (quotes), closed box 1, ibid.

38. Telcon, Laird and Kissinger, 15 Jan 1970, folder 8, box 3, HAK Telcons, NSC, Nixon Library; memo, Haig for Kissinger, 15 Jan 1970, folder 3, box 961, Haig Chron Jan 1970, ibid.

39. William Beecher, "Laird Says Defense Cuts Will Cost 1,250,000 Jobs," *New York Times*, 16 Jan 1970, 1; James Wieghart, "Defense Aim: Cut Another Half Billion, *New York News*, 16 Jan 1970, 9; George Wilson, "Cutbacks Detailed By Laird," *Washington Post*, 16

Jan 1970, 1; Fred Farrar, "Asks Armed Forces of Under 3 Million," *Chicago Tribune*, 3 Feb 1970, 8; ASD(PA) News release 83-70, 2 Feb 1970, folder Staff Meetings Jan–Mar 1970, box 14, Acc 330-77-0062, WNRC.

40. Annual Budget Message, FY 1971, 2 Feb 1970, *Nixon Public Papers 1970*, 46–47, 50, 54, 56.

41. Memo, William A. Morrill, Deputy Director for Programming, BoB, for recipients, 21 Mar 1970, folder AVAF–DPRC 69–70, box 37, Anderson, SMOF, WHSF, Nixon Library.

42. Annual Budget Message, FY 1971, cited in note 40.

43. New Obligational Authority covers funds authorized by Congress for various accounts. Total Obligational Authority represents authorized funds (NOA) plus loan authority, or financing adjustments. This is the authority to borrow money to cover the principal in loan accounts. TOA also includes unobligated budget authority from previous years and budget authority transferred from other appropriations.

44. HCA, Subcommittee on the Department of Defense, *Department of Defense Appropriations for 1971: Hearings*, 91st Cong., 2nd sess., 25 Feb 1970, table 1, pt.1:159.

45. SCAS, *Authorization for Military Procurement, Research, and Development, Fiscal Year 1971, and Reserve Strength: Hearings on S. 3367 and H.R. 17123*, 91st Cong., 2nd sess., 20 Feb 1970, pt. 1:57.

46. Arlen Large, "Democrats Assail Spending for Defense In TV Reply to State of Union Address," *Wall Street Journal*, 9 Feb 1970.

47. SCAS, *Authorization for … FY 1971*, 20 Feb 1970, 8.

48. Ibid., 8 (quotes).

49. Memo, Laird for Nixon, 27 Feb 1970, folder Work File Budget I, box 112, Acc 218-92-0029; Robert Keatley, "Pentagon Is Seeking Its Smallest Share of Budget Since Fiscal 1950," *Wall Street Journal*, 3 Feb 1970.

50. SCAS, *Hearings*, cited in note 45, 9–12, 23.

51. Ibid., 23–25.

52. Ibid., 97–101 (quotes, 98).

53. Ibid., 101–03.

54. Ibid., 150–52.

55. Ibid., 165.

56. HCAS, *Hearings on Military Posture*, 91st Cong., 2nd sess., 4 Mar 1970, HASC No. 91-53, pt. 1:6949.

57. Ltr, Laird to Rivers, 23 Mar 1970, w/ltr, Rivers to Laird, 5 Mar 1970 attached, folder 52, box 5, Records from SecDef Vault, Acc 330-74-142.

58. HCAS, *Hearings*, cited in note 56, 4 Mar 1970, 6950–51 (quote); Laird statement, 25 Feb 1970, HSCA, *Hearings*, cited in note 44, 203–04.

59. HCAS, *Hearings*, cited in note 56, 4 Mar 1970, 6957, 6964 (quote).

60. Ibid., 6962–64.

61. Ibid., 6961–62; HSCA, *Hearings*, cited in note 44, 205–06; ltr, Clifford to Senator Proxmire, 15 Jan 1969, attached to OSD(PA) News Release 43-69, 16 Jan 1969, folder GP Aircraft 1969, box 906, OSD/HO.

62. Packard testimony, 9 Mar 1970, HCAS, *Hearings*, cited in note 56, 7041.

63. Walter S. Poole, *Adapting to Flexible Response 1960–1968* (Washington, DC: OSD Historical Office, 2013), 205–09.

64. "Lockheed Seeks Year Stretchout on C5 Program," *Wall Street Journal*, 10 Feb 1970, 2.

65. Ltr, D. J Haughton, Chairman of Lockheed, to Packard, 2 Mar 1970, in HCAS, *Hearings*, cited in note 56, 5 Mar 1970, 6980–83 (quote); and Packard statements, ibid.; 9 Mar 1970, 7026, 7030.]

66. Statement by Sen. Milton Young R–ND), *Cong. Rec.*, 26 Aug 1970, S 14266.

67. Packard testimony, 9 Mar 1970, *Hearings*, cited in note 56, 7030–31.

68. Ltr, Packard to Rivers, 5 Jun 1970, folder 52, box 5, Records from SecDef Vault, Acc 330-74-142; John L. McLucas, *Reflections of a Technocrat: Managing Defense, Air, and Space Programs During the Cold War* (Maxwell AFB: Air University Press, 2006), 115–16; "C–5 History," <www.globalsecurity.org>, accessed 5 Apr 2007; P.L. 92-70, 85 Stat. 178.

69. *Cong. Rec.*, 29 Apr 1970, H 3621–22; *Cong. Rec.*, 23 Jun 1970, S 9547; Spencer Rich, "Pentagon Wins Tests on C–5A, Herbicides," *Washington Post*, 27 Aug 1970, A1.

70. Korb, *Fall and Rise of the Pentagon*, 12–13.

71. Ltr, Haughton to Packard, 2 Mar 1970, cited in note 64; HCAS, *Hearings*, cited in note 56, 9 Mar 1970, 7027–28, 7045–46.

72. Memos, Laird for Nixon, 30 May 1970, folder Strategy 5-8, box 28, Laird Papers, Ford Library; Kissinger for USecState et al., 13 Jun 1970, folder DPRC & Def Budget 1970 vol. 1, box 235, Agency Files, NSC, Nixon Library.

73. George C. Wilson, "Senators Cut Arms Funds $1.3 Billion," *Washington Post*, 16 Jul 1970, A1; William McGaffin, "27 Lawmakers seek defense budget cut," *Chicago Daily News*, 15 Jul 1970, 1.

74. White House Press Release, 18 Jul 1970, *Nixon Public Papers 1970*, 600–02; telcon, Kissinger and Laird, 4 Aug 1970, folder 4, box 6 HAK Telcons, NSC, Nixon Library.

75. Minutes, SecDef Staff Meetings, 6 Jul 1970, 3 Aug 1970: both in folder Staff Mtgs Jul–Sep 1970, box 14, Acc 330-77-0062.

76. Memo, Haig for Kissinger, 20 Jul 1970, folder DoD vol. 7, box 224, Agency Files, NSC, Nixon Library; Chalmers M. Roberts, "Defense Economizing Is Near the Bone," *Washington Post*, 18 Oct 1970 (quote), 1-F.

77. Ltr, Laird to Shultz, 30 Oct 1970, folder FY 71 Budget, box 84, ASD(C) Files, OSD/HO.

78. Telcon, Kissinger and Laird, 29 Oct 1970 (quotes), folder 4, box 7, HAK Telcons, NSC, Nixon Library; Rearden, *Formative Years*, 541.

79. Ltr, Laird to Rivers, 11 Sep 1970, folder FY 1971 Reclama, box 84, ASD(C) Files, OSD/HO.

80. Minutes SecDef Staff Meeting, 8 Sep 1970, folder Staff Mtgs Jul–Sep 1970, box 14, Acc 330-77-0062.

81. Memo, Lehman for Kissinger, 8 Oct 1970 (quote), folder DoD vol. 9, box 225, Agency Files, NSC, Nixon Library; Roberts, Washington Post, 18 Oct 1970, 1-F, cited in note 76.

82. Ltr, Laird to Russell, 12 Nov 1970, folder FY 71 Reclama, box 84, ASD(C) Files, OSD/HO.

83. SCA, Subcommittee, *Department of Defense Appropriations for Fiscal Year 1971: Hearings*, 91st Cong., 2nd sess., 20 Nov 1970, pt. 5:1–4.

84. Ltr, Laird to Mahon, 8 Dec 1970, folder FY1971 Reclama, box 84, ASD(C), OSD/HO. Laird's letter to Russell appears in *Cong. Rec.*, 29 Dec 1970, S 21371–76; *Cong. Rec.*, 16 Dec 70, H 11776.

85. *Laird Public Statements 1970*, 6:2626 (quote); Staff Reporter, "Panel's Defense Fund Bill," *Wall Street Journal*, 16 Dec 1970.

86. Telcons, Kissinger and Stennis, 11:25 a.m.; Kissinger and Mahon, 12:30 p.m.: both in 19 Dec 1970, folder 3, box 8, HAK Telcons, NSC, Nixon Library.

87. P.L. 91-668, 84 Stat. 2036–37 (1971).

88. *DoD Key Officials 1947–2004*, 86.

11. A Turning Point: The FY 1972 Budget

1. Robert C. Moot, "The Defense Budget," n.d., folder FY 1971 Budget, box 84, ASD(C) Files, OSD/HO; "Address by Moot," 30 Apr 1970, folder Financial Management, box 790, Subject Files, ibid.

2. Walter S. Poole, *The Joint Chiefs of Staff and National Policy, 1969–1972* (Washington, DC: Office of Joint History, Office of the JCS, 2013), 26–28, 91–92.

3. SecDef FY 1972–1976 Fiscal Guidance Memo, 12 Jan 1970, attached to memo, Packard for Wheeler, 13 Jan 1970, folder DPRC, box 84, Acc 218-92-0029, NARA II. The guidance was labeled a draft working paper.

4. Memo, Packard for Service Secretaries, CJCS et al., 15 Jan 1970, folder 80, box 7, Records from SecDef Vault, Acc 330-74-142, WNRC.

5. Memo, Packard for Service Secretaries, 28 Jan 1970, folder 72, box 6, Records from SecDef Vault, Acc 330-74-142.

6. Poole, *JCS and National Policy 1969–1972*, 38–44.

7. NSDM 16, 24 Jun 1969, <www.nixonlibrary.gov/virtuallibrary/documents/nsdm/nsdm_016.pdf>, accessed 13 Aug 2012.

8. Poole, *JCS and National Policy 1969–1972*, 27–30.

9. "Defense Planning 1972–1976," n.d., box 1, Moorer Diary, Acc 218-05-006, NARA II. The document bears the heading "CJCS EYES ONLY."

10. Memo, Packard for Service Secretaries, 24 Mar 1970, cited in memo, Lynn for Kissinger, 28 Apr 1970, folder Defense vol. 7, box 224, Agency Files, NSC, Nixon Library.

11. Memos, Lynn for Kissinger, 28 Apr 1970 (quotes, emphasis in original), folder Defense vol. 7, box 224; Lynn for Kissinger, 21 Mar 1970, folder DPRC & Def Budget 1970 vol. 1, box 235: both in Agency Files, NSC, Nixon Library; memo, Mayo for Nixon, 2 Jun 1970 (quote, emphasis in the original), folder Personnel-Official, box D18, Laird Papers, Ford Library; memo, Nixon for Heads of Executive Departments and Agencies, 25 May 1970, folder Expenditures, box A 71, Baroody Papers, Ford Library.

12. Minutes, DPRC Meeting, 17 Jul 1970 (quotes), folder 2, box H-100, H Files, NSC, Nixon Library

13. Ibid.; memo, Knowles for CSA et al., 21 Jul 1970, folder CM 36-70 to CM 61-70, box 1, Acc 218-92-0029.

14. Ibid.

15. Minutes, DPRC Meeting, 17 Jul 1970 (quotes); memo, Knowles for CSA et al., 21 Jul 1970: both cited in note 13.

16. Memo, Kissinger for Nixon, 26 Jul 1970, folder Haig Chron Jul 23–31, 1970, box 969, Haig Chron Files, NSC, Nixon Library; memo, Kissinger for DPRC, 4 Aug 1970, folder Work File Budget I, box 112, Acc 218-92-0029.

17. Memo, Kissinger for Nixon, 18 Aug 1970, folder NSC Mtg Def Budget 8/19/70 [1 of 2], box H-029, H Files, NSC, Nixon Library.

18. Memcon, NSC Meeting 19 Aug 1970, folder 7, box H-109, H Files, NSC, Nixon Library.

19. NSDM 84, 11 Sep 1970, <www.nixonlibrary.gov/virtuallibrary/documents/nsdm/nsdm_084.pdf>, accessed 13 Aug 2014.

20. Minutes, SecDef Staff Meeting, 14 Sep 1970, folder Staff Mtgs Jul–Sep 1970, box 14, SecDef Records, Acc 330-77-0062, WNRC; memo, Kissinger for Agnew et al., 14 Sep 1970, folder DoD vol. 8, box 225, Agency Files, NSC, Nixon Library; telcon, Kissinger and Moorer, 12 Sep 1970, folder 7, box 6, HAK Telcons, NSC, Nixon Library; Moorer Diary, 14 Sep 1970 (quotes), box 1, Acc 218-05-006. Gardiner Tucker provided Laird with an analysis of NSDM 84; see memo, Tucker for Laird, n.d., folder NSDM 84, box 1C, Laird Papers, Ford Library.

21. Memo, Moot for Laird, 13 Sep 1970 (quote, emphasis in original), attached to memo, Tucker for Laird, cited in note 19. For no readily apparent reason, Kissinger insinuated to Rear Admiral Robinson, the JCS liaison officer at the NSC, that Laird really wanted less money ($71 billion in outlays) than Kissinger ($74.5 billion) did. Robinson dutifully informed the chairman. Perhaps Kissinger sought to open a wedge between the secretary and the military, but his charge had no basis. At no point did Laird request *less* money than the president's guideline. See Moorer Diary, entry for 14 Sep 1970, cited in note 19.

22. Ltr, Laird to Shultz, 30 Oct 1970 (quotes), attached to memo, Shultz for Laird, 20 Oct 1970, folder Shultz, box 1C, Laird Papers, Ford Library.

23. Richard J. Levine, "Army, Navy, Air Force Setting Their Sights on the 'Peace Dividend,'" *Wall Street Journal*, 10 Nov 1970, 1; MBT–70, http://en.wikipedia.org/wiki/MBT–70>, accessed 4 Sep 2013.

24. Memo for the Record, FY 1972 Budget, 24 Oct 1970, box 1, Moorer Diary, Acc 218-05-006.

25. Minutes, SecDef staff Meeting, 9 Nov 1970, folder Staff Mtgs Oct–Dec 1970, box 14, Acc 330-77-0062.

26. Memo, Morrill for Shultz, 6 Nov 1970 (quote), attached to memo, Smith for Kissinger, 7 Nov 1970, folder DPRC & Def Budget 1970 vol. 2, box 235, Agency Files, NSC, Nixon Library.

27. Minutes, DPRC Meeting, 9 Nov 1970 (quotes), folder 4, box H-100, H Files, NSC, Nixon Library; Memo for the Record, 9 Nov 1970, folder Work File Budget II, box 112, Acc 218-92-0029; Moorer Diary, entry for 9 Nov 1970, box 1, Acc 218-05-006.

28. Memo, Packard for Kissinger, 12 Nov 1970 (quotes, emphasis added), folder Haig Chron Nov 13–18, 1970 [2 of 2], box 973, Haig Chron Files, NSC, Nixon Library; memo, Smith for Kissinger, 16 Nov 1970 (quotes), folder DPRC & Def Budget 1970 vol. 2, box 235, Agency Files, ibid.; Moorer Diary, entry for 9 Nov 1970 (quote), cited in note 27.

29. Memo for the Record, Budget Planning, 27 Nov 1970, folder Nov 1970, box 1, Moorer Diary, Acc 218-05-006.

30. Telcon, Kissinger and Laird, 14 Dec 1970 (quote), folder 2, box 8, HAK Telcons, NSC, Nixon Library; Minutes, SecDef Staff Meeting, 23 Nov 1970, folder Oct–Dec 1970, box 14, Acc 330-77-0062.

31. Moorer Diary, entry for 18 Dec 1970, box 1, Acc 218-05-006; memos, Laird for Nixon, 18 Dec 1970; Laird for Kissinger, 19 Dec 1970 (quote), attached to note, Haig to Kissinger, 21 Dec 1970, folder DoD vol. 10, box 226, Agency Files, NSC, Nixon Library.

32. Memo, Laird for Kissinger, 23 Dec 1970 (quote), attached to memo, Smith for Kissinger, 24 Dec 1970, folder DPRC & Def Budget 1970 vol. 2, box 235, Agency Files, NSC, Nixon Library; Minutes, SecDef Staff Meeting, 28 Dec 1970, Oct–Dec 1970, folder Staff Mtgs, box 14, Acc 330-77-0062.

33. Budget Message to Congress, 29 Jan 1971, *Nixon Public Papers 1971*, 80–95; Executive Office of the President, OMB, *The U.S. Budget in Brief, Fiscal Year 1972* (Washington, DC: Government Printing Office, 1971), 6–7 (quote), 30–31.

34. DoD News Release 72-71, 29 Jan 1971; table 10, 29 Jan 1971, Budget 1972–1973 notebook, Subject Files, OSD/HO.

35. Laird Statement on FY 1972–76 Defense Program and the FY 1972 Defense Budget Before SCAS, 15 Mar 1971, 1–3 (quotes); Laird testimony, 4–5 Mar 1971, HCA, Subcommittee on the Department of Defense, *Department of Defense Appropriations for 1972: Hearings*, pt. 1:194.

36. "Laird Statement," cited in note 35, table 1.

37. Memo, Laird for Service Secretaries et al., 21 Aug 1970, folder Reserve Forces 1970, box 1095, Subject Files, OSD/HO.

38. *Hearings*, cited in note 35, 437–39; Michael Getler, "'Twin' Navy, AF Planes Questioned," *Washington Post*, 29 Mar 1971, A1.

39. Korb, *Fall and Rise of the Pentagon*, 13. For information on the development of the TFX, see Kaplan et al., *McNamara Ascendency*, 466–73.

40. AF fact sheet, F–15, 19 Feb 1971 (quotes); Navy fact sheet, F–14, 19 Feb 1971: both in folder 46, box 4, Records from SecDef Vault, Acc 330-74-142; Getler, *Washington Post*, 29 Mar 1971, cited in note 38.

41. *Hearings*, cited in note 35, 439 (quote); Michael Getler, "Air War on Hill: 3 Planes for 1 Job?" *Washington Post*, 22 Mar 1971.

42. *Hearings*, cited in note 35, 202–04 (quote 203); ULMS fact sheet, 19 Feb 1971; B–1 fact sheet, 22 Jan 1971: both in folder 46, box 4, Records from SecDef Vault, Acc 330-74-142; George W. Ashworth, "Pentagon Cutbacks Stress A-reliance," *Christian Science Monitor*, 5 Jan 1971.

43. Michael Getler, "Arms Spending Critics Open Fire Today on New Bomber," *Washington Post*, 4 May 1971; Getler, "Arms Spending Critics Ask Scrapping of B–1," *Washington Post*, 5 May 1971.

44. Memos, Kissinger for Nixon, 26 May 1971 (quote); Nixon for Laird, 28 May 1971 (quote): both in folder DoD vol. 7, box 227, Agency Files, NSC, Nixon Library; Stennis quoted in Michael Getler, "The 'Reckless" Talk about Military Spending," *Washington Post*, 30 Sep 1971, 18.

45. Memo, Smith for Kissinger, 2 Jun 1971 (quotes), folder DPRC Mtg 15–17 Jul 1971, box H-103, H Files, NSC, Nixon Library; Michael Getler, "Defense Costs Peril Strategy," *Washington Post*, 19 Apr 1971.

46. Ibid.; George C. Wilson, "Congress Rebelling At Size of Military," *Washington Post*, 10 May 1971, 1.

47. See *Hearings*, cited in note 35, 306ff.

48. *Cong. Rec.*, 4 Jun 1971, S 8238.

49. SecDef Statement, n.d., 14 (quote), folder Staff Mtgs Apr–Jun 1971, box 14, Acc 330-77-0062.

50. Minutes, SecDef Staff Meeting, 14 Jun 1971, ibid.

51. Minutes, DPRC Meeting, 26 Apr 1971, folder 2, box H-118, H Files, NSC, Nixon Library.

52. Memo, Haig for the President, 10 Aug 1971, folder 3, box 1001, Haig Special File, NSC, Nixon Library.

53. ASD(C), FAD 691, 21 Jan 1972, Budget 1972–1973 notebook, OSD/HO.

54. ASD(C), FAD 698, 15 Dec 1971, Budget 1972–1973 notebook, ibid.; Staff Reporter, "Senate Panel's $21 Billion Weapons Bill Leaves Pentagon's Requests Nearly Intact," *Wall St Journal*, 5 Aug 1971, 4; "Senate Armed Services Panel Cuts $1.2 Billion From Pentagon Budget," *Washington Post*, 5 Aug 1971, A1; Michael Getler, "The 'Reckless' Talk About Military Spending," 30 Sep 1971; Spencer Rich, "House-Senate Conferees Agree on Defense Money," *Washington Post*, 22 Oct 1971; George Wilson, "Pentagon is Winning in Senate Budget War," *Washington Post*, 25 Oct 1971; Donald C. Winston, "Conferees Clear $21.3 Billion Defense Bill," *Aviation Week*, 15 Nov 1971.

55. Korb, *Fall and Rise of the Pentagon*, 61–62; Van Atta, *With Honor*, 308–09; *U.S. Budget in Brief FY 1972*, Glossary.

56. *DoD Key Officials 1947–2004*, 86.

12. The Enduring Commitment to NATO

1. Rearden, *Formative Years*, 474; Department of State, *American Foreign Policy, 1950–1955*, vol. 2 (Washington, DC: Government Printing Office, 1957), 814n1. The 12 nations were the United States, Great Britain, France, Italy, the Netherlands, Belgium, Luxembourg, Norway, Denmark, Canada, Portugal, and Iceland. Greece and Turkey acceded to the treaty in 1952 and West Germany in 1955.

2. Kissinger, "Central Issues of American Foreign Policy," *FRUS 1969–1976*, 1:35. For a discussion of NATO during the Johnson administration, see Drea, *McNamara, Clifford, and the Burdens of Vietnam*, chaps. 14 and 15. For an assessment of the Soviet decision to invade Czechoslovakia, see Jiri Valenta, *Soviet Intervention in Czechoslovakia, 1968: Anatomy of a Decision* (Baltimore: Johns Hopkins University Press, 1991).

3. Nixon's Address to the Bohemian Club, 29 Jul 1967 (quote), *FRUS 1969–1976*, 1:5.

4. Nixon, *Memoirs*, 370–75; memo, Buchanan for Nixon, 19 Feb 1969, *FRUS 1969–1976*, 1:60.

5. Kissinger, *White House Years*, 394, 399–400; Steven L. Rearden, *Council of War: The History of the Joint Chiefs, 1942–1991* (Washington, DC: National Defense University Press, 2012), 344–45; Klaus Schwabe, "Commitments to NATO and Domestic Politics," in *A History of NATO: The First Fifty Years*, Gustav Schmidt, ed., 3 vols. (New York: Palgrave, 2001), 2:231.

6. Memo, Warnke for Laird, 28 Jan 1969, folder NATO 2–3A, box 13, Laird Papers, Ford Library; OASD (SA) fact sheet, REDCOSTE, 12 Mar 1969, folder 66, box 6, Records from SecDef Vault, Acc 330-74-142, WNRC.

7. Kissinger, "Central Issues of American Foreign Policy," 35, cited in note 2; Phil Williams, *The Senate and US Troops in Europe* (New York: St. Martin's Press, 1985), 145, 156, 159–60, 162; "In Europe: Pull Back Starts for the U.S.," *U.S. News & World Report*, 27 May 1968; Drea, *McNamara, Clifford, and the Burdens of Vietnam*, 417–21.

8. Other treatments of NATO issues include Raymond L. Garthoff, *Détente and Confrontation: Soviet-American Relations from Nixon to Reagan* (Washington, DC: Brookings

Institution, 1985); Geir Lundestad, *The United States and Western Europe since 1954: From 'Empire' by Invitation to Transatlantic Drift* (New York: Oxford University Press, 2003); Ronald E. Powaski, *The Entangling Alliance: The United States and European Security 1950–1993* (Westport, CT: Greenwood Press, 1994); Matthias Schulz and Thomas Schwartz, eds., *The Strained Alliance: U.S.-European Relations from Nixon to Carter* (Cambridge: Cambridge University Press, 2010); Thomas Schwartz, *Lyndon Johnson and Europe: In the Shadow of Vietnam* (Cambridge, MA: Harvard University Press, 2003); and Andreas Wenger et al., eds., *Transforming NATO in the Cold War: Challenges Beyond Deterrence in the 1960s* (New York: Routledge, 2006).

9. Edward Drea, "The McNamara Era," in *A History of NATO*, Schmidt, ed., 3:192–95 (quote 195).

10. Poole, *JCS and National Policy 1969–1972*, 113.

11. CIA Intelligence memo, "Current Problems in NATO," 21 Jan 1969 (quote), folder NATO vol.1, box 254, Agency Files, NSC, Nixon Library.

12. ISA fact sheet, Strategic Evolution, 10 Mar 1969, folder 66, box 6, Records from Sec-Def Vault, Acc 330-74-142; Drea, *McNamara, Clifford, and the Burdens of Vietnam*, 389, 391; David P. Calleo, *Beyond American Hegemony* (New York: Basic Books, 1987), 54, 235n30; John G. McGinn, "NATO in the Aftermath of the 1968 Invasion of Czechoslovakia," in *A History of NATO*, Schmidt, ed., 2:200.

13. "NATO: Public Opinion Considerations, 31 Jan 1969 (quote), attached to memo, Ryan for Shakespeare, 7 Feb 1969, folder NATO vol. 1, box 254, Agency Files, NSC, Nixon Library; memo, Warnke for Nitze, n.d., folder NATO 1, box 13, Laird Papers, Ford Library.

14. Memo, Warnke for Laird, 30 Jan 1969, folder NATO 2–3A, box 13, Laird Papers, Ford Library; memo Warnke for Laird, 28 Jan 1969, cited in note 6.

15. Memcon, Laird and Schroeder, 4 Feb 1969, folder NATO 4–6, box 13, Laird Papers, Ford Library. The Nonproliferation Treaty is treated in detail in Drea, *McNamara, Clifford, and the Burdens of Vietnam*, 328–32.

16. Memos, Kissinger for Nixon, 19 Feb 1969; Bergsten for Kissinger, 24 Mar 1969: both in folder Germany vol. 1 through Apr 1969, box 681, CF–Europe, Nixon Library; memo, Bergsten for Kissinger, 9 Jul 1969, folder Germany vol. 3 Jul–Nov 1969, box 682, ibid. A recent treatment of this subject is Francis Gavin, *Gold, Dollars, and Power: The Politics of International Monetary Policy Relation, 1958–1971* (Chapel Hill: University of North Carolina Press, 2007).

17. Tab A, memo, Laird for Nixon, 20 Feb 1969, folder NATO vol. 1, box 254, Agency Files, NSC, Nixon Library; Poole, *JCS and National Policy 1969–1972*, 115–16.

18. Memo, Laird for Nixon, 20 Feb 1969 (quote), cited in note 17; Views of the JCS, 13 Mar 1969 (quote), attached to memo, Laird for Nixon, 1 Apr 1969, folder DoD vol. 2 4/69, box 220, Agency Files, NSC, Nixon Library.

19. Memo, Laird for Nixon, 20 Feb 1969, cited in note 17; Nixon, *Memoirs*, 370; memo, Kissinger for Nixon, 21 Feb 1969, folder Haig Chron Feb 16–28, 1969 [2 of 2], box 955, Haig Chron Files, NSC, Nixon Library; DoD News Release 305-69, 21 Apr 1969.

20. Memo, Laird for CJCS, 13 Mar 1969, folder NATO 11, box 13, Laird Papers, Ford Library.

21. Memo, Laird for Nixon, 20 Feb 1969, cited in note 17.

22. *Cong. Rec.*, 15 Apr 1969, S 3710; William Greider, "U.S. Aides Privately Grumble Over NATO Cut By Canada," *Washington Post*, 5 Apr 1969; Drew Middleton, "NATO Pondering Course As It Enters Third Decade," *New York Times*, 10 Apr 1969.

23. Memo, Kissinger for Nixon, 1 Feb 1969, folder NATO vol. 1, box 254, Agency Files, NSC, Nixon Library.

24. Memo, Laird for Nixon, 5 May 1969, folder 1, box H-037, H Files, ibid. The Athens guidelines are covered in Kaplan et al., *McNamara Ascendency*, 305–09. See also John Duffield, *Power Rules: The Evolution of NATO's Conventional Force Defense Posture* (Palo Alto, CA: Stanford University Press, 1995).

25. Memo, Kissinger for Nixon, 13 May 1969 (quote), attached to memo, Sonnenfeldt for Kissinger, 20 May 1969, folder NATO vol. 4-2, box 256, Agency Files, NSC, Nixon Library.

26. Memo, Laird for Nixon, 30 Jun 1969, attached to memo, Kissinger for Laird, 12 Jul 1969; ltr, Laird to Segers, 24 July 1969: all in folder NATO vol. 5, box 257, ibid.; memo, Laird for Kissinger, 4 Nov 1969, attached to memo, Kissinger for Laird, 10 Nov 1969, folder NATO vol. 7, box 258, ibid.

27. NSDM 12, 14 Apr 1969, folder NSDM 1–50, box 363, Subject Files, ibid.; memo Walsh for Kissinger, 23 Apr 1969, folder NATO vol. 4-2, box 256, Agency files, ibid.: memo, Packard for Service Secretaries et al., 10 Jul 1969, folder FY 71 Budget, box 84, ASD(C) Files, OSD/OH; Kissinger, *White House Years*, 394; ISA fact sheet, Offset, 11 Mar 1969, folder 6, box 66, Records from SecDef Vault, Acc 330-74-142.

28. Backgrounders, 28 and 29 May 1969, attached to memo, Nixon for Haig, 16 Jun 1969, folder NATO vol. 5, box 257, Agency Files, NSC, Nixon Library.

29. Memo, Osgood for Kissinger, 25 Mar 1969 (quote), attached to memo, Kissinger for Nixon, 29 Mar 1969, folder NATO vol. 2, box 255, Agency Files, ibid.

30. NSSM 65, 8 Jul 1969, folder NSC Mtg Europe 1/28/70, box H-026, H Files, NSC, Nixon Library.

31. Poole, *JCS and National Policy 1969–1972*, 114–15.

32. Ibid.; NSSM 84 Report, *US Strategies and Forces for NATO*, 5 Jun 1970, 21, folder 4, box H-045, H Files, NSC, Nixon Library.

33. Memo, UnderSecArmy for Packard, 7 Jul 1970 (quote), folder NATO 145–147, box 15, Laird Papers, Ford Library.

34. Memo, Sonnenfeldt for Kissinger, 20 Aug 1969 (quote), attached to memo, Sonnenfeldt for Kissinger, 8 Sep 1969, draft joint State/DoD msg to NATO capitals, n.d., attached

to memo, Hyland for Kissinger, 17 Sep 1969, folder NATO vol. 6, box 257, Agency Files, NSC, Nixon Library.

35. Memo, Laird for Kissinger, 5 Sep 1969 (quote), attached to memo, Sonnenfeldt for Kissinger, 8 Sep 1969, cited in note 34.

36. Memo, Sonnenfeldt for Kissinger, 8 Sep 1969, cited in note 34.

37. Memo, Richardson for Nixon, 8 Oct 1969, attached to memo, Kissinger for Richardson, 20 Oct 1969, folder NATO vol. 6, box 257, Agency Files, NSC, Nixon Library.

38. Memo, Kissinger for Nixon, 14 Oct 1969, attached to memo, Kissinger for Richardson, 20 Oct 1969; memo, Laird for Nixon, 5 Sep 1969: all ibid.; Talking Paper for DepSecDef and CJCS, 14 Jan 1970, folder NATO 84–87, box 14, Laird Papers, Ford Library.

39. Memo, Laird for Nixon, 19 Feb 1970, folder NATO vol. 8, box 259, Agency Files, NSC, Nixon Library.

40. Ltr, Rogers to Fulbright, 6 Mar 1970 (quote), attached to Senate Resolution 292 (quote); memo, Haig for Barie, BoB, 16 Apr 1970: all in folder BoB vol. 2-1, box 206: both ibid.; Williams, *Senate and US Troops*, 164.

41. Memo, Laird for Nixon, 19 Feb 1970, cited in note 39.

42. Memo, Kissinger for Nixon, 5 Mar 1970, attached to memo, Kissinger for Laird and Rogers, 14 Mar 1970, folder 2, box H-098, H Files, NSC, Nixon Library. Nixon initialed his approval on the memo Kissinger sent to him.

43. Memo, ISA for SecDef, 6 Apr 1970, folder 70, box 6, Records from SecDef Vault, Acc 330-74-142.

44. Memo, Laird for Kissinger, 17 Aug 1970, folder NATO vol. 9-1, box 260, Agency Files, NSC, Nixon Library; memo, Laird for CJCS, 17 Aug 1970, attached to memo, Laird for SecNav, 17 Aug 1970, folder NATO 153–157, box 15, Laird Papers, Ford Library.

45. Memo, Ware for Laird, 10 Sep 1970, attached to note, Packard to Tucker, n.d., folder NATO 165–168, box 15, Laird Papers, Ford Library.

46. Memo, Rogers for Nixon, 22 Sep 1970 (quote), attached to memo, Eliot for Kissinger, 25 Sep 1970, folder Haig Chron Sep 25–30, 1970, box 972, Haig Chron Files, NSC, Nixon Library. Rogers sent Laird a copy of his memo.

47. Nixon Remarks on European Trip, 4 Oct 1970, *Nixon Public Papers 1970*, 806 (quote); Chalmers Roberts, "Nixon Moves to Curb Hill on NATO Cuts," *Washington Post*, 9 Oct 1970, folder NATO 1970, box 96, OSD/HO.

48. Msg 4583, Madrid from the Presidential Party to State, 2 Oct 1970; draft memo, Kissinger for Laird et al., n.d., (quote): both attached to memo, Sonnenfeldt for Kissinger, 8 Oct 1970, folder NATO vol. 9-1, box 260, Agency Files, NSC, Nixon Library.

49. Kissinger, *White House Years*, 401; memo, Sonnenfeldt et al. for Kissinger, 9 Oct 1970, folder NSC Mtg European Security 10/14/70, box H-029, H Files, NSC, Nixon Library; Minutes, SecDef Staff Meeting, 12 Oct 1970, folder Staff Mtgs Oct–Dec 1970, box 14, Acc 330-77-0062, WNRC.

50. NSDM 84, 11 Sep 1970, folder NSDM, box 1C, Laird Papers, Ford Library.

51. Memo, Laird for Nixon, 14 Oct 1970, folder NATO 178–181, box 15, ibid.

52. Memo, Haig for Kissinger, 15 Oct 1970 (quotes), attached to memo, Haig for Smith, 16 Oct 1970, folder Haig Chron Oct 14–24, 1970 [2 of 2], box 972, Haig Chron Files, NSC, Nixon Library.

53. Memo, Kissinger for Laird et al., 27 Oct 1970, folder NATO 190–195, box 16, Laird Papers, Ford Library.

54. Memo, Lynn for Kissinger, 28 Aug 1970, folder Senior Review Group NATO 8/31/70 [1 of 2], box H-047, H Files, NSC, Nixon Library; NSSM 84 Report, US Strategies and Forces for NATO, 5 Jun 1970, 50 (quote), cited in note 32; Poole, *JCS and National Policy 1969–1972*, 197–200.

55. NSC Review Group Meeting, 16 Jun 1970, folder 6, box H-111, H Files, NSC, Nixon Library; memo, Lynn for Kissinger, 28 Aug 1970, cited in note 54.

56. Memo, Davis for Mitchell, et al., 22 Oct 1970, folder NATO 183, box 15, Laird Papers, Ford Library.

57. Memo, Packard for Kissinger, 12 Nov 1970, folder Haig Staff Memos 7/24/70 to 12/31/70, box 1002, Haig Special Files, ibid.; Chalmers Roberts, "U.S. to Weigh Troop Cuts in Europe," *Washington Post*, 12 Nov 1970, folder NATO, box 96, OSD/HO; JCSM-531-70 for Laird, 18 Nov 1970, folder NATO 207–211, box 16, Laird Papers, Ford Library; memo, Smith for Haig, 27 Nov 1970, folder NATO vol. 9-1, box 260, Agency Files, NSC, Nixon Library.

58. Memo, Kissinger for Nixon, n.d., folder Haig Chron Nov 13–18, 1970 [1 of 2], box 973, Haig Chron Files, NSC, Nixon Library; memo, Fischer for Shultz, 17 Nov 1970, attached to memo, Shultz for Kissinger, 23 Nov 1970, folder NSC Mtg NATO 11/19/70 [1 of 4], box H-029, H Files, ibid.

59. Memcon, NSC Meeting 19 Nov 1970, folder NSC Minutes 1970 [1 of 3], box H-109, H Files, ibid.

60. Memo, Nutter for Laird, 21 Nov 1970, folder NATO 212–215, box 16, Laird Papers, Ford Library.

61. NSDM 95, 25 Nov 1970, folder NSDM 51–96, box 363, Subject Files, NSC, Nixon Library; memo, Kissinger for SecState, et al., 9 Dec 1970, folder NATO vol. 9-1, box 260, Agency Files, NSC, ibid.

62. Memo, Laird for Nixon, 27 Nov 1970 (quotes), attached to memo, Kissinger for Nixon, 30 Nov 1970, folder DoD vol. 9, box 225, ibid. Nixon indicated his decision on this memo.

63. Minutes, Combined SRG and Verification Panel Meeting, 31 Aug 1970, folder SRG Minutes 1970 [3 of 5], box H-111, H Files, NSC, Nixon Library.

64. Michael Getler, "Laird Bars Cuts Now in NATO Force," *Washington Post*, 1 Dec 1970; John Goshko and Alfred Friendly, "Europeans Raise Share for NATO," *Washington Post*, 2 Dec 1970; Laird, interview w/newsmen, 1 Dec 1970, *Laird Public Statements 1970*, 6:2444–46.

65. Alfred Friendly and John Goshko, "Détente Tied to Strength," *Washington Post*, 3 Dec 1970; Goshko "NATO Bars Talks on Détente Until Berlin Problem is Solved," *Washington Post*, 5 Dec 1970.

66. Poole, *JCS and National Policy 1969–1972*, 123–25.

67. Memo, Nutter for CJCS, 18 Dec 1969, folder NATO 81–83; JCSM-2-70 for SecDef, 6 Jan 1970, folder NATO 84–87; ltr, Laird to Rogers, 8 Feb 1970, folder NATO 90–93; memo, Packard for CJCS, 8 Apr 1970 (quote), folder NATO 115–118: all in box 14, Laird Papers, Ford Library.

68. NSSM 92, 13 Apr 1970, attached to memo, Kissinger for SecState et al., 14 Apr 1970; memo, Hyland for Kissinger, 13 May 1970: both in folder NATO vol. 8, box 259, Agency Files, NSC, Nixon Library.

69. Talking Paper for MBFR Meeting on 31 Aug 1970, NSSM 92, folder NATO 164, box 15, Laird Papers, Ford Library.

70. Memo, Smith for Kissinger, 29 Aug 1970 w/attached Talking Points (quotes), folder Haig Chron Aug 22–31, 1970, box 971, Haig Chron Files, NSC, Nixon Library; Talking Paper for DepSecDef and CJCS, n.d., folder NATO 164, box 15, Laird Papers, Ford Library.

71. Minutes, SRG and Verification Panel Meeting, 31 Aug 1970, cited in note 63; Talking Points attached to memo, Smith for Kissinger, 29 Aug 1970; Talking Paper for DepSecDef, n.d.: both cited in note 70.

72. Memo for the Record, 29 Oct 1970, attached to CM-340-70 for CSA et al., folder NATO 190–195; Memo for the Record, 25 Nov 1970, folder NATO 217–219: both in box 16, Laird Papers, Ford Library.

73. Kissinger, *White House Years*, 400–02, 534; memo, Kissinger for Nixon, 15 May 1971, folder USSR vol. 13, box 715, CF–Europe, NSC, Nixon Library. Nixon explained his reasoning in written comments on this memo.

74. NSDM 108, 21 May 1971 (quotes), folder Haig Chron May 19–25, 1971 [1 of 2], box 980, Haig Chron Files, NSC, Nixon Library; Kissinger, *White House Years*, 402.

13. Change in East Asia

1. The Nixon Doctrine and NSDM 27 stating the 1½-war strategy are considered in chapter 3 as well as numerous secondary works. See for example, Kissinger's *White House Years*.

2. See Margaret MacMillan, *Nixon and Mao* (New York: Random House, 2007) for a recent account of Nixon's trip.

3. Poole, *JCS and National Policy 1969–1972*, 212–13; NSSM 69, 14 Jul 1969, folder NSSM 50–69, box NSSMs 50–122, OSD/HO.

4. Memo, Packard for Kissinger, 30 Jun 1970, folder NSSM 50–69, box NSSMs 50–122, OSD/HO; "The Joint Chiefs of Staff and National Policy 1969–1972" (MS), Historical Division, Joint Secretariat, Joint Staff, Mar 1991, 409–10, OSD/HO.

5. Memos, Smith for Kissinger, 18 Mar 1971; Kissinger for USecState et al., 30 Mar 1971: both in folder DPRC 1971, box H-098, H Files, NSC, Nixon Library. See also chapter 15 herein for more information on force planning.

6. Memo for the Record, Burrows, 29 Jul 1971, folder Jul 1971, box 3, Moorer Diary, Acc 218-05-006, NARA II; memo, Odeen for Kissinger, 7 Dec 1971, folder 3 [1 of 2] box H-104, H Files, NSC, Nixon Library.

7. "JCS and National Policy 1969–1972," 421–22.

8. Memo, Laird and Rogers for Nixon, 9 Feb 1972, folder 3 [2 of 2], box H-104, H Files, NSC, Nixon Library.

9. Memo, Odeen for Kissinger, 11 Feb 1972 (quote), folder 3 [1 of 2], ibid.; memo, Kissinger for Rogers and Laird, 16 Feb 1972, folder 83, box 7, Records from SecDef Vault, Acc 330-74-142, WNRC. Kissinger wrote his comments on Odeen's memo. The memo for Rogers and Laird conveys the president's decision.

10. "JCS and National Policy 1969–1972," 427–29.

11. Bundy, *Tangled Web*, 136–37; quotation from Art 3 of the Treaty of Peace with Japan, 8 Sep 1951, *American Foreign Policy, 1950–1955: Basic Documents*, 1:425–26.

12. NSSM 5, 21 Jan 1969, folder Japan-2, box H-022, H Files, NSC, Nixon Library; memo, Sneider for Kissinger, 29 Jan 1969, folder Ryukyu Islands [2 of 2], box 555, ibid.

13. Annex E, "Japanese Defense Forces," folder Japan-2, box H-022, H Files, NSC, Nixon Library; Poole, *JCS and National Policy 1969–1972*, 232–33.

14. Poole, *JCS and National Policy 1969–1972*, 232; Van Atta, *With Honor*, 290–91.

15. Memcons, 14 Nov 1967, *FRUS 1964–1968*, vol. 29, pt. 2:227–32, 230 (quote); 15 Nov 1967, ibid., 232–34; Annex D, "Okinawa—Basic Information, folder Japan-2, box H-022, H Files, NSC, Nixon Library; Kissinger, *White House Years*, 326.

16. Arnold G. Fisch Jr., *Military Government in the Ryukyu Islands, 1945–1950* (Washington, DC: U.S. Army Center of Military History, 1988), 3–5.

17. Van Atta, *With Honor*, 290–91; memo, Laird for Nixon, 20 Feb 1969, folder Japan-Okinawa 1–3, box 8, Laird Papers, Ford Library.

18. JCSM-184-69 for SecDef, 29 Mar 1969 (quote), folder Japan-Okinawa 1–3, box 8, Laird Papers, Ford Library.

19. Poole, *JCS and National Policy 1969–1972*, 233; memo, Haig for Kissinger, 2 Apr 1969, folder 3, box 956, Haig Files, NSC, Nixon Library.

20. Memo, NSC for SecDef et al., 29 Apr 1969, folder 4, box H-299, H Files, NSC, Nixon Library; memo, Walske and Nutter for Laird, 17 Mar 1969, attached to memo, Laird for Wheeler, 19 Mar 1969, folder Japan-Okinawa 1–3, box 8, Laird Papers, Ford Library.

21. JCSM-264-69 for SecDef, 1 May 1969, folder Japan-Okinawa 4–9, box 8, Laird Papers, Ford Library. Carl Walske was Laird's assistant for atomic energy.

22. NSDM 13, 28 May 1969 (quotes), folder Japan 1–5, ibid.; Van Atta, *With Honor*, 291; memo, Rogers for Nixon, 2 Jun 1969, folder Japan vol. 1, box 533, CF–Far East, NSC, Nixon Library.

23. Ltr, Laird to Rogers, 28 Jul 1969, folder Japan-Okinawa 4–9, box 8, Laird Papers, Ford Library.

24. Nixon, *Memoirs*, 389 (quote); *Haldeman Diaries*, 3 Jun 1969, 62 (quote); memo, Richardson for Nixon, 4 Jun 1969, folder State vol. 3, box 280, Agency Files, NSC, Nixon Library; Van Atta, *With Honor*, 292. Curiously, Kissinger (*White House Years*, 329) termed the leak helpful.

25. Memo, Wheeler for Packard, 24 July 1969, folder Japan-Okinawa 4–9, box 8, Laird Papers, Ford Library.

26. Minutes, SecDef Staff Meeting, 2 Jun 1969, folder Staff Mtgs Apr–Jun 1969, box 13, Acc 330-77-0062, WNRC; memo, Nutter for Laird, 30 Oct 1969 (quotes), folder 4, box 959, Haig Files, NSC, Nixon Library; msg, Tokyo 6309 to State, 1 Aug 1969, folder State vol. 3, box 280, Agency Files, NSC, Nixon Library.

27. Sneider memo, 30 Aug 1969 (quote), attached to memo, Haig for Kissinger, 3 Sep 1969, folder 2, box 958, Haig Chron Files, NSC, Nixon Library.

28. Van Atta, *With Honor*, 293; memo, ASD(SA) for SecDef, 19 Jul 1969, folder Okinawa 1–5, box 5, Laird Papers, Ford Library.

29. Ltr, Doolin to Haig, 17 July 1969 (quote), folder Okinawa Gas Incident, box 554, CF–Far East, NSC, Nixon Library; telcon, Kissinger and Laird, 17 Jul 69, HAK Telcons, ibid.; Robert Keatly, "Okinawa Mishap Bares Overseas Deployment of Chemical Weapons," *Wall Street Journal*, 18 Jul 1969.

30. Selig S. Harrison, "Okinawa Gas Leak Report Perils Sato's Treaty Plan," *Washington Post*, 20 Jul 1969.

31. Van Atta, *With Honor*, 292–93; DoD News Release 610-69, 22 Jul 1969 (quotes), *Laird Public Statements 1969*, 5:1973–74; memo, Packard for Moorer, 26 Aug 1969; ltrs, Richardson to Laird, 1 Oct 1969; Laird to Richardson, 22 Oct 1969 (quote): all in folder Okinawa 1–5, box 5, Laird Papers, Ford Library.

32. Van Atta, *With Honor*, 293; Statement by Cyrus Vance (quote) and fact sheet on R&D funding, both attached to ltr, Laird to Rep. Edith Green (D–OR), 25 Mar 1969, folder Chemical Biological Warfare (CBW) vol. 1 calendar 1, box 37, Laird Papers, Ford Library; memo, Laird for Kissinger, 30 Apr 1969, attached to memo, Kissinger for Laird, 9 May 1969, folder CBW vol. 1, box 310, Subject Files, NSC, Nixon Library; NSSM 59, 28 May 1969, folder Review Group Meeting 10/30/69, box H-040, H Files, ibid.

33. David I. Goldman, "The Generals and the Germs: The Army Leadership's Response to Nixon's Review of Chemical and Biological Warfare Policies in 1969," *Journal of Military History* 73 (Apr 2009): 540–43; "Dugway Proving Ground," <http://en.wikipedia.org/wiki/Dugway_Proving_Ground>, accessed 2 August 2014. For details of the warfare and testing program see Seymour M. Hersh, *Chemical and Biological Warfare: America's Hidden Arsenal* (Garden City, NY: Anchor Books, 1969).

34. JCSM-243-69 for SecDef, 23 Apr 1969, folder CBW vol. 1 Calendar 2, box 37; JCSM-535-69 for SecDef, 28 Aug 1969 (quote), folder CBW vol. 1 Calendar 3, box 37; JCSM-563-69

for SecDef, 12 Sep 1969, folder Okinawa 1–5, box 5; memo, Packard for Wheeler, 26 Aug 1969, folder Okinawa 1–5, box 5: all in Laird Papers, Ford Library.

35. Memo, ActingASD (SA) for Laird, 29 Apr 1969, folder CBW vol. 1 Calendar 2, box 37, ibid.

36. Memos, Laird for Wheeler, 24 Oct 1969 (quote); Laird for Resor, 24 Oct 1969 (quotes): both in folder Okinawa 6–7, box 5, ibid.

37. Memo, Nutter for Laird, 23 Aug 1969, attached to memo, Packard for Moorer, 26 Aug 1969 (quote), folder Okinawa 1–5, ibid.; JCSM-535-69 for SecDef, 28 Aug 1969, cited in note 34.

38. Memo, Beal for Laird, 6 Nov 1969, attached to memo, ASD(I&L) for Laird, 7 Nov 1969, folder Okinawa 8–9, box 5, Laird Papers, Ford Library.

39. Memos, ASD(I&L) for Laird, 7 Nov 1969; Beal for Laird, 17 Nov 1969 (quote): both ibid.

40. Statement and Remarks on Chemical and Biological Defense Policies, 25 Nov 1969, *Nixon Public Papers 1969*, 968–70.

41. Memo, Laird for Beal, 12 Jan 1970; listing of correspondence, 4 Feb 1970: both in folder Okinawa 10–13; memos, Beal for Laird, 10 Mar 1970; Laird for Kissinger, 2 Apr 1970: both in folder Okinawa 14–20; DoD News Release 384-70, 6 May 1970, folder Okinawa 24–26: all in box 5, Laird Papers, Ford Library.

42. Oregon Historical Society biography of Governor Tom McCall, <www.ohs.org/education/focus/governor-tom-mccall.cfm>, accessed 11 Nov 2008.

43. Ltr, McCall to Nixon, 5 Dec 1969 (quote), attached to ltr, Laird to McCall, 8 Jan 1970, folder Okinawa 10–13, box 5, Laird Papers, Ford Library; memo Beal for Laird, 12 Dec 1969 (quote); memo Laird for Nixon, 17 Dec 1969 (quote), both attached to memo, Haig for Pursley, 30 Dec 1969, folder Okinawa vol. 1, box 554, CF Far East, NSC, Nixon Library.

44. Memo, Boe for Ehrlichman, 16 Dec 1969 (quote), attached to memo, Haig for Pursley, 30 Dec 1969, folder Okinawa vol. 1, box 554, CF–Far East, NSC, Nixon Library.

45. Memo, Haig for Pursley, 30 Dec 1969, attached to ltr, Laird to McCall, 8 Jan 1970 (quote), cited in note 43; State of Oregon News Release 70-66, 15 Apr 1970; US District Court Oregon, summons in a civil action, civil action file no. 70-252, 21 Apr 1970: both in folder Okinawa 22–33, box 5, Laird Papers, Ford Library; AP, "Okinawa Asks U.S. To Remove Gas," *Washington Post*, 8 May 1970, folder Okinawa, box 189, OSD/HO; memo, Finn for Green, 20 May 1970, attached to memo, Kissinger for Laird, 8 June 1970 (quote), folder Okinawa vol. 1, box 554, CF–Far East, NSC, Nixon Library.

46. Memo, Holdridge and Behr for Kissinger, 24 Apr 1970, attached to memo, Kissinger for Hughes, 2 May 1970; memo, Finn for Green, 20 May 1970, attached to memo, Kissinger for Laird, 8 Jun 1970: all in folder Okinawa vol. 1, box 554, CF–Far East, NSC, Nixon Library.

47. Memo, Kissinger for Haldeman, 14 Aug 1970; Memo for the Record by Train, 18 Jul 1970; memo, Hughes for Ehrlichman, 27 May 1970: all in folder DoD vol. 8, box 225, Agency Files, NSC, Nixon Library.

48. Memo, Kissinger for Nixon, 1 Jun 1970, attached to memo, Kissinger for Laird, 8 Jun 1970 (quote); memo, Guhin for Kissinger, 1 Jul 1970: all in folder Okinawa vol. 1, box 554, CF–Far East. NSC, Nixon Library.

49. Memo, Guhin for Kissinger, 6 Jul 1970, attached to memo, Packard for Kissinger, 25 Jul 1970, ibid.; memo, Moorer for Laird, 13 Jul 1970, folder CM 36-70–CM 61-70, box 1, Acc 218-92-29, NARA II; memo, Kissinger for Haldeman, 14 Aug 1970, cited in note 47.

50. Memos, Haig for Pursley, 28 Aug 1970, folder Haig Chron Aug 28–Sep 8, 1970; Haig for Kissinger, 1 Sep 1970, folder Haig Chron Sep 1–7, 1970 [2 of 2]: both in box 971, Haig Chron Files, NSC, Nixon Library; memo, Haig for Kissinger, 2 Sep 1970, folder Haig Staff Memos 7/24/70 to 12/31/70, box 1002, Haig Special Files, ibid.; AP, "Pentagon Will Move Gases Off Okinawa," *Washington Post*, 16 Sep 1970; Weekly staff meeting notes, 31 Aug, 8 Sep 1970, folder Staff Mtgs Jul–Sep 1970, box 14, Acc 330-77-0062.

51. Van Atta, *With Honor*, 294–95; ltr, Laird to Ambassador at Large David Kennedy, 14 May 1971, folder Japan-Okinawa 27–33, box 8, Laird Papers, Ford Library.

52. Memo, Kissinger for Laird, 5 Dec 1970, folder DoD vol. 7; Fact Sheet, Operation Red Hat, n.d., folder DoD vol. 11: both in box 226, Agency Files, NSC, Nixon Library; Reuter, "Okinawa Cleared of Poison Gas," *Washington Post*, 11 Sep 1971.

53. *Nixon Public Papers 1969*, 953–57 (quote, 955).

54. JCSM-297-70, 18 Jun 1970, folder Japan-Okinawa 10–16; memo, Laird for CJCS et al., 7 Apr 1971, folder Japan-Okinawa 24–26: both in box 8, Laird Papers, Ford Library.

55. Selig Harrison, "U.S., Japan Sign Pact," *Washington Post*, 18 Jun 1971 (quote); JCS Fact Sheet, Okinawa Reversion, 8 Jul 1971, folder Jul 1971, box 3, Moorer Diary, Acc 218-05-006.

56. JCS Fact Sheet, cited in note 55; DoD Information Guidance Series, 7-4, Okinawa Reversion, folder Okinawa, box 189, Subject Files, OSD/HO; memo, Laird for Service Secretaries, 13 May 1972, folder Japan-Okinawa 27–33, box 8, Laird Papers, Ford Library.

57. Ltrs, Laird to SecTreas, 21 Jan 1971, and SecTreas to Laird, 3 Feb 1971, folder Japan-Okinawa 17–23; Laird to SecTreas, 16 Feb 1971 (quote), folder Japan-Okinawa 24–26: all in box 8, Laird Papers, Ford Library.

58. Memo, Laird for Nixon, 19 Jul 1971, folder DoD vol. 12 cont., box 227, Agency Files, NSC, Nixon Library; memo, Laird for Nixon, 24 Dec 1971, folder Japan-Okinawa 27–33, box 8, Laird Papers, Ford Library.

59. Memo for the Record, 31 Aug 1971, SRG Meeting on 27 Aug 1971, folder Aug 1971, box 3, Moorer Diary, Acc 218-05-006.

60. Van Atta, *With Honor*, 296–97. See Morton H. Halperin, "Okinawa Cession," *Washington Post*, 30 Nov 1969, for a contemporary analysis of the agreement; see also Bundy, *Tangled Web*, 139, 141.

61. Reardon, *Formative Years*, 260–64; Condit, *Test of War 1950–1953*, 41–45; James F. Schnabel, *Policy and Direction: The First Year* (Washington, DC: U.S. Army Center of

Military History, 1972), 7–12; Don Oberdorfer, *The Two Koreas: A Contemporary History* (New York: Addison-Wesley, 1997), 5–7, 9.

62. USecState Richardson talking points for NSC meeting, 14 Aug 1969, folder 6, box H-023, H Files, NSC, Nixon Library.

63. Ibid.

64. NSSM 27, 22 Feb 1969, folder NSC Mtg 4 Mar 1970, box H-027, H Files, NSC, Nixon Library; memo, USecState to President Johnson, 23 Dec 1968, *FRUS 1964–1968*, vol. 29, pt. 1:455–58.

65. Memo for the Record, WSAG Meeting, 8 Aug 1969, folder WSAG Minutes 1969 and 1970 [6 of 6], box H-114; Memo for the Record, WSAG Meeting 25 Aug 1969, folder 2, box H-071: both in H Files, NSC, Nixon Library.

66. Ltr, Im to Laird, 7 Jun 1969, folder Korea 20–23, box 8, Laird Papers, Ford Library.

67. Memcon, 1 May 1969, folder Korea vol. 1, box 540, CF–Far East, NSC, Nixon Library.

68. Ltr, Laird to Mayo, 3 May 1969, folder Korea 13–19, box 8, Laird Papers, Ford Library; memos, Kissinger for Laird et al., 23 May 1969; Laird for Kissinger, 24 May 1969: both attached to memo, Kissinger for Nixon, 26 May 1969 (quote), folder Korea vol. 1, box 540, CF–Far East, NSC, Nixon Library. Nixon wrote his comment on Kissinger's memo. Memo, Kissinger for Laird et al., 4 Jun 1969, folder Korea 13–19, box 8, Laird Papers, Ford Library; telcon, Kissinger and Mayo, 14 Jul 1969, folder 4, box 2, HAK Telcons, NSC, Nixon Library.

69. NSSM 27 Summary Paper, 4 Aug 1969 (quote), folder 5, box H-023; Richardson talking points, 14 Aug 1969, NSC Meeting, cited in note 62; memo, Kissinger for Chairman NSSM 27 Steering Group, 16 Sep 1969, folder NSC Mtg 3/4/70, box H-027: all in H Files, NSC, Nixon Library; "JCS and National Policy, 1969–1972," 473–75.

70. CINCPAC Views, n.d., attached to ltr, Laird to Rogers, 25 Sep 1969; ltr, Rogers to Laird, 7 Oct 1969: both in folder Korea 29–36, box 8, Laird Papers, Ford Library; "JCS and National Policy 1969–1972," 475.

71. Memo, Nixon for Kissinger, 24 Nov 1969 (quote), folder HAK/President Memos 1969–1970, box 341, Subject Files, NSC, Nixon Library; Kissinger for Nixon, 25 Nov 1969, folder Haig Chron Dec 9–16, 1969 [2 of 2], box 960, Haig Chron Files, ibid. Nixon's quotation (emphasis in original) is noted on Kissinger's memo.

72. Memo, Kissinger for Nixon, 12 Dec 1969, folder Korea vol. 2, box 541, CF–Far East, ibid.

73. Memo, Kissinger for Richardson et al., n.d., folder 5, box H-099, H Files, ibid. This memo and attached issue paper were prepared for a January 1970 meeting of the DPRC.

74. "JCS and National Policy 1969–1972," 477–81.

75. Memo, Holdridge for Kissinger, 21 Jan 1970, attached to memo, Holdridge for Kissinger, 22 Jan 1970, folder Korea vol. 2, box 541, CF–Country Files, NSC, Nixon Library; msg, Seoul 492 to Ambassador Brown, 31 Jan 1970, attached to memo, Haig for Kissinger, 9 Feb 1970, folder Haig Chron Feb 8–14, 1970 [2 of 2], box 962, Haig Chron Files, ibid.

76. NSSM 27 Final Report, 19 Dec 1969, folder Korea 37–39, box 8, Laird Papers, Ford Library; NSSM 27 Summary Paper, 4 Aug 1969, "U.S. Policy and Programs," n.d.: both in folder 5, box H-023, H Files, NSC, Nixon Library; "The Issues for Decision," n.d., folder 7, box H-047, ibid.

77. "U.S. Policy and Programs," n.d., cited in note 76.

78. Memo, Lynn for Kissinger, 4 Feb 1970, folder 7, box H-047; Minutes, NSC Review Group Meeting, 6 Feb 1970, folder 8, H-111: both in H Files, NSC, Nixon Library.

79. Memo, Lynn for Kissinger, 26 Feb 1970, folder Korea vol. 2, box 541, CF–Far East, ibid.

80. Memos, Richardson for Kissinger, n.d.; Kissinger for Nixon, 3 Mar 1970: both in folder NSC Mtg 3/4/70, box H-027, H Files, ibid.; Talking paper attached to memo, Ware for Packard, 4 Mar 1970, folder Korea 40–43, box 8, Laird Papers, Ford Library.

81. Memcon, 3 Mar 1970 (quote), folder Korea vol. 2, box 541, CF–Far East, NSC, Nixon Library; "JCS and National Policy 1969–1972," 481–82; Draft Minutes, NSC Meeting, 4 Mar 1970 (quote), folder 1, box H-110, H Files, NSC, Nixon Library.

82. Draft Minutes, NSC Meeting, 4 Mar 1970, cited in note 81.

83. NSDM 48, 20 Mar 1970; memo, Packard for CJCS, 27 Mar 1970: both in folder 70, box 6, Records from SecDef Vault, Acc 330-74-142.

84. "JCS and National Policy, 1969–1972," 482–83.

85. Msg 1550, State to Seoul, 28 Mar 1970; "US-ROK Consultations, n.d.: both in folder 70, box 6, Records from SecDef Vault, Acc 330-74-142; News Conference w/Packard, 18 Jul 1970, *Packard Public Statements 1970*, 2:640–43; AP, "U.S. Pullout Plan Upsets S. Korea," *Washington Post*, 14 Jul 1970; George Zucker, "Troop Cutback in Korea Definite, U.S. as Conference Begins," *Washington Post*, 22 Jul 1970; UPI, "GI Pullout From Korea to Proceed," *Washington Post*, 24 Jul 1970.

86. Ltr, Packard to Johnson, 12 Oct 1970; memo, Packard for Kissinger, 12 Oct 1970; memo Kissinger for Nixon, 21 Oct 1970; Army Manpower Planning, 2 Dec 1970, attached to memo, Smith for Kissinger, 10 Dec 1970: all in folder DPRC 1971, box H-098, H Files, NSC, Nixon Library.

87. Memo, Johnson for Nixon, n.d. (quotes), attached to memo, Haig for Holdridge and Kennedy, 19 Aug 1970, folder Haig Chron Aug 11–17, 1970 [2 of 2], box 970, Haig Chron Files, ibid.; Poole, *JCS and National Policy 1969–1972*, 230.

88. JT US-ROK Statement, 6 Feb 1971, in DOS *Bulletin*, 1 Mar 1971, 263; "JCS and National Policy 1969–1972," 484.

89. "Republic of Korea Forces in Viet-Nam," n.d. (quotes), attached to memo, Davis for Irwin et al., 18 Jun 1971, folder Vietnam 452–453, box 36, Laird Papers, Ford Library; memo, Laird for Nixon, 26 Jun 1971, folder Vietnam 454–460A, ibid.; Stanley R. Larsen and James L. Collins Jr., *Allied Participation in Vietnam* (Washington, DC: Department of the Army, 1985), 129–32.

90. NSDM 113, 23 Jun 1971, folder Vietnam 454–460A, box 36, Laird Papers, Ford Library.

91. Memo, Laird for Nixon, 26 Jun 1971, cited in note 89; memo, Kissinger for Nixon, 6 Jul 1971, attached to memo, Nixon for Laird, 10 Jul 1971, folder July 8–13, 1971 [1 of 2], box 983, Haig Chron Files, NSC, Nixon Library; Graham A. Cosmas, *MACV: The Joint Command in the Years of Withdrawal, 1968–1973* (Washington, DC: U.S. Army Center of Military History, 2006), 397.

92. Nixon, *Memoirs*, 544–45.

93. Telegram 161648, State to Embassy in Republic of China, 23 Sep 1969; memo, Kissinger for Nixon, 9 Dec 1969; Embassy telegram 3080 to Rogers and Laird, 17 July 1970: all in *FRUS 1969–1976*, 17:88–90, 143–45, 223–25.

94. Memo for the Record, SRG Meeting, 12 Mar 1971; DoD Position Paper, n.d.: both in *FRUS 1969–1976*, 17:271–74, 277–82.

95. Ibid., 389; US China Policy Outline and Key Issues, folder Briefings Korea [2 of 3], box H-023, H Files, NSC, Nixon Library; NIE 13-8-69, 27 Feb 1969, *FRUS 1969–1976*, 17:16–17; Poole, *JCS and National Policy 1969–1972*, 211.

96. NSSM 14, US China Policy, 5 Feb 1969, folder Briefings Korea [3 of 3], box H-023, H Files, NSC, Nixon Library; Poole, *JCS and National Policy 1969–1972*, 211–12; Minutes, SRG Meeting, 15 May 1969, *FRUS 1969–1976*, 17:31–39.

97. Memcons, de Gaulle and Nixon, 28 Feb, 1 Mar 1969 (quote), folder Memcon, box 1023, Presidential/HAK Memcons, NSC, Nixon Library.

98. SNIE 13-69, 6 Mar 1969, *FRUS 1969–1976*, 17:22–24; Poole, *JCS and National Policy 1969–1972*, 212; NIE 13-8-69, 27 Feb 1969, cited in note 95.

99. Memos, Kissinger for Nixon, 23 Jun 1969 (quote); Richardson for Kissinger, 21 Jun 1969, attached to memo, Haig for Kissinger, 26 Jun 1969: both in folder Haig Chron Jun 1969 [1 of 2], box 957, Haig Chron Files, NSC, Nixon Library; NSDM 17, 26 Jun 1969, folder PRC 1–3, box 20, Laird Papers, Ford Library.

100. Memo, Kissinger for Nixon, 30 Jun 1969, folder 4, box 392, NSC, Nixon Library; NSSM 63, 3 Jul 1969, *FRUS 1969–1976*, 17:41–42; Poole, *JCS and National Policy 1969–1972*, 213–14.

101. Minutes, SecDef Staff Meeting, 19 Jul 1971, *FRUS 1969–1976*, 17:461.

102. Memo, Laird for Kissinger, 13 Aug 1971, folder PRC 7–15, box 21, Laird Papers, Ford Library.

103. Memo, Moorer for Laird, 30 Aug 1971, folder Taiwan 7–14, box 21, Laird Papers, Ford Library.

104. "Joint Statement . . . ," *FRUS 1969–1976*, 17:812–16, 815 (quote); memo, Nixon for SecState et al., 6 Mar 1972, folder PRC 16–24, box 21, Laird Papers, Ford Library; memcon, 1 Mar 1972, *FRUS 1969–1976*, 17:825–26.

105. Memo, Odeen for Kissinger, 29 Mar 1972, *FRUS 1969–1976*, 17:860–63; memo, Laird for Kissinger, 16 Jun 1972, folder Taiwan 29–37, box 21, Laird Papers, Ford Library; memcon, 10 Aug 1972, *FRUS 1969–1976*, 17:1037–39.

106. Memo, Kissinger for Laird, 16 Oct 1972, folder Taiwan 38–42, box 21, Laird Papers, Ford Library; memo, Holdridge for Kissinger, 6 Oct 1972, *FRUS 1969–1972*, 17:1087–89.

107. Telegram, State to Embassy in Republic of China, 20 Oct 1972, 0045Z, *FRUS 1969–1976*, 17:1090–91; 1090n3.

14. The All-Volunteer Force

1. Beth Bailey, *America's Army: Making the All-Volunteer Force* (Cambridge, MA: Belknap Press of Harvard University Press, 2009), 1–4; Leighton, *Strategy, Money, and the New Look*, 407; David M. Kennedy, *Over Here: The First World War and American Society* (New York: Oxford University Press, 2004), 144–47; Bernard D. Rostker, *I Want You! Evolution of the All-Volunteer Force* (Santa Monica, CA: Rand Corporation, 2006), 28; Robert K. Griffith Jr., *The U.S. Army's Transition to the All-Volunteer Force, 1968–1974* (Washington, DC: U.S. Army Center of Military History, 1997), 9–10.

2. Rostker, *Evolution of the All-Volunteer Force*, 28–29.

3. Griffith, *All-Volunteer Force*, 10–12.

4. Ibid; Prados, *Vietnam*, 170–71, 200–01; George Q. Flynn, *The Draft, 1940–1973* (Lawrence: University Press of Kansas, 1993), 214–18.

5. Rostker, *Evolution of the All-Volunteer Force*, 30–31, 64; Griffith, *All-Volunteer Force*, 1, 19, 21; ltr, Rivers to Fitt, 17 Sep 1968; memo, Wool for Fitt, 13 Nov 1968; memo, Fitt for Assistant Secretaries of Military Department (Manpower and Reserve Affairs), 15 Nov 1968 (quote): all Rostker documents. Rostker's *Evolution of the All-Volunteer Force* includes a DVD containing digitized copies of over 2,300 primary source documents on which the work is based. The materials, consisting of government memos, letters, staff papers, and reports come from various collections, including the National Archives. Documents identified as "Rostker documents" come from this DVD.

6. Rostker, *Evolution of the All-Volunteer Force*, 33–36; CBS radio transcript, 17 Oct 1968, folder AVF 1–3, box 1, Laird Papers, Ford Library; Griffith, *All-Volunteer Force*, 12.

7. Ltrs, Anderson to Laird, 24 Dec 1968; Burns to Nixon, 6 Jan 1969; memo, Nixon for Laird, 29 Jan 1969 (quote): all Rostker documents; Griffith, *The All-Volunteer Force*, 12, 17–19; memo, Haldeman for Flanigan, 17 Feb 1969, folder EX FG 216 Selective Service begin–7/31/69, box 1, Subject Files, WHCF, Nixon Library.

8. Memo, Laird for Nixon, 31 Jan 1969, attached to memo, Moose for Kissinger, 1 Feb 1969, folder Volunteer Army, box 497, Subject Files, NSC, Nixon Library; ltr, Nixon to Laird, 6 Feb 1969 (quote), folder AVF, box 36, Laird Papers, Ford Library; Rostker, *Evolution of the All-Volunteer Force*, 62.

9. Memo, Laird for Nixon, 7 Feb 1969, folder Volunteer Armed Forces, box 36, Laird Papers, Ford Library.

10. Feulner, memo for the Volunteer Army File, 26 Mar 1969, folder Volunteer Armed Forces 3, box A101, Baroody Papers, Ford Library; "The Report of the President's Commission on an All-Volunteer Armed Force," Feb 1970, < http://www.mcrmc.gov/public/docs/library/allportfolios/1970_Report_of_the_Presidents_Commission.pdf>, accessed 12 Nov 2014. The other members were former congressman Thomas Curtis, DuPont executive

Crawford Greenewalt, Georgetown University law student Stephen Herbits, Notre Dame University president Theodore Hesburgh, Hampton Institute president Jerome Holland, Mayfair Mills president Frederick Dent, Phillips Academy headmaster John Kemper, and Roy Wilkins of the NAACP. Wallis was also president of the University of Rochester.

11. Bailey, *America's Army*, 24–25.

12. Ibid., 25; Rostker, *Evolution of the All-Volunteer Force*, 66–67; memo, Haig for Kissinger, 2 May 1969 (quote), folder Haig Chron May 1969 [2 of 2], box 956, Haig Chron Files, NSC, Nixon Library; "Presentation by Harold Wool," SecDef Staff Meeting, 10 Feb 1969 (quote), folder Staff Mtgs Jan 27 1969–Mar 69 (quotes), box 13, Acc 330-77-0062, WNRC.

13. Memo, Rossotti for Laird, 22 Sep 1969, folder AVF 16–18, box 1, Laird Papers, Ford Library.

14. Memo, Laird for Service Secretaries et al., 10 Apr 1969, folder AFV 1–3, box 1, Laird Papers, Ford Library; Griffith, *All Volunteer Force*, 30.

15. Rostker, *Evolution of the All-Volunteer Force*, 144–45.

16. OASD(MRA) Fact Sheet, Project Volunteer Organization, 12 Nov 1970, Rostker documents; Rostker, *Evolution of the All-Volunteer Force*, 145–46.

17. Rostker, *Evolution of the All-Volunteer Force*, 146–48.

18. Griffith, *All-Volunteer Force*, 25.

19. Charter of the Special Assistant for the Modern Volunteer Army, 31 Oct 1970, folder AVF 42–48, box 1, Laird Papers, Ford Library; Griffith, *All Volunteer Force*, 52–53; Hunt, *Pacification*, 91; Bailey, *America's Army*, 46. Secretary Resor signed the charter.

20. Griffith, *All-Volunteer Force*, 65, 101–02; Bailey, *America's Army*, 53–54; Van Atta, *With Honor*, 251–54. Montague had also served as Forsythe's deputy in CORDS. Memo, Wollstadt for Kelley, 16 Jan 1971, folder AVF 56–58, box 1, Laird Papers, Ford Library.

21. Griffith, *All-Volunteer Force*, 188–94 (quotes, 189); Bettie J. Morden, *The Women's Army Corps, 1945–1978* (Washington, DC: U.S. Army Center of Military History, 1990), 228–31.

22. Memo, Laird for Nixon, 3 Feb 1969, Rostker documents.

23. William Beecher, "Laird Hints Test of Draft Lottery Before War Ends," *New York Times*, 19 Feb 1969; 1; "Briefing on Manpower," 18 Feb 1969, *Laird Public Statements 1969*, 1:144–49 (quote, 146).

24. Rostker, *Evolution of the All-Volunteer Force*, 67–68.

25. Special Msg to Congress, 13 May 1969, *Nixon Public Papers 1969*, 365–68; Nixon, *Memoirs*, 391; Van Atta, *With Honor*, 245.

26. Spencer Rich, " Hill Expected to Delay Draft Reform Until '70," *Washington Post*, 6 Jul 1969; memo, Laird for Nixon, 29 Aug 1969, attached to memo, Cole for Haldeman, n.d., folder Draft Reform, box 319, Subject Files, NSC, Nixon Library; Van Atta, *With Honor*, 245–46.

27. Memo, Flanigan for Rose, 22 Aug 1969, folder EX FG 216 8/1/69–9/30/69, box 1, Subject Files, WHCF, Nixon Library; memos, Laird for Nixon, 29 Aug 1969; Kissinger for Nixon, 29 Aug 1969: both attached to memo, Cole for Haldeman, n.d., cited in note 27; DoD News Release 770-69, 19 Sep 1969, *Laird Public Statements 1969*, 6:2167–69; George C. Wilson, "Congress Prodded on Reform," *Washington Post*, 20 Sep 1969, A1; White House Press Release, 10 Oct 1969; memo for Nixon, 9 Oct 1969: both in folder EX FG 216 10/1/69–12/31/69, box 1, Subject Files, WHCF, Nixon Library.

28. *Washington Post*, 20 Sep 1969 (quote), cited in note 27; Statement About the Decision of the Democratic Leadership to Defer Consideration of Draft Reform, 30 Oct 1969, *Nixon Public Papers 1969*, 893.

29. Peter Milius, "Hill to Act on Draft, Yields to Yale Head," *Washington Post*, 6 Nov 1969 (quote, A11), A1; Spencer Rich, "Unit Seeks Accord on Draft Lottery," *Washington Post*, 11 Nov 1969, A1; "Draft Bill Signed, Lottery Starts Jan.1," *Washington Post*, 27 Nov 1969, A1; P.L. 91-124, 83 Stat. 220 (1969). Van Atta, *With Honor*, 246. Laird may have had some influence on Brewster. He was one of 15 university presidents invited for lunch at the Pentagon to get them to support a lottery system. Melvin Laird, interview by Alfred Goldberg and Richard Hunt, 15 Oct 2001, 33, OSD/HO.

30. Van Atta, *With Honor*, 246–48 (quote, 246); memo, Laird for Nixon, 8 Feb 1970, folder Vietnam, 144–149, box 33, Laird Papers, Ford Library.

31. Griffith, *All-Volunteer Force*, 30–31.

32. Memo, Brehm for Kelley, 12 Jul 1969 (quotes), folder AVF 10–15, box 1, Laird Papers, Ford Library; Griffith, *All-Volunteer Force*, 32.

33. Memo, Wollstadt for Kelley, 22 Dec 1969, attached to memo, Kelley for Laird, 24 Dec 1969 (quotes), folder AVF 20–24, box 1, Laird Papers, Ford Library.

34. Bailey, *America's Army*, 25–27.

35. Griffith, *All-Volunteer Force*, 34–35.

36. Memo, Court for Kissinger, 30 Jan 1970, attached to memo, Kissinger for Ehrlichman, 3 Feb 1970, folder DoD vol. 6, box 224, Agency Files, NSC, Nixon Library.

37. Griffith, *All-Volunteer Force*, 37–38. The Army's analysis was attached to memo, Lynn for Kissinger, 17 Mar 1970 (quotes), NSC Meeting 3-24-70, box H-027, H Files, NSC, Nixon Library.

38. Summary of Report of the President's Commission on AVF; 21 Feb 1970 (quote); White House Press Conference, 21 Feb 1970: both folder Gates Commission, box 1090, Subject Files, OSD/HO; Griffith, *All-Volunteer Force*, 33–36; Special to *The New York Times*, "Report on All-Volunteer Army," *New York Times*, 22 Feb 1970.

39. Memo, Kelley for Anderson, 27 Feb 1970 (quotes), attached to memo, Kelley for Brehm et al., 27 Feb, folder AVF 25–30; memo, Resor for Laird, 8 Mar 1970, folder AVF 31–33: both in box 1, Laird Papers, Ford Library.

40. Transcript, *Meet the Press*, 22 Feb 1970, *Laird Public Statements 1970*, 1:432–33, 437 (quotes): memo, Haldeman for Kissinger, 23 Feb 1970, attached to memo, Haig for

Haldeman, 9 Mar 1970, folder Haig Chron Mar 1–11, 1970 [1 of 2], box 963, Haig Chron Files, NSC, Nixon Library; memo, Resor for Laird, 8 Mar 1970 (quote), folder AVF 31–33, box 1, Laird Papers, Ford Library.

41. Ltrs, Friedman to Laird, 23 Feb 1970 (quote); Laird to Friedman, 4 Mar 1970 (quote): both in Rostker documents.

42. Memo, Laird for Nixon, 11 Mar 1970 (quotes), attached to memo, Lynn for Kissinger, 17 Mar 1970, cited in note 37.

43. Minutes, Preparatory Session for NSC Meeting, 20 Mar 1970, folder NSC Minutes 1970 [3 of 3], box H-110; memo, Kissinger for Nixon, n.d., folder NSC Mtg 3-24-70, box H-027: both in H Files, NSC, Nixon Library.

44. Memo, Davis for Office of Vice President et al., 23 Mar 1970, folder AVF 34–35, box 1, Laird Papers, Ford Library; memo, Mayo for Nixon, 26 Mar 1970 (quote), folder Volunteer Army, box 407, Subject Files, NSC, Nixon Library. See chapter 3 for a discussion of NSDM 27.

45. Minutes, NSC Meeting 24 Mar 1970, folder NSC Minutes 1970 [3 of 3], box H-110, H Files, NSC, Nixon Library.

46. Ibid.

47. Memos, Rogers for Nixon, 2 Apr 1970; Ehrlichman and Kissinger for Nixon, 8 Apr 1970; Cole for Kissinger et al., 9 Apr 1970; NSDM 53, 14 Apr 1970: all in folder Volunteer Army, box 407, Subject Files, NSC, Nixon Library. The president made his decision on 8 April and Kissinger put it in NSDM 53 on 14 April.

48. President's Special Msg to Congress on Draft Reform, 23 Apr 1970, *Nixon Public Papers 1970*, 394–98 (quote 395); E.O. 11527, 23 Apr 1970, 35 *Federal Register* 6571.

49. Griffith, *All-Volunteer Force*, 42–44.

50. Memo, Anderson for Ehrlichman, 13 July 1970 (quotes), folder AVAF Draft 1970, box 37 Anderson, SMOF, WHCF; memo, Haig for Kissinger, 2 Sep 1970, folder Haig Staff Memos 7-24-70–12-31-70, box 1002, Haig Special File, NSC: both in Nixon Library; *Cong. Rec.*, 22 Jul 1970, S 11908 (quote).

51. Ltrs, Timmons to Stennis, 21 Aug 1970; Laird to Stennis, 14 Aug 1970 (quote): both in folder Volunteer Army, box 407, Subject Files, NSC, Nixon Library.

52. Memo, Lynn for Kissinger, 13 Aug 1970, ibid.

53. Memo, Laird for Service Secretaries and CJCS, 12 Oct 1970, folder AVF 42–48, box 1, Laird Papers, Ford Library.

54. Ltr, Laird to Hebert, 20 Jul 1971, *Laird Public Statements 1971*, 5:1951–52; Rostker, *Evolution of the All-Volunteer Force*, 93–94; Van Atta, *With Honor*, 427–28. Rostker claims Laird was opposed to the establishment of the school; Van Atta presents Laird as always a strong backer. In an interview in October 2001, Laird recalled his close collaboration with Congressman John E. Fogarty (D–RI), chairman of the House Appropriations Subcommittee for Labor–HEW, noting they built the CDC (Center for Disease Control), expanded

the National Institutes of Health, and set up 12 regional cancer centers in the United States. See Laird interview, 11 Oct 2001, 8–9; and Van Atta, *With Honor*, 80–81.

55. Griffith, *All-Volunteer Force*, 47–48; memos, Resor for Laird, 3 Nov 1970; Beal for Laird, 6 Nov 1970: both in folder AVF 49–52, box 1, Laird Papers, Ford Library.

56. Special Msg to Congress, 28 Jan 1971, *Nixon Public Papers 1971*, 75–78.

57. Memo, Laird for Kissinger, 26 Dec 1970, attached to memo, Packard for Kissinger, 22 Jan 1971, folder AVF 56–58; memo, Laird for Kissinger, 26 Jan 1971, folder AVF 59–62: both in box 1, Laird Papers, Ford Library.

58. Memo, Laird for Kelley, 27 Dec 1971, folder Pursley Chron file 11/71 to 1/72, box 16, OSD records, Acc 330-75-104, WNRC.

59. Memo, Smith for Kissinger, 10 May 1971, attached to memo, Nixon for Laird, 24 May 1971, folder Draft Reform 1971, box 320, Subject Files; memos, Bennett to Haig, 17 Jul 1971 and 20 Jul 1971: both in folder FY73–74 Budget, box 146, HAK Office Files: all in NSC, Nixon Library.

60. Memo, Kissinger for Nixon, 14 May 1971, attached to memo, Nixon for Laird, 24 May 1971, cited in note 59.

61. Memos, Veatch for Schlesinger, 6 May 1971; Smith for Kissinger, 10 May 1971: both attached to memo, Nixon for Laird, 24 May 1971, cited in note 59.

62. Memo, Smith for Kissinger, 10 May 1971; memos, Bennett to Haig, 17 Jul 1971, 20 Jul 1971: all cited in note 59.

63. President's Statement, 28 Sep 1971, *Nixon Public Papers 1971*, 1008–09; P.L. 92-129, 85 Stat. 348. In his signing statement, the president lauded Senators Stennis and Smith and Congressmen Hebert and Arends for their leadership in securing final passage.

64. Memo, Laird for Kelley, 27 Dec 1971, folder Pursley Chron File 11/71 to 1/72, box 16, SecDef Records, Acc 330-75-104, WNRC.

65. Memo, Laird for Kelley, 6 Jan 1972 (quote), attached to memo, Haig for Kissinger, 12 Jan 1972, folder s Jan 1–21 , 1972, box 990, Haig Chron Files, NSC, Nixon Library; memos, Kelley for Laird, 3 Jan 1972; Laird for SecArmy, 11 Jan 1972: both in folder AVF 67–69, box 1, Laird Papers, Ford Library.

66. Memo, Laird for Nixon, 28 Jul 1972, folder AVF 70, box 1, Laird Papers, Ford Library; memo, Laird for Service Secretaries, 21 Aug 1970, folder Resrve Forces 1970, box 1095, Subject Files, OSD/HO.

67. Memos, Odeen for Kissinger, 27 Jul 1972, 5 Aug 1972, attached to memo, Kissinger for Nixon, 22 Aug 1972; memo, Odeen for Kissinger, 13 Nov 1972: all in folder Draft Reform 1972, box 320, Subject Files, NSC, Nixon Library. The quotation is from memo, Laird for Nixon, 28 Jul 1972, cited in note 66.

68. Memos, Odeen for Kissinger, 27 Jul 1972, 5 Aug 1972, attached to memo, Kissinger for Nixon, 22 Aug 1972, cited in note 67.

69. Program/Budget Decision 281, 5 Dec 1972, Rostker documents; Rostker, *Evolution of the All-Volunteer Force*, 180–82; Griffith, *All-Volunteer Force*, 197–99. Rostker mistak-

enly credits Packard with issuing the decision, but Packard had left the post of deputy in December 1971.

70. Memo, Kissinger for Nixon, 22 Aug 1972, folder Draft Reform 1972, box 320, Subject Files, NSC, Nixon Library; ltr, Laird to Stennis, 30 Sep 1972, folder AVF 71–72, box 1, Laird Papers, Ford Library; Griffith, *All Volunteer Force*, 170–71.

71. "Achieving the All-Volunteer Force," attached to memo, Greenberg for Kelley, 7 Dec 1972, Rostker documents.

72. DoD News Release 48-73, 27 Jan 1973, *Laird Public Statements 1973*, 264.

73. Memo, Richardson for Nixon, 23 Feb 1973, Rostker documents; DoD News Release 134-73, 21 Mar 1973 (quote), OSD Historical Office, comp., *Public Statements of Elliot Richardson, Secretary of Defense, 1973*, 1:256–57. Emphasis in original.

74. "Status of All-Volunteer Force, n.d., folder DPRC Meeting 8-17-73, box H-106, H Files, NSC, Nixon Library.

75. Laird interview, 18 Aug 1986, 9; Van Atta, *With Honor*, 433 (quote).

76. Rostker, *Evolution of the All-Volunteer Force*, 747–48.

77. Ibid., 746 (quote).

78. Bailey, *America's Army*, 4.

79. Melvin Laird, interview by Alfred Goldberg and Maurice Matloff, 29 Oct 1986, 32–33, OSD/HO.

80. Kennedy, *Over Here*, 17–18, 147.

15. Strategic Defense: ABM and SALT

1. Ltr, Nixon to Laird, 4 Feb 1969 (quote), *FRUS 1969–1976*, 12:26–28. Nixon made sufficiency his formal policy in June 1969 (NSDM 16). See also McGeorge Bundy, *Danger and Survival: Choices About the Bomb in the First Fifty Years* (New York: Random House, 1988), 549.

2. Poole, *JCS and National Security Policy, 1969–1972*, 33–35; NSDM 16, 24 Jun 1969, <www.nixonlibrary.gov/virtuallibrary/documents/nsdm/nsdm_016.pdf>, accessed 18 Nov 2014; Nixon, *Memoirs*, 415–16; President's News Conference, 27 Jan, 1969, *Nixon Public Papers 1969*, 19.

3. Van Atta, *With Honor*, 188.

4. Kissinger, *White House Years*; Laird statement before House Subcommittee on DoD Appropriations, "FY 1971 Defense Program and Budget," 35–36; Institute for Strategic Studies, *The Military Balance, 1969–1970* (London: 1971), 5–6.

5. *Military Balance*, 192; Laird Statement on FY 1972–76 Defense Program and the FY 1972 Defense Budget Before SCAS, 15 Mar 1971, 161; William Beecher, "Administration Ends Study of Global Nuclear Strategy," *New York Times*, 1 May 1969, 1. MIRV refers to a missile payload of two or more warheads that can engage separate targets; MRV, to

warheads that engage the same target. Roger Labrie, *SALT Handbook: Key Documents and Issues, 1972–1979* (Washington, DC: American Enterprise Institute, 1979), 710.

6. Bundy, *Tangled Web*, 83–86; John Newhouse, *Cold Dawn: The Story of SALT* (New York: Holt, 1973), 79–80; Kissinger, *White House Years*, 204–05; Donald R. Baucom, *The Origins of SDI, 1944–1983* (Lawrence: University Press of Kansas, 1992), 27. See also Drea, *McNamara, Clifford, and the Burden of Vietnam*, 369–70.

7. Baucom, *Origins of SDI*, 36–39; President's News Conference, 6 Feb 1969, *Nixon Public Papers 1969*, 71; NSSM 23, 20 Feb 1969, OSD/HO.

8. Laird, interview on CBS Radio and *Face the Nation*, 9 Feb 1969, *Laird Public Statements 1969*, 1:125–31; JCSM-111-69 for SecDef, 26 Feb 1969 (quote), folder ABM 1–3, box 27, Laird Papers, Ford Library.

9. Laird interviews, 29 Oct 1986, 25–27; 15 Oct 2001, 24–25; Kissinger, *White House Years*, 205.

10. Beecher, "Sentinel Project Halted by Laird Pending Review," *New York Times*, 7 Feb 1969; President's News Conference," 6 Feb 1969, *Nixon Public Statements 1969*, 70; *Haldeman Diaries*, 27; Robert C. Jensen, "Laird Hints Work Will Resume," *Washington Post*, 10 Feb 1969; "Face the Nation," 9 Feb 1969, *Laird Public Statements 1969*, 1:125–34.

11. Robert B. Semple Jr., "Nixon Staff Had Central Role in Mission Decision," *New York Times*, 19 Mar 1969.

12. Memo, Laird for Kissinger, 1 Mar 1969, folder Safeguard-ABM 4, box 27, Laird Papers, Ford Library; "Issues Concerning ABM Deployment," n.d., attached to memo, Kissinger for Nixon, 5 Mar 1969, folder 1, box H-021, H Files, NSC, Nixon Library.

13. Memo, J/PM for SecState, 2 Mar 1969, folder 1, box H-021, H Files, NSC, Nixon Library; memo, Laird for Kissinger, 1 Mar 1969, cited in note 12.

14. Memo, Smith for Packard, 26 Feb 1969 (quote); ltr, Packard to Smith, 4 Mar 1969 (quote): both in folder SALT, vol. 1, box 10, Laird Papers, Ford Library.

15. Minutes, NSC Meeting, 5 Mar 1969, folder 1, box H-109, H Files, NSC, Nixon Library.

16. Memcon by Dobrynin, 3 Mar 1969, in *Soviet-American Relations: The Détente Years, 1969–1972*, Edward C. Keefer, ed. (Washington, DC: Government Printing Office, 2007), 31–32.

17. Memo, Johnson for Rogers, 13 Feb 1969, folder 1, box H-021, H Files, NSC, Nixon Library; *Haldeman Diaries*, 38–40; Kissinger, *White House Years*, 205–07; "Statement of Carl Kaysen," 13 Mar 1969, folder ABM-System Vol. 2, box 840, ABM–MIRV, NSC, Nixon Library.

18. Editorial, "That antimilitary mood," *Life*, 21 Mar 1969 (quote); Kissinger, *White House Years*, 204–07, 205 (quote).

19. President's News Conference and President's Statement, 14 Mar 1969, *Nixon Public Papers 1969*, 208–19.

20. Intell note, INR to SecState, 24 Mar 1969, folder USSR vol. 1, box 709, CF–Europe, NSC, Nixon Library; ed. note, *FRUS 1969–1976, SALT I*, 32:14–15.

21. "MIRVs," <www2.gwu.edu/~nsarchiv/nsa/NC/mirv/mirv.html >, accessed 22 Feb 2002.

22. Memo, Haig for Kissinger, 11 Jun 1969, folder 1, box 957, Haig Chron Files, NSC, Nixon Library; Van Atta, *With Honor*, 190.

23. Memo, Smith for Kissinger, n.d., attached to memo, Smith for Packard, 14 Apr 1969; ltr, Smith to Packard, 22 May 69; memo, Richardson for Nixon, 22 May 1969, attached to memo, Kissinger for Laird, 27 May 1969: all in folder SALT vol. 1 Calendar 4, box 22, Laird Papers, Ford Library.

24. Ltr, Packard to Smith, 26 May 1969; memo, Packard for Kissinger, 30 May 1969: both ibid.; memo, Packard for Kissinger, 28 May 1969, folder ABM 10–12, box 27, Laird Papers, Ford Library.

25. Memo, Lynn for Kissinger, 28 Jul 1969, folder 5, box 845, NSC, Nixon Library; OASD (SA), "MIRV Issues," 21 Jun 1969, folder MIRV 1–3, box 10, Laird Papers, Ford Library.

26. Memo, Kissinger for Nixon, 23 May 1969, "Continued Congressional Interest in a Moratorium (quote):" folder Haig Chron May 1969 [1 of 2], box 956, Haig Chron Files, NSC, Nixon Library; Marquis Childs, "Laird-Helms Confrontation On ABM Is Being Sanitized," *Washington Post*, 9 Jul 1969.

27. Memos, Kissinger for Nixon, 23 May 1969; Packard for Kissinger, 30 May 1969, attached to memo, Kissinger for Laird, 27 May 1969: both in folder Haig Chron May 1969 [1 of 2], box 956, Haig Chron Files, Nixon Library; memo, Haldeman for Rogers and Laird, 2 Jun 1969, folder Personnel, box D19, Laird Papers, Ford Library.

28. SCFR, Subcommittee on International Organization and Disarmament, *Strategic and Foreign Policy Implications of ABM Systems: Hearings*, 91st Cong., 1st sess., 21 Mar 1969, 229.

29. Ibid., 183–84; memo, Kissinger for Nixon, n.d., *FRUS 1969–1976*, 12:101.

30. SCFR, *Hearings*, cited in note 28, 213–14.

31. SCA, Subcommittee, *Department of Defense Appropriations for Fiscal Year 1970: Hearings*, 91st Cong., 1st sess., 10 Jun 1969, 499.

32. Ibid., 508.

33. Memo, Butterfield for Nixon, 11 Jun 1969, attached to memo, Haig for Kissinger, 17 Jun 1969, folder Haig Chron Jun 1969 [2 of 2], box 957, Haig Chron Files, NSC, Nixon Library; President's News Conference, 19 Jun 1969, *Nixon Public Papers 1969*, 480; Warren Unna, "Nixon is Firm Against Compromise," *Washington Post*, 2 Jul 1969.

34. Memo, BeLieu for Nixon, 11 Jun 1969, attached to memo, Butterfield for Kissinger, 12 Jun 1969, folder 5, box H-127, H Files, NSC, Nixon Library; William Chapman, "Laird Held Redefining SS-9 Stand," *Washington Post*, 24 Jun 1969; John W. Finney, "Laird Narrows Scope of Warning on Soviet Threat," *New York Times*, 24 Jun 1969.

35. A sanitized version of the 23 June hearing was printed in SCFR, *Intelligence and the ABM: Hearing*, 91st Cong., 1st sess., 23 Jun 1969.

36. Laird Press Conference, 23 Jun 1969, *Laird Public Statements 1969*, 5:1787–88, 1789–1800.

37. Ltrs, Laird to Stennis, 8 Jul 1969 (quotes); Stennis to Laird, 2, 3 Jul 1969: both in folder Safeguard-ABM Calendar 1, box 27, Laird Papers, Ford Library.

38. Warren Weaver Jr., "Nixon Missile Plan Wins in Senate by a 51–50 Vote," *New York Times*, 7 Aug 1969; Spencer Rich, "Ban on Deployment Defeated, 51 to 49," *Washington Post*, 7 Aug 1969.

39. Laird interviews, 29 Oct 1986, 26; 15 Oct 2001, 25; Robert Pursley, interview by Alfred Goldberg and Richard Hunt, 30 Jul 2003, 10, OSD/HO; Van Atta, *With Honor*, 191–93, 192–93 (quote).

40. Memo, Nixon for Haldeman et al., 7 Aug 1969 (quotes), folder HAK/President Memos 1969–1970, box 341, Subject Files, NSC, Nixon Library; Bundy, *Tangled Web*, 88; William Chapman, "ABM Dispute Spurs Partisan Activity," *Washington Post*, 16 Jun 1969.

41. Laird interviews, 29 Oct 1986, 26; 15 Oct 2001, 25; Pursley interview, 30 Jul 2003, 10–11; Van Atta, *With Honor*, 191–93.

42. Bundy, *Tangled Web*, 86.

43. Memo, Haig for Kissinger, 22 Feb 1969, folder Haig Chron Feb 16–28, 1969 [1 of 2], box 955, Haig Chron Files, NSC, Nixon Library. Attached to Haig's memo were an update from ACDA on talks, a message to NATO, and the text that Rostow presented to Dobrynin. Newhouse, *Cold Dawn*, 138–39; Alfred Goldberg, ed., "History of Strategic Arms Competition 1945–1972, Part II" (OSD/HO, 1981), 734.

44. "Strategic Arms Limitation Talks," at <www.state.gov/www/global/arms/treaties/salt1.html>, accessed 2 Dec 2010.

45. Poole, *JCS and National Policy 1969–1972*, 81–83.

46. Ltr, Nixon to Laird, 4 Feb 1969, *FRUS 1969–1976*, 12:26-28; Poole, *JCS and National Policy 1969–1972*, 81–83; Van Atta, *With Honor*, 194; Newhouse, *Cold Dawn*, 159; NSSM 28, 6 Mar 1969, folder NSSM 17-31, box 16 NSSMs 1–49, OSD/HO.

47. Meeting of NSSM 28 Steering Committee, n.d., folder SALT vol. 1 Calendar 3, box 22, Laird Papers, Ford Library.

48. NSSM 28 Summary Report, n.d., folder SALT [2 of 2], box H-022, H Files; memo, Kissinger for Nixon, 10 Jun 1969, folder SALT Jun–Jul 1969 vol. 2, box 873, SALT: both in NSC, Nixon Library; memo, Smith for NSSM 28 Steering Committee, 26 May 1969, folder SALT vol. 1, box 22, Laird Papers, Ford Library.

49. JCSM-377-69 for SecDef, 17 Jun 1969, folder SALT vol. 1, Calendar 7, box 22, Laird Papers, Ford Library; memo Kissinger for Nixon, 10 Jun 1969, cited in note 47.

50. Ed. note, FRUS 1969–1976, 32:39–40; President's News Conference, 19 Jun 1969, *Nixon Public Papers 1969*, 473; memo Rogers for Nixon, 26 Jun 1969, attached to memo Haig for Sonnenfeldt, 3 Jul 1969, folder SALT Jun–Jul 1969 vol. 2, box 873, SALT, NSC,

Nixon Library; memo, Pursley for Laird, 2 Jul 1969, folder Notes Misc Mtgs, box 3, SecDef Records, Acc 330-75-104; White House Press Release, 5 July 1969, folder SALT Jul-Nov 1969, box 1247, Subject Files, OSD/HO; Van Atta, *With Honor*, 194–95.

51. "Strategic Arms Limitation Talks," n.d., attached to memo, Warnke for Laird, 25 Jan 1969, folder 4, box H-020, H Files; memo, Eagleburger for Kissinger, 28 Jan 1969, folder USSR vol. 1, box 709, CF–Europe: both in NSC, Nixon Library.

52. Minutes, NSC Meeting, 25 Jun 1969, folder NSC Minutes 1969 [3 of 5], box H-109, H Files; memo, Nixon for SecState et al., 26 Jun 1969, folder SALT NSSM 28, box H-023, H Files; msg Bonn 07775 to State, 12 Jun 1969; memo, Kissinger for Nixon, 10 July 1969; memo, Kissinger for Nixon, 21 Jul 1969: all in folder SALT Jun-Jul vol. 2, box 873, SALT: all in NSC, Nixon Library.

53. Minutes, NSC Meeting, 18 Jun 1969, folder 3, box H-109, H Files; NSDM 16, 24 Jun 1969, folder NSDM 1-50, box 363, Subject Files: both in NSC, Nixon Library.

54. Memo, Laird for Kissinger, 3 Jul 1969 (quotes), attached to memo, Sonnenfeldt for Kissinger, 4 Jul1969, folder SALT Jun–Jul 1969 vol. 2, box 873, SALT, NSC, Nixon Library.

55. Memo, Kissinger for Nixon, 15 Jul 1969, folder 3, box 957, folder Haig Chron Jul 1969 [1 of 2], Haig Chron Files; ltr, Packard to Kissinger, 17 Jul 1969, attached to ltr, Kissinger to Packard, 22 Jul 1969, folder SALT Jun–Jul 1969 vol. 2, box 873, SALT: all in NSC, Nixon Library; Bundy, *Tangled Web*, 91, 94, 95.

56. Poole, *JCS and National Policy 1969–1972*, 87–88.

57. Ltr, Nixon to Smith, 21 Jul 1969, folder SALT [1 of 2], box H-022, H Files, NSC, Nixon Library; Jonathan Haslam, *Russia's Cold War From the October Revolution to the Fall of the Wall* (New Haven, CT: Yale University Press, 2011), 262.

58. Memo, Tucker for Laird, 7 Nov 1969, folder SALT Oct–Nov 1969 vol. 4, box 874, SALT, NSC, Nixon Library; draft paper by Nitze, 6 Nov 1969, attached to memo, Tucker for Laird, 7 Nov 1969, folder SALT 90, box 24, Laird Papers, Ford Library; Beecher, "White House Debates Whether to Expand ABM in Budget Due in January," *New York Times*, 21 Dec 1969.

59. Draft Minutes of NSC Meeting on SALT, 10 Nov 1969, folder NSC Minutes 1969 [4 of 5], box H-109, H Files, NSC, Nixon Library.

60. NSDM 33, 12 Nov 1969 (quote), attached to ltr, Nixon to Smith, 12 Nov 1969, folder SALT 94–97, box 24, Laird Papers, Ford Library; ltr, Smith to Nixon, 9 Dec 1969, attached to memo, Haig for Sonnenfeldt and Lynn, 12 Dec 1969, folder Haig Chron Dec 9–16, 1969 [1 of 2], box 960, Haig Chron Files, NSC, Nixon Library.

61. Ltr, Laird to Stennis, 16 Sep 1969, folder ABM 19–25, box 27, Laird Papers, Ford Library; Memo for the Record, Packard, 8 Dec 1969, attached to memo, Wilson for Lynn, 8 Dec 1969, folder 3, box H-099, H Files, NSC, Nixon Library; Laird interview, 29 Oct 1986, 26.

62. Memo, Kissinger for Nixon, 30 Oct 1969, folder DPRC and Def Budget 1969, box 234, Agency Files; memo, Lynn for Kissinger 7 Nov 1969, folder 2, box H-099, H Files: both in NSC, Nixon Library.

63. Memo for the Record, Packard, 8 Dec 1969, attached to memo, Wilson for Lynn, 8 Dec 1969, folder 3, box H-099, H Files, NSC, Nixon Library; Beecher, "White House Debates," cited in note 58.

64. Memo, Starbird for Resor, 15 Dec 1969, attached to ltr, Packard to Kissinger, 16 Dec 1969, folder 4, box H-099, H Files, NSC, Nixon Library.

65. Ltr, Smith to Nixon, 30 Dec 1969 (quote), folder ABM System vol. 3, box 840, ABM–MIRV; memo, Smith for Nixon, 21 Jan 1970, folder DPRC 1971, box H-098, H Files: both ibid.

66. Telcon, Kissinger and Packard, 30 Dec 1969 (quote), folder 6, box 3, HAK Telcons; memo, Kissinger for Nixon, 22 Jan 1970 (quote), folder ABM System vol. 3, box 840, ABM-MIRV: both ibid. Nixon wrote a note to Kissinger in the margin.

67. Memo on the Safeguard System, 31 Dec 1969; JCSM-784-69 for Laird, 31 Dec 1969: both attached to ltr, Packard to Kissinger, 31 Dec 1969, folder ABM 30–31, box 27, Laird Papers, Ford Library.

68. Memo Packard for Kissinger, 2 Jan 1970 (quote), attached to memo Watts for Kissinger, 2 Jan 1970, folder ABM System vol. 3, box 840, ABM–MIRV, NSC, Nixon Library.

69. Memo, Kissinger for Nixon, n.d., attached to memo, Lynn for Kissinger, 6 Feb 1970, ibid.; Minutes, DPRC Meeting, 30 Jan 1970, folder DPRC Minutes [1 of 3], box H-118, H Files, NSC, Nixon Library.

70. Laird News Conference, 24 Feb 1970, *Laird Public Statements 1970*, 7:457–72, 458 (quote); ASD(PA) News Release 146-70, 24 Feb 1970, folder Continental Defense 1970, box 698, OSD/HO; Memo for the Record, Slocombe, 26 Feb 1970 (quote), folder 1, box 841, NSC, Nixon Library.

71. Memcon, SALT, 8 Apr 1970, folder 7, box H-109, H Files, NSC, Nixon Library; memo Laird for Nixon, 9 Apr 1970, folder SALT 152–154, box 25, Laird Papers, Ford Library; memo, Lynn for Haig, 9 Apr 1970, folder Haig Chron Apr 8–12 1970 [2 of 2], box 964, Haig Chron Files, NSC, Nixon Library.

72. NSDM 51, 10 Apr 1970, *FRUS 1969–1976*, 32:231–52.

73. Newhouse, *Cold Dawn*, 183–84; Haslam, *Russia's Cold War*, 262.

74. NSDM 69, 9 Jul 1970 (quote); NSDM 73, 22 Jul 1970 (quote); NSDM 74, 31 Jul 1970: all in *FRUS 1969–1976*, 32:310–13, 320–21, 326–37.

75. *Cong. Rec.*, 23 Jun 1970, S 9547; Donald C. Winston, "Defense Bill Keyed to ABM Fight," *Aviation Week*, 27 Jul 1970; Kissinger, *White House Years*, 546–47; ltr, Laird to Stennis, 18 Aug 1970, folder Safeguard ABM Calendar 3, box 18, Laird Papers, Ford Library.

76. Kissinger, *White House Years*, 550–51; Van Atta, *With Honor*, 199–200; Memo for the Record, SecDef Staff Meeting, 24 Aug 1970 (quotes), folder Staff Mtgs, Jul–Sep 1970, box 14, Acc 330-77-0062.

77. Memo, Packard for Kissinger et al., 13 Jan 1971, folder Safeguard Calendar 4, box 18, Laird Papers, Ford Library.

78. Memo, Smith for Kissinger, 15 Jan 1971, folder 1, box H-007, H Files, NSC, Nixon Library; Safeguard and Related Programs, 13 Jan 1971, attached to memo, Packard for Kissinger et al., 13 Jan 1971, cited in note 77.

79. Ltr, Laird to Kissinger, 27 Oct 1970 (quote), folder DoD vol. 9, box 225, Agency Files, NSC, Nixon Library; memo, Laird for Nixon, 27 Jan 1971 (quote), folder ABM 58–61, box 27, Laird Papers, Ford Library.

80. Memo, Allison for Moorer, 29 Jan 1971, folder 9, box 2, Moorer Diary, Acc 218-05-006, NARA II; NSDM 97, 8 Feb 1971, folder ABM 58-61, box 27, Laird Papers, Ford Library.

81. Memo, Belieu for MacGregor, 5 Apr 1971, attached to memo, Haig for Kissinger, 8 Apr 1971, folder Haig Chron Apr 8–12, 1971 [2 of 2], box 978, Haig Chron Files, NSC, Nixon Library.

82. Memo, Pursley for Haig, 17 Apr 1971 (quote), attached to memo, Haig for Lehman, 20 Apr 1971, folder Apr 19–23, 1971 [2 of 2], box 979, ibid.

83. Memcon by Smith, 19 May 1971; Conversation among Nixon, Laird, Kissinger, 19 May 1971: both in FRUS 1969–1976, 32:491–97; Remarks on SALT, 20 May 1971, *Nixon Public Papers 1971*, 648; memo Resor for Packard, 25 May 1971, folder Safeguard ABM Calendar 5, box 18, Laird Papers, Ford Library.

84. NSDM 117, 2 Jul 1971, folder 15, box 3, Moorer Diary, Acc 218-05-006; memo, Laird for Kissinger, 20 Jul 1971, folder SALT vol. 15 [1 of 3], box 881, NSC, Nixon Library; memo, Laird for Kissinger, 12 Jul 1971 (quote); JCSM 330-71 for SecDef, 13 Jul 1971: both in folder SALT 264–266, box 26, Laird Papers, Ford Library.

85. NSDM 120, 20 Jul 1971, folder NSDMs 97–144 1971, box 364, Subject Files, NSC, Nixon Library.

86. Memo, Nutter for Laird, 31 Jul 1971; JCSM-361-71 for SecDef, 31 Jul 1971 (quote): both in folder SALT 271–273, box 26, Laird Papers, Ford Library; memo, JCSM-366-71 for SecDef, 6 Aug 1971, folder 16, box 3, Moorer Diary, Acc 218-05-006.

87. Memo, Tucker for Laird, 30 Jul 1971, attached to memo Laird for Nixon, 2 Aug 1971, folder SALT 271–273, box 26, Laird Papers, Ford Library.

88. Memo, Laird for Nixon, 2 Aug 1971, cited in note 87.

89. Conversation among Nixon, Laird, JCS, et al., 10 Aug 1971, *FRUS 1969–1976*, 32:587–96; 588, 589, 591, 593 (quotes).

90. NSDM 127, 12 Aug 1971, ibid., 598–99.

91. Memo, Tucker for Laird, 2 Sep 1971, attached to memo, Laird for Kissinger, 4 Sep 1971, folder SALT 274–278, box 26, Laird Papers, Ford Library.

92. Memo, Laird for Nixon, 15 Sep 1971 (quote), ibid.; memo, Smith for Kissinger, 17 Sep 1971, folder SALT vol. 17 [1 of 2], box 882, SALT, NSC, Nixon Library.

93. Memo, Kissinger for Nixon, 20 Sep 1971, attached to memo, Nixon for Laird, 22 Sep 1971, folder SALT vol. 17 [1 of 2], box 882, SALT, NSC, Nixon Library.

94. CM-1232-71 for Laird, 28 Sep 1971 (quotes), folder SALT 279–282, box 26, Laird Papers, Ford Library; JSCM-484-71 for Laird, 1 Nov 1971 (quote), folder 5, box H-032, H Files, NSC, Nixon Library.

95. Memo, Laird for Kissinger, 29 Oct 1971, folder SALT vol. 17 [1 of 2], box 882, SALT, NSC, Nixon Library; "OSD Position Summary" attached to memo, Packard for Kissinger, 6 Nov 1971, folder SALT 11/3/71, box H-009, H Files, ibid.

96. Kissinger, *White House Years*, 1130. See also chapter 15 for a discussion of Trident.

97. NSDM 140, 15 Nov 1971; *FRUS 1969–1976*, 32:645–46.

98. Memos, Laird for Nixon, 18 Jan 1972 (quote); Odeen/Sonnenfeldt for Kissinger, 20 Jan 1972, both attached to memo, Nixon for Laird, 9 Feb 1972, folder SALT vol. 17 [2 of 3], box 882, SALT, NSC, Nixon Library.

99. Memos, Laird for Nixon, 18 Jan 1972 (quote); Odeen/Sonnenfeldt for Kissinger, 20 Jan 1972; Kissinger for Nixon 8 Feb 1972: all attached to memo, Nixon for Laird, 9 Feb 1972, ibid.; Kissinger, *White House Years*, 1130 –31.

100. Memo, Laird for Kissinger et al., 17 Feb 1972, folder ABM 58–61, box 27, Laird Papers, Ford Library.

101. JCSM-99-72 for SecDef, 6 Mar 1972, folder SALT 298–300, box 26, ibid.

102. Memo for the Record, NSC Meeting, 17 Mar 1972, folder NSC Minutes 1971– [2 of 5], box H-110, H Files. NSC, Nixon Library.

103. Memos, Laird for Nixon, 11 Apr 1972; Kissinger for Nixon, 18 Apr 1972: both attached to ltr, Nixon to Laird, 20 Apr 1972, folder SALT vol. 17 [1 of 3], box 882, SALT, ibid.

104. NSDM 164, 1 May 1972, *FRUS 1969–1976*, 32:801–03.

105. Kissinger, *White House Years*, 1130–31, 1148–50; Van Atta, *With Honor*, 197–99; Anatoly Dobrynin, *In Confidence: Moscow's Ambassador to America's Six Cold War Presidents (1962–1986)* (New York: Random House, 1995), 209, 213; memcon, 22 Apr 1972, Brezhnev and Kissinger, in *Soviet-American Relations*, Keefer, ed., 716–20.

106. U.S.-Soviet Treaty on Limitation of ABM Systems and Interim Agreement on Limitation of Offensive Arms, 26 May 1972, *FRUS 1969–1976*, 32:908–17.

107. Moorer Diary, 25 May 1972, folder 25, box 5, Acc 218-050-006; CM-1880-72 for Kissinger, 26 May 1972 (quote), attached to msg, Haig to Kissinger, 26 May 1972, folder Haig Chron May 21–31, 1972, box 993, Haig Chron Files, NSC, Nixon Library.

108. JCSM-258-72 for SecDef. 2 Jun 1972, folder SALT 318–321, box 26, Laird Papers, Ford Library.

109. Memo, Laird for SecArmy, 26 May 1972, folder Safeguard ABM Calendar 5, box 18, ibid.; memo, Odeen for Kissinger, 7 Jun 1972, folder DoD vol. 17, box 231, Agency Files, NSC, Nixon Library.

110. Newhouse, *Cold Dawn*, 265.

111. Van Atta, *With Honor*, 194, 196.

112. Conversation, Nixon w/Kissinger, and Haldeman, 9 Mar 1972, *FRUS 1969–1976*, 32:692–95.

16. Realistic Deterrence? The FY 1973 Budget

1. *U.S. Budget in Brief FY 1972*, 5 (quotes), 8; *Cong. Rec.*, 24 Jan 1972, H 187; "'A Very Good Year'—For Which Party," *Newsweek*, 31 Jan 1972, 62–64.

2. Memo, Laird for Nixon, "Strategy for Peace," 6 Nov 1970, attached to memo, Laird for Nixon, 7 Nov 1970, folder Defense Memo for President, box 241, Agency Files, NSC, Nixon Library; Strategy of Realistic Deterrence, Calendar of Documents, vol. 1, folder Strategy of Realistic Deterrence, box 15, Laird Papers, Ford Library. The calendar describes Baroody's memo.

3. "Strategy for Peace," 6 Nov 1970, cited in note 2.

4. Ibid.

5. Ibid.; memo, Smith for Kissinger, 10 Nov 1970 (quotes), folder DoD vol. 9, box 225, Agency Files, NSC, Nixon Library. Emphasis in original.

6. Memo, Nixon for Laird, 1 Dec 1970, attached to memo, Kissinger for Nixon, 25 Nov 1970, folder DoD vol. 9, box 225, Agency Files, NSC, Nixon Library. Nixon's handwritten comments appear on Kisssinger's memo.

7. Memo, Laird for Nixon, 16 Dec 1970, folder Strategy 15, box 28, Laird Papers, Ford Library.

8. Memo, Smith for Kissinger, 21 Dec 1970, folder DPRC & Def Budget 1970 vol. 2, box 235, Agency Files, NSC, Nixon Library.

9. Memo, Smith for Kissinger, 8 Jan 1971, folder DoD vol. 10, box 226, ibid. Quotes from Kissinger's handwritten comments dated 15 Jan 1971.

10. Memo, Smith for Kissinger, 30 Jan 1971, attached to memo, Kissinger for Laird, 3 Feb 1971, folder DPRC & Def Budget 1971, box 236, ibid.; memo, Seamans for Laird, 12 Feb 1971, folder Strategy 21-23, box 28, Laird Papers, Ford Library; memo, Smith for Kissinger, 20 Feb 1971, folder 4, box H-101, H Files, NSC, Nixon Library; Memo for the Record of 18 Feb 1971 Meeting w/Kissinger and Laird, 1 Mar 1971, folder Haig Chron Mar 1–6, 1971 [1 of 2], box 977, Haig Chron Files, NSC, Nixon Library.

11. JCSM-57-71 for SecDef, 9 Feb 1971, folder Strategy 18-20, box 28, Laird Papers, Ford Library.

12. Memo, Seamans for Laird, 12 Feb 1971, folder Strategy 21–23; memo, Chafee for Laird, 8 Feb 1971, folder Strategy 18–20: both ibid.

13. Assessment of Tentative Strategy Guidance, Chief of Staff, United States Army, n.d., attached to memo, Resor for Laird, 12 Feb 1971, folder Strategy 21–23, ibid.

14. Memo, Kissinger for USecState et al., 24 Feb 1971, folder CIA vol. 4, box 208, Agency Files, NSC, Nixon Library.

15. Memo, Packard for Service Secretaries et al., 10 Feb 1971, Planning Guidance Assumptions, folder 1, box H-102, H Files, ibid.

16. Memo, Packard for Service Secretaries et al., 16 Jan 1971, folder DPRC and Def Budget 1971, box 236, Agency Files, NSC, Nixon Library; memo, Packard for Service Secretaries et al., 10 Feb 1971, Tentative Fiscal Guidance, folder 1, box H-102, H Files, ibid.

17. JCSM-95-71 for SecDef, 3 Mar 1971, folder Vietnam 334-336A, box 35, Laird Papers, Ford Library.

18. Memo, Resor for Laird, 13 Apr 1971, folder Strategy 24–27, box 28, ibid.

19. Memo, Seamans for Laird, 13 Apr 1971, ibid.

20. Memo, Chafee for Laird, 12 Apr, 21 Apr 1971, ibid.

21. Memo, Smith for Kissinger, 27 Feb 1971 (quotes), folder DPRC and Def Budget 1971, box 236, Agency Files; memo, Smith for Kissinger, n.d., folder DPRC Mtg 3-22-71, box H-102, H Files: both in NSC, Nixon Library.

22. Memo, Morrill for Shultz, 20 Mar 1970, folder DPRC Mtg 3-22-71, box H-102, H Files; telcon, Shultz and Kissinger, 26 Apr 1971, folder 10, box 9, HAK telcons; memo, Smith for Kissinger, 23 Apr 1971, folder DPRC Mtg 4-26-71, box H-102, H Files: all in ibid.

23. Agenda and Talking Points for the April 26 DPRC Meeting, folder DPRC Mtg 4-26-71, box H-102, H Files, ibid.

24. Telcon, Laird and Kissinger, 10:15 a.m., 29 Mar 1971, folder 6, box 9, HAK Telcons, ibid.

25. Minutes, DPRC Meeting, 26 Apr 1971, attached to memo, Davis for Kissinger, 7 May 1971; memo, Kissinger for USecState, 28 Apr 1971 (quote): both in folder DPRC and Def Budget 1971, box 236, Agency Files, ibid.; Memo for the Record, 26 Apr 1971, folder 12, box 2, Moorer Diary, Acc 218-05-006, NARA II.

26. Memo, Kissinger for USecState et al., 26 Mar 1971, attached to memo, Haig for Kissinger, 25 Mar 1971, folder DoD vol. 11, box 226, Agency Files, NSC, Nixon Library.

27. Minutes, DPRC Meeting, 26 Apr 1971; memo, Kissinger for USecState, 28 Apr 71 (quote); Memo for the Record, 26 Apr 1971: all cited in note 25.

28. Revised Policy and Planning Guidance for the FY 73–77 Defense Program (quotes), attached to memo, Laird for Service Secretaries et al., 22 Jun 1971, folder DPRC Mtg 15–17 Jul 1971, box H-103, H Files, NSC, Nixon Library. Packard sent Laird's guidance to Kissinger; see ltr, Packard to Kissinger, 3 Jul 1971, folder DoD vol. 12, box 227, Agency Files, ibid.

29. Memo, Smith for Kissinger, 12 July 1971, folder DPRC Mtg July 15–17 1971, box H-103, H Files; memo, Laird for Nixon, 16 Jul 1971, attached to memo, Smith for Kissinger, 22 Jul 1971 (quotes), folder DoD vol. 12 cont, box 227, Agency Files: both in NSC, Nixon Library; memo, Welander for Moorer, 31 July 1971; Talking Paper, 21 Jul 1971: both in folder 15, box 3, Moorer Dairy, Acc 218-05-006; telcon, Kissinger and Moorer, 2 Aug 1971 (quote), folder 1, box 11, HAK Telcons, NSC, Nixon Library.

30. Minutes, SecDef Staff Meeting, 2 Aug 1971 (quotes), folder Staff Mtgs Jul–Sep 1971, box 14, AFPC and SecDef Staff Mtgs, Acc 330-77-0062, WNRC; DoD Background Paper for DPRC Meeting, 3 Aug 1971, folder 1, box H-104, H Files, NSC, Nixon Library; Memo for the Record by Moorer, 2 Aug 1971, folder 16, box 3, Moorer Diary, Acc 218-05-006; memo

for Director Plans and Policy, Joint Staff, n.d., folder DPRC and Def Budget 1971, box 236, Agency Files, NSC, Nixon Library.

31. Minutes, DPRC Meeeting 5 Aug 1971 (quotes), folder DPRC Minutes [2 of 3], box H-118, H Files, NSC, Nixon Library.

32. Ibid.

33. Memo, Kissinger for Nixon, n.d., folder 2, box H-032, ibid.

34. Memcon, NSC Meeting, 13 Aug 1971 (quotes), folder NSC Minutes 1971 [3 of 5], box H-110, ibid.

35. Address to the Nation, *Nixon Public Papers 1971*, 886–91; memo, Smith for Kissinger, 16 Aug 1971, folder DPRC and Def Budget 1971, box 236, Agency Files, ibid.; Minutes, SecDef Staff Meeting, 12 Oct 1971, folder Staff Mtgs Oct–Dec 1971, box 14, AFPC and Staff Mtgs, Acc 330-77-0062; Joan Hoff, *Nixon Reconsidered* (New York: Basic Books, 1994), 138–44.

36. Memo, Smith for Kissinger, 29 Oct 1971, folder DoD vol. 13, box 228, Agency Files, NSC, Nixon Library; memo, Welander for Moorer, 12 Nov 1971 (quote), folder 19, box 3, Moorer Diary, Acc 218-05-006; telcon, Kissinger and Shultz, 28 Oct 1971 (quote), folder 11, box 11, HAK Telcons, NSC, Nixon Library.

37. Memo, Smith for Haig, 26 Oct 1971 (quote), folder FY 73–74 Budget, box 146, HAK Office Files; NSC, Nixon Library.

38. Memo, Court for Kissinger, 23 Nov 1971, ibid.

39. Ltr, Kissinger to Laird, 2 Dec 1971, folder DPRC Mtg 12-8-71, box H-104, H Files, ibid.; telcons, Kissinger and Laird, 2 Dec 1971, 10:30 am, 10:34 am, 3 Dec 1971, folder 4, box 12, HAK Telcons, ibid.; "SLBM Initiative—Key Issues," n.d., folder OMB 1971, box 268, Agency Files, ibid.

40. Memo, Laird for Nixon, 8 Dec 1971 (quotes), attached to memo, Odeen for Kissinger, 11 Dec 1971, folder DoD vol. 14-2, box 229, Agency Files, ibid.

41. Memo, Odeen for Kissinger, 11 Dec 1971 (quote), cited in note 40.

42. Telcon, Nixon and Kissinger, 11 Dec 1971, 2:45 p.m., folder 6, box 12, HAK Telcons, NSC, Nixon Library.

43. Telcons, Kissinger and Shultz, 11 Dec 1971, 3:00 p.m., 5:15 p.m., ibid.

44. Telcon, Kissinger and Laird, 11 Dec 1971, 3:35pm, ibid.; telcon, Kissinger and Haldeman, 11 Dec 1971, folder HAK Closed Telcons, box 1, ibid.

45. Memo, Laird for Kissinger, 14 Dec 1971, folder Pursley Chron 11/71 to 1/72, box 16, SecDef Files, Acc 330-75-104; memo, Odeen for Kissinger, 16 Dec 71 (quote), folder DPRC and Def Budget 1971, box 236, Agency Files, NSC, Nixon Library; telcon, Kissinger and Laird, 16 Dec 1971, folder 7, box 12, HAK Telcons, ibid.

46. Ltr, Kissinger to Laird, 22 Dec 1971, attached to memo, Odeen for Kissinger, n.d., folder DoD vol. 15, box 230, Agency Files, NSC, Nixon Library.

47. Telcon, Kissinger and Laird, 23 Dec 1971 (quote), folder 8, box 12, HAK Telcons, ibid.; memo, Laird for Kissinger, 24 Dec 1971, attached to memo, Odeen for Kissinger, n.d., cited in note 46.

48. Memo, Kissinger for Laird, 4 Jan 1972 (quotes), attached to memo, Odeen for Kissinger, n.d., cited in note 46.

49. Annual Budget Message, 24 Jan 1972, *Nixon Public Papers 1972*, 78–85, 83 (quote); OMB, *The Budget of the United States Government, Fiscal Year 1973* (Washington, DC: Government Printing Office, 1972), 78; *U.S. Budget in Brief FY 1973*, 7; Statement by the President, 24 Jan 1972, folder Fed Budget FY 1973, box 792, Subject Files, OSD/HO.

50. *Budget of the United States Government FY 1973*, 270–82.

51. OSD(C), "Budget Facts FY 1973," n.d., folder Staff Mtgs Jan–Mar 1972, box 15, SecDef Records, Acc 330-77-0062.

52. Ltr, Stennis to Laird, 8 Dec 1971 (quote), folder DoD Budget FY 72, box 791, Subject Files, OSD/HO.

53. "Criticism of Budget Mounts; Military Spending, Deficit Hit," *Washington Star*, 25 Jan 1972.

54. *Cong. Rec.*, 24 Jan 1972, H 187–188 (quote); *Cong. Rec.*, 24 Jan 1972, S 401–403.

55. Michael Getler and George C. Wilson, "Laird to Press Rise in Spending," *Washington Post*, 16 Feb 1972; Mark R. Arnold, "Laird Seeks Record $83.4 Billion for Modernizing Arsenal, Lifting Salaries," *National Observer*, 26 Feb 1972; Minutes, SecDef Staff Meeting, 24 Apr 1972, folder Staff Mtgs Apr–Jun 1972, box 15, SecDef Records, Acc 330-77-0062.

56. *Cong. Rec.*, 24 Jan 1972, S 357–363; "McGovern's Defense Proposals: Drawing Attention," *Congressional Quarterly*, 24 Jun 1972; Korb, *Fall and Rise of the Pentagon*, 69.

57. *Washington Post*, 16 Feb 1972, cited in note 55; Korb, *Fall and Rise of the Pentagon*, 69; Minutes, SecDef Staff Meeting, 20 Mar 1972 (quote), folder Staff Mtgs Jan–Mar 1972, box 15, SecDef Records, Acc 330-77-0062.

58. "Trident II D–5 Fleet Ballistic Missile," <https://web.archive.org/web/20140220230123/http://www.fas.org/nuke/guide/usa/slbm/d-5.htm>, accessed 7 Nov 2014; Ray Moseley, "Pentagon Wants Whole New Submarine System to Foil Russians," *Philadelphia Bulletin*, 5 Mar 1972; Harry Levins, "Laird's New Arms Strategy," *St. Louis Post Dispatch*, 17 Mar 1972; Herbert Scoville Jr., "Laird's Latest Alarms," *New Republic*, 25 Mar 1972; Philip W. McKinsey, "U.S. defense budget draws fire from Congress," *Christian Science Monitor*, 17 Apr 1972.

59. Michael Getler, "AF Counterattacks Over Budget, Scorns Navy Fear of Soviet Fleet," *Washington Post*, 18 Mar 1972.

60. Memo, Laird for Nixon, 2 May 1972 (quote), folder Laird 3, box A75, Baroody Papers, Ford Library; George C. Wilson, "House Votes Against Cutoff of War Funds," *Washington Post*, 28 Jun 1972. Laird's memorandum did not make explicit whether the senators sought to cut budget authority, expenditures or both.

61. *Cong. Rec.*, 24 Jan 1972, S 357–363 (quote, S 357); *Cong. Quarterly*, 24 Jun 1972 cited in note 56; Korb, *Fall and Rise of the Pentagon*, 71.

62. SCA, *Foreign Assistance and Related Programs Appropriations for Fiscal Year 1973: Hearings*, 92nd Cong., 2nd sess., 5 Jun 1972, 858 (quote), 859–860; Alan Horton, "Laird flays McG 'white flag' Plan," *Washington News*, 7 July 1972; Orr Kelly, "McGovern Plan for Defense Emerging as Top Vote Issue," *Washington Star*, 7 Jul 1972.

63. SCA, *Foreign Assistance and Related Programs Appropriations for Fiscal Year 1973: Hearings*, 5 Jun 1972, 858–60; ltr, Laird to Proxmire, 5 Jul 1972, folder DoD Budget Jul 1972–, box 792, Subject Files, OSD/HO; Robert Sherrill, "SCRAM, SCAD, ULMS and other aspects of the $85.9-billion defense budget," *New York Times*, 30 Jul 1972; *Laird News Conference*, 6 Jul 1972, *Laird Public Statements 1972*, 7:2789–2800; 2790 (quote).

64. Orr Kelly, "Economic Impact of Defense," *Washington Star*, 11 July 1972; Korb, *Fall and Rise of the Pentagon*, 73–77; 74. Moot's analysis was also printed in the September 28, 1972 edition of *Commanders Digest*, a DoD newsletter.

65. ASD(C), "The Economics of Defense Spending," Jul 1972, folder Staff Mtgs Jul–Sep 1972, box 15, Acc 330-77-0062; *DoD Key Officials 1947–2004*, 80, 82.

66. Laird interview, 11 Oct 2001, 12.

67. Memos, Laird for Kissinger, 12 Jul 1972; Kissinger for Laird, 28 Jun 1972: both attached to memo, Odeen for Kissinger, 25 Jul 1972, folder DPRC and the Def Budget Jan–Jul 1972, box 237, Agency Files, NSC, Nixon Library.

68. Special Message to Congress, 26 Jul 1972, *Nixon Public Papers 1972*, 741–44.

69. Memo, Laird for Nixon, 31 Jul 1972; attached to memo, Odeen for Kissinger, 1 Aug 1972, folder DPRC and Def Budget Aug–Dec 1972, box 237, Agency Files, NSC, Nixon Library.

70. Orr Kelly, "Budget Lid Move Scored by Laird," *Washington Star*, 1 Aug 1972 (quotes); Laird press interview, 2 Aug 1972, *Laird Public Statements 1972*, 7:3025–26.

71. Laird's public statements about the budget ceiling resulted in a flurry of phone conversations between Weinberger and Kissinger, Laird and Kissinger, and Ehrlichman and Kissinger. See telcons, Kissinger and Weinberger, 2 Aug 1972 and 5 Aug 1972; telcons, Kissinger and Ehrlichman, 2 Aug 1972 (quote), 3 Aug 1972; telcons, Kissinger and Laird, 2 Aug 1972 (quote), 3 Aug 1972, 11:14 a.m., 12:05 p.m., 5:14 p.m.: all in folder 6, box 15, HAK Telcons, NSC, Nixon Library.

72. Telcon, Kissinger and Weinberger, 29 Sep 1972, folder 3, box 16, ibid.

73. Memo, Odeen for Kissinger, 6 Oct 1972 (quote), folder DPRC and Def Budget Aug–Dec 1972, box 237, Agency Files; memo, Odeen for Kissinger, 27 Nov 1972, folder FY 73–74 Budget, box 146, HAK Office Files: both in NSC, Nixon Library.

74. *Cong. Rec.*, 13 Sep 1972, H 8320–21; John W. Finney, "House Unit Votes $4.3 Billion Cut in Outlays," *New York Times*, 12 Sep 1972.

75. HCA, *Department of Defense Appropriation Bill, 1973: Report*, 92nd Cong., 2nd sess., 11 Sep 1972, H. Rept. 92-1389, 12–14; Finney "House Unit Votes Most of Weapons Sought," *Christian Science Monitor*, 12 Sep 1972; Finney, "House Unit Votes $4.3 Billion Cut in Outlays," cited in note 74.

76. SCA, *Department of Defense Appropriation Bill: Report, 1973*, 2nd Cong., 2nd sess., 29 Sep 1972, S. Rept. 29-1243; *Cong. Rec.*, 12 Oct 72, H 9770–71; *Cong. Rec.*, 13 Oct 1972, S 17963–66; ltr, Laird to McClellan, 5 Oct 1972, folder DoD Appropriation FY 73, box 793, Subject Files, OSD/HO.

77. "Statement About Decision to Sign 37 Bills," 28 Oct 1972, *Nixon Public Papers 1972*, 1054. The text of Public Law 92-570 is in 86 Stat 1184. Minutes, SecDef Staff Meetings 10, 16 Oct 1972, folder Staff Mtgs Oct–Dec 1972, box 15, Acc 330-77-0062.

78. "Radio Address on Defense Policy," 29 Oct 1972, *Nixon Public Papers 1972*, 1065–66.

79. OASD(C), "Appropriation Acts by Appropriation Title with Comparison to President's Budget Request, FY 1973," FAD 749/73, 9 Oct 1973, Box 826D, Subject Files, OSD/HO.

80. News Conference, 11 Oct 1972, *Laird Public Statements 1972*, 8:3356–58; memo, Odeen for Kissinger, 27 Nov 1972, folder FY 73–74 Budget, box 146, HAK Office Files; memos, Haig for Kissinger, 14 Dec 1972 (quote); Odeen for Kissinger, 19 Dec 1972 (quote): both in folder DPRC and Def Budget Aug–Dec 1972, box 237, Agency Files: all in NSC, Nixon Library; Minutes, SecDef Staff Meeting, 24 Oct 1972, 13 Nov 1972, folder Staff Mtgs Oct–Dec 1972, box 15, Acc 330-77-0062; memo, Kissinger for Nixon, 2 Aug 1972, attached to ltr, Nixon to Laird, 8 Aug 1972, folder DPRC and Def Budget Jan–Jul 1972, box 237, Agency Files, NSC, Nixon Library.

81. Minutes, SecDef Staff Meeting 10 Oct 1972 (quote), cited in note 77.

82. *DoD Key Officials*, 90.

17. Military Assistance

1. Van Atta, *With Honor*, 41–42.

2. Laird statement, HSC, *Department of Defense Appropriations for 1971: Hearings*, 91st Cong., 2nd sess., 25 Feb 1970, 56–57.

3. Ibid.; Drea, *McNamara, Clifford, and the Burdens of Vietnam*, 455–82.

4. Ltr, Johnson to Packard, 7 Feb 1969; Joint State-Defense DPM, 1 Feb 1969: both attached to memo, Earle for Packard, 10 Feb 1969, folder FY 1970 Budget, box 81, RG 330 Budget ASD(C) Files, OSD/HO.

5. See for example the comments of Rep. George E. Brown of California, *Cong. Rec.*, 27 Mar 1969, H 2487–88.

6. HCFA, *Foreign Assistance Act of 1969: Hearings*, 91st Cong., 1st sess., 24 Jun 1969, pt. 3:516–17 (quotes); memo, Laird for Service Secretaries et al., 19 Apr 1969 (quote), folder Foreign Mil Sales, box A 71, Baroody Papers, Ford Library; White House Press Release, 22 Dec 1969, folder Mil Assistance 1969, box 63, Subject Files, OSD/HO.

7. SCFR, *Foreign Assistance Act, 1969: Hearings*, 91st Cong., 1st sess., 15 Jul 1969, 91–92.

8. Memo, Kissinger for Nixon, 25 Mar 1969; memo, Kissinger for Nixon, 1 Apr 1969, attached to "List of Invitees, n.d.: both in folder Foreign Aid, box H-021, H Files, NSC, Nixon Library; Talking Paper for SecDef, attached to memo, Davis for Office of Vice

President et al., 27 Mar 1970, folder 25 NSC Mtg, box 2, Records from SecDef Vault, Acc 330-74-142, WNRC.

9. Memo, Nixon for SecState et al., 5 Mar 1970; Talking Paper, 27 Mar 1970: both in folder 25, NSC Mtg, box 2, Records from SecDef Vault, Acc 330-74-142; NSDM 76, 10 Aug 1970, attached to memo, Davis for recipients of NSDM 76, 11 Aug 1970, folder NSDM 51–96, box 363, Subject Files, NSC, Nixon Library.

10. President's Special Message to Congress, 15 Sep 1970, *Nixon Public Papers 1970*, 745–48.

11. Memo, Laird for Nixon, 10 Aug 1971, attached to ltr, Kissinger to Laird, 1 Sep 1971, folder DoD vol. 13, box 228, Agency Files, NSC, Nixon Library; Rearden draft, Occasional Paper 5, "Détente and Vietnam: The Laird Years," 8 Feb 2011, 16, OSD/HO.

12. Memo, Laird for Nixon, 10 Aug 1971, cited in note 11.

13. Memo, Kissinger for Nixon, 14 Jul 1970, *FRUS 1969–1976*, 4:337, 342.

14. Memos, Rogers for Nixon, 4 Aug 1970, ibid., 69–70; Rogers for Nixon, 19 Feb 1971, ibid., 116–119.

15 Memo, Kissinger for Nixon, 17 Mar 1971, ibid., 134–37; memo, Haig for Kissinger, 24 Mar 1971, folder Haig Chron Sep 21–28, 1971, [2 of 2], box 987, Haig Chron Files, NSC, Nixon Library.

16. Memo, Nutter for Laird, 12 Dec 1969, attached to memo, Laird for Nixon, 13 Dec 1969 (quotes), folder Taiwan 1-6, box 21, Laird Papers, Ford Library.

17. Memo, Mayo for Nixon, 26 Dec 1969, folder BoB vol. 1-1, box 206, Agency Files, NSC, Nixon Library.

18. Memo, Laird for Nixon, 12 Jan 1970 (quote), attached to note WW to HAK, 22 Jan 1970, folder DoD vol. 5, box 223, ibid.; DoD, "Military Assistance and Foreign Military Sales May 1973," 5, folder Military Assistance 1973, box 64, Subject Files, OSD/HO.

19. Memo, Bergsten for Kissinger, 7 Jul 1970, folder WSAG [3 of 5], box H-070, H Files, NSC, Nixon Library; Webb, *JCS and the War in Vietnam 1969–1970*, 194; Peter Braestrup, "Pentagon Asks Funds for Military Aid," *Washington Post*, 2 Apr 1970; Lewis Sorley, *Arms Transfers under Nixon: A Policy Analysis* (Lexington: University Press of Kentucky, 1983), 27–28.

20. Memos, Laird for Kissinger, 11 Sep 1970 (quote), folder DoD vol. 8; Laird for Kissinger, 14 Oct 1970, folder DoD vol. 9: both in Agency Files, NSC, Nixon Library.

21. Memos, Weinberger for Nixon, 26 Sep 1970, *FRUS 1969–76*, 4:79–82; Kissinger for Nixon 6 Oct 1970, ibid., 4:84–85.

22. Memcon, 18 Nov 1970, ibid., 4:98–102 (quote, 99); White House Press Release, 18 Nov 1970, *Nixon Public Papers 1970*, 1074–79.

23. HCA, *Supplemental Appropriation Bill, 1971: Hearings*, 91st Cong., 2nd sess., 25 Nov 1970, 1282ff; SCFR, *Supplemental Foreign Assistance Authorization, 1970: Hearings*, 91st Cong., 2nd sess., 10–11 Dec 1970, 83–85.

24. Ibid., 104–06.

25. HCAS, *Supplemental Appropriation Bill, 1971: Hearings*, 25 Nov 1970, 1282ff; SCFR, *Supplemental Foreign Assistance Authorization, 1970: Hearings*, 10–11 Dec 1970, 83–85; 103–06; House of Representatives, *Supplemental Foreign Assistance Authorization*, 91st Cong., 2nd sess., H. Rept. 91-1791, 21 Dec 1970, 1–2 (quote).

26. Memos, Bergsten/Smith for Kissinger, 18 Dec 1970; Packard for Nixon, 30 Dec 1970; Rogers for Nixon, 31 Dec 1970: all attached to memo, Smith for Kissinger, 4 Jan 1971 (quote), folder DoD vol. 10, box 225, Agency Files, NSC, Nixon Library.

27. SCFR, *Foreign Assistance Legislation, Fiscal Year 1972: Hearings*, 92nd Cong., 1st sess., 14 Jun 1971, 336; President's Special Message to Congress, 21 Apr 1971, *Nixon Public Papers 1971*, 564–68, 567 (quote).

28. Spencer Rich, "Rogers Goes Hunting New Foreign Aid Bill," *Washington Post*, 4 Nov 1971; Rich, "Military Aid Voted in Senate," *Washington Post*, 12 Nov 1971; Laurence Stern, "U.S. Military Aid Program is Embroiled in Major Controversy," *Washington Post*, 7 May 1972 (quote); "Foreign Aid: The Dawn of a New Era," *Newsweek*, 15 Nov 1971, 40–41.

29. Felix Belair Jr., "Senate, 65 to 24, Votes $1.5 Billion for Foreign Aid," *New York Times*, 12 Nov 1971.

30. Ltr, Laird to Shultz, 24 Nov 1971 (quote), attached to memo, Kennedy/Hormats for Kissinger, 6 Dec 1971, folder DoD vol. 14-2, box 229, Agency Files, NSC, Nixon Library.

31. "Concept for Security Assistance in Defense Budget," attached to memo, Kennedy/Hormats for Kissinger, cited in note 30.

32. "Precis of OMB Paper," (quote), attached to memo, Kennedy/Hormats for Kissinger, 6 Dec 1971, cited in note 30; memo, Kissinger for Nixon, 31 Jan 1972, folder DPRC and Def Budget Jan-Jul 72, box 237, Agency Files, NSC, Nixon Library.

33. Memo, Kissinger for Nixon, 31 Jan 1972, cited in note 32; memo, Kissinger for Laird, 17 Mar 1972, *FRUS 1969–1976*, 4:214–15.

34. Memo, Shultz for Nixon, 23 Dec 1971; memo, Kissinger for Nixon, n.d.: both in *FRUS 1969–76*, 4:183–86; 184 (quote).

35. Memo, Laird for Nixon, 4 Jan 1972 (quote), attached to memo, Kennedy for Kissinger, 4 Jan 1972, folder DoD vol. 15, box 230, Agency Files, NSC, Nixon Library; President's Special Message to Congress, 14 Mar 1972, *Nixon Public Papers 1972*, 412–13; DoD, "Military Assistance and Foreign Military Sales Facts," May 1973, 5, 17, cited in note 18.

36. "An Approach to a Flexible Arms Supply Policy," attached to memo, Nutter for Packard, 19 May 1970, folder Mid East 37–45, box 11, Laird Papers, Ford Library.

37. Memo, Hughes for SecState, 16 May 1969, folder USSR vol. 2 4/22/69, box 709, CF–Europe, NSC, Nixon Library; Drea, *McNamara, Clifford, and the Burdens of Vietnam*, 424–55; Kissinger, *White House Years*, 345; William Tuohy, "Arab Commando Aide Hints More Raids on Israeli Airliners," *Washington Post*, 2 Jan 1969.

38. Talking Paper for Laird and Wheeler by Warnke and Johnson, n.d., folder Mid East 1–5, box 11, Laird Papers, Ford Library.

39. CM-4542-69 for Laird, 6 Sep 1969, folder Mid East 13–17, ibid.

40. Ibid; memo, Nutter for Laird, 8 Oct 1969 folder Mid East 18–25, ibid.; A.D. Horne, Arms Aid Stressed by Israel," *Washington Post*, 26, Sep 1969; Horne, "Further U.S. Arms Aid Indicated by Mrs. Meir," *Washington Post*, 27 Sep 1969.

41. Memcon, Packard and Rabin, 21 Oct 1969; NSSM 81, 6 Nov 1969: both in folder Mid East 18–25, box 11, Laird Papers, Ford Library; "Israel's Requests for Military and Economic Assistance," 2 Jan 1970 (quote), folder 6, box H-041, H Files, NSC, Nixon Library; memo, Nutter for Laird, 8 Oct 1969, cited in note 40.

42. Memo, Nutter for Laird, 6 Feb 1970, attached to memo, Murphy for Packard, 9 Feb 1970, folder Mid East 26–34, box 11, Laird Papers, Ford Library; memos, Kissinger for Nixon, 10 Feb 1970, folder USSR vol. 5; 18 Feb 1970, folder USSR vol. 7: both in box 711, CF–Europe, NSC, Nixon Library; Options Paper, attached to memo, Packard for Kissinger, 25 Feb 1970, folder Mid East 35–36, box 11, Laird Papers, Ford Library.

43. Memo, Kissinger for Sisco, 2 Mar 1970, folder Haig Chron Mar 1–11, 1970 [2 of 2], box 963, Haig Chron Files, NSC, Nixon Library; Nixon, *Memoirs*, 479–81; memo, Rogers for Nixon, 3 Mar 1970 (quote), attached to memo, Kissinger for Laird, 13 Mar 1970, folder 70, box 6, Records from SecDef Vault, Acc 330-74-142.

44. Memo, Laird for Kissinger, 18 Mar 1970, folder Mid East 37–45, box 11, Laird Papers, Ford Library.

45. Memos, Kissinger for Laird, 23 Mar 1970; Kissinger for Laird, 13 Apr 1970: both ibid.; Laird for Kissinger, 6 Apr 1970, folder 70, box 6, Records from SecDef Vault, Acc 330-74-142.

46. "Talking Points on the Middle East," 6 Apr 70, folder 70, box 6, Records from the SecDef Vault, Acc 330-74-142; memo, Kissinger for Nixon, 18 Mar 70, folder Haig Chron Mar 12–20 1970 [1 of 2], box 963, Haig Chron Files, NSC, Nixon Library; Kissinger, *White House Years*, 569, 572 (quote).

47. Memo for the Record, Meeting of NSC Special Review Group, 21 May 1970, folder SRG Minutes 1970 [4 of 5], box H-111, H Files, NSC, Nixon Library; memo, Nutter for Packard, 26 May 1970; memo, Nutter for Laird, 21 May 1970: both in folder Mid East 37–45, box 11, Laird Papers, Ford Library.

48. Memo for the Record, Robert Pranger, 2 Jun 1970, folder Mid East 47–50, box 11, Laird Papers, Ford Library; Memo for the Record, Harold Saunders, 28 May 1970, folder SRG Minutes 1970 [4 of 5], box H-111, H Files, NSC, Nixon Library.

49. NSSM 93, 13 Apr 1970, folder Mid East 37–45, box 11, Laird Papers, Ford Library; memo, Rogers for Nixon, 5 May 1970, attached to memo, Kissinger for Nixon, 11 May 1970, folder Haig Chron May 1–12, 1970 [1 of 3], box 966, Haig Chron Files, NSC, Nixon Library.

50. Memo, Laird for Kissinger, 3 Jun 1970 (quotes), folder Mid East 47–50, box 11, Laird Papers, Ford Library; memo, Laird for Nixon 5 Jun 1970, folder Review Group Mid East 6/8/70, box H-045, H Files, NSC, Nixon Library.

51. Memo, Ware for Packard, 8 Jun 1970, folder Mid East 47-50, box 11, Laird Papers, Ford Library; memo, Hyland for Kissinger, 8 Jun 1970, folder USSR vol. 8 May 1970–Jul

1970, box 712, CF–Europe, NSC, Nixon Library; memo, Kissinger for Nixon, n.d., folder NSC Mtg Mid East 6/10/70 [1 of 2], box H-028, H Files, NSC, Nixon Library.

52. Editorial note, *FRUS 1969–1976*, 12:507–14; Memo for the Record, 10 Jun 1970, folder 7, box H-109, H Files; NSDM 66, 18 Jun 1970, folder NSDM 51–96, box 363, Subject Files: both in NSC, Nixon Library.

53. Memo, Rogers for Nixon, 9 Jun 1970 (quote), attached to memo, Nutter for Packard et al., 20 Jun 1970, folder Mid East 51–56, box 11, Laird Papers, Ford Library.

54. Conversation with the President, 1 Jul 1970, *Nixon Public Papers 1970*, 543–59; 557–58 (quotes).

55. Msg, Tel Aviv 3442 to State, 2 Jul 1970, attached to memo, Murphy for Laird, 6 Jul 1970, folder Mid East 51–56, box 11, Laird Papers, Ford Library; memcon, Kissinger and Rabin, 8 Jul 1970, folder 1, box 969; memo, Kissinger for Laird et al., 8 Jul 1970, folder Haig Chron Jul 7–10, 1970 [2 of 3], box 969: both in Haig Chron Files, NSC, Nixon Library.

56. Memo, Nutter for Laird, n.d. (quote), attached to memo, Clark for Pursley, 3 Jul 1970, folder Mid East 51–56, box 11, Laird Papers, Ford Library.

57. Minutes, NSC Senior Review Group Meeting, 9 Jul 1970 (quote), folder SRG Minutes 1970 [3 of 5], box H-111, H Files, NSC, Nixon Library; memo, Nutter for Laird, 9 Jul 1970, folder Mid East 57-61, box 11, Laird Papers, Ford Library.

58. Memcon, 21 July 1970, folder Mid East 57-61, box 11, Laird Papers, Ford Library.

59. Memo, Laird for Service Secretaries et al., 16 Jul 1970, ibid.

60. Memos, Laird for Rogers and Kissinger, 18 Jul 1970 (quotes); Saunders for Kissinger, 20 Jul 1970 (quotes): both in folder Israel vol. 5 22 May 1970–Jul 1970, box 607, CF–Middle East, NSC, Nixon Library; Van Atta, *With Honor*, 274–75.

61. Memo for the Record, 31 Jul 1970; memo, Nutter for Laird, 5 Aug 1970: both in folder Mid East 62–67, box 11, Laird Papers, Ford Library.

62. President's Remarks to Reporters, 31 Jul 1970, *Nixon Public Papers 1970*, 635–36; Kissinger, *White House Years*, 578–85; memcon, 5 Aug 1970, attached to memo, Kissinger for Rogers et al., 6 Aug 1970, folder Mid East 62–67, box 11, Laird Papers, Ford Library.

63. Memo, Kissinger for Nixon, 6 Aug 1970, folder Haig Chron Aug 1–10, 1970 [1 of 3], box 970, Haig Chron Files, NSC, Nixon Library; memcon, 5 Aug 1970, cited in note 62.

64. NSSM 98, 10 Aug 1970, folder Mid East 62–67, box 11, Laird Papers, Ford Library.

65. Minutes, NSC Special Review Group Meeting, 12 Aug 1970, folder SRG Minutes 1970 [3 of 5], box H-111, H Files, NSC, Nixon Library; Memo for the Record, 12 Aug 1970, folder Mid East 62–67; memo, Pranger for Packard, 14 Aug 1970, folder Mid East 68–75: both in box 11, Laird Papers, Ford Library.

66. Memcon, 15 Aug 1970, folder Haig Chron Aug 17–21, 1970 [2 of 2], box 970, Haig Chron Files, NSC, Nixon Library; Kissinger, *White House Years*, 587–88.

67. Kissinger, *White House Years*, 588–93.

68. Kalb and Kalb, Kissinger, 196–99; Van Atta, *With Honor*, 272–74; "Black September in Jordan," <http://en.wikipedia.org/wiki/Black_September_in_Jordan>, accessed 12 Nov

2014; memo, Robinson for Moorer, 8 Sep 1970, folder Sep 1970, box 1, Moorer Diary, Acc 218-05-006; Minutes, SecDef Staff Meeting, 8 Sep 1970, folder Staff Mtgs Jul–Sep 1970, box 14, AFPC and SecDef Staff Meetings, Acc 330-77-0062. Kissinger, *White House Years*, 600–631 provides a detailed examination of the crisis.

69. Minutes, Senior Review Group Meeting, 8 Sep 1970 (quotes), folder 6, box H-111, H Files; memo, Nixon for Rogers and Laird, 23 Sep 1970, folder box 608 folder 1, box 604–611: both in NSC, Nixon Library.

70. Memo, Packard for Nixon, 3 Oct 1970 (quotes); NSDM 87, 15 Oct 1970; memo, Nutter for Laird, 30 Nov 1970: all in folder Mid East 76–81, box 12, Laird Papers, Ford Library.

71. Memo, Laird for Nixon, 10 Dec 1970 (quotes), folder Mid East 83–87, ibid.; Minutes, SecDef Staff Meeting, 24 Aug 1970, folder Jul–Sep 1970, box 14, AFPC and SecDef Staff Mtgs, Acc 330-77-0062.

72. Memcon, 11 Dec 1970, folder Haig Chron Dec 9–23, 1970 [2 of 2], box 975, Haig Chron Files, NSC, Nixon Library.

73. Memo, Kissinger for Nixon, 26 Jun 1971, folder NSC Mtg 6/29/71, box H-031, H Files, ibid.

74. Memo, Laird for Nixon, 21 Jun 1971, folder Mid East 111–117, box 12, Laird Papers, Ford Library.

75. Memos, Kissinger for Rogers, 28 Dec 1971; Nutter for Laird, 30 Dec 1971: both in folder Mid East 143–149, ibid.

18. Looking Toward the Future: The FY 1974 Budget

1. Memo, Odeen for Kissinger, 5 Jan 1971, folder DPRC Mtg 10 Feb 1972, box H-105, H Files, NSC, Nixon Library.

2. Ibid.

3. Memo, Laird for Service Secretaries et al., 23 Oct 1971, folder 2, box H-104, H Files, NSC, Nixon Library.

4. Ibid.

5. Interim Force Planning Guidance for the FY 74–78 Five Year Defense Program, n.d., ibid.

6. Ibid.

7. JCSM-508-71 for SecDef, 22 Nov 1971, folder Strategy 30–32, box 28, Laird Papers, Ford Library.

8. Memo, Laird for Kissinger, 13 Nov 1971, attached to memo, Odeen for Kissinger, 11 Feb 1972, folder DoD vol. 16, box 230, Agency Files, NSC, Nixon Library.

9. Memos, Smith for Kissinger, 8 Nov 1971; Smith for Kissinger, 19 Jan 1972: both in folder DPRC Mtg 12-8-71, box H-104, H Files, NSC, Nixon Library.

10. Memo, Smith for Kissinger, 8 Nov 1971, cited in note 9.

11. Memo, Odeen for Kissinger, 19 Jan 1972, folder DPRC Mtg 8 Dec 1971, box H-104, H Files, NSC, Nixon Library; ltr, Kissinger to Laird, 28 Feb 1972, folder Miscellaneous Correspondence, box D17, Laird Papers, Ford Library.

12. Defense Planning for FY 74–78, n.d., folder 3, [2 of 2], box H-104, H Files, NSC, Nixon Library.

13. Memo, Shultz for Kissinger, 7 Feb 1972 (quote), folder DPRC Mtg 12-8-71, box H-104, H Files, NSC, Nixon Library.

14. Minutes, SecDef Staff Meeting, 14 Feb 1972, folder Staff Mtgs Jan–Mar 1972, box 15, Acc 330-77-0062, WNRC; "Federal Budget Projections," n.d., folder DPRC Mtg 2-10-72, box H-105, H Files, NSC, Nixon Library.

15. "Federal Budget Projections," cited in note 14.

16. Memos, Odeen for Kissinger, 7 Mar 1972, folder OMB 1971, box 268; Odeen for Kissinger, 15 Mar 1972, folder DoD vol. 16, box 230: both in Agency Files, NSC, Nixon Library.

17. Minutes, SecDef Staff Meeting, 14 Feb 1972, cited in note 14.

18. Memo, Odeen for Kissinger, 7 Mar 1972, cited in note 16.

19. Memo, Odeen for Kissinger, 9 Feb 1972, folder DPRC Mtg 2-10-72, box H-105, H Files, NSC, Nixon Library.

20. Minutes, SecDef Staff Meeting, 13 Mar 1972, folder Staff Mtgs Jan–Mar 1972, box 15, Acc 330-77-0062; memos, Laird for Service Secretaries et al., 9 Mar 1972; Odeen for Kissinger, 30 Mar 1972: both attached to ltr, Kissinger to Laird, 7 Apr 1972, folder DPRC and Def Budget Jan–Jul 1972, box 237, Agency Files, NSC, Nixon Library.

21. Memo, Odeen for Spiers et al., 21 Jul 1972, folder DoD vol. 17, box 231, Agency Files, NSC, Nixon Library.

22. Memo, Odeen for Kissinger, 18 Jul 1972, folder DPRC Mtg 7-26-72, box H-106, H Files, NSC, Nixon Library.

23. Memo, Pursley for Laird, 17 Jul 1972, folder Pursley Chron File May 1972–, box 16, Acc 330-75-104.

24. Memo, Laird for Nixon, 18 Jul 1972 (quotes), attached to ltr, Nixon to Laird, 8 Aug 1972, folder DPRC and Def Budget Jan–Jul 1972, box 237, Agency Files, NSC, Nixon Library; Minutes, SecDef Staff Meeting, 24 Jul 1972, folder Staff Mtgs Jul–Sep 1972, box 15, Acc 330-77-0062.

25. Minutes, SecDef Staff Meetings, 10 Jul 1972, 17 Jul 1972: both in folder Staff Mtgs Jul–Sep 1972, box 15, Acc 330-77-0062.

26. Van Atta, *With Honor*, 393; White House Conversations, 299-19, 10 Nov 1971; 18-47, 10 Jan 1972, Nixon Library.

27. Memo, Odeen for Kissinger, 22 Jul 1972; Issue Paper, n.d.: both in folder DPRC Mtg 7-24-72, box H-106, H Files; memo, Davis for Kissinger, 24 Jul 1972 (quote), folder DPRC and Def Budget Jan–Jul 1972, box 237, Agency Files: all NSC, Nixon Library; Minutes, SecDef Staff Meeting, 24 Jul 1972, folder Staff Mtgs Jul–Sep 1972, box 15, Acc 330-77-0062.

28. Memo, Davis for Kissinger, 24 Jul 1972, cited in note 27.

29. Ibid.

30. Telcon, Kissinger and Laird, 25 Jul 1972, 9:20 a.m., folder 4, box 15, HAK Telcons, NSC, Nixon Library.

31. Telcon, Kissinger and Weinberger, 5 Aug 1972, 12:35 p.m., folder 6, ibid.

32. Memcon, 7 Aug 1972, folder Haig Memcons Jan–Dec 1972 [2 of 3], box 998, NSC, Nixon Library.

33. Memo, Odeen for Kissinger, 29 Aug 1972, folder DPRC and Def Budget Aug–Dec 1972, box 237, Agency Files, NSC, Nixon Library.

34. Memo, Odeen for Kissinger, 8 Nov 1972, ibid.

35. Memo, Odeen for Kissinger, 9 Aug 1972, ibid.

36. Ibid.

37. Minutes, SecDef Staff Meetings, 16 Oct 1972; 24 Oct 1972; 30 Oct 1972, folder Staff Mtgs Oct–Dec 1972, box 15, Acc 330-77-062.

38. Minutes, SecDef Staff Meeting, 6 Nov 1972, ibid.

39. Memos, Odeen for Kissinger, 16 Nov 1972, folder DoD vol. 18, box 231, Agency Files; Odeen for Kissinger, 28 Nov 1972, folder FY 73–74 Budget, box 146, HAK Office Files; Odeen for Kissinger, 30 Nov 1972, folder DPRC and Def Budget Aug–Dec 1972, box 237, Agency Files; Kissinger for Nixon, 27 Dec 1972, folder DPRC and Def Budget Aug–Dec 1972, box 237, Agency Files: all in NSC, Nixon Library.

40. Minutes, SecDef Staff Meetings, 4 Dec, 18 Dec, 26 Dec 1972, folder Staff Mtgs Oct–Dec 1972, box 15, Acc 330-77-0062.

41. Radio Address, 28 Jan 1973 (quote); Annual Budget Message to the Congress, Fiscal Year 1974, 29 Jan 1973 (quote): both in *Nixon Public Papers 1973*, 30–41.

42. OMB, *The Budget of the United States Government, Fiscal Year 1974* (Washington, DC: Government Printing Office, 1973), 345.

43. Ibid.

44. Ibid.

45. Ibid.

46. Memo, Odeen for Kissinger, 14 Nov 1972, folder 3, box H-106, H Files, NSC, Nixon Library.

19. Fixing the Fraying Force

1. Ronald Spector, "The Vietnam War and the Army's Self-Image," in *Second Indochina War Symposium*, John Schlight, ed. (Washington, DC: Government Printing Office, 1986), 170 (quote); Cosmas, *MACV, Years of Withdrawal*, 232 (quote).

2. Cosmas, *MACV, Years of Withdrawal*, 220–25.

3. Ibid.

4. See for example, Christopher G. Appy, *Working Class War: American Combat Soldiers and Vietnam* (Chapel Hill: University of North Carolina Press, 1993), 7.

5. Johns, *Vietnam's Second Front*, 157, 171.

6. Drea, *McNamara, Clifford, and the Burdens of Vietnam*, 525–27.

7. Ibid., 525–31.

8. Ibid.

9. Hammond, *Military and the Media*, 171–72; Cosmas, *MACV, The Years of Withdrawal*, 232–33.

10. Memo, Bartimo for Fitt, 9 Nov 1967 w/attached Task Force Report on Drug Abuse, folder SEA-RS-32, Ronald Spector Files, CMH. Spector collected these files for a never-completed book on the U.S. soldier in Vietnam that would have been part of the U.S. Army series on the Vietnam War.

11. Memo, Bartimo for Fitt, cited in note 10.

12. Fact Sheet, "Drug Abuse," Laird Trip Notebook, 5–13 Jan 1971, OSD/HO; Hammond, *Military and the Media*, 171–72; Cosmas, *MACV, Years of Withdrawal*, 233; Fact Sheet, DoD Drug Abuse Control Committee, 5 Jan 1970, folder Drug Abuse 1970, box 35, Laird Papers, Ford Library; MRA Fact Sheet, "Use of Drugs by Servicemen,", 7 Mar 1969, folder 66, box 66, Records from SecDef Vault, Acc 330-74-142, WNRC; memo, Laird for CJCS, Service Secretaries et al., 25 Aug 1969, folder Drug Abuse 1969, box 35, Laird Papers, Ford Library; OASD(A), Report of Investigation, 5 Nov 1968 (quote), folder SEA-RS-16, Spector Files, CMH.

13. UPI, "Navy Ousts 3,800 Who Used Drugs," *Washington Post*, 21 Apr 1970, folder Drug Abuse 69-70, box 1102, Subject Files, OSD/HO; memo, Nixon for Kissinger, 13 Apr 1970 (quote), attached to memo, Kissinger for Laird, 14 Apr 1970, folder Vietnam Apr 1970, box 145, Vietnam Files, NSC, Nixon Library.

14. MACV msg MAC 14163, Abrams to McCain, 30 Oct 1970 (quote), folder Vietnam Sep–Oct 1970, box 25, Acc 218-92-0029, NARA II. Van Atta's biography only discusses Laird's reaction to the drug issue as Secretary of Defense.

15. Memo, Kelley for Service Secretaries et al., 27 Apr 1970; DoD Report on Drug Abuse in Vietnam, attached to memo, Laird for Nixon, 2 May 1970: both in folder Drug Abuse 1970, box 35, Laird Papers, Ford Library.

16. Memo, Kelley for Laird, 10 Aug 1970, ibid.

17. Ltr, Dodd to Laird, 13 Jul 1970; ltr, Schweiker to Laird, 22 Jul 1970: both in folder SEA-RS-41, Spector Files, CMH.

18. "Army Drug Users Offered Amnesty," *Washington Post*, 23 Jul 1970; Vera Glaser and Malvina Stephenson, "Laird Aiming to Torpedo Dodd's Show," *Washington Star*, 16 Aug 1970; Bernard D. Nossiter, "Army Trying to Reclaim GI Addicts," *Washington Post*, 21 Sep 1970.

19. DoD Directive 1300.11, 23 Oct 1970 (quotes); Senate Committee on the Judiciary, Subcommittee on Juvenile Delinquency, *Report of Proceedings*, 30 Oct 1970, folder SEA-RS-7, Spector Files, CMH.

20. Memo for the Record, 17 Dec 1970, folder Haig SEA trip Dec 1970 [4 of 4], box 1011, Haig Special Files, NSC, Nixon Library; "Drug Abuse," cited in note 14; memo, Laird for Moorer, 25 Jan 1971 (quote), folder Vietnam Jan–Feb 1971, box 26, JCS Records, Acc 218-92-0029; memo, Taber for Laird, 20 May 1971, folder Drug Abuse 1971, box 35, Laird Papers, Ford Library.

21. Memo for Laird, n.d., attached to memo, Gordon for Baroody, 14 Jun 1971, folder Drugs, box A70, Baroody Papers, Ford Library; memo, Krogh for Ehrlichman, 13 Apr 1971, attached to memo, Haig for Holdridge, 19 Apr 1971, folder Apr 19–23, 1971 [2 of 2], box 979, Haig Chron Files, NSC, Nixon Library.

22. Memo, Kelley for Laird, 5 Jun 1971; memo, Nixon for Laird, 11 Jun 1971 (quote): both in folder Drug Abuse 1971, box 35, Laird Papers, Ford Library.

23. Minutes, SecDef Staff Meeting, 7 Jun 1971, folder Staff Mtgs Apr–Jun 1971, box 14, AFPC and SecDef Staff Mtgs, Acc 330-77-0062.

24. President's Special Message to Congress, 17 Jun 1971, *Nixon Public Papers 1971*, 739–49.

25. Remarks About an Intensified Program for Drug Abuse Prevention and Control, 17 Jun 1971, ibid., 738–39; Remarks to Eastern Media Executives, 18 Jun 1971 (quotes), ibid., 755.

26. Memo, Laird for Service Secretaries and CJCS, 17 Jun 1971, folder Drug Abuse 1971, box 35, Laird Papers, Ford Library; Van Atta, *With Honor*, 337.

27. This section employs the historically appropriate term "black" in discussing race relations. As the *Oxford American Writer's Thesaurus* noted on page 85, "Black, designating Americans of African heritage, became the most widely used and accepted term in the 1960s and 1970s." The term was used in public discourse, media accounts, books, and government documents, and was commonly found in such phrases as "black pride" and "black power" that expressed racial pride, identity, and solidarity.

28. Ronald H. Spector, *After Tet: The Bloodiest Year in Vietnam* (New York: Free Press, 1993), 244–45; Hammond, *Military and the Media*, 176–77; Henry Maurer, *Strange Ground: An Oral History of Americans in Vietnam, 1945–1975* (New York: Henry Holt and Company, 1989), 240–41 (quotes). See also John Darrell Sherwood, *Black Sailor, White Navy: Racial Unrest in the Fleet during the Vietnam Era* (New York: New York University Press, 2007); James E. Westheider, *The African-American Experience in Vietnam: Brothers in Arms* (New York: Rowman & Littlefield, 2007); Elmo R., Zumwalt Jr., *On Watch: A Memoir* (New York: Quadrangle, 1976).

29. Memo, Brown for Nixon, 10 Mar 1969 (quotes) attached to memo, Laird for White House, 2 May 1969, folder Equal Opportunity 1, box 35, Laird Papers, Ford Library.

30. Ibid.; memo, Ehrlichman for Nixon, 19 Mar 1969, (quote), both attached to memo, Laird for White House, 2 May 1969, folder Equal Opportunity 1, box 35, Laird Papers, Ford Library; memo, Cole for Brown, 1 Apr 1969 (quote), attached to memo, Kissinger for Ehrlichman, 28 Oct 1969, folder Racial Problems, box 379, Subject Files, NSC, Nixon Library.

31. Memo, Brown for Ehrlichman, 15 Aug 1969, attached to memo, Kissinger for Ehrlichman, 28 Oct 1969, cited in note 31.

32. Memo, Laird for All Military Personnel, 2 May 1969, folder EEO, box A70, Baroody Papers, Ford Library.

33. "As Race Issue Hits Armed Forces," *U.S. News and World Report*, 1 Sep 1969; "Black Power in Vietnam," *Time*, 19 Sep 1969; "Pentagon Aide Finds Racial Unrest Up Among Viet GIs," *Washington Post*, 30 Nov 1969: all in folder DoD Integration 1969, box 1097, Subject Files, OSD/HO.

34. Van Atta, *With Honor*, 329–30; "Department of Defense Human Goals" (quotes).

35. "Equality of Opportunity," folder EEO, box A70, Baroody Papers, Ford Library.

36. Minutes, SecDef Staff Meeting, 12 Jan 1970, folder Staff Mtgs Jan–Mar 1970, box 14, AFPC and SecDef Staff Meetings, Acc 330-77-0062; Bennett, "Command Leadership," 8 Jan 1970 (quote), folder EEO, box A70, Baroody Papers, Ford Library; memo, Laird for Service Secretaries, CJCS, 28 Jan 1970 (quote), folder Equal Opportunity 1, box 35, Laird Papers, Ford Library.

37. Memo, Hedlund for Laird, 3 Feb 1969, folder Equal Opportunity 1, box 35, Laird Papers, Ford Library; Senate Committee on the Judiciary, Subcommittee on Administrative Practice and Procedure, *Equal Employment Opportunity Procedures: Hearings*, 91st Cong., 1st sess., 27–28 Mar 1969, 128–30.

38. Packard Statement to Subcommittee of Senate Judiciary Committee, 28 Mar 1969; DoD News Release 220-69, 27 Mar 1969 (quote): both in *Packard Public Statements 1969*, 2:351–90; DoD News Release 808-71, 22 Sep 1971, folder Equal Opportunity 4, box 36, Laird Papers, Ford Library.

39. Minutes, SecDef Staff Meeting, 3 Mar 1969, folder Staff Mtgs Jan–Jun 1969, box 14, AFPC and SecDef Staff Meetings, Acc 330-77-0062; memo, Laird for All Employees, 3 Apr 1969, folder EEO, box A70, Baroody Papers, Ford Library.

40. E. O. 11478, 8 Aug 1969; memo, Froehlke for CJCS et al., 7 Apr 1970, folder Froehlke 1, box A71, Baroody Papers; Reprint of the Labor Department order, *Federal Register*, 5 Feb 1970, folder EEO, box A70, ibid.; memo, Laird for Service Secretaries et al., 30 Jan 1970 (quote), folder Equal Opportunity 1, box 35, Laird Papers: all in Ford Library; Hoff, *Nixon Reconsidered*, 90–91.

41. Robert C. Seamans Jr., *Aiming at Targets* (Washington, DC: Government Printing Office, 1996), 171–72; Van Atta, *With Honor*, 331–32; Minutes, SecDef Staff Meeting, 9 Feb 1970, folder Staff Mtgs Jan–Mar 1970, box 14, AFPC and SecDef Staff Mtgs, Acc 330-77-0062.

42. DoD News Release 113-70, 10 Feb 1970 (quotes), folder EEO, box A70, Baroody Papers, Ford Library; Seamans, *Aiming at Targets*, 171–72; Van Atta, *With Honor*, 331–32; Minutes, SecDef Staff Mtg, 9 Feb 1970, cited in note 41.

43. Memo, Laird for Service Secretaries, 28 Jan 1970, cited in note 37; memos, McLucas for Laird, 18 Mar 1970; Chafee for Laird, 25 Mar 1970 (quote); Resor for Laird, 17 Mar 1970 (quote): all in folder EEO, box A17, Baroody Papers, Ford Library.

44. Memos, Froehlke for Laird, 5 Jun 1970; Laird for Kelley, 28 Jul 1970; Kelley for Laird, 28 Aug 1970: all in folder Equal Opportunity 2, box 36, Laird Papers, Ford Library.

45. Ltr, Wilkins to Laird, 28 Aug 1970, attached to ltr, Laird to Wilkins, 8 Oct 1970, ibid.

46. Ltr, Laird to Wilkins, 8 Oct 1970, cited in note 46.

47. Memo, Kelley for Laird, 12 Nov 1970, folder Equal Opportunity 2, box 36, Laird Papers, Ford Library.

48. DoD Directive 1100.15, 14 Dec 1970.

49. DoD News Release 564-71, 25 Jun 1971; DoD Directive 1322.11, 24 Jun 1971; memo, Kelley for Packard, n.d., all attached to memo, Packard for Service Secretaries, 24 Jun 1971, folder Equal Opportunity 4, box 36, Laird Papers, Ford Library.

50. Task Force Charter, 5 Apr 1972 (quote); memo, Buzhardt for Laird, 15 Jan 1972: both attached to memo, Laird for Kelley, 21 Jan 1972 (quotes), ibid.; memo, Laird for Service Secretaries, 7 Sep 1972 (quote), folder Equal Opportunity 5, box 36, Laird Papers, Ford Library.

51. Laird interview, "Today Show," 30 Nov 1972, *Laird Public Statements 1972*, 8:3536; Laird News Conference, 30 Nov 1972, *Laird Public Statements 1972*, 8:3538–45; memo, Lucy for Moorer, 30 Nov 1972, folder 3 box 6, Moorer Diary, Acc 218-05-006.

52. Memo, Wallace for Hughes, 17 Jun 1971, folder Equal Opportunity 3, box 36, Laird Papers, Ford Library; Van Atta, *With Honor*, 330–31; Nixon White House conversation 491-03, 28 Apr 1971, Nixon Library.

53. Morden, *Women's Army Corps*, 3–6; Mattie E. Treadwell, *The Women's Army Corps* (Washington, DC: U.S. Army Center of Military History, 1954), 4–7; Van Atta, *With Honor*, 333.

54. Morden, *Women's Army Corps*, 48–56, 71–72; Van Atta, *With Honor*, 333–34.

55. Morden, *Women's Army Corps*, 210–16, 223, 241; Van Atta, *With Honor*, 334; Bailey, *America's Army*, 141–42.

56. Morden, *Women's Army Corps*, 231; Van Atta, *With Honor*, 334–35.

57. Zumwalt, *On Watch*, 261–65; Van Atta, *With Honor*, 335–36; Nixon White House Conversation 578-08, 24 Sep 1971, Nixon Library.

58. Van Atta, *With Honor*, 335–36; DoD News Release 572-72, 7 Aug 1972, folder Equal Opportunity 5, box 36, Laird Papers, Ford Library.

59. Memo, Nixon for Heads of Executive Departments and Agencies, 21 Apr 1971, folder Equal Opportunity 3, ibid.

60. Memos, Laird for Service Secretaries et al., 6 Jun 1971; Laird for Nixon, 6 Nov 1971: both in folder Equal Opportunity 3, ibid.

20. Laird's Legacy

1. Van Atta, *With Honor*, 3–4; ltr, Laird to Nixon, 8 Nov 1972 (quote), folder Laird 3, box A75, Baroody Papers, Ford Library; Laird interview, 11 Oct 2001, 2, 3.

2. Ltr, Nixon to Laird, 17 Nov 72 (quote), folder SecDef Correspondence, box D17, Laird Papers, Ford Library.

3. In *White House Years*, 32–33, Kissinger pays unstinting tribute to Laird's skill and accomplishments as secretary.

4. Pursley interview, 30 Jul 2003, 3, 30.

5. Laird interview, 11 Oct 2001, 4.

6. Memos, Moot for Laird, 4 Dec 1972 (quote), folder Summary Paper Tab B, box 43; Foster for Laird, 26 Dec 1972, folder Taking Stock 5, box 29; Tucker for Laird, 30 Jan 1973 (quote), folder Taking Stock 13, box 29: all in Laird Papers, Ford Library.

7. Memo, Moot for Laird, 4 Dec 1972, cited in note 6; James Schlesinger, interview by Alfred Goldberg and Maurice Matloff, 1 Aug 1991, OSD/IIO.

8. *FRUS 1969–1976*, 32:2–6; memo, Laird for Kissinger, 13 Feb 1969, cited in *JCS and National Policy, 1969–1972*, 132–33; memo, Foster for Laird, 26 Dec 1972, cited in note 6.

9. Nitze, *From Hiroshima to Glasnost*, 302; *FRUS 1969–1976*, 32:692–95.

10. Memo, Foster for Laird, 26 Dec 1972, cited in note 6; memo, Shillito for Laird, 19 Dec 1972, folder Taking Stock 8, box 29, Laird Papers, Ford Library.

11. *DoD Key Officials*, 76, 78, 84, 88; Korb, Fall and Rise of the Pentagon, 94.

12. Laird interview, 11 Oct 2001, 12.

13. Ltr, Nixon to Laird, 17 Nov 1972 (quote), cited in note 2.

14. Van Atta, *With Honor*, 423–24; Pursley interview, 15 Aug 1997, 23, 25.

15. Memo, Moot for Laird, 4 Dec 1972, cited in note 6.

16. Memos, Laird for Kissinger, 22 Jan 1969; Kissinger for Laird, 25 Jan 1969: both in folder NSC-Org-1, box 40, Kissinger/Scowcroft Papers, Ford Library; memo, Laird for Service Secretaries, 12 Sep 1969, attached to memo, Pursley for DirDIA, 9 Jan 1970, folder Misc Corres, box D17, Laird Papers, Ford Library; telcon, Laird and Ehrlichman, 23 Dec 1971, folder Special Report for President tabs 1–18, folder 5 of 5, box 22–24, WHSF, SMOF, Young Files, Subject Files, Nixon Library; Laird, handwritten note entitled "Awareness of Problem," folder SecDef Correspondence, Box D17, Laird Papers, Ford Library; memos, Laird for Nixon,15 Mar 1971; Nixon for Laird, 8 Apr 1971: both in folder Staff Mtgs Apr–Jun 1971, box 14, Acc 330-77-0062, WNRC; Hersh, *Price of Power*, 207–08; Van Atta, *With Honor*, 224, 298, 300.

17. Telcon, Laird and Ehrlichman, 23 Dec 1971 (quote), folder Spec Report for Pres tabs 1-18, folder 5 of 5, box 22-24, WHSF, SMOF, David Young Files, Subject Files, Nixon

Library; Randolph, *Powerful and Brutal Weapons*, 19–20; Van Atta, *With Honor*, 302–03; Rodman, *Presidential Command*, 66–67; Laird, "Awareness of Problem," cited in note 16.

18. Cosmos, *MACV: The Joint Command, 1968–1973*, 397

19. Memo, Shillito for Laird, 19 Dec 1972, cited in note 12; memo, Gardiner for Laird, 30 Jan 1973, cited in note 8.

20. Clarke, *Advice and Support*, 511–22; Cosmas, *MACV: The Joint Command, 1968–1973*, 422–27.

21. Van Atta, *With Honor*, 481; Hunt, *Pacification*, 258–79; Kevin Boylan, "Goodnight Saigon: American Provincial Advisors' Final Impressions of the Vietnam War," *Journal of Military History* 78, no. 1 (Jan 2014): 233–70.

22. Van Atta, *With Honor*, 183; Webb, *JCS and the War in Vietnam 1969–1970*, 14–15.

23. Ltr, Nixon to Laird, 17 Nov 1972, cited in note 2.

24. Memo for President's Files, NSC Meeting, 8 May 1972, folder NSC Minutes 1971 [2 of 5], Box H-110, NSC, Nixon Library.

25. See Pursley's discussion on the ability of South Vietnam's forces. He answered a qualified yes to the question of whether the South Vietnamese were strong enough to survive. In his 30 July interview (pages 37, 41) he observed that the key to Vietnamization was the ability of the South Vietnamese to be willing to support themselves, to reach "a strong enough point . . . to confront the North Vietnamese now with an interminable confrontation."

26. Memo, Kelley for Laird, 11 Dec 1972 (quote), folder Summary Papers Tab C, box 43, Laird Papers, Ford Library

27. Memo, Foster for Laird, 30 Jan 1973, cited in note 8; memo, Froehlke for Laird, 8 Dec 1972 (quote), folder Taking Stock 1, box 28, Laird Papers, Ford Library. Kelley does not indicate whether the budget figures were TOA or expenditures.

28. Memo, Kelley for Laird, 11 Dec 1972, cited in note 25.

29. For Robert McNamara's doubts regarding his own actions in Vietnam, see his two works: *In Retrospect: The Tragedy and Lessons of Vietnam* (New York: Times Books, 1995) and *Argument Without End: In Search of Answers to the Vietnam Tragedy* (New York: Public Affairs, 1999).

30. Pursley asserts Laird's role was essential in these initiatives. See Pursley interview, 15 Aug 1997, 32, OSD/HO.

31. Van Atta, *With Honor*, 458–65; Kinnard, *Secretary of Defense*, 152; Pursley interview, 30 Jul 2003, 31, OSD/HO.

NOTE ON SOURCES
AND SELECTED BIBLIOGRAPHY

THE EXTRAORDINARILY RICH documentary collections from the Richard Nixon Presidential Library in Yorba Linda, California, and the Gerald R. Ford Presidential Library in Ann Arbor, Michigan, proved indispensable to this book. Part of the Nixon materials, the essential National Security Council (NSC) Files encompass the entire range of national security issues and include the formulation of policy and the positions taken by Nixon, Laird, and Kissinger. Telephone conversations that Kissinger had with the president, Laird, Rogers, and other important figures were transcribed, not verbatim but in sufficient detail to delineate the issues under consideration and the often conflicting positions taken by the principals. Of singular value are the chronological files of Alexander Haig. The H Files, the Institutional Files of the National Security Council, contain the complete record of various meetings. In addition to these materials, the president's tape recorded conversations offer unparalleled candor and detail.

After Laird left the Pentagon, he gave his papers to the Ford Presidential Library. This collection consists of documents on all the major issues that crossed the secretary's desk. Most of the records belong to Record Group 330 and illustrate the interaction between Laird, OSD, and the JCS. Also at the Ford Library are the papers of William Baroody, who drafted many speeches and policy papers for Laird.

Within the RG 330 records at the Washington National Records Center in Suitland, Maryland, are several valuable collections. The Records from the SecDef Vault comprise the documents that were kept in Laird's office. Equally valuable is the complete set of notes of the secretary's weekly staff meetings. Superbly transcribed by Eugene Livesay, these files show the issues that Laird emphasized with his assistant secretaries and the services. The files of Robert Pursley, also in RG 330, proved insightful.

Special mention needs to be made of the JCS records now stored in the National Archives in College Park, Maryland. Part of that collection is the remarkable diary kept by Admiral Thomas Moorer during his tenure as JCS chairman. As expected, it contains a listing of daily events but goes much further to include transcriptions of telephone and office conversations and copies of documents and memoranda. The diary indicates Moorer's behind-the-scenes maneuvering and his occasional mistrust of the White House and the secretary.

Finally, the archives of the OSD Historical Office provided a unique source of information on Defense budgets, congressional testimony, and press stories about defense issues. Two collections deserve separate mention: the files of the Assistant Secretary of Defense (Comptroller) contain an unparalleled collection of material about the Defense budget process; and the multiple volumes of the *Public Statements of Melvin Laird, Secretary of Defense,* and the *Public Papers of David Packard, Deputy Secretary of Defense,* compiled by the OSD Historical Office, include press conferences, speeches, interviews, and other public documents.

Primary Sources

Manuscript Collections

Gerald R. Ford Presidential Library and Museum, Ann Arbor, MI
>   William J. Baroody Papers
>   Kissinger-Scowcroft Files, 1969–1977
>   Melvin R. Laird Papers

National Archives and Records Administration (NARA) II, College Park, MD
>   Records of the U.S. Joint Chiefs of Staff, Record Group 218
>>   Records of the Joint History Office, Office of the Chairman of the Joint Chiefs of Staff
>>>   Accession 218-05-006, Admiral Thomas H. Moorer Diary
>>>   Accession 218-92-0029
>>>   Accession 218-98-33

Richard Nixon Presidential Library and Museum, Yorba Linda, CA
>   Henry A. Kissinger (HAK) Office Files
>>   HAK Administrative and Staff Files
>   Henry A. Kissinger Telephone Conversations (Telcons) Transcripts
>   National Security Council Files
>>   Institutional Files (H Files)
>>   Presidential Acquisitions File
>>>   Agency Files

Alexander M. Haig Chronological Files

Alexander M. Haig Special Files

Backchannel Files

Jon Howe Chronological Files

Korea: EC–121 Shootdown File

Lake [Anthony] Chronological Files

Name Files

Subject Files

Vietnam Subject Files

White House Central Files

Staff Member and Office Files

Martin P. Anderson Files

White House Special Files

Staff Member and Office Files

Harold Robbins Haldeman Files

President's Personal File

White House Tapes

Office of the Secretary of Defense, Historical Office, Washington, DC

Assistant Secretary of Defense (Comptroller) Files

Oral History Collection

Subject Files

U.S. Army Center of Military History, Washington, DC

Creighton Abrams Papers

Ronald Spector Files

Washington National Records Center, Suitland, MD

Records of the Office of the Secretary of Defense, Record Group 330

Accession 330-74-142, Records from SecDef Vault

Accession 330-75-104, SecDef Records

Accession 330-77-0062, Staff Meetings

Executive Branch Documents and Reports

Cole, Alice C. *The Department of Defense: Documents on Establishment and Organization, 1944–1978*. Washington, DC: OSD Historical Office, 1979.

Keefer, Edward C., et al., eds. *Soviet-American Relations: The Détente Years, 1969–1972*. Washington, DC: Government Printing Office, 2007.

Nixon, Richard. *Public Papers of the Presidents of the United States: Richard Nixon, 1969–1974*, 6 vols. Washington, DC: Government Printing Office, 1971–1975.

Office of Management and Budget [Bureau of the Budget]. *The Budget of the United States Government, Fiscal Year 1970*. Washington, DC: Government Printing Office, 1969.

———. *The Budget of the United States Government, Fiscal Year 1971*. Washington, DC: Government Printing Office, 1970.

———. *The Budget of the United States Government, Fiscal Year 1972*. Washington, DC: Government Printing Office, 1971.

———. *The Budget of the United States Government, Fiscal Year 1973*. Washington, DC: Government Printing Office, 1972.

———. *The Budget of the United States Government, Fiscal Year 1974*. Washington, DC: Government Printing Office, 1973.

———. *The U.S. Budget in Brief, Fiscal Year 1970*. Washington, DC: Government Printing Office, 1969.

———. *The U.S. Budget in Brief, Fiscal Year 1972*. Washington, DC: Government Printing Office, 1971.

———. *The U.S. Budget in Brief, Fiscal Year 1973*. Washington, DC: Government Printing Office, 1972.

Office of the Secretary of Defense. Historical Office. *Department of Defense Key Officials, 1947–2004*. Washington, DC: 2004.

———, comp. *Public Statements of Clark Clifford, Secretary of Defense, 1968–1969*. 4 vols.

———. *Public Statements of Melvin Laird, Secretary of Defense, 1969–1973*. 8 vols.

———. *Public Statements of David Packard, Deputy Secretary of Defense, 1969–1971*. 4 vols.

———. *Public Statements of Elliot Richardson, Secretary of Defense, 1973*. 5 vols.

Trask, Roger R., and Alfred Goldberg. *The Department of Defense, 1947–1997: Organization and Leaders*. Washington, DC: OSD Historical Office, 1997.

U.S. Department of Defense. *Department of Defense Annual Report for Fiscal Year 1968 Including the Reports of the Secretary of Defense, Secretary of the Army, Secretary of the Navy, Secretary of the Air Force*. Washington, DC: Government Printing Office, 1971.

———. *Department of Defense Annual Report for Fiscal Year 1969 Including the Reports of the Secretary of Defense, Secretary of the Army, Secretary of the Navy, Secretary of the Air Force*. Washington, DC: Government Printing Office, 1968.

———. *Department of Defense Annual Report for Fiscal Year 1970 Including the Reports of the Secretary of Defense, Secretary of the Army, Secretary of the Navy, Secretary of the Air Force*. Washington, DC: Government Printing Office, 1969.

———. *Department of Defense Annual Report for Fiscal Year 1971 Including the Reports of the Secretary of Defense, Secretary of the Army, Secretary of the Navy, Secretary of the Air Force*. Washington, DC: Government Printing Office, 1970.

———. *Department of Defense Annual Report for Fiscal Year 1972 Including the Reports of the Secretary of Defense, Secretary of the Army, Secretary of the Navy, Secretary of the Air Force.* Washington, DC: Government Printing Office, 1971.

———. *Department of Defense Annual Report for Fiscal Year 1973 Including the Reports of the Secretary of Defense, Secretary of the Army, Secretary of the Navy, Secretary of the Air Force.* Washington, DC: Government Printing Office, 1972.

U.S. Department of State. *Foreign Relations of the United States, 1964–1978.* 34 vols. Washington, DC: Government Printing Office.

Congressional Documents and Reports

U.S. Congress. *Congressional Record,* 1969–1973.

U.S. Congress. House. Committee on Appropriations. *Department of Defense Appropriations for 1970: Hearings,* 91st Cong., 1st sess., 1969.

———. Committee on Appropriations. *Department of Defense Appropriations for 1971: Hearings,* 91st Cong., 2nd sess., 1970.

———. Committee on Appropriations. *Department of Defense Appropriations for 1972: Hearings,* 92nd Cong., 1st sess., 1971.

———. Committee on Appropriations. *Hearings: Supplemental Appropriation Bill, 1971,* 91st Cong., 2nd sess., 1970.

———. Committee on Armed Services. *Hearings on Military Posture,* 91st Cong., 1st sess., 1969.

———. Committee on Armed Services. *Inquiry into the U.S.S. Pueblo and EC–121 Plane Incidents: Report,* 91st Cong., 1st sess., 1969.

———. Committee on Foreign Affairs. *Hearings: Foreign Assistance Act of 1969,* 91st Cong., 1st sess., 1969.

U.S. Congress. Senate. Committee on Appropriations. *Department of Defense Appropriations for Fiscal Year 1970: Hearings,* 91st Cong., 1st sess., 1969.

———. Committee on Appropriations. *Department of Defense Appropriations for FY 1971: Hearings,* 91st Cong., 2nd sess., 1970.

———. Committee on Appropriations. *Hearings: Foreign Assistance and Related Programs Appropriations FY 1973,* 92nd Cong., 2nd sess., 1972.

———. Committee on Armed Services. *Hearings: Nominations of Laird, Packard, and Darden,* 91st Cong., 1st sess., 1969.

———. Committee on Armed Services. *Authorization for Military Procurement, Research and Development, Fiscal Year 1970, and Reserve Strength: Hearings,* 91st Cong., 1st sess., 1969.

———. Committee on Armed Services. *Authorization for Military Procurement, Research and Development, Fiscal Year 1971, and Reserve Strength: Hearings,* 91st Cong., 2nd sess., 1970.

———. Committee on Armed Services. *Military Authorizations and Defense Appropriations for Fiscal Year 1971: Hearings,* 91st Cong., 1st sess., 1970.

———. Committee on Foreign Relations. *Hearings: Foreign Assistance Act, 1969*, 91st Cong., 1st sess., 1969.

———. Committee on Foreign Relations. *Hearings: Foreign Assistance Legislation, FY 1972*, 92nd Cong., 1st sess., 1971.

———. Committee on Foreign Relations. *Hearings: Strategic and Foreign Policy Implications of ABM Systems*, 91st Cong., 1st sess., 1969.

———. Committee on Foreign Relations. *Hearings: Supplemental Foreign Assistance Authorization, 1970*, 91st Cong., 2nd sess., 1970.

———. Committee on Foreign Relations. *Impact of the War in Southeast Asia on the U.S. Economy: Hearings*, 91st Cong., 2nd sess., 1970.

———. Committee on the Judiciary. *Equal Employment Opportunity Procedures: Hearings*, 91st Cong., 1st sess., 1969.

Published Memoirs and Papers

Bunker, Ellsworth. *The Bunker Papers: Reports to the President from Vietnam, 1967–1973*. Berkeley, CA: University of California, 1990.

Clifford, Clark M., and Richard Holbrooke. *Counsel to the President: A Memoir*. New York: Random House, 1991.

Dobrynin, Anatoly. *In Confidence: Moscow's Ambassador to America's Six Cold War Presidents (1962–1986)*. New York: Random House, 1995.

Haig, Alexander. *Inner Circles: How America Changed the World: A Memoir*. New York: Warner Books, 1992.

Haldeman, H. R. *The Haldeman Diaries: Inside the Nixon White House*. New York: G.P. Putnam's Sons, 1994.

Johnson, U. Alexis. *The Right Hand of Power*. Englewood Cliffs, NJ: Prentice Hall, 1984.

Kissinger, Henry A. *White House Years*. Boston: Little, Brown, 1979.

McLucas, John L. *Reflections of a Technocrat: Managing Defense, Air, and Space Programs During the Cold War*. Maxwell AFB: Air University Press, 2006.

Nitze, Paul H. *From Hiroshima to Glasnost: At the Center of Decision: A Memoir*. New York: G. Weidenfeld, 1989.

Nixon, Richard M. *RN: The Memoirs of Richard Nixon*. New York: Grosset & Dunlap, 1978.

Seamans, Robert C., Jr. *Aiming at Targets*. Washington, DC: Government Printing Office, 1996.

Westmoreland, William C. *A Soldier Reports*. New York: Doubleday, 1976.

Zumwalt, Elmo R. *On Watch: A Memoir*. New York: Quadrangle, 1976.

Interviews

Office of the Secretary of Defense, Historical Office, Oral History Collection, Washington, DC

Goodpaster, Andrew. Interview by Alfred Goldberg and Maurice Matloff. 19 January 1984.

Haig, Alexander. Interview by Alfred Goldberg and Ronald Landa. 14 February 1996.

Laird, Melvin. Interview by Maurice Matloff and David Trask. 18 August 1986.

Laird, Melvin. Interview by Maurice Matloff and Alfred Goldberg. 2 September 1986.

Laird, Melvin. Interview by Alfred Goldberg and Richard Hunt. 11 and 15 October 2001.

Laird, Melvin. Interview by Alfred Goldberg and Maurice Matloff, 29 October 1986.

Marshall, Andrew W. Interview by Alfred Goldberg and Maurice Matloff. 1 June 1992.

Moot, Robert. Interview by Alfred Goldberg and Richard Hunt. 26 October 2001.

Pursley, Robert. Interview by Alfred Goldberg and Richard Hunt. 30 July and 13 August 2003.

Pursley, Robert. Interview by Alfred Goldberg and Roger Trask. 15 August 1997.

Secondary Sources

Books

Ambrose, Stephen E. *Nixon: The Triumph of a Politician, 1962–1972*. New York: Simon and Schuster, 1989.

American Institute of Public Opinion. *The Gallup Poll: Public Opinion, 1935–1971*. Wilmington, DE: Scholarly Resources, 1978.

———. *The Gallup Poll: Public Opinion, 1972–1977*. Wilmington, DE: Scholarly Resources, 1978.

Anderson, David L., ed. *Shadow on the White House*. Lawrence, KS: University Press of Kansas, 1993.

Andrade, Dale. *Trial by Fire: The 1972 Easter Offensive, America's Last Vietnam Battle*. New York: Hippocrene Books, 1995.

Andrew, Christopher M. *For the President's Eyes Only: Secret Intelligence and the American Presidency from Washington to Bush*. New York: Harper Collins Publishers, 1995.

Appy, Christian G. *Working Class War: American Combat Soldiers and Vietnam*. Chapel Hill, NC: University of North Carolina Press, 1993.

Baucom, Donald R. *The Origins of SDI: 1944–1983*. Lawrence, KS: University Press of Kansas, 1992.

Berman, Larry. *No Peace, No Honor: Nixon, Kissinger, and Betrayal in Vietnam*. New York: Free Press, 2001.

———. *The Office of Management and Budget and the Presidency, 1921–1979*. Princeton, NJ: Princeton University Press, 1979.

Bowman, William, and Thomas Sicilia. *The All-Volunteer Force After a Decade: Retrospect and Prospect*. Washington, DC: Pergamon-Brassey's, 1986.

Braestrup, Peter, ed. *Vietnam as History: Ten Years after the Paris Peace Accords*. Washington, DC: The Wilson Center/University Press of America, 1984.

Brauer, Carl M. *Presidential Transitions: Eisenhower through Reagan*. New York: Oxford University Press, 1986.

Brown, Seyom. *The Crises of Power: An Interpretation of United States Foreign Policy During the Kissinger Years*. New York: Columbia University Press, 1979.

Bui, Diem, and David Chanoff. *In the Jaws of History.* Boston: Houghton Mifflin, 1987.

Bundy, McGeorge. *Danger and Survival: Choices About the Bomb in the First Fifty Years.* New York: Random House, 1988.

Bundy, William P. *A Tangled Web: The Making of Foreign Policy in the Nixon Presidency.* New York: Hill and Wang, 1998.

Calleo, David P. *The Imperious Economy.* Cambridge, MA: Harvard University Press, 1982.

Chester, Lewis, Godfrey Hodgson, and Bruce Page. *An American Melodrama: The Presidential Campaign of 1968.* New York: Viking Press, 1969.

Clarke, Jeffrey J. *Advice and Support: The Final Years, 1965–1973.* Washington, DC: U.S. Army Center of Military History, 1988.

Clodfelter, Mark. *The Limits of Air Power: The American Bombing of North Vietnam.* New York: London: Collier Macmillan, 1989.

Cohen, Warren I. *America in the Age of Soviet Power, 1945–1991.* Cambridge: Cambridge University Press, 1993.

Colby, William Egan, with James McCargar. *Lost Victory: A Firsthand Account of America's Sixteen-Year Involvement in Vietnam.* Chicago: Contemporary Books, 1989.

Colodny, Len, and Robert Gettlin. *Silent Coup: The Removal of a President.* New York: St. Martin's Press, 1991.

Cosmas, Graham A. *MACV: The Joint Command in the Years of Withdrawal, 1968–1973.* Washington, DC: U.S. Army Center of Military History, 2006.

Daalder, Ivo H., and I. M. Destler. *In the Shadow of the Oval Office: Profiles of the National Security Advisers and the Presidents They Served—From JFK to George W. Bush.* New York: Simon & Schuster, 2009.

Dallek, Robert. *Nixon and Kissinger: Partners in Power.* New York: Harper, 2007.

Davidson, Phillip B. *Vietnam at War: The History, 1946–1975.* Novato, CA: Presidio Press, 1988.

Davis, Vernon E. *The Long Road Home: U.S. Prisoner of War Policy and Planning in Southeast Asia.* Washington, DC: OSD Historical Office, 2000.

Destler, I. M. *Making Foreign Economic Policy.* Washington, DC: Brookings Institution, 1980.

———. *Presidents, Bureaucrats, and Foreign Policy: The Politics of Organizational Reform.* Princeton, NJ: Princeton University Press, 1974.

Dommen, Arthur J. *Laos: Keystone of Indochina.* Boulder, CO: Westview Press, 1985.

Drea, Edward J. *McNamara, Clifford, and the Burdens of Vietnam, 1965–1969.* Washington, DC: OSD Historical Office, 2011.

Duffield, John. *Power Rules: The Evolution of NATO's Conventional Force Posture.* Palo Alto, CA: Stanford University Press, 1995.

Eckes, Alfed, and Thomas Zeiler. *Globalization and the American Century.* Cambridge: Cambridge University Press, 2003.

Enthoven, Alain C., and W. Wayne Smith. *How Much Is Enough? Shaping the Defense Program, 1961–1969.* New York: Harper & Row, 1971.

Fedder, Edwin H. *NATO and Détente*. St. Louis, MO: Center for International Studies, 1979.

———, ed. *NATO in the Seventies*. St. Louis, MO: Center for International Studies, 1970.

Fisch, Arnold G., Jr. *Military Government in the Ryuku Islands, 1945–1950*. Washington, DC: U.S. Army Center of Military History, 1988.

Franck, Thomas M., and Edward Weisband. *Foreign Policy by Congress*. New York: Oxford University Press, 1979.

Gaddis, John Lewis. *Russia, the Soviet Union, and the United States: An Interpretive History*. New York: Wiley, 1978.

———. *Strategies of Containment: A Critical Appraisal of Postwar American National Security Policy*. New York: Oxford University Press, 1982.

Garfinkle, Adam. *Telltale Hearts: The Origins and Impact of the Vietnam Anti-War Movement*. New York: St. Martin's Press, 1995.

Garthoff, Raymond L. *Détente and Confrontation: American-Soviet Relations from Nixon to Reagan*. Washington, DC: Brookings Institution, 1985.

———. *Perspectives on the Strategic Balance*. Washington, DC: Brookings Institution, 1983.

Gavin, Francis. *Gold, Dollars and Power: The Politics of International Monetary Policy Relations, 1958–1971*. Chapel Hill, NC: University of North Carolina Press, 2007.

Goldstein, Martin E. *American Policy towards Laos*. Hackensack, NJ: Fairleigh Dickinson University Press, 1973.

Goodman, Allan E. *The Lost Peace: America's Search for a Negotiated Settlement of the Vietnam War*. Stanford, CA: Hoover Institution Press, 1978.

Greene, John Robert. *The Limits of Power: The Nixon and Ford Administrations*. Bloomington, IN: Indiana University Press, 1992.

Greenwood, Ted. *Making the MIRV: A Study of Defense Decision Making*. Cambridge, MA: Ballinger, 1975.

Griffith, Robert K., Jr. *U.S. Army's Transition to the All-Volunteer Force, 1868–1974*. Washington, DC: U.S. Army Center of Military History, 1997.

Haig, Alexander. *Caveat: Realism, Reagan, and Foreign Policy*. New York: Macmillan, 1984.

Halberstam, David. *The Best and the Brightest*. New York: Random House, 1972.

Halperin, Morton H., Priscilla Clapp, and Arnold Kanter. *Bureaucratic Politics and Foreign Policy*. Washington, DC: The Brookings Institution, 1974.

Hamilton-Merritt, Jane. *Tragic Mountains: The Hmong, the Americans, and the Secret Wars for Laos, 1942–1992*. Bloomington, IN: Indiana University Press, 1993.

Hammond, William M. *Public Affairs: The Military and the Media, 1968–1973*. Washington, DC: U.S. Army Center of Military History, 1996.

Hannah, Norman B. *The Key to Failure: Laos and the Vietnam War*. Lanham, MD: Madison Books, 1987.

Haslam, Jonathan. *The Soviet Union and the Politics of Nuclear Weapons in Europe, 1969–87*. Ithaca, NY: Cornell University Press, 1990.

———. *Russia's Cold War: From the October Revolution to the Fall of the Wall.* New Haven: Yale University Press, 2012.

Herring, George C. *America's Longest War: The United States and Vietnam, 1950–1975.* 2nd ed. New York: Knopf Press, 1986.

Hersh, Seymour M. *Chemical and Biological Warfare: America's Hidden Arsenal.* Garden City, NY: Anchor Books, 1969.

———. *The Price of Power: Kissinger in the Nixon White House.* New York: Summit Books, 1983.

Herz, Martin F. *The Vietnam War in Retrospect.* Washington, DC: Georgetown School of Foreign Service, 1984.

Hoff, Joan. *Nixon Reconsidered.* New York, NY: Basic Books, 1994.

Holst, Johan J., and William Schneider, Jr., eds. *Why ABM? Policy Issues in the Missile Defense Controversy.* New York: Pergamon Press, 1969.

Hunt, Michael H. *Ideology and U.S. Foreign Policy.* New Haven: Yale University Press, 1987.

Hunt, Richard A. *Pacification: The American Struggle for Vietnam's Hearts and Minds.* Boulder, CO: Westview Press, 1995.

Institute for Strategic Studies, *Military Balance, 1969–1970.* London: 1971.

Isaacs, Arnold R. *Without Honor: Defeat in Vietnam and Cambodia.* Baltimore: Johns Hopkins University Press, 1983.

Isaacson, Walter. *Kissinger: A Biography.* New York: Simon & Schuster, 1992.

Johns, Andrew L. *Vietnam's Second Front: Domestic Politics, the Republican Party, and the War.* Lexington, KY: University Press of Kentucky, 2010.

Jones, Frank Leigh. *Blowtorch: Robert Komer, Vietnam, and American Cold War Strategy.* Annapolis, MD: Naval Institute Press, 2013.

Kalb, Marvin L., and Bernard Kalb. *Kissinger.* Boston: Little, Brown, 1974.

Kaplan, Lawrence S., Ronald D. Landa, and Edward J. Drea. *The McNamara Ascendancy, 1961–1965.* Washington, DC: OSD Historical Office, 2006.

Kaplan, Morton A. *Vietnam Settlement: Why 1973, Not 1969?* Washington, DC: American Enterprise Institute for Public Policy Research, 1973.

Kennedy, David. *Over Here: The First World War and American Society.* New York: Oxford University Press, 2004.

Kimball, Jeffrey. *Nixon's Vietnam War.* Lawrence, KS: University Press of Kansas, 2002.

———. *The Vietnam War Files.* Lawrence, KS: University Press of Kansas, 2004.

Kinnard, Douglas. *The Secretary of Defense.* Lexington, KY: University Press of Kentucky, 1980.

Kissinger, Henry A. *Ending the Vietnam War: A History of America's Involvement in and Extrication from the Vietnam War.* New York: Simon and Schuster, 2003.

———. *Nuclear Weapons and Foreign Policy.* New York: Harper & Row, 1957.

Korb, Lawrence J. *The Fall and Rise of the Pentagon: American Defense Policies in the 1970s.* Westport, CT: Greenwood Press, 1979.

Labrie, Roger. *SALT Handbook: Key Documents and Issues, 1972–1979.* Washington, DC: American Enterprise Institute, 1979.

Lake, Anthony. *The Vietnam Legacy: The War, American Society, and the Future of American Foreign Policy.* New York: New York University Press, 1976.

Larsen, Stanley R., and James L. Collins Jr., *Allied Participation in Vietnam.* Washington, DC: Department of the Army, 1985.

Le Gro, William E. *Vietnam from Cease-fire to Capitulation.* Washington, DC: U.S. Army Center of Military History, 1981.

Leighton, Richard M., *Strategy, Money, and the New Look, 1953–1956.* Washington, DC: OSD Historical Office, 2001.

Lewy, Guenter. *America in Vietnam.* New York: Oxford University Press, 1978.

Lundestad, Geir. *The United States and Europe since 1945: From "Empire" by Invitation to Atlantic Drift.* New York: Oxford University Press, 2003.

MacMillan, Margaret, *Nixon and Mao.* New York: Random House, 2007.

Matusow, Allen. *Nixon's Economy: Booms, Busts, Dollars, and Votes.* Lawrence, KS: University Press of Kansas, 1998.

Maurer, Henry. *Strange Ground: An Oral History of Americans in Vietnam, 1945–1975.* New York: Henry Holt and Company, 1989.

Mobley, Richard A. *Flash Point North Korea: The Pueblo and EC–121 Crises.* Annapolis, MD: Naval Institute Press, 2003.

Momyer, William W. *Air Power in Three Wars.* Washington, DC: Air Force History and Museums Program, 1978.

Morden, Bettie J. *The Women's Army Corps: 1945–1978.* Washington, DC: U.S. Army Center of Military History, 1990.

Morris, Roger. *Richard Milhous Nixon: The Rise of an American Politician.* New York: Holt, 1990.

Moulton, Harland B. *From Superiority to Parity: The United States and the Strategic Arms Race, 1961–1971.* Westport, CN: Greenwood Press, 1973.

Nalty, Bernard C. *Air War Over South Vietnam, 1968–1975.* Washington, DC: Air Force History and Museums Program, 2000.

———. *The War Against Trucks: Aerial Interdiction in Southern Laos.* Washington, DC: Air Force History and Museums Program, 2005.

Neufeld, Jacob, and R. Cargill Hall, eds. *The U.S. Air Force In Space.* Washington, DC: Air Force History and Museums Program, 1998.

Newhouse, John. *Cold Dawn: The Story of SALT.* New York: Holt, 1973.

Nguyen, Llien-Hang T. *Hanoi's War: An International History of the War for Peace in Vietnam.* Chapel Hill: University of North Carolina Press, 2012.

Nye, Joseph S. *The Making of America's Soviet Policy.* New Haven: Yale University Press, 1984.

Osgood, Robert Endicott. *Retreat from Empire? The First Nixon Administration.* Baltimore: Johns Hopkins University Press, 1973.

Palmer, Bruce. *The 25-Year War: America's Military Role in Vietnam.* New York: Simon & Schuster, 1985.

Parmet, Herbert S. *Richard Nixon and His America.* Boston: Little, Brown, 1990.

Patterson, James. *Grand Expectations.* New York: Oxford University Press, 1996.

Perlstein, Rick. *Nixonland: The Rise of a President and the Fracturing of America.* New York: Scribner, 2008.

Pierre, Andrew J. *Nuclear Weapons in Europe.* New York: Council on Foreign Relations, 1984.

Poole, Walter S. *The Joint Chiefs of Staff and National Policy, 1969–1972.* Washington, DC: Office of Joint History, Office of the JCS, 2013.

Porter, Gareth. *A Peace Denied: The United States, Vietnam, and the Paris Agreement.* Bloomington, IN: Indiana University Press, 1975.

Powaski, Ronald E. *The Entangling Alliance: The United States and European Security, 1950–1993.* Westport, CT: Greenwood Press, 1994.

Prados, John. *Keepers of the Keys: A History of the National Security Council from Truman to Bush.* New York: Morrow, 1991.

———. *Vietnam: History of an Unwinnable War.* Lawrence, KS: University Press of Kansas, 2009.

Randolph, Stephen. *Powerful and Brutal Weapons: Nixon, Kissinger, and the Easter Offensive.* Cambridge, MA: Harvard, University Press, 2007.

Rearden, Steven L. *Council of War: The History of the Joint Chiefs, 1942–1991.* Washington, DC: National Defense University Press, 2012.

———. *The Formative Years, 1947–1950.* Washington, DC: OSD Historical Office, 1984.

Rochester, Stuart I., and Frederick Kiley, *Honor Bound: The History of American Prisoners of War in Southeast Asia, 1961–1973.* Washington, DC: OSD Historical Office, 1998.

Rodman, Peter. *Presidential Command: Power, Leadership, and the Making of Foreign Policy from Richard Nixon to George W. Bush.* New York: Knopf, 2009.

Roland, Alex. *The Military-Industrial Complex.* Washington, DC: American Historical Association, 2001.

Rostker, Bernard D. *I Want You! The Evolution of the All-Volunteer Force.* Santa Monica, CA: Rand Corporation, 2006.

Rothkopf, David J. *Running the World: The Inside Story of the National Security Council and the Architects of American Power.* New York: Public Affairs, 2004.

Safire, William. *Before the Fall.* New York: Doubleday, 1975.

Schieps, Paul J. *The Role of Federal Military Forces in Domestic Disorders, 1945–1992.* Washington, DC: U.S. Army Center of Military History, 2012.

Schlight, John, ed. *The Second Indochina War.* Washington, DC: Government Printing Office, 1986.

Schulz, Matthias, and Thomas Schwartz. *The Strained Alliance: US-European Relations from Nixon to Carter.* Cambridge: Cambridge University Press, 2010.

Schurmann, Franz. *The Foreign Politics of Richard Nixon: The Grand Design.* Berkeley: University of California Press, 1987.

Schwartz, Thomas. *Lyndon Johnson and Europe: In the Shadow of Vietnam.* Cambridge, MA: Harvard University Press, 2003.

Shaw, John M. *The Cambodian Campaign: The 1970 Offensive and America's Vietnam War.* Lawrence, KS: University Press of Kansas, 2005.

Sherwood, John Darrell. *Black Sailor, White Navy: Racial Unrest in the Fleet during the Vietnam Era.* New York: New York University Press, 2007.

Small, Melvin. *Johnson, Nixon, and the Doves.* New Brunswick, NJ: Rutgers University Press, 1988.

———. *The Presidency of Richard Nixon.* Lawrence, KS: University Press of Kansas, 1999.

Smith, Gerard C. *Doubletalk: The Story of the First Strategic Arms Limitation Talks.* Garden City, NY: Doubleday, 1980.

Snepp, Frank. *Decent Interval.* New York: Random House, 1977.

Sorley, Lewis. *Arms Transfers under Nixon: A Policy Analysis.* Lexington, KY: University Press of Kentucky, 1983.

———. *A Better War: The Unexamined Victories and Final Tragedy of America's Last Years in Vietnam.* New York: Houghton Mifflin Harcourt, 1999.

———. *Thunderbolt: General Creighton Abrams and the Army of His Times.* New York: Simon & Schuster, 1992.

———, ed. *Vietnam Chronicles: The Abrams Tapes, 1968–1972.* Lubbock, TX: Texas Tech University Press, 2004.

Spector, Ronald H. *After Tet: The Bloodiest Year in Vietnam.* New York: Free Press, 1993.

Stein, Herbert. *Presidential Economics: The Making of Economic Policy from Roosevelt to Reagan and Beyond.* New York: Simon and Schuster, 1984.

Stevenson, Charles, A. *The End of Nowhere: American Policy towards Laos since 1954.* Boston: Beacon Press, 1972.

Talbott, Strobe. *The Master of the Game: Paul Nitze and the Nuclear Peace.* New York: Knopf, 1988.

Thayer, Thomas C. *War Without Fronts: The American Experience in Vietnam.* Boulder, CO: Westview Press, 1985.

Thompson, Nicholas. *The Hawk and the Dove: Paul Nitze, George Kennan, and the History of the Cold War.* New York: Henry Holt and Co., 2009.

Thompson, Wayne. *To Hanoi and Back: The United States Air Force and North Vietnam, 1966–1973.* Washington, DC: Air Force History and Museums Program, 2000.

Thornton, Richard C. *The Nixon-Kissinger Years: Reshaping America's Foreign Policy.* New York: Paragon House, 1989.

Treadwell, Mattie E. *The Women's Army Corps*. Washington, DC: U.S. Army Center of Military History, 1954; 1991.

Van Atta, Dale. *With Honor: Melvin Laird in War, Peace, and Politics*. Madison, WI: University of Wisconsin Press, 2008.

Van Staaveren, Jacob. *Interdiction in Southern Laos, 1960–1968*. Washington, DC: Air Force History and Museums Program, 1993.

Volten, Peter M. E. *Brezhnev's Peace Program: A Study of Soviet Domestic Political Process and Power*. Boulder, CO: Westview Press, 1982.

Webb, Willard J. *The Joint Chiefs of Staff and the War in Vietnam, 1969–1970*. Washington, DC: Office of Joint History, Office of the JCS, 2002.

Webb, Willard J., and Walter S. Poole. *The Joint Chiefs of Staff and the War in Vietnam, 1971–1973*. Washington, DC: Office of Joint History, Office of the JCS, 2013.

Wenger, Andreas, et al., eds. *Transforming NATO in the Cold War: Challenges Beyond Deterrence in the 1960s*. New York: Routledge, 2006.

Westheider, James E. *The African-American Experience in Vietnam: Brothers in Arms*. New York: Rowman & Littlefield, 2007.

Willbanks, James H. *Abandoning Vietnam: How America Left and South Vietnam Lost Its War*. Lawrence, KS: University Press of Kansas, 2004.

Wolfe, Thomas W. *The SALT Experience*. Cambridge, MA: Ballinger, 1979.

Zaffiri, Samuel. *Hamburger Hill*. New York: Presidio Press, 1988.

Zeiler, Thomas. *American Trade and Power in the 1960s*. New York: Columbia University Press, 1992.

Articles

Berman, Larry. "The Office of Management and Budget That Almost Wasn't." *Political Science Quarterly* 92, no. 2 (1977): 281–303.

Burr, William, and Jeffrey Kimball. "Nixon's Secret Nuclear Alert: Vietnam War Diplomacy and the Joint Chiefs of Staff Readiness Test, October 1969," *Cold War History* 3, no. 3 (2003): 113–56.

Duscha, Julius. "The Political Pro Who Runs Defense." *New York Times Magazine*, 13 June 1971.

Halperin, Morton H. "The Decision to Deploy the ABM: Bureaucratic and Domestic Politics in the Johnson Administration." *World Politics* 25, no. 1 (1972): 62–95.

Hanhimaki, Jussi. "'Some More Smoking Guns'? The Vietnam War and Kissinger's Summitry with Moscow and Beijing, 1971–1973," *The SHAFR Newsletter* 32, no. 4 (2001): 40–45.

Hessman, James D. "DoD After Two Years of Laird." *Armed Forces Journal* 108, (21 December 1970): 32–34.

Hoff-Wilson, Joan. "'Nixingerism,' NATO, and Detente." *Diplomatic History* 13, no. 4 (1989): 501–26.

Kimball, Jeffrey. "'Peace With Honor': Richard Nixon and the Diplomacy of Threat and Symbolism." In *Shadow on the White House*, edited by David Anderson, 152–83. Lawrence, KS: University Press of Kansas, 1993.

Laird, Melvin R. "A Strong Start in a Difficult Decade: Defense Policy in the Nixon-Ford Years." *International Security* 10, no. 2 (1985): 5–26.

Small, Melvin. "Containing Domestic Enemies: Richard M. Nixon and the War at Home." In *Shadow on the White House*, edited by David Anderson, 130–51. Lawrence, KS: University Press of Kansas, 1993.

Spector, Ronald. "The Vietnam War and the Army's Self-Image." In *Second Indochina War Symposium*, edited by John Schlight, 169–86. Washington, DC: Government Printing Office, 1986.

Ware, Richard A. "The Pentagon's Office of International Security Affairs, 1969–1973," American Enterprise Institute for Public Policy Research, 1986.

Warner, Michael. "Reading the Riot Act: The Schlesinger Report, 1971." *Intelligence and National Security* 24, no. 3 (2009): 387–417.

Winston, Donald C. "Defense Bill Keyed to ABM Fight," *Aviation Week*, 27 July 1970.

Unpublished Paper
Gordon, Vance, et al. "Revolution, Counter-Revolution, and Evolution: A Brief History of the PPBS."